SAP PRESS e-books

Print or e-book, Kindle or iPad, workplace or airplane: Choose where and how to read your SAP PRESS books! You can now get all our titles as e-books, too:

- By download and online access
- For all popular devices
- And, of course, DRM-free

Convinced? Then go to www.sap-press.com and get your e-book today.

SAP S/4HANA®

 PRESS

SAP PRESS is a joint initiative of SAP and Rheinwerk Publishing. The know-how offered by SAP specialists combined with the expertise of Rheinwerk Publishing offers the reader expert books in the field. SAP PRESS features first-hand information and expert advice, and provides useful skills for professional decision-making.

SAP PRESS offers a variety of books on technical and business-related topics for the SAP user. For further information, please visit our website: *www.sap-press.com*.

Bhattacharjee, Desai, Narasimhamurti, Vazquez, Walsh
Logistics with SAP S/4HANA: An Introduction (2nd Edition)
2019, approx. 550 pp., hardcover and e-book
www.sap-press.com/4785

Mehta, Aijaz, Duncan, Parikh
SAP S/4HANA Finance: An Introduction
2019, approx. 425 pp., hardcover and e-book
www.sap-press.com/4784

Michael Jolton, Yosh Eisbart
SAP S/4HANA Cloud: Use Cases, Functionality, and Extensibility
2017, 334 pp., hardcover and e-book
www.sap-press.com/4498

Densborn, Finkbohner, Freudenberg, Mathäß, Wagner
Migrating to SAP S/4HANA
2017, 569 pp., hardcover and e-book
www.sap-press.com/4247

Devraj Bardhan, Axel Baumgartl, Nga-Sze Choi, Mark Dudgeon,
Asidhara Lahiri, Bert Meijerink, Andrew Worsley-Tonks

SAP S/4HANA®

An Introduction

Rheinwerk
Publishing

Editor Megan Fuerst
Acquisitions Editor Emily Nicholls
Copyeditor Julie McNamee
Cover Design Graham Geary
Photo Credit iStockphoto.com/155419717/© ithinksky
Layout Design Vera Brauner
Production Graham Geary
Typesetting SatzPro, Krefeld (Germany)
Printed and bound in the United States of America, on paper from sustainable sources

ISBN 978-1-4932-1775-5
© 2019 by Rheinwerk Publishing, Inc., Boston (MA)
3rd edition 2019

Library of Congress Cataloging-in-Publication Data
Names: Baumgartl, Axel, author. | Bardhan, Devraj, author.
Title: SAP S/4HANA: an introduction / Devraj Bardhan, Axel Baumgartl, Nga-Sze
  Choi, Mark Dudgeon, Asidhara Lahiri, Bert Meijerink, Andrew Worsley-Tonks.
Description: 3rd edition. | Bonn : Rheinwerk Publishing, 2018. | Includes
  index.
Identifiers: LCCN 2018041183 (print) | LCCN 2018044878 (ebook) | ISBN
  9781493217762 (ebook) | ISBN 9781493217755 (alk. paper)
Subjects: LCSH: SAP HANA (Electronic resource) | Database management. |
  Management information systems. | Business enterprises--Data processing.
Classification: LCC QA76.9.D3 (ebook) | LCC QA76.9.D3 B3935 2018 (print) |
  DDC 005.74--dc23
LC record available at https://lccn.loc.gov/2018041183

Contents at a Glance

Dear Reader,

If keeping your tech up to date feels like a race against the clock of ever-advancing technology, you're not alone.

We live in a world where constant system updates give consumers access to the latest and greatest features. Take smart phones: It seems like hardly a day goes by before I need to update apps ranging from Facebook to Uber. Still, it makes sense—industry standards and end user expectations are constantly increasing. In some respects, tech is racing to keep up with us.

Of course, SAP S/4HANA updates don't come around every day, but when they do, they can be game changing. With SAP S/4HANA 1809, industry insiders consider the suite to be increasingly mature, and our author team is ready to give you a tour. Coming from IBM and SAP, they showcase both the stable architecture and established processes and the brand new functionality you'll want to get your hands on.

What did you think about *SAP S/4HANA: An Introduction*? Your comments and suggestions are the most useful tools to help us make our books the best they can be. Please feel free to contact me and share any praise or criticism you may have.

Thank you for purchasing a book from SAP PRESS!

Megan Fuerst
Editor, SAP PRESS

meganf@rheinwerk-publishing.com
www.sap-press.com
Rheinwerk Publishing · Boston, MA

Contents

1   The Digital Transformation: An Introduction   29

2   Finance   79

3   Manufacturing

8   Analytics and Reporting

9   Industry Solutions

10   SAP S/4HANA Cloud

11   SAP S/4HANA and the SAP Landscape   339

12   SAP S/4HANA Architecture   389

13   Extensions with the SAP Cloud Platform   453

14   SAP Leonardo   473

17 Building the Business Case

18 Customer Case Studies

Foreword from Uwe Grigoleit

There is no denying that today's enterprises face challenging times. Uncertainty reigns, prompted by rapid political, economic, social, and technological change. The pressure on business leaders to make the right decisions in the face of this uncertainty has never been greater. At the same time, employees are being pushed to become more productive, work more efficiently, and learn to adapt faster to ensure the success of their organization in a digitally-disrupted landscape.

Businesses the world over recognize the radical reshaping of processes, products, and entire industries currently in progress. SAP S/4HANA is the intelligent ERP solution that with each new release increases the use of intelligent technologies and capabilities, such as machine learning, conversational AI, and predictive analytics, to support next-generation practices that enable our customers to build an intelligent enterprise.

Since its launch over three years ago, SAP S/4HANA has helped companies capture rapidly emerging opportunities and cope with equally fast-moving threats. Already, over 2,100 SAP customers are live with SAP S/4HANA. In fact, the first 1,000 customers implemented SAP S/4HANA during the first 2.5 years of its availability, and the second 1,000th customer milestone was achieved in less than a year.

Designed for in-memory computing, it provides the flexibility and responsiveness that companies demand, integrating disparate sources of data to enable true real-time insight and the ability to execute immediately. Companies that are deploying SAP S/4HANA as their digital core have a distinct advantage in today's marketplace.

With SAP S/4HANA, customers can implement a more agile IT landscape, dramatically reduce TCO, and support continuous innovation. SAP offers a consistent solution in any environment—cloud, on-premise, or hybrid—allowing customers to benefit in any scenario or combination that is right for them

When insight, flexibility, and responsiveness are critical to success—today and tomorrow—companies can't rely on yesterday's technology. I encourage you to explore the power of SAP S/4HANA, the real-time enterprise resource planning suite built on our advanced in-memory platform.

Uwe Grigoleit
Senior Vice President and General Manager of SAP S/4HANA, SAP SE

Foreword from Cameron Art

The great opportunity ahead…

I am delighted to pen a foreword to the next generation of *SAP S/4HANA: An Introduction*. The amount of innovation flowing into the space is not only creating a groundswell of momentum but also a multitude of opportunities. Momentum and excitement fills the SAP ecosystem and continues to bubble into new areas of opportunity. The expertise and talent that lies within that ecosystem is once again awakened by the new shot in the arm of energy and focus. That talent in turn is activating the clients of SAP, opening their eyes to the opportunity of SAP as a platform of digital reinvention and the necessity for those that are transforming their own client and employee experiences, business partner engagement, and even business models, taking advantage of the richness of contemporary online, mobile, virtual reality models. Successful businesses and business models are setting the bar for consumer expectations at an increasing height.

Every day we see the impact of this phenomenon on business models and industries. Consumers' expectations have shot skyward based on an expectation of deep engagement with products and services provided through technology. For individual companies, the focus is now becoming clearer. The mandate is to use the digital core to not only target, attract, and engage clients in new ways, but also importantly to connect that interest end to end through the core processes of manufacturing, distribution, and fulfillment to deliver fully on the heightened expectations.

The clearest vision of this digital reinvention is illustrated through IBM's long time business partner: SAP. SAP S/4HANA is bringing all the benefits of Internet technologies to everyday business. It allows clients to deliver all of those things that born-on-the-web companies have differentiated, *at scale*. It provides real-time visibility into operations, is available anywhere and anytime, is always on, and is flexible to meet a company's needs. It allows every business to compete and prosper.

We continue to be fortunate to partner with SAP in this digital revolution. This platform for business has allowed us to invest heavily our own R&D into the digital transformation journey. For many, the most efficient way to get started will be through our SAP S/4HANA Impact Assessment tool, and they'll find the quickest time to value through our Impact Industry Solutions. This highlights the quickest time to value for new transformation efforts built upon the digital core. A fast growing segment in parallel to this is our Bluefield Transformations. Bluefield Transformation is essentially a new way to approach the move to the digital core leveraging more of the existing footprints. In those clients where the configuration, the data, and the existing processes fit uniquely to the clients business models, we are seeing much interest in taking advantage of all the experience and work of the past again as a rapid start on the SAP S/4HANA journey. Within our practice, we will continue to push the envelope in R&D and investments to allow clients the most efficient path to this new paradigm of a digital foundation that enables front-office differentiation—all while making the path there based upon proven reliable tools, relying less on consulting hours and customization. Finally, we cap off all of this work with the continuation of our digital transformation partnership with SAP, bringing together the latest technologies in artificial intelligence, cloud, IoT, big data, blockchain, and cognitive computing to drive value for our clients.

This book provides a comprehensive introduction to SAP S/4HANA and how it can address and support the digital transformation your company. It covers all relevant aspects, from value scenarios to a full digital transformation roadmap. The authors use their experience from different industries and concrete examples of when and how to use SAP S/4HANA, in combination with lines of business solution from SAP, to show you how to support your digital journey. Between these pages, the authors provide you with practical information and project examples of how to approach the changes to your ERP landscape.

My hope for all readers is that you will find it as inspiring as I have. In this new digital world, we can change how it works for the benefit of all with our work. What businesses are capable of is changing due to technology. What governments are capable of is changing due to technology. What the world is capable of is changing due to technology. It is a time of great opportunity. IBM is honored to help our clients and our great partner in SAP go capture it!

Cameron Art
Managing Partner, Enterprise Cloud Applications, IBM Global Business Services

Preface

As the leading global packaged application provider, SAP supports the changing demands of its customer base by providing a solution that can support their organizations' needs. With the introduction of the SAP HANA database in 2010, SAP provided the ability to use in-memory capabilities to accelerate its business applications and to integrate transaction and reporting capabilities into a single database. In 2013, SAP made the move to using SAP HANA as the platform for all its business applications. In addition to the changes on the platform level, there was a significant move toward the consumption of "as a service" models. This allowed companies to reduce their implementation and maintenance costs and increase productivity with cloud-based deployment options.

SAP's acquisition of other companies such as SuccessFactors and Hybris (which is now SAP C/4HANA) has added functionalities needed to build an end-to-end digital platform. To simplify the processes and to address the demand of a more user-centric solution, SAP introduced SAP Fiori as part of the overall platform. The combination of those changes and capabilities led to a renovation of SAP ERP toward a new product line called SAP S/4HANA and led to a new way of implementing SAP products: SAP Activate.

Why Read This Book?

With all the changes introduced in the past years and the innovations that are coming alongside those changes, there is a need for more detailed information about and experience with SAP S/4HANA. We know that there is detailed information available for certain aspects of SAP S/4HANA, but we believe that other sources only cover a subset of the overall information and that only address a specific audience. With this book, we provide a comprehensive overview of the different aspects of SAP S/4HANA from industry, business, and technical perspectives.

We also share the experiences we've gathered in different client situations, as well as challenges and how to solve them, with concrete examples. In addition, we've identified a need to prepare customers for the digital transformation and to provide them with the right setup to make their business case from the strategic, organizational level on down to the technical and operational levels. We aim to close the gap at the strategic level by discussing concrete best practices and how to apply them.

This overview should help both new SAP clients and experienced SAP customers understand the different aspects of and changes to their environments.

Audience

This book is geared toward CxOs, business owners, enterprise architects, and project managers who want to get a consolidated overview of the value of SAP S/4HANA and the related products supporting the digital transformation. We cover the industry perspective and the implications, as well as the strategic, imperative results of the industry transformation. Because of this scope, we believe the book is relevant for all SAP-interested readers across all industries.

We also included information to help business teams understand SAP S/4HANA's functional capabilities (e.g., finance and logistics), as well as how the value scenarios improve day-to-day work.

On the other side, we look at the technical platform and the migration, upgrading, and deployment options that are useful for enterprise architects and project managers.

We want to encourage the readers of the book to take a closer look at the concepts we introduce and consider them in future transformation and implementation projects.

Structure of the Book

This reference book on SAP S/4HANA provides both a complete overview and important details on each topic. The structure guides you from a strategical level to a practical level and covers all key aspects of each topic. This book also serves as a compendium: You can pick it up at a specific chapter and read through that chapter for detailed information on a selected topic. Each chapter is complete as a standalone source. However, we recommend that you start from the beginning and work through the book because some chapters do refer to previous chapters and build on each other.

Chapter 1 provides an overview of the digital transformation and introduces its main drivers. It also describes the fundamentals of SAP S/4HANA, including the different editions and deployment options. We provide an overview of business value scenarios and how they support the digital transformation. Within the value scenarios, you'll see concrete optimization and savings potential. We wrap up with a high-level overview of the SAP S/4HANA architecture and deployment options.

In **Chapter 2**, we introduce the key functionalities of SAP S/4HANA Finance and how they address some key business challenges. This chapter also provides an overview of the SAP S/4HANA Cloud capabilities for finance, and an outlook of future capabilities that will be available with further releases.

Chapter 3 looks at the manufacturing capabilities of SAP S/4HANA with information on MRP Live, optimization of product master data, production planning (PP), and detail scheduling (DS). It also contains information on general process simplification, SAP S/4HANA Cloud functionality for manufacturing, and the outlook of manufacturing capabilities.

Chapter 4 covers the supply chain in SAP S/4HANA, from inventory valuation to embedded extended warehouse management and embedded transportation management. Once again, we conclude the chapter with an overview of the SAP S/4HANA Cloud capabilities for supply chain and a look at the future of the supply chain in SAP S/4HANA.

Chapter 5 looks at sales, marketing and commerce (which are often grouped together), and service management. Some highlights of this coverage include the sales order fulfillment cockpit, customer relationship management functionality, and optimized service master data management. We conclude with an overview of the SAP S/4HANA Cloud capabilities for sales, marketing and commerce, and service management, as well as the outlook for these capabilities.

In **Chapter 6**, we look at sourcing and procurement in SAP S/4HANA. Functionality covered includes operational purchasing, invoice and payables management, sourcing and contract management, and supplier analytics. To conclude, we'll continue our pattern of first discussing the available functionality in SAP S/4HANA Cloud for sourcing and procurement, before taking a look at the future outlook.

Chapter 7 rounds off our logistics-based chapters with coverage of research and development (R&D) and asset management. We'll look at SAP Innovation Management, SAP Project and Portfolio Management, SAP Commercial Project Management, and SAP Product Lifecycle Costing. We'll also examine a few areas of asset management, from maintenance planning and scheduling to maintenance operation and execution to mobile asset maintenance. To conclude, we'll provide an overview of both the SAP S/4HANA Cloud capabilities for R&D and asset management and the future outlook.

In **Chapter 8**, we discuss analytics and reporting in the context of SAP S/4HANA. We look at operational reporting, embedded SAP BW and SAP BPC, enterprise-wide reporting, cognitive analytics, and big data.

In **Chapter 9**, we look at three major industry solutions: SAP S/4HANA Retail for merchandise management, SAP S/4HANA for fashion and vertical business, and SAP S/4HANA Oil & Gas. We'll look at some technical simplifications and the functionality available within them.

Chapter 10 looks at SAP S/4HANA Cloud, discussing its value proposition, the current scope of the solution, and some tasks and considerations specific to its deployment. We also briefly cover extensibility options and the content lifecycle management process for SAP S/4HANA Cloud.

After we introduce SAP S/4HANA and its functional capabilities, we broaden your view in **Chapter 11** by introducing the extended functionality provided by the line of business (LoB) solutions outside the digital core (e.g., SAP SuccessFactors, SAP Ariba, SAP C/4HANA, and SAP Integrated Business Planning) and how they integrate with SAP S/4HANA. Therefore, we provide a high-level overview of the functional capabilities of these solutions and how they complement each other.

In **Chapter 12**, we explain the details of and the concept behind the SAP HANA platform and how it addresses the typical issues of an IT department and serves as the database for SAP S/4HANA. We get into the principles of the SAP HANA database concepts, scalability, virtualization, and operations. These features are being extended by security and user experience (UX) to complete the architecture.

Based on the fundamentals of the SAP HANA architecture, **Chapter 13** describes the extension possibilities of future SAP solutions and how SAP S/4HANA can be extended via in-app and side-by-side extensions. We also introduce SAP Cloud Platform and possibilities for Internet of Things (IoT) and SAP Leonardo as fundamental pieces of the digital value chain.

We'll dive deeper into SAP Leonardo in **Chapter 14**, discussing what functionalities are offered by key technologies such as IoT, machine learning, blockchain, and big data, and how they intersect with SAP S/4HANA. We'll also examine two use cases, to help envision how these technologies can be put into practice.

Next, **Chapter 15** helps you get prepared from a technical perspective for a move to SAP S/4HANA and provides the relevant prerequisites. We discuss the different implementation options and approaches, as well as the recommended housekeeping activities and relevant tools.

An essential part of a successful SAP S/4HANA implementation project is having the right approach and method. In **Chapter 16**, we explain the principles of the SAP Activate framework in the context of SAP S/4HANA and provide an overview of the available tools.

After we explain SAP S/4HANA and its benefits, architecture, principles, methods, and tools, we use **Chapter 17** to demonstrate how you can build your own business case. We also discuss what methods and tools should be used to make the right decision for your company.

In **Chapter 18**, we illustrate and prove the value of SAP S/4HANA with a review of concrete, real-world cases that show what benefits can be achieved.

Acknowledgments

Creating this book took a lot of work, so you can imagine that it couldn't be accomplished by a small group. We the authors want to say thank you to all of the supporters who helped us complete this book successfully.

First, we want to thank our families for helping us find the time and the peace to write this book. We also want to thank our friends and colleagues who helped us get this project done. We want to express our gratitude to Gairik Acharya, Nihal Ansari, Dharma T. Atluri, Subhajit Basak, Mike Beer, Dmitry Chaadaev, Supriya Das, Avijit Dhar, Aauyush Dhawan, Sean Freeman, Rahul Jha, Tomas Krozl, Debabrata Mandal, KJ Min, Shreayan Nandi, Silpa Polisetti, Dinesh Thigale, and Partha Trapathi for providing significant support to the author team and making significant contributions to some chapters.

We also want to say thank you to all of those who aren't mentioned by name but supported us in the book project.

And, last but not least, we really want to say thank you to Megan Fuerst and Emily Nicholls from SAP PRESS, who had patience with our team and provided encouragement and support.

—**Devraj Bardhan**, **Axel Baumgartl**, **Nga-Sze Choi**, **Mark Dudgeon**, **Asidhara Lahiri**, **Bert Meijerink**, and **Andrew Worsley-Tonks**

Chapter 1

The Digital Transformation: An Introduction

Now that the cloud, social, mobile, and big data are widely used, the digital transformation is moving to the next level: the intelligent enterprise. Organizations must continue to adapt and adopt new capabilities to stay in the game. This chapter describes what digital transformation and the "intelligent enterprise" really means, how to keep pace with changing requirements, and what value SAP S/4HANA brings.

Within the past 30 years, digitalization of the world has massively increased. It began with the Internet and the ability to instantly and digitally access information, and it continues to grow via the use of smartphones and social media, which connect us all on a global level and enable us to exchange information, interact, and stay connected. By 2020, an estimated 2.5 billion people will be connected on personal and business social networks worldwide. At the same time, an estimated 200 billion devices will be linked to each other via the Internet of Things (IoT). The use of machine learning and artificial intelligence (AI) is now part of every process; for example, with the use of natural language processing or sentiment analysis, there are new possibilities to improve processes or even create new business models.

For example, a smart home contains different IoT devices (e.g., smart thermometer, smart plugs, etc.) to control and monitor your home. These devices can be combined with data provided by weather data suppliers and enhancement services to control your home. From a business perspective, this IoT data can be used to extend or enhance current services to the consumer or even to build new business models.

To give another example, huge growth has occurred in the automatization of the manufacturing industry. According to the International Federation of Robotics (IFR), the demand for industrial robots increased by 48% from 2010 to 2014 and has increased exponentially over the past three years. In short, digitalization is everywhere, from the personal to the global economy.

These technological changes and the transformation toward digital aren't new to us. We adopt this on a consumer level as well as on a company level, and we're in the middle of the digital transformation. With the use of big data, cloud, social, and mobile, we established the basis to move toward the next maturity level of the intelligent enterprise. The intelligent enterprise will use new technologies, such as machine learning and AI, to come to the next level of automation with bots that help to execute processes in a no-touch way, where no interaction with a human being is needed.

In this chapter, we'll discuss exactly what the digital transformation and the intelligent enterprise are and what they mean for you or your industry. In addition, we'll discuss some business scenarios that can help you understand the value of SAP S/4HANA and how it's different from your current enterprise resource planning (ERP) solution. We'll end the chapter by briefly discussing the architecture and the different deployment options of SAP S/4HANA.

1.1   Digital Transformation and the Intelligent Enterprise

First, let's begin with some recent history of how the digital transformation started and how it's now maturing and influencing different business areas as we head toward the intelligent enterprise. Figure 1.1 shows the evolution of digitalization that began with individual digital products in the 1980s driving forward the industrial automation and has now matured into the ability to build completely new business models based on intelligent technologies.

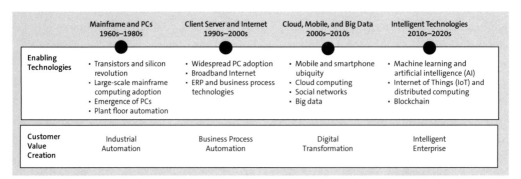

Figure 1.1 Road Map from Industrial Automation to the Intelligent Enterprise

These new business models include companies such as Amazon for commerce, Facebook for social media, and Uber and Lyft connecting different services and building collaborative networks.

Does this mean that traditional companies will no longer exist or are being taken over by the new challengers? For example, Google is aggressively going into the mobility space and engaging with autonomous cars. At the same time, German automotive producers BMW, Daimler, and Audi jointly acquired Nokia to extend their capabilities toward supported and autonomous driving. We see that though there is the potential for traditional companies to lose market share to new challengers, there is also a huge potential for them to extend their current market or market segments.

This shows one way in which traditional business models are being challenged. The digital transformation is driving existing businesses to accelerate their speed and to leverage digital potential. Although many traditional board members, such as the chief executive officer (CEO) and the chief information officer (CIO), see the digital transformation as a short-term topic that needs to realize benefits on a quarterly basis, we believe it's a continuous adoption process that goes beyond the here and now.

Equally, if it's a short- or long-term adoption process, all these changes have an implication for how companies will run their businesses in the future and how they need to adapt. This subsequently has implications for the ERP capabilities that will support companies in building their digital platform cores as a foundation to gain value from the digital transformation journey.

Returning to the question of what we mean by the phrase "digital transformation," we can see that it has different implications for different people, such as the following:

- For some, it's about technology as an enabler.
- For others, digital is a new way of engaging with customers.
- For still others, it represents an entirely new way of doing business and defining new business models.

Digital transformation and the intelligent enterprise aren't limited to these aspects, however. In the same way that you have different stakeholders within organizations, you'll find different interests and views on the same topic. In terms of how the digital transformation is influencing industries, companies, and consumers, we can define the term digital transformation as follows:

Digital transformation is the way in which businesses are being impacted by leveraging new technologies (e.g., cloud computing or process automation via robots) and how this affects the overall organization of a business. It's about hyperconnectivity and the utilization and interpration of new data that can provide better insight and generate predictable results to reimagine business models from procurement to sales and services and to improve the entire value chain.

Based on that definition, what are the fundamental pieces of the digital transformation? From a technical perspective, the following technical megatrends will have the biggest impact on business:

- **Cloud computing and services**
  Cloud computing accelerates time to value, drives higher adoption of new technologies, and connects value chains in real time. Although this has relevance for all CxOs (CEO, CIO, CDO, etc.), it's especially relevant to chief marketing officers (CMOs), who rely on accelerated time to value in this digital age. Organizations need to evaluate exactly which delivery models will help them innovate faster in today's digital economy. Most organizations already operate in a hybrid world in which cloud technologies interact with on-premise apps. Four key cloud models are relevant for customers:

  - **Infrastructure as a service (IaaS)**
    IaaS is an enterprise class-optimized infrastructure built using open standards. Businesses are leveraging IaaS (e.g., IBM SoftLayer) to get up and running in a matter of hours without significant capital expense.

  - **Platform as a service (PaaS)**
    PaaS provides an entire computing platform in the cloud, including hardware, software, and open application programming interfaces (APIs) to build new businesses and create new solutions. Examples include Apple, SAP Cloud Platform, and IBM BlueMix, with their range of APIs and services that will also be a disruptive platform for business. Another model of PaaS is managed PaaS for enterprise applications, in which customers move their on-premise platforms to public or private clouds (e.g., SAP HANA Enterprise Cloud, IBM C4SAP).

  - **Software as a service (SaaS)**
    SaaS is a mature trend, with offerings such as SAP Ariba providing solutions via the cloud. SAP is currently the leader in this area, with more than 80 million users leveraging SaaS. With SaaS growing more than 20%, we see more apps moving into the cloud. Although this trend is dominated by customer relationship management (CRM), procurement, and human resources (HR) solutions

(think SAP SuccessFactors), other solutions, such as SAP ERP, are also moving into the cloud.

– **Business process as a service (BPaaS)**
BPaaS enables business transformation. An example is outsourcing commodity business processes (e.g., payroll, expense payments) to a commercial "as a service" pricing model.

- **Mobile solutions and user experience (UX)**
In the digital era, being mobile-first and providing a first-class UX are essential technology components. The chief value of mobility for CMOs is having a readily available personal channel for customers. However, they also need to provide a consistent UX across all channels their customers use (e.g., in store, browser, mobile).

When consumers check out a vendor's offerings, they expect to search for products, read reviews, and experience standard pricing, whether they're shopping from their smartphone or laptop, by telephone, or in a brick-and-mortar store. Their purchase decisions and brand loyalty are heavily dependent on a positive buying experience. Businesses must now deliver an omnichannel experience through the customer journey.

Internally, design thinking is an essential part of today's digital transformation strategies. Design thinking is an effective way to structure complex tasks with an integrated method that takes both people and the collaboration between teams into account to generate extraordinary results. It also uses a six-phase iterative innovation process that considers the place as a factor to increase collaboration and effectiveness. The interaction with the end user and the usability and effectiveness play especially important roles in the adoption of a mobile solution.

- **Big data**
Big data, including extended sources of data beyond traditional systems of record (e.g., social media, IoT), is emerging as a key technology trend. However, it's the analytics performed on this data that add business value, that is, innovative insight directly answering business and industry pain points.

One of the major blocks of big data is the mining and interpretation of social business data to understand the individual, deepen relationships and connect, and communicate and share information across structured and nonstructured data from a variety of resources. In today's digital age, feedback (positive or negative) on a customer's product is essential information to provide the business with more insight.

- **IoT**

  For organizations across industries, IoT will become one of the biggest, richest sources of data. IoT is also the vehicle for delivering cognitive capabilities in products, services, and processes. Due to security, regulations, cost, or simply speed, a large portion of IoT data processing needs to happen at the edge, where data is created and where human interaction occurs.

  However, IoT presents a data-processing challenge. If we want to accomplish transformational outcomes, we can't continue to ignore IoT data at the network's edge. There is massive opportunity to be had, but IoT also presents a significant data challenge as the scale, complexity, and diversity of IoT data threatens to overwhelm traditional computing systems.

  Traditional programmable systems are designed to handle specific scenarios and data sets. Nevertheless, IoT data doesn't play by traditional rules. Images, videos, sounds, and machine-to-machine data all come together through IoT. All this data is then combined with data sources, such as social media, weather reports, and enterprise data, which provide additional context and relevancy that sharpen the value of insights.

- **Cognitive computing**

  Although big data (particularly its insights into data) is one aspect of technology enablers on the CMO agenda, cognitive computing is another emerging technology. Cognitive computing enables companies to rethink the role of nonhuman channels by allowing all channels to be "human-like" and even tailored to individual customers' desires. For example, cognitive computing can guide people through complex decisions, such as choosing tax-efficient investments or using natural language to learn about and advise a customer, all while considering an exhaustive set of options. For large companies, this can drive significant cost benefits while improving customer satisfaction. The following are possible scenarios and capabilities provided by cognitive computing:

  - Understand unstructured data through sensing and interaction
  - Reason about data by generating hypotheses, considering arguments, and reviewing recommendations
  - Learn from training by experts, from every interaction, and from continually ingesting data
  - Understand, learn from, and reason through data to reshape an organization's industry

Cognitive computing-enabled processes are key to unlocking the value of big data and provide additional information that helps to automate processes or make informed decisions. In analytics, we also see the move from traditional descriptive and diagnostic analytics (describes what happened and why it happened) to predictive analytics (describes what will happen) and cognitive analytics (describes what should be done and how you can make it happen). Cognitive computing can help make sense of the explosion of data created by the Internet of Everything (IoE), meaning that all different information sources, such as devices, sensors, smartphones, and so on, are being considered and used to extract valuable insights.

Digital transformation and the intelligent enterprise have different meanings to different people, but we still see a common agreement that technology is an enabler and a game changer for CEOs. It's clear that, due to the digital transformation, the business model is influenced by technology and has implications for the business strategy. This also makes a change in the influence of the CIO and the CIO's organization, as they must transform from pure service providers to the innovation drivers of a company.

This requires transformation from a reactive mode into a more proactive mode to support an organizational, platform, and skills shift. As the new role of the CIO organization is to envision possible business for the company to lead and extend its current business model by harvesting existing data and providing better customer insights, building the right platform to transform into a customer-centric organization is essential.

Driving Transformation toward an Intelligent Enterprise

Companies need to ask what they need to do, from a business perspective, to drive forward the digital transformation and ensure that there is a real benefit from their investments. In short, companies must ask themselves the following:

- Do we have a clear digital strategy?
- What capabilities are needed based on our digital strategy?
- Where can we boost our existing business model with digital?
- From which industries can we be disrupted? Are there other industries that break into our current business?
- What can we forecast? Are there any trends that could have an implication on our current business?

- Can we adopt from the industry as a fast follower and adopt the first-mover strategy from others?

These are the initial questions businesses need to answer to drive forward their digital transformation with the following objectives:

- Creating value with better customer insight and customer experience based on aggregating different sources of information and tailoring personalized offerings
- Extending the business and getting into new markets by leveraging all channels that are digitally enabled by the newest technologies
- Enhancing current products with digital services or information
- Improving time to market with new products by digitalization and automatization to increase efficiency and effectiveness
- Building up core capabilities on the business and technology levels to support the digital transformation

1.2   Business Value Scenarios

Most of you likely have an existing SAP solution in place and have invested a lot of money to ensure that it fulfills your current requirements. Some of you may be uncertain about the business value and the migration costs that come along with moving to SAP S/4HANA, but there is a huge opportunity to reconsider the current processes with a focus on the digital transformation and the ability to support the future creation of business models. Therefore, it's essential to understand the value SAP S/4HANA brings from a functional perspective, as well as the technical capabilities that must be embedded in your strategy to tailor an individual road map that fits your future business.

Looking at the impact of the digital transformation (see Figure 1.2), you'll see five different layers that need to be supported to achieve the highest transformation toward creating new business models.

How does SAP S/4HANA address those challenges? Platform speed is increased with the migration to SAP HANA as an in-memory database. Speed is also increased by simplifying the data model and reducing the redundant application data. Creating a single data source for end-to-end processes aids in decision-making, and simplified and improved processes are enriched by role-based, user-specific UX.

In addition, having a single data source and the ability to aggregate data on the fly, in combination with the storage of customer behavior from different sources, provides better insight into customer behavior. You can understand what customers may do, what they're doing right now, and what they've done in the past. All this information is available in real time and is part of the future digital platform with SAP C/4HANA. All these capabilities are provided as part of SAP S/4HANA and the supporting line of business (LoB) solutions that are tightly integrated to support the digital value chain.

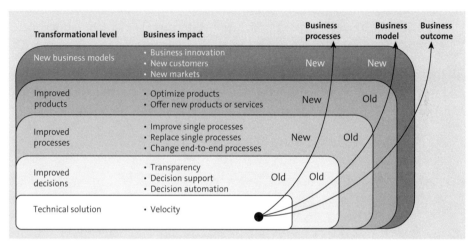

Figure 1.2 Digital Transformation Adoption Model

For the layers shown in Figure 1.2, we'll outline potential use cases to help you understand the value of SAP S/4HANA.

Let's begin with Figure 1.3, which contains a summary of the key innovations available in the current release. As you can see, it's in line with the digital transformation model and is based on the following three main changes:

- **Rearchitecting the in-memory platform**
  This supports the first four layers of the digital transformation model, from the technical solution up to improved products (Section 1.2.2). This is part of the SAP S/4HANA core solution and leverages the simplification of the technical architecture by combining online transaction processing (OLTP) and online analytical processing (OLAP) to drive analytics as part of the transactional processes. As an example, you can look at the decision-support cockpit for material requirements planning (MRP).

- **Responsive UX design**
  This supports improved decisions, processes, and products by providing a single-entry point for all customers and users (Section 1.2.1). It provides the capability to work from any device (e.g., smartphone, smart watch, etc.) and improves the effectiveness of users significantly with the redesign of transactions into user-centric SAP Fiori apps.

- **Unifying functionality in the core**
  This simplifies SAP S/4HANA and follows the principle of one as a key driver for simplification. The elimination of functional, technical, and data redundancies optimizes SAP S/4HANA and avoids complexity (Section 1.3).

All these changes have implications for the innovation capability of SAP S/4HANA and are the foundation for the different scenarios and simplifications in finance and logistics.

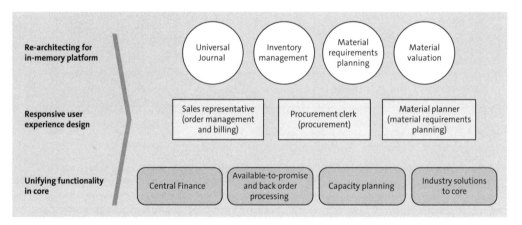

Figure 1.3 Key Innovations for SAP S/4HANA Enterprise Management

---

Note

You can create your own business scenario recommendations report based on your transaction usage. For a guide on how to do this, visit *www.s4hana.com/how-to-guide*. The report provides you with a detailed overview of the recommended business scenario, the relevance for your company based on the analyzed transactions, and the improved or relevant transactions that are affected. For illustrative purposes, a sample of an executive summary is shown in Figure 1.4.

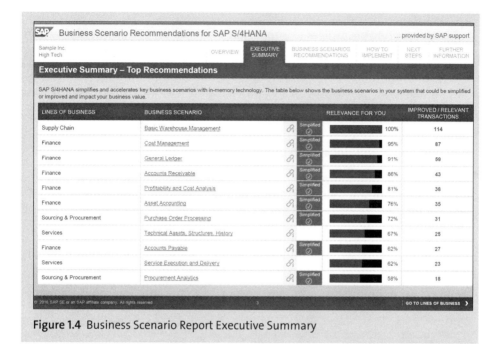

Figure 1.4 Business Scenario Report Executive Summary

Now, let's look at the three main areas in which SAP S/4HANA can add value to your business: through improved customer centricity and experience, increased customer insight and a better decision-making process, and a new digitally enabled supply chain.

1.2.1 Customer Centricity and Experience

As part of the digital transformation, the way users will access ERP solutions is different from the past. Users want access via different devices (e.g., mobile) in a simplified, user-friendly experience. In recent years, there has been a massive change in the behavior of specific target groups, such as Generation Y or Millennials; they're looking for a customized and focused UX that's simple to handle. Based on changing requirements and the future of digitally enabled enterprises, SAP decided to provide customers with a new UX called SAP Fiori. SAP Fiori applies the following new design principles to reimagine the UX:

- **Role-based**
  This design principle focuses on fulfilling individual working requirements.

- **Responsive**
  This design principle focuses on supporting every possible way of working—from desktop to mobile—to be responsive to customer needs.

- **Simple**
  This design principle focuses on only providing the user with what is essential and important.

- **Coherent**
  This design principle focuses on providing a fluid and seamless experience.

- **Delightful**
  This design principle focuses on satisfying users' needs and making an emotional connection.

With usage of SAP Fiori, there is a significant shift from the purely functional view that was available in the old SAP ERP to a role-based UX with a single entry point and a common design in SAP S/4HANA (see Figure 1.5) across business applications, whether cloud or on-premise.

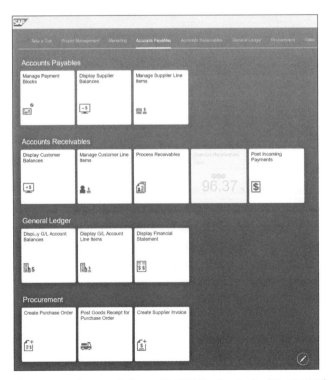

Figure 1.5 Role-Based View with SAP Fiori as Part of the SAP S/4HANA Cloud

From a strategy perspective, all new or existing SAP solutions will use SAP Fiori to harmonize the unified UX for SAP Ariba, SAP SuccessFactors, SAP C/4HANA, SAP Fieldglass, and both SAP S/4HANA and SAP S/4HANA Cloud.

Now, what's the real business value? Aside from the creation of a nice UI, SAP Fiori also affects how people work. This is evident in nonmonetary benefits such as the following:

- **Increased user satisfaction**
  The efficiency and effectiveness of work is increased because all applications can be accessed via a single-entry point with the same look and feel.

- **Increased customer loyalty**
  Using the unified UX (e.g., recruiting or procurement) increases both internal and customer loyalty.

- **Increased solution adoption**
  Reduced maintenance costs and user errors result from increased solution adoption.

Those nonmonetary benefits will lead to significant business results, such as the following:

- Gain productivity through the avoidance of errors, which will help free up additional team members for more productive work
- Save training costs through easier solution adoption, which will reduce the overall change management costs for implementation of new functionality

To give an example from an existing client, one food-delivery business improved its productivity by 60% after adopting the new processes based on SAP Fiori. Another customer eliminated training efforts due to the intuitive SAP Fiori design and the user-specific UI.

> **Note**
> SAP provides a tool to calculate the business value for selected scenarios at *www.sapcampaigns.de/us/UX_Calculator/*.

Based on the design principles described earlier, the changing UX strategy has the goal to support the simplification of the SAP S/4HANA solution, which is why SAP S/4HANA and SAP Fiori are tightly integrated. At present, not all SAP solutions are enabled fully with SAP Fiori, but solution development will continue. More SAP Fiori apps will be available in later releases that will simplify the overall solution. In addition, not all transactions are being replaced with SAP Fiori apps because there will be a move to a more role-based UX, and the processes will be streamlined and condensed to the necessary core functionality.

SAP S/4HANA Cloud is fully based on SAP Fiori, and accessing transactions via the SAP GUI for SaaS solutions isn't possible. Because only SAP Fiori apps can be used, this limits the functionality provided with SAP S/4HANA Cloud. As the product evolves and the simplification process continues, more processes will be supported by SAP Fiori apps. All this effort is based on the desire to reduce the redundancy on any level, ranging from the SAP HANA database up to the SAP Fiori UX.

The simplification process from SAP ERP to SAP S/4HANA doesn't just consist of the new UX design. Based on the simplification of the data model, redesign of the business logic, code pushdown, and role-based tailoring of the solution, there is also a process redesign coming along with the move to SAP S/4HANA.

SAP S/4HANA 1610 first supported 609 SAP Fiori apps, improved to support 890 apps in release 1709, and now supports more than 1,009 apps in release 1809.

If you want to realize the benefits of SAP S/4HANA, you should first look at the roles and the usage of the transactions to get a better understanding of where the best case for simplification or value realization resides. Second, you should look at the currently available SAP Fiori apps and review how they fit into your role requirements and where the gaps are. This will give you a good overview of the functionality your end users need and an understanding of what the current release covers.

> **Note**
>
> Not all users will be SAP Fiori users at the beginning, so you should plan for traditional SAP GUI users or a combination of both user types as well.

To identify currently available SAP Fiori apps, you can browse the SAP Fiori apps reference library (see Figure 1.6) at *https://fioriappslibrary.hana.ondemand.com/sap/fix/externalViewer/#*.

In the SAP Fiori apps reference library, you can select an area of interest to review the related available apps. All apps are assigned to different roles; for example, under **Accounts Payable Accountant**, there are apps available for **Create Manual Payment** and **Create Single Payment** (see Figure 1.7). You can see the details regarding app avail-ability, the required backend product, and any additional documentation. You can also take a detailed look via the list view and select different product suites for a quick glimpse.

If you want a recommendation based on your system usage, you can select this as an option within the library. A detailed guide on running an SAP Fiori relevance and readiness analysis is available at *https://bit.ly/2yRodkS*.

The results of the analysis provide a list of possibly relevant SAP Fiori apps based on your transaction usage, as well as the relevant prerequisites.

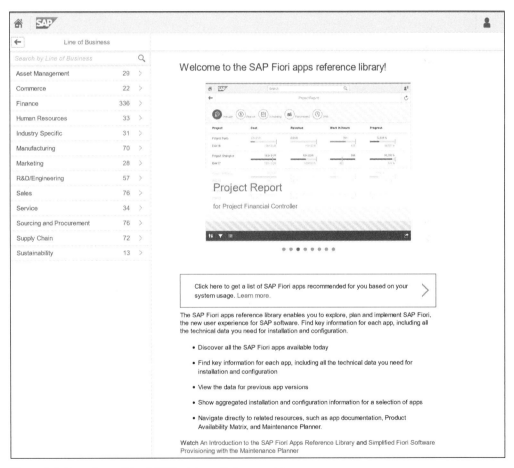

Figure 1.6 Overview of the SAP Fiori Apps Reference Library

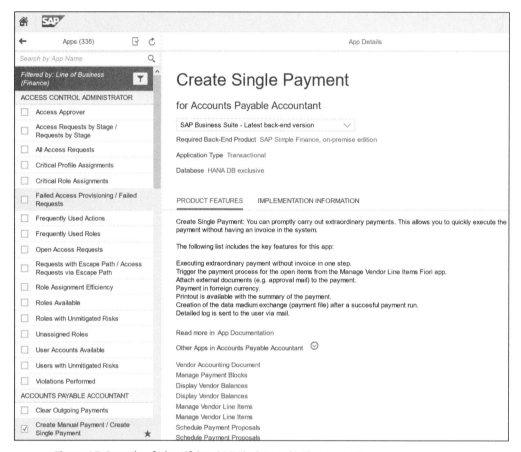

Figure 1.7 Sample of Identifying SAP Fiori Apps in Finance LoB

As a sample for the improved process time via SAP Fiori within SAP S/4HANA, let's look at the finance area to see how SAP S/4HANA Finance has been improved and simplified—in this case, for an account receivables accountant processing incoming payments (see Figure 1.8). Table 1.1 summarizes the differences between SAP GUI and the new SAP Fiori app available via SAP S/4HANA for posting received customer payments and cleared customer invoices. This process was traditionally handled by Transactions F-04, F-28, and FB05.

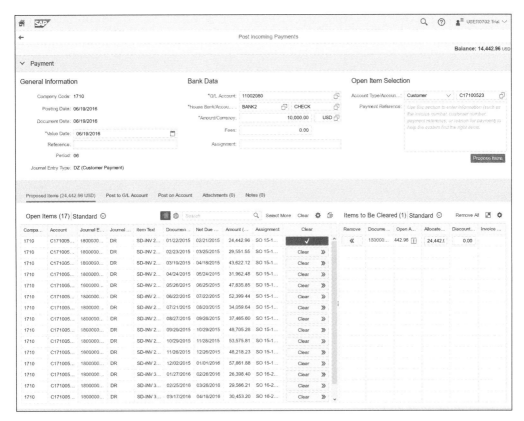

Figure 1.8 Clearing Invoices from Incoming Payments

SAP GUI (Traditional)	SAP Fiori (Simplified)	Improvement
Duration: 1:26 min	Duration: 0:59	31% reduction
Clicks: 27	Clicks: 17	37% reduction
Screen changes: 14	Screen changes: 2	86% reduction
Fields filled: 14	Fields filled: 7	50% reduction

Table 1.1 Comparsion of Activities and Savings between SAP GUI and SAP Fiori

As you can see, there is a significant improvement in running the clearing process via the SAP Fiori app, not only in the total duration but also in the change of screens and the information that needs to be entered manually. This is a simplification example that really demonstrates the value SAP S/4HANA brings with its unified UX.

In short, SAP Fiori isn't just about a nice UI; it's more about redesigning processes from an end-user perspective to be more efficient and to reduce costs. SAP Fiori can provide business value for your organization from a UX perspective, and there are tools available to identify the relevant business scenarios for your organization.

1.2.2   Customer Insight and Improved Decision-Making

As part of the digital transformation, it's not only important to improve the UX, as outlined in the previous section, but it's also become increasingly critical to better understand client behavior so that you can offer a tailored service or product. Therefore, it's essential to collect all necessary data, make the data available in real time, and create actionable results based on the analysis and prediction of data. With the transition to SAP S/4HANA, several changes enable you to provide better customer information and support the decision-making process. Due to the use of an in-memory database, the redesign of the data model, and the data footprint reduction that comes with SAP HANA, it's now possible to provide a single platform across the different solutions with one copy of the data and less integration effort.

SAP S/4HANA is designed to fulfill the end-to-end requirements of a digital value chain. It contains optimized, end-to-end processes that reside on a single data source, with SAP HANA as the digital backbone. It also contains IoT integration via SAP Cloud Platform, which allows companies to get insights and automatically initiate business processes from social media tools, as well as analyze structured and unstructured big data in real time.

This value chain is only possible because SAP S/4HANA also integrates SAP's existing portfolio of LoB cloud solutions, as follows:

- **SAP C/4HANA**
  This unified suite of cloud solutions manages the customer experience based on one trusted customer data model. It combines SAP's front-office cloud solutions with SAP S/4HANA powered by AI.

- **SAP SuccessFactors**
  This is the leading solution for human resource management.

- **SAP Integration Business Planning (SAP IBP)**
  This is SAP's platform for real-time supply chain planning that is built on SAP HANA and fully integrated with SAP S/4HANA.

- **SAP Fieldglass**

  This solution helps manage contingent labor.

- **SAP Ariba**

  This is the indirect material procurement network via which companies trade between each other in a fully digitized way.

- **SAP Concur**

  This business travel and expense management solution provides the best possible experience for the business traveler at the lowest possible cost for the company—and all fully integrated with the transactional system.

This portfolio enables customers to run their entire company digitally in a fully integrated manner. More information on the extended portfolio is provided in Chapter 11, which explains how those solutions fit into the overall strategy of SAP S/4HANA.

The step toward SAP S/4HANA and the plan to integrate all LoB solutions into a single data source combined with the capabilities of an in-memory database enables customers to move from a traditional, separated transactional and analytic data approach toward a unified one (see Figure 1.9). This significantly reduces the delay between the different data sources and enables customers to drive real-time analysis and make decisions on live data. You also can embed analytics as part of transactions to improve the process and provide better information based on real-time data instead of aggregating the data manually and spending additional time and manpower to produce outdated data.

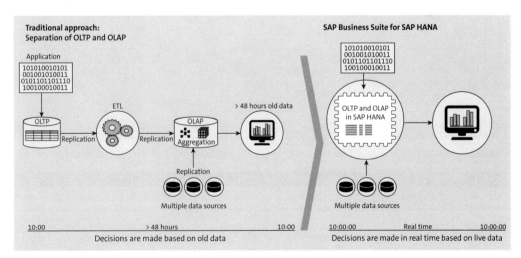

Figure 1.9 Integrating Real-Time Data Access for Improved Decision-Making

As shown in Figure 1.9, SAP S/4HANA provides all capabilities that are required from a digital platform. The redundant data limitation and the complex data models overview are gone, which enables you to conduct ad hoc and real-time analysis without data extraction and data loading.

As a concrete example, let's take a closer look at the work of an accounts receivable manager. If the accounts receivable manager wants to get an overview of the 90 days' receivables they are expecting sorted by the top 10 customers outstanding, they can easily access this information via an SAP Fiori app that provides detailed information for his entire customer base (see Figure 1.10). The reports available via SAP Fiori allow different user groups to get a detailed understanding of the finance data (e.g., auditors can drill down into the details of the overdue receivables and sort them by customer, company code, accounting clerk, etc.).

Figure 1.10 Overdue Accounts Receivables

Using this report, the accounts receivable manager can get a better overview of the top 10 customers and their behavior and then drill down into further details (see Figure 1.11). All this information provides transparency and helps companies improve their decision-making based on real-time financial data combined with on-the-fly reporting capabilities.

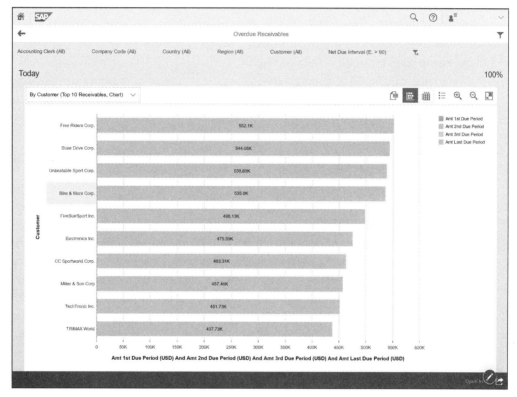

Figure 1.11 Overdue Receivables by Top 10 Customers

This example provides an overview of the key benefits of SAP S/4HANA based on the simplified data model, as listed here:

- **Real-time processing**
  Eliminate batch processing and data reconciliation through a single data pool.

- **Predictions**
  Discover and respond to future opportunities and challenges based on available/historical data.

- **Simulation**
  Simulate possible scenarios and explore the impact of business decisions on outcomes.

- **Responsive**
  Improve user satisfaction by reducing wait time through real-time access to data.

- **Drilldowns**
  Drill down into easy-to-use reports and analyze data at any level without exporting data.

- **Recommendations**
  Provide rule-based and instantaneous decision support that guides the user and text mining, and embed structured and unstructured data in one business process to ensure innovative business processes and business decisions.

1.2.3 Digitally Enabled Supply Chain

Section 1.2.1 showed how users are being empowered with people-centric UIs, and Section 1.2.2 showed how the simplification of a single data model with no redundant data is supported by SAP S/4HANA. Let's now look at the third piece of the puzzle: how logistics is changing due to the market trends that are driven through the digital transformation and how SAP S/4HANA addresses those topics. Although there are no changes to the processes themselves, there is a significant change in the way processes are executed more efficiently, as was shown earlier in Table 1.1. In logistics, the digital transformation has brought about significant changes; for example, consumers expect their orders to be fulfilled and shipped on the same day, so they can receive their product on the next day.

Another example is IoT and the collection of big data via sensors or other devices, which has huge implications for how companies monitor their supply chains. The rapid growth of collaborative networks is removing borders between suppliers and consumers, which has a big impact on how processes can be executed and improved.

The current SAP ERP system serves as a classical system of record to store your transactional data. The business user goes through different transactions for transparency into demand shortages, analyzes various reports, adds intelligence to the information, and then either prioritizes production or transfers goods from one plant to another to avoid shortages. With SAP S/4HANA, the business user gets away from the traditional system of record and leverages the core capabilities of the platform, such as IoT or business network connectivity, to obtain more detailed information and advanced analytical options that help him do his work more effectively.

To give a concrete example of the business value SAP S/4HANA provides in the logistics area, let's look at inventory management. The challenge of inventory management is to provide customers with the right products at the right time while simultaneously reducing storage and saving costs. In the past, to achieve transparency, you had to execute the backflush process (determining the number of parts that must be subtracted from the inventory) once a day, which led to inaccurate inventory in the system. With customers now expecting individualized and on-demand products and services, it's not feasible to work with outdated data that gives limited transparency into the available inventory, as this will lead to supply shortages and unsatisfied customers.

Most businesses are requiring real-time data in the entire supply chain to minimize the stock in warehouses and thus reduce total costs. With older ERP solutions, separate data is loaded from several sources, which takes too much time. Therefore, a simplified data model is needed to avoid redundant data and enable on-the-fly analysis to provide a detailed look inside the inventory and minimize the risk of deviations between physical inventory and virtual inventory. This is where SAP S/4HANA comes in.

Figure 1.12 illustrates the following classic inventory management process flow:

1. At 6:00 a.m., the stock is automatically entered via barcodes.
2. During the day, the inventory manager checks the virtual inventory available in his system. In this example, he checks the inventory at two-hour intervals, at 8:00 a.m., 10:00 a.m., and 12:00 p.m.
3. At 2:00 p.m., the stock is automatically entered via barcodes.
4. At the same time (2:00 p.m.), the inventory manager checks the virtual inventory again and gets a first view of the real values after the actualization of the information. This leads to a large deviation between the virtual and the real stock through, for example, production quality issues.

In this example, we have a high deviation between virtual and actual stock. To compensate for this difference and to prevent the production chain from stopping due to lack of parts, you must have safety stocks (see Figure 1.13). Safety stock is expensive because it requires additional costs (e.g., handling costs, space costs, etc.) on top of the stock itself. Therefore, it's essential to minimize safety stock.

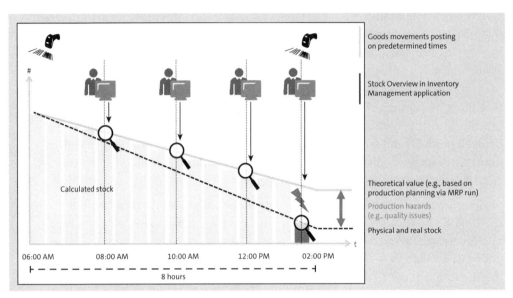

Figure 1.12 Classical Inventory Tracking

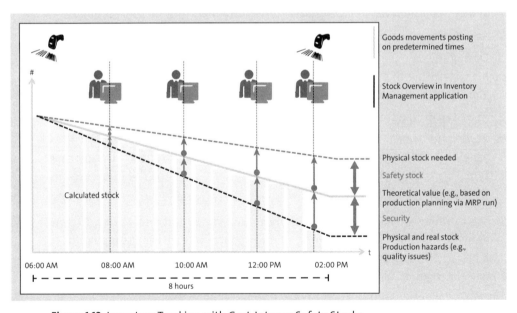

Figure 1.13 Inventory Tracking with Cost-Intense Safety Stocks

To avoid these deviations and to reduce the amount of safety stock, SAP S/4HANA enables you to reduce the difference between the theoretical and the real stock value. As shown in Figure 1.14, real-time inventory tracking allows you to enter values of stock in real time, so you can anticipate actions to compensate for the risks of production and reduce your safety stock.

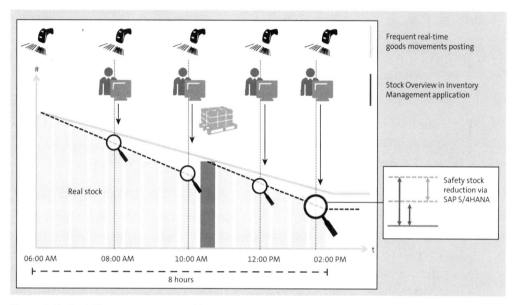

Figure 1.14 Real-Time Inventory Tracking

The foundation of this SAP S/4HANA simplification is the elimination of aggregates. In SAP ERP, the Materials Management (MM) inventory functionality is stored in table MKPF (header table) and table MSEG (line item table), with an additional 18 tables for quantities and values. Out of those tables, 11 aggregate tables have additional shadow tables for historical data (see Figure 1.15). All these tables are required to support reports such as report MB5B or report MMBE, among others. This all results in a great deal of redundant data, which was necessary before the possibilities of in-memory technology. With SAP S/4HANA, a new data model has been built that leverages the advantages of the in-memory columnar storage.

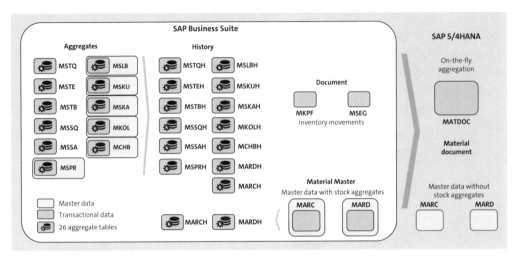

Figure 1.15 Inventory Management Changes from SAP ERP to SAP S/4HANA

With SAP S/4HANA, the single table MATDOC contains all the information formerly stored in all those various tables, which eliminates redundancy and provides you with better performance. Now that the aggregate tables have been replaced with Core Data Services (CDS) views, both on-the-fly calculations and compatibility with custom developments are supported. With these changes, SAP S/4HANA provides real-time processing of inventory postings and visibility of inventory values, so you can reduce your safety stock and manage smaller lot sizes moving through logistics operations—all leading to an overall cost reduction in your inventory.

Another example of optimization is found in the accelerated MRP available with SAP S/4HANA. As you can see in Figure 1.16, there is a huge simplification between the SAP ERP system and SAP S/4HANA. With SAP S/4HANA, you can now access your key performance indicators (KPIs) in real time. Due to increased transparency, there is a significant decrease in the amount of inventory you must keep on hand, which in turn results in cost savings.

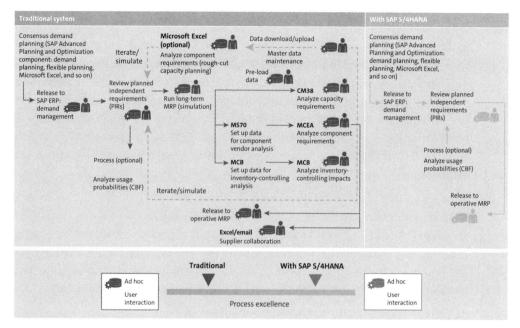

Figure 1.16 Accelerated Material Requirements Planning

A comparison between SAP ERP and accelerated MRP in SAP S/4HANA is shown in Table 1.2.

Traditional SAP ERP	SAP S/4HANA
No real-time planning due to elapsed time	Real-time system with KPIs instantly refreshed
Decisions based on "old" data, resulting in lower quality	Segment of one that reduces lot sizes down to single items
Lower forecast accuracy and attainment of promise date; increase in inventory	■ Focus on exception handling rather than standard processes ■ Inventory decrease with reliable ATP check

Table 1.2 Accelerated MRP Comparison between SAP ERP and SAP S/4HANA

1.3   Architecture at a Glance

In this section, we'll provide a first glance at the architecture concept of SAP S/4HANA to build a basic understanding that we'll build on in Chapter 12. As mentioned previously, the goal of SAP S/4HANA is the principle of one, which means the removal of redundant frameworks, technologies, data models, and application data. The guideline for a digital transformation platform is to focus on the essential and to reduce all overhead while leveraging the best technical possibilities to achieve a highly flexible solution for the digital era. To achieve this, we must take a closer look at the SAP architecture.

Within SAP, processes and features belong to a software component. All the relevant software components required for an SAP ERP 6.0 EHP 8 on-premise system are shown in Figure 1.17. As you can see, a lot of separate software components reflect the functionality available in the current release. The idea of components is to have the smallest possible unit that can be maintained separately to reduce maintenance and increase the ability to update smaller pieces of the overall solution separately.

As you can imagine, there are interdependencies between the different components that need to be considered; this adds additional complexity to the overall solution and its development. One of the goals of SAP S/4HANA is to remove these dependencies to come to one component with one deployment option.

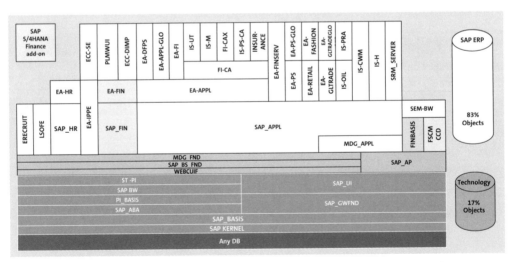

Figure 1.17 Overview of Software Components for SAP ERP 6.0 EHP 7 On-Premise

To follow the principle of simplification with SAP S/4HANA, the components that aren't essential need to be removed or merged, as shown in Figure 1.18.

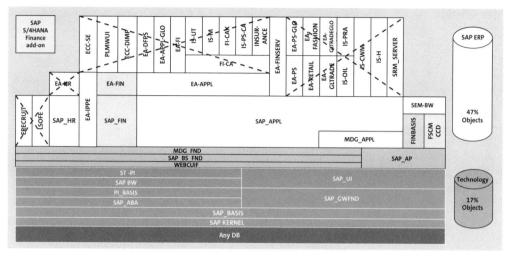

Figure 1.18 Reduced Objects Not Relevant for SAP S/4HANA Core Solution

SAP S/4HANA focuses on providing a baseline functionality around the areas of materials management (MM), sales and distribution (SD), customer services (CS), finance (FI), and controlling (CO). This leads to the simplified SAP S/4HANA core, which includes the baseline functionality. All other software components are removed to streamline the solution, as shown in Figure 1.19.

As you can see, SAP S/4HANA is built similarly to SAP ERP 6.0 EHP 8, but it's on a different code base. Both the original and the new code lines form the base for the different options illustrated later in Figure 1.21. This leads to some differences in the available functionality, as we'll discuss later in this section.

Now, we'll illustrate the high-level runtime architecture of SAP S/4HANA in Figure 1.20. On the highest level, technology stacks are illustrated with the incorporated technologies. At the top, the SAP Fiori shell layer represents all available technologies for users to work with, ranging from the Web GUI for SAP to SAP Fiori apps. Below that, you'll see SAP Gateway as an embedded component for the SAP S/4HANA ABAP stack for the cloud. For an on-premise SAP S/4HANA deployment, a separate UI front-end server is recommended.

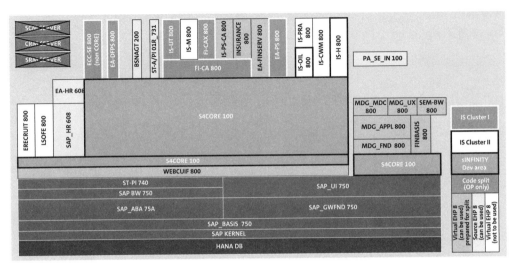

Figure 1.19 Software Components of SAP S/4HANA

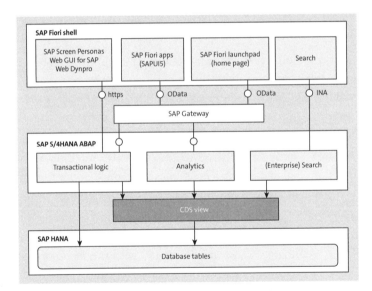

Figure 1.20 High-Level SAP S/4HANA Runtime Architecture

In the second layer, the SAP S/4HANA layer, you'll see two different options to consume SAP S/4HANA tables:

- Direct consumption via business logic inside transactional logic
- ABAP CDS views

CDS views are used to reduce the application logic and push down the code from ABAP into SAP HANA.

Based on the principle of one, several simplifications have been achieved, as follows:

- Simplifications of the data models for finance and inventory management
- Unification with Discrete Industry Mill Products (DIMPs) back to the SAP S/4HANA core application layer
- Simplification of long material number (LAMA) extending from 18 to 40 characters
- General deprecation process of around 70,000 main repository objects—for example:
  - Deprecation of Foreign Trade (SD-FT)
  - Remaining Beverage Solution (SD-SLS-PLL)
- One business partner via the customer vendor integration (CVI) as a single point of entry to create, edit, and display master data for business partners, customers, and vendors
- One single valuation via the Material Ledger (ML; no moving average price on table MBEW)
- One analytics approach:
  - Avoid embedded SAP Business Warehouse (SAP BW) based on redundant data
  - Avoid Logistics Information System (LIS)

> **Note**
>
> Further information on the top simplifications can be found on the SAP Community Network (*http://scn.sap.com/docs/DOC-70833*) and will be updated frequently.

As you can see in Figure 1.21, there are two different developments with separate code lines that supply the different product lines. Currently, classic SAP ERP can run on any database, including SAP HANA, and that supports the current functionality with some smaller functional enhancements and stabilization. As a second option, you can have classic SAP Business Suite on SAP HANA and activate the SAP S/4HANA Finance add-on. However, this is no longer recommended by SAP because SAP S/4HANA Finance 1605 is on support pack release only. No additional functional enhancement will occur. SAP S/4HANA is a flagship product that includes both finance and logistics functionalities and is the recommended target architecture. As the last piece of the product line, you can see SAP S/4HANA Cloud, which is recommended for companies with about 1,500 employees. It can also be used as a two-tier ERP product for larger corporations for their subsidiaries.

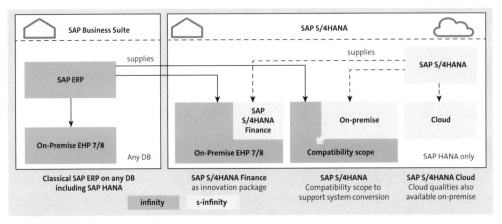

Figure 1.21 Overview of SAP Product Lines and Versions

SAP currently has a "cloud-first" strategy; because cloud solutions can be innovated and delivered faster, new functionality is usually available first in the cloud and then for the on-premise deployment options. To get a sneak peek at the next available functionality for your on-premise implementation, you can rely on the functionality provided with SAP S/4HANA Cloud. As shown in Figure 1.22, SAP S/4HANA is on a yearly cycle for new functionality, whereas SAP S/4HANA Cloud is on a quarterly cycle.

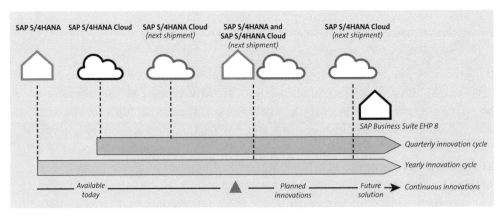

Figure 1.22 Release Cycle for SAP S/4HANA and SAP S/4HANA Cloud

1.4 Deployment Options

This section introduces the SAP S/4HANA deployment options—on-premise, public cloud, and single tenant (i.e., private) cloud—and outlines their relative merits and demerits to help you choose the right deployment model and the right cloud/cloud service providers. Currently there are two main solution options:

- On-premise SAP S/4HANA
- SAP S/4HANA Cloud

For both SAP S/4HANA and SAP S/4 HANA Cloud, there are various options to deploy the solution. To choose the SAP S/4 HANA version and deployment that is best for your organization, it's important to know about these options so you can optimize the overall IT landscape, minimize the initial costs of the SAP S/4HANA deployment, and have a balanced cost structure throughout the lifecycle of the landscape.

You have three main options for deployment: SAP S/4HANA, SAP S/4HANA Cloud, and a hybrid of the two, which can contain a two-tiered ERP model. In the following sections, we'll provide criteria for choosing among your different deployment options.

1.4.1 On-Premise

SAP S/4HANA contains the entire SAP ERP scope with simplifications in several core areas. When we talk about the entire SAP ERP core, there are some differences from the SAP ERP solution, which are highlighted in the simplification lists for every release. There may be some functions that are completely deprecated and have no substitute solutions, or there may be substitute solutions outside the core of SAP S/4HANA. The details for these functions are provided in the simplification list for each version of SAP S/4HANA released. Several additional functionalities have been incorporated into the SAP S/4HANA core, including the industry solutions and the major parts of the LoB solutions, such as SAP Extended Warehouse Management (SAP EWM) or SAP Transportation Management (SAP TM) (discussed in Chapter 4). For SAP S/4HANA, the release cycle for new functionality is annual and can be deployed on-premise or in the cloud with the IaaS model.

Your first decision is to choose the right SAP S/4HANA product version: SAP S/4HANA or SAP S/4HANA Cloud. When making this decision, you should consider the following primary aspects:

- **Licensing model**
  SAP S/4HANA follows the traditional licensing model. For SAP S/4HANA Cloud, the pricing follows subscription-based licensing, per the SaaS model.

- **Range of functionality**
  So far, on-premise SAP S/4HANA has the complete set of functions from SAP Business Suite/SAP ERP; however, they don't all use simplified code or the SAP Fiori frontend (refer to the simplification list for deviations from SAP ERP functions). SAP S/4HANA Cloud supports core functionality, including finance, manufacturing, professional services, sales, sourcing and procurement, supply chain, R&D engineering, HR, and asset management. (The scope of functions for SAP S/4HANA Cloud will be enhanced on a quarterly basis, and documentation of the SAP S/4HANA Cloud 1808 release is available at *https://bit.ly/2JFKG8i*.)

  Therefore, a customer who needs the full-blown SAP ERP functionality beyond what's provided by SAP S/4HANA Cloud needs to opt for the on-premise version or wait for SAP S/4HANA Cloud to reach a state at which it can cater to these functionalities. In fact, some major clients with significant SAP footprints are waiting for this to happen so they can adopt SAP S/4HANA Cloud.

- **Standardization versus flexibility**
  SAP S/4HANA provides complete flexibility to perform any customization to the standard solution as required by the customer's business processes. SAP S/4HANA Cloud, on the other hand, provides limited capability for customization. Thus, SAP S/4HANA Cloud is suited to those organizations that have the strategy to adopt standardized processes. They can adhere to the functionalities provided by SAP S/4HANA Cloud.

- **IT strategy in terms of usage of SaaS**
  The IT strategy for some major organizations is to adopt a SaaS model for all their IT solutions, even their ERP solutions. This might potentially drive them to adopt SAP S/4HANA, as long as it has the functionality they need.

- **Infrastructure and operations**
  For SAP S/4HANA, the client has complete control of the infrastructure, deployment, and maintenance schedule. For SAP S/4HANA Cloud, SAP provides the system and any service-level agreements for the nonfunctional requirements. SAP also must test the delta functions every quarter for a fixed number of days before updates are applied. Thus, the customer has no control over accepting version

upgrades. This has some advantage in terms of reduced maintenance, but companies must plan for the resources and effort needed for this continuous testing every quarter.

- **Implementation approach and timelines**
  The implementation for SAP S/4HANA Cloud is much faster due to the standardized process configurations, which include SAP Best Practices for implementation. Both new and existing SAP ERP customers only need to perform data migration, which is aided by migration tools and templates for different data objects. Deep technical skills aren't needed. For the on-premise implementation—both for the migration scenario and the new implementation scenario—technical knowledge and skills are mandatory for the team because there will be customer-specific scenarios and considerable customization. The timelines for the SAP S/4HANA adoption are also longer.

- **Costs**
  Costs are affected by several factors, including the reduced implementation timelines. However, because SAP S/4HANA Cloud is a SaaS model, the product licensing costs and the infrastructure and operational costs decrease. Because SAP S/4HANA Cloud has fewer customization capabilities, it also has the advantage of less maintenance overhead. Apart from the licensing model, the infrastructure investment and maintenance overhead can also be tackled through an IaaS adopted for SAP S/4HANA.

There can be certain constraints in terms of SAP S/4HANA Cloud adoption as well—for example:

- Regulatory compliance might compel the data to be on-premise, or the data might not be able to be taken outside the country, requiring in-country hosting of the data center.

- Organizations might have security concerns about the data being in the cloud, in the public domain, beyond the organization's firewall.

- The size of the database may be too large for the currently available cloud options for SAP HANA.

The second concern is gradually changing due to the knowledge that there are certain precautionary steps the customer should take and, of course, that cloud providers must follow standard security processes to be certified for productive usage by customers. Beyond the standard security features related to user authorization and authentication, data security and privacy controls in SAP products are available irrespective of being on-premise or in the cloud. From a physical security perspective, SAP data centers comply with the latest telecommunications industry standards, such as ANSI/TIA/EIA-942 Tier III or higher.

A summary of the service options is shown in Table 1.3.

	IaaS	PaaS	SaaS
Applications	N/A	N/A	X
Operating system and middleware runtime	N/A	X	X
Server, storage, and network	X	X	X
Service model	Computing resources available at lowest infrastructure component level	Application deployed on managed services	Consumed by end user, delivered through the Internet
Control over cloud service	<ul><li>Control over application, operating system, and updates</li><li>Limited control over network</li><li>No control over underlying physical infrastructure</li></ul>	<ul><li>Control over application deployed</li><li>Control over application-specific configuration on hosting environment</li><li>No control over underlying infrastructure</li></ul>	<ul><li>Limited user-specific configuration and customization</li><li>No control over software release and update</li><li>No control over underlying platform and infrastructure</li></ul>

Table 1.3 SaaS, PaaS, and IaaS Options Summary

After choosing the relevant product version, there are more decisions to be made. The on-premise version can be deployed in the cloud or on-premise, with options for multiple deployment models (the following terms will be explained in greater detail in Chapter 12):

- **Multiple Components on One System (MCOS)**
  In the same SAP HANA server, multiple SAP HANA databases along with the system identifier (SID) can be configured (e.g., development and quality environments).

- **Multiple Components in One Database (MCOD)**
  Multiple SAP components run on the same SAP HANA database.

- **SAP HANA Multitenant Database Containers (MDCs)**
  Multiple tenant databases are isolated in the same SAP HANA system.

- **Virtualization using smaller virtual machines (VMs)**
  Smaller VMs are used within the SAP HANA system, or logical partitioning is used.

Figure 1.23 shows the decision tree for choosing an SAP S/4HANA deployment.

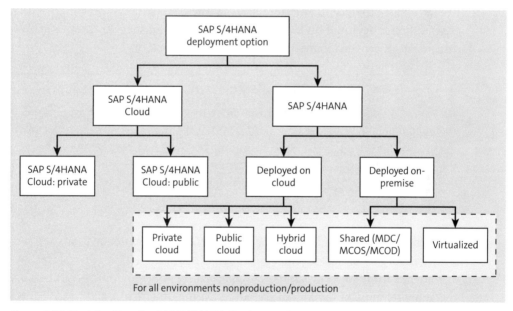

Figure 1.23 Decision Tree for SAP S/4HANA Deployment

There can even be a combination or a stacking option for these deployment models. Some options are provided by the specific hardware, including the processor. For example, IBM Power Systems machines with their proprietary processors can provide an MDC on top of a VM.

The customer's SAP HANA-related existing infrastructure setup, the database size requirements, and the nonfunctional requirements all affect the choice of deployment models for SAP S/4HANA. For example, your choice may be influenced by the following:

- If there are other applications that use the SAP HANA database, you might look at combining and sharing infrastructure to minimize costs.
- If the database size is too large, then the resource sharing options won't work out, at least for the productive environment. You might look at sharing the nonproductive environments, using one of the available options (e.g., MDC/MCOD/ MCOS) and virtualization or a combination of these options. The restrictions for such deployment options must be adhered to, which we'll discuss in Chapter 12. For example, there are products that can be deployed as MCOD for production per the whitelist provided in SAP Note 1661202. These restrictions don't apply if each application is deployed on its own tenant database, but they do apply to deployments inside a given tenant database (in an MDC scenario).

> **Note**
>
> There are additional SAP Notes for the different deployment scenarios (e.g., SAP Notes 2096000, 1681092, 2248291, and 2423367). SAP Note 2426339 (Support for SAP HANA 2 in SAP S/4HANA) is another important SAP Note, and the SAP HANA Master Guide (*http://help.sap.com/hana/SAP_HANA_Master_Guide_en.pdf*) should be referenced when deciding on the right deployment option for a combination of applications.

The deployment option can also be chosen based on SAP recommendations and considerations for the advantages and disadvantages of a given option. For example, SAP recommends using MDC for all the MCOS scenarios it fits and for MCOD because MDC supports most of the MCOD scenarios. On the other hand, all the SAP HANA applications deployed using MDC will share the same SAP HANA database. As a result, any SAP HANA database upgrade will impact all the applications at the same time. In addition, the high availability/disaster recovery (HA/DR) configuration will impact all tenant databases because they're part of the same SAP HANA database.

With SAP HANA 2.0, using MDCs will be the only operational mode for SAP HANA systems, so you'll no longer be able to operate a single-container system. Refer to SAP

Note 2423367 (Multitenant Database Containers Will Become the Standard and Only Operation Mode) for more information.

As another example, SAP supports multiple SAP HANA databases on the same system (the MCOS scenario), even for the production environment, but only for scale-up or single-host scenarios. For this option, sizing must be performed carefully, and proper volume testing is important before going live because contention for the system resources by the different components using the same system may lead to poor performance in production (see SAP Note 1681092). Your choice may also be influenced by the following:

- The underlying infrastructure from existing vendors and the scalability options for that hardware make a difference. Depending on the maximum available size, the workload can be virtualized to enable proper resource sharing.
- Nonfunctional requirements play an important role in the choice of deployment model—for example:
  - Responsiveness: This may determine whether any cloud deployment is an option for the productive environment. For high responsiveness, on-premise is the preferred option.
  - HA/DR time objective/recovery point objective: Certain options are better from a HA requirement point of view. If cloud providers can't cater to availability— say, more than 99.5%—or if such service-level agreements (SLAs) could have a high cost impact, then having the system on-premise might be the best choice. Another example of a cost-optimized HA option occurs when the system on which the secondary server is running can be shared with the nonproductive instances.
  - Disaster recovery: Having the DR set up in the cloud while the workload runs on-premise is a cost-effective option. Alternatively, your cloud partner should be able to provide and maintain a DR solution if the actual solution is also hosted on cloud.

For an organization that wants to use IaaS for the on-premise deployment of SAP S/4HANA, there are several options along with the management functions on top of these infrastructure services. The cloud vendors normally offer unmanaged IaaS, managed IaaS, or managed PaaS. The different types of services are shown in Figure 1.24.

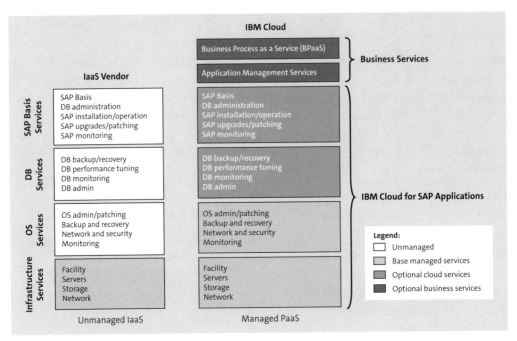

Figure 1.24 Service Options for IaaS and PaaS: Managed and Unmanaged

1.4.2   SAP S/4HANA Cloud

SAP S/4HANA Cloud uses an SaaS model and is maintained and operated by SAP in SAP's infrastructure. SAP S/4HANA Cloud is again available in two flavors: public and single tenant (private).

SAP S/4HANA Cloud, public option, has limited flexibility in terms of customization. It doesn't allow modification of standard objects but allows limited extension. SAP S/4HANA Cloud, single-tenant edition (otherwise known as the private option), allows a similar level of modification but more flexibility in terms of usage. For example, for the public version, the processes are only accessible through SAP Fiori apps. Thus, the challenge lies in the fact that functionalities available on simplified code without an SAP Fiori app won't be available on the public cloud. However, for the single-tenant version of the same product, these other processes are accessible through the SAP GUI.

For more details about the latest releases and the major processes available in SAP S/4HANA Cloud, see Chapter 10.

> **Note**
>
> More details about the features of each release can be found at *http://help.sap.com/s4hana*.

Before we discuss the single-tenant cloud and public cloud options in detail, let's first look at some items you should consider before deciding if your landscape and your business are ready for SAP S/4HANA Cloud.

Initial Considerations

You may start by asking yourself the following questions:

- Are all types of workload cloud-ready?
- How do we analyze the workload to check for cloud readiness?

There are methods to analyze the workload that cloud providers such as IBM or Microsoft can use to help organizations determine the feasibility. Some examples of the workload traits that determine their readiness for cloud adoption are listed in Table 1.4.

Not Ready for Cloud	Possibly Ready for Cloud	Ready for Cloud
■ Sensitive data ■ High degree of customization ■ Not virtualized software ■ Complex processes and transactions ■ Regulatory constraints ■ Complex software licensing ■ Tight integration with other on-premise systems	■ Information-intensive ■ Isolated workloads ■ Mature workloads ■ Nonproduction systems ■ Batch processing	■ Analytics ■ Infrastructure storage ■ Industry applications ■ Disaster recovery ■ Development, test, and training environments ■ Infrastructure compute ■ Business processes (e.g., CRM, HR, etc.) ■ Industry-vertical application ■ Web-hosted apps ■ Collaboration ■ Office applications

Table 1.4 Workload Cloud Readiness Analysis Sample

What about cloud adoption for SAP ERP, which is for many organizations the core transactional system supporting mission-critical business processes? Enterprise software such as SAP ERP is often at the core of the organization's business processes, and, today, SAP S/4HANA forms the digital core of the organization. Although these solutions don't see the type of seasonal variability experienced by other solutions, such as e-commerce sites, there are still demands for periodic scalability (e.g., testing environment for a project duration). Many other business drivers also hold true for these ERP solutions. There are some additional factors (see Figure 1.25) that show how the standard nondifferentiating processes can be moved to the cloud while differentiating solutions requiring heavy customization stay on-premise or in a single-tenant cloud. The other influencing factor is the regulatory compliance applicable for the organization, including country-specific rules.

The trend shows quite a move toward a hybrid adoption pattern for solutions such as SAP ERP. Before we discuss the hybrid model, however, we need to look at both the single-tenant cloud and the public cloud.

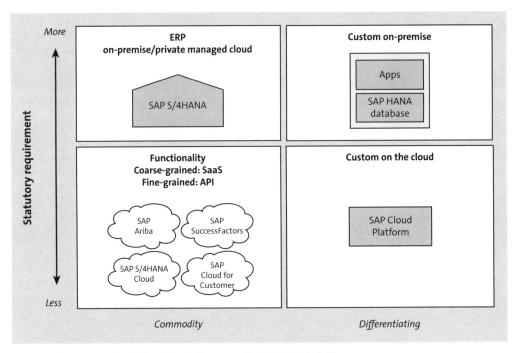

Figure 1.25 Cloud Decision Influencers for SAP ERP Solutions

Private Cloud

The advantages of private cloud deployment are as follows:

- The same level of security is used as for on-premise deployments because the environment is set up only for one customer and isn't shared.
- An initial investment is required to build the infrastructure, but the advantage is in the ability to effectively use that infrastructure (e.g., rapid provisioning, etc.) and reuse existing hardware.
- This is an especially good option for an IT landscape that has several systems and requires high-volume transactions with close integration with other systems.
- A few partners, such as IBM and HP, offer services to build a private cloud environment.

From an SAP S/4HANA perspective, this is just different model, but the same rules apply as for on-premise. In addition, the private cloud needs to use SAP-supported hardware and supported virtualization techniques.

Public Cloud

The advantages of a public cloud deployment are as follows:

- Cost savings is one of the major advantages for the public cloud option. There's no need to invest in infrastructure, and no up-front initial investment for capital expenditure (capex) is required; instead, it's a pay-for-usage model.
- This is a good model for all customers (even startups or individuals) unless there are other concerns or constraints, as mentioned earlier.
- Many public cloud offerings are available for SAP S/4HANA from SAP, as well as from partners such as IBM, Amazon Web Services (AWS), and Microsoft Azure.

From the SAP S/4HANA point of view, the cloud service needs to have official support status from SAP. From an overall perspective, however, the management requirement for the cloud infrastructure, the customer's responsibility, and the cloud vendor's responsibility should be clearly determined.

1.4.3 Hybrid Model

As mentioned earlier, not all workloads are the right fit for the cloud. Often, organizations must take a middle path and choose a hybrid model to optimize the cost and time benefits versus other considerations. In addition, though an organization can have a road map in place to move all applications to the cloud, this can be a multiyear journey.

For SAP S/4HANA, some organizations want to have nonproduction applications in the cloud but production on-premise. Some others want SAP BW on the SAP HANA system in the cloud but want SAP S/4HANA either on-premise or in a private cloud because critical business processes may have responsiveness requirements that need a data center in a physically closer location or may require a high-bandwidth connectivity. This will have a cost implication and may act as a deterrent to be in the cloud. Figure 1.26 shows examples of the different scenarios in which the environments of an SAP solution can be deployed all on-premise, in the cloud, or using a hybrid model.

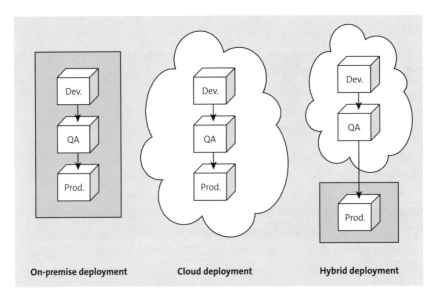

Figure 1.26 Hybrid Cloud Scenario Example

There can be several other use cases for hybrid cloud scenarios. The following list is a representative set and not exhaustive:

- Legacy and new landscapes are integrated.
- Systems of engagement are located in the cloud, while the system of record remains on-premise—for example, SAP Fiori or SAP Gateway on SAP Cloud Platform, which connects to a backend on-premise SAP S/4HANA.

- The variable load is offloaded—for example, a testing server or an upgrade project requiring a parallel landscape in the cloud.

- For an IT landscape with multiple SAP instances, the smaller instances (which should be closer to standard SAP solutions) can move to SAP S/4HANA Cloud, while larger ones with more customization can be on-premise. There can be several such combinations of the two-tier ERP landscape, including the possibility to combine SAP S/4HANA solutions and non-SAP HANA or non-SAP ERP solutions.

1.5   Cloud Vendor

The IT division of an organization adopting SAP S/4HANA needs to have an overall understanding of its business requirements. This understanding will lead to choosing the type of cloud adoption (private, public, or hybrid with cloud and on-premise) and the SAP HANA-based products that need to be deployed together with SAP S/4HANA, now or in the near future. These decisions will give the IT department an idea of what to look for in a cloud vendor. A single service provider might offer a business-centric SLA that is flexible, simple, and cost-effective, with an ability to respond to growth opportunities. Some of the major factors that must be kept in mind while choosing a cloud vendor are as follows:

- **Security, privacy, and compliance**
  Infrastructure should meet industry compliance standards, such as ISO 20000, 270001, and 9001; TIA Tier III; SOC1 (SSAE-16); and PCI DSS. You should feel confident that you can trust a cloud provider with your data.

- **Global presence**
  Look for data centers and network points of presence (POPs) for the cloud vendor across the globe for full control over data sovereignty and to minimize latency.

- **Scalability**
  Aim for a more scalable environment designed specifically for enterprise use with the ability to help better secure client-customized images and instances. The provider should have a robust portfolio of time-tested, enterprise-class solutions, including software, hardware, and services.

- **Reliability and high availability**
  Infrastructure should have redundancy and reliability built in, meaning that you're protected from the most common causes of application outage.

- **Support and service**
  You should find out what support and services are offered before selecting a vendor. If you need extra support and services from vendors to ensure your enterprise technology solutions run well, this should be taken into consideration.

- **Cost-effective**
  Cloud services (e.g., operating expenses [opex]) make infrastructure costs more predictable and offer organizations better cost control. Look for cost-effective, always-on instances, with the flexibility to spin up more as and when needed.

- **Thought leadership**
  The cloud vendor should architect and provide offerings based on IT Infrastructure Library (ITIL) best practices and industry-leading migration services to facilitate client transformation to the cloud. The vendor should have expertise in and best practices for managing and operating security-rich enterprise data centers around the world.

There are some additional aspects that can be considered as well. Accelerators will help provide required instances faster. For example, SAP HANA Enterprise Cloud, SAP's private cloud solution, has APIs and other integration adapters that help connect with on-premise SAP systems. SAP also has System Landscape Optimization (SLO) services for data migration to the cloud.

IBM has startup bundles/packages for SAP S/4HANA that enable clients to quickly get SAP HANA proof-of-concept (POC) and test environments up and running in the IBM Cloud. The POC instance can be set up quickly, in as little as three days. SAP also provides POC environments on SAP's public cloud for an SAP S/4HANA trial or demo through the SAP Cloud Appliance Library (*https://cal.sap.com/*).

1.6   Integration

The IT landscape with SAP HANA is typically a hybrid, with some components in the cloud, possibly some cloud-based SaaS solutions, and some on-premise components. There might be different deployment options for the different environments as well. Business processes can run between the SAP S/4HANA core and other solutions, including SaaS-based SAP solutions, such as SAP SuccessFactors, or SAP C/4HANA and SAP Ariba.

Thus, one of the challenges in this kind of environment is the integration aspect. Depending on the use case, multiple integration technology requirements might be in use. The different integration scenarios in a typical hybrid cloud landscape are shown in Figure 1.27.

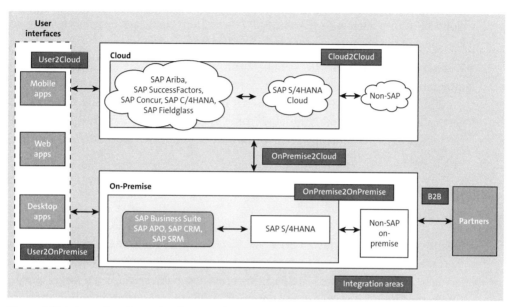

Figure 1.27 Integration Scenarios for SAP S/4HANA

For SAP S/4HANA Cloud, the required customer integration scenarios are deployed, configured, and activated in the cloud instances provisioned by SAP, or SAP provides self-configuration UIs so that customers can configure the solution. The content is integrated with SAP cloud solutions such as SAP SuccessFactors Employee Central, SAP Ariba, SAP Marketing Cloud, SAP Jam, and SAP Multi-Bank Connectivity, as well as third-party integration with Vertex for tax calculation. If there is a requirement to build new integration scenarios, SAP Cloud Platform provides the extension platform for SAP S/4HANA, in which new integration capabilities can be created using whitelisted APIs.

SAP S/4HANA hosted on-premise or on a cloud platform such as the SAP HANA Enterprise Cloud can be integrated with SAP's cloud solutions through standard integration content delivered by SAP either through SAP Process Orchestration or SAP Cloud Platform Integration. SAP Cloud Platform Integration is SAP's cloud integration middleware and is a SaaS product. Any other integration tool provided by a third party can also be used if it has the right kind of connectors for on-premise-to-cloud and cloud-to-cloud integration. For example, Dell Boomi can connect to several SaaS products, such as SAP SuccessFactors or Salesforce. Prior to SAP S/4HANA 1511, the integration components required for the SAP S/4HANA system had to be installed as add-ons. By 1709, SAP S/4HANA included native integration components for most cloud solutions, such as SAP Ariba, SAP Concur, SAP Fieldglass, SAP SuccessFactors, and most of the products under the SAP C/4HANA suite brand.

Web services or OData services enabled through SAP Gateway can also be used for integration. Some of the integration can use REST API calls from SAP S/4HANA to cloud solutions such as SAP Concur so that both getting data from that solution and getting it into the solution is initiated from SAP S/4HANA. For data movements, SAP Data Services, SAP Landscape Transformation, or SAP HANA smart data integration can be used.

1.7   Summary

In this chapter, we provided a brief overview of the digital transformation and the next maturity level moving toward the intelligent enterprise. We also explained the changes and implications on this transformation path because it's important to understand both where to act and how fast to act, which is reflected within the pace layered model.

We explained the key principles of customer centricity and experience, with SAP Fiori as the leading UX for SAP S/4HANA, as well as their possible benefits. We offered a brief overview of how SAP S/4HANA helps you achieve better customer insight and provides improved decision-making capabilities based on the SAP HANA platform. Along with the previous information, we discussed business value scenarios and the digitally enabled supply chain as part of SAP S/4HANA.

We illustrated a high-level overview of the SAP S/4HANA architecture and the principles behind SAP S/4HANA, as well as the simplifications that have been achieved from technical and functional perspectives, all to build a solid foundation for the following chapters.

We covered the different deployment options of SAP S/4HANA on-premise or in a private cloud and SAP S/4HANA Cloud, public option. When deciding on a flavor of SAP S/4HANA, especially for cloud deployment, you must keep in mind how it relates to the greater scheme of the IT landscape and IT strategy, as well as how it relates to the other SAP HANA products already in the landscape or in the adoption road map.

Migration services to facilitate client movement to the cloud also need to be considered to migrate current landscapes seamlessly in the cloud space. There are many variables to consider when choosing the right deployment strategy, but ideally this decision should be looked at from both a business perspective and an IT perspective to achieve immediate and long-term business goals.

In the next chapter, we'll move on to our first functional topic of focus: finance.

Chapter 2
Finance

The key features of SAP S/4HANA Finance address pain points identified by the various IBM CFO surveys held over the years, which is helpful input to fuel the business case for SAP S/4HANA Finance.

SAP S/4HANA Finance follows SAP's simplification strategy. The introduction of the SAP HANA database, which enabled real-time data, made it possible to rethink how to run financial processes. SAP S/4HANA Finance was the first area in which SAP offered these new functionalities, which we'll describe in this chapter in more detail.

In the following sections, we'll provide insight into the seven key pain points chief financial officers (CFOs) are experiencing and show how SAP S/4HANA Finance addresses these, which should help build the business case for implementing SAP S/4HANA Finance.

Furthermore, we'll talk in more detail about SAP S/4HANA Finance functionalities such as the Universal Journal, the Material Ledger (ML), some improved functionalities in asset accounting (AA), Cash Management, SAP Business Planning and Consolidation (SAP BPC) for SAP S/4HANA Finance, group reporting, profitability analysis (CO-PA), Central Finance, and the month-end close process. We conclude this chapter with a look at SAP S/4HANA Cloud's finance capabilities, and an assessment of the maturity of SAP S/4HANA Finance, its business case, and its outlook.

2.1 Industry Pain Points and SAP S/4HANA Benefits

In this section, we'll look at seven key pain points identified for which SAP S/4HANA Finance can provide relief, contributing value to your organization:

1. Driving integration of information across the enterprise effectively
2. Driving enterprise cost reductions
3. Measuring/monitoring business performance

4. Optimizing planning, budgeting, and forecasting

5. Executing continuous finance process improvements

6. Providing inputs for an enterprise strategy

7. Developing talent in the finance organization

Let's now explore these seven areas in more detail.

2.1.1   Integration of Information

Driving integration of information across the enterprise means that you have the governance in place to ensure common business processes and data definitions in your enterprise. You have all that information technically captured in one place—to use SAP's phrase, a *single source of truth*. This single place in your system environment can satisfy all your financial information needs and serves as the single source for all your interfaces as well. Many organizations are struggling with this; their finance departments can't reach their full potential because they can't provide required business insights.

Having only the technical ability for a single source of truth isn't sufficient, but from an organizational perspective, it's very important that the right governance structure is in place as well. To get to a single source of truth, an organization must have a clear idea of its financial reporting requirements. The organization must also have governance structures in place, such as business process ownership and business data ownership, to guarantee harmonized business processes and ensure that data is defined and captured in a common and consistent way across all business units. When the organization has all that governance in place, it then makes sense to have the technology as well to realize a single source of truth for finance via SAP's Universal Journal in the application landscape.

SAP ERP struggles in this area. Its financial capabilities contain multiple ledgers, such as the General Ledger (G/L), cost center ledger, profit center ledger, Material Ledger (ML), and the Profitability Analysis (CO-PA) ledger (see Figure 2.1). Due to all these different sources of financial information, reconciliation activities are required to make sure all the ledgers are synchronized.

With the introduction of SAP S/4HANA Finance, there is now just one ledger called the *Universal Journal* (captured in table ACDOCA), in which all details for actual postings can be found. Additional journals, such as the consolidation journal (table ACDOCC) and planning journal (table ACDOCP), caan be used to support, for example, consolidation and planning requirements.

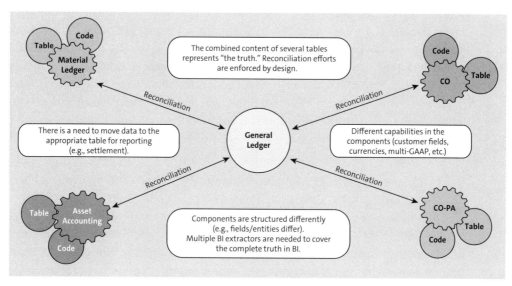

Figure 2.1 Challenge of SAP ERP Architecture: Various Ledgers

Consequently, you no longer have to consider where to report or interface your financial data from. The SAP S/4HANA Finance journals contain this disparate data, as shown in Figure 2.2.

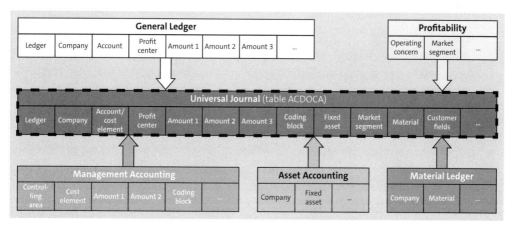

Figure 2.2 SAP S/4HANA Journals: Combining Information from Multiple Ledgers into Several Source Tables

2.1.2 Enterprise Cost Reductions

SAP S/4HANA's capability for in-memory processing using columnar databases shortens processing time significantly and eliminates the need for running processes in batches. Processes that you would normally run at period-end due to long running times can now be run on a daily or weekly basis. Because it contains all the actual data, the Universal Journal removes the need to reconcile SAP ERP Financials (FI) and Controlling (CO) data and provides you with visibility into, for example, work in progress (WIP) in real time. These abilities enable a *soft close*, meaning that you no longer need to wait to analyze your data after month-end close activities; you can analyze the data daily to steer the business. No reconciliation efforts are required because you're reporting from one single source of truth.

Due to the speed of SAP S/4HANA processing and the shift toward soft closes, a lower head count is required in the closing process. Capacity requirements are now more equally spread over the month rather than increasing dramatically at the end of the month. SAP S/4HANA Finance gives you access to very detailed data in real time, which helps you spot out-of-line situations immediately, minimizing costs of failure. Prompt remedial action is now possible, without waiting until the data is available after month-end. Reporting is simplified, fast, and multidimensional, making drill-down reports almost redundant. You no longer need to run operational reporting in a separate SAP Business Warehouse (SAP BW) environment, which has a positive impact on the speed of turning data into information and thus on the operating costs.

2.1.3 Measuring Business Performance

SAP S/4HANA provides better insight during the posting period because you'll have easy access to real-time profitability on a granular level. Because the introduction of the Universal Journal simplifies data structures, you can perform end-to-end analysis and define new responsibilities in many areas, including the following:

- **Predicting the future**
  You can simulate the impact of different business models on your profitability. With a single source of truth in place and SAP S/4HANA's speed, you can connect your data with external sources to anticipate the future.

- **Managing receivables**
  Having access to real-time data allows the sales and accounts receivable departments to work more closely together. Collection tasks are moved from back-office teams to sales representatives.

A sales manager with access to real-time open item data any place, anytime on his mobile device via SAP Fiori apps can discuss out-of-line situations more efficiently with customers and can document agreed-upon actions immediately. In addition, this information is visible to the accounts receivable department. SAP Fiori delivers a role-based, consumer-grade user experience (UX) across all lines of business, tasks, and devices and is the new way of accessing SAP S/4HANA information and executing your SAP transactions.

For a good example of how SAP Fiori can be used, consider the Process Receivables transactional app (shown in Figure 2.3). Using this app, you can access a list of receivables payable by an individual customer. You can then create promises to pay and dispute cases. You start the app either by entering a customer number directly or by searching for a customer.

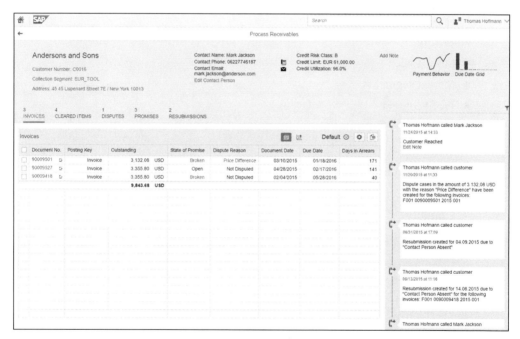

Figure 2.3 Cash Management with SAP Fiori Apps

SAP S/4HANA Finance allows you to have real-time access to your cash position. There is no data latency, meaning cash managers can perform their tasks on the real cash situation. Cash Management provides you with the following in real time:

- Financial statements
- Actual cash flow analysis
- Liquidity forecast

2.1.4   Optimize Planning, Budgeting, and Forecasting

With the introduction of SAP BPC for SAP S/4HANA Finance, a new, more user-friendly planning process is supported. SAP ERP provided different planning solutions for Cost Center Accounting, Profit Center Accounting, Internal Orders, and CO-PA. Reconciliation of all these solutions could cause problems and delays. SAP BPC for SAP S/4HANA Finance provides a single tool to plan the following elements:

- Profit and loss
- Revenue
- Pricing
- Cost of sales
- Market segments
- Profit centers
- Cost centers
- Activity cost
- Internal orders
- Projects
- Liquidity

Because all this planning data will be stored in a single data structure, reconciliations are no longer needed. Another benefit is that you can apply the same validations to the planning data, and that reporting will have the same look and feel. In fact, SAP created a single source of truth for financial planning data in table ACDOCP (Plan Data Line Items). Plan data isn't part of the Universal Journal as it contains actual data only. You still need to read two different tables if you want to run a plan/actual comparison report.

2.1.5   Continuous Finance Process Improvements

SAP S/4HANA is about not only the speed of the database but also the value SAP S/4HANA technology will bring to finance activities in general. SAP S/4HANA Finance allows you to run your processes faster, which enables faster planning, reactions, reporting, and analysis.

As stated in Section 2.1.3, SAP S/4HANA enables continuous insight into your financial figures; it allows you to shift from month-end activities to weekly or daily activities. Because actual FI and CO data live in a single table (ACDOCA), you can run, for example, your legal reporting and customer and market view reporting without needing to reconcile these reports. Using this single table also allows you to combine information from various areas into one report—for example, spend analysis by responsibility and profit and loss (P&L) by market segment, along with other dimensions, such as customer and material group or WIP analysis by relevant production order and cost center. SAP S/4HANA Finance extends the reporting and analysis capabilities that were previously only possible via SAP BW reporting.

SAP S/4HANA Finance provides new functionality as well, such as intercompany reconciliation, which is a great improvement in the financial close process. Intercompany reconciliation detects intercompany mismatches at an early stage, allowing you to have them corrected before the month-end close. It also performs the following tasks:

- Improves and accelerates automated matching
- Eliminates batch jobs (real-time analysis supports continuous intra-period process execution)
- Improves UX and enhances data drilldown to reduce the reconciliation effort
- Provides better process oversight via a new intercompany reconciliation dashboard

SAP also provides a very user-friendly goods receipt/invoice receipt (GR/IR) monitor that shows the goods receipt for which no invoice has been posted and vice versa.

SAP S/4HANA Finance also comes with the SAP Financial Closing cockpit for SAP S/4HANA, which allows you to centrally monitor and control closing tasks; enables automation of some manual steps, transactions, programs, jobs, workflows, and remote tasks; and allows owners to collaborate effectively during the closing process. It also offers best practices closing templates to streamline the closing process and supports audits by recording the output and history of all tasks performed and who performed them.

2.1.6   Provide Inputs to Enterprise Strategy

Today, companies are expected to produce more predictable financial results, eliminate surprises, and respond to market changes with more agility. To meet these expectations, finance functions must forecast with more precision, reduce cycle times associated with budgeting and investment, and shift from a retrospective statutory reporting view to one that is more forward-looking. Therefore, it's vital to be able to link your company's key performance indicators (KPIs) with your strategic objectives and to have a system in place that can show whether you're still on the right track and provide you the information to get on track again if necessary.

SAP S/4HANA Finance offers SAP BPC for SAP S/4HANA Finance, as well as the ability to integrate both operational/nonfinancial and financial information in a cohesive manner and to optimize the planning, budgeting, and forecasting processes. It also works with advanced analytics tools such as SAP HANA Live and SAP Crystal Reports, which are available to build real-time dashboards (which we'll discuss further in Chapter 8 on reporting and analytics).

It's important to drive integration of information across the enterprise via a robust infrastructure with common standards, data definitions, finance processes, and planning platforms. In other words, you should strive to implement a single source of truth for the financials processes.

However, successful finance organizations go a step further by integrating their organizations' strategic, operational, and financial planning to impact the overall business performance. SAP S/4HANA Finance can play a crucial role here, and the newly introduced Universal Journal is key to that goal.

Because you have easy and real-time access to your internal data via SAP S/4HANA Finance's Universal Journal, you can use this as a basis for simulating the impact on the business performance of potential new offerings by using SAP's advanced analytic tools, such as SAP Predictive Analytics. SAP Predictive Analytics also allows you to evaluate opportunities for stimulating your organic growth or the potential for mergers and acquisitions.

SAP Predictive Analytics can provide organizations with the ability to anticipate and shape their business, their customer relationships, competitive forces, and operational aspects. It enhances organizational performance by applying advanced mathematical modeling, deep computing, simulation, data analytics, and optimization techniques by using analytical engines, data mining, and statistical models that address specific business process areas. SAP S/4HANA Finance brings greater speed and agility to decision-making, with clear links to target performance outcomes, more reliable and accurate financial reporting, and greater visibility into the levers that drive performance. By combining your own internal data organized in SAP S/4HANA Finance's Universal Journal with external data sources, such as industry trends and the nature of the competition, you can better determine the most promising opportunities.

2.1.7   Develop Talent in the Finance Organization

Considerable skills are required to benefit from SAP S/4HANA's real-time data provision and to operate sophisticated analytical tools such as SAP Predictive Analytics. SAP S/4HANA Finance can help assess and improve business performance only with these sophisticated business analytics and the talent to interpret and use cross-functional information. However, acquiring the right technological and business know-how is only one of the issues CFOs must handle; many CFOs are preoccupied with more immediate challenges, such as whether their own finance teams are ready to weather the storm. Table 2.1 lists some finance workforce challenges and the opportunities available to address them.

Workforce Challenge	Workforce Opportunity
Finance skills are focused on transaction processing.	Transform competencies into more value-added activities to support the evolving role of finance.
Qualified professionals are wasting effort on activities that add less value.	Refine the skill mix to focus professionals on driving business value and innovation.
Data analysis is performed by management.	Develop junior employees in decision support.
The finance team is globally distributed.	Enable global collaboration.
Shared services expansion or relocation eliminates local roles.	Educate and redeploy top talent into retained organization roles.
The implementation of SAP ERP systems eliminates roles.	Expand transformation to train and educate top talent to develop value-adding capabilities.

Table 2.1 Finance Workforce Challenges and Opportunities

Workforce Challenge	Workforce Opportunity
Employee turnover is high.	Grow organically by defining new career paths.
Linear traditional career paths are eroding.	Chart multidimensional career paths to develop the leaders of tomorrow.
Employee development is informal.	Align learning and development programs to support the CFO agenda and future job roles.

Table 2.1 Finance Workforce Challenges and Opportunities (Cont.)

With new technology and new processes in place when using SAP S/4HANA Finance, training is typically restricted to how to use the tool to continue to perform jobs as before the SAP ERP implementation—essentially focusing on efficiency versus effectiveness. You should go beyond how to use the tool or module; for example, help develop critical thinking skills so that employees can leverage the tools to perform value-added analysis.

2.2   Key Functionalities

In this section, we'll introduce the most important functionalities of SAP S/4HANA Finance. Some of these, such as SAP BPC for SAP S/4HANA Finance and the Universal Journal, have already been part of our discussion but will be fleshed out in detail. We'll also discuss the ML, the new AA, Cash Management, group reporting, CO-PA, Central Finance, and the soft-close process enabled by SAP S/4HANA Finance.

2.2.1   Universal Journal

As stated in earlier sections, one of the key features of SAP S/4HANA Finance is the availability of a single source of truth for finance via the Universal Journal, captured in table ACDOCA. This table provides the following:

- One common view of financial and operational data is provided to help ensure enterprise-wide consistency and reduce reconciliation time and errors.
- Real-time data is available across all financial dimensions.

- A single line-item table contains full details for all applications for instant insight and extensibility.

- Data is stored only once, with no reconciliation needed by design.

- Fast multidimensional reporting is available without replicating data to SAP BW.

- If SAP BW is already in place, only one extractor is needed instead of many for financial data.

- From the ABAP program perspective, read access remains the same.

- SAP-provided compatibility views redirect the program to the new format in SAP HANA.

The power of the Universal Journal is that financial data that was spread over multiple tables in previous versions of SAP is now stored in a single table. Information from FI, CO, AA, ML, and account-based CO-PA is combined in a single entry in table ACDOCA to provide the benefits outlined in the preceding list. Keep in mind that costing-based CO-PA and special-purpose ledger tables aren't part of the Universal Journal table. It makes a lot of sense to explore the possibilities of account-based CO-PA before activating costing-based CO-PA and to prevent the use of special-purpose ledgers because both will jeopardize the single source of truth concept.

Furthermore, as discussed in Section 2.1.1, you can only benefit from a Universal Journal when your organization has a clear idea of its financial reporting requirements. You must also have the governance in place to guarantee harmonized business processes and to guarantee that data is defined and captured in a common and consistent way across all business units. You can only take full advantage of SAP S/4HANA Finance when you have a single source of truth for finance, that is, a single place in your system environment in which all data elements required for any financial reporting are defined in a consistent way.

The *coding block* can help determine what information needs to be managed. A coding block is used to document all reporting requirements for an organization, and it serves as the basis for setting up the design of the Universal Journal in SAP S/4HANA Finance. A coding block consists of business measures, represented by rows, and business dimensions, represented by columns, as shown in Figure 2.4. Measures are normally represented by the chart of accounts in your SAP system, and the dimensions are represented by posting details such as material, customer, channel, and so on. It's essential to understand that not all measures need to be recorded; for example, gross profit is a measure that is calculated based on the revenue and cost of goods sold (COGS) elements. The same applies for the measures as well. Not all dimensionality is required in the initial recording. Some dimensions can be derived based on the recorded elements later (e.g., by an allocation).

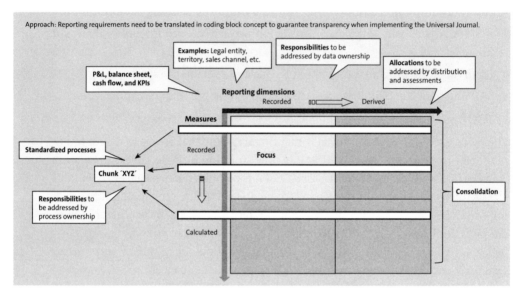

Figure 2.4 Coding Block Approach

All reporting requirements need to be broken down to fit this concept. All definitions should be in business terminology and not be linked to any system. For an example of a coding block, see Figure 2.5.

In Figure 2.5, the business measures and the related business dimensions are depicted clearly. For example, the **Land and buildings** account requires the following four business dimensions: **Legal entity**, **OpCO** (operating company), **RepCO** (reporting company), and **General Ledger account**.

After you have a coding block, you can use it to design how to depict your data in SAP. As stated earlier, a coding block consists of business measures (rows) and business dimensions (columns).

Measures are split into measures to be recorded and measures to be calculated. Measures to be recorded are normally represented by the chart of accounts in SAP. Measures to be calculated are a computation of the measures that are recorded (e.g., gross profit).

Account	Description	Movement specifications	Chunk ID	Chunk	Glossary ID	Legal entity	OpCO	RepCO	General Ledger account	Material (master)	Material group (e.g., brand, COGS type)
									DD	DD	DD
A10100	Land and buildings	M_PPE	130	ASSETS		x	x	x	x		
A10200	Plant and equipment	M_PPE	171	ASSETS		x	x	x	x		
A10700	Other operating assets	M_PPE	163	ASSETS		x	x	x	x		
A10800	Not employed in business operations	M_PPE	151	ASSETS		x	x	x	x		
A10000	Property plant and equipment		176								
A20910	Trademarks, patents, and licenses	M_INT	211	ASSETS		x	x	x	x		
A20920	Software	M_INT	189	ASSETS		x	x	x	x		
A20930	Internal developed intangible assets	M_INT	122	ASSETS		x	x	x	x		
A20980	Intangible intercompany assets	M_IGW	119	ASSETS		x	x	x	x		
A20990	Miscellaneous intangible assets	M_INT	144	ASSETS		x	x	x	x		
A20900	Other intangible assets	M_INT	158								
A20100	Goodwill	M_INT	112	ASSETS		x	x	x	x		
A20000	Intangible assets	M_INT	118								
A30910	Non-current derivative assets		146	OTHER ASSETS		x	x	x	x		
A30920	Securities		185	OTHER ASSETS		x	x	x	x		
A30990	Miscellaneous financial assets		143	OTHER ASSETS		x	x	x	x		
A30900	Other non-current financial assets		162								
A30200	Pension assets		168	OTHER ASSETS		x	x	x	x		
A30300	Deferred tax assets	M_TAX	95	OTHER ASSETS		x	x	x	x		
A30400	Investments in subsidiaries	M_INV	126	OTHER ASSETS		x	x	x	x		
A30600	Investments in associates	M_INV / ASS	125	OTHER ASSETS		x	x	x	x		
A30700	Loans to group companies	M_NON	134	OTHER ASSETS		x	x	x	x		
A30800	Non-current receivables		150	OTHER ASSETS		x	x	x	x		

Figure 2.5 Coding Block Example

Dimensions are split as well into dimensions to be recorded and dimensions to be derived. Dimensions to be recorded need to be supplied by the business transaction at recording time. For example, if we state that the revenue measure should contain customer and material as dimensions, a business transaction that triggers a revenue line should support it. If we also state that revenue should have channel as a dimension as well, and it can't be recorded at inception time, then we need an allocation to get revenue at the required level of reporting via an allocation.

Dimensions can be represented by SAP's organizational structural elements (e.g., company codes, profit centers, and functional area segments) or by master data elements—in many cases, as CO-PA dimensions. By plotting SAP solutions in the coding block, you can see exactly which SAP elements will be used for representing each part of the coding block, which should clearly indicate the requirements for any business transaction feeding the coding block.

In summary, the coding block will do the following:

- Provide a road map for how to depict real-life organizational structures as SAP ERP organizational structural elements.

- Determine what can be reported where (in which SAP module).

- Ensure consistency in mapping business requirements that relate to organizational structure elements.

If you have all that preparatory work in place, then it makes sense to use technology such as the Universal Journal in SAP S/4HANA to realize a single source of truth for finance in your application landscape.

Keep in mind that the introduction of the Universal Journal doesn't necessarily mean that the SAP modules needed for depicting your financial organization will change. You'll still set up AA, cost centers, profit centers, ML, and CO-PA—but you'll probably switch to account-based CO-PA, which under SAP S/4HANA is similar to costing-based CO-PA and is incorporated into the Universal Journal. The benefit of the Universal Journal is that it combines all the information stored in those various ledgers in the past into a single ledger entry. In addition, by combining FI and CO information in one table, there's no longer a need for cost elements. In SAP S/4HANA Finance, primary cost elements are replaced by G/L accounts. To support secondary cost elements as well, the G/L master record is extended by a special attribute indicating a secondary cost element.

In some SAP S/4HANA releases, the Universal Journal had some release restrictions regarding currencies and transfer pricing. As of SAP S/4HANA Finance 1605 and SAP S/4HANA 1610, in addition to the local and global currency, the Universal Journal supports eight freely definable currencies per ledger.

As of SAP S/4HANA 1709, full support for up to three parallel currencies is available in controlling (CO). This enables the ability to implement parallel currencies and valuations in CO and takes away the existing release restrictions for on-premise deployments of SAP S/4HANA Finance.

Furthermore, there are two options available for storing multiple valuations in FI. One is an approach in which every valuation is stored in a separate ledger—a parallel single-valuation ledger—so that there is a clear separation of posts and reports on a specific valuation (see Figure 2.6).

Ledger	Company	CURTP (local)	CURTP (global)	CURTP1	CURTP2	
0L	1000	10	30			Legal view
GR	1000	11	31			Group view
PC	1000	12	32			Profit center view

Figure 2.6 Currency Support in SAP S/4HANA Enterprise Management (Parallel Single Valuation)

In the other, multiple valuations are stored in a single ledger—the multivaluation ledger—as shown in Figure 2.7.

Ledger	Company	CURTP (local)	CURTP (global)	CURTP1	CURTP2	CURTP3	CURTP4
GL	1000	10	30	11	31	12	32

           Legal view   Group view   Profit center view

Figure 2.7 Currency Support in SAP S/4HANA Enterprise Management (Multivaluation)

These currency and ledger functionalities are part of SAP S/4HANA as of release 1503.

2.2.2   Material Ledger and Transfer Pricing

ML functionality has been present in SAP ERP for a long time as part of Product Costing (CO-PC). ML allows you to perform the following tasks in the system:

- **Parallel currencies**
  Without ML, stock values are stored in the system only in one currency. If you need to get stock reports in another currency, conversion is performed using the reporting date exchange rate. ML lets you valuate goods movements using the historical exchange rates. In SAP ERP, up to three parallel currencies can be defined in ML. The parallel currencies feature is required for stock valuation in countries with highly fluctuated local currency or in industries with standard currency stock units.

- **Parallel valuations**
  In addition to parallel currencies, the ML can maintain several valuations. These valuations can depict stock values from different views (legal, group, profit center), and values in each valuation can differ by addition or exclusion of certain values. This feature allows you to analyze stock values simultaneously from different perspectives. It's used by global companies to gain visibility into stocks from the following different perspectives:
  - Legal valuation (statutory and/or tax)
  - Corporate group valuation
  - Individual company segments/organizational units valuation (profit centers)

  In total, only three combinations of parallel currencies/parallel valuations can be defined in SAP ERP.

- **Periodic actual cost**
  During period-end, valuation of all goods movements is performed with the preliminary valuation price, which is normally the standard price for produced goods and the standard or moving average price for purchased materials. ML adds a feature to calculate periodic actual cost. In this case, all variances from the preliminary valuation of materials are collected in the ML. At period-end, revaluation of ending inventory and consumption can be performed with the determined actual price. Revaluation is possible using different rules for different valuations.

ML functionality used to be an optional feature in SAP ERP and was activated in the system only if one or several of the previously mentioned features were required. In this case, one or several ML features were activated with the respective configuration and process adjustments, which led to a vast number of different approaches to ML usage.

Because ML was an optional component in SAP ERP, it used a fully separate set of tables to store data. This led to two historical disadvantages of the ML:

- A need to reconcile values between ML and other functional components (most notably FI and Materials Management [MM])
- The absence of a comprehensive reporting tool for different material valuations because data was distributed among FI tables, MM tables, and ML tables

In SAP S/4HANA Finance, on the other hand, the goal is to have a single source of truth for the data with the ability to drill down to the required level of detail when needed. To achieve this goal, the table setup must be clear and simple, without data duplication and distribution. The historical ML setup didn't match the new concept because it was a rather complex separate module with its own tables. Therefore, SAP S/4HANA Finance introduced a single common solution for material valuation. This solution consists of mandatory ML functional components combined with architectural changes.

With mandatory usage of ML, it's no longer necessary to store values in inventory-valuation tables (e.g., tables EBEW, EBEWH, MBEW, MBEWH, OBEW, OBEWH, QBEW, QBEWH) in the table xBEW(H) namespace. Therefore, in SAP S/4HANA Finance, these tables are no longer updated to store transactional figures and only contain material master data attributes, leading to higher data integrity and higher throughput.

Contents of ML tables MLIT, MLPP, MLPPF, MLCR, MLCRF, MLCD, CKMI1, and BSIM are now stored in table ACDOCA. For materials that aren't relevant for actual costing, ML tables

MLHD, MLIT, MLPP, MLCR, and MLCD are no longer updated; instead, values are updated in table ACDOCA. For materials that are relevant for actual costing, tables MLHD, MLIT, MLPP, MLCR, and MLCD are updated (see Figure 2.8). To get the full picture of material valuation for both types of materials, compatibility views are used, which read from both tables.

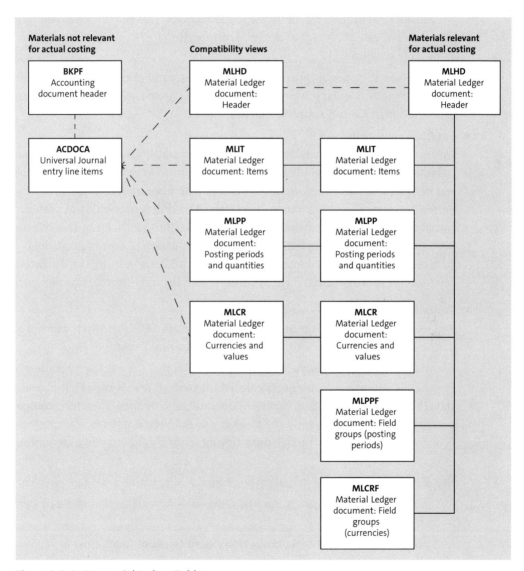

Figure 2.8 SAP Material Ledger Tables

The main ML features are updated and work in the following way in SAP S/4HANA Finance:

- **Parallel currencies**

  In SAP S/4HANA Finance, a single-currency setup must be used across all finance functionalities: FI, CO, and ML. This single-currency setup is defined once and used in the Universal Journal for all financial transactions. This provides a single view into material valuation and uses common reporting tools that are linked to the same table structures.

  As of release 1610 SP 01, previous limitations of parallel currencies in ML are excluded totally. Similar business functionality for up to three parallel currencies can be set up in ML and always reconciled with FI.

- **Parallel valuations**

  Due to changes in finance table architecture, the parallel valuation approach was redesigned in SAP S/4HANA Finance. The first solution to cover parallel valuation was delivered as part of release 1605 together with a solution to store additional currencies. A more stable solution that covered the full functionality available in standard SAP ERP was delivered as part of release 1610 SP 01. From this release, both transfer prices functionality and multiple valuation of cost of goods manu-factured (COGM) can be supported in the ML. This allows you to calculate actual product cost based on different accounting principles and internal requirements.

- **Periodic actual cost**

  Periodic actual cost is an optional feature of the ML in SAP S/4HANA Finance that can be used if the requirement to calculate periodic actual cost is in place.

  The main concern many have about using the ML is that the closing schedule will be complicated due to actual cost calculation steps. If actual costing isn't used, then the ML has no impact on closing or operational processes. Therefore, compa-nies not using the ML currently and that have no requirement to calculate periodic actual cost won't need to update their closing schedules and modify accounting policies.

  SAP also simplified the ML actual costing functionality in SAP S/4HANA Finance:

  - The number of ML closing steps was reduced as several sequential steps were combined into one.
  - A new Material Ledger cockpit was introduced to simplify ML closing process-ing.

2.2.3   New Asset Accounting

SAP released the new AA for the first time in SAP ERP 6.0 EHP 7. However, to use the new AA in SAP S/4HANA, the following business functions are required:

- ENTERPRISE_EXTENSIONS – EA-FIN
- ENTERPRISE_BUSINESS_FUNCTIONS – FIN_AA_PARALLEL_VAL

In SAP S/4HANA Finance, new AA is mandatory. There is no option to use the classic FI-AA functionality, and migration steps are incorporated into the SAP S/4HANA Finance migration. Data from classic FI-AA tables ANEK, ANEP, ANEA, ANLP, and ANLC is now stored in table ACDOCA, which means AA is fully integrated in the Universal Journal so there are no longer any redundant data store or reconciliation issues.

The main shift in SAP S/4HANA Finance is to move from batch processing to online processing. The goal is to perform as many process steps as possible not during the closing but during the period (this is a *soft close* process, which is discussed in more detail in Section 2.2.9). In the new AA, this is achieved to some extent with a new configuration setup for depreciation areas. In SAP S/4HANA Finance, it's not only the leading depreciation area that posts its values to the G/L online but also other depreciation areas. The leading valuation can be recorded in any depreciation area. It's no longer necessary to use depreciation area 01 for this. The system now posts both the actual values of the leading valuation and the values of parallel valuation in real time. The posting of delta values has been replaced; as a result, the delta depreciation areas are no longer required. This feature eliminates reconciliation issues between fixed assets and the G/L and increases transparency between depreciation areas and accounting principles. Several other improvements have been made as well:

- The need for a separate balance carryforward program for assets is eliminated because the AA subledger is fully integrated into the Universal Journal and therefore can be handled by the carryforward program for the Universal Journal (Transaction FAGLGVTR).

- The availability of the planned depreciation values for the new year in table ACDOCA after running the balance carryforward means the planned depreciation values are visible and reportable upfront to improve transparency. Changes to master data and related transaction data are visible in real time as well.

- Period-end closing can still be performed without correcting errors with individual assets. You have to make sure that all assets are corrected by the end of the year only so that depreciation can be posted completely.

- All acquisition and production cost (APC) changes in AA are posted to the G/L in real time. Periodical APC postings are no longer supported.
- Transaction types with restriction to depreciation areas are removed in new AA, and you can set the obsolete indicator in the definition of the transactions that were restricted to depreciation areas in the classic FI-AA.
- The depreciation posting logic has undergone changes as well. There are multiple changes on the selection screen of the program as follows:
  - Multiple company codes can now be executed at the same time.
  - Depreciation postings are allowed even if some assets aren't complete.
  - Depreciation postings are now at the asset level.

  These changes should reduce the reconciliation effort significantly and provide seamless reporting capabilities for all accounting principles. At the same time, the number of line items increases proportionally to the number of parallel accounting principles.

There are also other minor improvements and restrictions in the new AA compared to the classic FI-AA. These influence both the technical implementation and process change in SAP S/4HANA Finance and need to be analyzed prior to migration.

2.2.4   Cash Management

Cash Management processes were supported by SAP ERP prior to SAP S/4HANA Finance. Functionality was distributed between SAP ERP functional components, such as Bank Accounting (FI-BL) and SAP Financial Supply Chain Management (SAP FSCM), and wasn't focused on supporting central cash management and distributed processes.

With a strong business direction to move to central cash management, there was a need for an integrated product that would support integrated group and subsidiary cash management processes. SAP introduced Cash Management in SAP S/4HANA to address this requirement. This functionality changes the way companies can manage cash using SAP functionality and provides a set of functional innovations to support that.

Cash Management works only using the SAP Fiori user interface (UI). There is no option to use new functions via SAP GUI. Cash Management consists of several functionalities—Bank Account Management, Cash Operations, and Liquidity

Management—that support business requirements. We'll discuss these functionalities in the following sections.

Bank Account Management

Cash Management offers the ability to manage bank accounts centrally via Bank Account Management, which offers the following main features:

- **Management of bank accounts hierarchy**
  Bank accounts are presented hierarchically and are easily accessible by the central cash manager. Bank and bank account masters are master data and no longer Customizing data. Bank accounts can be grouped easily for cash pooling and reporting purposes.

- **Approval process for creating, changing, and closing bank accounts**
  The bank account managing process is now more business-oriented rather than IT-based. Approval flows are seamless and easy to maintain and execute, with no need to perform configuration steps. This includes setting defined fields, which can be maintained only after specific approval is obtained.

- **Cash position analysis on bank accounts instead of G/L accounts**
  There is no longer a need to check the balance of your G/L accounts representing your bank accounts; you can refer to the bank account itself.

- **Additional account attributes linked to bank account master data**
  Account attributes are now part of bank master data and bank account master data.

- **Integrated cash pooling and cash concentration functionality**
  This functionality is simplified and integrated into the bank account hierarchy.

For customers who don't want to use the full scope of the new features offered by Cash Management in SAP S/4HANA, it's possible to use Bank Account Management Lite. This option doesn't include workflow-based governance for opening, closing, and changing accounts; payment signatory; overdraft limit; review process; remote bank account support; bank hierarchy view and bank account group view; or bank contact person functions.

Cash Operations

Cash Management in SAP S/4HANA offers a new set of features to support daily cash operations. The following features are accessible via the new SAP Fiori UX and are designed to support the overall concept of central cash management:

- **Overall monitoring of bank statements**
  Monitors whether bank statements imported successfully.

- **Daily cash forecasts**
  Provides a forecast of today's closing balance.

- **Bank risk analysis**
  Analyzes deposit distribution in terms of bank ratings and identifies deposits in high-risk bank accounts.

- **Bank transfers and payments initiation**
  Makes bank transfers.

- **Approving and monitoring payments**
  Approves payments or bank transfers.

In the past, these features were part of the FI-BL and SAP FSCM modules. Now, they're combined under a similar UI and share a similar governance concept. In addition, a set of predefined analytical apps from the initial SAP Fiori launchpad provides an instant outlook over the company cash status and trends. From the top-level analysis, it's possible to drill down to the account level and the line-item level. The SAP Fiori UX offers more analytical possibilities than SAP GUI.

Liquidity Management

Reliable cash forecasts play a critical role in business operations. Sufficient cash must be available to support daily operations without excess cash lying in bank accounts uninvested.

SAP addresses the liquidity planning and management topic with the new Liquidity Management functionality that is part of Cash Management. It provides features to create and manage the liquidity plan of a company and compare actual figures against the plan.

As with all new Cash Management functionalities, Liquidity Management is designed to support a centralized cash management process. The entire process is controlled by the embedded SAP BPC engine and can be enhanced using its features. By default, it supports standard planning techniques such as the following:

- Creating the plan based on reference data
- Autofilling with reference or plan data
- Adjusting currency and hedging
- Tracking plan data entered by subsidiaries

Cash Management processes within SAP S/4HANA can be integrated with the corporate workflow so that notifications to update or review the plan are sent via email. The group cash manager can control the status of the cash forecast entered by subsidiaries. Entered forecasted data can be seen in planning reports to analyze cash-sufficiency levels and adjust cash forecasts if needed. The system issues alerts if there are significant differences between the current plan and the previous plan.

Based on the actual posted data, you can see an overview of daily cash inflows and outflows and analyze them for past weeks and months. Data is provided via the common SAP Fiori app, with the ability to drill down to a detailed level.

With SAP S/4HANA release 1809, it's now possible to create a snapshot of the historic cash position to allow a cash manager to do the following:

- Retain a historic snapshot of the cash position report for comparison with the current view.

- Compare yesterday's historic cash position with today's view to reveal the differences in actual cost and to optimize the future cash disposition for investment financing.

Some enhanced functionalities are provided in the following areas:

- **Cash position details**
  - Multiple-day view on one page
  - More dimensions (planning level, G/L account, summarization term, planning group)
  - Ability to personalize the layout for analysis
  - Simplified backend for better performance

- **Bank Account Management**
  - Improved usability for countries only using International Bank Account Numbers (IBANs)
  - Easier configuration of field status groups
  - Generation of correspondence to banks based on opening, changing, and closing activities

- **Liquidity Management**
  - Preconfigured Liquidity Forecast Details app

- **One Exposure from Operations**
  - Integration with SAP ERP Materials Management (MM) and Sales and Distribution (SD) modules
- **Liquidity Forecast**
  - Integration with real estate data

2.2.5   Business Planning and Consolidation

SAP Business Planning and Consolidation (SAP BPC) is the traditional solution of focus for a business' planning and consolidation tasks. SAP BPC is available in the following versions:

- SAP BPC for NetWeaver
- SAP BPC for Microsoft
- SAP BPC for BW/4HANA
- SAP BPC for SAP S/4HANA

The SAP BPC for NetWeaver and SAP BPC for Microsoft versions are use standard model, whereas SAP BPC for SAP BW/4HANA and SAP BPC for SAP S/4HANA use the embedded concept.

Before explaining the features of SAP BPC for SAP S/4HANA, it's important to understand the differences between the standard and embedded model. SAP BPC standard model mainly focuses on supporting the planning and consolidation function in a flexible and independent way. Often these solutions are operated and owned by the business function. They can operate in a stand-alone way but do need replicated master and transactional data, which might result in data inconsistencies/reconciliation issues.

If the business can live with a less flexible planning and consolidation solution, the embedded approach could be a better alternative. In this alternative, no data replication is required because it will use the existing tables of SAP ERP, SAP BW, or SAP S/4HANA. This ensures data consistency between the transactional reporting system and the SAP BPC reporting system because it's using the same source of data. This feature relates not only to transactional data and master data but also to a consistent way of rolling up summary data and the use of reporting hierarchies and attributes.

In this section, we'll explain the features of SAP BPC for SAP S/4HANA (which uses the embedded model type) that will guarantee consistency between both plan and actual data while at the same time facilitating real-time or live reporting of plan and actual results by using the Universal Journal as its basis. We'll also discuss Real-Time Consolidation features.

SAP BPC for SAP S/4HANA will contain predelivered SAP BPC content with real-time interaction with SAP S/4HANA transactional and master data, as depicted in Figure 2.9.

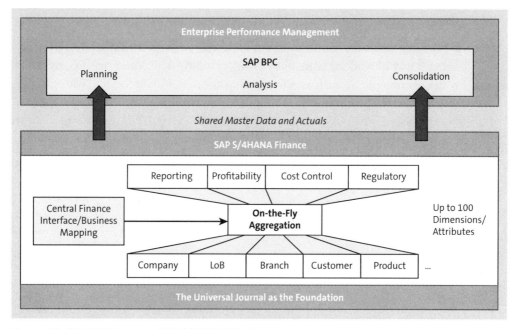

Figure 2.9 SAP BPC Based on SAP S/4HANA Technology

Using the Universal Journal in an SAP BPC context provides the following benefits:

- The speed of the SAP HANA database will improve the performance of planning and consolidation processes, such as intercompany eliminations and currency conversion.

- Access to master and transactional data via the Universal Journal will occur in real time without replication of the data to a special InfoCube first.

- Aggregation, planning, and consolidation can be performed on the fly.

Next, we'll explain the planning function of SAP BPC for S/4HANA followed by the consolidation functionality.

Planning

In the past, the planning process was performed mainly outside of the SAP ERP system, and ready-to-use data was uploaded to SAP ERP using the data structure of the respective functional component. Because very different planning areas and respective data structures are used, this usually happened outside the system.

SAP BPC for SAP S/4HANA offers an alternative to classic planning capabilities within the FI and CO modules. Along with UI improvements, this solution enables you to access actuals data and master data directly in SAP ERP without data replication.

All planning activities can be accessed via a Microsoft Excel frontend to provide a common way of working with and viewing planning data. There are no longer silos for the planning data, such as planning in CO-PA and planning for cost centers or profit centers; all planning data is contained in a real-time InfoCube in the local SAP BW installation, which is optimized for SAP HANA. Actual data and master data are accessed directly in real time without the replication that would be necessary in a standalone SAP BW system.

SAP BPC is still limited to financial planning, as depicted in Figure 2.10, and doesn't involve logistics planning yet, although integrating the two is on SAP's future road map.

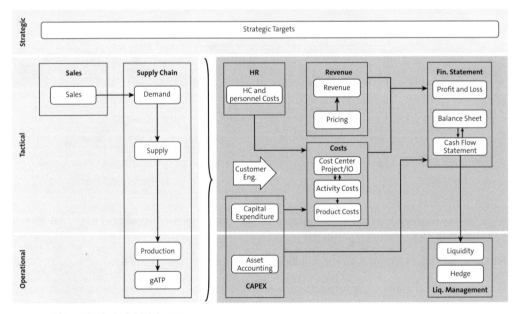

Figure 2.10 SAP BPC Scope

SAP BPC includes the following planning processes:

- Cost center planning
- Project/internal order planning
- Profit and loss planning
- Liquidity planning

SAP S/4HANA Finance delivers a set of predefined sample XLS workbooks for planning in Excel format. You can use these as a reference when creating your own set of workbooks. The following standard content is also included for each planning area:

- Monthly planning
- Yearly planning
- Standard functions for copy, lock, distribute, and so on
- Retraction to SAP ERP where relevant
- Plan versus actual comparison reports

Functions provided since SAP S/4HANA 1610 are described in Table 2.2.

Function	Description
Planning content	<ul><li>Sales planning on periods (basic)</li><li>New workbook to plan revenues: Material quantity × price = revenue</li><li>Activity price planning</li><li>New workbook to record the plan rate for an internal activity</li><li>Activity consumption planning</li><li>New workbook to record the expected quantity of a specific activity provided by a partner cost center</li><li>Fixed amount transfer planning</li><li>New workbook to plan for fixed amount transfers between cost centers</li></ul>
Predictive	Cost simulation (enhanced): Now possible to specify sender accounts and sender cost centers
Extensibility	Model extension tool: Shortens SAP BPC implementation by generating InfoObjects and so on for customer-specific planning dimensions

Table 2.2 SAP BPC Scope

Function	Description
Architecture	Planning persistency in table ACDOCP: Alternative plan data persistency designed for specific use cases
UI for SAP Analysis for Microsoft Office	Workbooks redesigned for SAP Fiori: The design of all planning workbooks adapted to meet SAP Fiori style guidelines

Table 2.2 SAP BPC Scope (Cont.)

The main advantages of SAP BPC for SAP S/4HANA are as follows:

- User friendly and flexible
- Hardware, resources, and time savings due to using the embedded model
- Aggregated detailed plan/actual comparisons and simulation capabilities

With SAP S/4HANA release 1809, you now have the ability to connect SAP Analytics Cloud to an on-premise planning environment. This will allow you to perform planning in a cloud environment first, with the ability to later feed this data in table ACDOCP without using the Excel import functionality.

Also, further improvements in plan data allocations have updated new universal planning persistency in the following ways:

- Allocation of planned costs for first scenarios
- Enhancement of data structures to better support the reporting of allocation results
- Simplification of rule definition for plan allocations
- Improved traceability of allocations

In the future, we expect that logistics planning functionality will be integrated with SAP BPC, which will make an integrated, enterprise-wide planning cycle possible.

Real-Time Consolidation

There are a few methods for performing consolidation in SAP S/4HANA: Real-Time Consolidation with SAP BPC for SAP S/4HANA, and the recently introduced SAP S/4HANA Finance for group reporting. We'll discuss Real-Time Consolidation with SAP BPC for SAP S/4HANA in this section; group reporting will be covered in next section.

In SAP S/4HANA, Real-Time Consolidation is available based on SAP BPC functionality as depicted in Figure 2.11.

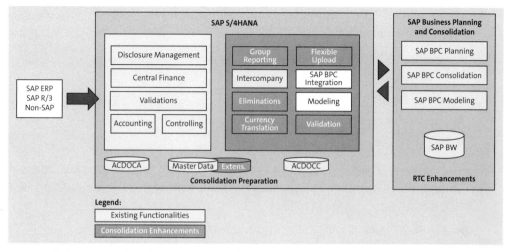

Figure 2.11 SAP BPC and Real-Time Consolidation

Real-Time Consolidation doesn't mean all consolidation functions, such as elimination and currency conversion, are executed in real time; instead, it means that SAP BPC has real-time access to the transactional and master data needed for consolidation without the need for replication inherent in the traditional consolidation solutions. This need for replication leads to data latency so that the consolidation system isn't as up to date as the underlying financial system.

In SAP S/4HANA, the Universal Journal stores all financial data in a single table: table ACDOCA. For Real-Time Consolidation, a similar SAP HANA table is introduced: table ACDOCC. Table ACDOCC has a similar structure as table ACDOCA but has some extra fields for the integration with SAP BPC. SAP HANA views support SAP BPC to read both table ACDOCA and table ACDOCC without the need for replication. This not only applies for the transactional data but also for reading the required master data.

SAP BPC for SAP S/4HANA offers the following functionalities for consolidation:

- Enhanced modeling function in SAP S/4HANA and access to planning data for consolidation
- Improved functionality for mapping operational charts of accounts and consolidation charts of accounts
- Integration with multicurrency accounting
- Validations at the source
- An advanced consolidation monitor

- Intercompany elimination and adjustments
- Currency conversion
- Balance carryforward
- Intercompany matching
- Account transformation
- Support for matrix consolidation and US eliminations
- Equity pickup (in a future release)

Furthermore, it supports SAP Analysis for Microsoft Office, SAP Fiori, and SAP Lumira, designer edition, as frontends. The main advantages of consolidation in SAP BPC for SAP S/4HANA are as follows:

- Merger of SAP BPC consolidation and SAP S/4HANA
- Read access to Universal Journal
- Read access to SAP S/4HANA master data
- Flexible data model
- Real-time access, resulting in data quality, speed, and transparency

Real-time access is a key improvement in SAP BPC for SAP S/4HANA. Not only does it allow postings to be checked at any time, but also any necessary adjustments can be made locally with immediate results. In addition, real-time access supports the single source of truth concept by allowing complete drill-through to the entity line items, rather than requiring multiple systems.

Furthermore, as of 1709, the capability to validate at the source (i.e., check the quality of the input at the source, rather than after replication to a consolidation system) is crucial to a continuous group close process as depicted in Figure 2.12.

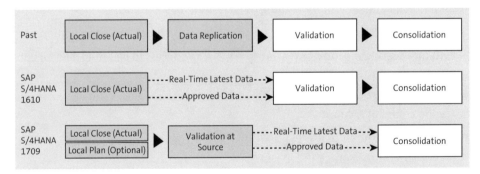

Figure 2.12 Validate at the Source

With SAP S/4HANA release 1809, a new consolidation tool was introduced: group reporting. At the time of writing (fall 2018), it looks like this will be the major strategic tool in the consolidation space going forward. We'll discuss group reporting further in the next section.

2.2.6   Group Reporting

One of the most important innovations delivered in SAP S/4HANA 1809 is the new solution for consolidation and group reporting. There are several legacy SAP products supporting consolidation and group reporting processes, including the SAP ERP-based Enterprise Controlling Consolidation System (EC-CS) module, SEM BCS, and SAP Financial Consolidation. On top of these legacy products, there are also several versions of SAP BPC available in the SAP product portfolio, as we saw in the previous section. In addition, SAP decided to develop a single SAP S/4HANA embedded consolidation and group reporting product for both on-premise and cloud deployment options, and which combines the most valuable elements from all the legacy SAP solutions available so far in this area.

Practically, we are talking about two versions of the same product:

- SAP S/4HANA Cloud for group reporting: Public cloud and subscription-based version that has been released for the first time with SAP S/4HANA Cloud 1705.
- SAP S/4HANA Finance for group reporting: On-premise or single-tenant cloud version of the product released in September 2018 as a part of SAP S/4HANA 1809.

Both new on-premise and cloud consolidation and group reporting solution versions share the same code line and provide similar functional capabilities. In this chapter we will focus on the on-premise version delivered in SAP S/4HANA 1809.

On top of the two versions of the consolidation and group reporting solution, there is also SAP Group Reporting Data Collection, which is an optional cloud-only product supporting collection of data for consolidation and group reporting purposes, including manual data collection using predefined data entry forms.

In this section, we'll take a look at the key concepts and capabilities of SAP S/4HANA Finance for group reporting.

Key Product Concepts

SAP S/4HANA Finance for group reporting aims to consolidate the most valuable elements from all the legacy solutions. The functional and process scope covers data collection, eliminations, currency translations, and reporting for statutory and managerial purposes. On top of core consolidation tasks, it also supports the reporting of nonfinancial data, preparation of notes for financial statements, and provides input for the disclosure management process.

SAP S/4HANA for group reporting works in real time, directly leveraging SAP S/4HANA transactional data from the accounting transactional engine of SAP S/4HANA (the Universal Journal). You can also import additional data for consolidation purposes from external financial systems or other sources. SAP S/4HANA for group reporting uses master data from SAP S/4HANA, and on top of that you can also have additional master data visible only at the level of consolidation layer—for example, profit centers—that can be useful when importing data from sources out of SAP S/4HANA with their specific characteristics.

Consolidation based on data from a core ERP system is a major change comparing to the most of legacy SAP solutions in this area—the consolidation engine is moving back to the core ERP system. This concept is not new; we have already seen a similar setup in SAP ERP and the EC-CS module.

What are the main benefits of consolidation and group reporting based on data from the core ERP system? First of all, you can combine consolidated data with operational data. From the group-consolidated level you can drill down to the lowest level of transactional details from each single consolidated unit. This means much better visibility of source data, and as a result also a much better level of transparency in reporting.

In many cases, you can also expect a lower TCO. You don't need to have a separate instance for the standalone consolidation system, and you also don't need to develop and maintain integration between this standalone system and SAP S/4HANA. There is just one environment to administer and maintain. It's also important to keep in mind that the new product provides the same user experience as the rest of SAP S/4HANA, including, for example, SAP Fiori applications, which makes it easier to learn for end users.

Finally, SAP S/4HANA for group reporting enables the concept of continuous accounting. In simplest terms, certain activities that in traditional consolidation are performed after the period-end closing, are shifted left on the time axis to the time before closing, in order to reduce the peak load of after-closing activities, and reduce the overall time required for the preparation of consolidated group reporting. The achieved time savings allow you to invest more time in value-adding analytical activities, as opposed to completing mechanical financial data processing tasks. These "shifted-left" activities include, for example, validations or intercompany reconciliations of receivables and payables.

Core Consolidation Capabilities

SAP S/4HANA Finance for group reporting delivers a comprehensive set of core consolidation capabilities. Let's explore these capabilities, as follows:

- **Data collection**
  SAP S/4HANA Finance for group reporting operates directly on the data from the Universal Journal. On top of that, you can collect data from external systems, which contains at least three options: You can upload data from a file, you can use an API to automatically integrate data from external sources, or you can enter data manually. Manual data collection for consolidation can be managed using the cloud SAP Group Reporting Data Collection solution, where you can define data entry forms for manual entries and corresponding validations. You can also leverage this tool for the collection of nonfinancial data and additional data required for financial statement notes.

- **Data release**
  Key users from the local consolidated entity can review, approve, and release the data for consolidation. At the moment of release, all the data gets a timestamp; any additional entries or changes after the timestamp are not taken into account in the current period consolidation. The data release process originates from SAP BPC for SAP S/4HANA.

- **Currency translation**
  There are two alternative methods available for currency translation; you can either translate values in foreign currencies at the level of consolidation layer, or you can inherit the exchange rate and corresponding translation from the original source document from the Universal Journal. Currency translation differences resulting from the use of different exchange rates can be presented as specific items in the statement with specific transaction types. There is also functionality supporting cleaning currency translation rounding differences that occur between the translation of single items and the translation of totals.

- **Manual entries**
  You can manually create adjusting entries at the consolidation level only.

- **Eliminations**
  SAP S/4HANA Finance for group reporting enables automatic eliminations of

intercompany receivables and payables, incomes and expenses, while also providing intercompany reconciliation reporting capabilities. There's also a log allowing you to identify what triggered an elimination, what the impact of this is, and more. The main missing element in this area is the automatic interunit elimination of profit in inventory—according to the SAP S/4HANA Finance product development road map, we can expect this element in year 2020.

- **Consolidation of investments**
  Limited automated consolidation of investments is possible, and enhanced functionality is planned to be delivered in next releases of the product. There is a rule-based model applied, similar to SAP BPC.

- **Planning**
  It's possible to consolidate plan data. Plan data is persisted in table ACDOCP (universal planning—introduced in SAP S/4HANA 1610, and already used in SAP BPC for SAP S/4HANA). In the future, it will be possible to incorporate into table ACDOCP plan data from different external sources (including import from file and SAP Analytics Cloud for planning).

- **Validations**
  You can run validations on the pre-consolidated values, consolidated values, translated figures, and more. The new product can run validations prior to consolidation, in order to identify potential issues before you start the actual group closing and consolidation process. There are pre-defined validation rules delivered in the system. Rules can be active or draft, and you can also define tolerance limits for validation rule variations.

- **Master data**
  In general, the same set of master data is shared between the SAP S/4HANA core functionality and group reporting. An additional advantage here over the legacy EC-CS module is in the case of consolidation of data originating from entities working in external systems. In SAP S/4HANA Finance for group reporting, you can create master data specific for these entities at the consolidation level only. For example, you don't need to keep profit centers that are specific for external entities only, and then make them visible for users in core SAP S/4HANA Finance; instead, the master data is visible at the level of consolidation system only.

- **Consolidation versions**
  Consolidations can be prepared based on different types of data (actual and plan) and, using specific control parameters, you can define how different consolidation tasks are performed.

Consolidation Monitoring

There are two main monitoring tools available in S/4HANA Finance for group reporting:

- **Data Monitor**
  Tool supporting data collection and preparation activities per a consolidation unit. The Data Monitor is delivered with a predefined list of tasks, including the release of SAP S/4HANA data, the collection of data (from external units), the validation of different types of data, and currency translation.

- **Consolidation Monitor**
  Tool supporting the execution of consolidation tasks, delivered in the form of dashboard presenting consolidation process status per consolidation group. It's similar to the Consolidation Monitor in the legacy EC-CS module or SEM-BCS solutions. As with the Data Monitor, we get the Consolidation Monitor with a predefined list of tasks.

In addition to the two monitors, there's also logs allowing you to track activities related to consolidation preparation.

There are several reporting engines available for use with SAP S/4HANA Finance for group reporting. We can use SAP Fiori analytics apps, an Excel add-in, or SAP Analytics Cloud. It's possible to establish live connections between SAP S/4HANA and SAP Analytics Cloud. This capability enables additional reporting possibilities, especially in relation to the comparison of actual and plan data.

There is a rich set of predefined reports on consolidation-relevant data, provided in the form of SAP Fiori analytical apps. These can be grouped into two main areas:

- **Local reports**
  Reports for the analysis of data before consolidation, including several versions of the balance sheet, P&L statement, cash flow report, and additional reports supporting the analysis of details in case of doubts related to the quality or accuracy of data.

- **Group reports**
  Reports focused on consolidated data and group analysis, including several versions of the consolidated balance sheet, consolidated P&L statement, cash flow, statement of comprehensive income, statement of changes in equity, and additional report supporting analysis of data details.

2.2.7   Profitability Analysis

SAP has made a clear statement with SAP S/4HANA Finance: the future direction of CO-PA is account-based. This follows SAP's plan for simplification and integration of SAP S/4HANA and the overall SAP solution portfolio. In the SAP S/4HANA context, SAP isn't speaking of account-based CO-PA anymore but calls it profitability analysis in the Universal Journal. Functional gaps, which differentiated costing-based CO-PA in the past, are now more and more incorporated into account-based CO-PA. Additional developments for account-based CO-PA soon will shorten the functional gaps of costing-based CO-PA that are still in place today.

The main decision factor regarding which functionality to select must be whether you need a common and integrated profitability model or a separate tool to calculate and analyze profitability. Although account-based CO-PA is tightly integrated with FI and is always reconciled, this could be undesirable in some business environments. In such environments, costing-based CO-PA is still a valid option.

In this section, we'll look at the two types of CO-PA before jumping in to how SAP S/4HANA has affected a number of CO-PA processes: COGS postings, valuations, top-down distributions, and production variances. We'll end with a brief look at some of the new quantity fields.

Costing-Based and Account-Based Profitability Analysis

As stated previously, there are two types of CO-PA possible in SAP:

- **Costing-based CO-PA**
  This type groups costs and revenues according to value fields and costing-based valuation approaches, both of which you can define yourself.

- **Account-based CO-PA (known as profitability analysis within the Universal Journal)**
  This type is organized into accounts and uses an account-based valuation approach.

You select CO-PA types during the Customizing of the operating concern in SAP. You can even select both types to be run in parallel, but fully parallel implementation is hard to achieve because all assignments, allocations, and reports are defined individually per CO-PA type. Parallel implementation places a heavy burden on system maintenance and creates big reconciliation problems without adding much business value.

As a result, in the past, SAP's recommendation was to use costing-based CO-PA as a main tool, with account-based CO-PA activated for reconciliation purposes with FI. In addition, there were functional gaps that made it preferable to use costing-based CO-PA over account-based CO-PA.

In SAP S/4HANA, additional functions are available in account-based CO-PA that were previously only possible in costing-based CO-PA. Of course, the new functionality isn't a copy and paste of the functionality in costing-based CO-PA because CO-PA must still be reconciled with FI.

In addition to new functional features, there are also architectural changes in SAP S/4HANA Finance. To keep constant reconciliation between FI and CO-PA, fields from CO-PA are now part of table ACDOCA. Account-based CO-PA and FI are now updated at the same time during the postings, which eliminates the need for reconciliation between these functional components.

With the addition of CO-PA fields to table ACDOCA, now it's possible to derive them during any P&L posting, not only during posting to CO-PA. There is an enhanced derivation in SAP S/4HANA Finance to derive characteristic values and post them to table ACDOCA during initial posting in real time, instead of waiting for period-end closing. For example, for cost posting to a customer project, the system will search for the settlement configuration to CO-PA contained in a work breakdown structure (WBS) element. If no settlement rule is found, the system will look for an assigned sales order to derive required characteristic values. If there is no settlement rule to CO-PA defined in Customizing, the system will look for derivation rules defined in Transaction KEDR, which now works for table ACDOCA postings.

Cost of Goods Sold Postings

There is a timing difference between COGS postings to FI and costing-based CO-PA. Posting to FI happens the moment a finished good is issued from stock, whereas posting to costing-based CO-PA happens at the moment of billing. COGS in CO-PA is derived from the VPRS condition (representing the COGS item) in the billing document or from a standard cost estimation using a CO-PA valuation. In the second case, you can split COGS based on standard cost estimate components and put the split information into different value fields. In FI, COGS is derived on the other side, from the material valuation view of the sold good.

The main disadvantages of this timing difference center on the following reconciliation problems:

- What if the good has been issued from stock, but the invoice isn't issued yet?
- What if the VPRS condition isn't correctly maintained in the SD pricing?
- What if the return of sold goods is performed in a different period?

All costing-based CO-PA business and technical issues pile up until the end of the month, and then the results can hardly be reconciled. This results in companies writing large manuals on how to track and handle different types of differences and introducing complex business controls.

Since SAP ERP 6.0 EHP 4, the system can post values to costing-based CO-PA at the moment of goods issue. However, few companies use this function because of the following restrictions:

- There is no option to split COGS into cost components.
- Not all characteristics available during goods issue are compared to billing; therefore, the profitability segment for COGS isn't posted to the same level as revenue.

In SAP S/4HANA Finance, SAP introduced a new function for account-based CO-PA that is intended to solve the problem of not being able to split COGS. Now it's possible to split COGS based on the cost components of the standard cost estimate and post this split to different G/L accounts. Posting occurs at the moment of goods issue, so values are always reconciled between FI and CO-PA. This is like CO-PA valuation based on the standard cost estimate in costing-based CO-PA. The difference here is that values are posted to accounts (because there are no value fields in account-based CO-PA).

However, the following restrictions remain, compared to costing-based CO-PA:

- Only one cost component structure assignment is possible; otherwise, double postings would result.
- There's no option to perform revaluation of cost components based on the actual price from the ML. Posting occurs for one COGS account in this case. SAP promises to deliver this function later.

As of SAP S/4HANA release 1709, an enhanced splitting procedure is available that allows users to perform splits of COGS accounts by cost component, not only for transactions related to sales orders but also for the following types of transactions:

- Stock transfers
- Intercompany sales

- Third-party sales
- Point-of-sale transactions
- Sales processes posted to internal orders
- Sales processes posted to projects

Because posting is performed at the moment of goods issue in account-based CO-PA, it's not posted with the same analytical details as a document from billing because CO-PA characteristics are derived from the sales order.

In addition, when you avoid differences between COGS values in FI and CO-PA, you receive differences between the billed quantity (revenue) and sold quantity (COGS) at the same time. In costing-based CO-PA, these were the same figures by definition. In account-based CO-PA, they can be different because they come from different sources.

Valuation

The valuation function is used to some extent by most companies that use costing-based CO-PA. In simple cases, this function allows you to split COGS according to cost components of standard or actual cost estimates. We touched upon this in the previous section and showed that in SAP S/4HANA Finance, this function is realized for account-based CO-PA.

A more complex valuation solution in costing-based CO-PA can be realized using the conditions and costing sheets. This functionality allows you to build dependencies among values posted to CO-PA and generate additional postings based on user logic. This is sometimes used for value field corrections, transfer prices treatment, and intercompany cases. The problem is that these additional CO-PA postings aren't depicted in FI and therefore pose reconciliation issues.

In SAP S/4HANA Finance, valuation functionality isn't available for account-based CO-PA. If there is a requirement to generate additional postings, the postings must be configured and created in SD and/or FI and only from there moved to CO-PA. This is possible because the SD pricing procedure uses similar functions to CO-PA costing sheets. Of course, this method requires more complex SD Customizing and additional G/L accounts, but, in the end, you'll receive more reconciled results.

For postings in FI, there is no such functionality as costing sheets, and additional postings must be generated using different methods. However, the underlying concept remains: there can't be postings in CO-PA that aren't reconciled with FI.

Top-Down Distribution

A long-lived misunderstanding is that top-down distribution isn't allowed in account-based CO-PA. In fact, top-down distribution is available in account-based CO-PA, but the processing instructions differ compared to costing-based CO-PA because there are no value fields in account-based CO-PA. When you select the **Value Fields** tab in Transaction KE28 for account-based CO-PA, you won't find the expected value fields and accounts (see Figure 2.13). You must select the value in the object currency and then combine it with the cost elements that store your revenues, for example, to make your distribution. That's a little bit more difficult than directly accessing one of the 200 value fields, but you definitely can set up selection logic to pick up the reference data you need to make the distribution.

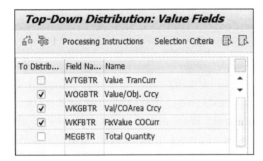

Figure 2.13 Top-Down Distribution Value Fields

Therefore, top-down distribution isn't really a differentiator of costing-based CO-PA; it can be used in account-based CO-PA as well.

Production Variance Allocation to Profitability Analysis

In costing-based CO-PA, it's possible to transfer production variances from variance calculations to CO-PA and segregate different variance types by different value fields. This functionality wasn't available previously in account-based CO-PA.

In SAP S/4HANA Finance, you can post production variances to different accounts based on the different variance categories. These accounts are then taken up to account-based CO-PA. Customizing is like the FI transfer structure, which is used for the same function in costing-based CO-PA (see Figure 2.14).

Splitting of Price Differences	PrDiff. Scheme	01	Main scheme

Splitting of Price Differences
- ▾ ☐ Splitting Scheme
  - • 🗁 Detailed Price Difference Accounts
- • ☐ Company Code Assignment

PrDiff. Scheme	01	Main scheme
CO Area	1000	
Chart of Accts	0010	
Scheme Line	0010	

Detailed Price Difference Accounts	
Description	Input price variance
Cost Elem. From	
Cost Elem. To	
CElem Group	
Category	PRIV
G/L Account	530000
☐ Default Ind.	

Figure 2.14 Detailed Price Difference Accounts

Additional Quantity Fields

It's a common business requirement to not only store the sales order quantity for financial analysis but also convert the quantity into the unit of measure (UoM) common across the product lines. Historically, in financial reporting, only quantities such as invoice quantity and delivered quantity are stored. This applies to account-based CO-PA also, for which quantities from FI are used.

In costing-based CO-PA, you can define additional value fields to store additional quantities and define rules for how to derive such quantities.

In SAP S/4HANA Finance, it's possible to define up to three additional quantity fields in the Universal Journal. The result is similar to what you could achieve with additional quantity value fields in costing-based CO-PA (see Figure 2.15).

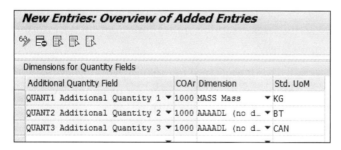

New Entries: Overview of Added Entries

Additional Quantity Field	COAr	Dimension	Std. UoM
QUANT1 Additional Quantity 1 ▾	1000	MASS Mass ▾	KG
QUANT2 Additional Quantity 2 ▾	1000	AAAADL (no d… ▾	BT
QUANT3 Additional Quantity 3 ▾	1000	AAAADL (no d… ▾	CAN

Figure 2.15 Customizing Additional Quantity Fields in Table ACDOCA

In addition, a business add-in (BAdI) is available in SAP S/4HANA Finance that allows you to influence UoM conversion as in costing-based CO-PA.

2.2.8   Central Finance

One of the implementation scenarios for SAP S/4HANA Finance is the Central Finance scenario. For customers that see the benefit of the new functionalities of SAP S/4HANA Finance but can't yet upgrade their legacy systems to SAP S/4HANA because they have a hybrid multi-ERP system landscape or because such an upgrade would be too complex, costly, or time-consuming, SAP offers Central Finance as a deployment option. Initially, Central Finance was seen as a scenario where just the finance functionality was positioned on an SAP S/4HANA box; however, more and more, we see that customers see Central Finance as a stepping-stone to a full-blown SAP S/4HANA system later. Therefore, it's important to realize that Central Finance has the capabilities of a full-blown SAP S/4HANA system but has some special business functions activated to be able to connect to a legacy system environment as well to replicate financial data in real time to a SAP S/4HANA Finance (Central Finance) environment.

This section explains the concept of Central Finance and how organizations can benefit from SAP S/4HANA Finance features, such as real-time central reporting based on the Universal Journal, the new UX available via SAP Fiori, and the improved functionalities of SAP S/4HANA Finance, without disrupting their existing application landscapes.

Central Finance Process

In the Central Journal concept (see Figure 2.16), legacy ERP systems (SAP and non-SAP) are connected via an SAP Landscape Transformation replication server to an SAP S/4HANA Finance system that acts as the central repository for financial data. The SAP Landscape Transformation replication server handles parts of the initial load and the new financial transaction updates.

Data (master data and transaction data) is replicated in real time from legacy systems to a central system via a Central Finance accounting interface using the SAP Landscape Transformation replication server, as depicted in Figure 2.17.

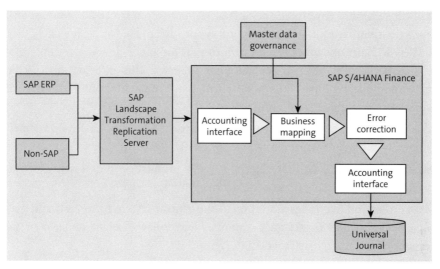

Figure 2.16 Central Journal Concept

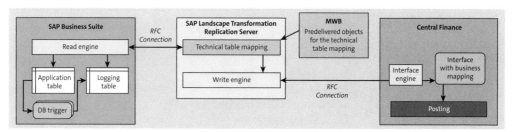

Figure 2.17 SAP Landscape Transformation Replication Server in the SAP S/4HANA Central Finance Context

The SAP Landscape Transformation replication server collects data written to databases in the source systems and feeds this data into the corresponding Central Finance accounting interface. The SAP Landscape Transformation replication server is used for the ongoing replication of data to Central Finance for both FI and CO postings. For the initial load of data, the SAP Landscape Transformation replication server is used to transfer CO postings. The initial load of FI data is managed via Customizing activities in the Central Finance system. The Central Finance process is as follows:

1. Central Finance offers integration with SAP Master Data Governance (SAP MDG) to access available mapping information there. Even if SAP MDG isn't in use, in the background, Central Finance uses the SAP MDG mapping tables that are available without installing SAP MDG (this doesn't require an SAP MDG license). The SAP

MDG license is only required if the SAP MDG application is used. If you use SAP MDG to distribute master data throughout your system landscape, it's likely that SAP MDG will already contain a lot of information about how master data elements map to each other in the different systems. This information can be accessed and doesn't have to be maintained again manually. Different types of master data are mapped in different ways:

– Master data such as company codes and company IDs must be either mapped manually as part of Customizing or mapped using SAP MDG.

– Master data relating to cost objects, such as production orders and internal orders, is mapped using the cost object mapping framework.

2. Business rules and mappings are set up in the central system to convert and harmonize incoming data from legacy systems. An overview of where to perform the different types of mappings is shown in Figure 2.18.

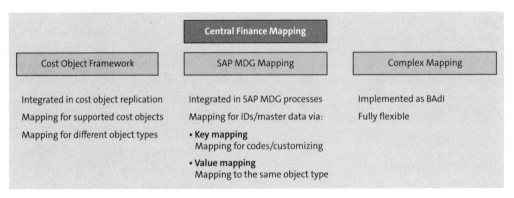

Figure 2.18 Business Rules and Mappings

3. In case of errors, the SAP Application Interface Framework can be used for corrections. This is a framework for interface implementation and error correction focused on business users. It provides user-friendly selection screens and is used to define three main interfaces:

– FI posting replication

– CO posting replication

– Cost object replication

4. The SAP S/4HANA Finance internal accounting interface transfers harmonized data to the format of the Universal Journal entry in the SAP HANA database.

5. The Universal Journal entry database in SAP HANA is then the underlying data platform on which SAP S/4HANA Finance operates.

By applying Central Finance as an implementation scenario, source systems are untouched and continue to work as before. You can then use the following functionalities to leverage SAP S/4HANA Finance capabilities:

- FI and secondary CO postings from several source systems are replicated in real time into a central SAP S/4HANA Finance system.

- With document drilldown to the original FI document in the source system using the Document Relationship Browser, you can see the document flow of an FI document. For example, you can navigate back from an FI document to the original sales order.

  You can also search for the reposted FI document using the company code, original document number, or fiscal year from the source system.

- Cost objects (production orders, product cost collectors, and internal orders) are replicated from source systems to the central system.

- A mapping functionality is available for harmonizing master data before posting into Central Finance.

- Existing master data mapping from SAP MDG is accessible (optional).

- Centralized error handling is handled with the error correction and suspense tool.

The real-time data flow is depicted in Figure 2.19.

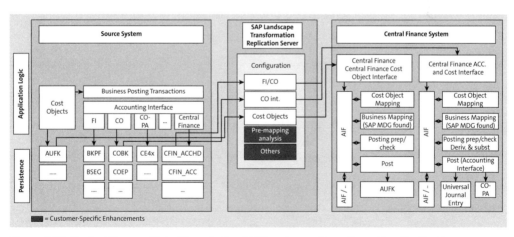

Figure 2.19 Central Finance Data Flow via the SAP Landscape Transformation Replication Server

Central Finance offers some reconciliation reports as well, as described in Table 2.3.

Level of Analysis	Report Name	Purpose
Level 1	FINS_CFIN_DFV_FI_DOC_COUNT Transaction FINS_CFIN_DFV_FI_NUM	FI Documents Count: Checks whether all FI docs have been replicated as expected.
Level 2	FINS_CFIN_DFV_FI_BAL_COMPARE Transaction FINS_CFIN_DFV_FI_BAL	FI Balance Comparison: Checks whether debit or credit amount per G/L account is the same in a source system and Central Finance system.
Level 3	FINS_CFIN_DFV_FI_DOC_COMPARE Transaction FINS_CFIN_DFV_FI_DOC	FI Documents Comparison: Checks whether all FI document line items for selected G/L accounts in a source system and Central Finance system sum to the same amount.
Level 1	FINS_CFIN_DFV_CO_DOC_COUNT Transaction FINS_CFIN_DFV_CO_NUM	CO Documents Count: Checks whether all CO (secondary posting) docs have been replicated as expected.
Level 2	FINS_CFIN_DFV_CO_BAL_COMPARE Transaction FINS_CFIN_DFV_CO_BAL	CO Balance Comparison: Checks whether debit or credit amount per cost element used in secondary postings is the same in a source system and Central Finance system.
Level 3	FINS_CFIN_DFV_CO_DOC_COMPARE Transaction FINS_CFIN_DFV_CO_DOC	CO Documents Comparison: Checks whether all CO document line items (secondary postings) for selected G/L accounts in a source system and Central Finance system sum to the same amount.

Table 2.3 Central Finance Standard Reconciliation Reports

Characteristics and Benefits

The key element in this Central Finance scenario is the Universal Journal. As stated before, to realize the single source of truth for finance, it's very important for an organization to have a clear idea of its financial reporting requirements. Next, the organization must have the governance in place to guarantee that business processes are harmonized and that data is defined and captured in a common and consistent way across all business units. Central Finance offers you an implementation scenario with the following characteristics:

- Headquarters can establish a single source of truth for more financial insight into what's happening in the company and with higher data quality due to built-in SAP ERP validations.

- You can harmonize your master data on the fly in the central system without having to undertake a large harmonization project throughout your entire system landscape (e.g., common central chart of accounts, single central controlling area, single central operating concern).

- You can establish a financial data warehouse that is updated in real time and fully reconcilable because it shares the same transactional data model as the source system (in contrast to SAP BW).

The Central Finance scenario can also offer you the following advantages:

- The benefit from the flexibility and speed of reporting of SAP accounting powered by SAP HANA (G/L, P&L, CO-PA)

- The ability to report your P&L on any dimension (e.g., down to the product level)

- The advantage of new reporting capabilities of SAP S/4HANA Finance (SAP Analysis for Microsoft Office and SAP Lumira, designer edition)

- A central place to prepare your consolidation and perform adjustment postings and allocations

- A central place to perform invoice verification using, for example, SAP Invoice Management by OpenText (Vendor Invoice Management [VIM]), as depicted in Figure 2.20.

In this scenario, VIM is connected to the Central Finance system where the required workflows and checks are executed in Central Finance and where, after approval, a posting is triggered in the source system that will be replicated to Central Finance.

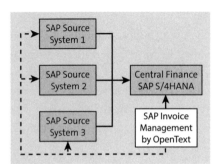

Figure 2.20 Central Invoice Verification

Table 2.4 describes the differences between Central Finance for central reporting and traditional SAP BW reporting to clarify the benefits of Central Finance.

Topic	Description	SAP BW System	Central Finance
System consolidation	■ SAP ERP instances ■ Non-SAP ERP instances	Yes	Yes
Centralized reporting	■ Finance reporting ■ Management reporting	Yes	Yes
Real-time business intelligence (BI)	■ Real-time reporting ■ Role/business user interaction	No	Yes
Central process execution	■ Closing-oriented (nonoperational) ■ Cross-client processes ■ Corporate/group processes	No	Yes
Big data	■ Exposed SAP-wide data attributes ■ Enclosure of external statistics	No	Yes
Predictive finance	■ Trends and forecasting ■ Correlation analysis ■ Classifications and decision trees	No	Yes

Table 2.4 Central Finance Scope

Topic	Description	SAP BW System	Central Finance
Integrated business planning	■ Embedded planning ■ Integrated business planning	No	Yes
Code innovation	■ Cash Management ■ FI-CO code pushdown ■ One logistical FI-CO document	No	Yes

Table 2.4 Central Finance Scope (Cont.)

Increasingly, the Central Finance scenario is used not only for central financial reporting alone but also for central finance processing and central Real-Time Consolidation as well:

■ **Corporate reporting and planning platform**
Central Finance serves as a facilitator for the single source of truth in the following ways:

– Across entities and units with harmonized master data

– Using the SAP S/4HANA Finance data model

– With new reporting tools and the speed of SAP HANA

■ **Centralization of processes**
The value of Central Finance processes includes the following:

– Standardization and harmonization

– Central control over cash flow and risks

– Simplified shared services functions

– Simplification of the IT landscape

■ **Real-Time Consolidation**
Financial consolidation in Central Finance includes the following characteristics:

– Based on a single source for legal and management consolidation

– Consistent internal and external reporting

– Reduced data redundancy

With release 1809, the following extra functions are also made available:

■ Transfer of the cost of goods sold split and price difference split for central profitability analysis

- Down payment processing for central payments
- Simulation and comparison reports for central profit center accounting
- A more efficient error correction tool to support repostings and reversals
- Increased flexibility and speed in the initial load process
- A finance data hub for Real-Time Consolidation via the replication of trading partner and profit center information within replicated postings (including the initial load)

Unified Central Finance System

Reporting is the first step on your path to a fully unified Central Finance system in a single SAP S/4HANA box, as depicted in Figure 2.21.

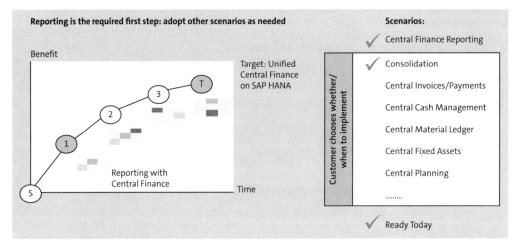

Figure 2.21 Reporting on a Unified Central Finance System

Central Finance is considered a stepping-stone to a full-blown SAP S/4HANA Enterprise Management system. We call this a "lift-and-shift" scenario. Keep in mind that Central Finance is a normal SAP S/4HANA system with the CFIN business function activated. This business function allows you to use the SAP Landscape Transformation replication server, SAP Application Interface Framework, and a light version of SAP MDG to map master data. It also provides some additional configuration features for the Central Finance scenario.

In this lift-and-shift scenario, a customer starts by connecting legacy systems to the Central Finance system to allow for central financial reporting. Later, they might start using Real-Time Consolidation as well and some financial transactions, such as central accounts receivable, central accounts payable, and central payments. After that, the customer will *lift* nonfinancial functionalities from the legacy systems and *shift* them to the Central Finance systems. By doing so, at the end of the lift-and-shift activities, the legacy system will no longer generate any financial transactions and will dry out. The reasons to use this scenario are as follows:

- Gaining SAP S/4HANA experience before a full migration
- Reducing uncertainty around SAP S/4HANA functionalities thanks to learning about them in small steps
- Mitigating risk by making the migration steps a lot smaller

Before you start implementing Central Finance, it's extremely important to envision the end-state of the business functions to position in Central Finance, as depicted in Figure 2.22.

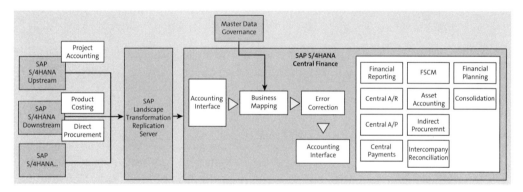

Figure 2.22 End-State Vision of Central Finance Functionalities

Doing this ensures that all the data elements you'll need in the future for reporting and processing are already replicated and stored in the Central Finance environment from the first go-live date because it won't be easy to add data elements to the Central Finance structure later. It's not like CO-PA where after you've updated the structure, you can regenerate the tables. In CO-PA this is possible because you're operating in the same system with access to the complete system. In Central Finance, however, the original source system is connected via System Landscape Transformation only.

Next, based on this end-state vision, you can check whether the functions you require in the end state are already supported by Central Finance; if not supported, you can find out when these functionalities are expected to be delivered by SAP based on the SAP road map for Central Finance, allowing you to develop an implementation plan based on that information. For example, you might want Central Finance to connect a source that uses a special ledger and isn't possible at the moment but is part of the future road map for Central Finance.

To summarize, we advise the following steps for defining your Central Finance architecture:

1. Define the structure of Central Finance by using the coding block approach.
2. Decide what business functions will be executed at end state on Central Finance.
3. Define a road map for moving functions to Central Finance (not necessarily a big bang approach).
4. Define best practice processes for these Central Finance functions using the latest technologies from SAP S/4HANA, robotic process automation (RPA), blockchain, and machine learning.
5. Connect sources to Central Finance (sources need to be made ready for connecting).

As you can see, a lot of prep work is needed before a Central Finance target architecture can be established. For the outlook of functionalities provided by Central Finance, see Section 2.4.

2.2.9   Real-Time Data and Soft Close

As stated previously, SAP S/4HANA Finance enables continuous insight into your financial figures in real time via the Universal Journal, which will have a huge impact on the financial closing process. One key feature of the Universal Journal is that it brings together FI and CO data in a single table. In SAP ERP, there was a strict border between the FI tables and CO tables that caused reconciliation issues between these tables and caused CO-related data (e.g., WIP) not to be visible in FI until, for example, a production order was settled at month-end.

Now, because all data for FI and CO is stored in table ACDOCA, WIP is visible immediately, which means financial reporting on WIP can be done anytime, anyplace, and anywhere. The settlement still must be run at month-end, but this will only be a kind of technical step now; all reporting on WIP will no longer be dependent on the settlement.

The same applies for profitability-related data. In SAP ERP, a derivation rule had to be applied to get profitability data on the required level of detail, and this data was only available in CO. Now, derivations are performed on the spot, making daily reporting on profitability possible. In addition, because all CO data is stored in one table, integrated reporting for these modules is possible.

Table ACDOCA combines ledger and subledger data in one table as well. The impact on fixed assets accounting is that, for example, all information for planned depreciations is visible in real time as well, so you don't have to run the monthly depreciation to have the accumulated depreciation values available for financial reporting. This information will have the correct cost center assigned to it as well, so the information needed for cost center reporting is also available immediately.

Consequently, many activities that were traditionally performed as part of the month-end close process are no longer needed or can shift to a process run during the month, which enables soft closes. Financial reporting is heavily impacted by this because most of month-end reports now can be run daily. This will effect on your financial workforce as well. A lot of activities in the past were based on transactional activities—that is, preparing the data to run a financial report at month-end. Because the data is already available in real time now, you no longer need people who can transact the data; instead, you need people who can use this data to perform predictive analysis. In the example of a traditional close shown in Figure 2.23, note the following challenges:

- Multiple batch run dependencies
- Batch-processing bottlenecks delaying downstream activities
- High effort needed to correct errors
- Solving complex issues delayed until after close
- Solutions made under extreme time pressure
- Delayed visibility on reporting

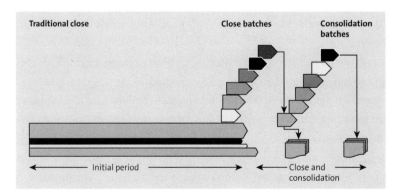

Figure 2.23 Traditional Financial Close

SAP S/4HANA Finance improves this in the following ways, as depicted in Figure 2.24:

- Elimination of batch job bottlenecks
- Continuous intercompany reconciliations
- Continuous financial reporting visibility
- Automation of routine tasks
- Full management visibility into the closing task via an SAP Fiori Financial Closing app

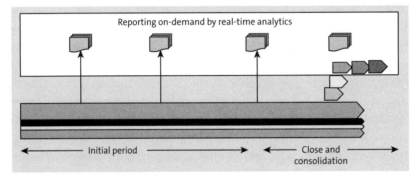

Figure 2.24 Financial Close with SAP S/4HANA Finance

In SAP S/4HANA release 1809, the following additional functionalities were delivered to improve the financial close process:

- **Margin analysis**
  Further enhancements have been added with SAP S/4HANA 1809 that enable a more complete, real-time margin analysis, including predictions through the following:
  - Real-time margin analysis that integrates with profitability information in the Universal Journal
  - Predictive accounting, which, unlike mathematics-based predictions, makes use of insights from expected revenue and expected expenses. The expected revenue is based on data derived from incoming sales orders, and the expected expenses are based on commitments. Predictive accounting provides forward-looking margin insights.
- **Universal allocation**
  The objective of universal allocation is to combine the various allocation functions under one umbrella. Combining FI and CO allocations, actual and plan data,

and simulation capabilities into one tool simplifies the allocation process dramatically. The current versions do not support activity allocation and settlements yet. This will be part of a future road map.

- **Treasury and Risk Management**
SAP Treasury and Risk Management and the area of collaborative finance operations is also improved. An example of collaborative finance operations is the innovations delivered via SAP Cloud Platform for the centralization of AR, which will support the following:
  - Automated credit integration of credit bureau rating information in SAP Credit Management
  - Customer fact sheet that provides access to AR data for the sales team or executives
  - Customer payments that will improve the collaboration with customers on open item clearing and allow customers to pay bills with bank transfers
  - Some basic coverage of foreign currency hedge management under US GAAP regulation

2.3   Finance in SAP S/4HANA Cloud

Next to the on-premise version, SAP delivers finance functions via a public cloud solution: SAP S/4HANA Cloud for Finance. SAP S/4HANA Cloud for finance differs from the on-premise solution in that fewer functionalities are part of the core solution, and the level of freedom for having your own settings is limited. However, the functionalities available in the cloud are consistently increasing on a quarterly release cycle.

The FI functions supported in SAP S/4HANA Cloud for finance are grouped into six main functions:

- **Accounting**
Functions/processes to support G/L accounting, accounts receivable (AR), accounts payable (AP), AA, inventory valuation, and integration to SAP Ariba and SAP Fieldglass.
- **Accounting and close operations**
Functions/processes to support period-end closing of maintenance orders, plants, projects and production orders, revenue recognition, advanced compliance reporting, statutory financial consolidation capabilities, and integration with SAP

Analytics Cloud for plan and consolidation data through read access to tables ACDOCP and ACDOCC.

- **Advanced financial operations**
  Functions/processes to support basic and advanced credit management, collection and dispute management, contract accounting, integration with the cash application, and direct debit and digital payments.

- **Contract and lease administration**
  Functions/processes to support lease-in, lease-out, and service contracts.

- **Cost management and profitability analysis**
  Functions/processes to support commitment management, overhead cost accounting, profitability and cost analysis accounting, and project financial control, as well as integration options for Central Finance.

- **GR/IR Reconciliation**
  SAP S/4HANA Cloud for goods and invoice receipt reconciliation is a solution that improves the GR/IR process by displaying all the required data on one screen so that the processing steps and statuses can easily be seen. In addition, it leverages machine learning techniques to propose the next steps for items that could not be matched, based on the status and situation of a purchase order item.

- **Treasury management**
  Functions/processes to support advanced Bank Account Management, advanced cash operations, bank integrations with financial services network, foreign currency management, hedge accounting, trade finance management, and so on.

All the processes in SAP S/4HANA Cloud are based on SAP Best Practices, which include preconfigured content and simplify the adoption of SAP S/4HANA Cloud for faster time to value. It's important to note that it only make senses for a business to consider SAP S/4HANA Cloud if it's willing to accept this standard way of working as described in SAP Best Practices.

The key piece is that best practices foundation, also called the baseline or core, which contains the already-mentioned ready-to-run business processes SAP delivers directly together with the product. As a consequence, SAP S/4HANA Cloud has business processes ready to run after you install. This baseline can be complemented with additional best practice packages, for example, around the UI and for finance (e.g., Cash Management), on top of the basic configuration of the SAP S/4HANA system. Further SAP S/4HANA Cloud options will be discussed in Chapter 10.

The same applies to operational reporting: if customers need additional reports based on SAP S/4HANA, the best practices for operational reporting describe how this can be done. For example, SAP S/4HANA Cloud comes with a standard chart of accounts, which you can change to your chart of accounts as long it can be mapped to the standard offered one. However, because reporting is not only dependent on the chart of accounts, it makes a lot of sense to check if all your financial reporting requirements can be satisfied by the cloud solution.

> **Note**
>
> For SAP S/4HANA Cloud for finance, it's important to make a distinction between self-service configuration that is done by the system integrator and expert configuration that needs to be done by SAP.

On top of the core functionalities, it's possible to connect to the SAP Cloud Platform for functionalities such as the following:

- **SAP RealSpend**
  Provide visibility and access to up-to-the-minute budget and spending information by connecting to SAP S/4HANA data in real time. Line managers can perform ad hoc spend analysis and other on-the-fly calculations, enabling live business processing.

- **SAP Financial Statement Insights**
  Flexibly analyze P&L in real time. Finance professionals can discover hidden trends and drive strategic decision-making by performing personalized ad hoc analysis of financial statements in real time. In SAP S/4HANA Cloud release 1808, SAP introduced smart alerts in SAP Financial Statement Insights. Smart alerts are able to detect unusual business situations in revenue and cost accounts and proposes explanations for these unusual business events.

2.4   Outlook

We still expect many finance functionalities to be added in the future, especially for Central Finance. In the first release of SAP S/4HANA Central Finance in April 2015, only G/L-level data was replicated to the Central Finance system. As a result, Central Finance could only be used for reporting balance sheets and P&L statements and as a single source for feeding SAP BW and financial consolidation systems. In SAP

S/4HANA Finance 1709, functions were delivered that allow the replication of clearing data for AR and AP items, as well and an additional replication scenario was added for open item management in Central Finance. We expect that Central Finance will be able to replicate in the end all subledger-level data as well, such as AP, AR, and assets, so it will be possible to position financial shared services on top of the Central Finance instance. In this case, financial shared service employees wouldn't have to log on to the various SAP ERP systems anymore but could perform their tasks based on the information stored in the Central Finance instance. In addition, Central Finance will make it possible to have the following capabilities available in real time:

- Central Cash Management and liquidity forecast position
- Central AR and AP processing, such as SAP Collections and Dispute Management and SAP Credit Management
- Central payments and reconciliation functions
- Central fixed AA
- Central closing based on soft-close principles
- Central intercompany reconciliation
- Central consolidation functionalities using the Universal Journal as a basis

In the long term, we expect that Central Finance will develop as the single source for all financial transactions, financial planning and consolidation, and reporting (see Figure 2.25).

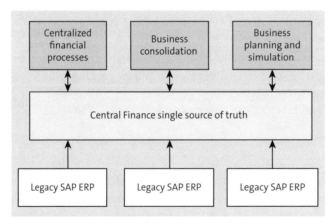

Figure 2.25 Expected Future Architecture of Central Finance

All of this will make the Central Finance implementation scenario interesting for companies that lack a strong centralization culture but are looking for more centralized and transparent finance operations. Therefore, Central Finance may be the right choice under the following conditions:

- If the short-term goal is limited to centralizing finance functions only
- If standardization of nonfinancial functions isn't required in the short term or isn't achievable due to lack of global governance
- If you can agree on a global coding block structure for FI
- If having G/L-level data only is acceptable in the short term
- If you want to use it as the single source for interfacing with your consolidation system
- If you accept the uncertainty of the SAP road map for supported functionalities

We also expect SAP to offer more functions to support the soft-close process. In addition, there will be a new concept for handling predictive data and a comprehensive overview report of all sales orders and their values for the time period regardless of the billing status.

2.5 Summary

In this chapter, we discussed how SAP S/4HANA Finance (on-premise and cloud) addresses the financial pain points and the key functionalities of SAP S/4HANA, such as the Universal Journal, new AA, SAP BPC, group reporting, and Central Finance, as well as the differences between SAP S/4HANA Finance on-premise and cloud. In the next chapter, we'll discuss SAP S/4HANA manufacturing functionalities in more detail.

Chapter 3
Manufacturing

In this chapter, we'll describe the key challenges for manufacturing. We'll then walk through SAP S/4HANA innovations for manufacturing and see how SAP S/4HANA can address existing pain points.

The focus of this chapter is on manufacturing, and we'll start with the key challenges that a chief supply chain officer (CSCO) and chief operations officer (COO) are facing within manufacturing. We'll discuss the SAP S/4HANA innovations within the manufacturing line of business (LoB) and describe the key benefits of SAP S/4HANA compared to the traditional SAP ERP system. We'll also take a look at the detailed SAP S/4HANA functionalities and outlook of SAP S/4HANA with regards to manufacturing.

3.1 Industry Pain Points and SAP S/4HANA Benefits

The roles of the CSCO and COO today are broader and more complex than ever. With roles no longer restricted to optimizing operations, such as planning, manufacturing, quality, sales, and delivery, today's digital economy and its continuous connectivity and information exchange (through the Internet of Things [IoT], social networks, etc.) are transforming business processes, business decisions, and business outcomes. Expectations from customers and partners have changed, too; they're becoming more demanding than ever.

What do these challenges mean for manufacturing? A material planner is responsible for hundreds of materials and is challenged with dozens of exceptions in a day. He must make sure there's enough supply to meet demand and identify and act on material shortages and other critical situations quickly.

The following are some of the key challenges in manufacturing today:

- Production planning and evaluation in traditional systems is time-consuming and labor-intensive. Due to the high volume of data, execution time for material requirements planning (MRP) runs long and needs to be scheduled in batch processes, either once a week or a few times a week. The material planner can't detect critical situations easily, and his day-to-day work often requires intensive manual analysis of the stock requirements list and data from multiple sources.
- Lack of real-time information causes inaccurate data for reporting and analysis, which results in the following:
  - Inaccurate production planning, causing incorrect inventory levels
  - Inaccurate capacity planning and leveling of resources
  - Insufficient information to detect and focus on critical situations only
  - Poor decision-making processes due to the lack of a real-time single view of materials and inefficient processes to evaluate solutions (need to navigate to multiple transactions)
  - Inability to minimize production risks across the networks (due to lack of complete and accurate manufacturing data)
- Many applications and disparate systems for different processes, creating different versions of truth and duplicated and scattered information.

Due to these challenges, the traditional system doesn't provide sufficient capabilities for companies to improve service levels and inventory accuracy, to avoid critical situations, and to drive revenue growth.

With SAP S/4HANA, enterprises can run advanced analytics at any point in time, at all levels of granularity in real time, and from a single system source, increasing supply chain visibility and transparency. They can now easily connect to people, devices, and business networks in real time and deliver new value in the digital economy. In addition, SAP S/4HANA offers capabilities to predict and simulate business outcomes that will allow enterprises to respond quickly and make better decisions.

With these core capabilities, CSCOs can now expand their digital transformations across the entire value chain to do the following:

- Improve collaboration with suppliers and customers.

- Deliver new and more personalized experiences to their customers, along with better services, due to a better understanding of customer demands and better integration between business processes.

- Manage their assets more effectively and drive new business insight through real-time information on big data. They now can leverage an open innovation platform to quickly integrate, extend, and build innovative SAP Fiori apps and embed device data across the value chain to create new business models.

With SAP S/4HANA, the innovations can be split into three different categories:

- **Rearchitecting the functional core**
  In this category, innovations have been made within the SAP S/4HANA core. The technology footprint has been optimized and modernized and online transaction processing (OLTP) and online analytical processing (OLAP) have been enabled, which allows the processing of on-the-fly reporting and analytics.

- **Responsive user experience (UX)**
  This category focuses on SAP Fiori, a role-based UX with a new responsive design. SAP Fiori apps can be run on any device and have been designed for exception-based issue handling.

- **Unifying the functional core**
  The focus for the third category is the elimination of redundancies, which have been built in to SAP Business Suite over the years, resulting in a simplified suite.

SAP S/4HANA resolves some of today's challenges and provides a single source of truth, as well as advanced analytics and insights via real-time data. With SAP S/4HANA, enterprises can truly become analysis-led and technology-enabled digital enterprises. You can make your supply chain more transparent and create a more agile environment in which you can predict and respond more rapidly.

Now, we'll provide a summary of the key challenges and pain points related to the area of manufacturing and see how SAP S/4HANA can resolve them.

Table 3.1 shows the key challenges for the CSCO in the manufacturing area and how SAP S/4HANA functionalities can address today's challenges.

Challenge for the CSCO	How SAP S/4HANA Can Help
Lack of visibility: ■ Lack of real-time availability of granular data to identify and analyze bottlenecks and improve planning and execution decisions. ■ Lack of tightly integrated supply chain capability to respond to variable market conditions. ■ Lack of a centralized demand and supply planning capability to create a forward vision. Use real-time market-related and customer-related data to predict and manage shifts in demand. ■ Lack of analytical insight to drive optimal performance of assets, facilities, and energy.	MRP cockpit improves the following: ■ Transparency of internal and external shortages across the entire enterprise. ■ Visibility of accurate inventory position across multiple plants. ■ Ability to track overall material flow and visibility over fast and slow runner inventories. ■ Increased visibility into capacities and bottlenecks. ■ Real-time stock alerts, based on current stock situation.
Increasing volatility in demand and supply: ■ Limited real-time and advanced analytics doesn't provide sufficient capabilities for CSCOs to predict demand and identify issues quickly. ■ Most processes requiring human intervention don't offer opportunities to automate specific tasks and have users focus on exception-based management.	MRP enterprises can be more resilient against supply and demand volatilities due to the following: ■ Real-time alerts of supply problems, improving transparency into critical situations. ■ Faster MRP runs to propagate demand information faster and allow quicker action in response to changes in demand and supply. ■ Prescriptive algorithms, such as decision support for changes in demand and supply. ■ Simulations and evaluations of supply alternatives. ■ Ability to manage and track change requests.

Table 3.1 Manufacturing Challenges and SAP S/4HANA Advances

Challenge for the CSCO	How SAP S/4HANA Can Help
Increased complexity: ■ Lack of support for using robotics. The usage of robotics continues to increase as new applications are found across the value chain from production to warehousing, distribution, and the customer. ■ Increased complexity due to globalization and the respective efforts to expand into new markets, seeking low-cost manufacturing locations and the need to offer new and innovative products and services.	Simplifications in the following processes: ■ Introduction of MRP area level, offering a more advanced and efficient logic and allowing more differentiation possibility in MRP. ■ Simplified subcontracting logic. ■ Simplified sourcing logic. ■ Several product master fields eliminated to avoid redundant setup. ■ Production planning and detailed scheduling (PP/DS) embedded into SAP S/4HANA, resulting in complexity in integration. ■ Extended solutions for complex manufacturing that are seamlessly integrated with the digital core.
Lack of collaboration: ■ Lack of collaboration between different departments due to different systems and lack of integration. Collaborative demand planning should establish flexibility in the planning process on different levels of aggregation with different groups of customers. ■ Lack of collaboration with external partners for support for co-development.	New functionality that allows for the following: ■ MRP cockpit for seamless collaboration between production and procurement departments. ■ Improved collaboration among R&D, sales, and manufacturing by creating seamless visibility into new product development projects, available and required capacities, and current sales figures and promotion budgets, as well as better integration of product design with manufacturing. ■ Improved integration between sales and production through the integrated available-to-promise (ATP) processes. ■ Improved collaboration through standard integration with SAP Integrated Business Planning (SAP IBP).

Table 3.1 Manufacturing Challenges and SAP S/4HANA Advances (Cont.)

In the next section, we'll look at the major functionalities that SAP S/4HANA has introduced for manufacturing.

3.2   Key Manufacturing Functionality

We'll begin this section with the product master and the key ways it has been optimized in SAP S/4HANA. Then, we'll describe the embedded production planning and detailed scheduling (PP/DS) functionality that was released as part of 1610. Next, we'll continue with MRP Live, the optimized MRP functionality. We'll also discuss complex manufacturing and demand-driven MRP, both added as part of 1709. Finally, we'll close the chapter with some insights on the latest innovations of release 1809 around production operations and engineering and the functionalities delivered for complex, discrete, and component assembly manufacturing.

3.2.1   Product Master Optimization

In SAP S/4HANA, one key change made to the product master is the extension of the material number to 40 characters. The related functionality for extended material numbers can be switched on; however, the technical Data Dictionary object contains this length of material number. This change doesn't represent any issues for a greenfield implementation and, in fact, paves the way for industry-specific content to be enabled within the SAP S/4HANA core release, such as for the automotive industry. In fact, the 40-character material number originated in the IS-Automotive extension.

Also in the realm of the product master, several fields in the MRP view won't be used any longer in SAP S/4HANA, such as storage location MRP, quota arrangement usage (procurement data), etc. There is also a new material type, SERV, for service materials, which is introduced for the product master for simplification purposes. Because not all fields and user departments are relevant for this type of material, these fields are hidden in SAP S/4HANA to produce a more simplified and leaner look. Before using, additional configuration for this material type is required.

3.2.2   Production Planning and Detailed Scheduling

Since release 1610, PP/DS can be accessed in SAP S/4HANA through manufacturing planning capabilities. This change will reduce integration efforts because integration with master data and work center resources isn't needed any longer, thus leading to more seamless master data and user interface (UI) harmonization.

You can perform the following via the included functionalities:

- Use the new Create Optimal Orders for Shipment app in SAP Fiori to order multiple materials in one purchase order and to optimize order quantities to best use the means of transport.
- Plan critical products (e.g., long replenishment lead time).
- Optimize and plan the resource schedule by taking the resource and component availability into account.
- Cover product requirements in procurement proposals for in-house production or external procurement.
- Create executable production plans.
- Perform constrained-based production planning.
- Make use of the reusable operation list for order scheduling.
- Improve personalization capabilities.
- Access the production scheduling board through a web-based graphical scheduling tool or new SAP Fiori app for PP/DS that allows access to some of the new functionalities in this list.

Figure 3.1 shows the traditional process in SAP ERP versus the reinvented process in SAP S/4HANA. With embedded PP/DS functionality, no core interfaces are required for master data; it's all shared within one system.

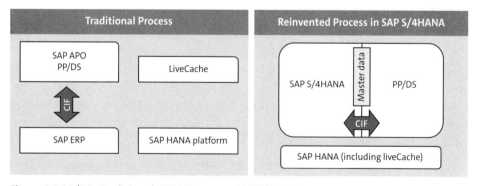

Figure 3.1 PP/DS: Traditional SAP ERP versus SAP S/4HANA

3.2.3   Material Requirements Planning

In the area of MRP, SAP S/4HANA offers *MRP Live*, an optimized MRP functionality in an SAP Fiori app. MRP Live offers several improvements, including real-time data and advanced analytics to improve material flow visibility and enable better decision-making for the material planner. With MRP Live, production planning can be performed based on real-time data, and stock situations can be analyzed based on the most up-to-date material and stock information. This will allow for a more accurate MRP run and reduce the lead time for planning. Users have access to real-time data that can be run on any device via SAP Fiori and for which the UI is fully adoptable based on the user role. Companies can analyze material flows in real time with single-query access to data. The rules that define shortages can be flexibly determined to provide insights into material shortages, and supply and demand can be presented in chronological order, showing the exact level of stock by day.

The system supports a real-time alert functionality based on the current stock requirements situation. This allows users to be proactive—rather than reactive—and take actions quickly to avoid critical situations. ATP confirmation to customers will be faster and more accurate. With the real-time data and analytics in SAP S/4HANA, users can monitor the standard processes in an efficient way and focus specifically on exceptions. Companies will have better control over their material availability, resulting in fewer stock-outs, decreased stock levels, and increased customer satisfaction.

The MRP cockpit is the main entry point for the material controller to identify disruptions in the material flow and review the impact of these issues quickly. MRP proposes solutions and provides simulation capabilities to support user decision-making, resulting in decreased material shortages.

With the Manage Material Coverage app, users can view the current material situations with availability details and solution suggestions by the system. The system will perform a rating for each solution to indicate the viability of the solution; a two-star rating resolves the issue, and a one-star rating resolves the issue partially. The user can preview the suggested solution, and the system will provide a simulated view of it, considering any possible constraints, such as maximum order quantities and inventory in supplying plants.

Figure 3.2 shows a display screen from MRP Live in which users can simulate and predict material situations.

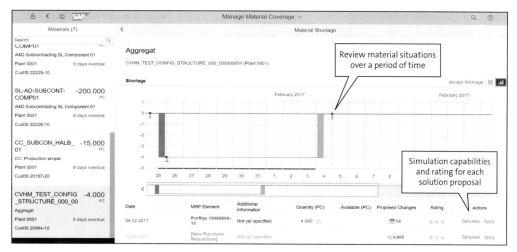

Figure 3.2 MRP Live Screen with Overview of Current Material Situations

In addition, in MRP Live, the MRP Dispatcher offers automatic determination and selection of planning mode for each material based on the functional requirements of the material. It offers a new mode and a classic mode, as follows:

- **New mode**
  Supports procurement and in-house production, delivery schedules, and configurable materials. This mode will be enhanced continuously in future releases.

- **Classic mode**
  Supports capacity planning and discontinuation. Special functionalities in MRP will remain in the classic mode, together with existing customer enhancements, which means there is no loss of functionality and special functionalities can be used immediately in a compatible way.

SAP S/4HANA significantly improves the performance of the MRP run (see Figure 3.3). In classic MRP, the application server must call the database table multiple times for each table one by one, and a lot of data has to be transferred and read by the application server. This causes performance issues, so executing an MRP run in the traditional system is a time-consuming process and often must be scheduled in batches to handle the data.

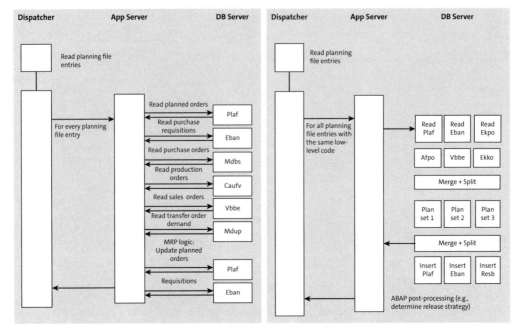

Figure 3.3 Classic MRP versus MRP Live

With SAP S/4HANA, the MRP run is significantly improved. With the parallelization functionality of SAP HANA, different tables can be read at the same time, and data from these tables can be transformed into a common structure, ignoring all the columns that aren't needed by MRP. The data in the database server is used to detect material shortages. MRP creates planned orders and purchase requisitions to cover these shortages, and these objects are again inserted into the database at one time. MRP Live can read material receipts and requirements, calculate shortages, and create planned orders and purchase requirements all in one database procedure. In SAP S/4HANA, an MRP run can be up to 10 times faster than in classic MRP, and users can run MRP as frequently as needed without system performance issues.

MRP Live offers the following business benefits:

- Increased visibility of material flow, improving efficiency and accuracy of production planning
- Proactive decision-making and ability to react quickly to demand changes due to improved analytics and real-time reports

- Flexibility in tailoring capacities and receipts to meet required quantities
- Real-time visibility of inventory levels and automation of procurement proposal creation

With MRP Live, SAP provides a product design that is lean and flexible. With the real-time analytics and decision support of MRP Live, material planners can now work more efficiently and focus more on exceptions and problem solving, rather than on standard operational tasks.

In release 1709 of SAP S/4HANA Enterprise Management, another major innovation for manufacturing has been added (and further optimized in release 1809), which is demand-driven MRP, delivered as an extended LoB solution for SAP S/4HANA.

This is a more personalized and dynamic way of replenishment planning. With the demand-driven MRP concept, companies can do the following:

- Manage buffers of components and semifinished products across the complete bill of materials (BOM).
- Prioritize existing demand and sales orders over forecasts.
- Reclassify and redetermine stock levels.
- Provide real-time prioritization of supply orders.

This functionality improves the overall transparency of the manufacturing process and offers decision support for MRP-related issues by providing detailed analytics based on lead time and consumption. With release 1809, the following additional features have been added:

- **Demand-driven overview page**
  Enables users on one screen to see all information related to different aspects of demand-driven replenishments, for example, buffer level management, and planning and execution of the replenishment.
- **Enhanced visibility and interactive planning capabilities**
  Enables material planners to sort the list of materials they are responsible for according to planning priority and on-hand stock status. In addition, they can interactively create and view open supply orders (for in-house and external) for a material.
- **Setting time-dependent buffer levels**
  Enables flexible setting of product "sunsetting" and support for seasonality and new product introductions.

Next to these new innovations, SAP S/4HANA offers MRP-related optimizations. In SAP S/4HANA, storage location MRP is no longer available; MRP can only be planned on the plant and MRP area levels. With the introduction of MRP areas, MRP requirements for different subcontractors can be differentiated within the same plant. MRP areas cover the same requirements for MRP on the storage location level (through MRP type ND or VB).

In the traditional MRP, SAP ERP doesn't create planning file entries on the storage location level. MRP in SAP ERP must plan all materials separately in the planned storage locations and plant levels every time inventory or an expected receipt is changed in a single separately planned storage location. In SAP S/4HANA, the system can create planning file entries on the plant and MRP area levels. There is no longer a need to set up MRP area-specific materials master data for every subcontractor.

SAP S/4HANA has also simplified the subcontracting and sourcing logic. In SAP ERP, there are three different ways of planning parts for a subcontractor:

- Planning subcontracting demand together with internal demand in the make-to-stock (MTS) planning section (SAP ERP 3.0 logic)
- Separating subcontracting demand and stock into single subcontracting planning sections (one section per subcontractor) and planning uncovered subcontracting demand together with internal demand in the MTS planning section (SAP ERP 4.0 logic)
- Planning the demand of every subcontractor separately by means of subcontracting MRP areas (SAP ERP 4.5 logic)

In SAP S/4HANA, the 4.0 logic was removed, and the 4.5 logic was simplified. In addition, the following is now true:

- Default parameters are used if MRP area-specific material master records don't exist.
- MRP areas for every subcontractor can be created.
- MRP area/supplier-specific material master data can still be created if required.

SAP S/4HANA offers a reduced set of sources of supply and a simplified sourcing logic. The following types of sources of supply are offered:

- **Production versions**
  Procurement type E (in-house production) or X (both procurement types).
- **Purchasing info record**
  Procurement type F (external procurement).

- **Delivery schedules**
  Procurement type F (external procurement).

- **Purchasing contract**
  Procurement type F (external procurement).

The following are some of the key simplifications in sourcing logic in SAP S/4HANA:

- Production versions are the only sources of supply for in-house production and are integrated into quota arrangements. In the traditional SAP ERP system, the source of supply for internal production was determined via a selection method in the material attributes of quantity, explosion data, and production version. A production version references a routing, and the routing is used to create production orders.

- In SAP S/4HANA, MRP only selects production versions that are neither **Locked for Usage** nor **Locked for Automatic Sourcing**, as opposed to **Locked** or **Not Locked** in SAP ERP. The new status **Locked for Automatic Sourcing** corresponds with the **Relevant for Automatic Sourcing** indicator in the purchasing info records. One production version can be defaulted for new planned orders and manually dispatched to proper lines/work centers.

- In SAP S/4HANA, you don't have to create a source list entry for purchasing info records that are relevant for MRP. A new indicator in the purchasing info records, **Relevant for Automatic Sourcing**, can be set for records that are relevant for MRP.

- Source lists aren't yet considered in the latest SAP S/4HANA releases, as a workaround quota arrangement can be used.

- You no longer need to set up material master attributes for consideration of quota arrangements for SAP ERP. In SAP S/4HANA, MRP will always consider quota arrangements.

3.2.4 Production Operations and Engineering

Since SAP S/4HANA release 1709, additional innovations in the area of production engineering and operations have been added to the manufacturing LoB. With these innovations, SAP wants to address some of the gaps between engineering and manufacturing by extending the SAP S/4HANA core functionalities to meet the requirements for digital manufacturing for a more integrated, collaborative, and automated computer systems around manufacturing processes. We'll now discuss some of the key innovations for manufacturing engineering and extended production operations that came with the latest releases:

- **Production engineering**

  Production engineering enables a smooth transition from product design to manufacturing. Some of the key features included are as follows:

  - Engineering cockpit that enables the hand over of master data to manufacturing BOMs and routing management.

  - 3D visual support for BOMs and work instructions, as well as process planning functionality, such as work instructions and definition of routing.

  - Intelligent change management capabilities and extended change impact analysis, enabling production engineers to view and analyze related objects during change evaluation.

- **Extended production operations**

  This functionality enables enterprises to manage their shop floor operations with automated monitoring and data collection to track and trace their products and perform root cause analysis. Key capabilities of this functionality are as follows:

  - Manage changes to production orders and related master data.

  - Manage the work queue and the information necessary to streamline operations.

  - Track and trace individual parts and part-specific genealogy by shop floor item.

  - Handle defects by doing the following:

    - Record a defect during production execution, including the root cause of the issue, and put objects (e.g., material, work center) on hold.

    - Respond to quality issues during the production of a serialized product or with a processed order.

    - Decide and take follow-up actions for the quality engineer for further defect handling.

  - Use improved capabilities for the model and unit of BOMs, routings, and production orders.

  - Integrate project net activity with production orders and leverage the BOM interface for versioned BOMs via enhancements in the area of major assemblies and installation kits.

  - Use an SAP Fiori app that supports the collection of inspection results in table format using characteristics:

    - To collect and perform measurements and checks.

    - For shop floor routing at the operation activity level.

- For form fields to work with instructions in the embedded data collection.
  - Use an SAP Fiori app that supports the work instruction process with embedded data collection of inspection characteristics and component information and carry out an operation activity in shop floor routing.

In the next section, we'll discuss the innovations for complex, discrete, and component manufacturing.

3.2.5   Complex, Discrete, and Component Assembly Manufacturing

SAP S/4HANA offers several enhanced functionalities specifically for discrete, component, and complex manufacturing. We'll address some of the key highlights available for 1809:

- **Complex assembly**

  This functionality is delivered as part of SAP S/4HANA production engineering and extended operations solution and provides seamless integration and a digital "thread" between product engineering for highly complex products and the SAP S/4HANA core through a unified systems of record. It offers the following:

  - A comprehensive planning capabilities for material requirements, production, and capacity planning
  - Capabilities for manufacturing process planning
  - Capabilities for change impact analysis
  - Capabilities to monitor shop floor operations with automatic issue detection, root cause analysis, and decision support
  - Capability to provide the full set of relevant information through the adaptive UI
  - Capability to work or run several operation activities at the same time for a production order or serialized product
  - Additional extensions for complex assembly, such as first article inspection, buy offs, and certifications

  SAP product engineering and extended operations for complex manufacturing can be extended with SAP digital manufacturing solutions.

- **Discrete manufacturing**

  Discrete manufacturing is the production of distinct products, such as office supplies, cars, and phones. All innovations mentioned previously in production engineering and extended operations are included in discrete manufacturing as well.

Additional innovations specifically for discrete manufacturing include the following:

- **Next generation grouping, pegging, and distribution (GPD) functionality**
  With this functionality, companies can connect MRP, PP/DS, earned value management, the as-built list, the complex assembly system management system, and ATP functionality to GPD. GPD provides serial number and simulation capabilities and enables users to experience optimized inventory management and finance functionalities.

- **Next generation, just-in-time (JIT) supplies to customers**
  This functionality is built for high-performance processing of summarized and sequenced JIT calls from customers. Users can use standard SAP Fiori apps for managing JIT-specific master data for monitoring and managing JIT calls. It leverages the simplified and optimized data model in SAP S/4HANA without any shared buffer usage.

- **Component manufacturing**
  The following capabilities are available for component manufacturing:

  - Demand-driven replenishment with buffer positioning and monitoring
  - Predictive MRP for long-term planning
  - Quality management defect handling and machine learning
  - ATP alternative-based confirmations with simple location substitute and product allocation monitoring
  - Two tier analytics by on-time delivery performance analysis
  - Capacity planning
  - Integration with the following solutions:
    - Embedded transportation management (TM) in SAP S/4HANA
    - SAP IBP
    - Embedded extended warehouse management (EWM) in SAP S/4HANA

In the next section, we'll review the SAP S/4HANA Cloud functionalities for manufacturing.

3.3   Manufacturing in SAP S/4HANA Cloud

In this section, we'll discuss the key functionalities for manufacturing that are covered by SAP S/4HANA Cloud, public option. SAP S/4HANA Cloud, public option, is available as a software-as-a-service (SaaS) solution and designed for businesses to provide an instant insight by using a single source of truth and real-time processes.

The manufacturing function within SAP S/4HANA Cloud can be divided into the following key areas:

- **Manufacturing engineering and process planning**
  We'll mainly discuss the following key features that are required during the engineering phase of a product, where you design and develop the product and continuously improve manufacturing equipment and production facilities: production BOM management and master recipe/routing management.

  In SAP S/4HANA Cloud, standard capabilities are provided to manage the BOM process. You create a complete, formally structured list of the components that make a product or assembly. Users can assign BOMs to a plant and use the monitoring and reporting capabilities within SAP S/4HANA to monitor multilevel BOM assignments and find BOMs for the components required to produce a material.

  For the management of master recipe and routing, features are offered to manage the objects and persons involved, model the production process using recipe/routing, and manage the production versions.

- **Production planning**
  In PP, the key features provided in SAP S/4HANA Cloud are centered around MRP and demand-driven replenishment. MRP includes all necessary functionalities that an MRP controller needs to ensure that sufficient supplies have been planned to cover requirements, monitor material shortage situations, and issue resolutions. Users can change and create planned individual requirements, perform MRP, monitor and manage supply and demand, and convert planned orders into production, planned, or purchase orders.

- **Manufacturing for the discrete industry**
  Discrete manufacturing provides standard production control and execution functionalities. We'll also highlight some of the key functionalities delivered for repetitive manufacturing and Kanban (JIT manufacturing/lean manufacturing, where scheduling is regulated through a board to track the production).

  The standard production control and execution functionalities for discrete manufacturing include those required, for example, for a production supervisor to manage and regulate the production process and the shop floor specialist to prepare and execute the production progress. Some of the key capabilities offered in SAP S/4HANA Cloud are as follows:

– Monitoring capabilities for the worklist and production orders

– Releasing production orders/process orders

– Executing production completion by setting the status of the production to **Complete** and completing the order settlement

– Picking and confirming the production order

Some additional features provided to accommodate the repetitive manufacturing and Kanban requirements are as follows:

– **Planning table**
This is the main operative planning tool that users can use to plan production quantities.

– **Repetitive manufacturing operations**
Examples include staging materials using the pull list, production confirmation, evaluations, and production reporting.

– **Kanban functionalities**
Examples include control cycle maintenance for Kanban production, status change (production confirmation), monitoring using the Kanban board, and the availability of various options for controlling cost accounting for Kanban.

- **Manufacturing for the process industry**
SAP S/4HANA Cloud provides some standard functionality for the manufacturing control and execution process. Some of these functionalities are very similar to the functionalities mentioned previously and provide companies with capabilities to monitor and adjust the worklist, release production orders/process orders, and monitor and execute production completion. For the production execution process, SAP S/4HANA Cloud offers monitoring capabilities for released production/process orders, performing picking, and confirming production.

- **Outsourced manufacturing**
In outsourced manufacturing, the key features provided are mainly for basic subcontracting and basic external processing:

– **Basic subcontracting capabilities**
Enables companies to plan materials that are produced by a subcontractor. During a planning run, subcontracting purchase requisitions or schedule lines for the material will be created, and subcontracting requirements will be created.

– **Basic external processing capabilities**

Enables companies to instruct a supplier or a subcontractor to process individual production. The system will check, during conversion of a planned order into production order, if it requires external processing. During scheduling, external processing can be taken into account to give you an overview of all information regarding the subcontracting process. It offers the capabilities to users to valuate externally processed operations and to determine a cost element.

SAP S/4HANA Cloud has a quarterly release cycle, so this list is always changing and not exhaustive.

3.4   Outlook

SAP will continue to add more predictive and machine-learning capabilities to provide better analytics for decision-making. In addition, more innovative manufacturing scenarios will be added, such as manufacturing 4.0 scenarios and production and replenishment scenarios. Table 3.2 lists the key innovations scheduled for manufacturing in future releases of 2019 and beyond.

Area	Future Innovations
Analytics	▪ Increased predictive and machine-learning algorithm to identify new patterns and detect process issues and root-cause analysis ▪ Prescriptive analytics capabilities ▪ New capabilities for boardroom-like UX with preconfigured content
Process innovations	▪ Improved process monitoring and decision support through predictive capabilities ▪ Artificial intelligence (AI) and machine-learning capabilities for production of master data and process optimization ▪ Intercompany and intracompany stock transfer order demand-driven scenarios ▪ Standardized API integration to enable innovative business processes on SAP Cloud Platform

Table 3.2 Outlook for Manufacturing with SAP S/4HANA

Area	Future Innovations
Manufacturing engineering	■ Extended scenarios for manufacturing 4.0 ■ Intelligent assistance for handling changes
Manufacturing planning	■ New demand-driven scenarios for production of individualized products and replenishments ■ SAP IBP integration with demand and supply ■ Plant simulation capabilities for capacity, purchasing, and financial planning
Distributed manufacturing	■ Manufacturing and execution processes integrated across the distributed supply network ■ IoT-based capabilities for track and trace of one-piece-flow manufacturing ■ New subcontracting scenarios for distributed supply networks ■ Improved collaboration capabilities, improving end-to-end traceability across the supply chain

Table 3.2 Outlook for Manufacturing with SAP S/4HANA (Cont.)

3.5   Summary

In this chapter, we discussed the key challenges within manufacturing and the SAP S/4HANA functionalities that will resolve and improve today's pain points. The highlights for manufacturing are as follows:

■ **Embedded PP/DS functionality**
A reduction in data complexity and optimized processes is due to all the functionality being embedded within the core. Less effort for building core interfaces is required.

■ **MRP Live**
This new MRP functionality will resolve today's major pain points. Companies can now run their MRP in a fraction of the time. Predictive and simulation capabilities also will enable better decision-making and less frequent stock-out situations.

■ **Several process and master data optimizations**
Due to several changes to the MRP process, processes and master data optimizations, such as optimized subcontracting processes and product master optimization, are available.

- **SAP product engineering and operations functionalities**
  These functions will help enterprises smoothly transition from product design to manufacturing and manage the shop floor activities in a more efficient and effective way.

- **Complex, discrete, and component manufacturing**
  SAP S/4HANA 1809 also addresses the different requirements and specifics for complex, discrete, and component manufacturing functionalities.

We also discussed the SAP S/4HANA Cloud functionality for manufacturing. This list is expected to continuously increase with frequent new releases.

The outlook for manufacturing is to increase the scenarios for various processes, such as scenarios for manufacturing 4.0 and more machine-learning and AI capabilities added to several processes. In the next chapter, we'll focus on the supply chain LoB.

Chapter 4
Supply Chain

In this chapter, we'll discuss how SAP S/4HANA Enterprise Management addresses the pain points and challenges related to the supply chain industry.

Let's switch our focus to the supply chain line of business (LoB) within SAP S/4HANA Enterprise Management. We'll review the industry pain points for the supply chain and explain what key SAP S/4HANA benefits will resolve today's pain points. Then, we'll discuss the SAP S/4HANA innovations in a more detailed way, starting with the simplified data model and material valuation.

Next, we'll discuss the embedded extended warehouse management (EWM) and embedded transportation management (TM) in SAP S/4HANA functionalities and their key benefits compared to the decentralized option. We'll also take a look at the improved catch weight management capabilities, quality management, and commodity management functionalities integrated into the SAP S/4HANA core.

We'll conclude this chapter with a look at the SAP S/4HANA Cloud supply chain functionality, planned innovations for the supply chain, and a summary of the SAP S/4HANA innovations that will resolve the pain points.

4.1 Industry Pain Points and SAP S/4HANA Benefits

In today's world, a company must meet three key demands: speed, individuality, and innovation. With the rise of new technologies, customer expectations have increased significantly. Customers have more specific product requirements and want the delivery of their orders as quickly as possible. In addition, with the heavy competition of today, customers have a lower threshold and can switch at any moment to another supplier or to someone who hasn't entered the market before.

Following are some of today's key challenges for supply chains:

- Increasing customer requirements cause companies to produce products adapted to individual requirements. Classic inventory planning can't keep up with the flexible accommodations or custom configurations that customers are expecting today.

- Lack of real-time reports on stock levels often leads to delivery delays and dissatisfied customers.

- Lack of transparency and real-time insights causes companies to struggle with data analysis.

Inventory management in SAP S/4HANA enables organizations to harmonize warehouse inventories and demand and supply planning, as well as use all data and analysis on a company-wide basis. Real-time processing of inventory postings and inventory values rather than overnight jobs can lead to a higher accuracy of inventory, increase in turnover, and reduced days of items in stock.

In addition, inventory management can take all production locations and external supply chains into account and can manage the changing demand for smaller lot sizes passing through entire logistics operations with all involved parties. Real-time information, including early error detection, creates precise where-used information per unit.

SAP S/4HANA allows real-time processing of inventory postings and visibility of warehouse inventory, resulting in the following business benefits:

- Improved on-time delivery
- Increased inventory turnover
- Reduced cost of inventory
- Single source of truth for inventory in one system
- Decreased stock levels due to increased transparency

The user experience (UX) offered by SAP Fiori enables users to access data anytime and anywhere. Within SAP Fiori, there are three types of SAP Fiori apps: transactional, analytical, and fact sheet.

Transactional SAP Fiori apps allow you to execute specific tasks and transactional activities. Those that are currently available for inventory management allow you to do the following:

- Post goods receipts (GRs) for purchase orders
- Transfer stock from one storage location to another storage location and make changes to stock type
- Manage stock by posting an initial GR or scrapping from stock

Analytical SAP Fiori apps are used to provide real-time insights and/or key performance indicator (KPI) information into specific parts of a process. Related to inventory management, an analytical SAP Fiori app is available for material document overview and stock overview (for a single material). It provides the user with an overview of inventory level and material postings at any point in time and on any device.

Fact sheet SAP Fiori apps allow users to quickly navigate to other related documents and provide links to follow-on processes. Fact sheets for inventory management are provided for the following:

- Goods receipt (GR)
- Goods issue (GI)
- Material

Table 4.1 describes the key challenges for the chief supply chain officer (CSCO) for the area of supply chain management and how SAP S/4HANA functionalities can address today's challenges.

Challenge for the CSCO	How SAP S/4HANA Can Help
Lack of visibility: - Lack of visibility of most-up-to-date stock levels (internal and extended supply chain). - Lack of real-time support to improve planning and execution decisions. - Lack of support to identify where and how many products are stocked, how to allocate stocks to improve the service levels and reduce logistics costs, and how to reduce waste along the supply chain.	SAP S/4HANA increases visibility using the following functions: - Real-time insights on inventory levels, improving accuracy. - Advanced available-to-promise (ATP), improving visibility into remaining noncommitted inventories, and possibilities to cover incoming customer orders. - Embedded EWM in SAP S/4HANA. - Embedded TM in SAP S/4HANA.

Table 4.1 Supply Chain Management Challenges and SAP S/4HANA Advances

Challenge for the CSCO	How SAP S/4HANA Can Help
Increasing volatility in demand and supply: ■ Limited system capabilities to provide real-time data to identify issues, to react to stock shortages, and to ultimately improve service levels and optimize processes.	Enterprises can be more resilient against supply and demand volatilities due to the following benefits: ■ Better real-time data and analytics, allowing enterprises to quickly identify issues and follow up. ■ Real-time alerts for the current stock situation and supply issues.
Increased complexity: ■ Complex data models for inventory management (various tables for stock status), increasing complexity in programming and decreasing throughput. ■ Inflexible valuation methods, not allowing different currencies, and complexity in table structures containing transactional data and master data attributes (decreased throughput).	SAP S/4HANA provides simplifications in the following processes: ■ Simplified data model for inventory management, reducing memory footprint. Only main tables remain, with no redundancies. ■ Simplified inventory valuation data model of one valuation method instead of two in the traditional SAP ERP system (inventory management and Material Ledger [ML]). In addition, transactional data is retrieved from the ML instead of stored in separate tables, increasing system throughput. ■ Embedded EWM in SAP S/4HANA, reducing complexity of interfaces and data setup. ■ Integrated quality management processes and increased efficiency achieved by optimizing quality inspection process.
Lack of collaboration: ■ Inability to view accurate inventory levels across different departments, resulting in different views, incorrect commitments to customers, and misalignment between departments.	SAP S/4HANA improves collaboration using the following: ■ Advanced available-to-promise (AATP), allowing better visibility into remaining noncommitted inventories and possibilities to cover incoming customer orders. ■ Increased collaboration among manufacturing, logistics, sales, and quality teams through embedded quality management and EWM processes.

Table 4.1 Supply Chain Management Challenges and SAP S/4HANA Advances (Cont.)

In the next section, we'll describe the key innovations in the supply chain and provide you with more details about SAP S/4HANA functionalities and how they can resolve the issues in the traditional system.

4.2   Key Supply Chain Functionality

In this section, we'll look at some of the major changes SAP S/4HANA brings to the supply chain—for example, the simplification of the materials management/inventory management (MM/IM) data model and the simplification of the inventory valuation data model.

We'll explore the embedded EWM and embedded TM in SAP S/4HANA, before concluding with a look at catch weight management, quality management, and commodity management functionalities.

4.2.1   Data Model Simplification

In SAP ERP, material documents are stored in two document tables, MKPF and MSEG. In addition, there are other tables that store aggregated actual stock quantity and material master attributes. On top of these, specific tables with aggregated actual stock quantity by stock type (e.g., sales order stock) also exist.

With SAP S/4HANA, material document data isn't stored in tables MKPF and MSEG any longer. Instead, it's stored in the new denormalized table MATDOC, which will contain the header and item data of a material document, as well as many other attributes. The tables for aggregated actual stock quantities don't exist any longer; instead, actual stock quantity will be calculated on the fly from the new material document table MATDOC. As a result, the new data model will work on the database level in an INSERT mode without database locks.

Figure 4.1 shows the traditional data model and the new simplified data model in SAP S/4HANA.

The key benefit of the SAP S/4HANA data model change is a significant decrease in aggregates and history tables (24 tables), resulting in the following improvements:

- Increased throughput due to fewer tables to be updated and thus fewer tables to be locked

- Better and faster reporting due to most information coming from just one table, MATDOC, and more flexibility because actual stock quantity data is calculated on the fly

- Flexible design for new stock types (no additional tables)

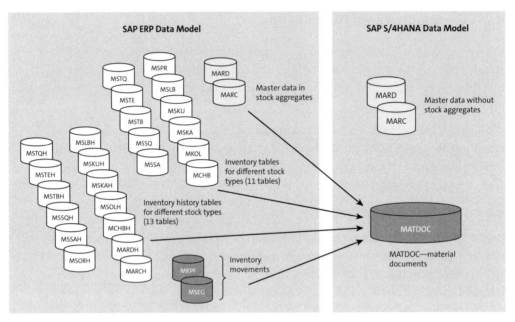

Figure 4.1 Inventory Management: Data Model Design

All aggregates tables will continue to exist in SAP S/4HANA. Through a redirect feature in SAP S/4HANA, any redundant table will be guided to the new table. Therefore, all customers' coding will continue to work in SAP S/4HANA as well.

4.2.2   Inventory Valuation and Advanced Available-to-Promise

In SAP ERP, the inventory valuation tables contain transactional and master data attributes. With SAP S/4HANA, this is simplified. The inventory valuation tables do still exist as Data Dictionary definitions as well as database objects. However, they will only be used to store material master data attributes. The transactional fields will be retrieved from the ML, which is mandatory in SAP S/4HANA. As a result, those fields aren't updated any longer in the original tables. The original tables will be updated less often, which will increase the system throughput.

SAP S/4HANA features scalable material valuation capabilities using only one ML. That way, customers can use multiple currencies and valuation methods per different accounting laws, such as generally accepted accounting principles (GAAP). In the traditional SAP ERP system, material valuation needs to occur on the IM level and the MM level.

Activation of the ML is mandatory in SAP S/4HANA, which enables improved and more flexible valuation methods in multiple currencies and parallel accounting standards. It also improves scalability of the business processes. In addition, the ML is a prerequisite for the use of actual costing.

With SAP S/4HANA, there is a simplification of the data model structure for inventory valuation. Data will now be stored mainly in the Universal Journal table ACDOCA.

SAP also provides functionality related to ATP, which is called *advanced ATP* (AATP). It combines the simplicity of the traditional SAP ERP system with the sophisticated back order and product allocation checks of SAP APO using an entirely new logic, making it more flexible and more user-friendly within one system.

The benefits of AATP compared to the traditional ATP functionality are as follows:

- Built for high-performance mass ATP checks
- Increased automation due to more flexible order confirmation rules and priorities
- New requirement classification for automatic exception handling
- Improved accuracy due to real-time inventory information
- Unified and simplified data all within one system

These benefits are supported by key functionality within AATP, which can be divided into three key areas of innovations:

- Back order processing (BOP)
- Product allocation
- Release for delivery

Now, let's explain each area in more detail.

Back Order Processing

The BOP functionality in SAP S/4HANA consists of four SAP Fiori apps that provide increased flexibility and enable the user to configure BOP rules, set up and schedule BOP runs, and monitor the results of the BOP run.

Figure 4.2 shows the available SAP Fiori apps that will enable users to set up the entire back order process, as follows:

- **Configure BOP Segment**
  This SAP Fiori app allows users to define their own sets of rules and to prioritize the distribution of supply when the demand of materials exceeds the available inventory.

- **Configure BOP Variant**
  This SAP Fiori app enables users to define a variant for BOP for automatic reschedule processing and materials rescheduling in case of limited supply. In a variant configuration, a combination of filters and prioritizers are assigned to a confirmation strategy for BOP.

- **Schedule BOP Run**
  This SAP Fiori app enables users to schedule a BOP run to occur at any point.

- **Monitor BOP Run**
  After the BOP run has been executed, this SAP Fiori app enables the user to display the result of the executed run, in either simulation or active mode, and show the confirmation status of requirements and any processing issues during the run.

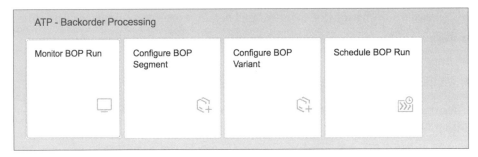

Figure 4.2 Back Order Processing

Within AATP BOP, there is a new concept for requirement classification that allows orders to be confirmed according to predefined criteria. There are five classifications (win, gain, redistribute, fill, and lose), each with its own rule for order confirmation prioritization. For example, the winner and the gainer have the highest priorities and will never lose their confirmed quantities, whereas the loser will always lose all the confirmed quantities to any of the other classifications. Figure 4.3 shows the five requirement classifications in BOP and their priorities for order confirmation.

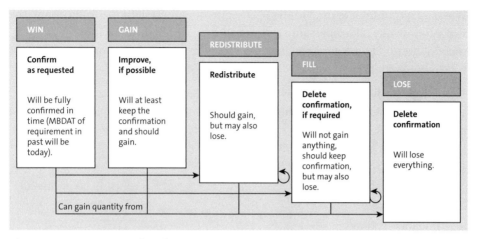

Figure 4.3 Requirement Classifications

Within the segment definition of the BOP variant, users can use a global filter (optionally) that can be restrictive or inclusive. Figure 4.4 shows an example of BOP without a global filter.

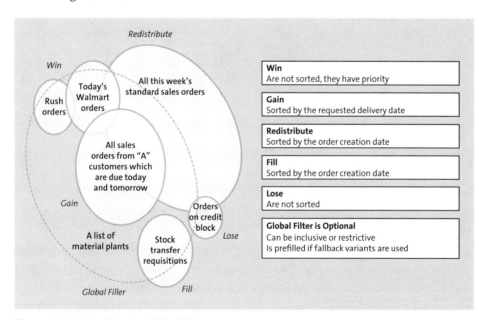

Figure 4.4 BOP without a Global Filter

When no global filter is used in the BOP segment definition of the BOP variant, the BOP run will only take orders into account that fall within the criteria of the BOP segment definition and will reschedule and reconfirm orders based on the priority of each requirement classification.

When a global filter is applied within the BOP segment definition, BOP first will account for orders that meet the segment definition, then a global filter will be applied that will restrict all the orders for BOP that aren't part of the global filter. Figure 4.5 shows an example of BOP with a restrictive global filter.

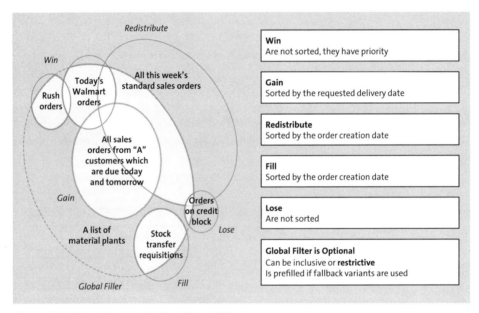

Figure 4.5 BOP with a Restrictive Global Filter

In the example in Figure 4.6, the global filter is the master filter, which will define the set of requirements to be included in BOP. The BOP segmentation definition is only used to cluster and prioritize requirements within the BOP variant.

After the BOP run has been executed, users can access the SAP Fiori app to monitor the result and see the orders that have been successfully (re)confirmed and the issues that occurred during processing, as shown in Figure 4.7. In this example, orders that are successfully confirmed have a green status (checkmark), and ones with issues have a red status (exclamation point).

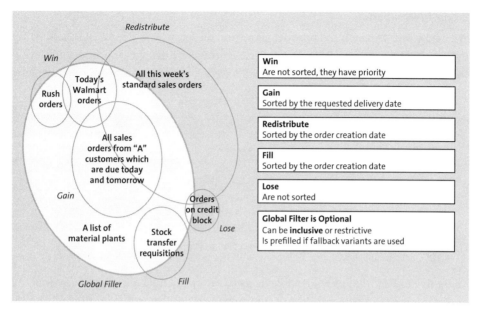

Figure 4.6 BOP with an Inclusive Global Filter

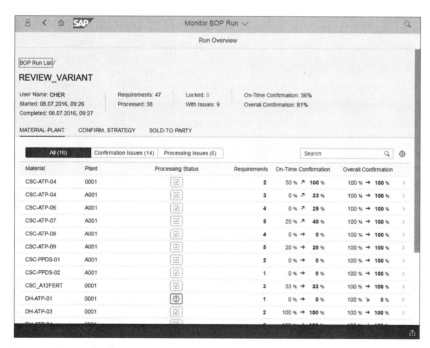

Figure 4.7 Result of a BOP Run

Product Allocation

We'll now walk through the product allocation design within the AATP functionality in SAP S/4HANA. As with BOP, SAP S/4HANA provides a design for product allocation that enables increased flexibility for users to set up product allocation rules by using five SAP Fiori apps, as shown in Figure 4.8.

Figure 4.8 Available SAP Fiori Apps for Product Allocation

These five SAP Fiori apps will enable users to set up product allocation functionality in a more flexible way compared to traditional SAP ERP, in which product allocation is set up through configuration. The details of each app are as follows:

- **Configure Product Allocation**
  This SAP Fiori app enables users to configure product allocation objects based on a variety of attributes at the sales order, material, plant, or customer level.

- **Manage Product Allocation Planning Data**
  This SAP Fiori app enables users to manage product allocation data. The user can view all data relevant to product allocation in one screen and can use group and aggregation capabilities to allow mass allocations and easy maintenance of characteristics and planned allocation quantities.

- **Manage Product Allocation Sequences**
  This SAP Fiori app enables sequential product allocation and combines multilevel supply constraints with an alternative source of supply.

- **Assign Product to Product Allocation**
  This SAP Fiori app allows users to assign a product allocation object to a product to support business decisions about whether and to what extent a sales order must be confirmed.

- **Product Allocation Overview**
  This SAP Fiori app provides an overview of characteristic value combinations, overloaded/under-/high-loaded periods, product allocation order items with subsequent drilldown options to relevant sales order, etc.

With release 1809, some additional enhancements have been made to the product allocation functionality, enabling increased flexibility by allowing custom fields users to add and display custom fields to the product allocation object header data in the Configure Product Allocation app and then use these fields during the product allocation process for stock transport orders as well. Additionally, it's now possible to automatically reorganize product allocation planning data and assignments after changing characteristics (e.g., deletion or reactivation) and combining values.

Release for Delivery

An additional key innovation within the AATP functionality that we'll describe is the Release for Delivery app, which enables the user to do the following:

- Review order confirmation situations and take timely actions on short-term supply and demand changes.

- Redistribute already-confirmed quantities to the order according to the company's prioritization strategy.

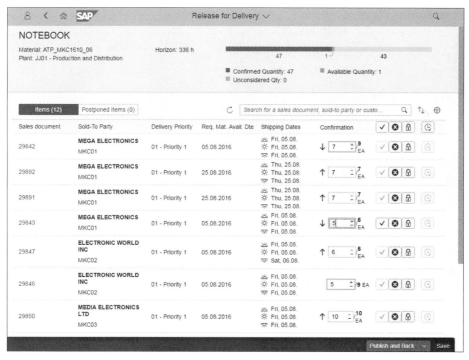

Figure 4.9 Release for Delivery App in SAP Fiori

- From release 1809, users can see dependencies on product allocation and delivery groups in the app. They have the ability to process items as part of a delivery group and validate the confirmation. Items constrained by product allocations can't be changed.

Figure 4.9 shows the Release for Delivery app, which enables users to review and redistribute order confirmation situations.

Alternative-Based Confirmations

Also, alternative-based confirmations (ABCs) is a new functionality (with two new SAP Fiori apps, as shown in Figure 4.10) introduced in 1809. ABC offers the substitution functionality for location, which is similar to SAP Advanced Planning and Optimization (SAP APO) global available-to-promise (GATP)'s location substitution.

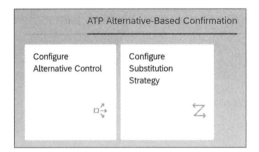

Figure 4.10 ATP Alternative-Based Confirmation

4.2.3   Extended Warehouse Management

Traditional warehouse management (WM) is available within SAP S/4HANA, and all existing business processes and functionalities will remain available. However, traditional WM isn't the target architecture; in the long term, it will be replaced by EWM. EWM has been embedded in SAP S/4HANA since release 1610, providing state-of-the-art warehousing capabilities within one system. With this functionality, SAP offers an additional deployment option for its customers to have EWM deployed within the core of SAP S/4HANA.

Figure 4.11 shows the available deployment options for WM.

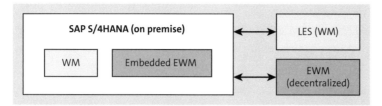

Figure 4.11 Warehouse Management Deployment Options in SAP S/4HANA

In the long term, SAP will continue to support and invest only in embedded EWM in SAP S/4HANA and decentralized SAP EWM, and a common core of functionalities within SAP EWM will evolve over time for both options. Decentralized SAP EWM, either integrated with SAP S/4HANA or SAP ERP, will remain a valid deployment option in the longer term for the following business reasons for customers:

- Risk mitigation
- Regional SAP EWM systems
- Multiple SAP ERP connections (e.g., some logistic service provider scenarios in which multiple SAP ERP systems need to be connected)

Embedded EWM in SAP S/4HANA will contain the scope of SAP EWM 9.4, and both deployment options will have an almost identical common core, covering the same business scenarios and processes with very few minor exceptions (e.g., multiple SAP ERP connections aren't possible in embedded EWM in SAP S/4HANA). The technical integration with SAP ERP will be different for embedded EWM in SAP S/4HANA and decentralized SAP EWM; however, the same integration will be used with other systems (e.g., SAP Global Trade Services [SAP GTS] or SAP TM). Embedded EWM in SAP S/4HANA will use the scope of SAP EWM 9.4 with a focus on simplification and reduction of redundant objects and data.

With embedded EWM in SAP S/4HANA, SAP provides the latest warehousing capabilities. The following are the high-level key benefits of this change:

- A single system
- Reduction of data redundancy
- Elimination of the Quality Inspection Engine
- Simplification

We'll describe these benefits in greater detail in the following sections.

A Single System

First, with embedded EWM in SAP S/4HANA, the integration with SAP S/4HANA core processes is simplified. Core interfaces are no longer required for master data objects, resulting in a reduction of data replication, which offers the following benefits:

- Reduced database footprint
- Reduced effort for monitoring and data alignment and thus less total cost of ownership (TCO)
- Simplification of system and data setup

Master data objects and actual data—for example, accounting objects and material values—are all contained within one system, allowing a direct read of data, increasing system throughput, and reducing system complexity. In the decentralized SAP EWM version, several almost identical Customizing tables exist between the SAP ERP system and SAP EWM. In embedded EWM in SAP S/4HANA, these redundant tables are reduced, resulting in a significant reduction of Customizing in SAP EWM.

In addition, with embedded EWM in SAP S/4HANA, the SAP Fiori launchpad is enabled, providing warehouse users with a similar UX as found with the SAP Fiori launchpad as the single point of access for all SAP Fiori apps.

We'll now describe the main details of these changes for each object:

- **Business partners**
  In the classic version of SAP EWM, core interfaces are needed to transfer business partners (customers/vendors) to SAP EWM, and these will be mapped to business partner objects in SAP EWM. SAP EWM uses different numbering, and due to differences in data objects, different address check routines need to be set up in SAP ERP and in SAP EWM. With embedded EWM in SAP S/4HANA, there will only be one business object (i.e., business partner), which will be used for both customers and vendors across different LoBs in SAP S/4HANA.

- **Material master**
  Like business partners, in embedded EWM in SAP S/4HANA, there's no need to transfer master data from the SAP ERP system to SAP EWM; instead, all the relevant data (e.g., various SAP APO tables) will be read through Core Data Services (CDS) views and used for SAP EWM. Embedded EWM in SAP S/4HANA also provides the additional benefit of support for 40-digit material masters.

- **Batch master**
  In embedded EWM in SAP S/4HANA, all relevant batch information will be available immediately for usage within SAP EWM. This offers users various benefits, such as the ability to manage batches with shelf life even without batch classifications and the ability to manage batches based on plant-specific attributes, addressing a limitation of SAP EWM 9.4.

Figure 4.12 shows the traditional scenario and the embedded EWM in SAP S/4HANA scenario for the three data objects.

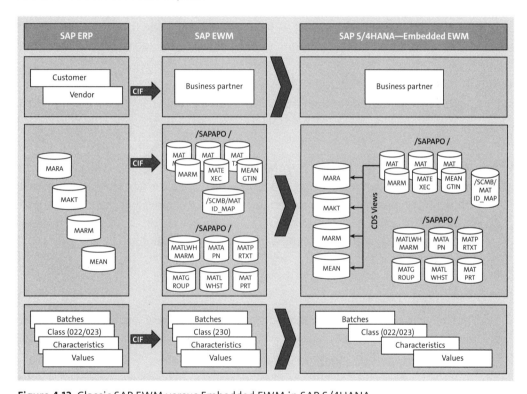

Figure 4.12 Classic SAP EWM versus Embedded EWM in SAP S/4HANA

In addition to the data objects discussed previously, the same principles apply for the following data objects:

- **Product valuation data and accounting data**
  Standard table MBEW is used to store material valuation data. Specific information from this table in the traditional scenario is transferred through remote function

calls (RFCs) into two tables in SAP EWM to store the material price and split valuation. In embedded EWM in SAP S/4HANA, all material values can be read directly in SAP S/4HANA from the main table MBEW.

In addition, only relevant accounting objects will be replicated in SAP EWM through RFCs; therefore, not all accounting-related information is available in SAP EWM. With embedded EWM in SAP S/4HANA, all accounting documents will be immediately available and can be accessed directly. There is no longer any need to replicate accounting objects.

- **Project stock**
  With embedded EWM in SAP S/4HANA, the existing table /SCWM/ERP_PSP with the mapping and conversion routine will be redundant because you can access standard table PRPS directly.

- **Dangerous goods/hazardous substances and phrases**
  No data replication through Application Linking and Enabling (ALE) is required. With embedded EWM in SAP S/4HANA, you have direct access to all standard tables.

With embedded EWM in SAP S/4HANA, several Customizing tables have been eliminated due to similar Customizing in SAP ERP. An example is table THUTYPE in SAP ERP for the handling unit (HU) type configuration and its equivalent in SAP EWM, table /SCWM/THUTYPE, with the exact same configuration. As a result, 12 different tables have been removed in SAP EWM, eliminating double data maintenance and the risk of data mismatch.

Reduction of Data Redundancy

The following changes have been made to optimize processes and reduce data redundancy:

- **Expected goods receipt (EGR) will no longer be used**
  With decentralized SAP EWM, EGR can be used to copy data from a purchase order or production order to the inbound delivery. Data replication occurs through a report in SAP EWM. With embedded EWM in SAP S/4HANA, EGR no longer exists and isn't needed because the inbound delivery can be created directly from the purchase order or production order with the most up-to-date information. Figure 4.13 shows the decentralized SAP EWM option versus the new embedded EWM in SAP S/4HANA version.

- **Delivery request (notification) and posting change request document eliminated**

  The delivery request (notification) document can be used for inbound and outbound processes to save and transfer all relevant information from a reference document to the delivery document. With decentralized SAP EWM, the delivery request (notification) document is skipped; instead, the delivery document in SAP EWM is created directly from either the inbound or outbound delivery document in SAP S/4HANA. Therefore, any functionalities in standard SAP EWM that are linked to the delivery request or notification document will no longer be available in embedded EWM in SAP S/4HANA.

The same applies for the posting change request document. In embedded EWM in SAP S/4HANA, the posting change document is created directly from the outbound delivery document.

Figure 4.14 shows the current process and the new option for both inbound and outbound processes.

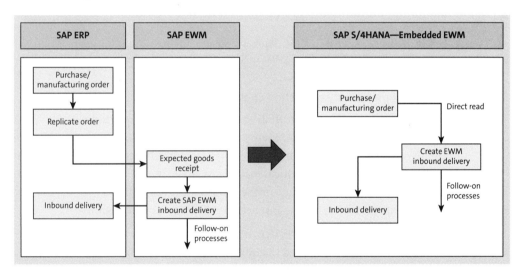

Figure 4.13 Expected Goods Receipt in Classic SAP EWM versus Embedded EWM in SAP S/4HANA

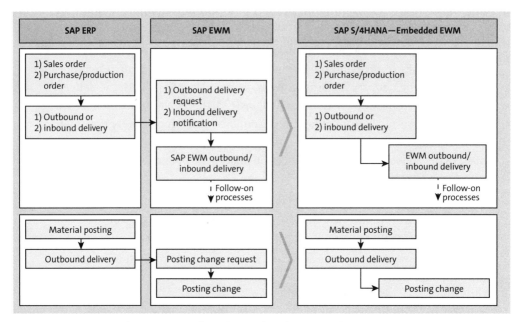

Figure 4.14 Delivery Request (Notification) and Posting Change Request Documents in Classic SAP EWM versus Embedded EWM in SAP S/4HANA

Elimination of the Quality Inspection Engine

The important new benefit of eliminating the Quality Inspection Engine is the result of reducing data redundancy. The Quality Inspection Engine had been used as a lean solution to support the quality inspection process and offered functionalities that provided flexibility for configuration inspection rules. In the classic SAP EWM scenario, inspection details are set up in the material master, and the inspection rule details are set up to determine the inspection relevance of a document.

With embedded EWM in SAP S/4HANA, no inspection setup is required in the material master; all details are captured in embedded EWM in SAP S/4HANA.

Due to the elimination of the Quality Inspection Engine, the process will be optimized significantly. In classic SAP EWM, the inspection process is as follows:

1. In SAP EWM, a GR of an inbound delivery is waiting to be posted.

Note

The trigger can also be at delivery creation or **In Yard** status.

2. Based on the inspection rules setup, the Quality Inspection Engine will determine whether it's relevant for the inspection process.

3. If yes, an inspection document is created and saved.

4. After release of the inspection document, the Quality Inspection Engine informs the SAP ERP system of the creation of an inspection document.

5. An inspection lot is created based on the inspection setup data in SAP ERP. The inspection document in the Quality Inspection Engine and inbound delivery is updated accordingly.

6. The inspection is executed, and details are recorded in SAP ERP.

7. The usage decision is also recorded in SAP ERP.

8. SAP ERP transfers the relevant inspection details to the Quality Inspection Engine, and the inspection document is updated.

9. Follow-up actions in SAP EWM are executed accordingly.

With embedded EWM in SAP S/4HANA, the inspection process is as follows:

1. In SAP EWM, a GR of an inbound delivery is waiting to be posted.

2. Based on the inspection rules setup, using the quality management functionalities in SAP S/4HANA, the system determines whether it's relevant for the inspection process.

3. If yes, the system determines the inspection setup data and creates an inspection lot.

4. The inspection is executed, and details are recorded in SAP S/4HANA.

5. The inspection details are recorded.

6. The usage decision is recorded.

7. In SAP EWM, follow-up actions are executed accordingly.

Simplification

Embedded EWM in SAP S/4HANA offers massive simplifications through reduction of redundant data and through leaner processes and fewer business documents. In addition, specific functionalities within the classic SAP EWM have been disabled or replaced to meet the SAP S/4HANA guidelines and vision. The following functionalities have been disabled/replaced:

- **SAP TM (freight order management [FOM])**
  The decision not to include FOM in embedded EWM in SAP S/4HANA arose mainly because TM offers enhanced functionalities and has been made available as an

embedded functionality within SAP S/4HANA. SAP TM is also offered as a sidecar solution. We'll describe embedded TM in SAP S/4HANA more detail in the next section.

- **Supply chain routing (SAP Supply Chain Management [SAP SCM] routes)**
  SAP doesn't want to offer routes in SAP ERP, SAP TM, and SAP SCM in the long run; therefore, the SAP SCM routes are disabled, and only SAP ERP routes are used.

- **Microsoft Silverlight UI replaced by SAPUI5 technology**
  The official end-of-support date for Microsoft Silverlight is October 5, 2021. Microsoft Silverlight will be replaced by SAPUI5 technology for the following four use cases:

  - Creating appointments
  - Monitoring appointments
  - Planning staging areas
  - Maintaining capacity

Due to the mentioned massive simplifications of embedded EWM in SAP S/4HANA, the effort required for basic setup of EWM has been reduced significantly and now includes only a third of the setup in the SAP EWM/SAP ERP integration guide.

Optimization and Monitoring

SAP is adding new innovations and apps in every release to optimize the warehousing processes and create better insights to reduce TCO and investments.

Let's start with the following enhanced and new SAP Fiori apps:

- **Enhanced Run Outbound Process app**
  Allows you to perform several outbound process-related activities into one app, such as cancellation of picking, warehouse tasks, and GI. It also allows you to manually create picking tasks.

- **Enhanced Change Inbound Delivery app**
  Enables all inbound delivery process activities to be executed from one single app, such as canceling GR, manually creating putaway tasks, reprinting HU labels, changing stock types, and displaying and canceling warehouse tasks.

- **Enhanced Product Maintenance app**
  Allows you to create, update, and mark product master data for deletion. In addition, you can archive product data and storage type data with other product data and enable warehouse product data search by warehouse number.

- **New Pack Outbound Deliveries app**
  This app is used for work centers to execute the following packing-related processes:
  - Packing of picked stock into a shipping HU
  - Packing of complete or partial item quantities
  - Printing shipping labels for HU
  - Capturing weight and connecting to scale
  - Creating and changing shipping HUs
  - Packing and shipping for batch managed and serial products
- **New Inventory Counting, Enabling Activation, Printing and Counting of Physical Inventory Documents app**
  This app can be used to capture result counts, capture quantities on bins, and capture HUs and sub-HUs, as well as include batch and serial numbers.

Additionally, the following new reports and enhanced functionalities are provided to monitor warehouse operations:

- **ABC Analysis report**
  Enables users to classify products based on historical warehouse task-related information with the option for the users to update the putaway indicator, section indicator, and cycle counting indicator, as well as specify ABC limits.
- **Storage bin-change logs**
  Enhanced to enable users to activate and create change logs for storage bins and view this information from the EWM storage bin master.
- **EWM warehouse monitor functionality**
  Enhanced to include new methods for users to create ad hoc product or HU warehouse tasks from a list of selected stocks and create ad hoc posting changes to change stock type, post to another product or batch, and release the stock from a customer order. A new monitor node and methods are also provided to simplify unassigning HUs to picked stock from an outbound delivery order.
- **Mass warehouse products creation and mass updates functionality to storage type data**
  This functionality includes the following:
  - Ability to retrieve a list of products with or without storage type or warehouse-specific data

- Enhanced methods to mass create warehouse and storage-type-specific data
- New selection options by material type and plant-specific data

Now that we've discussed all the EWM-specific functionalities, it's time to move on to the next key topic, transportation management (TM). Just like EWM, in the next section, we'll discuss all the key innovations from TM.

4.2.4   Transportation Management

With release 1709, embedded SAP TM basic and advanced shipping functionality were offered in SAP S/4HANA. They offer best-of-breed transportation functionalities, leveraging existing SAP TM, built within SAP S/4HANA. Just like the embedded EWM in SAP S/4HANA functionality, embedded TM in SAP S/4HANA is the target architecture and will replace the legacy SAP TM functionality brought over from SAP ERP in the long run. With embedded TM in SAP S/4HANA, SAP is following the principle of one: one set of master data within one system, with no more data redundancy.

Table 4.2 shows the differences in functionality between basic and advanced SAP TM. One additional note is that advanced TM requires an additional license.

Basic Shipping	Advanced Shipping
■ Main parts of the transportation network except trade lane, allocations, business shares, and resources ■ Freight agreements ■ Charge management, except air-specific charges, event-based charges, and consolidated charge calculation ■ Separate inboun /outbound freight order/ booking management (delivery-based) ■ Basic transportation planning ■ Transportation execution without event management ■ Freight settlement with agency billing ■ Direct tendering/subcontracting ■ TM output management ■ SAP BW analytics	■ Strategic freight management ■ Service product catalog/service order management ■ Advanced charge calculation ■ Combined inbound/outbound transportation process ■ Advanced transportation planning with optimization capability ■ Driver management ■ EWM integration ■ Group logistics ■ Embedded analytics with CDS views

Table 4.2 Basic and Advanced Shipping

Figure 4.15 shows the different options to deploy basic shipping functionalities within SAP S/4HANA. In the traditional SAP ERP system, basic shipping functionalities were offered through Transportation in SAP ERP (LE-TRA); however, in the longer term, this will be replaced by embedded TM in SAP S/4HANA. With the first option, SAP offers compatibility packs to enable users to continue using the existing transportation functionalities (which are based on LE-TRA) within SAP S/4HANA until end of life of the compatibility packs. The second option, available since 1709, is to use embedded TM in SAP S/4HANA. The third option is to deploy SAP TM as a sidecar.

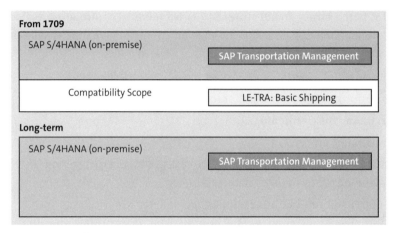

Figure 4.15 Different Deployment Options for Basic Shipping Functionalities

Key benefits of embedded TM in SAP S/4HANA are as follows:

- One system, leading to the following:
  - Harmonized master data, with no interfaces required (see Figure 4.16)
  - Harmonized Customizing
  - Harmonized transport scheduling
- Real-time embedded analytics
- SAP Fiori launchpad UI for SAP S/4HANA
- Integrated TM and EWM functionalities

Figure 4.16 shows the business partner and material master requirements for traditional SAP ERP and embedded TM in SAP S/4HANA.

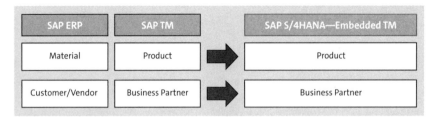

Figure 4.16 Integration of SAP TM with Traditional SAP ERP versus Embedded TM in SAP S/4HANA Functionality

Because SAP TM is the target architecture, SAP is planning to continue providing more innovations and functionalities for the enablement of TM core functionalities. Since release 1809, the following new innovations have been added:

- General functionalities added to the TM core, including the following:
  - Ability to perform cost distribution for forwarding orders
  - Internal settlement agreement
  - Export and import processing
  - Updates to the delivery, for example, in case of delivery splits, triggering GR/GI posting, planning status updates, dates, and so on
  - Creation of freight units out of scheduling agreements
- Integration to SAP Logistics Business Network, including the following benefits:
  - Integrated tendering and subcontracting processes from SAP TM to SAP Logistics Business Networks
  - Integrated carrier invoicing processes
  - Tour tracking capabilities, including functionality to initiate tour tracking and receive events from the outside world and calculate the estimated time of arrival based on real-time information
- Mixed pallet and load planning capabilities and optimization, including the following benefits:
  - Improved capabilities to create precision in building pallets by optimizing the physical positions of cartons on a pallet (considering stackability and orientation constraints of products)
  - Capabilities to put different products from the customer into one carton and stack products for different customers into one pallet

Next, we'll discuss the capabilities within catch weight management.

4.2.5   Catch Weight Management

Since release 1610, catch weight management functionality is integrated into the SAP S/4HANA core and can be used by activating the business functions for catch weight management. Catch weight management in SAP S/4HANA isn't identical to the former industry solution IS-CWM. Therefore, some features from the traditional architecture of IS-CWM won't be supported in SAP S/4HANA, and some additional changes in the new catch weight management functionality in SAP S/4HANA may have an impact on customer coding when converting IS-CWM to catch weight management in SAP S/4HANA. In this section, we'll describe the functionalities that are available in SAP S/4HANA catch weight management and also highlight those areas that aren't supported (yet) in SAP S/4HANA.

With catch weight management in SAP S/4HANA, companies can use a parallel, variable quantity in inventory management to valuate goods movement independently of their logistics quantity. The catch weight management solution is mainly used in the consumer products and the foods processing industry. Catch weight management provides the following functionalities:

- Capability to manage two independent units of measure (UoMs) throughout the main inventory management and in different LoBs (sales, purchase, production, inventory management)
- Full support for processing of BOM materials with advanced returns management
- Automated value correction by initiating handling of differences in parallel UoMs

Traditional IS-CWM functionalities that are no longer supported in SAP S/4HANA catch weight management include the following:

- Parallel unit of measure category "B" because it's unnecessary to store quantities in a second UoM without any depending functionality, and because category "B" is reserved for EWM in SAP S/4HANA
- Flexible material prices
- Screen sequences "CW" and "CE" delivered for the material master because they have been replaced by new SAP S/4HANA standard screen sequences
- Some attributes, such as /CWM/TOLGR and /CWM/TY2TQ

In addition to these functions that are no longer supported in SAP S/4HANA, there may also be business add-ins (BAdIs) and functions that can't be migrated to SAP S/4HANA. Since release 1709, SAP offers migration tools for clients to migrate their existing catch weight management solution into SAP S/4HANA.

4.2.6   Quality Management

In Section 4.2.3, we already highlighted some of the key innovations around EWM. One of the key optimizations with the embedded EWM in SAP S/4HANA is the elimination of the Quality Inspection Engine to create a leaner solution for the quality inspection process. In this section, we'll highlight some more quality management-related innovations in SAP S/4HANA.

The newest improvements provided for quality management in SAP S/4HANA are the new SAP Fiori apps that are provided to record quality inspection results and the improved analytics and monitoring capabilities:

- **Quality Results Recording app**
  Enables users to carry out and process several individual inspections at different intervals or during a particular event during production. It allows users to use inspection points during production or the inspection interval.

- **Defect Monitoring app**
  Users can record defects manually that need to be documented and rectified. This app allows users to identify the quality issues and evaluate the defect data for further follow up and determine the corrective actions to prevent the issue from reoccurring.

- **New Manage All Quality-Related Tasks app**
  Users can perform different quality-related activities all through one single app. Examples of these activities are task planning based on a general catalog for tasks, maintaining a general catalog, issue processing, text recording, and flexible and state-of-the-art worklists for monitoring quality tasks.

- **Manage Quality Level app**
  Provides the users with an overview page of the quality level of the material or material/supplier. This data is used to determine the inspection stage for the sample determination of the next inspection lot. This can be displayed in a worklist with the option for a graphical presentation enabling users to reset the quality level in the overview page.

In the next section, we'll discuss the last innovation area in the supply chain LoB (on-premise): commodity management.

4.2.7   Commodity Management

In earlier SAP S/4HANA releases, commodity management for sales, purchasing, and risk management was technically switched off, and, as a result, customers with these commodity business functions activated weren't able to convert to SAP S/4HANA. Since releases 1709 and 1809, the commodity management functionality has become available in SAP S/4HANA for sales, procurement, and risk application. The key functionality of SAP S/4HANA commodity management for sales, purchasing, and risk application include the following:

- **Commodity management for purchasing**
  With commodity management for purchasing, companies can manage their procurement processes for buying commodities and commodity-dependent goods. It can help them create commodity contracts based on market quotes, automate pricing calculations, and streamline the invoicing processes. Some of the key functionalities are as follows:
  - New entered price fixations (priced quantities in purchase and sales orders) can be automatically allocated to GR and deliveries.
  - Market identifier code isn't mandatory anymore when creating commodity forwards based on derivative contract specifications (DCS).
  - The commodity pricing engine can access commodity curves based on DCS to determine forecast market values for the DCS of commodity derivatives.
  - Swap rates can be used to determine exchange rate forecasts for currency conversions using exchange rate forecast routine.

- **Commodity management for sales**
  With commodity management for sales, companies can process and manage sales documents, deliveries and billing documents, or commodities and perform simple formula-based commodity pricing. Some of the key functionalities are as follows:
  - Commodity-related market data management: Use market data management based on derivative contract specifications or basis market data entered manually in the system and accessed by the commodity pricing engine.
  - Commodity pricing: Apply complex pricing formulas, rules, and conditions in all the sales documents for provisional billing and/or final billing.
  - Processing commodity sales transactions and documents: Commodity sales support the creation and processing of sales orders, sales contracts, and deliveries, as well as provisional, differential, and final billing documents.
  - Period-end valuation: This functionality is used for deliveries of commodities with GIs, where the commodity price is floating and a final invoice hasn't been posted yet either on or before the valuation key. Period-end valuation can be

used to calculate the accrual amount from the difference between an anticipated final invoice and the posted amount.

- **Commodity management for risk management**
  Commodity management for risk management enables companies to identify
  and quantify exposure to commodity price risks and mitigate risks with financial
  commodity derivatives. It helps companies comply with regulations and accounting standards that are applicable to financial derivatives. Users can create and
  update commodity risk positions in real time and provide a comprehensive
  insight into commodity risk positions by flexible positions and mark-to-market
  reporting. Some of the key functionalities include the following:

  - Risk reporting from purchase contract capture and subsequent documents to
    risk analysis.

  - Mark-to-market queries, including stock logistics documents and financial
    derivatives; unified mark-to-market reporting, including key figures for con-
    tract value and market value; and undiscounted mark-to-market valuations for
    stock, logistics documents, and financial derivatives.

  - End-of-day snapshot reporting and "current" data valuations.

You now have a better understanding of the latest innovations in SAP S/4HANA version for the supply chain LoB. In the next section, we'll discuss the supply chain functionalities that are available in the SAP S/4HANA Cloud, public option.

4.3   Supply Chain in SAP S/4HANA Cloud

We'll now discuss the key functionalities in the SAP S/4HANA Cloud, public option,
for supply chain. We can divide these key features into the following five areas:

- **Inventory management**
  The key functionalities that are available within SAP S/4HANA Cloud for IM are as
  follows:

  - Physical inventory/inventory count and adjustments capabilities, enabling
    users to perform periodic stock count and adjustment process. Users can gener-
    ate inventory count sheets and bock materials during physical count. Results of
    the count can be entered in the system and accepted.

  - Post goods movements, based on a standard list of movement types.

  - Display price change documents with the valuation of the material.

- Reporting and monitoring capabilities, providing users with a standard list of reports to, for example, identify overdue stock transfers and evaluate total stock of a material at a plant/storage location level. Users will also have the options to monitor and adjust inventory processes for day-to-day activities.

- **Logistics execution**
  Contains functionalities around inbound and outbound delivery processing, as follows:

  - Inbound delivery processing: This is the process that starts when the goods are shipped from the vendor's location and ends when the GR is done at the ship-to location. SAP S/4HANA Cloud provides standard inbound delivery processing functionalities to support this process. When users create a purchase order or a scheduling agreement, a goods receiving point is determined, followed by an inbound delivery and receipt.

  - Outbound delivery processing: Similar standard transactions are available in SAP S/4HANA Cloud, enabling users to create outbound deliveries based on a list of sales documents, display logs for the sales order or delivery, perform picking, print the picklist, and perform GI.

- **ATP**
  The ATP functionality offers the availability check and the BOP capabilities. With the availability check, companies can determine on which date and in which quantity a particular requirement can be fulfilled based on a specific checking rule and the current supply for a material. The BOP functionality enables users to reprioritize sales orders and stock transport orders and then perform automated mass availability checks in the case of limited stock to supply the available stock according to a specific inventory.

- **AATP**
  The AATP functionality offers the product allocation and release for delivery capability, enabling users to allocate material for a specific time period based on characteristic value combinations. The release for delivery functionality allows users to manually reprioritize sales orders and stock transport orders in the case of limited stock. After reprioritizing, the logistics process can be triggered.

- **Warehousing**
  SAP S/4HANA Cloud supports basic integration scenarios for logistics/warehousing processes with SAP EWM. The following integration scenarios are currently supported:

- Transfer of warehouse-related master data.
- Inbound processing scenario, which supports the inbound process from procurement, stock transport order, or customer returns.
- Outbound processing scenario, which supports the GI from sales order and stock transport order.
- Production supply and receipt from production, which supports the outbound delivery process from production and transfer of the delivery note to SAP EWM. In addition, the GR performed in SAP EWM will be transferred back to the SAP S/4HANA Cloud system for further processing.

More functionality is constantly being added to SAP S/4HANA Cloud; therefore, this list isn't exhaustive.

4.4   Outlook

As mentioned earlier in this chapter, embedded EWM and TM will be the target architecture; as a result, SAP has scheduled more innovations in these two areas. In addition, SAP will add more enhanced and predictive analytics, especially in the area of logistics, IM, and EWM. Machine learning and artificial intelligence (AI) will be introduced in several areas, such as quality management and IM, to improve process optimization.

Table 4.3 lists key innovations that are scheduled for the supply chain in future releases coming in 2019 and later.

Area	Future Innovations
Inventory management	■ New scenarios for demand-driven intercompany and stock transfers ■ Machine learning and AI for master data and process optimization
Logistics execution	■ New and improved analytics for shipping and receiving specialists ■ Improved KPIs and KPI monitoring capabilities to foster insight to action

Table 4.3 Key Innovations Planned in Supply Chain Areas

Area	Future Innovations

Transportation management	■ Industry requirements for the following:
	  – Retail
	  – E-commerce
	  – Direct store delivery (DSD)
	  – Bulk transportation
	■ Integration with advanced ATP
	■ Internet of Things (IoT) integration capabilities for track and trace
	■ Simulation capabilities for freight capacity
	■ Integration into external optimization/planning
	■ Integration into supply chain planning and SAP BW/4HANA
	■ Driver management

Quality management	■ Improved analytics of quality management data to provide insights to action ■ New SAP Fiori apps and pages for compliance management ■ Simplified inspection planning processes ■ Machine-learning capabilities for compliant processes with solutions proposals capabilities ■ Standardization of issue-resolution procedures
Extended warehouse management	■ Simulation and forecasting capabilities ■ Industry-specific extensions (e.g., automotive) ■ New scenarios for IoT ■ Enhanced analytics ■ Expanded warehouse automation ■ Extended e-commerce capabilities
Advanced ATP	■ Integration of ABC with product allocation and BOP

Table 4.3 Key Innovations Planned in Supply Chain Areas (Cont.)

4.5   Summary

In this chapter, we've shown the key pain points from our C-level executives and how SAP S/4HANA innovations can resolve some of these challenges. The innovations discussed in this chapter include the following:

- Simplified data model and table structure, reducing the complexity of both the data model and custom code implementation

- Embedded functionalities in SAP S/4HANA, such as EWM and TM, strengthening the back-office functionalities from the core and reducing complexity in the system landscape

- No redundant data and simplified processes because all processes are executed within one system (direct postings and no redundant documents, such as expected GR documents)

- Real-time analytics providing the most accurate information on inventory levels and ability for better decision-making due to improved visibility

- One material valuation instead of two (IM and ML), reducing complexity and redundant setup and information

- AATP enabling a high level of flexibility for users to implement ATP or product allocation scenarios

- Release for delivery supporting users in the case of ad hoc order-confirmation changes, providing an oversight of all the current order confirmation status

- Catch weight management, quality management, and commodity management functionalities

We also explored the key supply chain functionality offerings for SAP S/4HANA Cloud, as of fall 2018.

SAP will continue to provide innovations for the supply chain LoB. The areas of focus for next releases will be embedded TM, improved analytics, and machine-learning and AI capabilities.

In the next chapter, we'll move on to sales, marketing, commerce, and service management functionality in SAP S/4HANA.

Chapter 5

Sales, Marketing, Commerce, and Service Management

This chapter will focus on the industry pain points within the sales, marketing, commerce, and service management lines of business and will discuss the SAP S/4HANA innovations that help C-level executives address these key pain points.

In this chapter, we'll focus on three lines of business (LoBs): sales, marketing and commerce (which are often grouped), and service management. We'll start with a look at industry pain points and the benefits SAP S/4HANA offers. Then, we'll discuss the key functionalities for each LoB, starting with sales. For example, within sales, the highlights are the sales order cockpit and functionalities, such as condition contract settlement. As in previous chapters, we'll discuss each functionality in a more detailed way in later sections to provide a good understanding of what these functionalities have to offer.

Then, we'll discuss the functionalities within marketing and commerce and especially go into a little more detail for the embedded customer relationship management (CRM) and integration with SAP Billing and Revenue Innovation Management. Finally, we'll conclude the chapter with the functionalities SAP S/4HANA offers for service management, service master data maintenance, and service parts and service agreements management.

The final sections of this chapter will include a discussion of relevant SAP S/4HANA Cloud functionality, an outlook, and a summary for all three LoBs.

5.1   Industry Pain Points and SAP S/4HANA Benefits

The role of the internal sales representative has become increasingly challenging. Today, customers are more demanding than ever and expect a more personal approach to service. In addition, they want the most up-to-date information related to their orders and delivery timelines at any point in time. Expecting sales representatives to share information with them, listen to their feedback, and involve them in the order fulfillment process creates many challenges for the sales representative:

- **Lack of real-time data**
  Real-time data is necessary for managers to make more efficient order fulfillment decisions.

- **Advanced analytics**
  Lack of advanced analytics hinders the creation of a holistic view of the supply chain processes.

- **Integration**
  Better integration of the various components of the supply chain is necessary to identify risks and issues more quickly (e.g., stock shortages).

- **Collaboration with customers**
  Enterprises need to collaborate with their customers to improve and personalize the customer experience and thus drive growth.

SAP S/4HANA can support today's key challenges in sales. Its capabilities offer an internal sales representative a comprehensive overview of the current order fulfillment situation. Real-time data and on-the-fly analytics can be used for troubleshooting and decision-making purposes.

SAP S/4HANA can support the key challenges that chief supply chain officers (CSCOs) face today. Table 5.1 describes how SAP S/4HANA innovations can address the key challenges from sales, marketing and commerce, and service management perspectives.

Challenge for the CSCO	How SAP S/4HANA Can Help
Lack of visibility: ■ A traditional SAP ERP system doesn't provide capabilities for a holistic overview of the order fulfillment flow. ■ Lack of real-time visibility of accurate inventory levels results in incorrectly committed sales orders.	SAP S/4HANA provides the following: ■ Advances a single source of holistic transparency into sales order fulfillment issues on desktops and tablets. ■ Increased visibility for remaining noncommitted inventories and possibilities to cover incoming customer orders. ■ Sales order fulfillment cockpit for improved visibility of the order flow and allowing internal sales representatives to monitor and focus on exceptional cases. ■ Increased visibility through new and improved SAP Fiori apps for performance and order fulfillment management. ■ Improved visibility by using machine learning, predictive, and co-pilot capabilities in sales monitoring and analytics.
Increasing volatility in demand and supply and insufficient capabilities to meet the increasing customer demand due to the following: ■ Lack of order flow status and inability to track orders. ■ Insufficient system support to allow exception-based work. ■ Inability to have an accurate overview of stock levels.	SAP S/4HANA improves the process as follows: ■ Improved sales processes to help enterprises be more prepared for volatility in supply. ■ Improved customer retention by enhancing the flow of information on order status and tracking. ■ Accelerated complaints and returns management. ■ Exception-based working to monitor and react to shortages faster. ■ Clarification of issues effectively and efficiently by prescriptive decision support and facilitated collaboration. ■ Advanced available-to-promise (AATP) process with flexible rules to quickly reschedule orders based on customer and demand priorities with prescriptive decision support.

Table 5.1 Sales Challenges and SAP S/4HANA Advances

Challenge for the CSCO	How SAP S/4HANA Can Help
Increased complexity: ■ Complexity in document tables. ■ Inefficient and complex process to get order status flow or stock status; need to go through different screens or different sources to get the full status.	The following simplifications have been made: ■ One central master data object (business partner) is used for vendors, customers, and business partners. ■ SAP Global Trade Services (SAP GTS) replaces SAP Sales and Distribution (SD) foreign trade/customs. ■ SAP Credit Management replaces SD credit management. ■ Settlement management replaces SD rebates. ■ SAP Revenue Accounting and Reporting replaces SD revenue recognition. ■ Various document status tables were eliminated and moved to corresponding header and item tables. ■ Redundant document and rebate index tables were eliminated. ■ SD foreign trade will be replaced by SAP GTS as the central solution for foreign trade-related requirements. ■ Embedded CRM functionality will strengthen back-office activities in the core of the enterprise and reduce complexity due to all elements being embedded in one system. ■ Fully embedded service management processes within the core functionalities solution will reduce complexity in IT landscapes.
Lack of collaboration: ■ Lack of integrated view of the ATP situation. ■ Lack of integration with SAP CRM–related systems, resulting in an inability to view customer data to predict demand and act accordingly.	Better collaboration due to the following: ■ Improved integration of sales and production through the integrated ATP process. ■ Standard integration with the SAP S/4HANA extended solution SAP C/4HANA for improved collaboration. ■ Embedded CRM functionalities.

Table 5.1 Sales Challenges and SAP S/4HANA Advances (Cont.)

5.2   Key Sales Functionality

In this section, we'll discuss the SAP S/4HANA innovations for sales. Most of today's pain points in this area relate to the lack of real-time analytics and visibility across the entire order fulfillment process. We'll discuss how innovations such as the sales order fulfillment cockpit can help internal sales order representatives significantly in performing more efficient and effective work. Other areas of innovations are related to the condition contract settlement, which will enable enterprises to be more flexible due to the more rule-based and flexible architecture of the solutions.

5.2.1   Data Model Simplification

In SAP S/4HANA, various existing status tables have been eliminated, and all fields under these tables have been moved to the corresponding header and item tables for sales documents, deliveries, and billing documents. The document flow table has been simplified as well. Redundant document and rebate index tables have also been eliminated (see Figure 5.1).

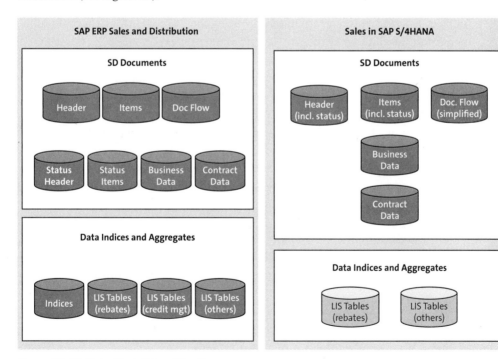

Figure 5.1 SD Data Model Simplification

With the changes in the data model, SAP S/4HANA offers the following key benefits:

- Lower total cost of ownership (TCO) due to data model simplification
- Reduced memory footprint (e.g., simplified document flow, elimination of index tables, fewer aggregates)
- Increased performance of SAP HANA queries and code pushdown (one SELECT statement instead of two SELECT statements; easier join for header/items, including status and business data)
- Increased robustness of rebate processing (no redundancies due to aggregates)
- Faster business outcomes with reduced operational cost
- Increased competitiveness with integrated, fast, and flexible business processes
- Higher employee productivity with focus on value-added tasks

5.2.2   Sales Order Fulfillment and Monitoring

SAP S/4HANA enables the user to monitor, manage, and collaborate on sales orders due for shipping and invoicing, allowing customers and company agreements to be fulfilled easily, on time, and accurately. By using the SAP S/4HANA sales order fulfillment cockpit facilitated by the SAP Fiori frontend user experience (UX), the sales representative can filter sales orders with issues and gain insight into the process execution. They can visualize issues over the entire end-to-end sales process in a single dashboard. Additionally, new innovations have been added to improve the overall sales order fulfillment analytics, enabling users to monitor order-to-delivery performance in a better way. In this section, we'll discuss the sales order fulfillment cockpit functionality and the additional key analytics for sales order monitoring.

Sales Order Fulfillment Cockpit

The sales order fulfillment cockpit in SAP S/4HANA offers the following business benefits:

- Enables visibility into order fulfillment
- Provides internal sales representatives the ability to focus on critical issues/exceptional cases
- Combines analytical insights with operational actions to allow internal sales representatives to run actions directly and track the progress at any point in time
- Improves collaboration with internal and external contacts to resolve issues

With the sales order fulfillment cockpit, companies can reduce their order-to-cash cycle time, increase their service level, and reduce outstanding payments. In the traditional SAP ERP system, the internal sales rep must check multiple reports for a holistic view of all related processes. Multiple issues in one order can't be detected easily in one step, creating a higher risk of undetected exceptions. Problem-related communication and decisions can't be tracked in the system, and reports need to be run multiple times.

In the sales order fulfillment cockpit, the user can immediately view all the sales order fulfillment issues on one screen categorized by sales order issues, delivery issues, supply chain issues, or billing issues. The SAP Fiori UX enables the user to drill down into each type of issue and immediately make corrections through the sales order fulfillment cockpit.

Figure 5.2 shows the sales order fulfillment cockpit with the number of issues for each category and the sales documents details visible.

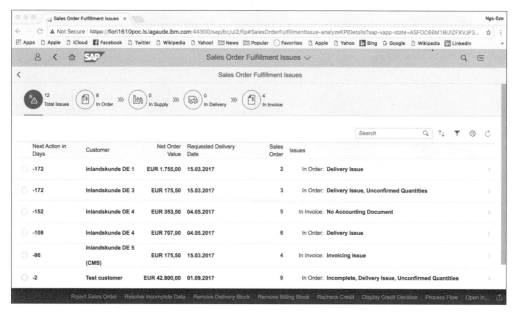

Figure 5.2 Sales Order Fulfillment Cockpit

Sales Order Monitoring

With the 1809 release, SAP has provided some key new features in the area of sales monitoring and analytics:

- The first SAP CoPilot functionalities have been applied to use natural language either by voice or text to track and display sales orders, for example, "Show me all sales orders from client xx."
- Natural language can be used to create a subsequent sales order from a quotation.
- Predictive analytics and machine learning capabilities can do the following:
  - Determine the quotation conversion probability and gain reliable insight into order probability and expected sales volume based on insights.
  - Monitor and analyze delivery performance to check customer fulfillment based on the customer requested delivery date.

Sales Orders, Billing, and Returns Management

In addition to the improved sales analytics and monitoring, some new enhancements and innovations have been added in the area of sales orders, billing, and returns management:

- New functionality has been added to the Track Sales Order app to enable users to do the following:
  - Execute mass transactions directly from the sales order list generated through the app.
  - Navigate from the "search result" list to the sales order details, where sales order fulfillment is graphically displayed.
  - View orders with issues and directly go to the sales order fulfillment cockpit to resolve the issues.
  - Reject sales orders and sales order items from the detailed view for the relevant sales order.
- Workflow approval capabilities for credit memo requests are provided, allowing users to display and manage the approval workflow for credit memo requests with the Inbox Approval app.
- Enhancements have been made to the Manage Sales Orders and Manage Sales Orders without Charge apps with new capabilities to perform mass changes at the header level.
- A new SAP Fiori app is available for managing incomplete sales orders with price differences with the customer expected price, including blocking and releasing these incomplete sales orders.

- Enhancements have been made to the Manage Customer Returns app, providing support to the users to do the following:
  - Return third-party products to the suppliers.
  - Conduct inspections at customer sites and have materials remain at the customer site.
- New features have been added for advanced returns management, enabling the following:
  - Processing of service materials, bills of materials (BOMs), and full products in the returns order and material inspection.
  - Entry of additional inspection fields in the return order and material inspection.
  - Support of legal requirements related to the refund of services related to a physical product when products and services have been sold together.

Enhancements and new features for billing and invoicing include the following:

- Upload functionality of billing document requests via Microsoft Excel for omni-channel convergent billing using the Manage Billing Document Request app.
- Easier scheduling of recurring billing document creation and billing jobs release through the use of rule-based data selection.
- Enabling users to set relative rules that specify the period for billing.
- Enabling users to specify variable date rules, for example, to bill all the billing due list documents with a billing date before the first of the month on the fifth of the same month.
- Enhancements to the Manage Billing Document app with new functionality to perform billing document split analysis or compare two billing documents and view what has caused the document split.
- The My Sales Order Overview app provides users with information such as sales order data and performance figures to highlight the areas where actions are needed using actionable cards in a dashboard format.

5.2.3 Condition Contract Settlement

In SAP S/4HANA, SD rebates are replaced by the condition contract settlement process, followed by the settlement management process. This means that all existing rebate agreements can only be processed up until the end of the validity date and then closed by a final agreement. Customers with SAP CRM trade promotion management (TPM) who want to integrate their existing TPM scenarios with SAP S/4HANA will have to use SD rebate processing, which has been optimized for the database footprint. Consider the following key differences between condition contract settlement and the SD rebate agreement functionality:

- With condition contract settlement, SAP provides a central solution for customer and vendor conditions. In the traditional solution, all customer rebate–relevant billing documents are stored in table VBOX. For changes that needed to be applied retrospectively, this table will need to be updated through a separate transaction (Transaction VBOF), and all billing documents in this table would be locked at the same time. The other issue is the size of the table; this table could contain millions of entries required for rebate calculation.

- In condition contract settlement, there is no longer any table VBOF equivalent. Rebate settlement-related information doesn't need to be stored in a table; instead, rebate conditions will be applied instantly. In addition, condition contract settlement enables the user to use multiple data sources for rebate settlements. Traditionally, this can only be done based on the billing documents.

Figure 5.3 shows the traditional SD rebate agreement versus the condition contract settlement.

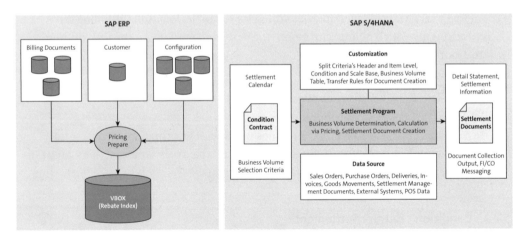

Figure 5.3 SAP ERP versus SAP S/4HANA Customer Rebates

The key benefits of condition contract settlement are as follows:

- A flexible and state-of-the-art solution for settlement scenarios in which users can determine business volume sources based on flexible and definable criteria that can be configured in Customizing
- Designed for high performance (with SAP HANA)
- Enables new and innovative rebate scenarios to be set up thanks to its open architecture

5.2.4   Foreign Trade

In SAP S/4HANA, SAP GTS replaces SD foreign trade/customs. The foreign trade/customs functionality won't be available any longer in SAP S/4HANA; SAP GTS is the successor of this requirement. SAP GTS (previously provided as an external service installed as an additional instance) can be natively integrated with SAP S/4HANA. Letter of credit, legal control, export control, and preference management in foreign trade/customs aren't available any longer in the material master; instead, the SAP GTS-based functionalities are used. SAP GTS offers additional functionalities for import management and export management. For intrastat reporting, a customer can leverage the functionality within SAP S/4HANA.

Prior to conversion, careful analysis of all currently used foreign trade processes is needed. If the customer uses a third-party foreign trade system, it's possible that an adjustment will be needed from the respective third-party foreign trade system; alternatively, SAP GTS can be connected to SAP S/4HANA to run the respective foreign trade processes.

5.2.5   Credit Management and Revenue Accounting

SAP Credit Management (FIN-FSCM-CR) replaces SD credit management in SAP S/4HANA. SAP provides tools to migrate to SAP Credit Management, which contains several elements:

- Configuration data
- Master data
- Credit exposure data
- Credit decision data

On the revenue accounting side, SAP Revenue Accounting and Reporting replaces SD revenue recognition. SD revenue recognition isn't available in SAP S/4HANA. Instead, SAP S/4HANA functionality should be used that supports the new revenue accounting standard according to International Financial Reporting Standard 15 (IFRS 15) and adopted by local generally accepted accounting principles (GAAPs).

5.3   Key Marketing and Commerce Functionality

Let's turn our attention to key innovations in marketing and commerce.

With SAP S/4HANA, the core SAP CRM functionality is brought into the core of your enterprise. With this change, SAP communicates a clear split between front-office and back-office activities by strengthening the back-office activities through the embedded CRM functionalities. Enterprises can choose to integrate SAP S/4HANA with extended solutions as well, such as SAP Sales Cloud and SAP Service Cloud to bring more functionalities to the front-office end. In addition, SAP S/4HANA also offers integration with the SAP Billing and Revenue Innovation Management solution.

5.3.1   Customer Relationship Management

With embedded CRM, SAP has headed in a new product direction. Traditionally, SAP CRM and SAP ERP are separated; between the two systems, there are many duplicate functionalities, such as quote management, pricing management, and order and contract management. The integration between the two systems is rather complex; replication efforts in both systems is required to move and transfer the appropriate information between both systems.

With SAP S/4HANA, SAP offers rich CRM functionality in the core with seamless integration and low TCO, with the end goals of optimizing the processes in the back office (SAP S/4HANA) and simplifying the processes in the frontend with SAP C/4HANA. Figure 5.4 illustrates how the traditional scenario is changed by this new production direction.

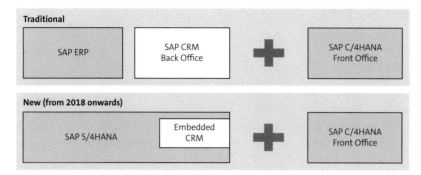

Figure 5.4 Traditional Back-Office and Front-Office Scenario versus New Scenario

With the first release of CRM functionalities into SAP S/4HANA, SAP brings the key service management-related functionalities into the core of SAP S/4HANA.

Key benefits of embedded CRM in SAP S/4HANA are as follows:

- Simplified landscape and operations due to being embedded within the SAP S/4HANA core, thus reducing interfaces and middleware systems
- Reduction of functional redundancies
- Data harmonization
- SAP Fiori 2.0 UX

The current scope for embedded CRM in SAP S/4HANA includes the following:

- Service core functionality, as follows:
  - Service contract management
  - Install base management
  - Service quotation management
  - Case management
  - Integration with SAP Leonardo for ticket and email categorization
- Sales core functionality, as follows:
  - Activity (tasks and appointments)
  - Calendar
  - Lead
  - Opportunity

- Replication-free and harmonized master data for the following:
  - Functional locations
  - Product bundles
- System consolidation via the SAP Fiori launchpad integration mode

Now that we have a better understanding of the embedded CRM scope, let's have a look at SAP Billing and Revenue Innovation Management functionalities in SAP S/4HANA.

5.3.2   Billing and Revenue Management

SAP Billing and Revenue Innovation Management is the SAP solution that enables enterprises, especially in the telecom and utilities industries, to process high volumes of transactions while enjoying increased flexibility and better integration with the different components of the offer-to-cash cycle.

In SAP S/4HANA, contract accounts receivable and payable (FI-CA) is integrated with SAP Biller Direct. With this integration, enterprises can offer their end customers a solution in which they can view their account status, receive invoices, and make self-service payments online. The SAP Biller Direct functionality isn't the target architecture within SAP S/4HANA, but it will still be available for now. In addition, master data replication, such as for business partners and contract accounts, is supported from FI-CA to SAP-convergent charging as joint replication, which means only the master data related to provider contracts that are received in FI-CA will be replicated.

As of release 1809, the following existing solutions aren't yet available in SAP S/4HANA:

- Billing and invoicing of consumption data isn't possible within SD and FI-AR but will only be available in FI-CA. Therefore, replication of provider contracts and the automatic creation of contract accounts without existing contract accounts in SAP CRM isn't possible.
- The Common Object Layer Framework, used to transfer data among SAP CRM, SAP convergent charging, and SAP ERP, will not be provided any longer. With SAP S/4HANA, this functionality will be redundant, as the transfer of data will be performed directly.

With the available integration with SAP S/4HANA, enterprises will now have more flexibility and scalability, leveraging the benefits of the SAP Billing and Revenue Innovation Management solution and integrating with SAP S/4HANA. Companies will now have the ability and flexibility to create new business models and leverage the following functionalities in FI-CA:

- Pricing simulation
- Subscription order management
- Billing, receivables, and collections
- Transaction pricing
- Usage metering

5.4   Key Service Management Functionality

In this section, we'll discuss the functionalities provided by SAP S/4HANA for the service management area. Most importantly, beginning with release 1610, enterprises can now leverage the SAP S/4HANA core to perform full end-to-end service management processes. Let's walk through the key functionalities that will enable enterprises to perform their service and service master data management processes, the management of spare parts, and service agreement processes.

5.4.1   Optimized Service and Service Master Data Management

SAP first offered service management functionalities with SAP S/4HANA release 1610. For service master data management, the following functionalities are available:

- **Technical assets and structure history**
  This includes the master data maintenance of details relevant to the customer for the maintenance of installed equipment at the customer site, such as customer location, call center, field service, depot repair, and so on. Within the master data setup, you can provide relevant hierarchical and relationship structures for increased visibility. You also can view the history related to changes to service maintenance activities and master data changes.

- **Service task lists and catalogs**
  SAP S/4HANA provides a service task list with a sequence of individual tasks, including the required resources, tools, and materials to complete maintenance service requests. Through service catalog functionality, enterprises define and standardize a set of activities as a predefined service offered to their customers.

- **Service maintenance plan and event scheduling**
  This includes the automatic scheduling of service maintenance tasks based on

available time and resources, determined by real-time data. With SAP S/4HANA, companies can plan predictive and preventive services based on a predefined and automatically scheduled maintenance plan.

5.4.2   Service Parts and Service Agreement Management

SAP S/4HANA offers foundational capabilities to enable enterprises to fulfill key processes around service parts and service agreement management. The key functionalities can be divided into the following subprocesses:

- **Service management**
  Within the service management area, enterprises can now capture the different service management processes in SAP S/4HANA. During service initiation, all relevant tasks related to the service will be captured, and requirements such as resources and parts requirements will be defined to allow planning and scheduling of the service.

  With SAP S/4HANA, field service engineers and service management departments now have access to the most up-to-date data related to the service history and the service requirements to be able to deliver and execute the service. After the service is successfully fulfilled, billing information can be retrieved instantly from all relevant sources, and monitoring capabilities will be provided to ensure tracking of timely billing and service revenue.

- **Service parts warehousing and fulfillment**
  Within SAP S/4HANA, several analytical apps are available to provide instant data on the available inventory and full integration with the core functionalities of SAP S/4HANA. This will enable enterprises to increase efficiency in the planning, procurement, and warehousing of parts.

- **Service agreement management**
  This includes the handling of service agreements across different industries. SAP S/4HANA enables companies to support different types of service agreements, such as service contracts and warranties. Within the service agreements, companies can capture all relevant information related to the service, such as the type of service and the scope, which conditions are applied to the agreements, and how the service will be executed.

5.5   Sales, Marketing, Commerce, and Service Management in SAP S/4HANA Cloud

We'll now discuss the available SAP S/4HANA Cloud, public option, features for sales, commerce, marketing, and service management. In the latest SAP S/4HANA Cloud release 1808, no functionalities have been made available yet in the area of commerce, service management, and marketing. Therefore, in this chapter, we'll mainly discuss the capabilities that are available in the area of sales, such as the following:

- **Sales contract management**
  These functionalities enable companies to create, change, and list contracts. You can also use the available lists/reports to display, for example, expired contracts, completed contracts, and so on. SAP S/4HANA Cloud offers you advanced analytics to track contract fulfillment rates, focus on contracts with the highest value, and further drill down to the contract details if needed.

- **Sales order management and processing**
  SAP S/4HANA Cloud supports multiple order scenarios that are also available in SAP S/4HANA on-premise. Some examples of scenarios that are available in SAP S/4HANA Cloud are the following:
  - Sell from stock
  - Sales order processing with down payment
  - Inquiry processing
  - Quotation processing
  - Consignment processing
  - Make-to-order (MTO) sales processing
  - Free-of-charge delivery processing
  - Listing

  Credit management functionality is available to enable companies to set credit limits for their customers. This credit check will be performed at the moment of creation or change of the sales documents. The system takes the total receivables, the open items, and the credit value of the sales document into account while performing the credit check.

- **Sales billing**
  In addition, in the area of sales billing, SAP S/4HANA Cloud offers the following standard scenarios:

- – Debit/credit memo processing
- – Billing document processing
- – Omnichannel convergent billing
- – Invoice list processing

- **Claims, returns, and refund management**
  This feature enables companies to process customer returns, creating return orders with or without reference to either invoice or sales order. A return material authorization form is forwarded to the customer and attached to the incoming goods. A return delivery note is created with reference to the return order, and when the goods have physically arrived, it will be received into stock. A credit memo will then be sent to the customer. SAP S/4HANA Cloud also enables users to implement workflows to optimize the approval process for internally created credit memo requests.

- **Sales monitoring and analytics**
  This feature offers you different capabilities to check and monitor the status of the sales orders. Some key functionalities are available for the following processes:
  - – Managing duplicate sales documents
  - – Managing incomplete documents
  - – Analyzing incoming sales orders (e.g., monthly trends and net amounts of sales orders) and filter and report sales orders based on various criteria (e.g., year, month, sales organization)
  - – Comparing planned versus actual sales

Keep in mind that given SAP S/4HANA Cloud's quarterly release cycle, this isn't a complete list of every available functionality.

5.6   Outlook

Table 5.2 outlines the direction and planned future innovations for sales, marketing and commerce, and service management. Some of the key innovations scheduled for the upcoming releases are related to embedded CRM to enhance the core SAP S/4HANA functionalities with more SAP CRM capabilities and machine-learning capabilities for order processing.

Area	Current Planned Innovation
Sales	<ul><li>Machine-learning and natural language-processing capabilities within order and billing processes</li><li>Improved integration functionalities for the integration of third-party products and customer developments</li><li>New capabilities to create customer-specific reports</li><li>Improved capabilities to create queries and reports for key performance indicator (KPI) monitoring in a simpler way</li></ul>
Marketing and commerce	<ul><li>Improved UX, such as new apps for SAP Billing and Revenue Innovation Management</li><li>Improved real-time analytics</li><li>Adoption of machine-learning and artificial intelligence (AI) capabilities and predictive models</li><li>Collaborative invoice cockpit for product bundles, incorporating converging billing</li></ul>
Service management	<ul><li>Additional sales core functionalities and further enhanced service core functionalities based on SAP CRM add-ons, such as the following:<ul><li>Lead and opportunity management</li><li>Activity, tasks, and territory</li><li>Call lists</li></ul></li><li>Integration with SAP S/4HANA order management functionality</li><li>Complaint and in-house repair</li><li>Basic field service</li><li>Improved UX and introduction of SAP CoPilot</li><li>Improved analytics (e.g., to increase efficiency for sales operations)</li></ul>

Table 5.2 Outlook for Sales, Marketing and Commerce, and Service Management with SAP S/4HANA

5.7 Summary

In this chapter, we discussed the pain points and challenges in sales, marketing and commerce, and service management. We walked through the key innovations in sales, such as data model simplification and the sales order fulfillment cockpit, and covered how new functionalities such as predictive analytics, machine learning, and co-pilot functionalities can help enterprises reduce complexity, improve sales order–fulfillment visibility, and be more flexible when setting up new sales scenarios and rebate agreements.

In marketing, commerce, and service management, the key innovation in SAP S/4HANA is the embedded CRM functionality, which makes SAP S/4HANA a stronger core for back-office activities when paired through standard integration with extended solutions, such as SAP Billing and Revenue Innovation Management. For service management, SAP offers a full end-to-end solution within the core to enable service master data management and service parts and service agreement management.

We closed the chapter with a discussion of the SAP S/4HANA Cloud functionality for sales and a look ahead at possible innovations for sales, marketing and commerce, and service management.

In the next chapter, we'll focus on the sourcing and procurement LoB.

Chapter 6
Sourcing and Procurement

In this chapter, we'll address C-level pain points specifically in the sourcing and procurement area and see how SAP S/4HANA can help C-level executives resolve these challenges.

This chapter focuses on sourcing and procurement by discussing the challenges in this area and how SAP S/4HANA can help address them. We'll then provide details about SAP S/4HANA innovations and the future innovations and direction for the sourcing and procurement line of business (LoB). We'll discuss these key functionalities in the different areas of sourcing and procurement, which includes operational purchasing, invoice and payables management, sourcing and contract management, and supplier evaluation and analytics. In the 1809 release of SAP S/4HANA, new machine learning capabilities were added to the sourcing and procurement LoB, enabling intelligent procurement for enterprises. We'll also explore these functionalities in a more detailed way.

6.1 Industry Pain Points and SAP S/4HANA Benefits

One of the key challenges within sourcing and procurement today is the technical complexity of the landscape related to the previous solutions introduced for procurement, such as SAP Ariba, SAP Supplier Relationship Management, and SAP Supplier Lifecycle Management. Different systems are providing operational, tactical, and strategic activities, resulting in many challenges in aligning data across systems and supporting the data.

In addition, challenges in today's enterprise resource planning (ERP) systems are related to the following:

- Lack of visibility to view the entire purchasing flow and lack of real-time data to provide accurate inventory levels

- Insufficient capabilities in the system to enable users to search for and view purchasing information efficiently

- Inability to use advanced analytics to better understand and react to changes in the environment

- Lack of integration between systems, forcing users to go in different systems via different user interfaces (UIs)

With the introduction of SAP S/4HANA Enterprise Management, some of the traditional challenges are being addressed in the following ways:

- Leveraging the Ariba Network to overcome the complexity of supply chains and to provide a system that functions as a single point of interaction

- Enabling self-service purchasing using SAP Ariba

- Integrating SAP Supplier Lifecycle Management functions with collaboration tools for a more efficient and tighter collaboration with business partners to reduce time to market, increase flexibility in the context of volatile demands, and increase supply chain visibility

- Introducing a simplified process using one data object for purchasing requirements, which helps to shorten process cycle times

- Using built-in transactional or strategic analytics, for example, through improved contract monitoring or supplier evaluation reporting

SAP S/4HANA provides a streamlined view of all procure-to-pay processes and gives you the visibility and insights you need to make strategic decisions or to optimize the procure-to-pay processes. With the new system capabilities combining online analytical processing (OLAP) with online transaction processing (OLTP) on the same SAP Fiori screen, drilling down into the lowest level of detail with real-time exposure gives performance providers a compelling value proposition to exploit. In the following subsections, we'll discuss the most important new functionalities introduced with SAP S/4HANA Enterprise Management for the sourcing and procurement space.

Table 6.1 lists the key challenges for the chief supply chain officer (CSCO) for the sourcing and procurement area and how SAP S/4HANA functionalities can address today's challenges.

Challenge for the CSCO	How SAP S/4HANA Can Help
Lack of visibility: • No single view of the entire purchase order flow. • Lack of real-time data to provide accurate inventory levels. • Limited search capabilities; users go through different screens (or even different systems) to view data related across contract worklists and contract and supplier data. • Users access different systems to view different data across the entire flow.	Improved visibility and transparency with the following: • Ability to track purchase order flow. • Visibility of accurate inventory position across multiple plants. • Dynamic and flexible search feature across contract worklists with capability to navigate directly to contract and supplier fact sheets. • One system for purchasing of all direct materials, indirect materials, and services with a harmonized UI.
Increasing volatility in demand and supply: • Lack of an integrated view of the process doesn't provide sufficient support to enterprises to be more prepared for volatility in demand and supply. • Lack of analytics.	SAP S/4HANA for sourcing and procurement helps reduce the impact of volatility in supply with the following: • Standard integration for SAP Ariba for a more efficient procurement process. • Advanced analytics to identify discounts and pricing opportunities for better supply planning.
Increased complexity: • Technical complexity of the landscape due to different solutions for different parts of the processes. • Challenges aligning data across different systems.	Complexity is reduced by the following: • One-step management of contracts and use of self-service requisitioning for procurement. • One central master data object (business partner) for vendors, customers, and business partners. • Standard integration with SAP Ariba for more optimized processes and a single source of truth.

Table 6.1 Sourcing and Procurement Challenges and SAP S/4HANA Advances

Challenge for the CSCO	How SAP S/4HANA Can Help
	<ul><li>Machine-learning capabilities to improve efficiency and complexity of processes for users, for example, automatic proposal of material group and reduction of free text item due to auto proposal for creation of new catalog item.</li><li>Smart buying capabilities using natural language.</li><li>Central procurement for system landscapes with multiple ERP systems.</li></ul>
Lack of collaboration:<ul><li>Lack of integration between different systems to provide a single source of truth.</li><li>Inability to view an entire material flow for in-house production and procurement production.</li></ul>	Collaboration is enhanced with the following:<ul><li>Ability to secure many-to-many networked collaboration with trading partners.</li><li>Seamless collaboration between production and procurement departments via the MRP cockpit.</li><li>Standard integration with SAP S/4HANA solutions such as SAP Ariba to improve collaboration.</li></ul>

Table 6.1 Sourcing and Procurement Challenges and SAP S/4HANA Advances (Cont.)

6.2   Key Sourcing and Procurement Functionality

In this section, we'll walk through the key SAP S/4HANA innovations in sourcing and procurement. We'll start with the innovations in the operational purchasing and provide some examples of SAP Fiori apps that will enable companies to perform operational procurement processes more efficiently. Then, we'll discuss the key functionalities for invoicing, sourcing, and contract management, before taking a look at innovations in supplier evaluation and analytics. Finally, we'll examine the impact of machine learning and intelligent procurement.

6.2.1   Operational Purchasing

Several key changes to the operational procurement processes will be employed within the SAP S/4HANA Enterprise Management core in the following areas: self-service procurement, collaboration, UI changes, and purchase order output.

In the traditional SAP ERP system, there are no real-time insights for the operational purchaser to perform daily tasks. Decisions are made based on outdated data, and there is no real-time key performance indicator (KPI) reporting, which makes improving the service level challenging.

With SAP S/4HANA, users can get real-time insights and KPIs immediately. The operational purchaser can do his job based on the most up-to-date information, and, at any point in time, users can run real-time KPI reports to get insight on their performance. SAP S/4HANA offers the following real-time KPI reports:

- Purchasing and invoicing spend
- Contracts
- Purchase order average delivery time
- Supplier information

SAP S/4HANA provides the operational purchaser a holistic view of activities within operational procurement. Real-time analytics facilitates the purchasers being able to react directly to spend exceptions or overdue purchase order items.

In addition to this, with SAP S/4HANA release 1809, the central procurement hub functionality has been added to enable enterprises to centrally manage all their key activities around purchasing, contract management, and sources of supply management.

The **Procurement Overview Page** (Figure 6.1) provides all companies with all their relevant KPI information in one screen, enabling them to immediately see their current performance without running multiple reports as in the traditional SAP ERP system. They can immediately see exceptions and act on them.

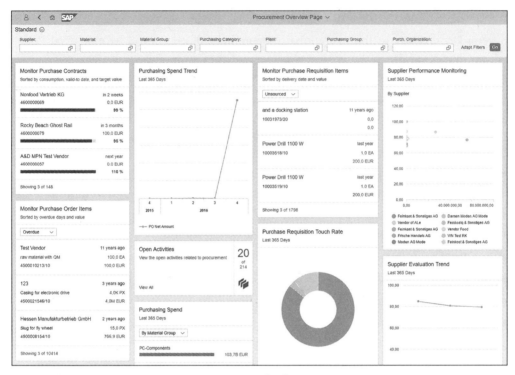

Figure 6.1 Procurement Overview Page with All Procurement KPIs on One Screen

Figure 6.2 shows an example of one of the standard KPIs for purchase order average time. This app enables the strategic buyer to monitor performance and follow up with the supplier proactively based on available statistics. Like other analytical SAP Fiori apps, it offers users several views for display, such as the following:

- **By Supplier**
- **By Material Group**
- **By Plant**
- **By Purchasing Category**
- **By Document**

Self-service requisitioning is a relatively new capability in SAP S/4HANA. The self-service procurement processes have been simplified by consolidating the shopping cart and purchase requisition objects into a single structure based on the purchase requisition. The basic process of requisition, approval, purchase order creation, and goods receipt is facilitated by the UI changes, described in the next section.

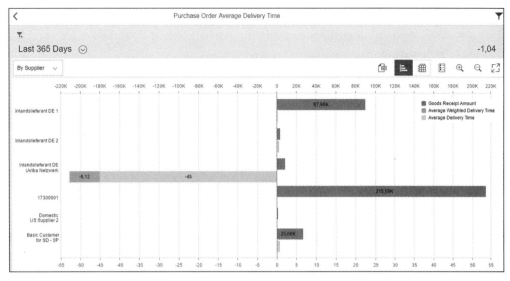

Figure 6.2 KPIs in the Purchase Order Average Delivery Time App

With SAP S/4HANA, customers have integrated catalog functionality within the purchasing requisition SAP Fiori apps based on the Enterprise Search functionality. The SAP ERP self-service procurement business function is made obsolete with the SAP S/4HANA core deployment.

In the traditional system, a user must go through multiple screens to find and assign sources to purchase requisitions. The creation of purchase orders is often performed through a batch input report. In SAP S/4HANA, all tasks to search, find, and assign a source of supply, as well as create a purchase order, can be handled from one screen. The system automatically proposes the available sources of supply to the purchaser. This significantly increases the efficiency and the speed of the purchaser when assigning supplies to the purchase requisitions. In addition, a new SAP Fiori interface has been introduced to convert purchase requisitions to purchase orders. Transaction ME57 is still available through SAP GUI.

The creation of manual purchase orders in SAP S/4HANA is supported by several capabilities to improve efficiency:

- Users can select previous purchase orders or sources, such as a template, thus minimizing errors and improving efficiency.

- Several fields are prefilled based on the selected supplier or material type.
- A draft purchase order is created automatically when sessions are lost, and it's retrieved automatically when logged on again.

Several additional SAP Fiori apps are delivered to manage this streamlined procurement process:

- **Create Purchase Requisition app**
  The Create Purchase Requisition app enables users to select products from different catalogs and create a purchase requisition. It offers the ability to create free text descriptions for items in the purchase requisitions. Improved search capabilities let users easily and efficiently find relevant catalog items.

- **My Purchase Requisitions app**
  The My Purchase Requisitions app (see Figure 6.3) offers users a single app to check the status of purchase requisitions and all other information relevant to purchase requisitions. You can filter based on predefined criteria and go to display or change mode to make changes to purchase requisitions directly from this SAP Fiori app. It offers procurement in a single app as a go-to point for all·purchase requisition-related information and follow-up activities.

- **Post Goods Receipts app**
  With the Post Goods Receipts app, users can directly post received goods with reference to the purchase order.

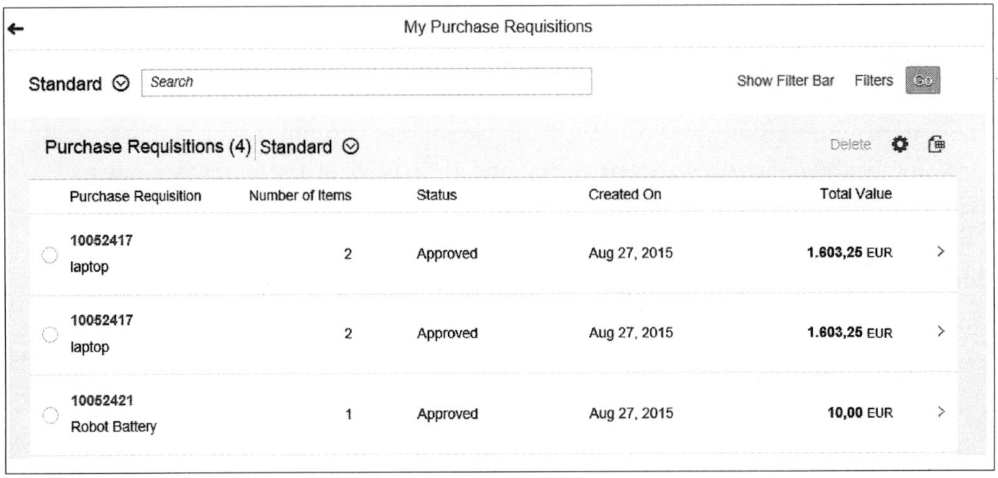

Figure 6.3 My Purchase Requisitions App

The Ariba Network is currently only available for use with SAP ERP 6.0 and forms a core part of the SAP S/4HANA release. SAP Ariba integration can be performed via one of three distinct methods (see Figure 6.4):

- Direct integration of SAP S/4HANA through standard output management
- SAP Process Orchestration (on-premise)
- SAP Cloud Platform Integration (cloud deployment)

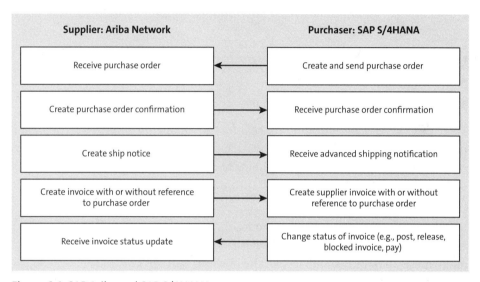

Figure 6.4 SAP Ariba and SAP S/4HANA

With SAP S/4HANA, a new output management approach is in place. By design, the new output management includes cloud qualities, such as extensibility enablement, multitenancy enablement, and modification-free configuration. Therefore, the complete configuration differs from the configuration used when output management is based on table NAST. The new configuration is based on the Business Rules Framework plus (BRFplus), which is accessible for customers. In SAP S/4HANA, the target architecture is based on Adobe Document Server and Adobe Forms only. For the form-determination rules (along with other output parameters), the BRFplus functionality is used (in this sense, in combination with the message determination). Output management based on table NAST is no longer supported for new documents in purchase orders. Purchase orders that are migrated from legacy systems and for which table NAST-based output has been determined can be processed with this technology. For all new purchase orders, the new output management is used. Therefore, in procurement for purchase orders, there is a need to adapt the configuration settings related to output management.

6.2.2 Invoice and Payables Management

Organizations face several challenges within accounts payable (AP) processes that should be addressed with systemized solutions in the future:

- Slow invoice processing, leading to late payments and endangering supplier relations
- Lack of visibility into invoice and payment data
- Slow invoice/payment approvals
- High percentage of exceptions that require manual handling

There's a change of authorization concept for the supplier invoice. In the past, when posting invoices for a specific company code, the user was checked to ensure he was authorized for any plant. Now, the system checks the authorization for the company code in general. If an item is changed with a purchase order reference, the specific plant is checked.

In line with the change in the data model, the business partner is now the primary business object, meaning the business partner transactions are now used to complete the creation or maintenance of the business partner. This will allow a holistic view of the business partner for all applications. However, in terms of managing the configuration, certain constraints exist when dealing with the business partner object; for example, the customer vendor integration (CVI) mapping and business partner number ranges must be considered across multiple application areas.

The traditional SAP ERP system has redundant object models for master data. With SAP S/4HANA, the business partner approach is now capable of centrally managing master data for business partners, customers, and vendors. In a business relationship, the business partner can assume other business partner roles and—in this case, with SAP S/4HANA—the general data, which is independent of a business partner's function or application-specific extensions, need not be created again. This prevents data from being created and stored redundantly.

As a result, the standard IDoc type for vendor master integration, CREMAS, is discontinued and not available within an SAP S/4HANA system. Therefore, the replacement technology for business partner replication via service-oriented architecture (SOA) must be used.

6.2.3   Sourcing and Contract Management

The processes from a sourcing and contract management perspective that are delivered within the first releases of SAP S/4HANA are streamlined and mostly based on the standard SAP ERP transactional processes, facilitated through the same SAP Fiori apps that have been available since the first release of SAP S/4HANA.

The processes and transactions available within the SAP S/4HANA core components related to sourcing processes are limited to the standard request for quotation (RFQ) and quotation transactions from SAP ERP.

The contract management functions that are present within the SAP S/4HANA initial releases are the same as those contained within the SAP Business Suite powered by SAP HANA and enabled by SAP Fiori.

There are three main SAP Fiori apps that enable operational contract management:

- **Purchase Contract app**
  Displays basic information about a contract (Figure 6.5).
- **Contract Line Item app**
  Shows details about a contract item and allows users to navigate from this screen to other transactions to make changes to contract items directly.
- **Manage Purchase Contracts app**
  Delivers an analytical view of contract usage, status, and validity. It enables users to search and display all contract-related information and verify the status of contracts immediately through a single screen. From this SAP Fiori app, you can navigate to other transactions.

The contract management processes are facilitated through these SAP Fiori apps, which deliver a display-only view of the standard SAP ERP data structures for contracts.

A set of SAP Fiori apps for establishing and managing purchasing info records is used within the SAP S/4HANA core component, allowing for an overview of the various sources of supply for a material across plants and purchasing organizations. The Manage Sources of Supply app provides a list display of the purchasing info record and links to SAP Fiori fact sheet apps for displaying purchasing info records.

For complex source-to-contract functions, we recommend SAP Ariba.

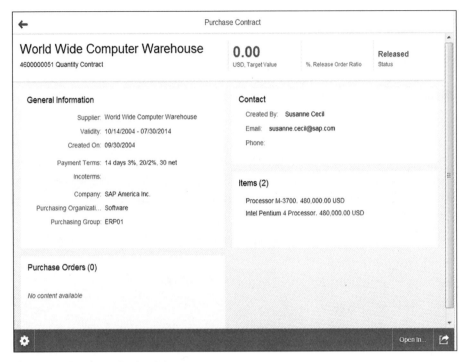

Figure 6.5 Purchase Contract App

6.2.4   Supplier Evaluation and Analytics

With the initial release of SAP S/4HANA Enterprise Management, SAP has made the move to incorporate the following three core business functions from the SAP Supplier Lifecycle Management solution within the latest releases of SAP S/4HANA:

- **Supplier portfolio management**
  Strategic procurement activities such as supplier categorization are now enabled through the portfolio management business function. Specifically, strategic buyers can classify and manage their supply base within purchasing categories. The integration components for Dunn & Bradstreet (D&B) integration also are included in the SAP S/4HANA core delivery.

  With SAP S/4HANA, suppliers can be classified based on various criteria, such as spend, strategic importance, risk, and so on. Companies can define internal activities to track supplier performance and view and analyze supplier information. This gives companies transparency in their supplier portfolios based on these classifications and reduces risks by identifying low-performing suppliers.

- **Supplier evaluation**

  Supplier evaluation and performance management processes can be initiated and managed across the supplier base by strategic buyers.

  In the traditional system, no real-time data was available due to the volume of the data, causing a lack of transparency and decision support. In SAP S/4HANA, the full question library and survey management functionality is available for use, so business user input on supplier performance can be evaluated and included as input for supplier management activities, with additional improvements in SAP S/4HANA:

  – Questionnaires definable directly in SAP S/4HANA

  – Monitor and search flexibility for evaluation responses and ability to navigate to response details

  – Ability to create evaluation requests and distribute to appraisers

  Figure 6.6 shows an example of a supplier evaluator response in SAP S/4HANA.

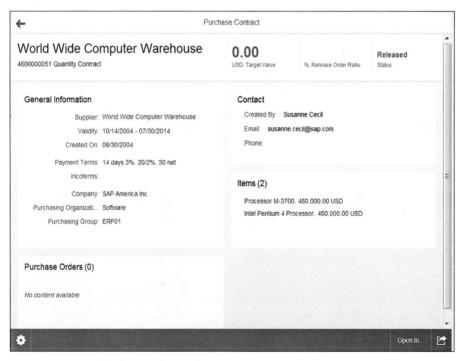

Figure 6.6 Example of a Supplier Evaluation Response

- **Collaboration and activity management (integration with SAP Jam)**
  Increased collaboration functions are enabled for purchasing users to communicate and collaborate with internal parties through activity integration with SAP Jam. The sell-side components and functionality aren't yet available in the initial release, so relevant sell-side integration with suppliers isn't yet possible.

In addition, several new SAP Fiori apps have been developed for use with SAP Supplier Lifecycle Management functions:

- Task processing for management of internal collaboration activities
- Completion of supplier evaluation surveys by internal users
- Supplier activity management
- Supplier lists and portfolio statuses
- Supplier appraisal
- Supplier portfolio and category management
- Purchasing categories created, managed, and assigned to supply base
- Management of supplier evaluation processes by the strategic buyer, including evaluation of results

The SAP GUI transactions for vendor masters are made obsolete in line with the data model change in SAP S/4HANA. The business partner is now the primary business object for both vendor and customer master data, so business partner transactions will be used to create or maintain business partners.

6.2.5   Intelligent Procurement by Machine Learning

With release 1809, the first machine-learning capabilities have been added to the sourcing and procurement processes and the first steps have been made to the intelligent enterprise. These initial processes selected for machine-learning capabilities are mainly focused on automation and exception handling processes such as the following:

- Increased invoice automation processes and efficient invoice monitoring processes are provided for exception handling with machine-learning capabilities (e.g., to identify issues immediately).
- Usage of free text is reduced because the system using machine-learning capabilities will automatically propose new catalog items.

- SAP S/4HANA automatically proposes material groups to use when free-text items are used in purchase requisitions.

- When materials are used without a source of supply, SAP S/4HANA automatically proposes the available options using machine learning.

The innovations listed are just the selected machine-learning capabilities for the most recent release of SAP S/4HANA. SAP will continue to build these capabilities through helping enterprises to become an intelligent enterprise by uniting human expertise with machine insights.

6.3   Sourcing and Procurement in SAP S/4HANA Cloud

SAP S/4HANA Cloud, public option, offers all the key processes for companies to execute their sourcing and procurement activities. In this chapter, we'll divide the features into different areas and explain for each area what processes and functionalities are included, as follows:

- **Sourcing and contract management**
  SAP S/4HANA Cloud offers companies all the required functionalities to execute their sourcing and contract management activities. They can manage the source lists to specify the allowed sources for a material plant and manage the info records to specify certain information about the material/supplier, such as pricing information. Other features include quota arrangements, RFQs to a supplier, and supplier quotations comparisons. From a contract management perspective, standard functionalities are available to manage purchasing contracts as scheduling agreements.

- **Operational procurement**
  The following key features are included for operational procurement:
  - Self-service requisitioning: SAP S/4HANA Cloud enables you to copy purchase requisitions, select products from catalog or by free text, use the shopping on behalf functionality, process purchase orders, and process confirmations.
  - Requirements processing: The functionalities provided here are apps to manage purchase requisitions and use the workflow for either the automatic, one-step, or two-step approval. SAP S/4HANA Cloud offers a mass change capability to enable users to trigger mass changes for specific values.

- Purchase order processing: Similar to purchase requisitions, SAP S/4HANA provides standard apps to allow users to manage purchase orders through a single app, making mass changes to purchase orders and monitoring the follow-on processes.

- Service purchasing and recording: The features that are available here are service purchasing, for example, for consulting services, managing service entry sheets to record the services that have been performed (manually or automatically via timesheets) and finally the approval process of all the entry sheets.

- Purchase order collaboration: Features are included for collaboration with your suppliers via the Ariba Network or an external supplier system. The process supported are sending purchase orders (including attachments), receiving confirmation and advanced shipping notifications (ASNs), sending goods receipts, and monitoring capabilities, such as troubleshooting errors in outbound messages.

- **Invoice management**
  The Managing Supplier Invoice app (with reference to purchase order items) is a single app that will give you all the relevant information to monitor status and determine follow-up actions. It offers functionalities to upload invoice documents, manage supplier invoice lists, and support the invoicing processes from consignment stock and the down payment processes for purchase orders.

- **Supplier management**
  For the supplier management process, SAP S/4HANA Cloud offers two key features: (1) classification and segmentation of suppliers to enable companies to assess and classify their suppliers at regular intervals, and (2) the supplier evaluation, where a questionnaire can be sent out to appraisers to evaluate suppliers.

- **Central procurement**
  Central procurement gives companies the capability to integrate SAP S/4HANA Cloud with other ERP systems in the client's system landscape to offer centralized procurement processes over the entire system.

- **Procurement analytics**
  The procurement overview provides you with all the operational and analytical procurement information on a single page. It offers users a set of actionable operational and analytical cards that can be easily rearranged as needed, and filters are provided as required to drill down to the needed information. In addition, monitoring capabilities enable users to quickly identify and navigate to the related apps

to resolves issues, such as overdue purchase orders, scheduling agreement items, and missing supplier confirmation.

With every quarterly release, SAP S/4HANA Cloud incorporates more functionality. Therefore, it's always valuable to check back in to see what's available.

6.4   Outlook

Table 6.2 lists key innovations scheduled for sourcing and procurement in releases for 2019 and beyond.

Area	Current Planned Innovation
Sourcing and contract management	■ Conversational voice interfaces and machine-learning capabilities (for all areas) and data prediction capabilities
Supplier evaluation and analytics	■ Holistic supplier and category monitoring ■ Improved supplier monitoring
Invoice and payables management	■ Improved machine-learning capabilities to optimize invoice process
Operational purchasing	■ Machine learning for automation of purchase document approvals ■ Auditing of procurement collaboration with blockchain

Table 6.2 Outlook for Sourcing and Procurement with SAP S/4HANA

6.5   Summary

SAP S/4HANA resolves some of today's C-level key challenges by helping you improve your supply chain visibility and transparency through better monitoring tools and real-time data. With embedded advanced analytics, companies now can run advanced analytics at any point in time to react quickly to changes in their environment and have better insights for negotiation.

In this chapter, we discussed how simplified processes and data, reduced complexity, and standard integration with SAP Ariba allow more optimized processes, a single source of truth, and improved collaboration capabilities, such as many-to-many secured network collaboration with trading partners. We also looked at the machine-learning capabilities that will continuously be added to SAP S/4HANA core capabilities as a step toward an intelligent enterprise.

In the next chapter, we'll take a look at our final major functional areas of interest: research and development and asset management.

Chapter 7
Research and Development and Asset Management

This chapter addresses functionalities such as SAP Product Lifecycle Management and SAP Portfolio and Project Management that fit under the umbrella of research and development and asset management to extend SAP S/4HANA functionality. We'll cover topics that are driving digital transformation in this area.

Few companies can rest on their laurels and cease product development. For example, pharmaceutical companies might need to develop new products or a new active pharmaceutical ingredient to alleviate health-related problems faced by society—but even in other industries, such as banking, companies are using research and development (R&D) to create new product or services.

Consequently, an organization's R&D area has two broad goals: to improve a product portfolio and to improve processes or operations. Companies can improve their product mix by introducing new products and segments or by improving their existing product lines to differentiate themselves from the competition. They can improve processes or operations by making workflow changes to reduce costs or reduce rejections in the production line or by making changes in operations for overall cost reductions. This requires an organization to focus on and institutionalize R&D.

Similarly, an organization's asset management function is focused on getting the maximum use out of an existing asset. It considers questions such as how to manage an asset in a way that avoids unplanned outages or how to improve in-house prediction capability to minimize the impact of assets' downtime on supply chain capability. Another aspect of asset management is putting tools into the hands of technicians so that errors are minimized during maintenance, as well as providing tools such as 3D visualizations and augmented reality to deployed workforces.

SAP has taken this challenge and created products in this area so that the digital journey of an organization can be fruitful. In this chapter, we'll introduce tools within SAP S/4HANA and other products for R&D and asset management, highlighting existing and expected key features and discussing how these products can be used to fulfill important product- or process-related objectives. We begin with a discussion of industry pain points and the challenges faced by chief supply chain officers (CSCOs), and then focus on R&D products and asset management products.

7.1   Industry Pain Points and SAP S/4HANA Benefits

R&D is an important support function for each industry; it helps an organization offer products and processes based on its customers' requirements. Some of the key trends visible across industry are increasing speed of disruption, diminishing returns in R&D, constant innovation as a growth driver, and management of investment in both R&D and in the existing product portfolio.

For example, consider the following common pain points that many organizations wrestle with:

- Consumer requirements are changing at an ever-increasing pace. An organization needs to understand these requirements and offer suitable products and processes to meet customer needs.
- Organizations need to institutionalize their innovation road map so that customer requirements can be fulfilled.
- Companies must align R&D processes and resources to improve time to market for innovative products at an optimized cost.
- Collaboration with various stakeholders in the innovation process is essential.

SAP Innovation Management provides transparency from idea generation to offering innovative products and processes to the market. It also engages employees to contribute meaningfully with fewer irritants while integrating fully with product development. SAP also offers an intuitive user experience (UX) in cloud and on-premise solutions, which can be accessed around the clock via mobile devices and desktops.

In addition, asset management is an important function in all organizations, especially when the key success factor of the industry depends on efficient utilization of assets, such as in the airline industry. In the current environment, the R&D industry faces some pain points, such as the following:

- Unplanned downtime, outages, reduced asset availability, and reduced asset reliability
- Low return on investment (ROI) for assets, lack of complaint and risk management, and inefficient maintenance spend
- Inaccurate asset master data, which can cause incidents and inefficiency
- Data and information stored in multiple systems
- Decision-makers and technicians lacking the right knowledge at hand

To transform, the business and organization must prioritize the following:

- Managing cost, risk, and performance holistically
- Balancing capital expenditure and operating expenditure and moving toward total expenditure
- Monitoring and predicting performance of assets, people, and processes
- Bringing operation data into a business process context
- Collaborating with other stakeholders, such as manufacturers, service providers, and engineering and procurement suppliers
- Integrating with sensors and other Internet of Things (IoT) objects

SAP has worked toward addressing these pain points and toward a strategic initiative by providing maintenance management in SAP S/4HANA Enterprise Management. SAP has included additional capabilities for asset operation and environment, health, and safety in add-ons and has also provided other product suites such as SAP Master Data Governance (SAP MDG), SAP Predictive Maintenance Services, SAP Asset Intelligence Network, and SAP Mobile Asset Management.

SAP S/4HANA will resolve some of today's C-level challenges. It will help technicians and engineers become mobile users and will improve decision-making capability through the improved UX, embedded analytics, and contextual help. Some of the key challenges in asset management for CSCOs in the asset management area are described in Table 7.1.

Challenge for CSCO	How SAP S/4HANA Can Help
Needs a preventive maintenance solution for more uptime for production equipment	Use of predictive analytics services in conjunction with better UX will help improve uptime.
Lack of system mobility for work that must be complete on-site	Mobile applications such as the SAP Work Manager and the SAP Inventory Manager will help overcome such challenges.
Requires improved collaboration and connectivity	Use of IoT and its integration with SAP S/4HANA and the asset intelligence network will help in this area.

Table 7.1 CSCO Challenges in Asset Management

7.2   Key Research and Development Functionality

Outside of the core of SAP S/4HANA, SAP offers four major products in the R&D area that complement an organization's R&D functionality:

- SAP Innovation Management
- SAP Portfolio and Project Management
- SAP Commercial Project Management
- SAP Product Lifecycle Costing

These products may require additional licenses beyond SAP S/4HANA. In the following sections, we'll discuss each product in turn.

7.2.1   SAP Innovation Management

SAP Innovation Management is a product powered by SAP HANA that is available separately either in the cloud or on-premise. This product can be installed standalone and/or integrated with ERP systems such as SAP S/4HANA, with SAP Portfolio and Project Management, with SAP Jam, and with other software.

SAP Innovation Management has a user-friendly user interface (UI) for desktop or mobile. This product can be used during your idea-generation and conceptualization phases. SAP Innovation Management can help you run campaigns for idea generation either globally or locally. It can also help you evaluate, process, and add ideas to portfolios. These ideas can be further developed as a project and managed in SAP Portfolio and Project Management; they also can be managed in SAP Commercial Project Management.

The following are key features of SAP Innovation Management:

- Evaluate the most promising ideas with the help of a stage-gating process.
- Engage employees in the innovation process and reward employees.
- Collaborate with various stakeholders in the innovation process.

The business value of innovation management can be derived where innovation can be institutionalized and improve the quality of the innovation pipeline, as shown in Figure 7.1. An organization can also leverage experts and its subject matter expert network through the expert finder.

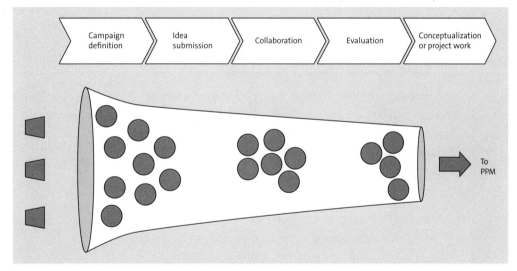

Figure 7.1 Scope of SAP Innovation Management

7.2.2 SAP Portfolio and Project Management

SAP Portfolio and Project Management is on-premise software that can be used standalone or can be integrated with an ERP system, such as SAP S/4HANA. This product can also integrate with third-party (non-SAP) human resources (HR) and financial software through remote function calls (RFCs). It can be used to manage the portfolios of projects created after idea evaluation and conceptualization.

SAP Portfolio and Project Management helps project managers achieve the following objectives:

- Align portfolios with business goals and strategy.
- Gain visibility into entire portfolio and key performance indicators (KPIs).
- Manage portfolios, including projects, programs, and services.
- Effectively manage innovation projects using structuring, scheduling, and visualization.
- Support different implementation models, such as Six Sigma, Phase Gate, Critical Path, and Product and Cycle Time Excellence.
- Incorporate all HR resources and financial resources.
- Perform resource management.
- Track portfolio project details, such as baseline, forecasted, and actual costs.
- Perform real-time what-if analyses to simulate various situations and changes.

7.2.3   SAP Commercial Project Management

SAP Commercial Project Management can be used whenever R&D services are being provided to clients as a service. As a tool that can be used to analyze investment alternatives and to track project budgets, milestones, and delivery, SAP Commercial Project Management facilitates the following:

- Get real-time access to project data.
- Generate project status reports using embedded analytics.
- Accurately forecast quantity, cost, and revenue.
- Unify financial management through the project lifecycle.
- Accurately identify and track project issues.
- Manage change requests, including approvals and rejections.

SAP Commercial Project Management allows you to monitor projects when provided to clients as a service. It has collaboration features that can be used to collaborate with suppliers of various inputs and services, as well as manage risk. The change management functionality is useful for project managers; it helps track all the changes coming to projects and manages associated risks. The project finances can be monitored and tracked with various deliveries.

In release 1809, several improvements to existing SAP Fiori apps for SAP Commercial Management, as well as new SAP Fiori apps, have been created:

- **Project Cost Overview app**
  This app has been enhanced to allow the user to easily monitor and compare planned costs with actual costs. The user has the ability to monitor the variance and costs for each individual line item. Also, it's possible to view cost details for multiple projects or work breakdown structure (WBS) elements from different projects and hierarchies in one overview.

- **Monitor Project Procurement app**
  This new SAP Fiori app enables the user to monitor purchase orders and purchase requisitions that are associated with project or WBS elements.

- **Create Change Requests and Report Issues apps**
  These new SAP Fiori apps report project issues and create change requests for the project. Users can use this new app to leverage a simpler change request approval process using the overall status. This is an addition to the already-existing change approval process.

7.2.4 SAP Product Lifecycle Costing

SAP Product Lifecycle Costing is an on-premise product with a UI that has a similar look and feel to Microsoft Excel. This software is built on SAP HANA and can be used to cost products during the engineering phase—which is particularly useful for products created under the engineer-to-make principle.

Let's look at some of the key features offered in SAP S/4HANA for product engineering during the R&D and pilot stages. From there, we'll highlight some key features and SAP Fiori apps and provide a bit more detail:

- Modern and real-time cost calculation engine powered by SAP HANA
- Flexibility to handle calculations using manual overrides and recalculation
- Target costing
- Version and what-if simulations
- Custom attributes, fields, and formulas
- Multiple costing sheets
- Local master data and integration with Microsoft Excel
- Time-dependent prices and rates

- Inbound integration with SAP ERP, Excel, and other applications using application programming interfaces (APIs)
- Export to Excel and other applications using APIs
- Pricing selection for components and activities
- Support for multiple currencies
- Support for overhead calculation
- Analytics and reporting for various costs and comparison of different versions

With release 1809, an engineering cockpit has been introduced that enables users to get an overview of engineering changes and progress for the various objects.

In addition, the manage engineering change functionality offers monitoring capabilities for change processes on a regular basis and gives them the ability to create new changes to certain events. It has an enhanced workflow and configuration capabilities that enable a flexible workflow configuration and integration of responsibility management. Change processes can be automated that are driven by workflow functionality.

With advanced variant configuration, users can access several SAP Fiori apps to get an overview for variant configuration. They can navigate directly to other objects, such as locked variant configuration objects, recent configuration simulations, and so on. They have the ability to open a list report of the configuration objects and immediately navigate to the app to maintain the object.

The business value of this product lies in getting the right costing for new or engineered products. This will help an organization reduce product costs and reduce time to market for the new product.

7.3   Key Asset Management Functionality

In the following sections, we'll examine a few areas of asset management, including maintenance planning and scheduling, maintenance operation and execution, and mobile asset maintenance.

7.3.1   Maintenance Planning and Scheduling

Asset resource scheduling is a new feature in SAP S/4HANA. Its key capabilities include the availability of KPIs to monitor and balance the work center load. The maintenance planner can analyze the work center load and view work order operations.

SAP Multiresource Scheduling also can be used as an add-on for SAP S/4HANA. SAP customers can tap into a few additional features here, such as the Scheduler Workplace. Schedulers can now use a graphical planning board with a drag-and-drop feature, manual and automatic planning, visualization of clocking data, and alert monitoring in SAP Multiresource Scheduling. This means that schedulers can plan for employees, contractors, work centers, and equipment and tools, along with resource placeholders.

SAP S/4HANA offers the Maintenance Planning Overview app in SAP Fiori, which is a role-based and personalized entry page for maintenance planners to monitor the progress of various maintenance activities that impact asset availability and reliability. Some of the key capabilities enabled are as follows:

- Monitoring of new maintenance requests or malfunction reports to support users in their planning activities
- Monitoring of orders that are still in preparation with details that help maintenance planners create detailed and consistent maintenance orders
- Monitoring of planned orders during execution, which supports a successful closing by removing all issues that may come up during execution
- Analytics for critical factors in a chosen time period and enabling the users to see this in figures and colored charts
- Navigation capabilities to edit documents that have been identified as critical or contact person responsible

As of release 1809, there are also enhanced object pages, which allow users to do the following:

- Find maintenance plans and items.
- Find measuring points and documents.
- Immediately see all relevant insights and take actions on order and operation projects, as well as find notification, maintenance orders and operations, and task lists.

Furthermore, a damage analysis and analytical lists overview page helps maintenance planners and engineers easily identify repeatedly failing object parts, defects, and main causes that will hinder reliable use of equipment and functional location. It will also help them quantify the failing technical objects or group of technical objects and give them the ability to identify the causes for repair that take the most time.

In addition, standard integration with SAP Asset Intelligence Network has been provided for the following:

- Equipment and functional locations from SAP S/4HANA with equipment and locations from SAP Asset Intelligence Network
- The display of content in SAP Asset Intelligence Network, received from business partners within an object page from enterprise asset management
- Navigation of object pages for equipment and functional locations to assets and equipment in SAP Asset Intelligence Network

7.3.2   Maintenance Operation and Execution

In maintenance operation and execution, changes include improvements in UX, improvements in analytics, and use of mobile applications. Earlier, in SAP ERP, only vendor codes, material groups, and cost elements were displayed in the maintenance order. Now, the description is added so that users can understand these codes. Additionally, the **Maintenance Activity Type** field is now available in maintenance notifications and maintenance plans.

Selecting and deselecting objects now is easy from the maintenance order, in which **Select All** or **Block Selection** options are available. In SAP ERP, users had to select objects individually. Simplified order views enable navigating to overview pages of preceding or follow-on orders to create, change, or display plant maintenance (PM) orders. Follow-on orders can be created from the **Operation** tab of PM orders.

Now, measurement documents can be viewed from the application, allowing you to create, change, and display equipment, and create, change, and display functional location.

Maintenance plan call details can be viewed from the change order, operation transaction, and change PM orders transaction. Material availability checks can also be determined from the maintenance order. The planning plant can be used for filtering the deadline-monitoring transaction.

7.3.3   Mobile Asset Maintenance

Mobility in asset management now includes three products: SAP Work Manager, SAP Inventory Manager, and SAP Asset Manager (planned for future releases).

SAP Work Manager can be used to complete the work order and provide access to asset details, such as history, location, work order details, and materials needed. SAP Work Manager also can be used create notifications and work orders, display master data and measurement documents, install and dismantle equipment, and perform linear asset management and uploading and downloading of attachment and inspection rounds.

SAP Work Manager can be integrated for geotagging using additional components. It has an embedded visual enterprise viewer, augmented reality, and a meter-management component.

SAP Inventory Manager can be used to manage cycle counts, issues, receipts, and transfers. It supports warehouse management (WM) and inventory management (IM) functionalities.

As mentioned, SAP Asset Manager is planned for future releases.

7.4   R&D and Asset Management in SAP S/4HANA Cloud

In SAP S/4HANA Cloud, public option, several key features are provided in the area of R&D and asset management.

For R&D, SAP S/4HANA Cloud (as of release 1808) only offers functionalities in the area of enterprise portfolio, project management, and project monitoring. At this point, the release of R&D functionalities in SAP S/4HANA Cloud is one of the lesser developed lines of business (LoBs). Within this LoB, functionalities are available for users to define projects and the underlying elements to use for accounting structures for subsequent accounting tasks, such as cost planning, actual costs, and revenue collection or settlement. Key features here include the following:

- Maintenance of template projects
- Maintenance of operative projects
- Generation of project settlement rules
- Reporting of project costs and budgets
- Project monitoring, for example, overview of projects, and creating and assessing project-related collaborations

In the area of asset management, SAP S/4HANA Cloud (as of release 1808) only provides functionalities around PM. With these functionalities, companies can plan and perform the maintenance of operational systems, such as the following:

- **Technical asset management**
  Allows users to manage data throughout the entire lifecycle of technical assets.
- **Maintenance execution**
  Allows users to perform planned and unplanned maintenance activities.
- **Maintenance planning, scheduling, and dispatching**
  Allows users to perform accurate planning and scheduling to ensure minimum disruption to the operation of an asset.
- **Asset information system**
  Allows users to analyze the performance of assets and asset management systems.

With the key features for SAP S/4HANA and SAP S/4HANA Cloud now explained, we'll discuss the future outlook for R&D and asset management in the next section.

7.5   Outlook

In general, in the R&D space, the focus will be on engaging multiple stakeholders and on making those interactions interesting through gamification features, such as leaderboards, points and badges, feedback, and voting.

Table 7.2 lists the key innovations scheduled for R&D for future releases in 2019 and beyond.

Area	Planned Innovations
Employee suggestion box	- Evaluation request - Create and assign evaluation request - Request acceptance and completion date - Monitoring of evaluation result
Open innovation	- Company-wide voting - Voting on any campaign from within the company or from external stakeholders - Campaign milestones - Definition of additional campaign milestones

Table 7.2 Outlook for R&D

Area	Planned Innovations
Continuous improvement	■ Idea-management view ■ Flexibility of ideas view list ■ Campaign results ■ Summarization of idea results ■ Ideas list view enhancement ■ Add action to idea list ■ Vote aging ■ Compute score with aging as a factor

Table 7.2 Outlook for R&D (Cont.)

On the asset management front, we anticipate developments in using business context and sharing operational data, using benchmarks and intelligent services, and more complete coverage of the asset lifecycle—for example, asset optimization and simulation—with deeper integration with SAP ERP, SAP S/4HANA, SAP Service Cloud, and SAP CRM. In addition, integration with the Internet of Things (IoT) will become a standard feature and can't be ignored.

Table 7.3 lists key innovations scheduled for asset management for future releases in 2019 and beyond.

Area	Current Planned Innovation
Asset strategy and performance	■ Proactive maintenance strategy planning with integration with SAP Integrated Business Planning (SAP IBP) and third-party content library for planning and forecasting for the assets in the supply chain ■ Maintenance budget planning ■ Collaborative inventory and spare parts optimization
Maintenance planning and scheduling	■ Comprehensive scheduling of resources using individual resource assignments ■ Asset management resource scheduling in the cloud ■ Integrated scheduling using workforce management (SAP Multiresource Scheduling and SAP S/4HANA)

Table 7.3 Outlook for Asset Management

Area	Current Planned Innovation
Maintenance execution	▪ UX enhancement through adding quick action buttons, searches, and object pages in maintenance plans, task lists, measurement points, and measurement documents ▪ Simplified test equipment calibration by eliminating the need for maintenance plans, maintenance orders, and confirmations
Environment, health, and safety	▪ Assistance for workers and environment, health, and safety specialists to access their data from any device ▪ Use of predictive and real-time analytics to improve safety and risk management ▪ Support of a central database for various pollutants ▪ Management of change as an embedded functionality in SAP S/4HANA
Asset networks—asset information and collaboration	▪ Collaborative work order management to enable joint scheduling and confirmation of planned work ▪ Equipment as a service for renting and booking ▪ Support for additional industry standards and content ▪ Resale of content and best practices ▪ Integration with SAP IBP
Asset networks—asset information governance	▪ Support for additional objects on demand ▪ Enhancements to the asset information workbench
Asset networks—SAP Predictive Maintenance Services	▪ Dynamic maintenance scheduling using constraint-based optimization ▪ Library of ready-to-use machine-learning content per asset type ▪ Fingerprint similarity analysis for assets ▪ Support for edge computing ▪ Prescriptive maintenance ▪ Package management for root-cause analysis ▪ Diagnostics trouble code analytics ▪ Collaboration exploration

Table 7.3 Outlook for Asset Management (Cont.)

7.6   Summary

SAP S/4HANA and other associated products in the R&D space can be used stand-alone or in conjunction with other products. Not all products may be required by an organization, so each company should evaluate products to consider whether they align with their requirements and IT strategy.

SAP Innovation Management will be useful during initial phases and can engage all employees. When employees are engaged and have visibility into ideas, they become motivated, which is important for an organization. SAP Portfolio and Project Management is useful for management of multiple projects, programs, and services. The insight into the portfolio of projects and its alignment with the organization's strategy is an important outcome of the software. SAP Commercial Project Management is another tool provided by SAP to reduce cost and time to quotation for projects provided to clients as a service. SAP Product Lifecycle Costing is important during the product engineering phase and can be used to reduce the product cost and time to market. Its UI is like Excel's, although it doesn't currently produce an Excel sheet.

The asset management functionality in SAP S/4HANA is enhanced by improving the UX, adding functionality in SAP Fiori apps, adding display fields for the codes, and simplifying some options, such as selecting and deselecting rows. New products such as SAP Asset Manager will be added in future releases. In addition to improvement in core asset management and SAP Multiresource Scheduling, additional products such as SAP Predictive Maintenance Services and SAP Asset Intelligence Network will help an enterprise transform from reactive to preventive. The addition of maintenance features in SAP IBP will help organizations plan for maintenance impacts on supply chain planning.

In the next chapter, we'll move on from the LoB topics with a look at analytics and reporting in SAP S/4HANA.

Chapter 8
Analytics and Reporting

This chapter provides the current options for reporting in SAP
S/4HANA. We'll touch on various products from SAP for analytics,
such as embedded SAP Business Warehouse (SAP BW), embedded
analytics, and embedded SAP Business Planning and Consolida-
tion (SAP BPC), as well as data and data lakes.

SAP S/4HANA forms the digital core of an IT landscape (current or future) for an SAP customer. To make the digital transformation of an enterprise effective, that is, to create an intelligent enterprise, it's imperative to have the power of analytics behind the decisions. When the time comes to choose analytical tools, selecting the right product—from the right backend reporting tool to the frontend dashboard and integration tools—from among several options can cause a lot of confusion in the minds of the analytics and enterprise architecture teams. Where to invest, how to estimate the future of existing investments, and how to cater to different types of data requirements are some of the key questions we'll address here.

Based on the usage or the type of data on which analytics is carried out, we can classify the reports into the following two categories:

- **Operational reporting**
  Operational reporting deals with the transactional data at real time or near real time, either in the transactional system itself or in another system where this data is replicated. Now, with the advent of advanced tools, advanced analytics are also possible. These reports will help businesses make quick decisions and changes.

  For example, with operational reporting, a plant manager can see in real time which production orders have been completed in the past seven days or the production cost of a particular product.

- **Enterprise-wide reporting**
  Enterprise-wide reporting leverages data from multiple sources across the enterprise and performs reporting and analytics across functional areas and systems.

The data may be at different levels of granularity. Enterprise-wide reporting can also be used for historical data analysis and trend analysis.

For example, if the chief financial officer (CFO) of an organization wants to have a glimpse of the overall budget spent across all markets for a particular brand and then drill down to particular markets, countries, or periods, such analytics would typically be done through the enterprise data warehouse.

Note

While the gaps between operational analytics and enterprise-wide analytics are going to decrease gradually, we still see the trend to keep different systems for different types of reporting.

In this chapter, we describe the various options from SAP available today for different use cases and different source data in the context of a landscape with an SAP S/4HANA core.

8.1   Evolution of Analytics

From the perspective of seeking insights, the world of analytics has changed from descriptive analytics to cognitive analytics. Some basic operational analytical requirements have been consistently present, such as finding out which vendor performed well to meet all key performance indicators (KPIs) related to timely delivery, what sales orders are to be delivered in the next seven days, what inventory is available for a given material across warehouses/storage locations, and so on. In recent years, the analytics requirements have become diverse, and with the maturity of the analytics tools, various types of analytics came into being.

Figure 8.1 shows the six stages of data analytics. Let's walk through each stage:

❶ **Data acquisitions (sometimes called data foundations)**
At this early stage, the focus is on integrating data sources and on addressing data governance.

❷ **Descriptive reporting**
The emphasis is on creating a single source of truth for reporting/structured KPIs.

❸ **Data exploration**
This stage involves "democratizing analytics" and facilitating access to quick insight.

❹ **Predictive modeling**

This stage creates actionable insights and tests hypotheses.

❺ **Prescriptive modeling**

This stage embeds analytics into the decision-making processes.

❻ **Cognitive computing**

This stage allows you to elevate the analytics experience for maximal business benefits, serving up real-time insight at key points of engagement.

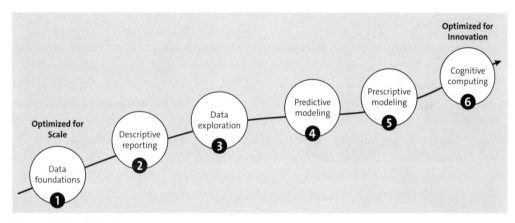

Figure 8.1 Analytics Journey

Now, with the advent of new types of data—its inflection point being the huge amount of social media and their pervasiveness in building the opinions of the masses—the intelligence of the instruments (along with the options to get data from smart meters in real time) provides new challenges to the analytics world. Moreover, the challenges are increasing every day. Thus, the next step in Figure 8.1 (data exploration) depicts different data that needs to be explored.

Then comes the predictive analytics, which is based on different types of algorithms, depending on the data type and its variance. The predictive analytics lead the way for the prescriptive variety, through which a clear set of instructions can emerge for analyzing the data based on an event trigger. For example, if the data set for some related parameters for a piece of equipment shows a specific trend, then the predictive analytics may specify at which point the equipment will break down; hence, predictive maintenance will be triggered before such an alarm level. The prescriptive analytics will suggest actions to mitigate such a breakdown point altogether. Therefore, prescriptive analytics is a combination of predictive and descriptive analytics and helps determine whether to act and, if yes, what actions to take. This is of course a bigger umbrella and can even use the next genre of analytics, which leverages cognitive computing.

For all these types of analytics, actionable insights are achievable with vastly differing types of data, including structured and unstructured; high volumes of data; data within the enterprise; or data combining outside intelligence or information. Reporting now can be agile, with hugely improved performance with many types of flexible analyses and with a much-improved user experience (UX) with SAP Fiori or SAP Fiori-like (SAPUI5-based) apps.

Figure 8.2 shows the overall analytical landscape for an enterprise where the operational reporting uses embedded analytics in SAP S/4HANA. Analytical SAP Fiori apps can also be used on top of the SAP S/4HANA data. SAP analytics tools, such as SAP Analytics Cloud or the on-premise tools of the SAP BusinessObjects Business Intelligence (SAP BusinessObjects BI) suite, can enable additional dashboards and visualization. The data is replicated to SAP BW/4HANA to meet the enterprise-wide reporting requirements. This system works as part of the data lake as well (see Section 8.6.1 for more information on data lakes) because it can pull the data from Hadoop. It can also combine the data from Hadoop with the data from other systems through SAP Vora.

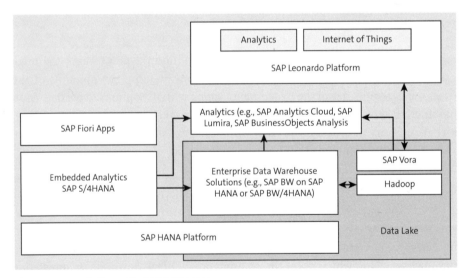

Figure 8.2 Analytics with SAP S/4HANA

SAP Leonardo also provides services for analytics, as well as services for integrating big data, such as Internet of Things (IoT) data (the data feed from sensors or connected systems), which we'll discuss in detail in Chapter 14. This data can be stored in Hadoop as well.

Finally, the cognitive analytics using Watson application programming interfaces (APIs), which can be exposed using the IBM Cloud platform, can also be integrated. Further cognitive computing, including sentiment analysis, image recognition, and more, can be leveraged to gain insight from data as well. Still, this is just one example of one variation of the analytics landscape; there can be several other such variants.

In this chapter, we'll introduce various products from SAP in the analytics area and touch on the types of analytical activities they support for SAP S/4HANA customers. We'll also touch on the concepts of big data and data lakes.

8.2   Operational Reporting

The classic examples of descriptive analytics are the different types of operational reporting required on top of the transactional system data. Traditionally, in the pre-SAP HANA days, operational reporting was required to be run on the SAP ERP system itself, taking data from the transactional SAP ERP system. When the data was too much to handle, this data was replicated to the SAP BW system, aggregated, and then reported against.

For any reports that had to be run in SAP ERP and that dealt with huge amounts of data, the only option was to run these reports in batches. Batch job failure was a common issue, resulting in daily frustrations of IT support and an inability to take some business actions in a timely manner. Think of a large retail customer that needs to move stock from the inventory at the warehouse to the stores in the morning based on a batch job-based report of the store inventory. If the batch job fails, the entire business is impacted in multiple ways: the stock sits in the warehouse, increasing the inventory carrying costs; the trucks are underused; and the stores have no stock, resulting in dissatisfied customers. The same situation can be completely turned around by SAP HANA-based reporting, which will take seconds to execute. These stock reports can be generated every day and on demand, thereby planning and executing the stock movements from the warehouses to the right stores in a timely manner.

Exception reporting for situations such as excess inventory after running materials requirement planning (MRP) could be run in batches on the traditional SAP ERP systems. However, with the advent of SAP HANA, reporting has become a lot easier, can be run in real time, and doesn't require any batch runs or any other data ware-housing tools. There are a few options to create these operational reports, which are discussed in the following sections. In particular, SAP Analytics Cloud can be lever-aged for both operational as well as other type of reports (see Section 8.3.4).

8.2.1   ABAP-Based Reports

The traditional ABAP-based operational reports should be run via the main process-ing involving the larger data set in the SAP HANA database layer (code pushdown) via ABAP Core Data Services (CDS) views. The frontend can use SAP Fiori apps (for stan-dard views) or SAPUI5 for custom views, which can consume the CDS views.

8.2.2   Embedded Analytics

Embedded analytics is a set of analytical features directly embedded in the SAP S/4HANA system to work on top of the transactional data. This is the most popular way of performing operational reporting in the current SAP S/4HANA world, and it doesn't require additional installations or licenses.

Let's consider the architecture of embedded analytics. The virtual data model (VDM) in the form of CDS views (which we'll discuss in Chapter 12) forms the base of this ana-lytics. The architecture is as follows:

- Visualization layer, which consists of the following:
  - SAP Fiori
  - SAP analytics products (visualization)
- Analytics layer, which consists of the following:
  - Embedded analytics
  - SAP Analytics Cloud/SAP Lumira/SAP BusinessObjects Analysis, and so on
- Access layer, which consists of the following:
  - OData
  - Transient analytical queries
- Virtualization/modeling layer, which consists of the following:
  - CDS views
- Persistence layer, which consists of the following:
  - SAP S/4HANA

SAP has classified many tools under the umbrella of embedded analytics. The classification is based on the user type, as well. Figure 8.3 from SAP depicts the current set of tools and the types of users who would use them.

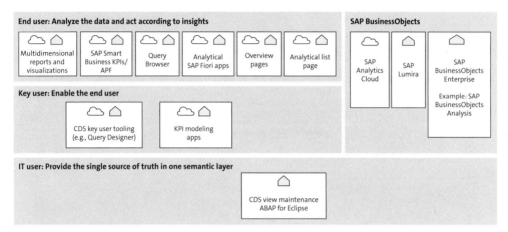

Figure 8.3 Embedded Analytics Tool Overview

Now, let's discuss the key embedded analytics tools and how they operate on the transactional data of the underlying SAP S/4HANA system.

Multidimensional Reports and Visualization

This type of reporting is again accessible through SAP Fiori apps, has the ABAP Web Dynpro application as its backend, and exposes analytical CDS views. These reports are very similar to the analytical SAP Fiori apps both in terms of look and feel and in their use of configurable key figures and dimensions.

SAP Smart Business KPIs and the Analysis Path Framework

SAP Smart Business applications can display the business KPIs calculated based on the transactional data in your SAP S/4HANA system. The KPI Modeler is used to configure these KPIs, and you can create the tiles in the SAP Fiori launchpad, which shows the analytical SAP Fiori apps for a KPI. A KPI is the first entity that needs to be created, and the data source of that KPI is the SAP HANA view or the corresponding OData service. A few analytical apps support drilling down to the next set of visualizations.

Figure 8.4 shows how an app has been configured and which CDS view it uses in the KPI Modeler.

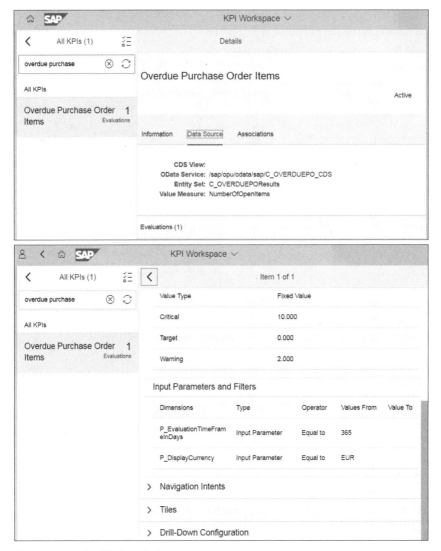

Figure 8.4 Embedded Analytics Reporting Example

The Analysis Path Framework (APF) is the framework in SAP Fiori through which you can configure interactive, chart-oriented, analytical drilldown apps. APF-based apps enable the user to view and analyze the data of several KPIs from different data sources. Users can interactively explore data step by step from different perspectives to analyze and investigate root causes. In each analysis step, you can investigate

KPIs/measures and select relevant data to filter the information provided in subsequent steps. By combining different analysis steps and applying filters, you interactively create your own flexible analysis path.

Query Browser

The Query Browser tool displays the results of a query based on CDS views. As shown in Figure 8.5, it's available through an SAP Fiori app. The Query Browser displays the available CDS views, and the user can choose to display and execute any of the CDS views after they are configured.

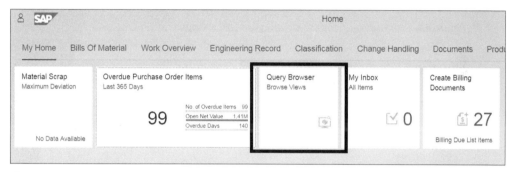

Figure 8.5 Query Browser Tile in SAP Fiori Launchpad

Analytical SAP Fiori Apps

Analytical SAP Fiori apps provide role-based insight into the KPIs of your business processes. These can be configured on top of SAP S/4HANA, consuming VDMs, and set up as tiles in the SAP Fiori launchpad, as shown in Figure 8.6. The SAP Fiori launchpad shows the apps that are applicable for a specific user role.

Thus, these apps provide real-time information about large-volume data via a simplified frontend for better monitoring and hence offer better control of these KPIs. You can configure several predelivered KPIs and insight-to-action scenarios, or you can create new ones based on the KPI modeling framework. These apps consume OData services, which can be generated from the ABAP CDS views. These apps have dimensions and measures, and you can apply filters on certain configurable fields. For example, Figure 8.7 shows open purchase orders for multiple vendors over a set period. In this case, the period is set to last 365 days, but it could be set for a week or a month, for example. In the top-left corner, you can see that **Plant** is one of the filter criteria for the app. The bottom screenshot in Figure 8.7 shows the results of applying that filter.

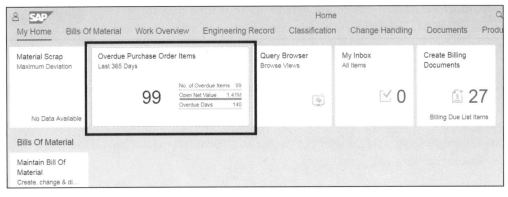

Figure 8.6 SAP Fiori Launchpad Showing Analytical Apps

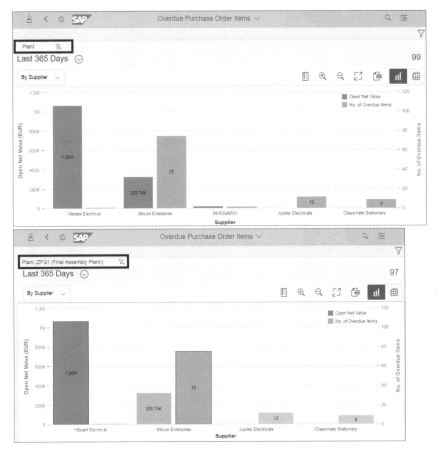

Figure 8.7 Analytical App Example: Overdue Purchase Order

Overview Pages and Analytical List Page

In an SAP Fiori-based embedded analytics environment, it's important to understand that apps follow certain design principals per the SAP Fiori floorplan design. As such, user transitions start from the home page in the SAP Fiori launchpad (which is based on roles, so only relevant apps appear), move to an overview page on which the user has an overview of an analytical app and his responsible areas, and then move to the analytical list page, which is helpful to list the relevant items and can be filtered per requirements. The user will then typically navigate to the actual object page from the list page to take necessary actions.

Note

For more information about embedded analytics and SAP Fiori 2.0, we recommend the following blog post: *http://bit.ly/2xFZboi*.

8.2.3   Native SAP HANA Applications

Now, we'll touch on the native SAP HANA applications because they cater to different types of reporting or different types of analytical scenarios and are important to the analytical landscape.

When it comes to operational reporting, we can create data models from SAP HANA Live views or CDS views from SAP S/4HANA or any other system through SAP Landscape Transformation replication server or other replication tools, such as SAP HANA smart data integration, SAP HANA smart data access, or SAP Data Services, designed for getting the data into the data model in near real time and building the reports out of this sidecar.

There are several such examples of operational reporting out of native SAP HANA applications. For example, a UK-based retail company had several hundred warehouses and stores across the world. By running inventory reports across these warehouses and stores, it now has much better planning of stock movements from the right stores to the right warehouses, so stores have the right stock, thus ensuring that customers get what they require when they require it. All of this results in satisfied customers, better sales, and optimized inventory costs and stock movement planning.

Other reports were created for tracking the operational costs for manufacturing its products and cost optimization. Another report shows the intrastat VAT report for goods movement across European countries. There are thousands of these use cases, with companies employing applications that use new data models or reuse part of the SAP ERP data models and gather data from disparate sources.

This product has advanced analytics capabilities and can integrate Predictive Analysis Libraries (PALs), which are in the SAP HANA platform itself, or other libraries, such as the R library for predictive models.

8.2.4 Embedded SAP Business Warehouse and SAP Business Planning Consolidation

Online analytical processing (OLAP) capabilities were introduced in the form of embedded SAP BW in SAP ERP as of SAP NetWeaver 7.0. Now, with the advent of SAP S/4HANA, it plays a more significant role as a feasible alternate for providing analytical insights. SAP BW (OLAP engine) is included in the SAP S/4HANA system and is known as embedded SAP BW. However, we don't recommend implementing this option as a full-fledged enterprise data warehouse. Instead, this option is for those multidimensional reports that need a percentage of the SAP S/4HANA data to be replicated to the OLAP engine. A good rule of thumb mandates that 20% of the total overall data volume of the system should include data replicated from SAP S/4HANA or integrate data from other sources or planning applications.

Embedded SAP BW relies on a separate authorization concept. Authorizations from SAP Business Suite on SAP HANA or SAP S/4HANA don't apply; if you require these authorizations, they must be mapped separately.

Embedded SAP BW can be installed either on the same client as the SAP S/4HANA system or on a separate client, depending on the scenario (e.g., if the embedded SAP BW requires data replication from another source, SAP recommends installing it on a separate client).

There are two main advantages of using embedded SAP BW. First, SAP S/4HANA CDS views are automatically exposed as operational data provisioning (ODP) transient InfoProviders and can be used in the SAP Business Explorer (SAP BEx) Query Designer to define custom queries. The SAP BEx queries should be based on SAP S/4HANA embedded analytics CDS consumption/query views. Second, you can add SAP BW functionality without using SAP BW modeling objects.

A different use case scenario would use the embedded SAP Business Planning and Consolidation (SAP BPC) functions for planning purposes, running on the embedded SAP BW. This requires a separate license. Thus, SAP BPC for SAP S/4HANA is an add-on on top of embedded SAP BW; this model frees you from performing any data loading because it leverages the underlying data in SAP S/4HANA. It comes with prebuilt content, such as a series of InfoProviders, input-ready queries, and planning functions and workbooks based on SAP Analysis for Microsoft Office. This content covers the following planning areas:

- Cost center planning
- Internal order planning
- Project planning
- Cost of sales planning
- Profit center planning
- P&L planning
- Market segment planning
- Balance sheet planning
- Liquidity planning

SAP has delivered multiple SAP Analysis for Microsoft Office workbooks; once activated, they can be consumed directly out of the box. You also can set up standard and custom reports to compare planned versus actual data, taking the data from the underlying SAP S/4HANA transactional system.

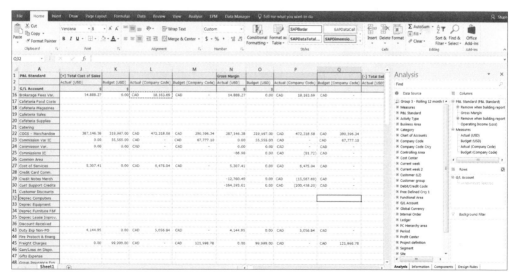

Figure 8.8 Planned versus Actual Comparison with Embedded Analytics in SAP S/4HANA

Figure 8.8 shows an embedded analytics-based app that compares actual sales against planned sales for each profit center and breaks down various components along the same lines.

8.3   Enterprise-Wide Reporting

The enterprise-wide reporting options have broadened, creating some doubt in clients' minds about which option to invest in further, especially if they've invested heavily already into some older products, such as SAP BW on SAP HANA. The right choice depends on each client's landscape scenario. A simplified decision tree is shown in Figure 8.9. Real-world scenarios may be more complex, and more factors may need to be considered, including integration with various sources of information and integration with different types of libraries for algorithms.

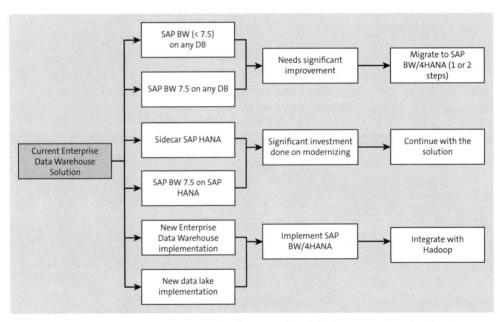

Figure 8.9 Sample Decision Tree for Choosing the Right Data Warehousing Tool

Example
Consider a client who implemented SAP BW a decade ago. The company may have done some technical upgrading but never leveraged the new features and the

simplified data flows of an SAP BW 7.5 solution. Now, the client decides to move to the SAP HANA database and wants to choose the right product and the right road map. The cleaner option may be to implement a new SAP BW system from scratch. However, that wouldn't be a practical approach. The business may see no substantial benefit for such huge investments and may not even have the budget or skills in their organization. The easier option for them would be to migrate to SAP BW/4HANA and, in the process, change the data flows and optimize the solution.

8.3.1   SAP HANA Enterprise Analytics

SAP HANA enterprise-related analytics uses the SAP HANA platform, and its applications are known as native SAP HANA applications. One usage scenario for this product is as a data mart. When this product became available, some SAP customers started implementing their enterprise-wide reporting on this platform, some clients used it in a hybrid mode with their SAP BW on SAP HANA solutions, and others started a journey to consolidate their reporting on the SAP HANA platform.

Although this platform uses the three types of SAP HANA views—attribute views, analytic views, and calculation views—SAP is strongly encouraging customers to use only calculation views when modeling analytical requirements. In fact, SAP even provides tools to convert other views to calculation views, from SAP HANA 1.0 SP 10 onward. Figure 8.10 shows an example of a calculation view for a scenario. The graphical model was created by dragging and dropping multiple functions, such as the union and joins from multiple projection views.

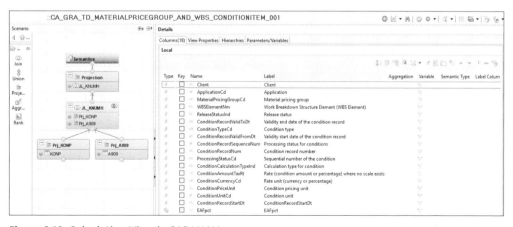

Figure 8.10 Calculation View in SAP HANA

8.3.2   SAP Business Warehouse on SAP HANA

The classical SAP BW was the first SAP application to move to the SAP HANA database, but since then, it has evolved into a more powerful data warehousing product with SAP BW 7.5 on SAP HANA. Layered Scalable Architecture (LSA) was once the recommended architecture for SAP BW before SAP HANA, but a new architecture is recommended for SAP BW on SAP HANA: LSA++.

Let's understand the transition from LSA to LSA++. LSA was introduced in SAP BW to provide a flexible and comprehensive framework for designing data flows. This helps ensure a structured approach of SAP BW implementation with better accuracy, scalability, completeness, and maintainability. The data in LSA moves through various layers before being made available for reporting.

LSA stores data in multiple layers and often redundantly. On one hand, this improves performance, scalability, and maintainability, but, on the other hand, it increases the time for data loading and increases the size of the SAP BW database. However, with the power of SAP HANA, some of these layers can be omitted, and an even simpler architecture can be developed. SAP has developed LSA++ with the following objectives:

- Keeping the number of persisted storage layers to a minimum:
  - Reduces data-loading time and makes near-real-time data replication possible using SAP Landscape Transformation.
  - Reduces the size of the SAP HANA database.
- Reporting from any layer:
  - In SAP HANA, the data is stored in column-based tables, and data resides in main memory, so reporting is very fast from any table-like structures; only dimensionally modeled objects aren't necessary for reporting performance.
  - Helps with near-real-time acquisition of data if sourced via real-time replication.

In LSA++, most reporting is done through advanced DataStore objects, which almost eliminates the need for InfoCubes, except for special cases, such as noncumulative key figures and planning applications.

The key advantages of this architecture lie in its simplified design and implementation, with fewer layers and hence fewer SAP BW objects, resulting in better maintainability. It also ensures reduced data redundancy and data footprint, reduced data latency, and improved performance. LSA++ also makes it possible to have near-real-time reporting.

8.3.3   SAP BW/4HANA

SAP BW/4HANA is the latest data warehousing product from SAP, and it's built for SAP HANA-optimized processes and leverages the SAP HANA platform. Note that in terms of product versions, SAP BW/4HANA isn't a successor of SAP BW but rather a new product altogether. Hence, it doesn't support all the old SAP BW objects but still uses the similar concepts of InfoObjects, InfoProviders, and CompositeProviders to merge data from SAP BW InfoProviders with data from SAP HANA views and open operational DataStore (ODS) views to integrate data sources into SAP BW/4HANA. SAP BW/4HANA has its own standard content for SAP S/4HANA.

SAP BW/4HANA supports LSA++ (discussed in the previous section), with some additional nuances. There's a lot of commonality in terms of features and functions between SAP BW 7.5 on SAP HANA and SAP BW/4HANA, and most of the features introduced earlier in SAP BW 7.5 (or earlier versions such as SAP BW 7.3) are available in SAP BW/4HANA.

Let's consider some of the enhanced features leveraged in both SAP BW 7.5 and SAP BW/4HANA:

- The advanced DataStore object is the new persistence object used in SAP BW/4HANA. InfoObjects still manage their own persistence. It's possible to perform queries and reporting on this layer without undergoing any transformation.

- Open ODS views are reusable SAP BW data warehouse semantics on field-based structures.

- Virtual data marts (using CompositeProviders that combine InfoProviders or Open ODS views) and logical warehousing are powerful functions with several advantages. Thus, unless it's required (e.g., in multiple queries with high frequency), you don't need to load data in the SAP BW system and can instead use a logical data warehouse with virtual integration of data. Sometimes, a combination of approaches for physical data load and virtual data integration is required.

- Integration of different data sources is possible using Open Hub services because SAP BW/4HANA has an open architecture. New extraction services, such as the operational delta queue (ODQ), make it possible for data to be loaded or replicated to an advanced DataStore object directly. Integration with SAP HANA smart data integration also means that many new adapters are available, which makes it simple to include data sources such as Twitter and Hadoop.

- Code pushdown to the SAP HANA layer improves the system performance to a large degree and reduces the ABAP application layer to a slimmer version.

- Data tiering is the concept of storing data depending on various factors, such as data temperature, regulatory compliance, and so on, in different storage types. Data temperature is a way to label data based on recency, frequency of usage, and other business needs. Because SAP HANA uses main memory and hence is high performing, there is a high cost associated with this memory usage, which thus must be optimized. Therefore, data that's less frequently required can be stored in other storage, such as in extended tables in the SAP HANA dynamic tiering solution (non-SAP HANA database) or in Hadoop (for cold data). However, this data can be brought into SAP HANA as and when required. SAP BW/4HANA comes with an adapter for Hadoop, which can be used as near-line storage.

Note that the suite of SAP BEx tools, such as Query Designer, Analyzer, Web Analyzer, and Web Application Designer, isn't supported for SAP BW/4HANA. SAP's recommendation is to move to SAP Analytics frontend tools, including SAP Analytics Cloud.

8.3.4   SAP Analytics Cloud

SAP Analytics Cloud is a software-as-a-solution (SaaS) for SAP analytics that includes business intelligence, predictive analytics, and planning and is built on SAP Cloud Platform. SAP provides business content for several industries and LoBs with this solution; in fact, the SAP Digital Boardroom solution is available on top of SAP Analytics Cloud. SAP Analytics Cloud can connect to data sources such as SAP S/4HANA, SAP BW on SAP HANA, or SAP BW/4HANA on-premise or SaaS solutions, either online or through data replication.

Figure 8.11, Figure 8.12, and Figure 8.13 give an example of profitability analysis, viewed through the SAP Digital Boardroom. In SAP Analytics Cloud, you can organize the related visualizations in a user story and then add the stories to the agenda in the SAP Digital Boardroom.

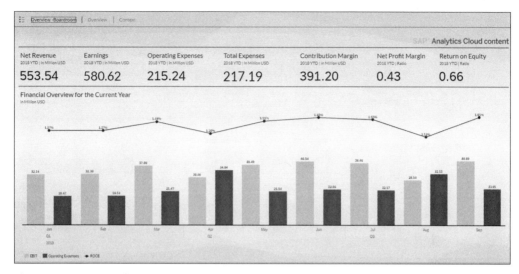

Figure 8.11 SAP Digital Boardroom Storyboard Part 1

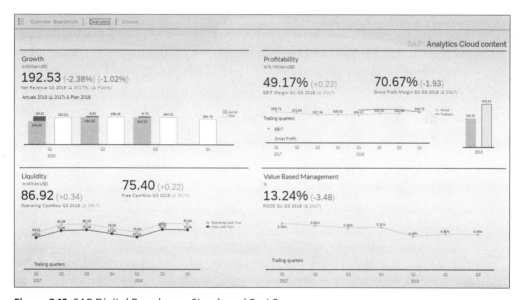

Figure 8.12 SAP Digital Boardroom Storyboard Part 2

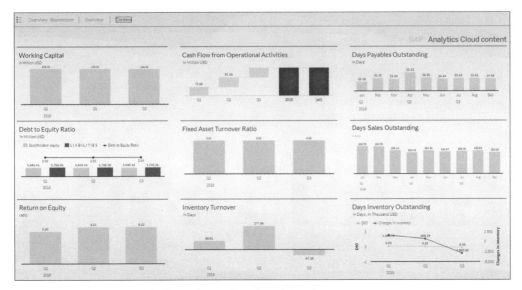

Figure 8.13 SAP Digital Boardroom Storyboard Part 3

Figure 8.11, Figure 8.12, and Figure 8.13 show the charts that slice and dice the data and show profit margins and gross revenue breakdown per business entity, profitability breakdown by legal entity, net profit and trend by business segment, drilling down to related KPIs per country, and then drilling down to further details of plan versus actual costs and profits per chart of accounts.

SAP Analytics Cloud now has several standard content items for SAP S/4HANA for several industries and LoB solutions. It also has content stories taking data from SAP SuccessFactors, such as HR General or HR Recruitment, and from SAP Ariba, such as spend management.

> **Note**
>
> To get up-to-date information on the business content provided in the current version, visit *www.sapanalytics.cloud/learning/business-content/*.

Next, we'll discuss how to solve the analytical puzzle for a hybrid environment, which is becoming quite common in large enterprises.

8.4   Reporting in a Hybrid Landscape

Reporting and analytics environments for hybrid landscapes are becoming quite complex, as the options for various products, even within the SAP landscape, increases. Making the right choice for the right reporting platform for each piece of the application landscape is quite a difficult task now.

When it comes to hybrid landscapes, an example of which is shown in Figure 8.14, one of the options is to use the analytical content that comes out of the box for each product, for example, for SAP Ariba Spend Analysis, SAP SuccessFactors Workforce Analytics, and embedded analytics for SAP S/4HANA. SAP Concur has also its own dashboards, including self-service reporting.

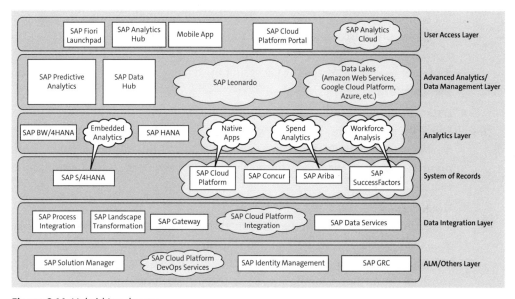

Figure 8.14 Hybrid Landscape

For enterprise analytics, a solution such as SAP BW/4HANA is used if it's a greenfield implementation. If the client has an existing SAP BW solution, the company may take different paths to SAP HANA though SAP BW on HANA or by converting to SAP BW/4HANA through the standard SAP migration path. Every other analytics solution that requires data from multiple systems can be orchestrated either on SAP Analytics Cloud or in a native SAP HANA analytics app while the frontending can be through the dashboarding functionalities of the SAP Analytics Cloud.

Figure 8.14 is a representative figure of some of the tooling options available in a combined or hybrid on-premise and cloud platform for the various layers, whether it's the system of records, the analytical systems, or the data management layer.

It's important to consider a few aspects while creating the analytics strategy for such hybrid landscapes:

- **Build versus reuse**
  Build analytical reports only if they don't come out of the box of any of the applications existing in the landscape or if they have high licensing costs. The creation of custom analytics has a high total cost of ownership (TCO). In addition, speed of adoption is faster if out-of-the-box solutions are leveraged.

- **Data reuse**
  Try to minimize data replication unless complex calculations or combining data from multiple sources are required. In addition, if there is an SAP BW on HANA and a native or side-by-side SAP HANA instance sharing the same SAP HANA database, it's better to cross-leverage the views and the data between applications built on these platforms.

- **Data volume**
  Live data connections, say from SAP Analytics Cloud, can have a performance impact, especially if the connections are getting data from a different cloud or on-premise system. Hence, data retrievals need to be restricted to the minimum required.

- **User access**
  Most of the reports used in the line functions for operational analysis should be available typically in the SAP Fiori launchpad, if that's the frontend being used. It only makes sense for a focused analytics team to have specific user access built, which can be on cloud portals or even on the SAP Analytics Hub.

- **Self-service analytics**
  Support of self-service analytics for the advanced users should be provided.

- **Operations**
  In terms of operations, the roll out of analytics can be done in phases and should consider the organization's maturity in terms of its usage. In addition, the support needs to be well structured with the right processes so that the end user doesn't face problems when support is needed for reports provided by different applications.

- **On-premise versus cloud**

  Last but not the least, there are analytics solutions now from SAP that run on-premise while others run on the cloud. The analytics landscape should be a right mix that leverages both options. If there is high volume of data to be brought from source systems that are on-premise, or if heavy processing must be done on the data, it may make sense to use the on-premise analytics solution. However, if there are quite a few SaaS instances already being used or even native analytical applications that need to be built using the SAP HANA platform, it may be worthwhile to have the SAP Analytics Cloud solution. Sometimes, it may be a combination of both types of solutions with heavy-duty enterprise analytics done on-premise, and easier, lightweight analytics requiring faster deployment done on the cloud or at least the frontend solution can be based on the cloud.

Thus, when choosing the analytics strategy, it's good to have an idea of the types of analytical functions that are typically required for that industry and then lay down the basic patterns and the recommended tools to be used for each pattern.

In the next section, we'll delve into some of the advanced analytical concepts, such as cognitive analytics.

8.5   Cognitive Analytics

The analytics world benefits from advances in artificial intelligence (AI), in part because services can now be consumed directly, which enables us to advance beyond the world of structured data. Although AI is a very broad term, the cognitive (or learning) capabilities of systems are growing.

Cognitive systems are built to emulate the cognition capabilities human beings possess to learn from their surroundings. Cognitive analytics based on natural language processing and machine-learning capabilities, for example, are now showing insights into different types of nontraditional data and helping to create meaning from big data, including social media data, data from sensors or the IoT, geospatial data, and so on. These insights will help drive responses to users in a personalized manner, by taking in data and analyzing and understanding the geospatial and temporal context for users. It's easy to imagine where this kind of cognitive analytics will make an impact, from the medical services field to efforts to combat terrorism and beyond.

SAP has come up with machine learning under the auspices of SAP Leonardo, which provides additional intelligence and enables what is now known as the intelligent enterprise.

Some of other major players are developing new functionality in this area as well. For example, IBM's Watson APIs can be used in conjunction with any mashup platform to provide advanced analytics. IBM Cloud is the platform from which these APIs are available. IBM's Conversation API introduces a natural language interface for applications such as virtual agents or chat bots to automate interactions with end users, and Tone Analyzer is a service that employs linguistic analysis to detect emotional, social, and language tones in written documents, even down to the sentence level.

Note

You can find more details about Watson APIs and related use cases at *www.ibm.com/watson/products-services/*.

In Chapter 14, we'll discuss the new machine-learning services provided as part of the SAP Leonardo platform. You can use these services in a similar way to those used by the Watson APIs; the ways your SAP S/4HANA system consumes data are very similar. Of course, when planning for any implementation, you should take into consideration how mature these services are at this point and the effort of training users on the APIs.

Cognitive analytics considers various types of data from various sources and uses advanced cognitive functions to derive the right interpretation of such data. Let's consider a few examples: Imagine that you can measure the sensor data from a car for acceleration rate, frequency of braking, road conditions, weather, traffic, case history of traffic infractions, and so on to draw conclusions about an individual driver's driving patterns. This helps during any investigation of an accident and related insurance claims. Similarly, for connected cars, you can use analytics to determine when a car needs maintenance based on run time rather than a fixed number of miles or months.

Another example might be the automatic detection of cyber threats. Cyber threats are a great cause of concern because they cause huge losses of productivity and revenue and because they're difficult to predict; there's no way to manually read and analyze the huge volumes of structured and unstructured data that security analysts need to process every day. AI and machine learning allow systems to learn continuously by constantly analyzing billions of data points to detect patterns and even predict attacks before they occur.

For a third example, you can measure the condition of any piece of equipment in a manufacturing line at runtime through sensor data coming from the sensors or the control systems, and thus optimize the maintenance activities and reduce planned and unplanned downtime. This could then trigger the creation of a work order for a maintenance activity, predict a faulty part replacement, and create a requisition for that spare part in the backend SAP S/4HANA system.

From these analytics, some prescriptive steps—such as creating a maintenance order for a piece of equipment, creating a work order for production, changing the campaign parameters for a new product, increasing oil well production, or triggering a faulty product recall from social media analytics—are created that need to be fed back into the transactional system.

In the next section, we'll dive into big data analytics and discuss both data lakes and SAP Data Hub, which also houses SAP Vora, because these serve some of the important aspects of data hosting and data preparation for analytics to work on.

8.6   Big Data Analytics and Data Lakes

In a data lake, data from different sources are brought together in such a way that it's cleaned, its source is identified, it follows common business semantics for an organization, and it's made accessible to the right users for further analytics, often in a self-service mode.

The concept has evolved along with the advances of the big data concepts, because this big data brings new challenges to the world of analytics in terms of unstructured data types, very high volumes of data/streaming data, and events that need to be used as triggers for some analysis of that data. In the following sections, we'll look at data lakes, big data, and SAP Vora.

8.6.1   Data Lakes

The term *data lake* has suddenly gained a lot of popularity and is applied to mean different things. The following are some of the key motivations behind the data lake concept:

- Data needs to be analyzed, but huge amounts of data makes it difficult to store in high performance and advanced analytical systems, such as SAP HANA; the storage cost would be extremely high, and not all the data is important to store in this way. This then requires data storage beyond the data warehousing systems, such as SAP BW on SAP HANA or SAP BW/4HANA, and more cost-efficient yet easy-to-integrate systems, such as Hadoop clusters.

- An infrastructure is required that can store these analytical repositories without dependency on a specific data format. In other words, you need an infrastructure that can handle structured, unstructured, or semistructured data.

- The data lineage from the source system should be traceable. This is also useful for regulatory compliance.

- You need to enable business users to use the data for self-service analytics.

- Application rationalization needs data to be in a well-architected format in a few systems, rather than all over the landscape with several different types of data warehousing solutions and visualization tools and even more custom-built solutions, which make maintenance a nightmare for IT and ease of use a nightmare for business users. A structured approach makes it possible to use the data in a publish-subscribe mode.

- The data will eventually move into the transactional systems and hence needs to be of guaranteed quality; thus, the governance framework plays an important part.

- Proper metadata management capability is important for analysts to understand the data they're consuming and a must-have for the data governance processes and data management processes.

Figure 8.15 shows how the data lake sits in an application landscape and interacts with other systems and how users interact with it.

Now you know why you need data lakes. Next, let's discuss how to make them.

The theory behind the data lake concept is that the data repositories at the core of the data lake should be designated to fit the criteria we've just defined. Each organization must formulate the data management and data governance principles they want to follow and include the metadata model to use, which should be easy to extend and have a set of semantics that is common across the business. The data repositories include the traditional data warehouse systems and have options to store unstructured or semistructured data. In an SAP environment, this means including an existing (or migrated) SAP BW on SAP HANA system or a newly implemented SAP BW/4HANA system along with Hadoop clusters.

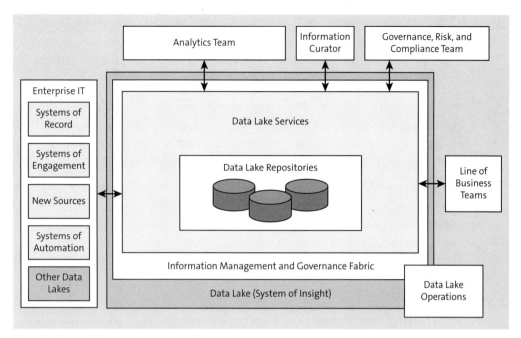

Figure 8.15 Data Lake

The data lake needs to be connected to the data sources throughout the enterprise through suitable governance—thus ensuring consistency and controllability of data. This can be assured by using integrated services and through implementation of workflows to ensure suitable governance and data quality as and when required, depending on the source and type of data. SAP HANA has these integration services, and many of these functions are also provided by SAP Data Services.

In addition, the data lake needs to have access control, monitoring, and audition capabilities to ensure proper governance and compliance.

The outer edge of Figure 8.15 shows the various users of the data lake:

- The analytics team is a group of users, including data scientists, responsible for carrying out the advanced analytics across the data lake.

- The information curator is responsible for the management of the data catalog, which will be used by users to find the relevant data elements within the data lake.

- The governance, risk, and compliance team is responsible for defining the overall governance program of the data lake and any associated reporting functions to demonstrate compliance.

- The data lake operators are responsible for the day-to-day operations of the data lake.

- The line of business (LoB) users might have roles such as the manufacturing line users, finance users, sales team, and so on.

Let's turn our attention to another important SAP product: SAP Vora, which plays an important role in the big data analytics area, on top of the Hadoop layer. This will help explain what the reference architecture for data lakes can look like in the SAP world.

> **Note**
>
> For more details on data lake architecture and design principals at IBM, see *Designing and Operating a Data Reservoir* (Chessell et al., IBM Redbooks, 2015; *http://www.redbooks.ibm.com/Redbooks.nsf/RedpieceAbstracts/sg248274.html?Open*).

8.6.2   SAP Vora

SAP Vora is a distributed computing solution that is deployed on Apache Hadoop and Spark clusters. It doesn't require any additional hardware. Because it provides a semantic layer on your big data, which is stored in the Hadoop layer and provides integration with the SAP HANA platform, you can run combined analytics across enterprise and Hadoop data.

All operations in SAP Vora can be accessed, executed, and extended through SAP HANA. SAP Vora itself can handle different types of data from different sources through open-source applications and libraries and provides high-performance sophisticated analytics against relational, time-series, graph, and JavaScript Object Notation (JSON) data. SAP Vora can also handle hierarchies, enterprise-ready calculations, and currency conversion, and it provides support for units. It has a simple web-based UI and supports SQL for querying data on Hadoop. Advanced users, such as data scientists, can leverage programming languages, for example, SQL, Python, Scala, C++, and Java, and can create mashups from different data sources.

From the user's perspective, SAP HANA and SAP Vora act as a single system with joint query optimization and automatic storage decisions that caters to big data analytical needs.

8.7   SAP Data Hub

SAP Data Hub is SAP's data operations management tool (DataOps). Initially SAP Data Hub 1.0 was released as an on-premise version, but now, as of September 2018, it's available as a platform-as-a-service (PaaS) and an SaaS model. The version released on October 2, 2018, is SAP Data Hub 2.3. SAP Data Hub has a strong integration with the enterprise systems, such as SAP S/4HANA, SAP BW/4HANA, SAP C/4HANA, and so on.

Its architecture is cloud-ready, containerized, and can be run on any platform that supports Kubernetes. This includes managed cloud services of Amazon Web Services, Google Cloud Platform, and Azure; private clouds or on-premise installations (e.g., Suse CaaSP); and the Cisco Container Platform for SAP Data Hub. In addition, from this version, machine learning has been integrated to the solution, the impact of which is highlighted later in this section.

SAP Data Hub was created to cater to the growing demands of handling multiple sources of data from various sources, to combine data from data lakes and enterprise data, and to prepare data for further analytics and orchestrate data.

The three pillars of the SAP Data Hub function are as follows:

- **Data pipeline**
  A data pipeline is the sum of the steps required for moving data between systems, for example, copying data from the source, moving it from on-premise to the cloud, transforming data, combining data from other sources, and so on. The job of the data pipeline is to ensure that these steps all happen reliably to all data in an automated way. The design and implementation of these data pipelines requires manual intervention. Typically, these steps used to require different software, but now, they can be managed entirely through the SAP Data Hub.

- **Workflows**
  Workflows orchestrate processes and data flows across different type of systems that may be using different type of technologies.

- **Governance**
  SAP Data Hub provides data governance, determines what kind of metadata is available in the different systems and who accesses what data, takes care of data security in cloud-based solutions, and so on.

Note that SAP Data Hub doesn't persist any data. Data processing is done at the source system only.

The key features of this solution are the following:

- **Data discovery**
  Understand the data by deep diving into different systems, including metadata management. SAP Data Hub features govern/manage the metadata, understand which format and state the data is in, determines the data lineage, and also combines the data from the different systems. A metadata crawler goes through the connected systems to collect this information. After publishing, the metadata is visible in the metadata catalog. The metadata search function helps to get data from a table, dimension, column, and so on.

- **Modeling**
  SAP Data Hub 2.3 provides a unified modeling interface via the SAP Data Hub Modeler. This interface provides the following:

  - Workflow pipeline operators: Data transfers (SAP HANA/SAP BW), Spark Jobs, and so on.
  - Remote sources orchestration: SAP BW process chain, SAP Data Services job, and SAP HANA flow graph.
  - Structured data transformations: Projections, aggregations, joins, unions, and cases.
  - Data masking: Mask out, numeric generalization, pattern variance, and so on.
  - Validation rules: Basic and custom functions.

- **Ingestion and integration**
  As shown in Figure 8.16, integrations with other systems are possible through connection with other tools from SAP, including SAP HANA smart data integration and SAP Data Services. They are part of the process chain where the integration tools actions are considered. The new version available from October 2018 has a connectivity framework that can connect to several databases and enterprise applications using native connectivity. This framework is evolving to accommodate more and more such connections. It can also connect to services such as the machine learning services of the SAP Leonardo platform. Ingestion to SAP Vora for streaming data has also undergone optimization.

- **Monitoring**
  Monitoring reveals what's going in the landscape and pipeline status, and makes it possible to deep dive into data processing issues.

Figure 8.16 shows the architecture of this product and its two components:

- **Application layer**

  This layer is installed on SAP HANA and is executable, with applications such as metadata catalog, scheduling and monitoring, policies, and so on. Here, the end user can do the end-to-end design for data management at design time.

- **Distributed runtime**

  This is executed where the data is residing, on the layer where data is persisted. Then the results of this data can be moved to the next environment for further processing. Distributed runtime runs on the Kubernetes cluster. Integration is possible to several systems, including SAP and non-SAP systems. SAP Vora is container-based as a Docker container and is executable. It may or may not use Hadoop. The connectivity framework connects all of the different types of connected systems, especially the integration tools of SAP and third-party products, and has connectivity to cloud-based data storage as well.

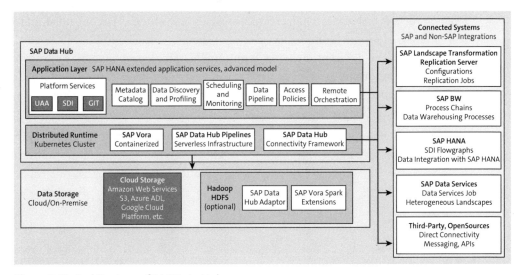

Figure 8.16 Architecture of SAP Data Hub

Note

More details on SAP Data Hub can be obtained at *https://help.sap.com/viewer/p/SAP_DATA_HUB*.

8.8   Summary

This chapter touched on the different types of analytical requirements that can arise in an enterprise. It also covered the various products available from SAP today that can be leveraged for different analytical needs of an enterprise running SAP S/4HANA as its digital core. The area of operational reporting has undergone a sea of changes with the advent of SAP HANA and the embedded analytics features of SAP S/4HANA.

We also covered the SAP Data Hub, which, although it doesn't directly churn out analytics, plays an important role because it manages the more structured data from enterprises, from IoT use cases, and from other big data platforms, including data lakes. With the data being handled in a streamlined way, doing analytics on this data, combining various types of data, and deriving the interpretations of data becomes easier.

We also touched on some of the aspects to keep in mind while choosing the right tools for the right use cases when creating an analytics strategy. We concluded that a combination of products and services—rather than any single product—is needed, depending on the different analytics requirements and various types of users. In addition, it's important to leverage the built-in analytics that each of the enterprise components, such as SAP S/4HANA, provides so that creation of newer reports or analytics is controlled.

Let's now move on to Chapter 9 where we'll discuss industry solutions based on the industry-to-core strategy.

Chapter 9
Industry Solutions

In this chapter, we'll touch on solutions for industries such as retail, fashion, and oil and gas. We'll compare some of the features and high-lights of each of the industry solutions.

SAP has delivered industry-specific solutions for several industries, and some of them are built into the core of SAP S/4HANA. SAP has moved several of its industry solutions to the SAP S/4HANA core to enable multiple industry solutions to run on the same instance without causing a conflict. This new approach is often referred to by SAP as the *industry-to-core* concept.

In this chapter we'll look at three of the most widely used industry solutions: retail, fashion, and oil & gas. Retail and Oil & Gas solutions were first released in 1610, followed by Fashion, which was released in 1709. For all three, a lot of additional functions have been released in 1809.

9.1 Retail

The official name of the latest product for retail is SAP S/4HANA Retail for merchandise management. In the following sections, we'll focus only on the retail-specific changes that make a difference compared to legacy SAP for Retail.

SAP S/4HANA Retail for merchandise management covers all relevant end-to-end merchandise management processes for retailers, and can also bring substantial advantages for SAP customers who run their core business in an industry other than retail. For example, telecom operators typically run a chain of customer service locations at which you can not only sign a new contract with your operator but also buy a new mobile phone or a battery charger. In the past, it was difficult—sometimes even impossible—to combine cross-industry operations with retail industry solutions in the legacy SAP ERP system. For example, a fashion company had to run its textile manufacturing on an IS-Mill system and manage direct sales in retail stores in a separate IS-Retail system.

SAP S/4HANA Retail can be activated in parallel with other industries, such as SAP S/4HANA Oil & Gas. It is also planned that, in the future, the solution will be able to work together with several business function sets that weren't feasible in SAP for retail—for example, for catch weight management.

Note

For detailed information about the possible coexistence of SAP S/4HANA Retail with other industry solutions, refer to SAP Note 2616967 (Coexistence of SAP S/4HANA Retail for merchandise management/SAP S/4HANA for fashion and vertical business and other industry solutions in SAP S/4HANA).

9.1.1   Technical Simplifications

As shown in all elements of SAP S/4HANA, efforts have been made in SAP S/4HANA Retail to reduce the backend complexity of the system. Although not all elements discussed in the following list are specific to SAP S/4HANA Retail, we've attempted to provide the most relevant simplifications for this industry, as follows:

- **Software component architecture**
  In the legacy system, activation of IS-Retail was a complex process requiring you to switch on industry extension ISR_Retail (SAP Retail) and enterprise extension EA-RET (Retail). There were also some additional retail functionalities that were included in Enhancement Packages (EHPs).

  SAP has removed EA-RET and the content of business function set ISR_Retail (SAP Retail). Retail coding is now a part of the SAP S/4HANA single core software component (S4CORE). Activation is much easier than in SAP ERP and is no longer exclusive; enterprise business function ISR_RETAILSYSTEM (Retail) can be activated in parallel to other industries. Some more generic parts of the Retail functionality are available even without activating it.

- **Customer vendor integration (CVI)**
  Customer and vendor masters were handled separately in SAP ERP, and using business partners was optional (with some exceptions). In SAP S/4HANA, the business partner (Transaction BP) is the single point of entry to maintain master data for business partners, customers, and vendors.

The specific transaction codes used to maintain customer/vendor master data separately from SAP ERP aren't available in SAP S/4HANA. At the same time, the main legacy tables for customer (table KNA1) and vendor (table LFA1) data remain in SAP S/4HANA.

- **Sites and business partners**
  In SAP for Retail, each site had the role of a customer and also could have the role of a vendor (optionally). Therefore, each site master had a customer master record assigned and sometimes also a vendor master record. In the legacy system, it wasn't possible to have business partners for customers/vendors assigned to retail sites.

  In SAP S/4HANA, business partner harmonization becomes available for the site (every customer/supplier record must have a business partner as a leading entity). There is a new BP role with a new role category for sites (BPSITE). There are also new business partner groupings for different types of sites (distribution centers, stores, franchisees, etc.).

  During the conversion from SAP ERP to SAP S/4HANA Retail, there is a special migration program to execute that will create business partners for all customers/vendors assigned to sites. There will be one business partner created per site, with a role C or with both roles C and V.

  There is one central maintenance option for maintaining addresses for business partners, including geolocation data for a retail site. This used to be possible in two ways: via site maintenance and via business partner maintenance. Both options were independent of each other and not synchronized. As of 1610 FPS 01, there is one central maintenance option: via business partner.

  Note that receiving points and departments are no longer maintained in the site maintenance transaction but are maintained only through the business partner maintenance function. This change should be addressed in the site/business partner distribution process.

> **Note**
>
> For more details on sites, refer to SAP Note 2310884 (SAP S/4HANA Conversion for Site Master).

- **Harmonization of retail article and material**
  The long-term target of SAP is to harmonize both material and retail articles as

283

product master data. SAP S/4HANA 1610 took the first small step in this challenging journey.

In the past, the method of storing characteristic valuations of variants of a generic article and a configurable material were different. Now, in SAP S/4HANA, both are harmonized; a generic article will be assigned to a configuration class, which will provide variant-creating characteristics for this article. The side effect of this simplification is a complex, three-step migration procedure that must be performed during the transition to SAP S/4HANA (premigration activities in SAP ERP, data transformation during downtime, and postmigration activities in SAP S/4HANA).

There is also a common, harmonized SAP Fiori app (Manage Product Master app) for products (materials) and articles management.

> **Note**
>
> For more details on generic article harmonization, refer to SAP Note 2339010.

- **User experience**
  SAP S/4HANA Retail delivers new and enhanced SAP Fiori applications to manage retail-specific business processes. Starting from the first SAP S/4HANA Retail release 1610, there has been a comprehensive set of SAP Fiori apps for in-store merchandising. In SAP S/4HANA 1709 FPS 01, two additional SAP Fiori object page-type apps were released: Retail Promotion and List Products. These apps brought a significant improvement to the work experience of store associates and store managers, who now are able to more effectively perform their daily and periodic tasks. They can use different types of devices including not only PC, but also tablets or mobile phones; most of these devices provide barcode scanning capabilities, which is essential in many in-store merchandising activities.

9.1.2   Available or Changed Functionality

In this section, we'll cover some of the functionality available in SAP S/4HANA Retail. Because covering the full scope of this functionality could fill a book itself, we'll focus our attention on those elements that have changed dramatically from what was available in SAP for Retail and on newly added functionality. Some of the most relevant elements are as follows:

- **Material Ledger (ML) and stock valuation**
  In SAP ERP, it wasn't possible to use the ML and actual costing in the IS-Retail

system. This limitation was driven by system performance reasons; in retail, there might be hundreds of thousands of articles, which could "kill" the system due to complex ML processing. As a result, this limitation caused compliance issues in certain countries in which having such types of valuation is a legal statutory requirement.

Now, in SAP S/4HANA, the ML is the single and obligatory engine of stock valuation, and SAP HANA in-memory processing speed eliminates all kinds of performance limitations. The functionality is managed by business function ISR_RETAIL_MATERIAL_LEDGER, which is soft-switched when there are retail articles identified in the system.

In the material master, we have new (from the retail point of view) ML accounting views, where we can see material valuation data in company code currency, including the total stock value at sales price (new in ML), plus valuation data in up to two additional parallel currencies. There are six ML views available: current, previous, and last previous year periods, and future, current, and previous costing runs.

- **Replenishment**
  There are also significant changes in the replenishment area. The main (classic) replenishment transaction, Transaction WRP1, and multistep replenishment transactions (Transaction WRFE, etc.) aren't available any longer. As an alternative, SAP proposes two options. First, use the materials requirements planning (MRP) functionality instead. The second option is the rapid replenishment and planning workbench (Transaction WRP1R), which is available in SAP S/4HANA but listed as no longer strategic. Rapid replenishment offers much better performance than classic replenishment, even in SAP ERP on non-SAP HANA databases, but, at the same time, it adds some process/functional limitations (e.g., you can't use rapid replenishment for external sites, e.g., vendor-managed inventory [VMI] processes).

  Another currently available option is the use of SAP Forecasting and Replenishment—a part of SAP Supply Chain Management (SAP SCM)—but this isn't in the target architecture either. This option also requires an additional SAP license, integration, and so on.

  For now, SAP is evaluating the option of developing the future strategic replenishment solution as a consuming application on the SAP Customer Activity Repository.

- **Catch weight management**

  In SAP S/4HANA 1610 FPS 01, the initial generic version of catch weight management was introduced with certain limitations (e.g., only new implementations, i.e., no migration is yet possible from the legacy IS-CWM to SAP S/4HANA catch weight management—and retail scenarios aren't supported yet).

  What's required is the possibility of using SAP S/4HANA catch weight management in retail scenarios. The current lack of such an option in SAP ERP in combination with retail is one of the pain points of IS-Retail customers running grocery stores (with articles such as meat or cheese). Unfortunately, catch weight management and SAP S/4HANA Retail are still not compatible, and may not be activated in a system at the same time. For the current status, please refer to SAP Note 2612327 – BF Conflict added for Retail towards Catch Weight Management.

  > **Note**
  >
  > For the detailed list of restrictions for catch weight management, refer to SAP Note 2671323 (SAP S/4HANA CWM 1809: Restriction Note).

- **Seasons Workbench**

  The legacy IS-Retail season functionality isn't available in SAP S/4HANA Retail. The same applies to season fields in the article master in the **Basic Data** view. There are new fields—**Season Year**, **Season**, **Collection**, and **Theme**—in the **Basic Data 2** view. Finally, seasons aren't defined in the configuration any longer; instead, SAP S/4HANA provides a Season Workbench application (Transaction FSH_SWB).

- **SAP Fiori-enabled in-store merchandising**

  In S/4HANA Retail, the entire in-store merchandising process has been SAP Fiori-enabled. The following SAP Fiori apps are available for store associates and managers:

  - Look-up Retail Products: Provides real-time access to product data to support store clerks in providing answers to customer's questions. The scope of information provided includes stock availability information (also in nearby stores, and as of 1709 FPS 01, also in graphical map format), and information about available variants (for example, color and size). Enhancements in SAP S/4HANA 1709 includes a feature displaying current, future, and past promotions and bonus buys, as well as current, future, and past deliveries of the product.

  - Receive Product: Provides functionality to post received products from internal or external vendors. This app can work in trusted or detailed mode.

- Order Product: Provides product ordering functionality. This app was already available in release 1610, but it was limited to purchase requisitions only. As of SAP S/4HANA Retail release 1709, this app has been extended by adding integration with SAP Forecasting and Replenishment. Order proposals originating from SAP Forecasting and Replenishment can be reviewed and adjusted as needed. Integration also covers transfer of information about exceptions and their priorities from SAP Forecasting and Replenishment, which can be displayed in the app's detail view.

- Transfer Products: New application from release 1709 that supports issuing stock transfer orders. Store associates can initiate the transfer of products from one store to another store, outlet, or to a distribution center (for example, after the end of sales season for a certain type of article). Each transfer order can be categorized using reason codes. Mobile devices can be used to scan the product (handling unit) barcode, to print the content label for the receiving site, and to print the shipping label for the carrier.

- Retail Promotion: Displays key information about the promotion, including the promotion ID, name, promotion period, administrative data, promotion attributes, status, participating stores, and products in scope.

- Count Product/Manager View: Supports cycle counting, physical inventory, and monitoring the progress of the counting process.

- Print Labels: Prints product labels.

- Adjust Stock: Supports real-time stock adjustments and ad hoc counting of products.

- Transfer Stock: Provides functionality to transfer stock from one location to another.

- Perform Store Walk-Through: Supports the execution of task lists related, for example, to inventory corrections.

As of SAP S/4HANA release 1809, the Transfer Products app has been enabled for radio frequency identification (RFID) processing. This app can process data received from an RFID antenna, and the transfer of products can be registered through RFID tag scanning. Previously available scanning of product barcodes remains supported as an equal alternative method and can be used as needed. The advantage of the new RFID-based solution is that you can read multiple tags in a single reading step, versus time consuming barcode item-by-item scanning.

On top of above listed in-store merchandising applications, there are also new SAP Fiori object pages, which provide an overview of most important information about an object, and direct access to the most important functions related to an object from a single screen. As of SAP S/4HANA 1709, there are object pages available for retail objects including product, site, and allocation. In SAP S/4HANA 1809 a new Promotion Data object page was added.

As of SAP S/4HANA 1809, there is a new List Products app. This app allows you to view and create listing conditions for a product, which define assortments and time periods in which a product will be listed. You can run listing simulations for a product and adjust the results before actual listing.

- **Structured articles with full products**

  Historically, there were two types of bill of materials (BOMs) in SAP S/4HANA Retail: full products with empties (for example, a bottle of beer consisting of a bottle (returnable) and beer [beverage content]), and structured articles including prepacks, displays, and sales sets. It was not possible to combine both types of BOMs.

  Starting from SAP S/4HANA 1709, it's possible to create structured articles (such as sales sets, prepacks, displays, and stands) with full products, including returnable empties with deposits (bottles, crates, etc.). This makes supply chain operations more effective by allowing the empty components to be items of the BOM. For example, as a structured article with full products, we can handle merchandise such as a mixed pallet with different types of beer in crates (bottles and crates are returnable materials here), or a sales (gift) sets consisting of a bottle of beer and a glass (bottle is returnable).

- **Merchandise distribution—single recipient purchase orders**

  This is a new process introduced in SAP S/4HANA 1809 that simplifies and speeds up merchandise distribution to a network of stores—namely processes such as cross-docking or flow-through in distribution centers. Retailers send a collective purchase order to a vendor with sub-items defining the breakdown of quantities for each store. For that purpose, a Supplementary Logistics Services article is required, which has to be assigned to the actual article being ordered. In the next step, the vendor sends a single delivery to the retailer's distribution center, which contains products packed separately according to the final recipients (which are stores in this case). This practically eliminates the step of repacking the goods in the distribution center, which brings time- and cost-saving benefits. It's a mirror image of another new process—pack separately – ship together—which is described in

Section 9.2.5, and which allows a vendor or a manufacturer to deliver goods packed separately according to the customer's requirements.

- **SAP Leonardo Machine Learning in GDSN data processing**
  This is another new innovation delivered in SAP S/4HANA 1809. Retailers are now using the Global Data Synchronization Network (GDSN) to obtain product information data from manufacturers or distributors. By leveraging machine learning powered by SAP Leonardo, we can improve the data quality and enrich the data with SAP-specific characteristics of the product in the GDSN inbound data processing. For example, based on learning from the historical data in the system, you can automatically assign product characteristics such as material group, unit of measure, or the price group.

9.1.3 Removed and Nonstrategic Functionality

Several elements of the SAP for Retail functionality are no longer available in SAP S/4HANA Retail. The list includes different types of features and functionalities—for example, prepack allocation planning, retail short text replacement (plant to site, material to article, etc.), perishables planning, retail ledger, or retail-specific SAP Fiori fact sheets for article, site, allocation, promotion, and bonus. In some cases, alternative solutions are available; however, in other cases, SAP has stated that there is no equivalent functionality available in SAP S/4HANA and that SAP will investigate whether such functionality will appear in a future release.

For some removed functionalities, there are other SAP products that offer the desired functionality (e.g., planning can be found in SAP Merchandise Planning and SAP Assortment Planning).

In addition, several elements of legacy SAP for Retail functionality are still available in SAP S/4HANA but are defined as no longer "strategic." Typically, these are functions that have been transferred to other SAP products for the retail industry (e.g., SAP Customer Activity Repository or SAP Forecasting and Replenishment) and likely won't be further developed in the core SAP S/4HANA Retail for merchandise management product. In some cases, a new (replacement) functionality is planned in future releases of SAP S/4HANA. For example, retail sales forecasting is still available in SAP S/4HANA, but the strategic direction for forecasting in retail is unified demand forecasting, which is a part of SAP Customer Activity Repository.

> **Note**
>
> You can find further information and the complete list of notes describing retail functionalities that are no longer available in SAP Note 2371618 (S4TWL—Retail Functionality Not Available Anymore).
>
> You can find further information and a list of SAP Notes describing retail functionalities that have been designated as no longer strategic in SAP Note 2371605 (S4TWL—Retail Functionality Not Strategic Anymore).

9.1.4   Retail Integration

In this section, we'll discuss several possible aspects of integration of SAP S/4HANA Retail for merchandise management with other selected software components from SAP that are dedicated to the retail industry.

SAP S/4HANA can be the target of data distribution from standalone SAP Master Data Governance (SAP MDG) for the following data:

- Customers and vendors (standard SAP MDG business partner)
- Articles (SAP MDG, retail and fashion management extension by Utopia)

SAP MDG can be also installed on top of SAP S/4HANA. The new version of SAP MDG, retail and fashion management extension by Utopia, includes the article scenario in SAP S/4HANA.

SAP S/4HANA Retail can be also integrated with SAP Commerce (formerly known as SAP Hybris Commerce). SAP offers a solution to integrate back-end SAP systems with SAP Commerce and SAP Data Hub, called SAP Hybris Commerce, integration package for SAP for Retail. As of the version 2.4 this integration solution provides for the integration of SAP S/4HANA on-premise with SAP Commerce (versions 1709 and 6.4, respectively), covering retail functionalities.

One of the foundational elements of SAP architecture supporting an omnichannel retail model is SAP Customer Activity Repository. SAP Customer Activity Repository consuming applications will offer the same integration possibilities as their underlying SAP Customer Activity Repository release.

Omnichannel Promotion Pricing (OPP) is a new functionality in SAP Customer Activity Repository for the centralized calculation of product price. In SAP Customer Activity Repository, the central Price and Promotion Repository (PPR) is mastered and made available for other consuming applications like Promotion Pricing Service

(PPS). Promotions can be maintained via SAP Promotion Management or via the new SAP Fiori Manage Promotional Offers app.

There are two basic deployment models available for OPP:

- Central: PPS in SAP Customer Activity Repository is called directly from the application like SAP Commerce, for example.
- Local: prices are sent from PPR in IDocs to a local price repository that is stored in an application like SAP Commerce, for example. A local repository has the same structure as a central repository in SAP Customer Activity Repository, but it contains a limited set of price and promotion data that are relevant for the local use.

In the price calculation process, OPP leverages contextual information, including a list of items in the shopping basket, discount coupons, and loyalty schemes. Based on this information, OPP identifies available promotions and applies them to the shopping basket.

The main advantage of the OPP engine is that it provides a single PPR, as well as single price calculation engine for all sales channels and applications. For many retailers, several PPRs and different price calculation engines were major obstacles in implementing the omnichannel sales model. SAP Customer Activity Repository with OPP can be a solution to this pain point. An additional benefit is the reduced effort to maintain price and promotion data (only once in OPP versus separately in each system and engine), and lower total cost of ownership (TCO). Note that OPP doesn't aim to replace the pricing engine in SAP S/4HANA; items like sales taxes or delivery costs should still be calculated by the sales and distribution (SD) pricing procedure.

A new element available since SAP S/4HANA 1709 is that PPS in SAP Customer Activity Repository can be remotely called from SAP S/4HANA Enterprise Management directly from the sales order level. It's also possible to apply more complex promotion and pricing rules (mix and match).

OPP is integrated into the SAP S/4HANA pricing procedure via the condition value formula *317 OPP: call PPS*. PPS is automatically called via this formula, and as a result the PPS in SAP Customer Activity Repository calculates the values and returns the results to the sales order in SAP S/4HANA. The results are saved in corresponding condition records in SD Sales Order, and in parallel the received information is persisted in the sales order header text.

Last but not least, SAP S/4HANA Retail for merchandise management can be integrated with SAP Forecasting and Replenishment, which is a part of SAP SCM.

9

9.2   Fashion

One of the major SAP S/4HANA innovations delivered in release 1709 was fashion industry enablement. The official name of the product is SAP S/4HANA for fashion and vertical business. This release brings significant benefits to vertically integrated companies, who can now manage and operate their fashion sourcing, distribution, and retail activities as one integrated business. Further functionalities supporting fashion manufacturing were released in SAP S/4HANA 1709 FPS 02 (May 2018).

The first foundational fashion-related elements were introduced with SAP S/4HANA release 1610, but they were focused on fashion retail only (e.g., season processing). In SAP S/4HANA release 1709, we get much more, including fashion wholesale enablement, and as of 1709 FPS 02, also manufacturing. The main sales pitch of SAP S/4HANA for fashion and vertical business is the "vertical solution" that covers and integrates fashion manufacturing, wholesale, and retail processes within a single SAP S/4HANA system.

To use some of the fashion-specific functions, you need to activate certain retail and fashion business functions in your SAP S/4HANA system (ISR_RETAILSYSTEM and other ISR_RET* business functions). For the supply assignment functionality, you need to activate the SUPPLY_ASSIGNMENT* business functions. Some fashion-specific functions are available in SAP S/4HANA core without such an activation.

Fashion-specific functionalities are accessible in SAP S/4HANA through the **Fashion for Vertical Business** menu which can be called with Transaction W1OM. We'll explore these functionalities in the following sections.

9.2.1   Demand and Supply Segmentation

Segmentation helps to better manage supply and demand streams in the supply chain model. This benefit is delivered through separation of stock, segmentation of customer demand, and definition of the optimal relationship between them both. Certain products can't or shouldn't be shipped from one site to another for several reasons of different natures. Supply and demand are matched in the segmentation strategy, in which we define which segment of demand can consume supply from a given supply segment.

This isn't a new functionality—segmentation has been available in legacy products—however, in fashion in SAP S/4HANA, it has been quite significantly modified (e.g., it has been decoupled from the stock protection functionality, described in an upcoming section).

There are two types of segmentation:

- **Logical segmentation**
  This is based on logical characteristics of the product, for example, sales channels in which products should be available, regions, markets, and so on.

- **Physical segmentation**
  This is based on physical characteristics of the product, for example, quality characteristics, country of origin, and so on.

When we compare the segmentation against the legacy SAP Fashion Management product, you can see that in SAP S/4HANA, most of the segmentation settings and characteristics can be maintained in application transactions, without touching the SAP configuration. To put it another way, the effort has been shifted from system administrators to key users.

In a typical segmentation setup process we can identify the following steps:

1. **Define characteristics and values**
   Segmentation information is built based on classification characteristics. The characteristics that can be used for segmentation must belong to the characteristics group "characteristics for segmentation" (SGT_SAP-C Segmentation) and carry certain attributes (for example, data type CHAR character format).

2. **Define segmentation structure**
   The segmentation structure is a combination of characteristics' segments. Once the segmentation structure is released for use (locked), it can't be changed anymore. You can define segmentation structures in Transaction SGTS (Segmentation Structure Maintenance).

3. **Define segmentation strategy**
   A segmentation strategy contains business rules defining what is allowed and what is not, including values and combinations of supply and requirement segments. You can define segmentation strategies in Transaction SGTC (Segmentation Strategy Maintenance). In the initial SAP S/4HANA for fashion and vertical business release 1709 FPS 02, only 1:1 and N:1 segmentation strategies were supported (1:1 = one requirement segment matches to only one supply segment; N:1 = multiple requirement segments match to one supply segment). More strategies (N:M and 1:N in MRP and supply assignment) have been delivered in SAP S/4HANA 1809. In this release, there is also a new Transaction SGT_SETUP, allowing you to

9

maintain both segmentation structure and strategy in a simplified way in a single transaction (separate Transactions SGTS for segmentation structure and SGTC for segmentation strategy remain available).

4. **Assignment of strategy to the product**
   Segmentation can be activated at the article level, so you can decide to use segmentation for selected articles or types of articles only. Note that this can be decided only at the initial stage, when there are no stock movements with the article. Alternatively, you can migrate an existing non-segmented article to a new one, which will be segmented. Segmentation data is maintained in the article master in the Basic Data 2 view.

> **Note**
>
> As of SAP S/4HANA release 1809, you can directly assign a segmentation strategy to a material in Transaction SGT_SETUP (Define Segmentation Setup).

When the last task is completed, every business transaction related to the article (for example, purchase requisition, purchase order, stock transport order, sales order, etc.) will follow the segmentation strategy and predefined rules, and carry the segmentation information.

Segmentation information can be entered manually, can be proposed (defaulted) by the system, or can be restricted. For the latter two options, there is a tool to determine default or restricted segment values. Defaulted or restricted segment values can simplify the user interaction in activities related to segmented articles, and/or reduce the number of segment data errors. You can default segment values specific for transactions (purchase order, sales order, etc.), context-specific (for example, org structures), or other. This tool, called the Default Segmentation tool, was released in SAP S/4HANA 1709, with no corresponding functionality in the legacy SAP Fashion Management or SAP Apparel and Footwear solutions.

You can use segmentation in a lot of transaction types in several process areas:

- **Procurement**
  Segmentation can be enabled across the entire procurement process, including purchase requisitions, purchase orders, purchase contracts, stock transport orders, inbound delivery, and Logistics Invoice Verification (LIV).

- **Sales**
  All the key sales documents, including inquiries, quotations, sales orders, contracts, deliveries, and billing documents, are segmentation enabled. In case of document creation with reference, the segmentation data is inherited from the reference document. You can also have segmentation-specific pricing with segmentation-specific condition types. And, of course, you can run segmentation-specific available-to-promise (ATP).

- **Inventory management (IM)**
  Segmentation can be used in goods movements, reservations, retail stock overview, and physical inventory.

- **Warehouse management (WM)**
  Transactions, such as transfer requirements, transfer orders, replenishments, or count results, have been enhanced with segmentation data (parameter Stock Segment).

- **Manufacturing**
  Segmentation can be used in production orders.

As you can see in this list, virtually all the key processes are enabled for segmentation, and segmentation information can be persisted in all key types of a business document. You can also have segment-specific weights and/or volumes defined in the article master.

As of SAP S/4HANA 1809, segmentation has also been enabled in advanced return management (ARM) functionality.

Last but not least, segmentation is also reflected in reporting. As of SAP S/4HANA release 1809, segmentation information is available in the Stock Overview report (Transaction MMBE), which is one of the most widely used inventory management reports. In this report, you can display stock at segmentation level. When a material is relevant for segmentation, then you can define the stock segment range as the report selection criteria.

9.2.2 Advanced Available-to-Promise

Advanced ATP (AATP) is the new SAP S/4HANA availability check engine, which is extra licensed in a regular SAP S/4HANA Enterprise Management product. For SAP S/4HANA Fashion, it's included in the license, as a required engine for the stock protection/product allocation functionality.

The new SAP S/4HANA AATP engine consists of four key elements:

- **Product availability check**
  This new, faster, and more effective availability check is optimized for SAP S/4HANA. As of release 1709, it supports segmentation.

- **Product allocations**
  This feature allows you to define stock allocations to ensure that the product demands from the most important customers and sales channels are fully met. This part of AATP is used in the fashion industry stock protection process.

- **Back order processing (BOP)**
  The classic ATP followed "first come, first serve" logic, which isn't sufficient for many omnichannel fashion retailers. In SAP S/4HANA AATP, demand has been labeled with five confirmation strategies (win, gain, redistribute, fill, lose), allowing you to define more sophisticated logic supporting prioritization of more important sales channels and customers. In SAP S/4HANA for fashion and vertical business, BOP has been merged with the fashion-specific supply assignment functionality.

- **Release for Delivery**
  The last element of AATP is a new SAP Fiori app that can be used to change sales order confirmations before creating outbound deliveries. Typically, this application can be used to perform last-minute quantity adjustments to eliminate or reduce issues related to shortages of products to be delivered.

In SAP S/4HANA release 1809, there are further enhancements in product allocations, BOP, and Release for Delivery, as well as a new functionality element called alternative-based confirmations (ABCs), allowing you to, among other things, determine the delivery plant based on defined key performance indicators (KPIs).

9.2.3   Stock Protection/Product Allocation

Stock protection, which is actually a concept or a business process rather than a functionality, allows you to prevent competition (sales cannibalizing) between sales channels and to optimize the supply process. Stock protection avoids the situation where stock has been consumed by low-priority sales channels or customers at the cost of product nonavailability for strategically important customers. From a technical point of view, this business process is supported by SAP S/4HANA AATP engine with product allocation functionality (this must be activated in the AATP Customizing, and, once activated, you can't return to the legacy product allocation solution).

The stock protection process had been available already in the legacy SAP Fashion Management product; however, it was based on different engines and concepts. It used segmentation to define sales plan attributes, and PIRs to define requirements per channel. In the SAP S/4HANA version, stock protection is decoupled from the stock segmentation, and it doesn't use PIRs anymore. In SAP S/4HANA, stock protection level is flexible and can be defined based on aggregated levels (e.g., material group or a set of materials); however, if needed, it can be also defined for single articles as well. Finally, from a technical point of view, stock protection is a part of the SAP S/4HANA core, so, theoretically, it's available for not only fashion customers but all customers.

Stock protection setup in SAP S/4HANA fashion and vertical business is enabled in the Product Allocations SAP Fiori app. This process is realized in four steps:

1. **Configure product allocation**
   In this step, you define product allocation objects (PAOs), which include characteristics value combinations. For each PAO, you define the quantity unit of measure in which we will plan, period type (daily, weekly, monthly, or quarterly), time zone, and indicate whether the maintained product allocation object should be valid for sales orders and/or stock transport orders. After defining these parameters, you can select characteristics values for stock protection (for example, distribution channel or customer number).

2. **Manage product allocation planning data**
   In this step, you maintain product allocation quantities for the defined PAOs (combinations of characteristic values) for the assigned time periods. These quantities can be downloaded to Excel, maintained, and uploaded back to the Product Allocations app. Uploading from third-party external systems is also possible.

   The current product plan/consumption/available/confirmed situation is also presented in this app in the form of bar chart.

3. **Manage product allocation sequences**
   In this step, you maintain the sequence of product allocations (prioritize in what sequence the system should look for quantities to fulfill the incoming order).

4. **Assign product to product allocation**
   In this step, you activate product allocation for products (per material/plant combination) and assign products to product allocation data.

9.2.4   Supply Assignment

Supply assignment functionality (formerly known as ARun) facilitates fixed assignments between requirements and supply elements, which remain valid until the creation of the outbound delivery. It's a real link in the SAP S/4HANA system database with assignment of supply to demand, which can't be overwritten by another rerun of ATP, and it disappears only after the outbound delivery is created.

There are several assignment scenarios possible; for example, we can assign the following:

- Customer's sales order to a stock in warehouse.
- Customer's sales order to a purchase order sent to vendor.
- Customer's sales order to a stock transport order between distribution centers.

In the SAP S/4HANA system, supply assignment and BOP have been merged into a single functionality based on the AATP) solution. Supply assignment is available in the SAP S/4HANA core solution not only for fashion, but for every customer. However, from the licensing point of view, it's a part of SAP S/4HANA for fashion and vertical business.

> **Note**
>
> To use the supply assignment functionality in SAP S/4HANA on top of the generic retail and fashion business function (ISR_RETAILSYSTEM), you need to activate two more assignment-specific functions: SUPPLY_ASSIGNMENT_01 and SUPPLY_ASSIGN-MENT_RETAIL_01.

The supply assignment functionality is fully SAP Fiori enabled; there are apps to create assignments, view the results, and compare between combinations.

In the legacy SAP Apparel and Footwear and SAP Fashion Management solutions, this functionality has been known under the name ARun, and there were several differences. In SAP Apparel and Footwear, ARun was activated at the global level. In SAP S/4HANA for fashion and vertical business (as in SAP Fashion Management), ARun is an optional feature that can be activated at the article/site level. The same applies to the assignment of batches: these are also optional and also activated at the article/site level. The release procedure has been decoupled from supply assignment and runs independently now in SAP S/4HANA.

Another fashion-specific element is Insight to Action (ITA), which is a reporting and manual maintenance tool (Supply Assignment Workbench) for assessing the end-to-end assignment situation, identifying and verifying exceptions (release check part), and initiating the required exception-related actions, such as manual adjustments, assignments, unassignments, and so on (manual actions part). This functionality can be leveraged when immediate corrective actions are required, for example, manual assignments to rush orders. The similar allocation legacy tool—ARun Optimizer/Workbench—has been sunset.

ITA can be also leveraged in the Inbound Delivery for Outbound Delivery (IFO Assignment) process. In this scenario, inbound goods can be directly used in shipping outbound orders (regular sales orders, stock transport orders, or free-of-charge orders), which eliminates the need to store the goods in the warehouse. The created outbound deliveries for orders are assigned to inbound deliveries in the ITA tool. IFO Assignment is available as of SAP S/4HANA 1809.

In SAP S/4HANA 1809, there are also two new analytical SAP Fiori apps that support supply assignment functionality:

- Supply Demand Overview (Detailed Analysis): Enables the presentation of overall supply, demand, and supply assignment situation.
- Supply Demand Overview (Flexible Analysis): Offers the functionality described in the previously described app, additionally allowing users to flexibly select dimensions such as plant, material group, customer group, and measures for open demand quantity, open supply quantity, assigned quantity, delivered, etc. This is similar to characteristics and value fields in classic Profitability Analysis (CO-PA).

Both new apps present data being analyzed in tabular and/or graphical (chart) formats, and they offer flexible filtering options that allow you to select data by plant, distribution channel, or generic article. The results of the analysis can be downloaded to Excel.

Supply assignment can work with standard and retail master data (material/plant or article/site).

9.2.5 Pack Separately – Ship Together

Pack separately – ship together (PSST) allows you to bundle sales order items for consolidated deliveries/shipments. It was introduced for the first time in SAP S/4HANA 1709 for fashion and vertical business. In PSST, you create logical grouping rules and then use these rules to group sales order items that need to be delivered/shipped together. Rules are typically defined by customers based on their business requirements.

Note that PSST isn't aiming to optimize the logistics operations, warehousing, or transport management processes of the company that is managing these processes in SAP S/4HANA for fashion and vertical business; it's purely focused on customer requirements related to consolidations of shipments, which can be driven by optimization of customer's logistics operations, warehousing, and so on.

PSST is activated at the sales document type and sales area levels. It can be deactivated at the item category level. After rule definition (Transaction FSH_PSST_GRA) and assignment to business partner (customer) master records (Transaction BP – Sales Area – Retail Additional Data), PSST grouping can be leveraged in the execution of supply assignment (ARun) and in the creation of outbound deliveries. PSST groups are assigned to sales order items in PSST Assignment and Monitor (Transaction FSH_PSST_MONITOR). As of release 1809, the PSST functionality is also available for stock transport orders.

9.2.6   Material Requirements Planning and Planned Independent Requirements

Planning in SAP S/4HANA for fashion for vertical business is based on planned independent requirements (PIRs) and MRP Live. We will briefly describe these two functionalities in this section.

Planned sales figures are typically prepared based on the analysis of actual sales figures from one or more previous sales seasons. PIRs are estimated figures that are entered or imported to SAP S/4HANA for fashion and vertical business. These estimated figures have to be distributed across different characteristics like color or size, based on distribution curves, for example. Planned sales figures must be also be distributed across time periods in order to answer the capacity limits related to different types of operations. You can create PIRs in Transaction FSH_PIR (generic article level) or in Transaction MD61 (at variant level). Quantities entered in Transaction FSH_PIR are distributed across all the variants based on predefined rules (distribution curve, current ratio, equal distribution, and consumption ratio).

A new MRP Live transaction (Transaction MD01N) provides an optimized MRP run performance. MRP functionality has been completely rewritten in order to implement application logic in SQL-script, which runs on the database server, enabling it to leverage SAP HANA database capabilities for parallel processing. MRP Live analyzes the entered PIRs and sales orders and, based on this information, creates supply elements to cover the demand. The practical outcome includes stock proposals, which can be purchase requisitions or purchase orders. MRP Live uses segmentation with 1:1 or N:1 relationships between requirement and stock segmentation.

As of SAP S/4HANA 1809, we have access to an additional functionality related to planning—cut-off calendar. Sales seasonality impacts both vendor delivery times and internal purchasing processing times; at the beginning of a season it can be significantly different comparing to the end of season. In order to more efficiently manage transactions in high demand seasons, vendors can define cut-off dates (dates by when purchase orders must be placed at vendor) in order to guarantee the delivery within the corresponding staging time. Cut-off dates are maintained in Transaction FSH_COD. A cut-off calendar is taken into account by MRP in creating purchase requisitions. On top of MRP, this functionality is also supported in ATP and in manual transactions like purchase requisitions.

9.2.7   Fashion Manufacturing

After the initial release of SAP S/4HANA for fashion and vertical business (1709), marketing materials from SAP said that "complete vertical integration is the vision of SAP S/4HANA for fashion and vertical business." At that stage, that was only the vision, due to a big gap at the beginning of the business chain, there was no fashion manufacturing in the scope of the solution. Manufacturing in SAP S/4HANA for fashion and vertical business was delivered in 1709 FPS 02 earlier than initially announced (originally expected in SAP S/4HANA release 1809 FPS 00), and it has helped to transform the vision to a product that actually covers the entire process scope of a vertically integrated fashion company.

Bills of materials (BOMs) in SAP S/4HANA for fashion and vertical business are called at the generic article level, which is created with average usage of materials that are required for base size. In variants for different sizes, you can define different usage of materials; for variant size S, you need less material than for variant size XL. It can be maintained based on quantity distribution profiles, which will define the usage for each size according to the predefined rules. On top of this there is also the zero quantity option, which allows you to skip certain components in selected variants; for example, you can have special color versions with or without an embroidery. Components can be also segmentation-dependent; again, as an example for segment A, you can have the same T-shirt version with a heat seal, and another segment B without a heat seal.

Routing in SAP S/4HANA for fashion and vertical business in most cases applies to all variants of a generic article, so it's called at the generic article level. There might be variances, for example, alternative routing versions for different segments. If you look at an example of a T-shirt, then in Segment A, you'll have an operation to apply the heat seal; in the routing for Segment B, such an operation won't be required.

Production versions determine which BOM will be used in combination with which routing to produce an article. In SAP S/4HANA, production versions are assigned in mass processing Transaction C223.

Most of the production planning and execution activities can be managed from the Production Control Workbench (PCW; Transaction FSH_PCW). In SAP S/4HANA for fashion and vertical business, production orders require several variants to manage article characteristics, such as different sizes and colors. MRP Live will create individual planned orders per variant, which can be grouped together as the master planned orders. Master planned orders can be converted into master production orders, which again will group orders for several production variants of a single generic article. In the background, however, you'll always have individual production orders for each variant.

> **Note**
>
> In the background, BOMs and routings are stored separately for each article variant.

Markers are templates which define the optimized placement of all the pattern pieces that create the clothing product. Markers are assigned to master planned and master production orders in the Production Control Workbench. After indicating the sizes of articles that you want to produce, the system will display all the applicable markers from which you can choose to be assigned. The size of the marker is required to plan the number of plies of fabric that will be consumed in the execution of a production order. Marker information can either be imported from an external computer-aided design (CAD) marking system or entered manually in the marker master data maintenance Transaction FSH_MARKERS.

Master planned and master production orders can group production variants of only one generic article. In certain cases, you need to bundle production of more than one generic article, for example, a suit that consists of trousers and a jacket. In such a case you might need to cut both items from the same fabric in a single operation based on a single marker. To do so, in the Production Control Workbench, select **Master Order for Trousers** and **Master Order for Jacket**, and create from them a single combined master order for a suit. Similarly to regular orders, combined orders support segmentation and season determination.

As of SAP S/4HANA release 1809, it's possible to perform partial conversion of master planned order or combined planned order to generate the master production order or the combined production order for partial quantity.

It's a common business practice in the fashion industry to use subcontracting in the manufacturing process. Therefore, the subcontracting cockpit functionality has been enhanced by segmentation. The subcontracting cockpit functionality provides an overview of the subcontracting process, including all the material movements to or from the subcontractors, as well as an insight into operations at the subcontractor if needed.

9.2.8   Protected Species Management and Preference Management

In the fashion industry, some products or parts of products are made of materials of animal origin like silk or fur. Protected Species Management (PSM) enables the enhancement of article master textile composition data with details of endangered/ protected species identity via the PSM code. PSM also prevents international trade transactions that aren't in line with international regulations (Convention on International Trade in Endangered Species of Wild Fauna and Flora – CITES). Each transaction involving products made of materials originating from endangered or protected species must be accompanied by a special CITES license.

Preference Management enables the indication of the origin of goods with reference to specific trade agreements between the European Economic Community (EEC) and countries that treat certain goods with reduced or exempt import duties. Reduced or exempt customs duties have an impact on the financial results of the company, and therefore should be taken into account in planning supply chain operations.

Both PSM and Preference Management functionalities are not new; they were already included in the legacy SAP Fashion Management product. In SAP S/4HANA for fashion and vertical business, both are available as of release 1809.

9.2.9   Data Migration from SAP Apparel and Footwear

SAP Apparel and Footwear is the legacy SAP solution for the fashion industry, and compared to the other legacy solution (SAP Fashion Management), there are more significant conceptual, process, and data model differences between this product and SAP S/4HANA for fashion and vertical business. Therefore, direct conversion from SAP Apparel and Footwear is not possible. The only possibility of transformation from SAP Apparel and Footwear to SAP S/4HANA is reimplementation, which involves the migration of data.

SAP provides an SAP Apparel and Footwear data migration solution based on the SAP S/4HANA migration cockpit, which is a standard migration tool embedded in SAP S/4HANA Enterprise Management. The solution enables the migration of master data and transactional data (open transactions) from the legacy SAP Apparel and Footwear system to the SAP S/4HANA scenario. The migration scope, on top of the generic master and transactional data objects, also includes fashion-specific objects such as season or segmentation data. The migration scope doesn't cover any configuration data, which has to be manually maintained in the target SAP S/4HANA for fashion and vertical business system. In case of a fairly common co-deployment of SAP Apparel and Footwear with SAP IS-Retail, the retail part isn't covered with SAP Apparel and Footwear Data Migration—it needs to be converted or migrated in a separate step.

> **Note**
>
> At the time of writing (fall 2018), SAP Apparel and Footwear data migration based on the SAP S/4HANA migration cockpit is available in restricted shipment mode only, and is focused on fashion wholesale data scope (i.e., manufacturing is not included). If you want to use the SAP S/4HANA migration cockpit for data migration from SAP Apparel and Footwear, please contact SAP. Unrestricted availability and coverage for manufacturing data is expected in 2019.

Data from the legacy SAP Apparel and Footwear system can be delivered in the provided Excel spreadsheets, or direct communication can be established to obtain data leveraging remote function calls (RFCs). For more details about the SAP S/4HANA migration cockpit, please refer to Chapter 15.

9.3 Oil & Gas

Full enablement of the oil and gas industry functionality has been delivered on SAP S/4HANA, including a simplified data model for SAP S/4HANA Oil & Gas for hydrocarbon management and new features introduced for SAP S/4HANA Oil & Gas for hydrocarbon management and the Trader's & Scheduler's Workbench.

In the latest release at the time of writing (SAP S/4HANA 1809), significant progress has been made in delivering the core functionality within the oil and gas industry, with advancements in several areas and optimization of the data model. An oil and gas industry client generally would find that the core functionality to operate the business both upstream and downstream is present in this release, but there are several areas in which specific consideration should be made, as outlined in the following sections.

9.3.1 Technical Simplifications

With the introduction of SAP S/4HANA release 1610, a new simplified hydrocarbon product management data structure was introduced, which provided the backbone for the oil and gas functionalities both upstream and downstream. This simplification rationalized the data structure for the oil additional quantities tables MSEG01 and MSEG02 into a combined table MATDOCOIL. This resulted in the removal of 16 oil inventory aggregated tables that can now be calculated on the fly, vastly reducing the IS-Oil data footprint in SAP S/4HANA. This new simplified data model (Figure 9.1) has provided the foundation for future innovation within the SAP S/4HANA Oil & Gas industry solution.

Many benefits are delivered through this rationalized data structure; for example, processing time is reduced because there is no longer any aggregation required, there are fewer inconsistencies within the additional quantities table, and high-speed evaluation across material document information is possible. This allows the innovation delivered within this latest release to be used for upstream operations management (UOM) group enhancements, allowing new UOMs to be added to a UOM group with minimal impact on existing data.

One of the key considerations for a system conversion to SAP S/4HANA 1809 (with respect to oil-specific data) is the need to perform data migration activities due to the transformation from deprecated tables MSEG01 and MSEG02 into the new table structure.

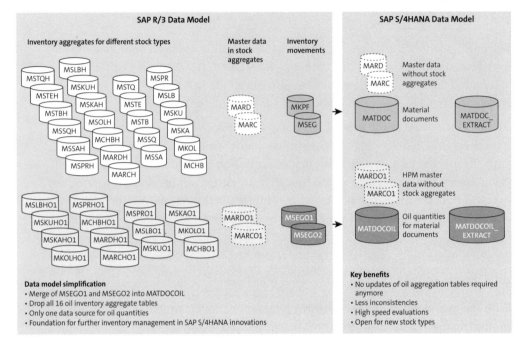

Figure 9.1 Data Model Simplification

The key to this SAP HANA-optimized aggregation for additional oil quantities is the new indexing format; this means that individual additional quantities are stored in separate columns within table MATDOCOIL and are then referenced within table MATDO-COIL_INDEX. This has a significant impact on any customized code that may have been developed within a system; previous interrogation of tables MSEGO1 and MSEGO2 relied on a header and item approach.

Clearly, the rationalized and optimized data model provides many SAP HANA-related performance benefits, but the data migration and custom code remediation related to any system conversion for an oil and gas customer should not be underestimated. The custom code remediation required for processing inbound or outbound movements or terminal automation system (TAS) integration when interacting with the new hydrocarbon product management data model would be particularly significant; this is an area likely to affect several oil and gas customers and should be evaluated in detail.

9.3.2   Upstream and Downstream

Upstream Oil & Gas functionality is well supported in the latest release of SAP S/4HANA, with all core IS-Oil functionality enabled with compatibility pack deployment, as well as several enhancements in specific upstream solutions. In SAP S/4HANA 1709, SAP S/4HANA Oil & Gas for upstream revenue management functionality was delivered with enhanced SAP HANA-based analytical content.

For customers on previous versions of SAP S/4HANA, SAP S/4HANA Oil & Gas for upstream revenue management is available via limited compatibility packs that can be combined with SAP S/4HANA Finance 1503 or 1605—for example, SAP S/4HANA Oil & Gas for upstream operations management, SAP S/4HANA Oil & Gas for upstream contracts management, and SAP S/4HANA Oil & Gas for upstream revenue management.

A specific enhancement has been delivered with the SAP S/4HANA 1610 release for upstream to provide enhanced functionality for UOM groups. This functionality allows a single UOM group to be enhanced with additional UOM groups in a seamless way, with tooling provided to update the additional oil quantities table. This is a significant improvement in functionality and allows new and changing business requirements to be reflected in existing data easily.

In 1709, a revamped SAP S/4HANA Oil & Gas for UOM was released. The enhancements and simplifications include exploration and production data collection and analysis, extracted products volume allocation, product ownership analysis (partner share, royalty share, etc.), a network modeler to simulate and graphically present the network structure and related allocation processes, and forecasting SAP Fiori apps. Customers running legacy SAP Upstream Operations Management functionality should monitor the changes for inclusion of this component.

On the other side, the SAP S/4HANA Oil & Gas downstream functionality currently delivers more innovation and optimization, now including supply chain visualization, which includes visualization of open shipments, relevant inventory, and associated alerts in a geospatial presentation. However, there are some key consideration in terms of target architecture components.

Core IS-Oil modules, such as Trader's and Scheduler's Workbench; Transportation and Distribution (TD); Tariffs, Duties, and Permits (TDP); and Marketing, Accounting, and Pricing (MAP), are delivered with some innovations in usability but little significant change in functionality, except for optimizations centering on the new hydrocarbon product management data model. There are some considerations regarding custom code remediation for existing customers that want to migrate; for example, the deprecation of table KONV (replaced with table PRCD_ELEMENTS) in the pricing area can provide significant areas of complexity for a migration.

The key area for evaluation in the SAP S/4HANA solution for downstream business is located around the functionality to manage service stations. The previous Marketing Retail Network (MRN)/Service Station Retailing (SSR) functionality is provided in compatibility packs only, and, unfortunately, not everything is available for everyone; old SSR functionality is available as a universal compatibility pack. The new SAP S/4HANA Oil & Gas for retail fuel network operations functionality is available only as a limited compatibility pack, so it can be combined with SAP S/4HANA Finance 1503 or 1605 only.

In general, these issues are addressed within the additional add-on component S4SCSD (Supply Chain Secondary Distribution) released with FPS 02 in May 2017, the functionality of which is detailed in the next subsection. However, it does include the full deployment of SAP S/4HANA Oil & Gas for retail fuel network operations.

9.3.3   Trader's & Scheduler's Workbench

The Trader's & Scheduler's Workbench is one of the key areas of innovation of the SAP S/4HANA 1610 release, delivering increased supply chain visibility through an optimized planning functionality. Despite this innovation, the core functionality within the Trader's & Scheduler's Workbench for master data, nomination, and ticketing is the same as that of the traditional IS-Oil solution, leading to little impact on a client migrating from an existing SAP ERP system.

There are three core aspects of the Trader's & Scheduler's Workbench functionality delivered within SAP S/4HANA:

- **Regional Inventory Dashboard**
  The Regional Inventory Dashboard is a new SAP Fiori app that provides inventory analysis on a graphical basis and provides alert monitoring, allowing the user to filter and display stock alerts. Direct integration is provided from the Regional Inventory Dashboard to the Inventory Planning Workbench.

- **Nomination Planning Workbench**
  The Nomination Planning Workbench is a Web Dynpro application that provides multimaterial and multilocation planning from one easy-to-use screen. A mass update feature is provided, allowing the user to quickly adapt nomination quantities and generate what-if scenarios to share with fellow schedulers.

- **Inventory Planning Workbench**
  An enhanced Inventory Planning Workbench providing real-time planning capabilities and next-generation what-if analysis and simulations allows business users to evaluate stock positions and react to alerts for inventory issues. Specific enhancements in FPS 02 are also delivered, including versions, global variants, global alerts, time-based constrains, global simulations, and OData service enablement.

Most of the enhancements and simplifications to the SAP S/4HANA Oil & Gas solution have been delivered for the Trader's & Scheduler's Workbench. The following SAP Fiori apps provide new features and enhancements:

- **My Nominations app**
  Schedulers can monitor nominations, access information, and set up new schedules, as well as add their own editable fields and append backend tables.

- **Regional Inventory Overview app**
  Users can set up alerts, monitor terminals, view stock information, and take actions on alerts and issues via the integrated Inventory Planning Workbench. An update was provided for an additional alert framework to match the enhanced global alerts in the Inventory Planning Workbench. You can also generate a heat map that presents only alert symbols (without inventory numbers).

- **Mass Change Events app**
  Users can monitor event changes, create and maintain nomination events, and perform mass change events for multiple nominations.

9.3.4   Transportation and Distribution

SAP has delivered a fully enabled transportation and distribution solution. The core shipment functionality that has existed within IS-OIL is retained, and the processing involved with shipment scheduling, load confirmation, and delivery confirmation follows the same structure as in previous SAP ERP releases.

SAP envisages integration directly between transportation management and bulk oil shipments to provide enhanced logistics scheduling and tracking functionality. However, the shipment object is retained in SAP S/4HANA and provides the basis for this integration.

The key point of simplification that must be evaluated by clients is the previous functionality for freight shipment costing that was delivered through the Logistics Execution – Transportation (LE-TRA) component, which isn't the target architecture within SAP S/4HANA. Instead, freight cost settlement functionality within SAP Transportation Management (SAP TM) is the solution of choice and will be available as an extended separately licensed solution embedded within SAP S/4HANA. However, this integration isn't delivered currently for optimized bulk oil shipments and is on the road map for future innovation.

9.3.5   Secondary Distribution

SAP has released a new SAP S/4HANA-based product called SAP S/4HANA Supply Chain for secondary distribution, which is an add-on for SAP S/4HANA that allows users to manage telecom sales, data collation, and retail fuel network operations, as follows:

- The telecom sales functionality of SAP S/4HANA Supply Chain for secondary distribution helps users manage sales transactions and process documents such as quotations, sales orders, or contracts. It provides access to reference data such as sales history transactions, credit limit information, or notes created for a specific customer. It's possible to integrate telesales with SAPphone to perform automatic customer searches by phone number or to make outbound calls.

- Data collation is a process of posting complex logistics business processes through the entry of reference data only, completing the process afterward by finishing the adjusting and follow-up documents that provide actual ex post volumes for loading, sales, and unloading. SAP S/4HANA Supply Chain for secondary distribution also offers functionality to integrate data interfaced from external partners, such as depots, through Application Linking and Enabling (ALE)/IDocs or flat files. Received data packages can be verified, converted, and passed to data collation.

- SAP S/4HANA Oil & Gas for retail fuel network operations helps manage and monitor the network of fuel stations and related inventory (replenishment) and financial (cash payments, credit cards, clearing) activities. It can support different fuel station ownership models, such as dealer-owned, company-owned, and hybrid combinations.

9.4 Outlook

SAP is continuously delivering innovations and simplifications for both upstream and downstream areas.

Oil and gas downstream innovations will include new SAP Fiori apps released for My Nomination Tickets and TSW Tickets, and a new mobile offline ticketing app available as part of the multichannel ticketing framework. The Inventory Planning Workbench will be enhanced via the new alerting framework functionality.

Improvements will also come in the solution integration area. SAP S/4HANA Oil & Gas will be integrated with SAP Commodity Management, and the Trader's & Scheduler's Workbench will be integrated with SAP Integrated Business Planning (SAP IBP) for demand.

In the upstream area, we expect only one change—but a very important one, especially for upstream customers from the United States: integration of SAP S/4HANA Oil & Gas for upstream revenue management with SAP S/4HANA Oil & Gas for upstream operations management.

9.5 Summary

This chapter introduced three different industry solutions: Retail, Fashion, and Oil & Gas. You should now have a good understanding of these solutions, including their benefits and features, as well as some of their restrictions.

In the next chapter, we'll move away from on-premise SAP S/4HANA with a discussion of SAP S/4HANA Cloud.

Chapter 10
SAP S/4HANA Cloud

This chapter introduces SAP S/4HANA Cloud and outlines its relative merits and functional gaps to help you choose the right SAP S/4HANA version for your company.

Software-as-a-service (SaaS) isn't a new concept. It has been proven, adopted, and successful over the past decade. SAP S/4HANA Cloud offers all the benefits of an SaaS offering, such as low total cost of ownership (TCO), no hassle keeping up with upgrades, and limited liability. The highest value SAP S/4HANA brings is access to best practices and the agility that comes with its connection to the ecosystem around the SAP S/4HANA digital core. The SAP S/4HANA system contains core functionality such as record-to-report, order-to-cash, and requisition-to-pay, but it also incorporates the latest innovations, such as machine learning. The SAP Fiori user experience (UX) is designed to make changes easy for users who've been working with SAP GUI for decades.

In this chapter, we'll provide an overview of SAP S/4HANA Cloud. We'll begin by discussing the value proposition of SAP S/4HANA Cloud before discussing the current scope of the solution. We'll also provide a high-level look at what an SAP S/4HANA Cloud deployment looks like, its extensibility options, and its content lifecycle management approach.

10.1 Value Proposition

When it comes to SAP S/4HANA Cloud, the first question to ask is which organizations are the best candidates for it. The obvious answer to this question seems to be small and medium enterprises (SMEs) with lean operations, but this is only partially true. SAP's official road map for SAP S/4HANA Cloud is aggressive, adding huge amounts of functionality in a short period of time, which may lead to bringing even large accounts with high complexities into the public cloud. There is ongoing innovation in terms of supporting additional country versions and languages. Currently, a good candidate for SAP S/4HANA Cloud is any firm that has more than 1,500 employees and is in the process of reimplementing SAP or beginning a greenfield implementation. For larger firms, the two-tier model is recommended, in which complex or highly customized systems at the corporate level are either on-premise or in a private cloud, while subsidiaries can be in a public cloud. The subsidiaries in this case are at liberty to be more innovative and flexible—this can be particularly useful when subsidiaries are in a different country from their parent company.

The private cloud is hosted on a single tenant that provides flexibility similar to an on-premise option, and users have access to IMG activities. The private cloud also supports many industry solutions and has multiple country and language support options compared to the public cloud. The new release cycle is annual, compared to quarterly releases for the public cloud. In this section, we're focusing only on SAP S/4HANA Cloud, public option. Section 10.4 covers the SAP S/4HANA Cloud, single tenant edition (otherwise known as the private option). We'll also talk about the transition path from single tenant to multitenant.

Figure 10.1 and Figure 10.2 depict the decision process to choose a solution in the public cloud, in the private cloud, or on-premise. Figure 10.1 shows the process for new customers, while Figure 10.2 shows the process for existing SAP customers. In these figures, BYOL stands for bring your own license.

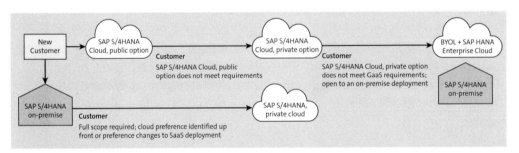

Figure 10.1 New Customer Deployment Options

This shows how new customers can choose between the on-premise SAP S/4HANA version or SAP S/4HANA Cloud version. In the SAP S/4HANA Cloud version, they can choose the private cloud version if the functionality or industry support isn't adequate for the public version. If even this version doesn't meet their requirements, they can opt for the public cloud hosting option on SAP HANA Enterprise Cloud or opt for the on-premise version. If they choose the SAP S/4HANA on-premise version, they can opt for it to be hosted on the cloud.

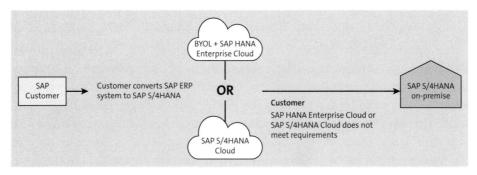

Figure 10.2 SAP Customer Deployment Options

For existing SAP customers, they can check if the SAP S/4HANA Cloud version meets their requirements, in which case, they can go for an SAP S/4HANA Cloud implementation; otherwise, they have to go for conversion to SAP S/4HANA either on-premise or on SAP HANA Enterprise Cloud.

The overall value proposition for SAP S/4HANA Cloud can be summarized as follows:

- Go-live in weeks
- Quarterly updates
- Fit-to-standard implementation approach
- Machine learning and artificial intelligence (AI) capabilities
- Digital assistant
- Predictive analytics
- In-memory database
- Real-time insights
- Native integration
- Available across all devices
- Reduces the complexity of the digital agenda using best practices
- Faster innovation due to new releases of machine learning, automation, or AI technologies occurring in the cloud before on-premise

10.2   Core Functional Capabilities

Initially, SAP S/4HANA Cloud had multiple editions, including SAP S/4HANA Marketing Cloud (hybrid option), SAP S/4HANA Finance Cloud, SAP S/4HANA Professional

Services Cloud, and SAP S/4HANA Manufacturing Cloud. These are now merged into a single offering: SAP S/4HANA Cloud. Along with core finance functionality, it also offers optimized order-to-cash, streamlined procure-to-pay, accelerated plan-to-product, project services, manufacturing and supply chain management, asset management, and integration with SAP SuccessFactors Employee Central for HR processes. It also provides functionality for master data management. SAP S/4HANA Cloud also has integration with SAP Extended Warehouse Management (SAP EWM) and, for finance, some add-ons are supported. Innovation using machine learning has been incorporated to help with SAP Cash Application. Figure 10.3 illustrates the scope of SAP S/4HANA Cloud.

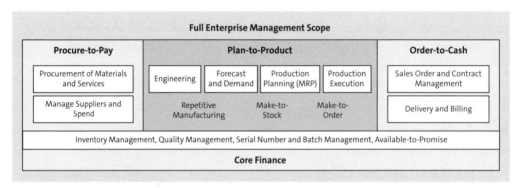

Figure 10.3 SAP S/4HANA Cloud Full Enterprise Management Scope

SAP S/4HANA Cloud doesn't have any add-ons or functionality for specific industries such as retail, oil and gas, utilities, and so on, although it has some functions for professional services in the 1808 version. Customers who require such functionality will need to keep using those functions in their existing SAP ERP system while moving the core functions to SAP S/4HANA Cloud. As part of the future road map, SAP will be building some of these industry solutions on SAP Cloud Platform. SAP S/4HANA Cloud provides a basic set of functionalities; after evaluation, if this isn't sufficient, then customers need to choose SAP S/4HANA instead.

Currently, the other choice in case the client either wants to go for a cloud-based solution but needs the functions from the SAP S/4HANA on-premise version, they can choose SAP S/4HANA Cloud, single tenant edition. For details on this version, see Section 10.4.

As of version 1811, SAP S/4HANA Cloud has been localized for the following countries: Australia, Austria, Belgium, Brazil, Canada, China, Denmark, Finland, France,

Germany, Hong Kong, Hungary, India, Indonesia, Ireland, Italy, Japan, Luxembourg, Malaysia, Mexico, Netherlands, New Zealand, Norway, Philippines, Poland, Romania, Saudi Arabia, Singapore, South Africa, South Korea, Spain, Sweden, Switzerland, Taiwan, Turkey, UAE, United Kingdom, and United States. In upcoming releases, SAP plans to add support for Russia and Portugal.

Currently, as of version 1811, SAP S/4HANA Cloud supports the following languages: Arabic, Bahasa (Malaysia), Chinese (simplified), Danish, Dutch, English, Finnish, French, German, Hungarian, Italian, Japanese, Korean, Norwegian, Polish, Portuguese, Romanian, Russian, Spanish, Swedish, Turkish, and traditional Chinese.

Table 10.1 shows the end-to-end business processes that are covered under SAP S/4HANA Cloud version 1808 and the core functional capabilities that support them.

Business Process	Available Functionalities
Idea to design	■ Project control ■ Compliant product lifecycle management
Procure to pay	■ Operational purchasing ■ Collaborative sourcing and contract management ■ Inventory management ■ Invoice and payables management ■ Supplier management ■ Procurement analytics
Plan to production	■ Basic production planning ■ Basic production processing ■ Inventory management ■ Maintenance management
Order to cash	■ Order and contract management ■ Inventory management ■ Receivables management
HR connectivity	■ Time recording
Core finance	■ Accounting and closing operations ■ Contract and lease management ■ Cost management and profitability analysis ■ Treasury management

Table 10.1 Functions Available in SAP S/4HANA Cloud 1808

Business Process	Available Functionalities
Offer to project	■ Contract to cash ■ Time and expense management ■ Professional services management

Table 10.1 Functions Available in SAP S/4HANA Cloud 1808 (Cont.)

> **Note**
>
> For a deeper look at core functional capabilities for specific lines of business (LoBs) in SAP S/4HANA Cloud, refer to our functional chapters earlier in this book. For finance, see Chapter 2; for manufacturing, see Chapter 3; for supply chain, see Chapter 4; for sales, marketing and commerce, and service management, see Chapter 5; for sourcing and procurement, see Chapter 6; and for R&D and asset management, see Chapter 7.

Every quarter, feature enhancements are added to the scope. Several application programming interfaces (APIs) or OData services get added, apart from the introduction of intelligent features. For example, a Solution Explorer feature is now available, as shown in Figure 10.4, which can be found at *https://bit.ly/2yUduWv*.

The Solution Explorer allows you to browse or find solutions and related resources.

In addition, SAP S/4HANA Cloud offers a What's New Viewer, as shown in Figure 10.5. For each version, the What's New Viewer displays the new features and functions that have been added or changed.

> **Note**
>
> More details about the features of each release can be found at *https://help.sap.com/viewer/product/SAP_S4HANA_CLOUD*.
>
> In addition, at any time, the What's New Viewer provides information about the latest release of any product. For SAP S/4HANA Cloud, go to *https://bit.ly/2AiWdqT*.

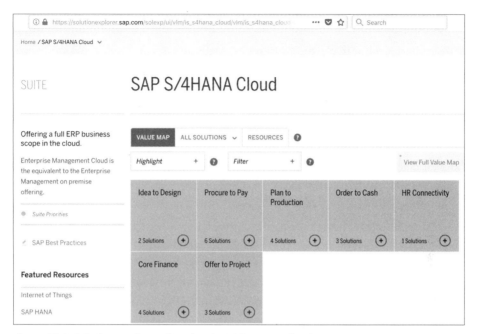

Figure 10.4 Solution Explorer Showing SAP S/4HANA Cloud

Line of Business	Solution Area	Solution Capability	Title	Short Description	Type	Scope Item	Application Component	Available As Of	Available In
				Cloud					
				• Ability to assign multiple licenses to one schedule line					
				See More					
Cross Applications			Define Withholding Tax Accumulation for Plants	This feature enables you to define if your plant accumulates the withholding tax in integration with TaaS (Tax as a Service). See More	New	BD9, BNX	FI-LOC-LO-BR	SAP S/4HANA Cloud 1808	Valid only for Brazil
Cross Applications			Hedge Accounting for FX Forward supporting IFRS 9	The scope item now includes the following: • Update Release Dedesignation Request process step in Appendix for cancellation of dedesignation request • Reclassification at Deviant Reclassification Date is provided for the reclassification of Balance Sheet Crossover. It is maintained in the Balance Sheet Recognition field in the Designation Splitting sub-area on the Hedge Accounting I tab of the Hedging Area • The automated designation of an FX transaction into a hedging relationship	Changed		FIN-FSCM-TRM	SAP S/4HANA Cloud 1808	

Figure 10.5 What's New Viewer

10.3   Deployment

With the background in place, let's move on to discuss the available tools, processes, typical project lifecycle, content lifecycle management, and extensibility options that will keep the system robust under the quarterly innovation cycle and still provide flexibility where needed to customize. We established the general deployment options in Chapter 1 (on-premise, cloud, or a hybrid model). Now, we'll dive deeper into the deployment specifics for SAP S/4HANA Cloud.

The best place to start is with the SAP Activate Roadmap Viewer, which provides the structure in detail with an in-depth view of the project phases: discover, explore, realize, and run.

It also provides more than 100 accelerator items, including templates for the project plan and communication plan, roles and responsibilities for various teams, quality gate questionnaires to check readiness for the next phase, test scripts, data migration, presentations on understanding concepts and processes, and—last but most important—training aides. The second-most-important tool is the SAP Best Practices Explorer, which helps users understand the predefined processes. These are industry-agnostic but work for all core requirements in finance, order-to-cash, procurement, project services, and so on. Becoming familiar with these two tools is a mandatory exercise, and this preparation can be started at any time without any investment because these resources are available free of cost. The only prerequisite is to have an S-user ID for complete access to the accelerators.

10.3.1   Fit-to-Standard

With the new direction focusing purely on business processes rather than on configuration and respective transaction codes, it's important to know about the available business processes to scope the solution.

The lesson learned from various teams that worked on the SAP S/4HANA Cloud implementation is that the fit-to-standard approach is the key—but at the same time, it can become a bottleneck if not enough time is spent on the process. The fit-to-standard process can be divided into the following steps (see Figure 10.6):

❶ Customer team familiarizes themselves with the best practice tools and resources.

❷ Review best practice process flows.

❸ Demonstrate business scenarios and concepts.

❹ Discuss how the standard processes fit with customer requirements.

⑤ Identify and collect required configuration to be activated to enable the required processes.

⑥ Enable customer on execution of scenarios from a usability perspective.

The fit-to-standard process starts in the discovery workshop and remains an important factor in the explore phase. The initial fit-to-standard workshop is crucial; customers need to be very sure that SAP S/4HANA Cloud is the best option and that the standard processes with limited extensibility will suffice for their business needs. This decision can't be made during the fit-to-standard exercise in the explore phase because the customer will have already committed to SAP S/4HANA Cloud at that point by signing up for a subscription.

Figure 10.6 shows that fit-to-standard doesn't become relevant only in the explore phase; it needs to be started in the discovery phase for successful implementation of the project.

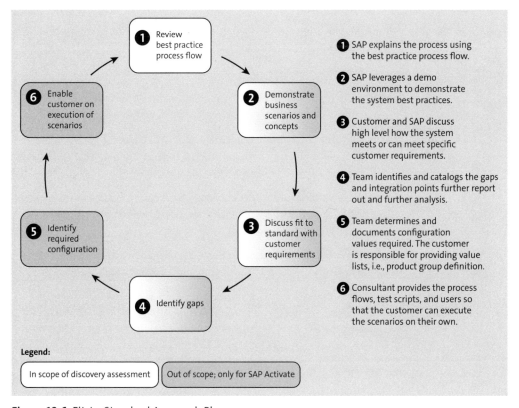

Figure 10.6 Fit-to-Standard Approach Phases

10.3.2   Deployment Resources

There are more than 100 documents (templates/resource documents) available through the SAP Activate Roadmap Viewer. Table 10.2 describes a few of the accelerators that can help during each phase of the SAP S/4HANA Cloud deployment.

Phase	Accelerator	Benefits
Discover	Enterprise support value map	Identification of enterprise service options, tools, and expertise for business needs
	Readiness check	Analysis of software prerequisites, infrastructure requirements, custom code adaption, and so on
	SAP Roadmap	Solution and product road map to help customers design their own road maps
	Simplification list	Understand business processes for simplification and the impact on current business processes
Prepare	Agile team roles and responsibilities	Project org charts for functional, nonfunctional, and architecture teams
	Project plan templates	Detailed sample project plan
	Project status report	Useful for daily updates to go over schedules, scope, risks, budget, and issues
	Quality gate checklists	Helps identify any risks or disturbances in the organizational and operational structure before moving to the next phase
	Security baseline template	Security operations map, including infrastructure security, code, setup, and overall compliance for audit
Explore	Automated data migration design template	Documents the technical design of an automated data migration solution
	Checklist—configuration and maintenance of storage infrastructure	Validation of technical architecture: technical performance optimization (TPO) and storage subsystem optimization service
	Custom Development Management Cockpit	Custom guidelines for development

Table 10.2 Templates and Resources from SAP Activate Roadmap Viewer

Phase	Accelerator	Benefits
	Data migration strategy and approach sample	Defines objectives of data migration, strategy, and approach, including deliverables
	Data governance	Training documents on data governance
	Model company	Set of accelerators with complete best practices and configuration for different industries, LoBs, process models, and more for an on-premise or cloud-hosted SAP S/4HANA system
	Functional test plan template	High-level functional test plan to make sure you meet all the business and technical requirements, including service levels
	Functional and implementation design template	Design template for automated data migration solution
	How to approach: Fit/gap workshop	Fit/gap analysis workshop process and preparation
	Rapid data migration	Methodology and conversion scenarios
	Scope and Effort Analyzer	SAP Solution Manager: Understand change impact, test scope, and related efforts
	Signoff template	Phase acceptance and closure: Make sure phase deliverables and expectations are met (approvals)
Realize	Continuous quality check (CQC) OS/DB migration check	Continuous migration check
	Documented procedure for integration validation	Integration validation based on product, solution, and operations standards
	Service component information	Company code transfer, client transfer, and system merge
	Enhancement template	ABAP custom development (workflows, reports, interfaces, conversions, enhancements, forms [WRICEF])
	WRICEF inventory template	WRICEF inventory with details about complexity for interfaces, report conversion, and so on

Table 10.2 Templates and Resources from SAP Activate Roadmap Viewer (Cont.)

10

Phase	Accelerator	Benefits
Deploy	CQC OS/DB migration check	Continuous quality check
	CQC for implementation	Continuous migration check, other CQCs for implementation, TPO, and upgrade
	Primary Customer Center of Expertise (CCOE) checklist	Primary certification checklist

Table 10.2 Templates and Resources from SAP Activate Roadmap Viewer (Cont.)

A two-week trial is available at no cost to gain familiarity with the interface, scope items, and SAP Fiori apps. A starter system is available in the explore phase that's preconfigured and has required test data. The system is key to performing the fit-to-standard analysis and creating a list of backlog items. In addition, note that at any given point, only two systems (e.g., starter and Q-systems or Q-system and P-system) are available. Although the scope items are determined in the starter system, the changes can't be moved to the Q-system. The Q-system isn't preconfigured, and the scope items must be selected and configured through the Self-Service Configuration User Interface (SSCUI) app. The users are defined in the SAP Cloud Platform Identity Authentication service and then imported into the starter system.

The landscape availability is shown in Figure 10.7. The provisioning of the starter system, activation of the Q-system, and transports to the P-systems are managed by SAP.

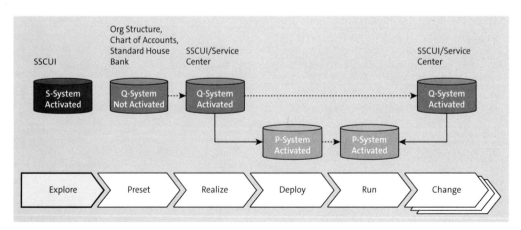

Figure 10.7 Starter System, Q-System, and P-System Landscape

Figure 10.8 illustrates the usage of the tools in different phases. The starter system has the required test data. The Automated Test Tool app is an enhanced tool in which each step is executed and the results recorded, including screenshots. This expedites testing of the end-to-end processes and helps meet regression-testing requirements.

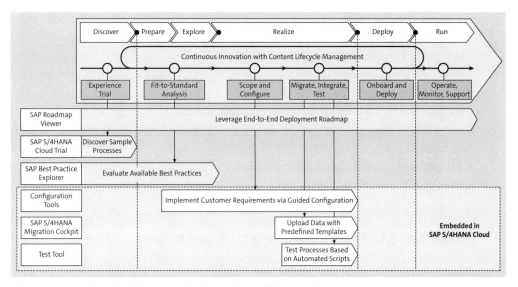

Figure 10.8 Tools and Their Usage in SAP Activate Phases

10.3.3   SAP Best Practices Explorer

The SAP Best Practices Explorer helps create faster time to value via best practice business processes that are robust and adhere to regulations and compliance. These are available for the entire scope of the solution and are classified in groups such as finance, application platform and infrastructure, asset management, database and data management, and so on. The full list is available in the content library. Detailed flow diagrams and test scripts are available for each process to help reduce the documentation effort and aid in consistency for testing.

A complete list of the best practices for SAP S/4HANA Cloud is available from the SAP Best Practices for SAP S/4HANA Cloud Content Library.

> **Note**
>
> SAP Best Practices are accessible on the web, but you may need an S-user ID to access and download them from *http://bit.ly/2frCb2o*.

10.3.4   Self-Service Configuration User Interface

The Manage Your Solution app provides easy access to configure your solution (scope), make changes, migrate data, and manage testing. It also provides access to training resources. Because there is no IMG or Transaction SPRO available in the public cloud, all the required configuration is performed through the guided configuration.

The guided configuration is available through the Manage Your Solution app, in which a user can scope/select business processes. After the business processes are selected, the respective SAP Fiori apps are available to the user with the related assigned roles. It's possible to make preapproved changes using in-app accessibility and manage changes through the extensibility cockpit. The Manage Your Solution app also provides access to manage the test processes and run automatic test scripts. A data migration interface is also provided, and data migration is carried out with the templates provided as accelerators.

10.4   SAP S/4HANA Cloud, Single Tenant Edition

SAP S/4HANA Cloud, single tenant edition (also known as private cloud), is a special option of a SaaS model that has currently more features and functions than the SAP S/4HANA Cloud, public option, and also more flexibility. In this case, the customer has a cloud version of SAP S/4HANA, but it's a dedicated instance specifically for that customer. There is also an SAP Activate methodology for this version of SAP S/4HANA. The advantages of this option are as follows:

- The solution provides the scalability of the cloud.
- The functionalities available for this version are the same as the SAP S/4HANA on-premise option, with full industry support and language support, as provided by the on-premise version.
- This option follows a subscription-based licensing, similar to the SAP S/4HANA Cloud.
- The deployment architecture includes a dedicated system landscape but on the cloud.

- The constraints that the SAP S/4HANA Cloud provides in terms of customization aren't limiting in this case (except SAP modification). The SAP S/4HANA extensibility framework can be used for any extensions, and there is a full extensibility option.

- There is an impact in terms of the TCO when compared with the SAP S/4HANA Cloud, public option. However, the functionality matching is an important criterion.

- It allows full expert configuration of the IMG and allows full extension of the SAP S/4HANA solution, but it doesn't allow any SAP code modification.

- It allows greenfield implementation but with data and configuration migration options. There is no option to build the system using system copy, however.

- Full integration with public cloud systems as well as on-premise systems is possible.

- While this option has new versions every 6 months, the customer has the flexibility to opt for the upgrade every 12 months and also to specify the timelines for the upgrade.

- The system governance is shared between SAP and the customer.

- While the lifecycle management for release upgrades along with support and features packs is included in SAP's scope, testing isn't.

In the following sections, we'll explore possible reasons why a business would choose SAP S/4HANA Cloud, single tenant edition, versus the SAP S/4HANA Cloud, public option, and some tips for a smooth migration from a private to public cloud setup.

10.4.1   Criteria for Choosing SAP S/4HANA Cloud, Single Tenant Edition

Because the SAP S/4HANA Cloud, single tenant edition, has more associated TCO and the innovations in SAP S/4HANA Cloud, public option, are released much earlier, you are likely questioning when to choose this version of the SAP S/4HANA solutions.

Following are some of the factors that make clients choose this version:

- There are regulatory constraints for using the public cloud version of any solution. Hence, the customer chooses the single tenant cloud option because the software can be installed in a dedicated tenant specific to this customer.

- The SAP S/4HANA Cloud, public option doesn't support the customer's industry solution.

- Some of the functionality required by the customer isn't there in the public cloud version but exists in the single tenant version because this is the same solution as the SAP S/4HANA on-premise version.

- The customer has customization requirements for the solution that can't be supported by the public cloud version.

- If the client has a huge workload, it may lead to performance issues, including latency, if the public cloud version is used, whereas it may be easier to install the single tenant cloud version in a dedicated system landscape on a cloud infrastructure.

- If the customer wants to migrate the existing configuration and data, that is only possible through a greenfield implementation with data and configuration migration to a SAP S/4HANA Cloud, single tenant edition.

For many organizations looking to adopt SAP S/4HANA now, SAP S/4HANA Cloud, single tenant edition, with a future migration path to SAP S/4HANA Cloud, public option (also known as multitenant edition) might be the optimal choice. Organizations with one or more of the following priorities should consider this route:

- A greenfield SAP S/4HANA implementation with a move back to a more standardized approach.

- Cloud-first strategy, including ERP SaaS, but with comprehensive business scope requirements that can't be completely covered by SAP S/4HANA Cloud, public option, as is.

Broadly, the considerations for your choice of SAP S/4HANA includes the following four dimensions, as shown in Figure 10.9:

- Scope
- Governance
- Standardization
- Costs

When we look at the additional evaluation criteria that would determine the right choice, including a comparison to SAP S/4HANA on-premise or private cloud, there are a number of additional considerations. See Figure 10.10.

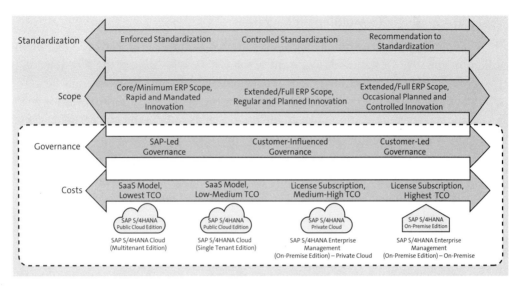

Figure 10.9 SAP S/4HANA Cloud, Public Option Dimensions

Consideration Area	1.	2.	3.	4.
System Landscape	●	●	◕	●
Implementation Methodology/Framework	●	●	●	●
Configuration Approach	◑	◑	●	◑
Modification/Customization Flexibility	●	●	◔	◔
Add-ons	●	●	◔	◑
Fit-to-Standard	◑	◑	●	◕
Project/Implementation Duration	◔	◑	●	◕
Licenseing/Cost Model	◔	◔	●	●
Support for SAP S/4HANA	◔	◑	●	◕
Conversion/Migration	●	●	◔	◔
Release Cycle for New Innovation	◑	◑	●	◕
Integration	●	●	◑	●
Localization	●	●	◑	●
Industry Solutions	●	●	◔	●
Non Functional Requirements	●	◕	◑	◕
User Interface	●	●	◑	●

○ Worst ⇨ Best ●

1. SAP S/4HANA Enterprise Management (On-Premise Edition) – On-Premise

2. SAP S/4HANA Enterprise Management (On-Premise Edition) – Private Cloud

3. SAP S/4HANA Cloud (Multitenant Edition)

4. SAP S/4HANA Cloud (Single Tenant Edition)

Figure 10.10 SAP S/4HANA Evaluation Matrix

10.4.2   Single-to-Multitenant Migration

Sometimes, the customer may want to move to the SAP S/4HANA Cloud, public option, to get a standard cloud-centric solution. Maybe most of the functionality is provided by SAP S/4HANA Cloud, public option, but a few functions may be in the road map that aren't yet there. Then the customer may, as an interim measure, go for the single tenant edition, with an intention that as soon as the public cloud version releases these features, they can move to the public cloud version.

The path of migration for the customer solution on SAP S/4HANA Cloud, single tenant edition, to the SAP S/4HANA Cloud, public option, will depend on how the single tenant implementation has been done. If the implementation is close to the standard, adhering to some basic rules provided by SAP, then a migration to the SAP S/4HANA Cloud, public option, is possible.

But if the implementation uses full flexibility in terms of customization of whatever is permitted in the single tenant edition, then there is no direct migration path to the public cloud option, and a greenfield implementation is the only possible way currently.

The golden rules that SAP has provided as recommendations for SAP S/4HANA Cloud, single tenant edition, implementation are listed here for easy reference:

1. **Fit-to-standard approach**
   To realize a process in the cloud, customers need to look at the standard process first and see if that process can be adopted. Any deviation or change should be done only if it's mandatory for optimizing the value of the business process.

2. **SAP Best Practices**
   Use SAP Best Practices published in SAP Best Practices Explorer (*https://rapid.sap.com/bp/*) as well as partner best practices. However, the restrictions need to be adhered to, for example, it's not recommended to use client 000; rather, copy configuration content from client 000 into a new client and then activate the best practices content based on business requirements. In addition, currently there is no methodology for adopting a model company from partners, if the partners have created some similar model companies. If a company needs to combine the SAP Best Practices with partner best practices, some manual intervention is required to selectively transport the partner best practices, which is difficult because of potential master data difference.

3. **Ensure cloud-like integration**
   Using whitelisted APIs and following SAP Activate guidance is recommended.

4. **Ensure cloud-like extensions**
   Use whitelisted APIs, side-by-side extensions, and in-app extensions, but don't use source code modification.

5. **Transparency on deviation**
   The customer needs to know each and every extension and integration points to ensure that the customer has a fair idea about the option that will be available for the road map to multitenancy.

Choices you make in implementation of the single tenant edition will affect the effort for moving to the public cloud or multitenant version.

In addition to these golden rules, the following practical considerations for implementation of SAP S/4HANA Cloud, single tenant edition, and safeguarding the migration to the multitenant edition need to be taken into account:

- **Resources**
  It is recommended that SAP practitioners (project managers and functional consultants) implementing SAP S/4HANA Cloud, public option (multitenant) should be certified. This certification recommendation is also applicable for SAP S/4HANA Cloud, single tenant edition. At a minimum, SAP practitioners should have training in the disciplines, approach, and methods for the implementation of SAP S/4HANA Cloud, public option. This will help enforce standardization and will prevent deviation from a pathway to the multitenant edition at a future time. SAP consultants need to unlearn the habits of past legacy and on-premise implementations, and move to an SaaS mindset.

  From a developer aspect, the skills and approach for custom developments need to transfer to a side-by-side application extension development on SAP Cloud Platform, with limited in-app extensions based on the golden rules for SAP (see Chapter 13). This should be the new approach for any SAP S/4HANA Cloud implementation, regardless of the version.

- **Governance**
  Through change control functions, it's necessary to ensure strong governance and design authority discipline (for clients, system integrators, and SAP practitioners). As the custodians of the single tenant design, they must ensure that the rules are being adhered to, and they must have the power to push back on deviation that could lead to complexities for a future multitenant migration.

- **Road map**
  It's important to ensure regular alignment with SAP on the multitenant road maps and any new single tenant golden rules.

10.5   SAP CoPilot

SAP CoPilot is a new product that works on top of SAP S/4HANA and helps automate some of the business process execution. It serves as the digital assistant and bot integration hub for the enterprise and enables a humanized UX for the customer's SAP application, creating objects and performing transactions through conversation. It can be used on mobile devices or in an SAP application.

While there are several different tools available in the market on collaboration and on digital assistance (e.g., Siri), SAP CoPilot provides these capabilities working on an enterprise application such as SAP S/4HANA.

For the 1808 version, SAP CoPilot supports chat, including solo chat with private thread, collaboration through multiple invitees to the chat, and sharing information via screenshots, images, video links, notes, and messages. You can add business objects that SAP CoPilot uses with some machine learning to recognize the notes. When the screenshot or the object is attached, you can navigate to the original object. An example of an SAP CoPilot search is shown in Figure 10.11.

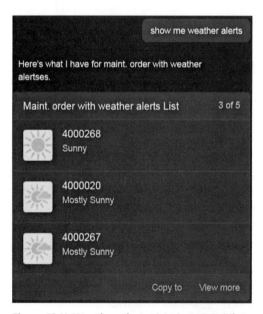

Figure 10.11 Weather Alerts List via SAP CoPilot

In addition, one of the uses of SAP CoPilot is to interact using natural language with the digital assistant to perform actions such as creating a purchase requisition or approval or asking for information to use in an enterprise search. It can even integrate with other commercially available assistants, such as Google Home, to talk to SAP or SAP SuccessFactors (beta version in 1808).

SAP CoPilot also has the bot integration hub feature that enables it to manage, train, and expose the bot functionality in different channels, such as Slack. Thus, there is no longer a need to build a bot for every channel. Using this feature, you can integrate bots from SAP Conversational AI, a collaborative platform for building, training, and deploying bots. SAP has the road map to integrate with other similar frameworks as well.

> **Note**
>
> Slack is a collaboration tool for teams to work together on specific topics. SAP CoPilot got the beta version for its integration with Slack in 1808.

SAP CoPilot can be customized for each customer by training through the SAP CoPilot skill builder, which includes new context without any coding.

> **Note**
>
> For more information on SAP CoPilot, visit *https://bit.ly/2OzFVmb*.

10.6   Extensibility

It's important to understand how gaps in functionality in SAP S/4HANA Cloud can be fulfilled through the extensibility options. There are several tools you can use to extend SAP S/4HANA Cloud functionality, as follows:

- **Extensibility cockpit**
  From version 1708, there is an extensibility cockpit to easily manage the in-app extensibility (forms, fields, business logic) and maintain the inventory of these changes.

- **SAP API Business Hub**
  SAP API Business Hub provides a detailed understanding of the interface development and available APIs for connecting to other cloud solutions, such as SAP Ariba, SAP Fieldglass, SAP SuccessFactors, SAP Concur, and so on.

- **SAP Cloud Platform**
  SAP Cloud Platform is available to create new apps and to provide side-by-side extensibility.

- **Custom CDS Views app**
  The Custom CDS Views app provides already-designed Core Data Services (CDS) views to create ad hoc reports and interface with other SAP and third-party solutions.

SAP S/4HANA Cloud, single tenant edition, supports the following extensibility options:

- **SAP enhancements**
  Adding functionality without modifying the source SAP code can be achieved using the standard SAP enhancement framework, which enables business add-ins (BAdIs) or user exits. The impact is that for every innovation cycle upgrade, these enhanced functions have to be tested.

- **Key user extensibility**
  This includes extensibility in the user interface, field, table, business logic (through code or business rules), reports (including extensibility for data sources, queries, standard settings of KPI and reports), end-user personalization and reports, and form and email templates. These can be achieved in a similar way that an on-premise SAP S/4HANA solution is extended, including in-app extensions.

Finally, if some SAP standard code modifications are required, because this isn't supported, the only option is to either use the first option or go for side-by-side extensions in the SAP Cloud Platform.

> **Note**
> For more information on extensibility, see Chapter 13.

10.7   Content Lifecycle Management

The SAP S/4HANA Cloud solution is managed and maintained by SAP. Releases are planned for each quarter starting in February of each year (Feb/May/Aug/Nov). At present, releases are available in two upgrade cycles, or "waves." There's a two-week period between the releases for quality assurance (QA) and production. The objects changed by in-app and side-by-side extensibility are managed efficiently, and there's no impact on such configuration after the releases. Figure 10.12 shows the SAP S/4HANA Cloud upgrade cycle.

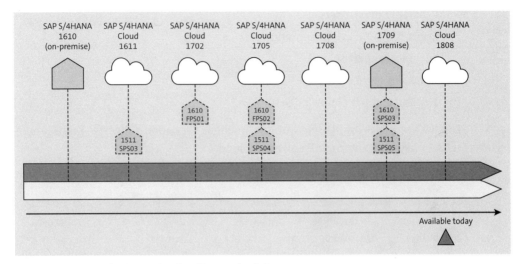

Figure 10.12 SAP S/4HANA Cloud Delivery Schedule

After you sign up for a subscription, a customer engagement executive (CEE) is assigned by SAP to make sure the processes are followed and to provide support for the fit-to-standard workshops and provisioning of the systems. With SAP Enterprise Support, a customer success manager (CSM) is assigned to provide support for extensibility, new releases, and any technical issues encountered during the project lifecycle. The key roles within the realm of content lifecycle management are as follows:

- **Customer engagement executive**
  - Post-sales relationship management
  - Strategic governance
  - Commercial management and renewals
  - Solution adoption/consumption measurement
  - Business outcomes and value delivery
- **Customer success manager**
  - Deployment success
  - Solution/release guidance
  - Mission-critical support

- Engagement review
- Quarterly scorecard delivery
- **SAP/partner expert services**
  - Consulting and implementation services
  - Technical expertise
  - Proactive service delivery
  - Key and end-user knowledge transfer

Table 10.3 provides an overview of the timelines for content lifecycle management for SAP's new content for SAP S/4HANA Cloud.

Use Case	Description	When	User Interaction	Activation Mode
Implementation project	Initial implementation	Any time	On user demand (e.g., phase change)	Initial activation (full activation)
Change project	Change project			Delta activation via upgrade procedure
Updates	Content corrections	Every two weeks	Automatic transparent delta (without user interaction)	Delta activation via upgrade/scope extension procedure
Improvements/upgrades	Continuous content improvement and adaptation	Each quarter		
New scope	Additional scope items and countries		On user demand	

Table 10.3 SAP S/4HANA Cloud Content Consumption Use Case Schedules

The maintenance schedule for SAP S/4HANA Cloud for all customers is as follows:

- Quarterly upgrade is performed as follows:
  - (Q) quality system is upgraded to latest release during first weekend after the release-to-customer (RTC) date.

- (P) production system is upgraded during the third weekend after the RTC date.
- (S) starter system for customers with no (P) system yet is upgraded during the second weekend after the RTC date.
- Each customer is notified six weeks prior to (Q) system upgrades.

There are no exceptions to this schedule; all customer instances are updated every quarter.

10.8   Summary

In this chapter, we looked at the features of SAP S/4HANA Cloud. Although adopting SAP S/4HANA Cloud provides value in terms of using innovative technology as well as providing the capability to interface seamlessly with other SAP and non-SAP cloud offerings, its greatest value lies in the opportunity to rethink your business and turn business ideas into reality with SAP S/4HANA as the center of digital transformation and support from the ecosystem built around it.

When deciding whether to implement SAP S/4HANA Cloud, keep in mind how it relates to the greater scheme of the IT landscape and IT strategy, as well as how it relates to other SAP HANA products already in the landscape or in the adoption road map. Migration services to facilitate client transformation to the cloud also need to be considered to migrate seamlessly into the cloud space. There are many variables to consider when choosing the right strategy, but this decision ideally should be looked at from both a business perspective and an IT perspective to achieve immediate and long-term business goals.

In the next chapter, we'll place SAP S/4HANA in context with the rest of the SAP landscape, and see how it integrates with other SAP solutions.

10

Chapter 11
SAP S/4HANA and the SAP Landscape

This chapter addresses the growing SAP portfolio of products to build the "intelligent suite" and deliver intelligence across value chains. We'll cover the SAP products that are required to build the "intelligent enterprise" outside the SAP S/4HANA core solution and address functional overlaps and synergies for a complete picture.

Now that you understand the key innovations SAP S/4HANA provides for finance and logistics, let's take a closer look at the extended SAP portfolio that is being provided to transform your company into an intelligent enterprise. All the solutions are modular, addressing a specific functional process chain, and can be run as independent standalone solutions. But to leverage their full potential, they can be integrated and work seamlessly together to deliver intelligence across the different value chains.

Figure 11.1 provides you with an overview of the full SAP landscape and products that enable you to build your processes with the advantages of the intelligent suite. The true value comes with the end-to-end integration of the processes to reflect your value chains.

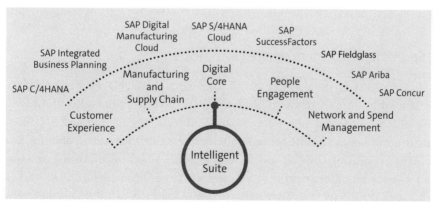

Figure 11.1 Overview of the Intelligent Suite

The intelligent suite will be achieved by providing you with a consistent user experience (UX) across the entire portfolio to increase efficiency and empower your employees. The intelligent suite provides you with out-of-the-box integration of the different products using the integration functionality of SAP Cloud Platform as part of the digital platform (for more details, see Chapter 13). In addition, you can easily extend your solutions and enrich them with intelligent workflows and processes (for more details about extending SAP S/4HANA, see Chapter 13).

Aside from SAP S/4HANA as the digital core, there are currently four other areas provided as part of the intelligent suite:

- **Network and spend management**
  Simplify your procurement and sourcing strategy with SAP Ariba. In addition, manage your contingent workforce with SAP Fieldglass, and control your travel and expense costs with SAP Concur.

- **People management**
  Optimize your human resource (HR) processes with SAP SuccessFactors.

- **Manufacturing and supply chain**
  Optimize your supply chain with SAP Integrated Business Planning (SAP IBP). In addition, optimize performance and elevate production quality and efficiency with SAP Digital Manufacturing Cloud.

- **Customer experience**
  Fully integrated end-to-end support is provided for your lead-to-cash processes with SAP C/4HANA integrated into the SAP S/4HANA.

In the following sections, we'll give an overview of each product, its functional capabilities, and how it fits into the overall SAP portfolio.

11.1   Sourcing and Procurement: SAP Ariba

The SAP Ariba software-as-a-service (SaaS) suite contains the biggest business commerce network to offer real-time collaboration between buyers and sellers. SAP Ariba is SAP's strategic sourcing and procurement solution embedded in SAP S/4HANA. Because the SAP S/4HANA suite contains all core functionalities and capabilities, SAP recommends reviewing the end-to-end requirements when transforming procurement to lay out which scenarios are being supported by SAP S/4HANA, SAP Ariba, SAP Fieldglass, or SAP Concur, or a combination of those products to fulfill the end-to-end requirements.

Currently procurement is organized into five functional blocks:

- Operational procurement with supplier collaboration
- Collaborative sourcing and contract management
- Supplier management
- External workforce management
- Services procurement

In the following sections, we'll take a closer look at each process.

11.1.1   Sourcing and Contracts

The sourcing process focuses on the management of electronic requests for information (RFIs), requests for quotation (RFQs), and requests for proposal (RFPs). At the same time, sourcing also conducts process compliance, reverse auctioning, and reporting against business key performance indicators (KPIs). The contract process focuses on the management of contracts (e.g., expiration) and conducting authoring compliance.

The main areas of sourcing and contracts in which SAP Ariba stands out are as follows:

- **Spend analysis**
  Good spend visibility is very important for companies, but not all companies have it. Traditionally, spend visibility has incorporated data aggregation, dashboards, and reporting, but with SAP Ariba Spend Analysis, companies can access commodity classification, supplier enrichment, market intelligence, and integrated spend management. SAP Ariba Spend Analysis will provide accurate ideas to make decisions such as improving the pipeline, increasing purchasing with suppliers, reducing inventory costs, mitigating supplier risk, and so on. Therefore, SAP Ariba Spend Analysis makes spend management more effective through data enrichment, 3D visibility for true spend intelligence, robust analytic tools, and native integration with sourcing, contract management, supplier information, performance management, and procure-to-pay.

- **Supplier discovery**
  One of SAP Ariba's strengths is supplier discovery. The Ariba Network can be used to search for new potential suppliers. Suppliers are required to introduce their commodities with a unique code (United Nations Standard Products and Services

Code [UNSPSC]), which enables customers to reach out to suppliers. Suppliers must pay to be available in the Ariba Network, unless a customer invites a supplier to an RFx, in which case, no extra costs (e.g., license costs) are charged to the supplier.

- **Supplier lifecycle performance**
  SAP Ariba Supplier Lifecycle and Performance provides comprehensive tools to help you onboard, qualify, segment, and manage supplier performance more effectively. Integrated into your procurement processes, it lets you drive spending to preferred suppliers and scale compliance for your entire supply base using an array of key capabilities. The key capabilities of SAP Ariba Supplier Lifecycle and Performance are as follows:

  - Unified vendor data model in the cloud provides a single accurate supplier record.

  - Supplier self-service in the cloud via Ariba Network makes it easy for suppliers to self-maintain their own information.

  - Flexible matrix for supplier qualification and segmentation lets you manage suppliers based on specific parameters.

  - Full integration with other SAP Ariba procurement applications supports speed and consistency throughout the entire procurement business.

- **Strategic sourcing**
  The Ariba Network enables SAP Ariba sourcing to have a very agile and rapid way of creating and managing RFx or auctions. Customers have detailed information about responses from suppliers that were invited to RFx or auctions, as well as real-time contact with those suppliers.

  Strategic sourcing incorporates capabilities such as sourcing projects with the ability to embed best practices for sourcing processes, approvals, and collaboration, as well as RFx and auctions management using electronic template-based event support for RFI, RFP, and RFQ. SAP Ariba supports multiple auction types, savings pipelines and tracking, decision support and optimization, integrated customer support, and out-of-the-box integration with spend visibility, discovery, contracts, suppliers, and procure-to-pay.

- **Contract management**
  SAP Ariba Contracts manages all organization agreements and subagreements on an integrated SaaS platform. In addition, SAP Ariba Contracts creates workflows during contract creation and maintenance, leverages prebuilt best practices

templates and workflows, and improves collaboration with suppliers. Contract lifecycle management provides organizations the opportunity to put their users in charge of contract maintenance. A contract repository is available for contract users in SAP Ariba. In the contract details, you can also add clauses to the clauses repository.

11.1.2   Requests and Purchases

Request processing focuses on strategic requisitioning capabilities, such as collaborative requisitioning and approvals, supplier onboarding, and catalog management, among others. The buying process focuses on order routing, spot-buy capabilities for noncontract spending, purchase order generation, and supply chain execution.

The main areas of requests and purchases in which SAP Ariba stands out are as follows:

- **Collaborative requisitioning and approvals**
  The Ariba Network enables multiple suppliers to collaborate. It works with catalog and noncatalog items, supports a spot-buy functionality, and enables collaborative configuration of complex items. The approval phases include four steps: precollaboration, begin collaboration, end collaboration, and postcollaboration.

- **Catalog management**
  With the Ariba Network, there are three types of items in a catalog: standard catalog, noncatalog, and punch-out catalogs. A *punch-out catalog* is a special version of a supplier's web catalog that's connected to the procurement system of a purchasing organization. Punch-out items behave the same way as catalog items in that a supplier can have one or more links to the punch-out catalog. Catalog kits enable adding multiple, bundled products with one click.

- **Order routing and notices**
  Among other order-routing functionalities, orders are transmitted through the Ariba Network, exported to SAP S/4HANA or SAP ERP, copied, dispatched manually, and combined.

- **Spot buy**
  Indirect materials, such as one-offs or emergency purchases that usually need rapid processing, can be bought using SAP Ariba's spot-buy capability. These suppliers are referred to as "long-tail" or one-off suppliers. Approved suppliers can be found in the SAP Ariba Spot Buy Catalog, which follows corporate policies and

11

ensures secure payment and shipment of goods. Typically, these nonsourced goods make up to 15% of the overall indirect spend.

- **Supply chain execution**
  Efficient supply chain execution is one of the important competitive key differentiators of the global and outsourced economy. Companies are asked to collaborate with all trading partners through a single global solution across multiple processes and geographies in real time. SAP Ariba Supply Chain is based on the Ariba Network, connecting all systems and stakeholders, collaborating effectively with multiple tiers of suppliers, and trading with partners at the same time in direct materials procurement. It manages all relevant processes, including consigned inventory, rolling delivery schedules, and contract management. SAP Ariba users can respond to changes in supply and demand in real time and identify errors using configurable business rules with automated validation and reconciliation.

- **Guided buying**
  The SAP Ariba guided-buying capability is a persona-based application offering nonprocurement professionals a single place to search for goods and services, making purchases with little to no involvement from the procurement department.

  The guided-buying capability captures organizations' purchasing policies and uses them to guide casual users and functional buyers to the outcomes they need. Users know right away when a policy is violated, rather than finding out after submitting a request. An example guided-buying screen is shown in Figure 11.2.

  Following are some of the key features of guided buying:
  - Guided buying targets exclusively casual users and functional buyers.
  - Guided buying focuses on the ultimate UX: smart, simple, and quick.
  - Guided buying targets no-touch or low-touch procurement.
  - Guided buying doesn't replace the purchase-to-pay (P2P) or sourcing functionalities but offers a better, simpler, and guided functionality for a specific subset of users who don't require all of the additional capabilities that the aforementioned modules offer.
  - Guided buying can also be an entry point for users to other SAP Ariba modules, such as those that handle sourcing and procurement.

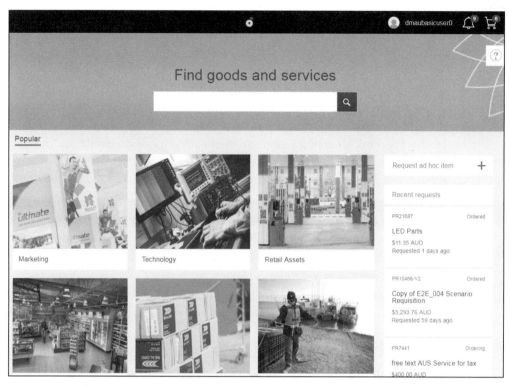

Figure 11.2 Guided Buying Landing Page

11.1.3   Invoices and Payments

Invoice processing focuses on digitizing invoices into an electronic format, which contains process steps such as delivery, matching, validating, and approval of invoices. SAP Ariba proactively converts suppliers submitting paper invoices to an electronic process after they reach a certain volume threshold, reducing the expense of paper as a positive side effect.

Payment processing focuses on synchronizing the delivery with electronic payments to eliminate risks and inefficiencies.

The main areas of invoicing and payments in which SAP Ariba stands out are as follows:

345

- **Invoice automation**
  Buyers have taken a series of approaches to automate their invoice processing. The invoice workflow for accounts payables (AP) streamlines the capturing, processing, matching, and finally approving of all invoices. Business users of SAP Ariba Invoice Management can create their own workflows tailored by categories of spend, suppliers, or other business-crucial variables. Invoicing can be performed easily and anywhere by email or smartphone, supporting remote and line-level invoice approval. It supports monitoring of both transaction details and supplier performance.

- **Invoice reconciliation**
  SAP Ariba's payment capability allows for simple supplier reconciliation. Invoices are matched either two ways or three ways. In the two-way scenario, after receipt, both the supplier invoice and the corresponding purchase order are matched, validated, and finally reconciled. In the three-way scenario, the purchase order receipt is considered as well. Invoices aren't changed; instead, a copy of the invoice is created and changed. Validation is performed on both the header and line item level by comparing amounts for each level to each other's document. In a final step, amounts are paid.

- **Discount management**
  With the SAP Ariba Payables discounting capability, suppliers are supported if requesting discounts from their buyers, enrolling in net or discount terms, and offering and accepting dynamic discounts. Buyers are supported in the ongoing management of discounts.

- **Working capital management**
  Usually, suppliers face challenges with inconsistent payment terms such as rigidly initiated payment terms from buyers. SAP Ariba's payment capability manages and extends payment terms of the working capital, which usually strategically results in reduced days sales outstanding (DSO) on the supplier side or extended days payable outstanding (DPO) on the buyer side.

- **Business-to-business (B2B) payments**
  A secure partner is engaged to capture, manage, and maintain sensitive supplier bank information to bridge the gap between invoicing and payment. Payment control is improved at a lower cost of processing. At the same time, the risk of fraud associated with payments is minimized.

- **Expense reimbursement**
  Travel expense reimbursement (through SAP Concur) provides all employees with the functionality to enter, calculate, approve, and finally reimburse expense types, such as mileage for private cars used, meals, accommodation/hotels, and local and public transport.

- **Bank automation**
  SAP Ariba's payment capability eliminates the need to maintain supplier bank account information because bank account data is stored in an external IT environment. Supplier payment inquiries are reduced when paying suppliers automatically.

- **SAP Ariba invoice conversion service add-on (ICS)**
  This solution facilitates conversion of paper invoices to cXML (including OCR) using a process that includes validation. A service provider managed by SAP Ariba receives paper invoices by mail or electronic invoices via email and converts them to cXML (an electronic format) for posting to the Ariba Network. The buyers can also scan the invoices themselves or use their own service providers to scan and send the images to SAP Ariba.

- **SAP Ariba open invoice conversion service add-on (open ICS)**
  This is like ICS, but the main difference is that the buyer's service provider (e.g., OpenText) handles the scanning and OCR and generates the cXML format. SAP Ariba works with the buyer and the service provider to integrate the provider's invoice-conversion solution with the Ariba Network.

11.1.4 SAP Ariba and SAP S/4HANA

SAP's strategy for procurement is divided into two blocks. Operational transactions (materials management, purchase order, operational contract, etc.) are part of SAP S/4HANA Enterprise Management, and strategic collaboration is covered by the LoB solutions from SAP Ariba, SAP Fieldglass, and SAP Concur, as shown in Figure 11.3. This creates a set of hybrid solutions that reflect the demand of today's organizations and that leverage the advantage of SAP Ariba and SAP S/4HANA integration. Strategic sourcing is executed in the SAP Ariba applications; best-value bids are finalized and result in a contract with price terms. The following scenario shows that SAP Ariba and SAP S/4HANA work perfectly in a fully integrated way:

- With the SAP Ariba Catalog, contract terms and pricing can be enforced at the catalog item level, driving compliance and resulting in realized savings.

- SAP Supplier Relationship Management (SAP SRM) users can punch out to the SAP Ariba Catalog to search for items and then complete their purchase order process in SAP SRM.

- After purchase order execution in SAP SRM, the purchase order is sent over to the supplier via the Ariba Network for fulfillment and invoicing.

From a licensing perspective, it's possible to have a licensing model for the pure cloud scenarios (with SAP Ariba as the procurement engine integrated into SAP S/4HANA) or for hybrid scenarios (SAP S/4HANA from end to end).

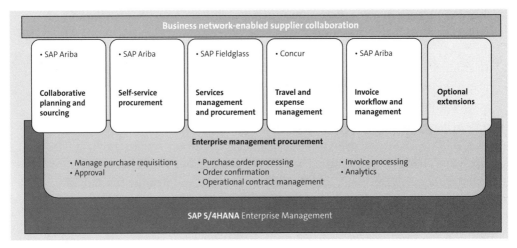

Figure 11.3 SAP S/4HANA Suite and LoBs

From a technical integration perspective, a lot of prepackaged integration content or best practices are already available in SAP Rapid Deployment solutions. As shown in Figure 11.4, there is already a lot of integration content available. New in version 1808 is the integration of SAP S/4HANA Cloud with SAP Ariba Buying and Invoicing. All of the available SAP Best Practice content and the SAP Ariba portfolio can be found at *https://bit.ly/2JIJ9hL*. Table 11.1 shows the scenarios that are now being supported with the SAP S/4HANA Cloud 1808 availability.

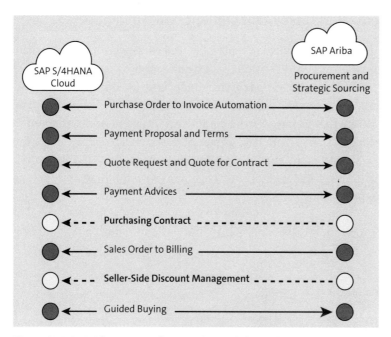

Figure 11.4 SAP S/4HANA and SAP Ariba Predelivered Integrations

Product	Scenario
Ariba Network	SAP Ariba Commerce Automation integration
	SAP Ariba Quote Automation integration
	SAP Ariba Payables integration
SAP Ariba Sourcing	SAP Ariba Sourcing integration with operational procurement
SAP Ariba Buying and Invoicing	SAP Ariba Buying and Invoicing integration

Table 11.1 Available SAP Best Practices for Integration with SAP Ariba Solutions

According to SAP's future road map for SAP S/4HANA integration, there will be further integration content to ensure a rock-solid and tight integration with the LoB solutions from SAP Ariba. If customers now want to move toward SAP S/4HANA, they can already start using SAP Ariba products to put real strategic sourcing in place.

11.2   Contingent Workforce Management: SAP Fieldglass

SAP Fieldglass is the leader in services procurement and contingent workforce management, and it completes the SAP portfolio for external services, such as contingent workers, statement of work projects and services, independent contractors, and specialized talent pools. The main SAP Fieldglass solution is a cloud-based vendor management system (VMS) that automates the complete contingent and statement of work (SoW) labor lifecycle (see Figure 11.5). As part of the overall SAP S/4HANA strategy, SAP Fieldglass completes the exciting SAP SuccessFactors and SAP Ariba portfolio, and it gives customers total workforce management with full-time and contract workers in a single platform.

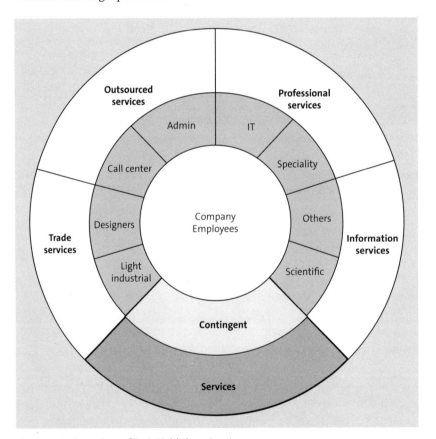

Figure 11.5 Overview of SAP Fieldglass Services

11.2.1 Vendor Management System

SAP Fieldglass supports the full lifecycle of a service engagement, from creating the RFx to evaluating the service provided (see Figure 11.6). It provides the capability to support complex projects with multiple SoWs and supports clients through the lifecycle from sourcing to engaging, managing, and invoicing.

The SAP Fieldglass VMS enables users to do the following:

- Use the decision wizard as a guide though the different engagement types and support the best worker composition from temporary workers to consulting services.

- Create requisitions easily that cover the essential parts of a job posting to support hiring managers in their processes.

- Perform approvals outside the tool via email and cover multiple levels of authorization. These can be tied to different types of rules, such as financial limits or departments/functions.

- Establish distribution lists of top-performing suppliers, and, from there, establish stepwise distribution to second- or third-tier providers. This enables users to assign specific or important job postings/categories to preferred suppliers to increase quality.

- Use the candidate review to get a quick side-by-side comparison of candidates, build shortlists, track the whole history of candidates, and get guidance on the candidate's price.

- Improve the quality and experience of new workers with action items and checklists though the onboarding and offboarding functions. This also provides transparency to the project management office.

- Adjust the time and expense functionality to the organization's needs to reflect different types of workers.

- Convert approved time sheets into an invoice that supports legal/tax requirements and discounts via the automatic invoicing function.

In addition, there are business intelligence and administrative tools that support the overall process and provide needed transparency.

From an integration point of view, there are currently more than 800 integration points available and standard integrations into some LoB solutions from SAP. The overall platform is based on an n-tier J2EE architecture and is delivered as a multitenant SaaS solution hosted by SAP Fieldglass itself.

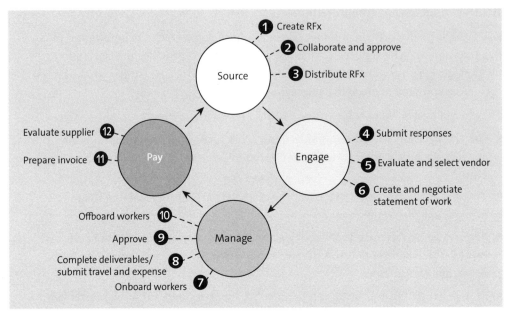

Figure 11.6 Typical Overview of Service Engagement Lifecycle

11.2.2   SAP Fieldglass and SAP S/4HANA

SAP Fieldglass follows the same strategic direction as the other cloud-based solutions outlined earlier in Figure 11.3. Its focus is on services procurement and contingent labor; from a strategic perspective, it will be the go-forward solution for services procurement within the SAP solution stack. Therefore, tight integration with other business networks products, such as SAP Ariba and SAP SuccessFactors, is required.

Currently there are different possibilities to integrate SAP Fieldglass into SAP S/4HANA to support authorization and authentication (users, single sign-on [SSO]), exchange master data (e.g., business units, cost center, etc.), and transactional data (worker, time sheets, etc.). A good source for integration scenarios is the SAP Best Practices Explorer. A concrete example is the standard integration scenario (see *https://rapid.sap.com/bp/#/browse/packageversions/BP_S4H_FG*) to support the automation of the integration in between SAP S/4HANA and SAP Fieldglass from requisition to billing and payment of contingent resources.

Figure 11.7 shows a typical process flow with its integration points illustrated to address seasonal skill shortages and provide required staffing to the projects. In this scenario, master data (cost center, internal order, and organizational information) is being retrieved from SAP S/4HANA, and transactional data (invoices) is being sent from SAP Fieldglass to SAP S/4HANA Finance to process invoicing.

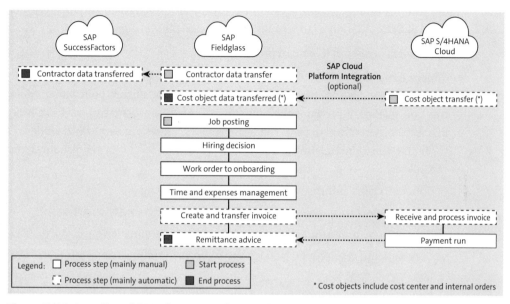

Figure 11.7 Integration of SAP S/4HANA and SAP Fieldglass

From a licensing perspective, SAP Fieldglass can be run as a separate solution with a separate license model that isn't part of the SAP S/4HANA license. If a customer is going to implement SAP S/4HANA, there is no conflict and no direct implication. Companies that want to implement SAP Fieldglass can start with an existing ERP system; integration scenarios and packages are already available.

11.3   Travel and Expense Management: SAP Concur

SAP Concur is a solution that combines and integrates overall spending into three major blocks: Concur Travel, Concur Expense, and Concur Invoice. The central principle is that all connected information can be managed in one place and provide transparency into overall spending. SAP Concur integrates with numerous third-party solutions and apps, from Airbnb and United Airlines to Uber and Starbucks.

11.3.1   Spend Management

All information used to plan a trip and to organize travel is captured within Concur Travel, even if it's captured offline by a travel agent working with SAP Concur. All this information is exchanged with Concur Expense and flows into an employee report, which makes it much easier for employees to create their expense reports.

The portfolio consists of five main products:

- **Concur Expense**
  Provides full visibility into spending and the ability to ensure policy and regulatory compliance. It provides the capability to synchronize a credit card as a baseline for the generation of claims. It also provides a nice and easy UX to guide you through the expense-claiming process. It consists of the following products and capabilities:
  - Concur Expense for the overall expense management
  - Concur Detect to audit expenses and avoid fraud and compliance issues
  - Concur Drive to document and control expenses around driving
  - Concur Request to provide you with workflows for request and approval before booking the travel
  - Budget to provide transparency for the actual costs and supports the overall budget planning
  - Payment solutions to automate and simplify the payments toward your employees and vendors
  - Bill statements to integrate company bill statements with Concur Travel and Concur Expense to simplify the purchasing card process
- **Concur Travel**
  Uses the same easy UX as Concur Expense and simplifies online travel reservations and booking. As noted, this booking tool is tightly integrated with Concur Expense and feeds information to Concur Expense as a baseline for expense reports. The current products around Concur Travel are as follows:
  - Concur Travel to provide employees with a central tool for travel booking
  - Concur Hipmunk to support smaller business with travel and expense management addressing companies that don't need the full SAP Concur suite or aren't ready to use it

- Concur Request to provide you with workflows for request and approval before booking the travel

- Concur TripLink to capture travel and spend and use machine learning to match them against each other to easily integrate them in your travel management

- Concur Locate to locate and connect to your employees, for example, for emergency warnings

- **Concur Invoice**
Accelerates and simplifies the invoicing of expenses and reduces invoice costs significantly. It helps automate invoices and provides transparency into your overall travel and expense spending. Concur Invoice consists of the following:

  - Concur Invoice to ease the full process from capturing invoices to payment

  - Concur Request to provide you with workflows for request and approval before booking the travel

  - Payment solutions to automate and simplify the payments to your employees and vendors

- **Data platform and analytics**
Delivers data and tools to control spending. Interactive dashboards, reports, and alerts provide a real-time view into how much is being spent and who's spending it. It has been expanded to support the full SAP Concur product suite and serves as the reporting backbone for SAP Concur. The following capabilities are included:

  - Budget to provide transparency for the actual costs and support for the overall budget planning

  - Analytics to provide insights based on the aggregated data that is being provided in near real time and to help you to make the right decisions

  - Intelligence to provides you with reports and information that help you make the right decision even on a persona level, as well as to help you set up a flexible reporting structure that monitors your budget and daily spends

- **SAP Concur mobile app**
The mobile app complements the web-based solution to make it possible to manage expenses and perform travel or invoice approvals from a mobile device.

The current strategy to enhance SAP Concur is to support partners building solutions on top of the platform that are preconfigured or provide integration packages to support the end-to-end process. These solutions are available through the SAP App

11

Center where partners list their products. The support covers different processes in the overall customer journey, including booking cars and trains, ordering food, and providing extensions for finance and HR. Customers can use these features easily, which increase efficiency and saves money.

From the overall integration perspective, SAP Concur solutions are interconnected with each other and can be integrated where necessary. The main goal is an integration into all SAP products across the full SAP portfolio. While there has been a lot of effort to integrate Concur Expense and Concur Invoice into SAP's HR and financial solutions as part of the digital core strategy, the effort in both areas continues to achieve a full coverage of customers' requirements. An integration of SAP Analytics Cloud with the data acquisition connector to Concur Expense is currently available but is planned to be expanded with new data platform APIs to Concur Expense, Concur Invoice, Concur Travel, Concur TripLink, Concur Hipmunk, and Concur Budget to allow budget planning for the end of 2018 and the beginning of 2019.

11.3.2   SAP Concur and SAP S/4HANA

Similar to the two previous products discussed, SAP Concur is aimed to complete and extend the intelligent suite toward travel and expense management. From an implementation perspective, there are no limitations for SAP S/4HANA. The integration path is the same for customers running SAP ERP Human Capital Management (SAP ERP HCM) and SAP ERP Financials (FI) on separate instances and on a single instance, or for customers running SAP S/4HANA Finance, or any combination of these. From an integration perspective, SAP shared that standard integration packages that support FI and payroll postings will be available in a future release that supports integration scenarios via SAP Cloud Platform or SAP Process Orchestration. The integration of SAP Concur in SAP S/4HANA currently supports Concur Expense and Concur Invoice for employee master data, cost objects, financial postings, payroll integration (for restricted use cases only), and General Data Protection Regulation (GDPR) compliance. For additional information around integration on SAP S/4HANA Cloud with SAP Concur, see the following blog at *https://bit.ly/2PgFrBM*.

From a financial perspective, SAP Concur is available with a separate license and isn't being considered in the SAP S/4HANA license model.

11.4   Human Resources: SAP SuccessFactors

As part of the digital core strategy, SAP SuccessFactors is the default HR functionality of SAP S/4HANA. Mobile-enabled with a modern UX, SAP SuccessFactors includes a complete set of core HR options with payroll, tightly integrated talent management solutions, robust workforce analytics and planning, and social collaboration tools.

This cloud HR suite is a highly scalable SaaS solution that offers various ways to extend existing process functionality beyond what's available out of the box. Standard solution configuration capabilities are supported with the ability to create new objects and business rules with the Metadata Framework (MDF) and create new applications with SAP Cloud Platform.

Further, standard integrations between SAP SuccessFactors and SAP S/4HANA are available to ensure that SAP SuccessFactors Employee Central is truly the next-generation core HR system of record for employee data.

Let's look at SAP SuccessFactors functionality in more detail in the following sections.

11.4.1   Employee Data

SAP SuccessFactors Employee Central is the core HR component of the SAP Success-Factors solution. It captures employee and organizational data, and it's built around the concept of self-service for HR professionals, managers, and employees.

SAP SuccessFactors Employee Central is an enterprise-grade, event-based transactional system with full workflow support. It includes position management, time-off management, global benefits, and reporting on employee and organizational data, as well as compliance and auditing. It also includes SAP SuccessFactors Employee Central Payroll, which is provided as an SAP-hosted solution based on SAP's long-established on-premise payroll engine.

11.4.2   Talent Management

SAP SuccessFactors has a broad array of talent management and related analytics functionality:

- **SAP SuccessFactors Recruiting**
  SAP SuccessFactors Recruiting combines the functionality from SAP Success-Factors Recruiting Management and SAP SuccessFactors Recruiting Marketing. It

provides a comprehensive recruiting solution that supports attracting, engaging, and selecting better candidates in an efficient way and then measuring the results of the recruiting process. SAP SuccessFactors Recruiting Management is a mobile and socially enabled applicant-tracking system that allows companies to select and hire the best talent faster. SAP SuccessFactors Recruiting Marketing is a social recruiting marketing platform that allows companies to attract and engage quality candidates via state-of-the-art social solutions, custom career sites, and analytics to measure the efficiency of various recruitment channels used in recruiting marketing campaigns.

- **SAP SuccessFactors Onboarding**

  This solution for new hires and hiring managers improves time to productivity, job satisfaction, and new hire retention. It guides and empowers new hires to access SAP SuccessFactors solutions by which they can fill in required new hire forms, access documentation, become acquainted with their new teams, enroll in and complete initial training, set initial goals, and use social collaboration tools that will help them become familiar with the new work environment.

- **SAP SuccessFactors Learning**

  This is a comprehensive learning management system that supports social and mobile learning to ensure compliance and development of talent with an enhanced learning experience. SAP SuccessFactors Learning enables managing, developing, and deploying instructor-led, offline, and formal and social online training.

  The SAP SuccessFactors Learning content service allows you to focus on learning quality and strategies while eliminating the need for hosting learning content and managing content infrastructure, security, delivery, and updates of learning content.

- **SAP SuccessFactors Performance & Goals**

  This is a performance management and goal-setting solution that allows you to create an aligned and high-performing workforce. Goal management enables you to communicate company strategy, create meaningful individual and group goals across the company, and assign/cascade them to employees so that they can support company business goals and strategy. Goals execution and progress can be measured in real time. SAP SuccessFactors Performance & Goals delivers various types of evaluations, performance assessments, and performance calibration; it streamlines the performance appraisal process and helps managers by providing tools (writing and coaching assistant, legal scan) and content that ensure a meaningful and compliant performance review and feedback process. Employee performance in relation to business goals is measured and can be integrated with the company reward system.

- **SAP SuccessFactors Compensation**
  This is a comprehensive compensation management solution that helps to retain top talent by supporting a pay-for-performance strategy and process. Compensation management allows you to create reward budgets with flexible approvals workflows, and budget spending monitoring is supported by analytics. It also enables you to create compensation plans with various pay components, including basic pay, bonuses, and stock. Part of SAP SuccessFactors Compensation is the variable pay module that supports very complex bonus programs based on performance results from multiple employee assignments within the company. Compensation enables a pay-for-performance reward culture by supporting reward pay based on performance results. Compensation calibration helps to make better compensation decisions with the support of objective ratings and ultimately helps to retain top talent and increase employee productivity.

- **SAP SuccessFactors Succession & Development**
  This solution supports succession planning and career development planning and allows you to identify, develop, and retain talent throughout the organization.

  Succession management allows you to identify key positions in the organization and nominate potential successors for those positions while monitoring their readiness to fill the role. The objective is to plan for staffing changes and ensure the readiness of nominated successors. Career development planning allows you to create development plans, track development activities for employees and nominated successors, and align learning activities with identified competency gaps to ensure that employees and successors will be ready to take on new future roles within the company. It improves motivation with continuous development and career planning; employees can track their preferred roles and monitor their readiness based on the competency levels required to progress to the role. A comprehensive talent search engine, a nine-box grid performance-potential matrix, and talent calibration are also provided.

- **SAP SuccessFactors Workforce Analytics**
  This is a comprehensive analytics and reporting solution that allows you to create reports and dashboards (with trend analysis) with aggregated data and with the ability to drill down to deeper levels of detail. It comes with a set of predefined

11

metrics and KPIs across core HR and talent modules. SAP SuccessFactors Workforce Analytics supports reporting on external data sources and can be connected to multiple systems to create cross-functional reports and dashboards. These reports and dashboards can be delivered to managers and business leaders in the form of published reports and easily consumable insights with a combination of core HR, talent, and non-HR data. SAP SuccessFactors Workforce Analytics enables access to industry benchmarks so that companies using the solution can compare themselves with industry peers across various metrics.

- **SAP SuccessFactors Workforce Planning**
  This solution addresses an organization's need to plan the future workforce based on business need and trends. It's a strategic workforce planning tool based on a long-term planning approach (as opposed to a short-term, operational planning approach) to match the required workforce to projected future workforce demand in terms of cost and skills. Based on available workforce data and benchmarks, the solution allows you to assess the company's readiness to execute various strategies (i.e., talent and reward strategies), forecast the impact of business decisions (i.e., mergers and acquisitions, development of new product lines), mitigate the risk, and take specific actions that the solution proposes from a library of strategies and actions. Multiple what-if scenarios can be modeled based on set parameters to analyze cost impacts. Predictive capabilities are available to support capability analysis in the context of current trends.

11.4.3   SAP SuccessFactors and SAP S/4HANA

From SAP's perspective, SAP SuccessFactors (as opposed to an SAP S/4HANA version of SAP ERP HCM) is the go-forward human capital management solution for SAP S/4HANA and the go-forward solution for the HR category within SAP's diversified cloud strategy. With adoption of the SAP HANA platform for foundation, integration, analytics, and application development, and with SAP Fiori for UX, the SAP SuccessFactors suite is the firmly established solution in the SAP solution portfolio and the future SAP S/4HANA road map.

SAP S/4HANA delivers significant simplifications and innovations compared to the previous-generation SAP ERP solution in which the SAP ERP HCM component resided. After the acquisition of SAP SuccessFactors, the adoption has been quadrupled for SAP customers using SAP SuccessFactors. This originally led to the strategic direction from SAP not to do a simplification or add additional new functionality in

SAP ERP HCM. But according to the latest information, SAP wants to support customers that are running on a different pace and build a new on-premise HCM option that is based on the SAP ERP HCM functional scope. The objective from SAP is to integrate the new option alongside SAP S/4HANA by 2023, with maintenance planned at least through 2030. It's also planned to support the migration toward the new solution with SAP migration tools to ease the adoption of the new functionality.

The SAP SuccessFactors solution can be integrated easily from the data and process perspective with on-premise and other cloud systems via prepackaged and SAP-maintained integrations, predefined integration templates, and APIs and custom integrations. Although customers have multiple options available for integrating SAP SuccessFactors with other solutions, SAP's preferred solution for SAP Success-Factors integration middleware is SAP Cloud Platform Integration, an integration-as-a-service (IaaS) platform specifically designed to support integration of SAP's range of cloud solutions with other on-premise and cloud systems. SAP is significantly investing in extending the range of prepackaged integrations with SAP cloud applications and other vendors' solutions. As illustrated in Figure 11.8, a set of integration content is currently available for the integration of SAP S/4HANA Cloud and SAP Success-Factors to serve the integration of employee and employment data.

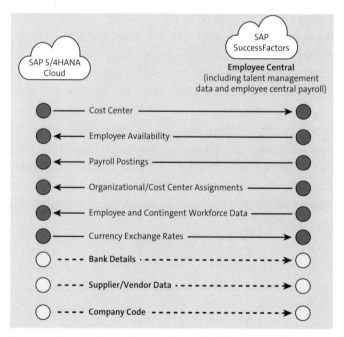

Figure 11.8 Predelivered Integration SAP S/4HANA and SAP SucccesFactors

For companies using on-premise SAP ERP HCM that want to implement talent management solutions, SAP SuccessFactors is an obvious choice because no enhancements are planned for talent management on-premise solutions. For companies that want to implement an HR information system with SAP, the SAP ERP HCM on-premise solution is still a viable option (i.e., it will still be tweaked for specific industry regulations, compliance localizations, and language support); however, from the long-term strategic perspective, SAP SuccessFactors Employee Central is a safer route.

In the end, companies that want to implement SAP S/4HANA or SAP S/4HANA Cloud that also require a human capital management suite will likely focus on the SAP SuccessFactors solution due to the current and planned SAP investment level and innovation in cloud human capital management solutions, as follows:

- Prepackaged integrations are available now via the SAP Best Practices Explorer (*https://rapid.sap.com/bp/*), so companies can connect SAP SuccessFactors Employee Central with SAP S/4HANA Cloud and SAP Success Factors Employee Central integration with SAP S/4HANA. Integration capabilities are available via SAP Cloud Platform web services, via SAP Process Orchestration for SAP S/4HANA, and via SAP Cloud Platform and web services for SAP S/4HANA Cloud. Additional information on how to integrate SAP S/4HANA Cloud with SAP SuccessFactors Employee Central can be found at *https://bit.ly/2D5bfm0* or *https://bit.ly/2PHIen1*.

  Companies that want to implement SAP S/4HANA, are using SAP ERP HCM on-premise, and aren't yet ready to implement SAP SuccessFactors can continue to use SAP ERP HCM running in a separate instance or a single instance together with SAP S/4HANA. SAP has plans for prepackaged integrations to enable both scenarios.

- One SAP road map for SAP S/4HANA Cloud and SAP S/4HANA integration will likely expand in the areas of employee integration, time sheet integration, total workforce integration with SAP Fieldglass, SAP SuccessFactors Employee Central, SAP ERP HCM, and SAP Ariba for the integration of contingent workforces. Detailed information on the available integration scenarios for SAP S/4HANA is available at *https://bit.ly/2AQWMZz*.

11.5   Customer Experience: SAP C/4HANA

In the age of digitalization, the demand for a customer-centric and everywhere-accessible buying experience is increasing. As part of SAP's strategy for the intelligent enterprise, the transformation of the backend functionality is already in place with SAP S/4HANA as the digital core.

With SAP C/4HANA, SAP delivers a unified suite of cloud solutions that manage the customer experience based on one trusted customer data model. It combines SAP's front-office cloud solutions with SAP S/4HANA powered by artificial intelligence (AI).

It provides a tight integration of the frontend processes into the backend to enable an end-to-end lead-to-cash process (see Figure 11.9). This customer-focused strategy is being complemented by the previous SAP Hybris products as well as from the acquisitions around Gigya, Callidus Cloud, and others.

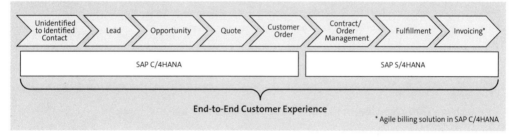

Figure 11.9 End-to-End Integration from Lead-to-Cash

With SAP C/4HANA, SAP addresses the following three customer requirements:

- **One consistent experience**
  Provide a consistent experience across any device or touchpoints customers have anywhere in the world.
- **Customer centricity**
  Tailor offerings around customer preferences, understand customer needs and demands as expected today, and create a 360-degree view of your customer.
- **Data protection**
  Provide a trustful relation to your customers and their data and ensure that data is being stored securely and isn't misused.

As illustrated in Figure 11.10, the portfolio of SAP C/4HANA includes five cloud solutions:

- SAP Commerce Cloud
- SAP Customer Data Cloud
- SAP Marketing Cloud
- SAP Sales Cloud
- SAP Service Cloud

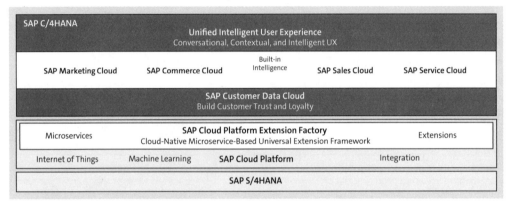

Figure 11.10 Overview of SAP C/4HANA Integrated into SAP S/4HANA

All the existing and acquired products by SAP are now being unified and rebranded to reflect the evolutionary change toward an integrated customer experience. To give you a better understanding of which previous subproducts now belong to which products, Table 11.2 breaks down the mapping of different products.

New SAP Name	Previous Products Included
SAP Marketing Cloud	■ SAP Hybris Marketing ■ SAP Hybris Customer Attribution ■ SAP Hybris Loyalty ■ SAP Hybris Digital Asset Management by Open-Text
SAP Commerce Cloud	■ SAP Hybris Commerce Cloud

Table 11.2 Overview of SAP C/4HANA Product Clusters to Previous Product Names

New SAP Name	Previous Products Included
SAP Sales Cloud	<ul><li>SAP Hybris Cloud for Sales</li><li>SAP Revenue Cloud</li><li>Callidus Cloud</li></ul>
SAP Service Cloud	<ul><li>SAP Hybris Cloud for Service</li><li>SAP Customer Engagement Center</li><li>SAP Hybris Knowledge Central by MindTouch</li><li>SAP Core Systems</li><li>SAP Callidus Cloud</li></ul>
SAP Customer Data Cloud	<ul><li>SAP Hybris Profile</li><li>Gigya</li></ul>

Table 11.2 Overview of SAP C/4HANA Product Clusters to Previous Product Names (Cont.)

As a portfolio, these offerings are fundamentally centered on customer engagement and commerce. All offerings include a combination of digital strategy, implementation services, and support services, which are integrated across multiple channels.

Today, business is about more than just business-to-business (B2B) or business-to-consumer (B2C) activities. The new buzzword is *customer-to-business* (C2B). Empowered customers are reshaping how business works and are expecting a new, deeper kind of engagement and experience. Consider the cases of Woolworths and Blockbuster: once dominating forces, they were forced into decline after failing to adapt fast enough to significant changes in technology and being unaware of how influenced these changes should be by the perceived experience of the customer. Organizations are now starting to put customer experience at the core of their digital focus in the absence of physical stores via virtual style advisers, for example, and have hence secured a strong following. C2B is about understanding and acting on customer signals and derived trends, building relationships, and delivering experiences that make customers ask for more. Customer engagement is reshaping industry dynamics and how businesses are run. The SAP C/4HANA portfolio can empower businesses to take control of their digital transformation journeys and preempt their customers' behavior to secure the most appropriate response and to keep them engaged.

In this section, we'll discuss the offerings behind SAP C/4HANA and the different products behind it.

11.5.1 Marketing

The evolution of the digital economy has seen a change in buyer behavior, and marketers have been challenged to keep up. The trend is toward contextual marketing, which systematically delivers mass personalization of customer interactions by leveraging insights about each individual customer to shape the customer's experience as each interaction unfolds. Contextual marketing allows marketers to engage customers in an intelligent way that nudges them toward a purchase rather than distracting them if they're already on that path.

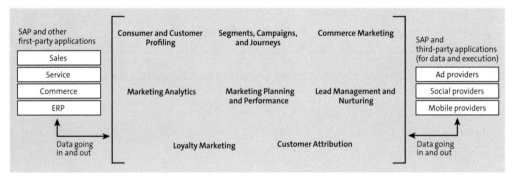

Figure 11.11 SAP Marketing Cloud Functions and Preconfigured Scenarios

As illustrated in Figure 11.11, SAP Marketing Cloud comes with a set of preconfigured scenarios that are ready to use and go beyond customer relationship management to help marketers develop the full context of individual customers and deliver highly personalized content and interactions at every stage of the customer journey. It also helps marketers understand the performance of all marketing activities to optimize resources, drive customer advocacy, and stimulate growth with the following capabilities:

- **Consumer and customer profiling**
  Capture and enrich customer profiles across all sources into a single view to gain deeper insights, understand your customer's journey, and turn this information into actionable business.

- **Segmentation and campaign management**
  Identify, target, and engage with the customers at the right moment and personalize the messages across multiple channels.

- **Commerce marketing**
  Enrich your commerce strategy with a personalized shopping experience based on

an extended marketing profile that supports the personalization of web shops, context-relevant product recommendations, and enriched personal profiles by capturing clickstreams.

- **Marketing planning and performance**
  Manage the growing operational complexities facing marketers and enhance your company's ability to orchestrate and optimize internal and external marketing resources.

- **Marketing analytics**
  Optimize your marketing and respond quickly to new opportunities with real-time performance insights.

- **Marketing lead management**
  Nurture your contact base, hand over qualified potential buyers and monitor success, driving closer collaboration between marketing and sales.

- **Loyalty management**
  Convert customers to loyal advocates by using a digital ready and seamlessly integrated program leveraging location-based marketing, mobile wallets, and insights into loyalty performance.

- **Customer attribution**
  Organize data to align with your business needs, gain insight into the performance of each marketing touchpoint, and immediately react to opportunities for growth. Get a better understanding of what's really triggering customer engagement.

The integration between SAP Marketing Cloud and SAP Commerce Cloud now enables additional functionalities to leverage SAP marketing campaigns and SAP marketing target groups to dynamically personalize the SAP Commerce Cloud storefront. This helps you better understand customer behavior and intent and personalize the shop with special recommendations or campaigns to increase the close rate on the store or enhance the core products with supplements.

11.5.2   Commerce

Industries across the globe are investing in commerce and backend systems to meet the demands of today's increasingly sophisticated customers. Companies from all sectors are seeking backend systems that provide an integrated view of their core business processes.

SAP Commerce Cloud offers the following features:

- Fully integrated solution for commerce, sales, and service
- Cloud catalog and storefront access for agents
- Customer and address data synchronization
- Integrated customer ticketing system
- Integrated assisted service module

Together, these key features enable businesses that run SAP Commerce Cloud to do the following:

- Enable personalized customer engagement
- Improve customer relationships
- Make sales processes more efficient
- Provide exceptional customer service across channels
- Gain a 360-degree view of customers

The integration of SAP Commerce Cloud with other SAP solutions provides a standardized, ready-to-use framework that connects SAP Commerce Cloud's omnicommerce capabilities with SAP products, including SAP S/4HANA; SAP Product Configuration; and SAP Marketing Cloud applications. This means that implementation partners no longer need to build integrations from scratch. With fewer custom configurations, the integrations can be implemented faster and at lower cost. It offers integration options in several areas, including transfer of master data, integration with SAP Marketing Cloud and SAP Customer Activity Repository, and solution and services configuration, to name a few.

Alongside these key features, several accelerators are available for SAP Commerce Cloud: B2B, B2C, China, and several industry-specific accelerators.

11.5.3   Sales

SAP Sales Cloud is a full cloud solution based on the previous SAP Hybris Cloud for Sales and SAP Revenue Cloud products enriched by the acquired Callidus Cloud solutions (see Figure 11.12). Callidus Cloud is targeted to help companies sell more, win more, and increase profitability. Referring to Figure 11.12, it's addressing mainly the core sales force automation and consists of two different products:

- **Callidus Cloud sales and performance management (SPM)**
  The SPM functionality includes the commission and incentive management for

direct/indirect business alongside the full lifecycle from order to payment. It supports the SAP C/4HANA suite to simplify the design of compensation plans and the modeling and planning of territories. SPM can easily design compensation plans, run reports on top of it, analyze sales performance, and adjust plans on the fly.

- **Callidus Cloud configure, price, and quotation (CPQ)**
  Callidus CPQ enhances the SAP C/4HANA portfolio within the quotation process with the ability to configure complex products supported by a pricing engine that can use complex pricing for direct and indirect as well as channel-specific pricing that considers tiered pricing customer-specific pricing. It allows the integration of approval workflows as well as the enhancement toward up-sell and cross-sell opportunities.

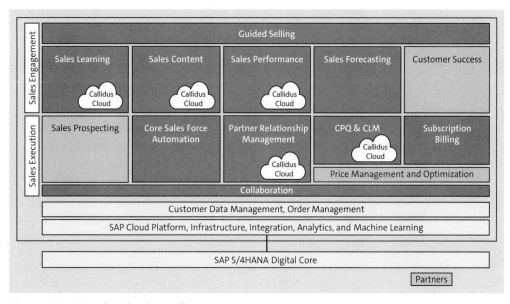

Figure 11.12 SAP Sales Cloud at a Glance

As shown in Figure 11.12, SAP Sales Cloud covers more than sales force automation and spans across the full customer lifecycle from lead to cash, including all after-sales processes from up-sell/cross-sell to renewal to support customer sales support. In the following, we outline the capabilities that are being provided:

- **Learning management**
  Ramp, onboard, and get new sales representatives in front of the customer faster

with online course builder, assessments, learning paths or gamification, and leaderboards.

- **Sales content**
  Create more meaningful customer engagements by providing a single source of truth, product playbooks, or customer-specific deal rooms available as offline content for your mobile.

- **Sales performance management**
  Provide real-time territory quota and planning, including the management of compensation plans and the provisioning of incentive leaderboards.

- **Pipeline management and sales forecasting**
  Automate and digitize the capturing of all deal activities to allow sales representatives to focus on the right customers and spend more time in customer conversation. You can highlight deals at risk or changes to the existing pipeline so that sales representatives can directly focus and increase the win rate.

- **Partner relationship management**
  Capability to provide a holistic view of all channel partners, including identification of the most productive partners and initiation of incentive programs or certification support.

- **Configure price quote and contract lifecycle management**
  Support the full lead-to-order process by supporting fast, complex quoting, margin protection, and customer- and channel-specific pricing/discounting. Contract management is supported with role-based contract templates and preapproved clause libraries. Contracts can be fully negotiated in an online workspace supporting approval workflows and signature as well as contract storage and management. This reduces the friction and builds customer confidence and trust.

Together, these capabilities build SAP Sales Cloud as a frontend layer to personalize and improve customer experience with SAP S/4HANA. For the integration of the SAP C/4HANA suite to SAP S/4HANA, there will be prepackaged content available that supports the full lead-to-cash process.

11.5.4   Services

The SAP Service Cloud is the single point of entry for the different service organizations, such as customer service, field service, or service management. It supports a personalized customer service experience and helps you to engage with customers on every channel. Currently, SAP Service Cloud supports the following different service types and roles (see Figure 11.13):

- **Self-service capabilities**
  Self-service portals are provided with integrated AI chat bots (powered by SAP Conversational AI) for collaborative service ticket resolution, along with gamification, customer feedback, and contextual service.

- **Customer contact center**
  Omnichannel engagement capabilities are available via phone, chat, email, and other channels, which are supported by interaction handling (history, orders, etc.) and agent guidance (scripting). All of these functions can be integrated into the Callidus Service Suite and the existing functionality, as well as in SAP Knowledge Central by MindTouch.

- **Field service management**
  Support is provided for the crowd service functionality to find an available technician in real time. Field service analysis and dashboards as well as field service knowledge management capabilities are also available.

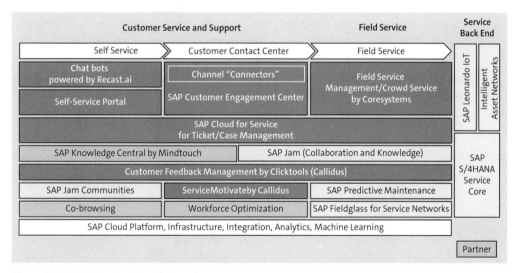

Figure 11.13 SAP Service Cloud Overview

From an end-to-end process view (interaction-to-resolution), the current available backend integration is available regarding spare parts, registered products, warranty, contracts, and billing processes. According to the current road map, this will be extended in the future toward an enhanced customer 360-degree experience that will allow customers to request, schedule, and manage their service requests and improved service schedule based on real-time road conditions. Further down the road, there will be a tighter integration into the finance, logistics, and HR backend processes to ensure an end-to-end picture supporting the full portfolio.

11.5.5   Customer Data

The SAP Customer Data Cloud solution is a fundamental element of SAP C/4HANA as it's the only industry solution with a consent-based data model. It helps to set the right foundation of trust with your customer and the personal data of the customer, as it provides transparency and control of the personal data to address privacy and compliance issues.

On May 25, 2018, the European Union applied a new regulation, GDPR, that must be applied to any global entity that is processing personal data belonging to an EU citizen.

With GDPR in place, individuals have the right to be informed about their data, access the data, request to erase the data, and get transparency and control about their personal profile. This must be put in the context of the collected data about your profile, location, social, devices, and other information that are being collected. If companies fail to address those topics, they will lose customer trust as well as risk being fined for noncompliance.

With SAP Customer Data Cloud, it's possible to manage consent throughout the lifecycle of a customer by defining present policies, maintaining accurate consent, and enforcing consent to downstream systems to provide user control, transparency, and the ability to manage preferences in a self-service. All of this can be done via the three capabilities/solutions of the SAP Customer Data Cloud (see Figure 11.14):

- **SAP Customer Identity**
  Identify and engage customers across channels and devices. This solution provides a frictionless point of entry across brands, regions, and digital properties as it enables a light registration process to enable an easy onboarding enhancement throughout the customer journey. This is supported by registration as a service (RaaS) as well as a secure identification of customers from any touchpoint via social media login or SSO capabilities. It also captures customers' registration to

improve conversions and protects against fraud and theft, for example, Distributed Denial of Service (DDoS) attacks.

- **SAP Customer Consent**

  Build trusted customer relationships based on transparency and control. It presents and captures customers' consent in a simplified and easy-to-use way, including version management and an audit log. It integrates into the downstream applications and enforces consistent consent management that can be handled by a customer self-service preference center. This helps to ensure GDPR compliance alongside the full process chain.

- **SAP Customer Profile**

  Powers trusted digital experience with customer data, as it transforms the customer identity into a single unified record for each customer that can be used to orchestrate specific attributes with any application, data, or service. It's possible to govern profiles alongside the customers' lifecycle according to the consent records and preferences supported by a an analytics functions to analyze and optimize customer experience and drive higher customer value.

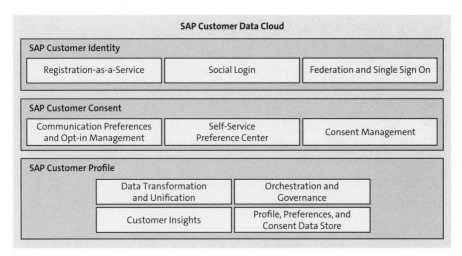

Figure 11.14 Key Capabilities of SAP Customer Data Cloud

11.5.6   SAP C/4HANA and SAP S/4HANA

SAP C/4HANA extends the SAP S/4HANA suite for customer-centric activities. Because SAP C/4HANA consists of several subproducts, it has a separate license model that isn't included in the SAP S/4HANA license. You can purchase and run most of the products separately. Nevertheless, they are tightly integrated; for example, SAP Marketing Cloud is built on SAP HANA and leverages the full capabilities of the platform.

Implementation of SAP C/4HANA products isn't dependent on SAP S/4HANA, but it can complement the implementation in different scenarios; for example, you can integrate SAP Sales Cloud into SAP S/4HANA to support the lead-to-cash process and not only lead-to-order.

From an integration perspective, several scenarios will be available in future releases that aren't yet confirmed and assigned to any release.

11.6   Master Data Management: SAP Master Data Governance

So far in this chapter, we've primarily discussed the cloud-based solutions that complement the SAP S/4HANA core, but it's important to switch gears for a moment to cover SAP Master Data Governance (SAP MDG). Beginning with SAP S/4HANA 1610, SAP MDG is embedded into SAP S/4HANA, in addition to being available on any database (including the SAP HANA database).

SAP MDG helps organizations enable governance processes for master data, ensure data quality, and remove data duplication. Master data can be created, changed, and approved centrally in SAP MDG and distributed to enterprise-wide systems. It's now available in two versions—one as an SAP NetWeaver-based product built on top of SAP ERP and the other as the SAP MDG running on SAP S/4HANA. In both cases, SAP MDG can be deployed as a hub model or in its embedded version with the core SAP enterprise application.

This product works in conjunction with other products in the following ways:

- **For data quality**
  We can use products such as SAP Information Steward or SAP HANA smart data quality to analyze data quality. SAP HANA smart data quality has the additional capability to enhance the data quality as well via cleansing, address enhancements, and geospatial data enrichment. With the advent of the microservice architecture on top of Cloud Foundry on SAP Cloud Platform, we have the potential to use SAP Data Quality Management, microservices, for location data.

- **For integration or extract, transform, load (ETL) purposes**
  SAP Data Services has multiple features for ETL functions, data quality enhancements (e.g., automated cleansing or address enrichment), and even data consolidation through identification of duplicates. SAP HANA smart data integration and SAP Cloud Platform Integration for data services have strong integration capabilities. They have similar integration capabilities, although SAP HANA smart data integration has additional data quality-related features.

The SAP HANA smart data quality and SAP HANA smart data integration have improved features and functions with SAP HANA 2.0. For example, the adapters in SAP HANA smart data integration can now support virtual IPs, and there are some new adapters: Apache Impala, Camel JDBC, PostgreSQL Log Reader, and so on.

SAP HANA smart data quality now has the following new features, which improves the **Cleanse** node:

- Create suggestion lists to output a list of valid address components for those records that weren't matched to the directory data.

- Choose to cleanse SAP Business Suite address data and assign content types designed for SAP Business partner data models.

- Override country settings, such as casing, diacritics, and formatting.

- In the **Geocode** node, assign coordinates that represent points of the address depending on the need based on improvements for SAP Web IDE.

SAP MDG 9.0 comes with prebuilt master data models for business partners (supplier and customer), materials, FI-related master data (e.g., profit center, profit center hierarchy, cost element/hierarchies, cost center, cost center hierarchy, and General Ledger [G/L] accounts), and other master data from partners for enterprise asset management, retail, and fashion management. With every release, SAP develops more content for the data models.

SAP MDG also allows consolidation of master data in a governed manner. In this scenario, data can be loaded into SAP MDG; duplication checks and data merges are now possible.

Here the duplication check rule is configured with certain parameters for the customer master and gets triggered when a requester requests a new customer. Figure 11.15 shows the SAP Fiori launchpad tab for consolidation of a business partner. The first step to start the consolidation process is to set up the importing configuration for a particular source. The figure also shows the process that has been set up for consolidation, which can include several steps, using the Create Consolidation SAP Fiori app. Figure 11.16 shows the consolidation run outcome.

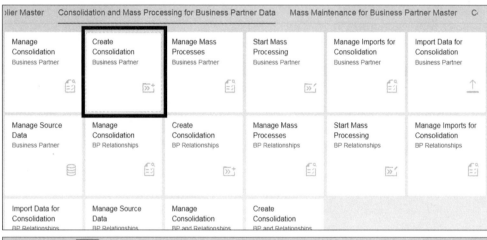

Figure 11.15 SAP MDG Consolidation Cockpit and Consolidation Process

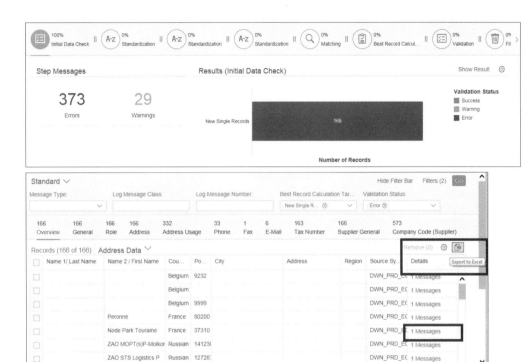

Figure 11.16 SAP MDG Consolidation Run Outcome

The following features make SAP MDG the master data governance tool of choice for SAP-centric landscapes:

- Built-in data models are available as well as the possibility of extending standard data models and creating new data models for master data objects.

- The UX is improved with Web Dynpro-based UIs and an increasing number of SAP Fiori-based UIs.

- Requests for master data creation normally undergo approval cycles; with SAP MDG, different types of workflows are easily enabled with validation rules through Business Rules Framework plus (BRFplus), and ABAP workflows and parallel workflows are also possible.

- After the change request for a master data creation/change is approved, it's distributed to the downstream systems using the Data Replication Framework via standard Application Linking and Enabling (ALE) technologies, but other integration technologies, such as web services, are also supported. SAP MDG provides out-of-the-box integration capabilities with SAP S/4HANA, SAP Ariba, and SAP Commerce Cloud.

- Analytics for process KPIs are also available for SAP HANA databases.

- Data quality enhancements are possible through integration with SAP Data Services or SAP Information Steward or for SAP HANA-based SAP MDG using SAP HANA platform services for quality enhancements.

- For the same master data, SAP MDG's key mapping concept maps the unique identifier for a system to the unique identifier in SAP MDG.

SAP MDG can be deployed on-premise or in the cloud. There are a couple of things to think about when it comes to SAP MDG and SAP HANA:

- SAP MDG can support co-deployment with SAP S/4HANA *and* be deployed as a hub model that distributes data to SAP S/4HANA (as shown in Figure 11.17).

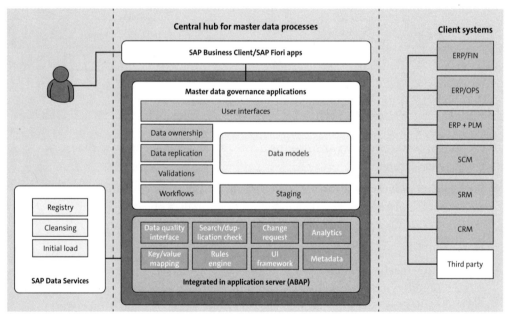

Figure 11.17 Sample Landscape with SAP MDG

- The key mapping function of SAP MDG can play an important role in Central Finance deployments to map financials master data from different systems.

- The consolidation scenario works better on SAP HANA, especially for large volumes of data.

- You can use the SAP HANA smart data integration service to connect to various source systems.

- SAP HANA smart data quality services offer evolving data quality enhancement capabilities, such as address cleansing and records matching.

With SAP MDG embedded in SAP S/4HANA since release 1709, there are some scope enhancements for the business partner, supporting documents, payment cards, and so on. The materials data model has also been enhanced to include shelf-life data and service parts management. With SAP S/4HANA 1809, there have been improvements in the master data consolidation and mass processing (creation/deletion) as well for classification data and business partner relationships. Some additional SAP HANA-based analytics are also included for data quality-related functions as well as enhancement in the functions available through SAP Fiori apps.

Some changes have been made in the classification of material master (UX change) functionality, and better support is provided for classification of supplier/customer. In addition, logging of actions such as the business partner blocking/deletion/read access helps in GDPR activities. SAP also provides several APIs, for example, the search and integration APIs. But the feature that deserves special mention (although it may require an additional license) is the SAP Data Quality Management microservices feature created on top of SAP Cloud Platform.

As of the time of writing (fall 2018), SAP MDG has multiple vendor and partner assignments to the business partner object. This can be done during consolidation, data duplication identification, and golden record creation, and it helps with mass processing of master data as well. This is possible only for SAP MDG running on SAP S/4HANA and not on SAP ERP. Further changes in consolidation features include following:

- The ability to delete records during best record calculation in consolidation. When downloading master data in Excel, manually enhancing and uploading again as mass processing will trigger validations again.

- Classification data can be changed during mass processing, and search and display of changes in active records is also available.

- Material search now happens by default through SAP HANA search.

- Newly added customers or vendors can be used like references for business partners and can be added within the same change request.

In finance master data, central governance of internal orders has been added to the governance and maintenance process, the data model, the integration from SAP MDG as IDocs or web services into SAP ERP or SAP S/4HANA, and the processing of the these interfaces at the receiving inbound systems.

There is now a joint UI for maintaining G/L accounting, including the cost element, and the integration is also at the interface level. Hence, the cost element changes can be replicated to SAP through the G/L master IDoc/service-oriented architecture (SOA) service. SOA services for Contract Accounts Receivable (FI-CA) elements are now available for loading into SAP MDG or replicating to SAP S/4HANA.

End-to-end integrations will be provided for master data across different systems, beyond just data replication (e.g., removing duplicates on SAP Ariba and in SAP MDG). Additional analytics will also be provided, such as the time series/current status trends for data quality and governance processes. Additional process analytics, such as SAP Fiori apps, have already been released in 1809 as dashboards and analytical list pages.

SAP MDG is integrated with SAP S/4HANA Cloud as well, enabling data quality enhancements for vendors and customers (business partner).

The road map for SAP MDG has a few interesting features planned, such as features to cope with data at a much larger scale because data sources are multiplying thanks to the IoT, social media integration, and so on. Thus, other systems could be used in conjunction with SAP MDG, for example, the SAP Data Hub, which provides the central design time and pushes execution on data lakes (e.g., through KAFKA to the Hadoop data lake). In addition, like other products, there is a plan to create the SaaS solution for master data management.

Note

You can refer to the details of the SAP Data Quality, microservices, at the following site: *https://bit.ly/2qxhV4L*.

This blog gives useful information about the microservice and related videos: *https://bit.ly/2LFaEfn*.

11.7 Supply Chain Planning: SAP Integrated Business Planning

SAP Integrated Business Planning (SAP IBP) is a cloud-based planning solution that rolled out as a native SAP HANA solution. In the following sections, we'll discuss the functionality available in each of SAP IBP's individual solutions:

- SAP IBP for sales and operations
- SAP IBP for demand
- SAP IBP for inventory
- SAP IBP for response and supply
- SAP Supply Chain Control Tower

We'll end this section by discussing SAP IBP in the context of SAP S/4HANA.

11.7.1 Sales and Operations Planning

The purpose of the sales and operations planning process is to balance demand and supply and to plan at a high level by involving all stakeholders, including marketing and finance and the operations team.

Key aspects of SAP IBP for sales and operations are as follows:

- **Planning**
  A cross-functional operations plan is delivered using demand and supply algorithms while considering the impact on inventory, service levels, and profitability. The financial impact on planning is taken into consideration to help make decision-making faster and easier. Planning involves functions for sales, marketing, supply, and finance.

- **Combining company strategy with customer and product strategy**
  A company's financial plan is translated to align with the marketing/product management group and demand planning. This strategy combination also helps formulate demand-driven planning based on key customer inputs.

- **Consistent data model**
  SAP IBP for sales and operations has close integration with SAP S/4HANA and the ability to provide a single source of truth. The data model can provide a single set of numbers for all areas of operations planning across the supply chain, and real-time analytics helps with faster decision-making.

- **Effective collaboration**
  Close integration with SAP Jam helps promote effective collaboration among stakeholders with good transparency in decision-making during the whole lifecycle of the planning process.

- **User interface**
  Using Excel for planning via an add-on is a big advantage for user communities; using an Excel worksheet provides comfort and familiarity when handling planning data.

A high-level depiction of SAP IBP sales and operations, collaborating with other functions, is shown in Figure 11.18.

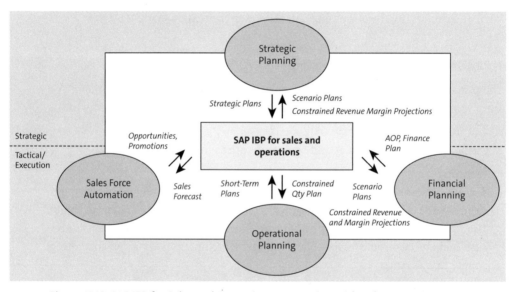

Figure 11.18 SAP IBP for Sales and Operations Interacting with Other Functions

11.7.2   Demand Planning

SAP IBP for demand contains all the traditional demand planning features and includes newer features, such as demand sensing, which will be useful for the business/supply chain that can adapt to a changing demand situation on a short-term basis. Overall, SAP IBP for demand is still maturing, mainly in the area of product lifecycle planning.

SAP IBP for demand has the following features:

- **End-to-end demand planning for mid- and long-term planning**
  This helps perform traditional demand planning using different statistical algorithms, very much like SAP Advanced Planning and Optimization (SAP APO).

- **Demand sensing**
  Demand sensing is a forecasting method with the capability of demand signal management, leveraging new mathematical techniques and near-real-time information to create/adjust a forecast on a short-term basis, based on the current realities of the supply chain.

- **Automated alerts**
  Automated alerts are provided for monitored situations for which forecast accuracy targets aren't met.

- **Collaboration**
  SAP IBP for demand can collaborate and communicate about the most recent, updated, and accurate demand plan.

11.7.3   Inventory Planning

SAP IBP for inventory helps optimize inventory norms across the supply chain. Its algorithm is adopted from SmartOps. Inventory targets are set up in such a way that the overall inventory carrying cost for the whole network is minimized while achieving required service levels for the customer. The variability due to uncertainty in a network leads to an increase in safety stock. This further results in building of safety stocks in every pocket of the supply chain node, which ultimately increases costs.

SAP IBP for inventory's multi-echelon model optimizes the internal service levels of each upstream stage and calculates the impact on each downstream stage using stochastic mathematics.

11.7.4   Response and Supply Planning

SAP IBP for response and supply can help an organization plan supply and respond to orders received. It can also help analyze orders missed or rescheduled due to various factors. This means that an organization can work toward removing such bottlenecks.

SAP IBP for response and supply (see Figure 11.19) helps an organization plan supply using unconstrained heuristics or optimize a supply plan using the optimizer. This capability works on time-series data and supports order-based supply planning, such as generation of production, procurement, and transport orders for distribution. Other features include unconstrained planning and constrained priority-driven heuristics planning. Optimization-based planning of individual orders is in the road map for future implementation. You can generate allocation to available-to-promise (ATP) and reschedule sale orders. SAP IBP for response and supply's order-based data model can be replicated in near real time from SAP S/4HANA.

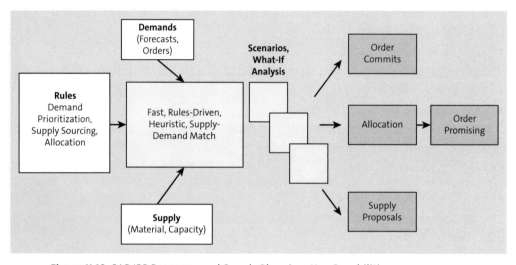

Figure 11.19 SAP IBP Response and Supply Planning: Key Capabilities

Supply planning can be used to plan supplies using either unconstrained heuristics or an optimizer in a constraint planning situation. With the optimizer, you can optimize the supply planning situation using either a profit maximization or cost minimization algorithm. It integrates requirements from demand, considers the norms determined using inventory optimization, produces rough-cut capacity planning requirements, and allows for procurement planning in a supply chain. The user can review and work on the scenarios using either Excel or SAP Fiori apps, which means that it can be viewed on mobile devices, tabs, and in a browser. It also allows for what-if scenarios and enables users to work in an Excel interface from end to end, starting from master data maintenance and batch job scheduling and moving through evaluation of planning scenarios and updating/manipulating planned requirements.

Response planning helps prioritize sales orders by ranking customer orders by priority via creating rules. Optimization-based ranking is in the product road map and will be available in the future. It also helps perform what-if analysis for an order coming in the future or an unforeseen event on the supply side. After a potential solution is determined and finalized, this functionality can be used to update the plan. The gating factors are analyzed, which will help an organization view various constraints in the supply chain and plan for longer-term solutions. For example, if the gating factors say that due to overload in a resource, most orders are rescheduled, an organization can plan to augment the capacity of that work center and improve the supply capability.

Supply and response planning can be used to perform the following processes in the supply chain management landscape:

- **Supply planning**
  - Capture inputs, such as demand and supply
  - Sequence demand by priority
  - Constrained planning run
  - Scenario planning using what-if analysis
  - Create or update supply planning and allocation

- **Response planning**
  - Capture inputs, such as sales orders, shipments, and allocation
  - Sequence demand by priority
  - Constrained planning run
  - Scenario planning
  - Update supply proposal or order confirmation
  - Analyze gating factors for long-term bottleneck removal

- **Demand prioritization**
  Depending on business requirements, orders can be prioritized based on rules. The rules can be created and changed easily. This helps in prioritization of orders; thus, an organization will always fulfill high-priority orders first.

- **Constrained forecasts**
  The planning process can anticipate orders and perform constrained planning based on the constraints from resource capacities, supplier commitment of orders, material availability, and lead time.

11.7.5 Control Tower

SAP IBP has good built-in analytics in SAP Supply Chain Control Tower. The key enablers of SAP Supply Chain Control Tower are end-to-end monitoring, alerts, and collaborative environments. We can analyze data in the same dashboard, extracting from demand, supply, inventory, and so on, and no additional data processing/extraction for any other analytics tool is needed. This helps with real-time tracking and decision-making by monitoring KPIs for the business. Some benefits of the SAP Supply Chain Control Tower include the following:

- All functions of SAP IBP use the same data from the SAP HANA database on the cloud. This helps users make decisions based on a single source of truth.
- Embedded analytics allows analysis of planning results.
- Simulation can help clarify various assumptions.
- High usability is achieved due to advanced UIs and because users feel comfortable handling their data in Excel. The same planning output can be saved in an offline workbook and sent to other stakeholders.
- SAP Supply Chain Control Tower includes the ability to collaborate using SAP Jam.
- Integration is available using SAP Cloud Platform Integration, SAP Data Services, and SAP HANA smart data integration.
- Near-real-time integration is provided with SAP S/4HANA and reuse of data for reducing redundancy.

SAP IBP for sales and operations integrates with all other supply chain planning processes to provide the following:

- A collaborative approach for better transparency among all stakeholders and planning functions
- Well-connected key processes
- Financial integration/financial visibility into planning
- Built-in analytics

11.7.6 SAP Integrated Business Planning and SAP S/4HANA

SAP provides the SAP IBP license only on the cloud using a SaaS model, but SAP S/4HANA is available both in the cloud and on-premise. Both can be integrated using SAP Cloud Platform Integration and SAP HANA smart data integration depending on the nature of the data. Note that SAP IBP can be operated only using SAP Fiori apps;

there is no access to SAP GUI as the same is available for SAP S/4HANA along with SAP Fiori apps. Most of the transaction data between SAP IBP and SAP S/4HANA is integrated in SAP IBP in time-series data via SAP Cloud Platform Integration except for orders in SAP IBP response via SAP HANA smart data integration. The integration isn't online or in real time, but it can be set up in near-real-time mode. Both new dimension products are built on the SAP HANA platform, so they're expected to work faster than traditional relational database management system (RDBMS) products. However, both products are maturing, and as customers slowly adopt them, we can see the effectiveness of the integration aspects between these two products in large and complex business environments in days to come.

11.8 Summary

This chapter provided an overview of the overall SAP portfolio and the LoBs that extend the SAP S/4HANA core solution to complete the requirements of the intelligent enterprise.

We introduced SAP Ariba and discussed the sourcing and procurement portfolio and how it relates to SAP S/4HANA Enterprise Management. We also discussed possible hybrid procurement scenarios and how the overall procurement portfolio fits together. We provided an overview of SAP Fieldglass and the capabilities of the VMS for contingent workforce and service procurement, and then reviewed the capabilities of SAP Concur for travel and expense management as an extension to SAP SuccessFactors. From there, we segued into a more detailed view of the SAP Success-Factors functional capabilities and how they fit into SAP S/4HANA and the other LoB solutions.

Then, we looked at the new SAP C/4HANA suite as a complementary front-office suite extending SAP S/4HANA toward an integrated customer experience ranging from SAP Marketing Cloud to SAP Customer Data Cloud to ensure GDPR compliance.

We detoured briefly to cover how SAP MDG fits into the SAP S/4HANA portfolio. As of SAP S/4HANA 1709, the embedded SAP MDG functionality will help organizations handle critical governance processes for master data.

This is a good starting point to take a closer look at the SAP S/4HANA architecture in the next chapter.

Chapter 12
SAP S/4HANA Architecture

This chapter provides information about the architecture of SAP S/4HANA, including some details of the underpinning SAP HANA platform and the SAP S/4HANA digital core.

The SAP S/4HANA architecture is based on the SAP HANA database, and it primarily uses an SAP Fiori-based user interface (UI). The architecture can support both online transaction processing (OLTP) and online analytical processing (OLAP) data. It largely consists of simplified data models from the SAP Business Suite; these simplifications ensure that no aggregation or index tables need to be persisted in the database.

In this chapter, we describe the SAP S/4HANA architecture, including data models, SAP HANA platform architecture, deployment models, and application lifecycle management (ALM). We also cover the SAP S/4HANA core, including how the other components complement this core and how the user experience (UX) has changed with the advent of the current SAP Fiori UX.

12.1 The Journey from SAP ERP to SAP S/4HANA

In this section, we'll talk about the evolution of the SAP product from the SAP Business Suite to the latest product, SAP S/4HANA. We'll also discuss the architecture of SAP S/4HANA, including how it forms the digital core of the modern enterprise, and the triggers for adopting SAP S/4HANA.

12.1.1 The Evolution of SAP S/4HANA

SAP launched the SAP HANA appliance in late 2010 to cater to high-volume, real-time operational analytics. Next, SAP released the SAP HANA database in 2011, with SAP Business Warehouse (SAP BW) powered by SAP HANA. At present, both products have evolved for many clients and are used to cater to the overall analytics portfolio.

In 2013, SAP released the SAP Business Suite powered by SAP HANA, which provided faster transaction processing, as well as reporting capabilities. Up to this point, running your SAP Business Suite on SAP HANA was the same as running your SAP Business Suite on any other database, with the same data structure and almost the same code base. The only basic difference was that the code handling high volumes of data was being pushed down to the SAP HANA database layer.

With this release, supporting products evolved; for example, the SAP HANA Live views presented the same semantic layer for each product, like SAP ERP. These views were leveraged to create operational reporting, either on SAP HANA in one of the side-by-side scenarios in which SAP Business Suite ran on any database, or in an SAP Business Suite on SAP HANA scenario. (We discussed operational reporting in Chapter 8.)

Currently, the SAP HANA Live views are used only in native SAP HANA applications, whereas Core Data Services (CDS) views are used in both native SAP HANA (version 10 and up) and SAP S/4HANA applications, as we'll explain in the next few paragraphs. SAP HANA Live views for SAP Business Suite on HANA continue to exist, but there is no migration possibility of these to the SAP S/4HANA world.

In 2015, SAP introduced SAP S/4HANA as a completely new product, which is, as discussed previously, based on the simplified data model of the SAP HANA database, a changed code base, and an SAP Fiori-based UI for many of the processes.

ABAP-based CDS views are used to access the underlying data model, and the code generated for these views is executed in the database layer. Now there are multiple versions of the SAP HANA platform with the release of SAP HANA 2.0. (For more details on the analytics product suite, see Chapter 8.)

What does the overall SAP S/4HANA architecture look like? At the core, the new simplified data models are represented as the physical tables. The SAP S/4HANA business functions read/update data into these data models, and there are virtual data models (VDMs) based on CDS views built on top of these physical tables. Of note, even in SAP S/4HANA 1809, not all the data models of the SAP ERP core have been transformed into simpler models at one time. This simplification is still evolving.

As shown in Figure 12.1, a VDM is a structured representation of SAP HANA database views. Originally, VDMs referred to the SAP HANA Live view for SAP Business Suite.

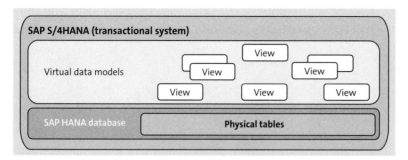

Figure 12.1 Virtual Data Model

CDS views are reusable views that serve as semantic data models not only to expose the underlying data into the operational reporting layer but also to provide additional functions, such as views with aggregation, analysis, and union (combining multiple selections into one result set) functions. CDS views can be created on top of tables or views. From SAP NetWeaver 7.4 on, CDS views are objects created in the ABAP layer. Before that, these views were built in the SAP HANA database layer and consumed in the ABAP layer as native SAP HANA objects. An example of the results of a query based on a CDS view is shown in Figure 12.2.

Figure 12.2 CDS Query Sample Result

The underlying technical innovation for the SAP S/4HANA architecture shown in Figure 12.3 is the SAP HANA platform, which uses the in-memory SAP HANA database.

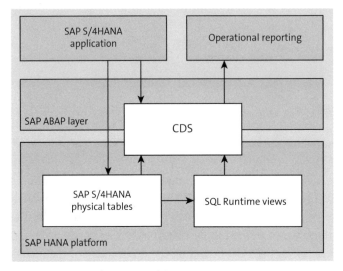

Figure 12.3 SAP S/4HANA Architecture

Before SAP NetWeaver AS ABAP 7.4 SP 05, CDS was available only in the design-time and runtime environments of SAP HANA. Now, the CDS concept is also fully implemented in SAP NetWeaver AS ABAP, whereas the code execution is pushed down to the database. Thus, CDS can be handled in the ABAP layer using the same transport mechanisms as other ABAP artifacts.

CDS views are of three main types:

- **Basic CDS views**
  These views are built on top of database tables/views and are used for some basic joins and calculations. Models are highly reusable.

- **Composite CDS views**
  These views use the basic views as a source and build complex logic per business requirements. Multiple basic and other composite views can be merged as well. Models are reusable.

- **Consumption CDS views**

  These views are used to make information available for consumption by SAP Fiori-based apps (e.g., Query Browser), KPI Modeler, SAP BusinessObjects reporting tools, and more.

An example of how CDS views can be built up from base views is shown in Figure 12.4.

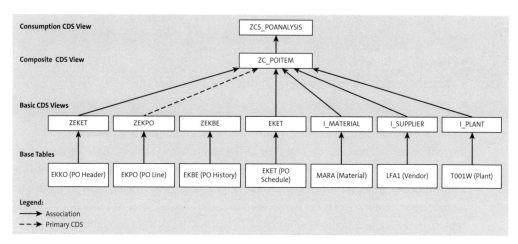

Figure 12.4 Schematic Diagram of CDS Views Relationship Model

You can look up a CDS view in the SAP S/4HANA system by running report RUTDDLS-SHOW2.

Note

Useful information on CDS views can be found at the following websites:

- *http://bit.ly/2x3SSuh*
- *http://bit.ly/2fkqOVl*

The simplification in the data model will result in a reduction in the database size as the number of redundant tables and the data to be stored in them diminishes with increasing simplification.

Some examples, as we saw in Chapter 2, are found in the finance area, in which the following physical tables no longer exist, replaced by views:

- Table ANLC: Fixed Assets: Cumulative Values
- Table BSAD: Index for Customers (Cleared Items)
- Table BSAK: Index for Vendors (Cleared Items)
- Table COSP: Cost Totals of External Postings
- Table COSS: Cost Totals of Internal Postings
- Table FAGLSBSAS: Index for G/L Accounts—New G/L (Cleared Items)
- Table FAGLBSIS: Index for G/L Accounts—New G/L
- Table GLT0: General Ledger Totals
- Table GLT3: Summary Data Preparations for Consolidation
- Table MLCD: Material Ledger

Another example of data model simplification in the finance area is for the Universal Journal entry in accounting. The new Universal Journal table ACDOCA provides real-time data from this single journal. As of 1610, there have been data model simplifications in other areas such as material management as described in Chapter 3, where transactions related to materials movement are all captured in table MATDOC table, replacing redundant tables MKPF and MSEG. No other major data model simplifications have been enabled up to SAP S/4HANA 1809.

> **Note**
>
> For more information on the Universal Journal, see Chapter 2, Section 2.2.1.

The data model simplification is possible because of the SAP HANA database capabilities. Figure 12.5 shows the table simplification from SAP ERP to SAP S/4HANA.

There is an evolving road map (available at the SAP Service Marketplace under **Improvements & Innovations · SAP Roadmaps · Cross Topics · SAP S/4HANA**) that SAP has provided to show how the different pieces of the SAP Business Suite will be integrated together gradually to optimize data usage and minimize data replication across various products. The core of this innovation is the SAP HANA platform, which we'll cover in detail in Section 12.2.

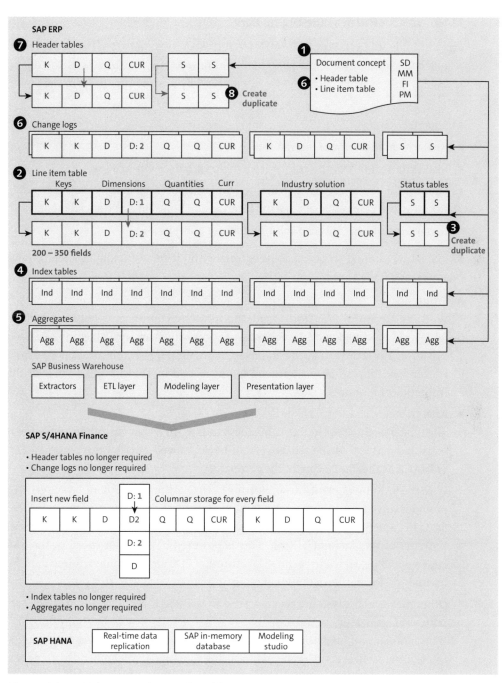

Figure 12.5 SAP S/4HANA: Changes in Tables

395

12.1.2   SAP S/4HANA as the Digital Core

Chapter 1 talked about how SAP S/4HANA forms an integral part of the IT digitalization agenda for many clients. To understand how SAP S/4HANA acts as the digital core, let's discuss what IT capabilities are needed by any product to form the digital core:

- Superlative UX
- Analytics at the point of interaction
- Real-time visibility of the enterprise to help with decision-making
- Support for various types of structured and unstructured data, as well as big data from various sources, including the Internet of Things (IoT) and social media
- Integration of best-of-breed solutions across boundaries

SAP S/4HANA has all these capabilities, qualifying it to be the digital core of your business, as detailed here:

- **Frontend**
  With the advent of SAP Fiori Cloud, the frontend components required include SAP Fiori launchpad and SAP Gateway services, which are available on SAP Cloud Platform. The SAP Fiori apps can have the SAP S/4HANA core component as the backend system. Thus, the backend is untouched by the changes to any of the frontend components.

- **Analytics**
  The type of agility required by a business today—in which customers expect personalized services, delivered now—can be supported only by the power of SAP S/4HANA as the digital core of the company.

  With the SAP HANA platform supporting both OLAP and OLTP data, SAP S/4HANA provides advanced analytical capabilities that weren't possible with traditional SAP ERP. SAP S/4HANA can perform real-time analytics on transactional data at the time of the data entry itself. This is powered by the high speed of the SAP HANA database, which uses the VDMs through CDS views on the required data for its analysis. Primarily, operational reporting can be used with this setup.

  Other means of analysis are also available to SAP S/4HANA, depending on the scenario and availability of the tools. For example, SAP S/4HANA has built-in hybrid transactional and analytical applications, such as SAP Smart Business cockpits, multidimensional reports and analytical SAP Fiori apps, and embedded analytics, which includes the Query Browser and Query Designer tools. For other types of enterprise-wide analytics, SAP S/4HANA supports SAP BW and SAP BW/4HANA for data extraction. Other analytics options and architecture are covered in Chapter 8.

- **Business components**
  SAP S/4HANA Enterprise Management serves as the foundational solution of the SAP S/4HANA business suite. This solution is built on the SAP HANA platform with user interactions via the SAP Fiori apps, forming the core of the business processes of the digital enterprise.

Some other solutions are being integrated into this core to make use of the common data model and reduce data replication across system components. Let's discuss a few of these changes in the following section.

12.1.3 Integration of SAP Products in SAP S/4HANA

SAP is in the process of integrating full or partial solutions in the SAP S/4HANA core on-premise version, including industry solutions. The SAP road map provides indicative timelines and plans, and can be found at the following URL: *https://www.sap.com/india/products/roadmaps.html.*

The following are the current state of such integrations:

- Already in SAP S/4HANA 1511, several industry solutions became part of the SAP S/4HANA core (e.g., Consumer Products, Mill Products, Utilities, etc.).

- In SAP S/4HANA 1610, most functions of the industry solutions for Retail and for Oil & Gas are also included.

  In version 1709, more functions for these industries were included, along with several SAP Fiori apps and CDS views. In addition, completely new functionality for agricultural contract management was included in the core.

- With version 1809, industry solutions for Utilities, Retail, and Fashion are included in the core.

- Extended warehouse management (EWM) is part of SAP S/4HANA 1610.

- SAP Advanced Planning and Optimization (SAP APO) is completely replaced by multiple solutions. Part of the functionality is covered by the cloud-based (SaaS) solution SAP Integrated Business Planning (SAP IBP). The production planning and detailed scheduling (PP/DS) and global available-to-promise (GATP; now known as advanced ATP [AATP]) functions are available and integrated with the SAP S/4HANA core in the 1610 release. The complementary solution for SAP APO, IS-CWM (catch weight management in the Consumer Products industry solution) was made available in SAP S/4HANA 1610. However, the solution isn't exactly the same, nor is a conversion possible from an earlier IS-CWM solution to SAP S/4HANA (see SAP Note 2358928). This feature was enhanced in the 1709 release to remove some of the constraints that were in the solution in the earlier version.

> **Note**
>
> As of fall 2018, SAP is focusing now on the "intelligent enterprise," which consists of the intelligent suite with SAP S/4HANA as the core. It's enabled through artificial intelligence (AI) and machine learning, process automation, intuitive UX, and advanced analytics. These technologies are supported by the digital platform provided by SAP Cloud Platform and by the data management layer. This also results in a more seamless integration between the SAP S/4HANA core and the surrounding applications.

In more recent SAP S/4HANA releases (1709 and 1809), some of the features in these line of business (LoB) solutions have been enhanced or newly included, as follows:

- Breakdown analysis and report and repair malfunction in SAP Enterprise Asset Management, including related SAP Fiori apps.
- SAP Commercial Project Management is now delivered as part of SAP S/4HANA and no longer as an add-on.
- SAP Transportation Management (SAP TM) is now embedded in SAP S/4HANA and the order integration with TM has been simplified. Thus, deliveries are created according to the results of transportation planning, and transportation requirements are created and updated based on delivery documents.
- EWM has been enhanced with load planning integrated with TM, optimized pallet planning, stock consolidation, and other functions.
- Embedded compliance in SAP S/4HANA has been added from a governance, risk, and compliance (GRC) perspective, with some basic functions.
- Many SAP Fiori apps in the procurement and finance areas have been added.
- Variant configuration (covered in detail in Chapter 7).
- Enhancements have been made in functions in environment, health, and safety (EHS) and quality management.
- For SAP Product Lifecycle Management, several changes have been made (refer to Chapter 7).

- SAP Master Data Governance (SAP MDG) now comes as embedded MDG in SAP S/4HANA (refer to Chapter 11).

- For SAP Customer Relationship Management (SAP CRM), details of the features available are mentioned in the feature scope description at the SAP Help Portal (*http://help.sap.com/s4hana*).

- SAP C/4HANA is the new solution for customer relationship management for a 360-degree view of customers. The portfolio has united the previous SAP Hybris cloud components with the same branding brush and has brought seamless integration with the SAP S/4HANA core. The unification has happened though a common data model, similar user experience from campaign to billing, extensions though the SAP Cloud Platform extension framework, and additional intelligent services provided by SAP Leonardo.

Other cloud-based solutions—SAP Ariba, SAP SuccessFactors, SAP Fieldglass, SAP Concur, SAP Cloud for Customer, SAP Financial Services Network, and third-party solutions, such as Vertex for tax calculation—can be integrated with the SAP S/4HANA core through various middleware products, including SAP Cloud Platform Integration, SAP Process Orchestration, or web services. SAP S/4HANA provides built-in support for some of these cloud solutions (e.g., SAP SuccessFactors and SAP Concur) since version 1610. More interfaces were made available in 1709; for example, exchange rates, a band master interface for SAP SuccessFactors Employee Central, and order data replication between SAP C/4HANA and SAP S/4HANA. In addition, built-in integration was provided in 1709 for SAP Ariba. With 1809, the following new interfaces were provided:

- SAP Ariba integration with materials management functionality in SAP S/4HANA for guided buying, enabling employees to choose or search from the Guided Buying catalog and add to a shopping cart. This cart is replicated in SAP S/4HANA, where a purchase requisition is created. The shopping cart also shows the subsequent documents created in SAP S/4HANA.

- Invoice integration between SAP Fieldglass and SAP S/4HANA enables an optimized workforce.

- Integration of SAP Manufacturing Execution with production operation functionality in SAP S/4HANA makes it possible to gather shop floor intelligence, enables a batch size of one, supports handover from engineering to manufacturing, and provides state-of-the-art production execution. There are some additional key features which this integration has provided, helping to gain further operational efficiency, especially for discrete manufacturing.

- Integration of Trader's & Scheduler's Workbench with SAP Integrated Business Planning (SAP IBP) for Oil & Gas enables the creation of nomination global simulations from SAP IBP in SAP S/4HANA and also sends physical inventory data from SAP S/4HANA to SAP IBP using the OData service provided.

- Several APIs are provided for sales; for example, sales orders, credit/debit memo requests, customer returns, pricing procedures, condition types, billing document requests (read, delete, and reject), and so on.

- New SOAP APIs in sourcing and procurement for Supplier Invoice – Create, Reverse, Send Status Update Notification, as well as purchase-order related APIs for Create, Write, Delete, Purchase Order – Send Status Update Notification, Send/Receive Notifications for Item History Updates, Purchase Requisitions – CRUD operations.

- Several asynchronous outbound SOAP services are now available that enable the transfer of procurement-related master data and configuration data to an external system. Also, SOAP APIs for service entry sheets are available with the Lean services functionality.

- Supply chain functionality has interfaces for inbound/outbound/return delivery's CRUD operations.

> **Note**
>
> Further details regarding changes in features and functionality with SAP S/4HANA version 1809 can be found at the following URL: *https://bit.ly/2CBfEwy*.

12.1.4   The Road Map to SAP S/4HANA and Innovations

For the IT department of an enterprise, the road map for SAP S/4HANA adoption depends heavily on the status of the IT landscape, especially the SAP footprint, and the short-term and medium-term focus areas. Let's discuss how the road map can be designed with a few example scenarios.

Triggers

Certain events trigger the evaluation of SAP HANA in its different forms, but here we'll talk only about those events that directly affect SAP S/4HANA considerations. You might begin considering the implementation of SAP S/4HANA under the following circumstances:

- **Business needs**

  Businesses may need functionalities that are available only in SAP S/4HANA—for example, a real-time operational report that influences business decisions. Businesses also may have certain pain points that can be solved by migrating to or implementing SAP S/4HANA. For example, there may be a consolidation scenario in which several large ERP systems need to be consolidated into a single large ERP system where all the business processes are aligned to the standard processes and are supported by a cutting-edge technology platform. This could be an existing system consolidation exercise or the result of a merger and acquisition. It could even be a divestiture in which part of the functions and data are removed, and the business wants to align the remaining solution with the latest SAP solution, which is SAP S/4HANA Enterprise Management.

- **Greenfield implementation**

  Many clients implementing or reimplementing SAP ERP tend to start with the latest version of SAP S/4HANA Finance (e.g., 1605) or SAP S/4HANA Enterprise Management (e.g., 1809 or 1709). For more information, see Chapter 15.

- **Technology drivers**

  There can be several technology drivers for an SAP S/4HANA adoption evaluation, including total cost of ownership (TCO) reduction through infrastructure footprint reduction or landscape simplification.

- **Hardware considerations**

  For many clients, the SAP HANA road map evaluation is triggered by a hardware refresh cycle. Instead of keeping the traditional hardware, they select hardware to support the SAP HANA platform so that they don't need to invest in the hardware for a reasonably longer period. Thus, they get the latest innovations of the database and, at the same time, have a future-proof solution. Many such clients like to go step by step and opt to migrate to an SAP Business Suite on SAP HANA solution to start.

- **Future-proofing**

  The SAP technology platform and making it ready for innovations is a driver for customers who need the platform to enable their business process innovation.

- **End of life (EOL)**

  EOL issues for SAP ERP versions can be drivers to cause some SAP customers to think about the latest product versions of SAP S/4HANA.

- **Upgrades**

  Upgrades can be important trigger points for many clients because they can be such cumbersome IT projects.

Inhibitors

Just as there are several triggers for an SAP S/4HANA adoption, there are some deterrents to a fast adoption of SAP S/4HANA. Some companies have decided to adopt only the SAP S/4HANA Finance functionalities, whereas others opt for the whole scope of the SAP S/4HANA solution.

Behind these choices, the most important consideration is that SAP S/4HANA is a new product that is still evolving. The end state in terms of the functionality for SAP ERP and industry solutions support is yet to be reached for the SAP S/4HANA Enterprise Management solution.

The other factor is that some large clients want to see how other companies of similar size and industry are faring with their SAP S/4HANA solutions before taking the plunge. SAP S/4HANA has made the foray into the market as of Q1 2015, and many companies have now completed their SAP S/4HANA implementation and are reaping the benefits already. The adoption of SAP S/4HANA has picked up quite a bit in the last few years, and this factor has become an accelerator, rather than a deterrent.

For some SAP customers that have huge databases, the hardware size limitations and the high costs for the large size can also act as deterrents. Typically, the existing uncompressed OLTP database (non-SAP HANA platform) is reduced by a factor of 5 to 10 when moved to SAP HANA. Even then, however, the existing database size and its rate of growth may be prohibitive, considering the current constraint in the scale-up and scale-out architecture and hardware availability. Some of these SAP customers are also considering archiving solutions, which take time to implement.

Some clients have an IT strategy to move completely into the cloud and are contemplating a SaaS solution such as SAP S/4HANA Cloud. However, SAP S/4HANA Cloud doesn't have all possible functionalities yet. Thus, several clients are playing a "wait and watch" game—waiting for more success stories, waiting for the SAP S/4HANA product to stabilize or at least have a clearly defined road map, or waiting for the entire simplification to be completed—before they embark on the SAP S/4HANA journey. Some clients are also adopting interim steps to prepare for the SAP S/4HANA journey, such as performing the SAP S/4HANA impact assessment on their existing solution and archiving projects. The SAP Business Suite on SAP HANA migration might also be a stepping-stone for some businesses.

With that said, most clients are building up their digital transformation road maps with SAP S/4HANA as the digital core and are at least assessing their current investments and the current state of their SAP ERP systems and other SAP products, while considering that some of these SAP products would be merged into the SAP S/4HANA core or moved to a cloud-based solution.

Decision Factors

When a client wants to evaluate its SAP S/4HANA road map, there are major factors to consider, as shown in Table 12.1. The table shows a sample for a greenfield implementation scenario in which the SAP customer is evaluating three options: SAP Business Suite on any database, SAP Business Suite on SAP HANA, and SAP S/4HANA. (*High*, *Medium*, and *Low* designate the degree to which the product matches with the customer's high-level requirements.)

Decision Factors	SAP Business Suite on Any Database	SAP Business Suite on SAP HANA	SAP S/4HANA
Functionality requirement	High	High	Medium
Solution stability	High	High	Medium
Costs (implementation, licensing, etc.)	Medium	Medium	High
Infrastructure costs	Medium	Medium	Medium
Innovation (big data analytics, IoT, etc.)	Low	Medium	High
Data volumes handling	Low	High	High
Speed of implementation	Medium	Medium	High

Table 12.1 Sample Set of Factors for Evaluation of SAP S/4HANA Adoption

This table, of course, provides only a simplistic view. In practice, the evaluation will be very different for different clients, and the weighting of different factors will vary with the client's focus or the primary driver for such an evaluation. Some clients want to be at the leading edge of innovation in their IT strategy, and they are more willing to take risks, whereas others want to have a more balanced strategy. This also can drive the weight placed on different factors under consideration.

The migration scenarios are even more complex because there needs to be detailed evaluation of the existing solution impact and the impact on the business processes subsequent to the migration to SAP S/4HANA. Details of the migration scenarios are covered in Chapter 15.

We also need to consider that with SAP S/4HANA, the functions of the transactional and analytical systems are being blurred, and there will be a similar impact on the different IT departments supporting the solutions. Thus, an enterprise needs to have an overall SAP HANA adoption strategy, including SAP S/4HANA and other products on SAP HANA based on their landscapes or requirements—for example, SAP BW on SAP HANA, SAP BW/4HANA, native SAP HANA, SAP Leonardo (refer to Chapter 14)—for support of IoT, machine learning, big data, or solution extensions for SAP Success-Factors or SAP C/4HANA; the list is long.

A final important aspect is that SAP is concentrating all the innovative solutions and inclusion of major functions within the SAP S/4HANA core (e.g., basic EWM, TM, master data management, etc.) and also creating the intelligent enterprise through solutions on SAP Leonardo. Therefore, even if there is no other business driver, there can be two major reasons to move to SAP S/4HANA: application consolidation (provided functionality is supported) and also not to be left behind in the innovation game in the areas where the company's core capabilities lie.

One thing is clear, however—SAP HANA adoption isn't a question of *if*, but *when*.

12.2   SAP HANA Platform

The SAP HANA platform for real-time analytics and applications makes it possible to combine the OLAP and OLTP worlds. This platform provides various capabilities or services and is the core that several SAP products leverage, including SAP S/4HANA. Before expanding into these capabilities, let's spend a little more time discussing the SAP HANA database.

12.2.1   SAP HANA Database

At the core of the SAP HANA platform is the SAP HANA database. The features that make this database the core for other products to leverage are discussed in the following sections.

In-Memory Storage

The capacity of main memory in servers has been increasing in leaps and bounds over the past few years, and such high memory is also becoming much more affordable. The advantage of in-memory operations on data is the huge speed difference when compared to accessing data from the drive. As an example, in-memory data can be accessed 100,000 times faster than data can be accessed from a spinning hard disk. In addition, the main memory is connected to the CPU through a high-speed bus, whereas the hard drives are connected through a chain of buses and controllers.

Columnar Storage and Row Storage

Relational databases organize data in tables that can store the data records in rows or columns. In SAP HANA, most tables are *columnar*, except for the system tables. Traditional row databases store data in a row as one "bundle." Although this leads to very good performance during write operations, its efficiency is lower during read operations. If the table has too many columns, and you need to extract the data only from some of those columns, classical row databases still need to read complete rows and then discard the unnecessary data. Because columnar databases store data for each column separately, they can retrieve only data from columns that were really required to deliver the response, avoiding unnecessary read operations.

In summary, the advantages for data selection are as follows:

- Only the relevant columns of the table need to be accessed when a query is run.
- Projections are efficient.
- Any column can be an index. Thus, a single-column index isn't persisted on the disk; instead, it's generated when the table loads. If it's a multicolumn index, this is persisted on the disk, so manual maintenance of secondary indices is no longer required.

There are certain disadvantages of a column-store table (e.g., insert-updates aren't easy), but these can be circumvented. For example, insert-updates are accelerated using a special table structure with a delta mechanism that minimizes the impact of write performance on columnar tables. However, delta operations such as the delta merge are memory- and CPU-intensive, with spurts of disk I/O load (while persisting the data). When tables become huge, the performance can be impacted. Hence, table sizes need to be kept under control through partitioning.

Note

More details about delta merge operations are available at *http://bit.ly/2y8HpZ0.*

Compressed Data

In SAP HANA, columnar storage makes different types of data compression possible. For example, table data is massively *compressed* in such a way that the data movements are minimized without increasing the CPU load for decompressing the data. Each column of the table undergoes this compression, which involves allocating consecutive numbers to distinct column values. This is known as the *dictionary* for each of the distinct columns. Hence, storage of such numbers is typically much smaller and helps to compress the data. A simple example is shown in Figure 12.6 to illustrate a column table and its dictionary.

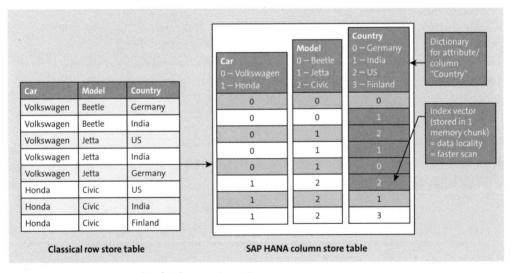

Figure 12.6 Example of Columnar Data Store

Other advanced compression algorithms are also applied on each column. The SAP HANA database determines the suitable algorithm to be applied to each of the columns and reevaluates this algorithm based on the data in the table. Columnar storage together with data compression makes database querying many times faster.

The data requirements of modern-day enterprise applications or data warehouse solutions may be much greater than those of single systems provided by hardware vendors. Parallel processing and partitioning overcomes this limitation.

Leverage Massively Parallel Processing

A single processor now has multiple cores or processing units, which increases the processor performance through parallel processing of its different cores. Each core can process each column, and this makes parallel processing simpler and more effective. Systems can be multiprocessors, thereby making more parallel operations possible. This again increases the overall system performance massively.

Leverage Partitioning

Partitioning normally is used in a scale-out architecture environment, but it can be used for a single-host environment as well. The data can be divided and placed into clusters of servers, forming a distributed database. Alternatively, the individual database tables can be placed on different servers within the cluster. If some of the tables are larger than a single server can hold, it can be split into several partitions with a group of rows per partition (horizontal), while each partition resides on a separate server within the cluster. This feature helps in quickly analyzing large amounts of data and handling complex calculations.

The column tables in the SAP HANA database are restricted to two billion records in a nonpartitioned table. If a table crosses this limit, the database will issue an error or the entire database can fail, as we've witnessed firsthand for one client. In such cases, partitioning is the only way out, unless of course the table contents can be truncated (e.g., log tables of which older data isn't required). The table can be split into partitions containing a set of rows determined by algorithms such as hash partitioning, round-robin, or partitioning by a range (e.g., by year). A combination of these algorithms can be used for multilevel partitioning. Partitioning, directly and indirectly, helps to increase the performance of the database for reading as well as writing through delta merge operations. Further information about partitioning in SAP HANA can be found in SAP Note 2044468.

For optimizing queries on partitioned tables in SAP HANA, static partition pruning is used. To do so, the query optimizer analyzes the WHERE clause of queries to determine whether the filters match the given partitioning specification of a table. Because this partitioning specification didn't change in SAP HANA SPS 02, static partition pruning was used. SPS 02 uses dynamic partition pruning, which is content-based and takes place at runtime based on the existence of statistics; it helps avoid the need to access and load into memory partitions, which aren't required. Other options to optimize performance are to use load distribution and the minimization of inter-host communication.

SAP HANA's performance depends on the innovations produced by processors and hardware vendors. The columnar structure allows the database to deploy a dedicated processor core for each column (or column partition). This enables databases to use massive parallel processing for individual queries and leads to significant acceleration compared to processing a query with a single core.

For example, as of September 2018, the Cisco, Fujitsu, Hitachi, and Lenovo servers can support up to 6 TB of scale-up for SAP Business Suite powered by SAP HANA or SAP S/4HANA, and HP supports up to 20 TB of scale-up, as well as scale-out in the appliance models. Cisco, Fujitsu, Hitachi, and Huawei provide 8 TB of scale-out for SAP S/4HANA. The latest information regarding the hardware capacity of various providers which are certified by SAP can be found here, and should be referenced for any size-related decisions: *https://bit.ly/2QKZOzs*.

With the Intel Skylake processor, Fujitsu and Lenovo can support 12 TB of scale-up for SAP S/4HANA/SAP Business Suite on SAP HANA; other hardware providers, such as Cisco, Dell, and HP, have also adopted this processor. As of October 2018, Cisco supports 12 TB in both scale-up and scale-out modes, while HP supports 20 TB under certified appliances.

Note

Some examples of SAP HANA on IBM Power systems are available at *https://sapon-power.wordpress.com*. The performance outcome for the Haswell CPU from Intel and how it's been used in servers is explained in a blog at *https://blogs.saphana.com/2015/06/29/impact-of-haswell-on-hana/*, and details about the Broadwell servers are explained in a blog at *https://blogs.saphana.com/2016/06/06/new-intel-xeon-broadwell-processor-boosts-sap-hana-scalability-performance-new-highs/*.

12.2.2   Virtualization

The SAP HANA platform (from SPS 05 onward) has supported virtualization technology to host multiple separated SAP HANA instances that run on separate virtual machines (VMs). This virtualization of the underlying server(s) can be performed for SAP S/4HANA, which helps to abstract the hardware layer and increase use of the hardware, thereby reducing TCO.

Figure 12.7 shows a configuration for Multitenant Database Containers (MDCs; explained in Section 12.2.6) on a virtualized environment.

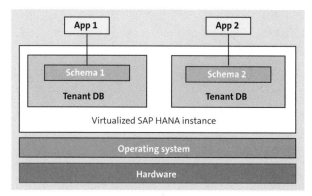

Figure 12.7 Virtualized SAP HANA System

Note

For any virtualization, SAP provides guidelines at *http://archive.sap.com/documents/docs/DOC-60312*.

These guidelines should be followed along with the best practices/recommendations of the hypervisor vendor.

The current virtualization options are as follows, as of September 2018, per SAP Note 1788665:

- Software-level virtualization options (hardware vendor–independent options):
  - VMware vSphere 5.5 (also for production)
    - VM limits: 64 vCPU, 1 TB RAM
    - Single-VM – General availability (GA; refer to SAP Note 1995460)
    - Multi-VM support of SAP HANA SP07 (and later releases) running on VMware vSphere 5.5 in production GA (refer to SAP Note 2024433)
    - SAP BW on SAP HANA scale-out – GA (refer to SAP Note 2157587; included only for the sake of completeness)

- VMware vSphere 6.0 (also for production)
  - VM limits: 4 VMs, 4TB RAM
  - SAP HANA SPS 11/12 (or later releases) for production single-VM and multi-VM use cases and nonproduction scale-out (refer to SAP Note 2315348)
- VMware vSphere 6.5 (also for production)
  - Single/multiple VMs supported from SAP HANA 1.0 SPS 12
  - Limits: 128 vCPUs on 4 sockets (4 sockets on up to 8 socket hardware), and 4 TB of RAM (refer to SAP Note 2393917)
- SLES KVM – Production support for SAP HANA 1.0 SP12 onwards (refer to SAP Note 2607144)
- Redhat KVM – Production support for SAP HANA 1.0 SP12 onwards (refer to SAP Note 2599726)
- Nutanix
- XEN (nonproduction only)
  - In GA with SAP HANA SPS 12 (or later releases) for production single-VM and multi-VM use cases for up to 4 TB of main memory (Big Data Warehouse [BDW])
  - Hitachi LPAR 2
  - SAP HANA SPS 07 (or later releases) for production and nonproduction use cases
  - Single- and multi-VM scenarios (see SAP Note 2063057)
- Hardware vendor-dependent options:
  - SAP HANA on Power – GA (refer to SAP Note 2230704)
  - In GA for single-VM and multi-VM scenarios with up to 8 logical partitions (LPARs) on one server
  - Hardware-based partitioning
    - HP nPartitions – GA (refer to SAP Note 2103848)
    - Fujitsu PPARs (physical partitions) – GA (refer to SAP Note 2111714)
    - Lenovo FlexNode – GA (refer to SAP Note 2232700)
  - Others
    - Hitachi LPAR 2.0 – GA (refer to SAP Note 2063057); in controlled availability (CA) for single- and multi-VM scenarios on full and half-sockets (HSW, BDW)
    - Huawei FusionSphere 3.1, 5.1 – CA (refer to SAP Notes 2186187 and 2279020)

- Huawei FusionSphere 3.1 with SAP HANA SPS 09 (or later releases) for production and nonproduction

Also, keep the following in mind for virtualization:

- As part of GA, SAP supported only scale-up scenarios for SAP S/4HANA, not scale-out. However, this has changed with SAP HANA 2.0 SP 00 and SAP S/4HANA 1610 FPS 01, for which scale-out is also supported.
- Sizing guidelines from SAP and vendor recommendations need to be followed for each VM, with no CPU/memory overprovisioning.
- The "SAP HANA Guidelines for Running Virtualized" file and the vendor-specific best practices document need to be followed for configuration and overall setup of the virtualized environment.
- There is a performance impact on the virtualized SAP HANA environment compared to a nonvirtualized environment. For example, SAP has mentioned a performance benchmark of less than 12% degradation for most tests in a virtual environment against a bare metal deployment, but there were outliers as well.

Note

The byte order in SAP HANA 1.0 on IBM Power is Big Endian; in SAP HANA 2.0 on IBM Power, the byte order is Little Endian.

For your choice of SUSE Linux distribution, SUSE Linux Enterprise Server 12 SPS 01 and above exclusively support Little Endian byte order on the IBM Power platform.

It's important to check the SAP guidelines for virtualization and the features and constraints available for the specific products used for virtualization; these are constantly evolving.

Note

Regarding restrictions when migrating SAP NetWeaver systems from SAP HANA 1.0 to SAP HANA 2.0 on IBM Power, see SAP Note 2429277 (Migrating an SAP NetWeaver-Based System from an SAP HANA 1.0 Database to an SAP HANA 2.0 Database on IBM Power). When upgrading from SAP HANA 1.0 on Power to SAP HANA 2.0 on Power, a full data migration is required. Backups from SAP HANA 1.0 on Power aren't compatible with SAP HANA 2.0 on Power (see the **What's New** release notes for SAP HANA 2.0 at *http://bit.ly/2wYirxx*).

For details on guidance and tools available for the migration, see the *SAP_HANA_ System_Migration_en.pdf* document attached to SAP Note 2551355 (SAP HANA Platform 2.0 SPS 00 Release Note). For best practices for SAP HANA on Power, visit *www.ibm.com/support/techdocs/atsmastr.nsf/WebIndex/WP102502*.

The concept of virtualization can be applied to the hardware for SAP HANA, which is available as an appliance or through the SAP HANA tailored data center integration (TDI) approach. The SAP HANA journey started with the appliance delivery model, in which the entire product was delivered as a preconfigured set of software components on top of preconfigured hardware components supplied by SAP-certified hardware partners. However, with the TDI approach, which again evolved over the years, you have the flexibility of using different hardware components (e.g., storage, network, and servers) from different vendors to integrate SAP HANA into the client's data center (on-premise or cloud). The components used in a TDI approach are shown in Figure 12.8. Restrictions are applicable, including the requirements to use SAP-certified hardware, storage, and configurations.

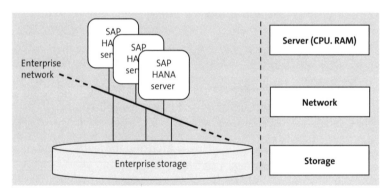

Figure 12.8 Tailored Data Center Integration Components

The TDI model is delivered in the following four phases:

1. **Shared enterprise storage**
   Customers can reuse their enterprise storage solutions for their SAP HANA deployments, but they need to choose from the list of certified storage vendors (found at *http://global.sap.com/community/ebook/2014-09-02-hana-hardware/ enEN/enterprise-storage.html*).

2. **Network**
   A customer can reuse its existing network solution in its enterprise. For example,

the customer can include its networking infrastructure and network components in its data center, such as routers, bridges, and switches for SAP HANA cluster internode and cross-site communication. For network solution guidelines, see SAP Note 1943937 and see SAP HANA TDI—Network Requirements at *https://scn.sap.com/docs/DOC-63221*.

3. **Entry-level SAP HANA E5 systems**

   Customers can choose the following cheaper CPU model: Intel Xeon E5 v2/v3 with more flexibility (restrictions: maximum two sockets, single-node only, with no support for scale-out).

4. **SAP HANA on IBM Power**

   Whereas the preceding option provides support to customers considering alternative hardware with its own processors, SAP HANA on IBM Power is supported only under the TDI model. Currently, the maximum memory (RAM) supported for production are for SAP BW on SAP HANA and SAP BW/4HANA at up to 16 TB RAM/LPAR with the ability to scale-out up to 16 nodes, and for SAP Business Suite on SAP HANA and SAP S/4HANA at up to 24 TB RAM/LPAR with the ability to scale-out up to 4 + 1 nodes (SAP S4/HANA only). Refer to SAP Central Note 2055470. The latest data can be checked at *https://bit.ly/2QKZOzs*.

5. **SAP HANA TDI – workload-driven sizing**

   Till the workload-driven option came in, customers had to use reference configuration with a fixed CPU-RAM ratio. This led to, in most cases, over-estimation of system resources leading to higher hardware cost with less CPU utilization. This option became available from Q3 2017. As of fall 2018, this option is available only for Intel Xeon E7 v4 (Broadwell), v5 (Skylake), and IBM Power 8. Now, the customers can do workload-driven sizing for CPU and memory instead of memory-driven sizing by running a report for SAP Business Suite on HANA or SAP S/4HANA (refer to SAP Note 1872170 – Business Suite on HANA and S/4HANA Sizing Report). For new installations, we can use SAP's Quick Sizer tool. However, note that there are constraints in taking this approach (refer to SAP Notes for recommendations and constraints).

Note

Refer to SAP Notes 2399995 and 2235581 for hardware requirements for SAP HANA 2.0 and for operating systems.

Sizing approach information can be found at *http://bit.ly/2qAhJBR*.

More details on the different options and the corresponding features can be found at *https://scn.sap.com/docs/DOC-63140.*

FOR TDI options and detailed documentation, refer to *http://bit.ly/2OljbMg.*

For a complete FAQ, visit *http://bit.ly/2qOo909.*

12.2.3   Scalability

The SAP HANA database can be scaled up or scaled out, and the technique to apply depends on whether SAP S/4HANA, SAP BW on SAP HANA, or native SAP HANA is running. We'll talk more about this after we explain the underlying concepts.

Until recently, SAP used reference configurations whereby SAP HANA systems required a specific CPU-to-RAM ratio. We'll discuss some examples in the next paragraph (please note that these data are liable to change frequently and it's best to consult the SAP guidelines for sizing). For more information, refer to "Availability and Scalability" of the SAP HANA Administration Guide available on the SAP Help Portal at *https://help.sap.com/viewer/p/SAP_HANA_PLATFORM.*

For SAP Business Suite or SAP S/4HANA, it's 768 GB per socket for the production environment. For the latest CPU model (Broadwell, released by Intel in June 2016), it's 1 TB of RAM per socket, allowing you to reach 8 TB of RAM on an eight-socket server. The CPU-to-RAM ratio for older CPU generations is much lower. The CPU-to-memory ratio as of September 2018 has increased to 1.5 for SAP Business Suite on SAP HANA per socket. Now, the recommendation is to configure 28 cores per socket on SAP HANA-certified Skylake processors 8180(M) and 8176(M). However, these recommendations are continuously changing, based on newer hardware innovations.

Scale-up has a single-host architecture in which a single system is built up from as many resources as feasible.

Specific hardware vendors support specific maximum levels of memory. For example, at the time this book was written, multiple vendors, such as IBM, Lenovo, Cisco, HP, SGI, Fujitsu, and Hitachi, support different levels of scale-up memory.

The scale-out architecture is created by clustering together smaller SAP HANA systems into a cluster database with shared storage, creating a multihost environment.

This architecture is supported in GA for SAP BW on SAP HANA, which supports a different CPU-to-RAM ratio. Because the size of a single server is limited to 4 TB, this was used for SAP Business Suite or SAP S/4HANA applications only for a high-availability configuration until SAP HANA 1.0. However, with SAP HANA 2.0, scale-out is supported in SAP HANA for transaction systems, so this constraint is no longer applicable. High-availability configuration details are covered in the next section.

The scalability of the SAP HANA architecture continues to improve with innovations from vendors such as IBM with IBM Power Systems and its own processors, other hardware companies using Intel processors, and the evolution of the processors themselves. The recommendation is to first scale-up to increase the memory in the single server up to its physical limits and then, for larger systems, scale-out; that is, add more servers in the SAP HANA system.

With SAP HANA 2.0 SPS 00, the scale-out option is now supported for SAP S/4HANA 1610 FPS 01 and beyond for memory scale-out.

Some important recommendations SAP has provided (see SAP Note 2408419) should be followed for the scale-out architecture:

- Dedicate the scale-out hardware to exactly one SAP HANA instance; that is, don't make use of Multiple Components in One System (MCOS) setups in which multiple SAP HANA database instances are installed on the same hardware. The reason for this recommendation is that compared to scale-up, the performance of scale-out systems is even more dependent on the behavior and load on all hardware components, including the storage and internal network components.

- When operating the SAP HANA database in MDC mode, you should only operate a single-tenant database. The reason for this is the same as for the previous recommendation.

- Don't operate multiple SAP applications within one SAP HANA database or within one tenant database (multiple components on one database [MCOD]). The methodology for table grouping and table distribution has been designed for running a single SAP application within the database. If you operate multiple applications within one database, this produces less favorable table grouping/distribution results.

The hardware configurations for the scale-out depend on the vendor and should be checked against the right nodes (e.g., an IBM Power-based node), as follows:

- **Power 8**

  The maximum of 176 cores and 24 TB used by a single SAP HANA (scale-up) must not be exceeded. For analytic workload (e.g., SAP BW), 192 cores and up to 16 TB can be used.

- **Power 9**

  The maximum of 24 cores and 4 TB used by a single SAP HANA 2.0 (scale-up) must not be exceeded. For analytic workload (e.g., SAP BW), up to 1.5 TB can be used. Refer to SAP Note 2188482.

Note

A list of SAP-certified SAP HANA hardware is maintained in the directory at *http://global.sap.com/community/ebook/2014-09-02-hana-hardware/enEN/appliances.html#categories=SoH*.

You can find further information in SAP Notes 2075461 and 1950470.

12.2.4   Recoverability

Recoverability of a database means that in the event of a database failure, the deployment is restored to the point at which the failure occurred. This is one of the most important considerations for a transactional system such as SAP S/4HANA and must be planned for properly.

Because the SAP HANA platform uses most data in-memory for best performance, in the case of a power failure, this data may be lost. However, there is persistent storage as well to protect against such failures. During normal operations, data is stored from the memory to the disk at regular intervals. This creates a *savepoint* (see Figure 12.9). In addition, logs are written for any change in data after each operation. The log data is also saved to the disk after each transaction commit. Therefore, in the case of a power failure, the database can be restarted like any other database and takes into account this log data after the last savepoint. This helps to maintain the database consistency.

Recoverability, in turn, is closely linked to the term *availability*. Availability indicates the operational continuity of the system and is measured as a reverse function of system downtime, expressed as a percentage. There are two other aspects that may be needed for the SAP HANA database in the case of a disk or data center failure: *high availability (HA)* and *disaster recovery (DR)*.

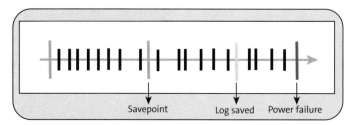

Figure 12.9 Persistence in SAP HANA

SAP states that HA "increases the failure tolerance within one data center by providing a fast switch over to an operational state of the SAP HANA database." HA indicates a set of techniques and plans for business continuity in case of server failure. DR is the process of recovering operations at a different data center after a server failure that is due to a site or data center failure.

There are two key performance indicators (KPIs) associated with recovery:

- **Recovery point objective (RPO)**
  RPO refers to the maximum permissible period during which data may be lost between the last backup and the system crash.

- **Recovery time objective (RTO)**
  RTO refers to the maximum possible time elapsed between the system unavailability and the system being operative again.

The following subsections describe the various options for making a system HA and/or DR. These options have different RPOs, RTOs, and costs.

Backup and Recovery (High Availability/Disaster Recovery)

Backups are necessary for database restoration in case of disk failures, to restore the database to an earlier point in time, or for database copy. Backups need to be made for data and log volumes and can be manual or automated. SAP HANA also synchronizes the data backup across multiple nodes and services without manual intervention. All services that require data to be persisted are backed up. Data backup happens when the database is running, and transactions are stopped only for a very short time when the backup is initiated. There are various options to perform a data and log backup, which can be configured through SAP HANA Studio:

- Backing up to file systems—for example, to a Network File System (NFS) share (SAP Note 1820529).

- Backing up to a third-party backup server through implementation of the Backint for SAP HANA application programming interface (API) by an SAP-certified third-party agent. Refer to SAP Note 2031547 for an overview of SAP-certified third-party backup tools and the associated support process.

- Backing up as a storage snapshot to external storage.

Recovery from these backup options is possible with the following alternatives:

- Recovery to the most recent state using data backup or storage snapshot and using the log backups post for that backup point and entries if still available in the log area.

- Recovery to a specific point in time by using the data backup or storage snapshot from that point in time and the log backups post for that backup point and entries if still available in the log area.

- Recovery using data backup or a storage snapshot at a specific time but without log backups for the time thereafter and without any log entries beyond that point.

During recovery, the SAP HANA database is shut down. The progress and the actions can be initiated and checked using SAP HANA Studio. For this option, the costs are comparatively lower, but it has an RPO greater than zero and a high RTO.

SAP HANA Storage Replication (Disaster Recovery)

This option enables continuous replication of all persisted data, including the data and the redo log of every committed transaction to a remote, networked storage system on a secondary site (see Figure 12.10). Several vendors offer this storage replication option. In some of these SAP-certified solutions, the SAP HANA transaction at the primary site is completed only when the SAP HANA transaction log at the primary site is replicated in the backup site. This is known as *synchronous storage replication* and can occur only if the two sites are within 100 kilometers of each other with a fraction of a millisecond round-trip latency.

If a full system failover is needed, the system administrator attaches a passive system to the secondary storage and ensures that there is no data corruption from both systems writing to the same storage. The SAP HANA system is then restarted to complete the restore process. This mechanism has an advantage over the backup-restore mechanism because RPO is much lower in this case, although there is an additional requirement in terms of network bandwidth and decreased latency between the primary and secondary storage sites. This option has medium costs associated with it with near-zero RPO (zero RPO for synchronous replication) and medium RTO.

The disadvantage of storage replication is that if there is any corruption to persistence for any reason, the corruption is also replicated.

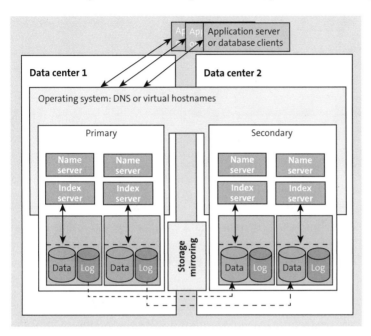

Figure 12.10 Storage Replication

SAP HANA Host Auto-Failover (High Availability)

In this scenario, an existing single-node or scale-out setup is extended by additional server nodes called *standby nodes*. Although SAP HANA supports multiple standby nodes, it's typical for only one additional node to be used. This standby server can take over in case one or more regular hosts become unavailable. If one host fails, the standby host automatically takes over by gaining access to the data and log volumes of the failed host. Thus, the standby server needs access to all the database volumes, which is accomplished by a shared network storage server. Figure 12.11 shows a configuration for host auto-failover.

The standby host is connected to this storage either through a distributed file system or by using vendor-specific solutions via the SAP storage connector API to dynamically detach and mount networked storage when the failure occurs. Note that all services are moved to the standby server when the failover happens at the host server level. This failover happens automatically without any external cluster manager but doesn't happen in the case of a single service failure.

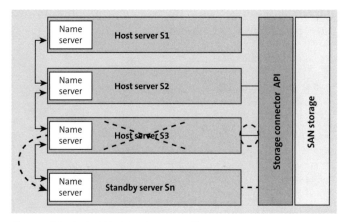

Figure 12.11 SAP HANA Host Auto-Failover

There are some useful techniques to maintain data consistency and to ensure that the primary and standby hosts aren't active at the same time and thus avoid allowing the recovered host and the standby servers to write to the data in parallel.

This option for HA has medium associated costs, zero RPO on committed transactions while in-flight transactions are lost, and medium RTO. RTO depends on the database size as the data needs to be loaded into memory. It's a good option for scale-out systems as it keeps the costs down, and only one additional server (or VM) is required.

SAP HANA System Replication (High Availability/Disaster Recovery)

System replication uses the N + N mode. For every SAP HANA server with N nodes, there is another similar server with the same number of nodes as the secondary. In this setup, the two databases (primary and secondary) can be located close to each other. Alternatively, the secondary database can be at a remote location as a DR option as well, but a reliable link is required between the two sites. The configuration is shown in Figure 12.12.

This option employs the live replication mode. In this mode, the services of the secondary SAP HANA system constantly communicate with that of the primary system, and all the data and logs of every transaction from the primary system are replicated and typically stored in the database in the secondary system with the same system identifier (SID) and instance number. The data commit in the primary system even can be set up to be complete only on persisting this replication log in the secondary system.

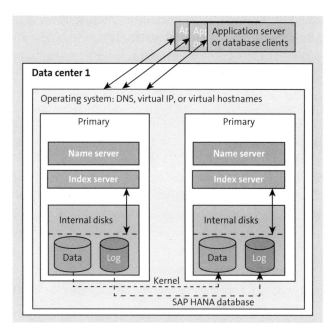

Figure 12.12 SAP HANA System Replication

There are a few options for how the data commit in the primary system can be set up depending on the log transmission and its writing to memory or persisting in storage to be synchronous or asynchronous. The replication modes are as follows:

- **Synchronous**
  The secondary system sends an acknowledgment only after saving/persisting the data. This mode can run with a full sync option, which means that log write is successful when the log buffer has been written to the log file of the primary and the secondary instance. In addition, when the secondary system is disconnected (e.g., because of network failure), the primary system suspends transaction processing until the connection to the secondary system is reestablished. No data loss occurs in this scenario.

- **Synchronous in-memory**
  The secondary system sends an acknowledgement as soon as it receives the data.

- **Asynchronous**
  The primary system doesn't wait for acknowledgement from the secondary system.

Note that synchronous modes are very much dependent on latency. Thus, high latency can seriously impact the performance and therefore should be used only when both databases are connected by low-latency networking.

There are two operation modes for system replication:

- **Delta shipping**

  To avoid ever-growing logs, data snapshots are shared from the primary system to the secondary system at regular intervals. In addition, the primary system shares status information about the column tables stored in the main memory. The secondary system loads these tables into memory. This is called a preload. In the case of a failure, the cluster manager initiates live replication mode in full operation for the secondary server. The secondary system, with preloaded column tables, will only load the row tables and replay the last transaction logs to operate as the primary system.

- **Log replay**

  The secondary system can instantly replay the log, thereby diminishing the delay in takeover to near zero.

The other consideration in this option is about the connections from the database client that are configured to reach the primary server. There are two options for diverting these connections to the secondary server after the failover. SAP NetWeaver connects to SAP HANA via the Database Shared Library (DBSL). One option is to use a virtual IP address to access the database host and the database instance on that host. Alternatively, the Domain Names Service (DNS) can offer virtual hostnames. This HA option has the highest cost but the lowest RTO and RPO.

The main difference between delta shipping and log replay is internal mechanics: Delta shipping sends logs to be saved to disk (not applied to data) and at regular intervals sends deltas of all block changes that happened since the last delta. For recovery, logs need to be replayed. The advantage is the low memory consumption; the secondary system can be used for nonproduction (QA). In log replay, this is different; all logs are applied to the secondary database, thus requiring reduced network traffic between the systems and reducing RTO. However, as the memory requirement is greater, using the secondary system for nonproduction becomes difficult.

For DR, the secondary system or storage must be in a remote location.

For SAP HANA 2.0, this option has received a boost with faster initial load from primary to secondary systems through multiple streaming (up to 32 streams). It also has faster disk to memory with up to 32 threads in parallel load and can have continuous access to business data while the primary system is in restart mode.

Databases with SAP HANA 1.0 SPS 11 and SPS 12 can upgrade to SAP HANA 2.0 directly. However, keep in mind that SAP HANA 1.0 on IBM Power needs to be converted from Little Endian to Big Endian.

An interesting load-balance feature SAP HANA 2.0 brings to the fore is the ability to enable read-intensive operations (say, from an operational report or an analytics dashboard) between a primary and secondary instance of SAP HANA with the active/active-read-enabled mode. There is also now a consolidated log backup file to make it easier for third-party tools to back up data.

> **Note**
>
> All the options for HA/DR have their advantages and disadvantages. More information can be found in SAP Note 2057595 (FAQ: SAP HANA High Availability).
>
> More details on operations mode and the constraints are found in the SAP HANA Admin Guide under **Availability & Scalability** · **Configuring SAP HANA System Replication**.

On-premise deployments of SAP S/4HANA use the standard SAP NetWeaver HA/DR functions. The SAP HANA HA mechanisms along with the SAP NetWeaver ABAP stack's latest features are evolving to provide a zero-downtime maintenance approach.

> **Note**
>
> The detailed steps of the SAP HANA database backup or recovery processes are described in the Technical Operations for SAP NetWeaver found on SAP's website. For SAP S/4HANA release information, go to *http://help.sap.com/s4hana*.

12.2.5   SAP HANA Operations

SAP provides different tools for performing SAP HANA operations such as installation, ongoing maintenance, monitoring, and lifecycle management. Because these tools are for the SAP HANA database, they are applicable for the SAP S/4HANA landscape as well. The main tools are listed here:

- **SAP HANA Studio**
  This tool is used for SAP HANA development and administration and is a favorite of system administrator experts. In future SAP road maps, the other web-based tools are more likely to be continued. Currently, however, SAP HANA Studio complements some of the other tools, such as the SAP HANA cockpit.

- **SAP HANA cockpit**
  A single SAP HANA database is administered and monitored from this web-based cockpit. This cockpit provides an SAP Fiori-like UI that has all the relevant activities or alerts grouped together nicely, as shown in Figure 12.13. This cockpit can be accessed via *http://<host>:<port>/sap/hana/admin/cockpit*.

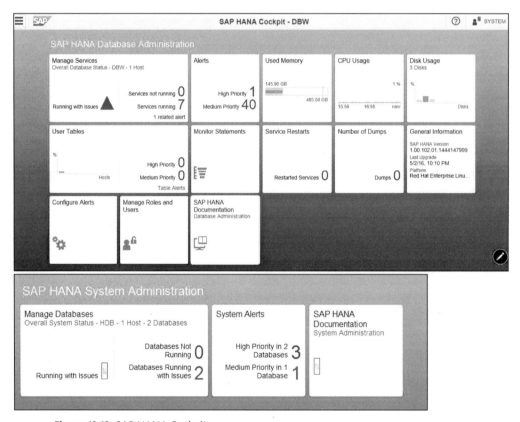

Figure 12.13 SAP HANA Cockpit

This cockpit provides basic administration and monitoring capabilities but also provides additional capabilities in terms of managing multitenant instances, including availability, resource usage, and performance for tenant databases. Each tenant database can be started, stopped, and deleted, and information about usage and alerts is also provided. The cockpit enables you to analyze the database status, including CPU usage and memory consumption for each service, as well as analysis of crash dumps. You can also configure and monitor various alerts as part of the Alerts SAP Fiori apps in the SAP Fiori launchpad.

The cockpit also provides options to perform additional activities if optional components are installed, such as SAP DB Control Center.

- **SAP DB Control Center**
  This web-based tool is used for monitoring the entire landscape of databases, including SAP HANA. This provides an overall status for the different databases in terms of their health, performance, availability, and capacity. It provides alert mechanisms as well for each system. As mentioned earlier, this tool can be accessed from the SAP HANA cockpit also.

- **SAP Solution Manager**
  SAP Solution Manager is now an essential part of the SAP landscape in all project phases. SAP Solution Manager provides a multitude of functions in the entire system landscape management and monitoring area. There are several resources for usage and configuration of SAP Solution Manager available from SAP. SAP Solution Manager 7.2 provides support for the SAP Activate methodology (covered in Chapter 16) for the SAP S/4HANA solution implementation.

  SAP Solution Manager 7.1 and beyond provides specific monitoring for SAP HANA. Various support packs have added functionality around SAP HANA monitoring as well. The big jump, of course, is in SAP Solution Manager 7.2, which is required for the proper usage of the SAP Activate methodology (see Chapter 16 for more details) for an SAP S/4HANA implementation. SAP Solution Manager 7.2 provides an SAP Fiori UX, following SAP's uniform UI strategy.

  SAP Solution Manager supports SAP HANA in all phases of the application management lifecycle (depending on the SAP Solution Manager version), including the following major functions:

12

- **Build SAP Like a Factory**
  - Central transport mechanism and change control
  - End-to-end test management with a central test plan
  - End-to-end solution documentation, including support for SAP Activate
- **Run SAP Like a Factory**
  - Database administration
  - End-to-end root-cause analysis
  - System monitoring
  - Monitoring of all core operations entities
- **Continuous quality checks (CQCs)**
  - During build, implementation, and configuration checks
  - During run and SAP EarlyWatch Alert
  - Best practices—for example, configuration, performance/sizing, and troubleshooting

Focused Insights for SAP Solution Manager also helps to do analysis through data that is collected, correlated, and analyzed. These insights are organized in three levels: operation, governance, and strategic. The strategic level is for the CXOs or executives and can show an IT scorecard containing quality of service, business continuity, service efficiency, and service capacity. In addition, it includes application performance against target service levels. The governance level is for the IT managers and can be used to show service level reporting, monitor and obtain best practice reports for KPIs, and track project progress. The operational level is for the experts and has the operations control center to display data in various granularities with drilldown capability (to do root-cause analysis), real-time status setup based on alerts, and so on.

Figure 12.14 and Figure 12.15 show how SAP HANA system monitoring can be performed from SAP Solution Manager and an SAP EarlyWatch Report generated from SAP Solution Manager. After you open the SAP Solution Manager work centers (run Transaction SM_Workcenter in SAP Solution Manager, in which all the technical monitoring has been configured), and go to the **Technical Monitoring** tab, you'll see the alert inbox, from which you can choose different types of alerts. In this case, the **Database Alerts** have been chosen. Similarly, from the **Technical Monitoring** tab, you can choose **Automated Reporting** to see the SAP EarlyWatch Alert report. You can choose the report for a solution run for a date or date range and see the detailed report as shown in Figure 12.15.

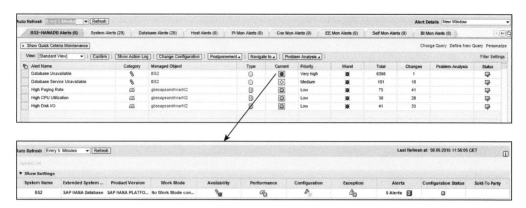

Figure 12.14 Alert Status in SAP Solution Manager

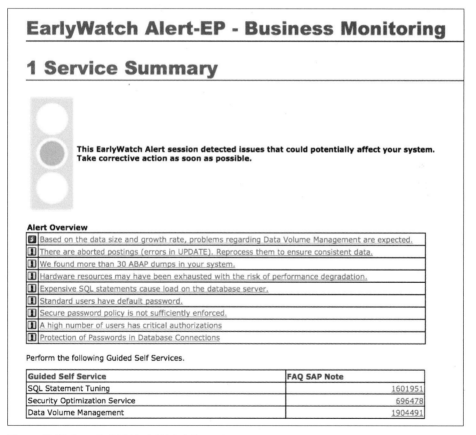

Figure 12.15 Sample SAP EarlyWatch Report

Technical monitoring is used during the run phase, for which SAP has provided many configurable KPIs for each of the SAP HANA databases in the landscape. Some examples are shown in Figure 12.16. In the SAP Solution Manager work centers, under the **Technical Monitoring** tab, choose **System Monitoring** to see a list of databases you can monitor. Choose the SAP HANA database to monitor, and it will show up on the following monitoring screen, along with the details, based on the KPIs configured.

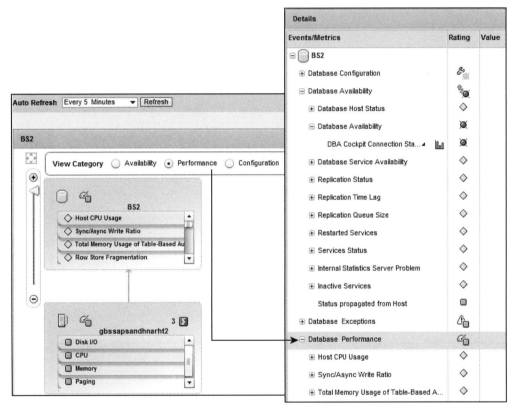

Figure 12.16 Technical Monitoring: SAP HANA Technical KPIs

SAP Solution Manager can be used to do end-to-end business process monitoring. There are a host of possible operations with business process monitoring that are available as apps under the SAP Fiori launchpad **Business Process Monitoring** tile, as shown in Figure 12.17.

Let's deep dive into some of the specifics of business process monitoring, as shown in Figure 12.18.

Figure 12.17 Business Process Monitoring in the SAP Fiori Launchpad

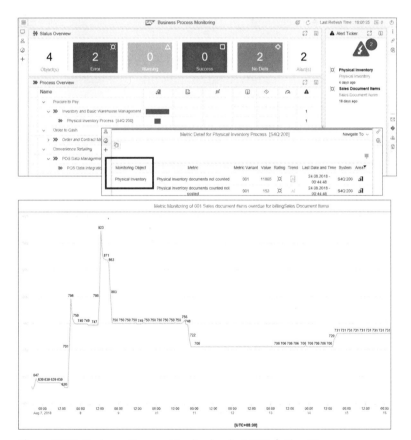

Figure 12.18 Business Process Monitoring in SAP Solution Manager

Several scenarios have been set up for monitoring, including the monitoring object. For example, in **Procure to Pay · Inventory and Basic Warehouse Management · Physical Inventory Process**, physical inventory is the monitoring object, whereas under **Order to Cash · Order and Contract Management · Sales Documents**, items overdue is being monitored. There are some alerts coming from the **Physical Inventory** process. Also, we can see the metric monitoring of the KPI set. For example, in Figure 12.18, metric monitoring of **Sales document item overdue for billing** is shown as a time graph.

- **SAP Landscape Management**
  This tool, which is used to simplify and automate centralized management and operations of SAP systems in both the physical and virtualized infrastructures, supports SAP S/4HANA provisioning and management (SAP Landscape Management 3.0 SP 07 as of Q3 2018). You can access the SAP DB Control Center and cockpit via SAP Landscape Management. Mass operations for multiple systems/instances can be performed through SAP Landscape Management, including support for system dependencies. The key features of this tool are the following:
  - SAP system clone, copy, refresh, and rename framework
  - Automatic sync between two SAP Landscape Management systems for multisite setups
  - System replication operations for SAP HANA
  - End-to-end monitoring of SAP systems and infrastructures
  - Visualization of the entire system landscape
  - Intersystem dependency framework
  - Single system and mass operations (e.g., starting and stopping)
  - Template based execution for operations
  - Scheduling operation and provisioning templates
  - Relocating systems from one host to another
  - User-configurable dashboards
  - Reporting
  - Application server installation and uninstallation
  - Diagnostics agent installation and uninstallation
  - Custom instances, operations, and hooks

Companies that provide virtualization capabilities use similar tools for fast provisioning of instances and operations.

With SAP HANA 2.0, the SAP HANA cockpit has become the most important tool for simplified enterprise-wide administration and monitoring for multiple SAP HANA databases because it can monitor multiple KPIs in one view. It also has simplified configuration of HA/DR options, such as the system replication setup. Other improved functions include detailed information about system crashes and thread execution and better user and role administration.

12.2.6 SAP HANA Logical Deployment Options

There are several logical deployment options for the SAP HANA database, such as the MCOD, MCOS, and MDCs scenarios. The steps for choosing the right deployment option need to be planned in advance for any SAP HANA implementation and need to take into account the support scenarios for that option as described in the various relevant SAP Notes.

In the following list, we'll look at each scenario in turn:

- **MCOD**
  This option entails multiple SAP HANA applications running on a single SAP HANA database, as shown in Figure 12.19. SAP supports this option in the productive environment for those packaged applications and scenarios listed in the whitelist for SAP S/4HANA included in SAP Note 2248291. For example, SAP MDG can be deployed with SAP S/4HANA 1511 (for SAP S/4HANA 1610 onwards, SAP MDG is embedded in SAP S/4HANA) in the same schema and supporting access to the same data sources.

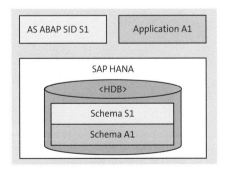

Figure 12.19 MCOD Scenario

The disadvantages in this scenario are as follows:

- SAP HANA can't execute backup on a smaller than database-level scale. Thus, it's not possible to back up data sets separately for each of the applications deployed. If data restoration is required, both data sets must be recovered to the same point.
- It's not possible to control performance on the data set level.

These same features can be advantageous for the following scenarios:

- If two data sets are closely related, and consistency between the two data sets is a must, this consistency is enforced implicitly; thus, the first point in the preceding list becomes an advantage.
- If there are "intensive" joins between the two data sets, then MCOD might lead to much better performance because both data sets are sharing the same processes and no cross-process data transfers are required.

- **MCOS**

  In this option, multiple SIDs are on a single SAP HANA hardware unit, as shown in Figure 12.20. Per SAP Note 1681092, this deployment is supported for production systems only for a single host or scale-up scenario. Earlier, support was only offered for nonproductive systems; now, production support for MCOS is valid for SPS 90 or higher in both single-node and scale-out scenarios (per SAP Note 2408419).

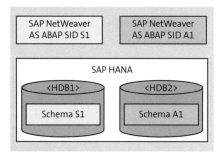

Figure 12.20 MCOS Scenario

- **MDC**

  This feature has been available in SAP HANA since SPS 09 and allows multiple, isolated instances of the application to be hosted in a single SAP HANA system. In this scenario, there is a central database used for system administration and one or more MDCs, called *tenant databases*. These tenant databases have their own parameters, backup/restore setups, and separate user management and application data. This configuration is illustrated in Figure 12.21.

The administration layer for the central database or system database contains the landscape topology information, system-wide parameter settings, and resource management for all tenant databases, including CPU and memory, as well as owning the complete backup of all databases. Although MDC supports the tenant databases being spread across multiple nodes in a scale-out scenario (refer to Section 12.2.3), current constraints (which can be found in SAP Note 2408419) make it possible for SAP S/4HANA to be deployed only in a single node in an MDC system. SAP Notes 2096000 and 2104291 are relevant for this feature.

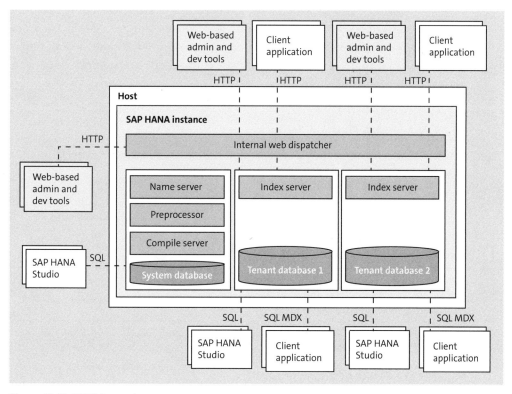

Figure 12.21 MDC Scenario

In all of these options, there are certain considerations with respect to the sizing of the overall hardware. For MDC, for example, the recommendation is to size each of the applications and then use additive sizing for the overall system. MDC is a new technology, so a practical approach needs to be taken by installing a few applications and carefully monitoring their resource utilization and performance before proceeding to further deployments. The same additive sizing approach needs to be taken for other scenarios as well, such as MCOD.

Furthermore, the potential impact on performance of applications on each other needs to be taken into consideration while planning. Plans for proper stress and volume testing need to be made before going live to monitor performance in each of these scenarios. For an MCOS scenario, SAP recommends using the resource management features of SAP HANA, such as parameters controlling memory limits, influencing CPU utilization, and so on.

With SAP HANA 2.0 SPS 01, MDC has become the only standard and only operation mode (see SAP Note 2423367), so you can't use a single-container system. For a new installation or an upgrade, the multi-container mode will have one default tenant database (for an upgrade, this tenant database corresponds to the single container of the earlier version).

12.2.7 SAP HANA Platform Services

The SAP HANA platform provides several built-in services, as depicted in Figure 12.22.

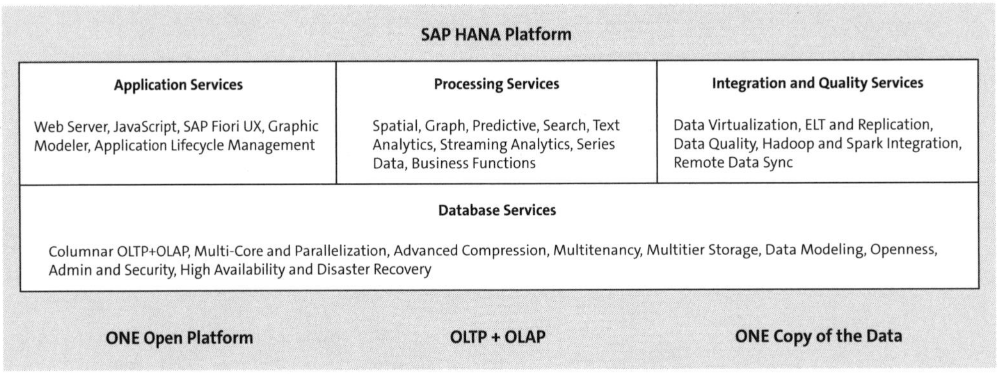

SAP HANA Platform		
Application Services	**Processing Services**	**Integration and Quality Services**
Web Server, JavaScript, SAP Fiori UX, Graphic Modeler, Application Lifecycle Management	Spatial, Graph, Predictive, Search, Text Analytics, Streaming Analytics, Series Data, Business Functions	Data Virtualization, ELT and Replication, Data Quality, Hadoop and Spark Integration, Remote Data Sync
Database Services		
Columnar OLTP+OLAP, Multi-Core and Parallelization, Advanced Compression, Multitenancy, Multitier Storage, Data Modeling, Openness, Admin and Security, High Availability and Disaster Recovery		
ONE Open Platform	**OLTP + OLAP**	**ONE Copy of the Data**

Figure 12.22 SAP HANA Platform Capabilities

Let's walk through each of the categories of the SAP HANA platform services:

- **Application services**
  One of the remarkable aspects of the SAP HANA platform services is that they enable coexistence of the web server and the database in the same system, reducing

data movements. These services provide built-in tools to develop, version control, bundle, transport, and install applications. In addition, there are options to use application servers and web servers with JavaScript support and HTML5 UI libraries, which enable deployment of SAPUI5-based UIs. These application services support several open development standards such as SQL, HTML5, JavaScript, Java Database Connectivity (JDBC), Open Database Connectivity (ODBC), and JavaScript Object Notation (JSON) using Eclipse-based or web-based development environments. They also support OData services, which are RESTful APIs following open protocols.

- **Processing services**
  These services enable applications dealing with different data types and vastly differing data characteristics. The services can include text analytics, predictive analytics using the Predictive Analytics Library (PAL) or integrating with the R library, search, and so on. They have a spatial engine that stores spatial data in ways similar to those used for other data types, that works on the different types of spatial data with spatial functions such as area, that leverages geo content such as maps, and that integrates with external geo-coding services because they support open standards compliance (Open Geospatial Consortium).

- **Integration and quality services**
  These services support data replication and data access from various types of database and file systems, both on-premise and in the cloud. Live data streams can be captured to help in adopting IoT scenarios and for analysis of IoT data. Connection to Hadoop through various means (e.g., Spark, Hive, HDFS, and MapReduce) is possible through the integration services. In addition, the integration services enable querying any other data sources, such as IBM DB2, Netezza, Oracle, Microsoft SQL Server, Teradata, SAP HANA, SAP Adaptive Server Enterprise (SAP ASE), and SAP IQ through SAP HANA smart data integration or SAP HANA smart data access.

- **Database services**
  These services leverage the capabilities of the SAP HANA database's following core features:

  - As an RDBMS database, it supports atomicity, consistency, isolation, and durability (ACID) transactions.

  - OLTP and OLAP data handling enables running transactions and real-time operational reporting on the same set of data on the same system.

  - Complex query handling is possible for huge amounts of data without the need for database tuning or aggregation.

12

- Queries are handled at high speeds without the need for indices.

- Multiprocessing of data allows the same operation to be performed across multiple data points.

- The database supports nonuniform memory access (NUMA), which means that the CPU processes its own memory faster than remote memory. This optimization helps support large nodes and supports several types of deployment models, as was covered in Section 12.2.6.

- Data modeling is supported.

- Data is accessible through open standards such as JDBC, ODBC, JSON, and OData.

- The standard security model is supported.

- Third-party administration tools can be used.

- The SAP HANA database supports various kinds of data lifecycle management. One is dynamic tiering of data in which data is stored based on usage, in memory, in disk, or in an archiving tool such as SAP IQ. The other is data aging. Data aging is available at an application level for SAP ERP Financials (FI) documents, Universal Journal entries, and material documents in SAP S/4HANA 1511. More information on data lifecycle management is provided in Section 12.6.

There have been some changes to the development features or tools of the SAP HANA platform. Some of the key changes are as follows:

- **SAP Enterprise Architecture Designer**
  This is a tool available as of SAP HANA 2.0 SP 00 that can be used to create business process diagrams (via Business Process Model Notation [BPMN] 2.0), physical data models representing database and generation, enterprise architecture diagrams, process maps, and requirements lists. This helps system architects capture, analyze, and present the organization's landscapes, strategies, requirements, processes, data, and other artifacts in a shared environment.

- **SAP Web IDE**
  The SAP Web IDE now supports GitHub features, HTML5-based module templates, and several enhanced SAP HANA tools.

- **Hierarchy functions under SAP HANA, spatial edition**
  SAP HANA provides a public hierarchy SQL interface with table functions of hierarchy generation and navigation.

- **Search, text analysis, and text mining**

  There are several functions available from SAP HANA 2.0 in these areas. For example, search rules can run in batch-processing mode, with functions to perform comparisons between two sets of data, dynamic search rule sets, data filtration on date-type fields, and similarity calculation with fuzzy search. The Text Analysis SQL API enables text analysis functions to be performed on any inputs, even beyond data stored in the SAP HANA database.

- **SAP HANA External Machine Learning (EML) Library**

  This is a new application function library (AFL) introduced in SAP HANA 2.0 SPS 02 to support the integration of Google TensorFlow with SAP HANA. The EML Library makes use of the open-source gRPC remote procedure call package to call predefined TensorFlow models remotely that have open-source libraries for machine learning.

> **Note**
>
> Dynamic tiering isn't generally supported for SAP Business Suite on SAP HANA or for SAP S/4HANA as of SAP HANA SPS 12 (the central note for dynamic tiering is SAP Note 2563560).

12.3   SAP S/4HANA Security

The security strategy for SAP S/4HANA should be part of the overall landscape security strategy, including authentication and authorization. This includes user provisioning with the correct roles so that the right users can perform their relevant tasks and have the option to access systems through single sign-on (SSO). There also needs to be audit logging so that a trace is available for critical user actions. Other aspects of security include encryption, network security, data center security certifications, General Data Protection Regulation (GDPR) compliance, and more.

The SAP HANA platform provides unified security options from both the database perspective and the analytics engine perspective, as shown in Figure 12.23.

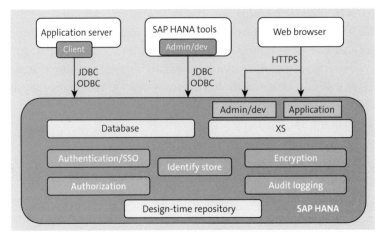

Figure 12.23 SAP HANA Security Model

The key security functions of the SAP HANA database are as follows:

- **Authentication and SSO**
  SAP HANA supports basic authentication using a username and password for both types of access, either through JDBC/ODBC access from the application server to the SAP HANA database or through HTTP access used by web clients directly talking to the SAP HANA extended application services (XS) engine.

  SSO can be set using various means that are typically used in SAP environments, such as Kerberos, Security Assertion Markup Language (SAML), SAP Logon and assertion tickets, and security certificates (e.g., X.509), depending on the access through web clients, GUI clients, and so on.

- **User and role management through the identity store**
  For logon, users must exist in the identity store of the SAP HANA database. Roles and privileges can be assigned to users and can be catalog or repository roles.

- **SAP HANA authorization**
  This can include the following privileges:
  - Database access privileges
  - Application privileges
  - Repository privileges

- **Encryption**
  Encryption can be at the communication, data, or data backup level:

- Data volume encryption is used to encrypt the data persisted in the database. However, when data is loaded in memory, it's decrypted. Thus, the data in memory isn't encrypted.
- For certain applications that need encryption as part of security from an application perspective, the internal encryption service is available—for example, for storing credentials used by SAP HANA for outbound interfaces.
- A Secure Store in File System (SSFS) instance is used to securely store internal root keys in the file systems.
- With SAP HANA 2.0, additional encryption capability is provided for full native data at rest, including redo logs, dynamic tiering data, and more. There is also enhanced encryption key management, which enables changing the root key of the application encryption service used.

- **Audit logging**
  This includes logging of critical events for security and compliance—for example:

  - User, role, and privilege changes and configuration changes
  - Data access logging
  - Read and write access (tables, views) and execution of procedures
  - Firefighter logging—for example, for support cases

On-premise deployments of SAP S/4HANA generally rely on the user management and authentication mechanisms provided with the SAP NetWeaver platform—specifically, SAP NetWeaver AS ABAP and the SAP HANA platform. Therefore, the security recommendations and guidelines for user administration and authentication as described in the SAP NetWeaver AS ABAP Security Guide and SAP HANA platform also apply to SAP S/4HANA.

A few example scenarios and the type of permissions required in each case are shown in Figure 12.24.

The following are some examples of user provisioning for the different layers of the application:

- **SAP Fiori apps—usability layer**
  These apps require user provisioning in the frontend server as well as the backend server. User provisioning for the SAP Fiori apps is performed manually in SAP Gateway, and the corresponding frontend roles are assigned. Depending on the type of SAP Fiori apps used, the roles need to be assigned in the ABAP frontend, ABAP backend, and SAP HANA database.

- **SAP S/4HANA—application layer**
  User master data and roles are created in SAP S/4HANA for the end users and IT team. Role assignment needs to be performed for the users. Authorizations will be provided to users based on the job roles they'll perform in the organization.

- **SAP HANA database—database layer**
  The user provisioning for the SAP HANA database will be carried out manually. As for the SAP Fiori apps (analytical app and fact sheets app), users may need access (privileges) in the SAP HANA database, depending on the configuration requirements of the specific SAP Fiori apps.

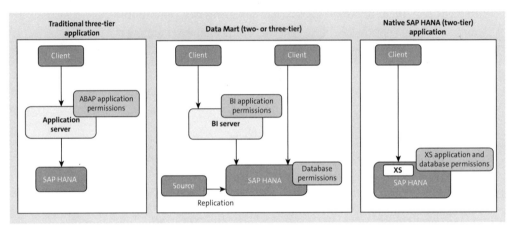

Figure 12.24 SAP HANA User Scenarios

With SAP HANA 2.0, there is now a provision to manage authorization through Lightweight Directory Access Protocol (LDAP) groups. In addition, there are additional authentication and user-management capabilities for SAP HANA extended application services, advanced model (XSA) scenarios, such as application-to-application SSO.

An important change that has been brought in is to cater to GDPR compliance. This new GDPR of the EEA (EU + Iceland, Liechtenstein, Norway) applies to all organizations that process personal data of EEA and UK individuals regardless of where the organization is located. The law has been in force from May 25, 2018. As an outcome of this law, reading/writing/changing/storing of personal data requires specific handling and impacts IT applications. Thus, to cater to GDPR compliance, some functionalities need to be included in each SAP product:

- Ability to identify and report data, including personal data and system-inherent consent management
- Improved data retention and deletion functionalities
- Product-specific technical and organizational security measures

The last includes logging, specific role logic and rights logic, encryption, and data masking, which may assist you in maintaining appropriate security to protect personal data.

> **Note**
>
> As of SAP S/4HANA 1709 FPS 02, changes are included to handle these special considerations. However, for existing SAP S/4HANA clients to avoid upgrades, they need to refer to SAP Note 2590321 (*https://bit.ly/2JgsUs9*). This note covers links for the help documentation for all the steps/actions to be taken for each of the SAP components.

12.4   SAP S/4HANA Core Data Models

When SAP S/4HANA was first introduced, it included SAP S/4HANA Finance (then known as SAP Simple Finance) module with a new code base. With SAP S/4HANA 1511, the new code base has extended to cover several business processes in logistics and operations. The new code base was on top of the simplified data models, which had removed the redundant data in terms of the aggregate tables. This simplification of the data models continued with SAP S/4HANA 1610, including changes in the sales and distribution (SD) area.

Before SAP HANA came into the picture, aggregate tables such as table BSEG and table BKPF were required to have faster reporting. Database operations were more complex because every time the transactional tables (headers, items, and sometimes subitems) were updated, these aggregate tables had to be updated, too. The design of the data model was to boost the performance of the reports while aggregating this data during reporting, which could leverage the aggregate tables instead of the detailed transactional tables.

Now, with the advent of SAP HANA, creating this aggregation in runtime is fast and easy. This simplification is leveraged in the data models that now do away with many of the tables and have a consolidated table for each major area, such as financials and logistics (see Chapter 2 through Chapter 7).

This simplified data model has quite an impact on the database size as the data volume to be persisted diminishes. There is an impact on custom code as well. The migration effects are discussed in Chapter 15. From an implementation perspective, when writing any custom code, you need to consider mapping the fields from the new combined table, such as table ACDOCA in finance or table MATDOC for material documents, instead of using multiple tables as were used earlier. There are additional considerations in terms of using CDS views or generating CDS views using the Business Function Library (BFL) for functions implemented on the SAP HANA database layer.

Note

For details about custom-coding aspects, visit *http://bit.ly/2k3H5I5.*

12.5   User Interface and User Experience

We've mentioned that SAP S/4HANA acts as the digital core for your business; one of the premises of being the digital core is to have processes be user-centric and accessible through intuitive UIs. This is made possible using *SAP Fiori apps*, which are SAPUI5 applications built on HTML5 technology (primarily) that can be rendered in any browser on any device—mobile, tablet, or desktop. These applications provide an intuitive UI and a seamless UX for business processes that otherwise would have required clicking through several screens of one or more transactions. SAP has also introduced SAP CoPilot, which uses machine learning to provide further enrichment in UX through intelligent assistance. More details about SAP CoPilot can be found in Chapter 10.

The focus of the SAP Fiori apps is to provide an improved UX through the following traits:

- Role-based UIs (the SAP Fiori launchpad can present apps as *tiles*, organized based on a user's role)
- Responsive framework (themes, personalized menus)
- Simplified UI for business processes
- Intuitive interactions

SAP provides a standard set of SAP Fiori apps on various platforms, but most require the SAP HANA database. SAP Fiori apps currently have three main business functions:

- **Transactional apps**

  For transactional processing (for the SAP HANA database or any other database).

- **Analytical apps**

  For analytical capabilities, including dashboards for KPI analytics (only for the SAP HANA database).

- **Fact sheet apps**

  For searching structured or unstructured data, including contextual navigation between related objects (requires the SAP HANA database).

Consult SAP's website for a list of all the SAP Fiori apps currently available. SAP has also published a detailed SAP Fiori road map for SAP S/4HANA and for SAP S/4HANA Cloud.

Figure 12.25 shows how SAP Fiori apps can be accessed through the SAP Fiori apps reference library (*www.sap.com/fiori-apps-library*). The set of SAP Fiori apps can be filtered by different criteria, one of which is product version. Within the set of SAP Fiori apps for a product version, the apps are also grouped by user role, as shown in Figure 12.25.

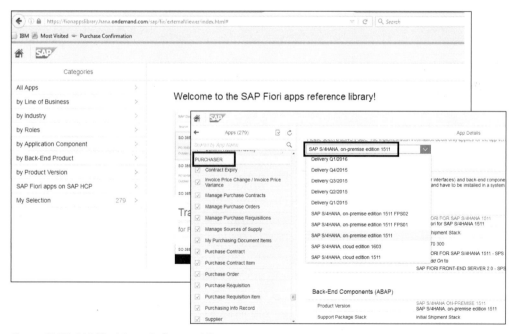

Figure 12.25 SAP Fiori Apps Reference Library

The product features and the details of the technical implementation are provided for each SAP Fiori app selected, as shown in Figure 12.26.

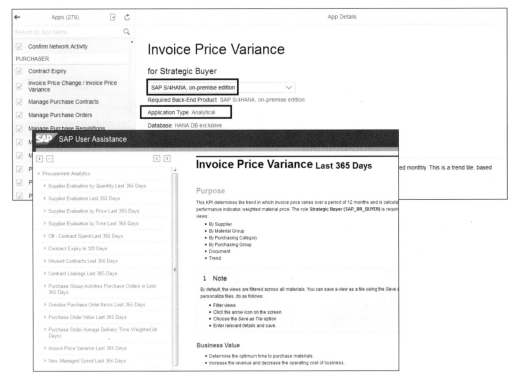

Figure 12.26 SAP Fiori App Details

SAP has created the standard SAP Fiori apps with user-centric designs, and they all can be accessed through the SAP Fiori launchpad. An SAP Fiori app, when accessed from the UI through the SAP Fiori launchpad or through a URL, retrieves data using OData services, which expose the backend data. The OData services are RESTful APIs generated by the SAP Gateway server from the backend Business Application Programming Interfaces (BAPIs) or function modules. A RESTful API is a web service API that follows the Representational State Transfer (REST) architectural style, which follows a few architectural constraints, such as stateless, client/server-based, uniform interface, and so on.

Now, with the advent of SAP Fiori Cloud, the SAP Fiori launchpad and the frontend components can be hosted in the cloud on SAP Cloud Platform. Extensions to these standard SAP Fiori apps can be made through the SAP Cloud Platform. The SAP Gateway component can still be on-premise or hosted in the cloud via SAP Cloud Platform. A subset of SAP Fiori apps is currently available within SAP Fiori Cloud.

The architecture of an SAP Fiori app, with SAP S/4HANA as the underlying application layer, is shown in Figure 12.27.

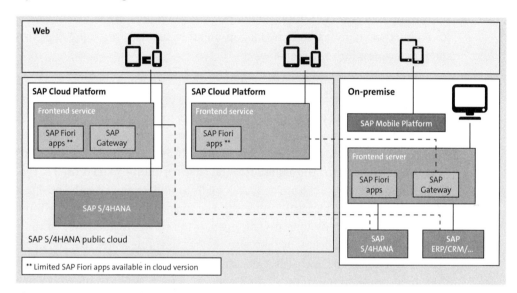

Figure 12.27 SAP Fiori Architecture

With SAP Fiori 2.0, the UX has been improved further. The user can see three areas on the screen after logging in to the SAP Fiori launchpad:

- **Notifications**
  Action items pertaining to that user in that specific role are displayed.
- **Me area**
  User details are provided, including favorites or commonly used apps/app finder.
- **Viewport**
  The main content is displayed in the middle of the screen.

12.6 Data Lifecycle Management

Managing data well now plays an even more important part than before because SAP HANA database costs are higher and scalability has limitations, as mentioned earlier.

In addition, business requirements don't call for availability of all data for all time periods in the main memory of SAP HANA.

There are three options for data management:

- To minimize data in SAP HANA through archiving, move data to an external store that can serve as an archiving solution, such as SAP IQ.

- For certain use cases, the data need not be stored in SAP HANA at all but can be stored in other solutions, such as Hadoop, and then accessed through SAP HANA smart data access into SAP HANA.

- For data in SAP HANA, the options for data management are as follows:
  - *Data aging*: This is a concept in SAP HANA that governs data through aging via two concepts—data resident time and business rules. Although this option is available to several technical objects, such as IDocs, application logs, workflows, and so on, few business objects in SAP S/4HANA Finance support this feature. Data aging is achieved through horizontal table partitioning and is used to separate hot data (current) from cold data (old). To understand how the business rules play a part in this partitioning, think of finance documents that are more than three months old but are still open. If the resident time is set to three months for these documents, because the business rule states that the document status can't be open, these documents can't be moved to the "cold" area. From a data-access perspective, this division is transparent to the user when viewed from an SAP Fiori app, for instance.
  - *Dynamic data tiering*: This is more relevant for the business warehousing or analytical use cases. Here, data is again divided based on usage into the following:
    - Hot data in memory.
    - Warm data stored in/accessed from disk.
    - Extended disk-based columnar tables.
    - Multistore tables. With SAP HANA 2.0, there is another type of database table, apart from the extended table—the multistore table. This table is a multipartitioned SAP HANA columnar table in which one part of the data remains in SAP HANA memory while the other part resides in the extended storage for the dynamic tiering.

For SAP Business Suite on SAP HANA or SAP S/4HANA, data aging is expected to play an important role as the number of business objects supported gradually increases.

However, the data aging framework of the SAP Business Suite and SAP S/4HANA currently doesn't support using dynamic tiering. Individual applications of the SAP Business Suite family may support dynamic tiering in an application-specific way. You'll need to refer to the respective application documentation to find the details.

Dynamic tiering requires an additional license. SAP HANA dynamic tiering provides the ability to create and process disk-based, columnar database tables known as extended tables, in addition to the traditional column- or row-oriented in-memory tables of the SAP HANA database. Similar to in-memory tables, extended tables are first-class database objects with full ACID compliance. All database requests regarding extended tables are integrated into SAP HANA's transactional context. Dynamic tiering is embedded into most SAP HANA operational processes, such as standby setup and backup and recovery.

Some interesting features have been released with SAP HANA 2.0. For example, in the system replication modes (synchronous/asynchronous), certain configurations are supported for two- or three-tier replications. Two-tier system replication has one secondary system per one primary system. For backup/recovery, a certain portion of the memory is reserved for log threshold. In the virtualization, SAP HANA dynamic tiering can also be virtualized by co-deploying in the same VM. The query performance for cross-store data sets has been enhanced by caching the data set resulting from the join between the data from the in-memory and dynamic tiering tables and reusing this cached data. See SAP Note 2298303 (SAP HANA dynamic tiering 2.0 SP 02 release note or later) for more details.

12.7   Development and Operations

Because SAP S/4HANA is quickly becoming the digital core of a modern enterprise, leveraging *development and operations* (coined as DevOps) is a key imperative. The key tenets behind the philosophy of DevOps, as represented in Figure 12.28, are as follows:

- Breaking down the silos between different teams and functions (e.g., LoBs, development teams, infrastructure teams, quality teams, etc.) to minimize handoffs among them, thereby improving efficiency, reducing loss of information, and increasing speed of delivery
- Increasing automation of activities across the software development lifecycle to increase speed and reduce errors

- Gathering and acting on feedback from both internal and external stakeholders to continuously improve and adapt rapidly to changes

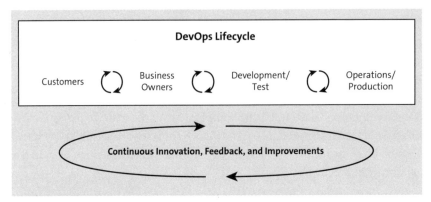

Figure 12.28 How DevOps Operates

Figure 12.29 shows that continuous business process planning results in new requirements, continuous development and testing, releasing/deployment, monitoring, and feedback, which again triggers business process planning, all running in continuous cycles.

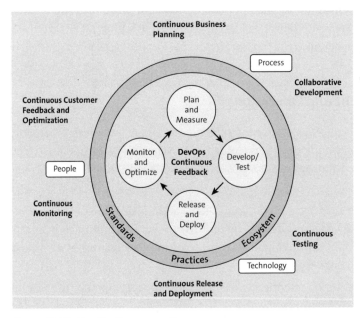

Figure 12.29 Continuity among Processes

If we translate this to the SAP S/4HANA world, the process model ideally should be generated automatically from requirements. From the process models, there can be automated creation of business process hierarchies, automation in coding, and automatic generation of test scenarios and test scripts. Finally, there should be automated monitoring of the business process after it's live, and the feedback for any additional requirements should flow back to the original requirements—and the cycle starts again. Thus, there's a need to have continuous *everything* and as much automation as possible in each of the phases. In the ABAP world, not all these processes and automations are seamless, and a single tool can't provide all solutions. SAP Solution Manager and its new component, Focused Build for SAP Solution Manager, helps with many of the steps, including integration with testing tools or process model generation tools.

Like all new SAP products, Focused Build for SAP Solution Manager has an SAP Fiori-based interface that is role-based and shows the relevant information in the tiles depending on the user's role. A sample cockpit is shown in Figure 12.30, along with the readiness dashboard, which provides real-time information about the status of every aspect of the project.

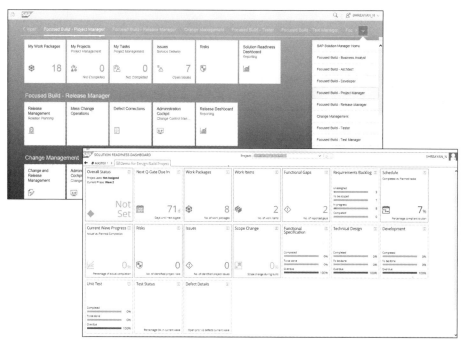

Figure 12.30 Focused Build Cockpit on SAP Solution Manager 7.2

Now, let's describe briefly how the DevOps phases mentioned earlier in Figure 12.29 are supported in SAP Solution Manager:

- **Continuous business planning**

  SAP Solution Manager 7.2-based requirements management or SAP Solution Manager 7.2's Focused Build project management for agile methodology caters to this need (see Figure 12.31). At this phase of the project, the SAP Activate methodology, with its prebuilt content, acts as an accelerator.

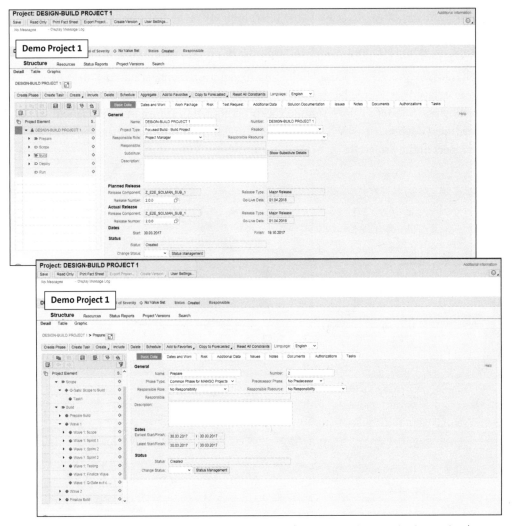

Figure 12.31 Focused Build: Sample Agile Project (Leveraging the Standard Template)

- **Collaborative development**
  This is possible through SAP Solution Manager's custom code lifecycle management or through SAP Cloud Platform, which provides a collaborative environment. One of the key areas for SAP S/4HANA is to use SAP Cloud Platform as the platform for extension (covered in Chapter 13).

- **Continuous testing**
  There are several tools for continuous testing, including SAP Solution Manager–based automated testing and third-party tools such as Worksoft, Panaya, and SmartShift. Defect management can be handled through SAP Solution Manager or through other tools, such as the HP Quality Center.

- **Continuous release and deployment**
  SAP Solution Manager's Change Request Management (ChaRM) tool can be configured to handle this. ChaRM can be integrated with the work packages defined in Focused Build for SAP Solution Manager if it's been set up for the requirements-gathering phase. Some automation in deployment can be achieved through advanced functions in the SAP HANA cockpit, as well as through various virtualization tools for environment provisioning.

- **Continuous monitoring**
  This is addressed through SAP Solution Manager's KPI monitoring, as well as through technical monitoring and business process monitoring (as explained earlier in Section 12.2.5).

- **Continuous customer feedback and optimization**
  This also can be handled through standard SAP Solution Manager features, including incident management and business KPI monitoring through business processing monitoring.

Now, let's look at how SAP Cloud Platform supports DevOps through its features, functions, and integrations. Some services in SAP Cloud Platform serve as extension platforms for SAP S/4HANA and for SAP SaaS solutions such as SAP SuccessFactors (discussed further in Chapter 13). These services and tools provide support for DevOps in this platform (see Figure 12.32). The GitHub repository serves as a source code versioning tool for Java, SAP HANA XS, SAPUI5, and SAP HANA models. Users will use the SAP Web IDE to set up a project and add its code to the GitHub repository. Tools such as Maven are used for unit-testing Java applications. More details about the Cloud Foundry, which now forms the basis of SAP Cloud Platform, are provided in

Chapter 13. The solutions lifecycle management (SLM) service helps to bundle different components of a solution based on different technologies into an archive called a *multitarget application archive* and then deploy them.

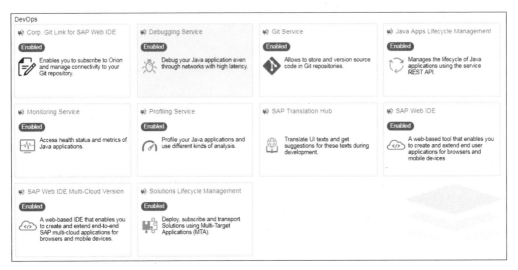

Figure 12.32 SAP Cloud Platform Services Supporting DevOps

There are still gaps in terms of end-to-end support of DevOps through a single platform in SAP. Several products and IT services companies are trying to bridge the existing gaps related to the automation and to break the silos, and often a DevOps initiative will run in parallel to an SAP S/4HANA project.

12.8   Summary

In this chapter, we touched on the drivers for the SAP S/4HANA evolution, all the major technical concepts, and the architecture behind the SAP S/4HANA solution, including the SAP HANA platform services, the SAP HANA database, and the various logical deployment options. We also covered SAP S/4HANA as the digital core, including the SAP Fiori frontend and the road map to SAP S/4HANA, complemented by the other evolving solutions from SAP.

In the following chapter, we'll take a look at your extension options with SAP Cloud Platform.

Chapter 13

Extensions with the SAP Cloud Platform

SAP Cloud Platform has advanced from being a platform that supports an individual customer or industry-specific extension strategy toward an enabler for the intelligent enterprise that supports the extensions of SAP S/4HANA and line of business solutions into an integrated smart business.

In this chapter, we'll explain the importance of the SAP Cloud Platform as part of the overall SAP strategy extending SAP S/4HANA as the digital core as well as extending additional functional areas, such as people management and customer experience. We'll start explaining the business advantages of SAP Cloud Platform and how you can use it to gain competitive advantage. After that, we'll provide a high-level overview of the SAP Cloud Platform capabilities followed by an overview of the different extensibility options. At the end of the chapter, we'll outline the connection between the SAP Cloud Platform and SAP Leonardo and how both fit together.

Let's start by discussing how SAP Cloud Platform enables business driven-development.

13.1 Business-Driven Development

From the beginning, SAP has helped clients use enterprise resource planning (ERP) solutions to standardize their business across the whole company and automate their operations. Today, most of these companies aren't starting with a greenfield implementation because they've already achieved a certain level of business automation. Therefore, most of the clients face integration challenges as well as customer-specific extensions that are required to reflect the differentiating aspect of the company to gain a competitive advantage.

With the rise of cloud computing, big data, Internet of Things (IoT), and machine learning over the past several years, data is becoming an immensely valuable for gaining a competitive advantage. With these new technologies, there is a need for a strong governance to maintain cloud-based solutions and provide restricted options to extend and customize SAP S/4HANA. The same is true for other cloud-based LoB solutions, such as SAP SuccessFactors and SAP Cloud for Customer.

Companies now need to go one step further from a business process automation to achieve the next level of business and become an intelligent enterprise. SAP's approach for the intelligent enterprise is to keep a stable core solution and provide the possibility to create competitive advantage through custom built extensions. Therefore, SAP provides end-to-end tools for key users and consultants to make smaller adjustments without worrying about any implications on the maintainability.

A key enabler for implementing intelligent processes is a data-driven digital platform that can combine structured and unstructured data and consists of the SAP Cloud Platform and the SAP HANA Data Management Suite (see Figure 13.1).

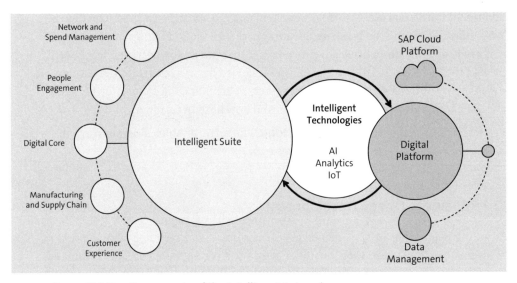

Figure 13.1 Key Components of the Intelligent Enterprise

With the SAP Cloud Platform, customers can connect, integrate, and orchestrate data as well as extend business processes of SAP S/4HANA as the digital core for the full intelligent suite. This will be enabled through application programming interfaces

(APIs) and microservices within the intelligent suite and will empower companies to integrate across heterogeneous environments.

The digital platform is a fundamental part of the intelligent suite as all technologies of SAP Leonardo will be available as a service for the SAP Cloud Platform to build solutions that can leverage artificial intelligence (AI), machine learning, IoT, blockchain, and advanced analytics.

From a business perspective, there are four different use case categories (see Figure 13.2) where SAP Cloud Platform can help businesses gain a competitive advantage. In the following sections, we'll describe them with concrete examples.

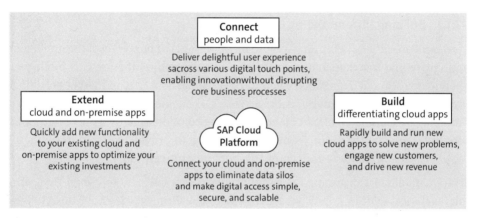

Figure 13.2 Key Use Cases for SAP Cloud Platform

13.1.1 Connecting People and Data

One of the challenges clients are facing today is to provide the right data tailored to the relevant role and responsibility everywhere at any time with a modern digital user experience (UX).

One typical scenario is that existing information from an SAP S/4HANA system need to be made available to different user types, for example, a field sales representative needs access to his leads, opportunities, and customer accounts, whereas a purchaser need access to approve contracts and orders, and track their status. Those scenarios are already available with SAP Fiori Cloud and can help customers adopt the intuitive SAP Fiori UX by leveraging the prepackaged content and services in the cloud. In this scenario, you would typically use the data/content from an existing SAP S/4HANA or SAP Business Suite and expose it via SAP Fiori Cloud. The SAP Cloud Platform will be required to develop, extend, and run SAP Fiori in the cloud.

Another example for connecting people and data could be the enablement of a field technician that is working at the client site and needs access to different types of data, for example, access to technical information, assigned tasks, customer data, and so on. This scenario can be addressed with the development of a mobile app that provides the required data to the different field teams in a tailored and easy-to-use way. The solution development can be done with the SAP Cloud Platform SDK for iOS that enables users to build business apps that leverage all features of an iOS device, such as location services or authentication via face recognition or Touch ID while providing secure access to SAP S/4HANA data.

13.1.2 Building Differentiating Cloud Apps

As described earlier, clients now want to move toward the next level of the intelligent enterprise and leverage and enhance their existing investments with intelligent technologies. Today companies need to be flexible and adjust to market behaviors quickly to gain a competitive advantage. This is where the SAP Cloud Platform comes into play by helping you build on your existing solutions and data and extend this information with, for example, machine learning, to provide you with insights on how you can differentiate your company from the competition.

The SAP Cloud Platform supports various types of new business solutions, for example, analytical solutions that leverage the existing real-time data of SAP HANA to provide insights to cross-sell and upsell opportunities for specific products and services that enhance the size of an initial business. Another example is sentiment analysis for social media (Twitter) where companies can check if they have positive or negative feedback. This scenario can be easily achieved with the SAP Cloud Platform Twitter integration package that allows you to load data into the SAP Marketing Cloud to assess, analyze, and take actions for the specific products or services.

A recent customer example is an existing logistics company that wanted to make its services available through online traders so that it can be easily consumed. The company implemented the SAP Cloud Platform API Management service to offer its services and functions to partners via APIs, such as address verification or delivery date check. This enabled the logistics provider to build a new business model that extended its current business reach and allowed new revenue streams because the company can now offer value-added services to its partners that are serving the end customers.

13.1.3 Integrate Apps and Data

As outlined at the beginning of this chapter, most clients today aren't starting on a greenfield; rather, they need to integrate into their existing solutions or build on top of them. Especially with the transition toward the cloud, it's essential to avoid application or data silos and support hybrid scenarios (see Figure 13.3). In addition, it's important to support the integration between cloud solutions, between cloud and on-premise solutions, and toward external partners or public authorities. Those scenarios fall into the following five categories:

- **Orchestration of processes across cloud and on-premise solutions**
  For end-to-end scenarios, ensure the integration flow between the different applications; for example, for a lead-to-cash process, you need to cross different solutions, such as Callidus Cloud, SAP Commerce Cloud, and SAP S/4HANA, to build the process. This integration flow is enabled via standard integration packages in the SAP Cloud Platform.

- **Data integration, data access, and data quality**
  Ensure availability of data from different sources and maintain business continuity with accurate and trustworthy data.

- **Integration of IoT**
  Integrate IoT devices and data into your processes or workflows and consume them with the SAP Cloud Platform capabilities.

- **Digital omnichannel access**
  Provide a seamless UX across the different channels while using SAP Cloud Platform experience maker to not only ensure consistent UX but also improve the overall experience through integrated and simplified flows.

- **Event processing**
  Assess and analyze events in real time and trigger actions based on the results to allow for, for example, the processing and maximized benefits of IoT data.

The example shown in Figure 13.3 is a typical external integration scenario. In this case, it's mandatory for the client to pass electronic invoice information to the tax authority because an approval from the tax authority is required for every outgoing invoice. This requirement can be fulfilled with the eDocument Framework as part of SAP S/4HANA leveraging SAP Cloud Platform integration to pass the information in a predefined structure. This reflects an integration scenario between an on-premise solution and a public authority.

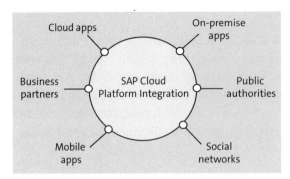

Figure 13.3 Integration Requirements Covered by SAP Cloud Platform

13.1.4 Extending Core and Software-as-a-Service Solutions

The most common scenarios for the SAP Cloud Platform are to reflect the individual requirements from a client via an extension of a LoB solution, the extension of the digital core, or an integration between both. Those extensions could be done in the following example scenarios:

- On a process level where a core process starts in SAP S/4HANA and is tightly integrated into a third-party solution or a custom built solution
- When SAP S/4HANA data is made available for people who don't use SAP S/4HANA
- Tailoring SAP Fiori-like apps for SAP S/4HANA to provide a seamless UX that increases the productivity of the employee
- An aggregation of data from different sources to build insights alongside the process chain

An example is a professional service client that uses the core functions of SAP S/4HANA Cloud to manage its projects, uses SAP SuccessFactors to manage the HR data, and integrates both systems to build a new process that reflects its requirements, for example, time-sheet recording, utilization tracking, or operational reporting with the SAP Cloud Platform. We'll see these scenarios more and more, where clients are using core functions of SAP S/4HANA and LoB solutions to build their individual solution on top with the SAP Cloud Platform.

But using extensions isn't just for clients; it's also a very powerful approach for SAP Partners to use the SAP Cloud Platform and build their industry/LoB-specific solutions in a side-by-side model to cover functional whitespaces or enhance existing functionalities. Within the SAP Partner program, there is a dedicated program that supports the building of SAP Partner intellectual property. It supports the partner in the ideation, solution build, and commercialization of SAP Cloud Platform-based solutions. More information can be found at *www.sap.com/buildbetter*.

Currently there are more than 1,500 partner apps available that extend either SAP S/4HANA or a LoB solution such as SAP SuccessFactors or SAP Ariba. For example, one of the solutions, "Ingentis org.manager [web] for SF" simulates new org structures based on your existing SAP SuccessFactors data. It's an easy-to-use application because you can use drag-and-drop functionality to simulate the reorganization. This solution is built on the SAP Cloud Platform and is tightly integrated into SAP Success-Factors as it could be launched directly through the SAP SuccessFactors UI via single sign-on (SSO). An overview of the available SAP and partner solutions that complement or extend existing core processes can be found at *www.sapappcenter.com*.

Now that we've looked at the different possibilities and use cases to support the different business requirements with SAP Cloud Platform, we'll provide you with an overview of the SAP Cloud Platform and the different extensibility options for SAP S/4HANA or any other SAP Cloud solution.

13.2 SAP Cloud Platform

The SAP Cloud Platform is a platform-as-a-service (PaaS) that allows you to build, extend, and integrate SAP solutions around the intelligent suite. It provides you with technical and business capabilities that help you to rapidly perform developments and enrich them with specific services, for example, IoT integration to enhance existing functions. It provides support to different programming languages, for example, Java and JavaScript, and provides core development tools that help you quickly start to develop and manage your solutions.

As shown in Figure 13.4, the SAP Cloud Platform is a central element of the intelligent enterprise that provides the glue between the elements of the SAP portfolio and provides the functionality to build, extend, or integrate applications. It provides you with the following different programming models for application development:

- HTML5
- XSJS
- Java
- Node.js

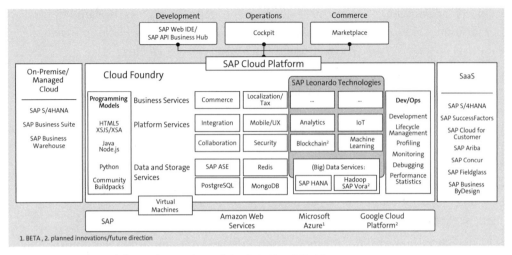

Figure 13.4 High-Level Overview of the SAP Cloud Platform

SAP Cloud Platform also provides you with a runtime container and a set of services for your use. It offers you the capability to integrate into SAP and non-SAP systems and to take advantage of real-time in-memory capabilities with the persistence in SAP HANA. When working with SAP Cloud Platform, there are several tools available:

- **Eclipse Integrated Development Environment (IDE)**
  Develops and deploys applications to perform operations such as user management, logging, and so on.

- **SAP HANA Web-based Development Workbench**
  This Web IDE is used for end-to end application development in SAP Fiori and SAPUI5. The SAP HANA Web-based Development Workbench is part of the design-time tools that help you become more efficient. With its layout editor (drag-and-drop tools), wizards, and templates, you can create starter applications with only a few clicks that require no further installation.

- **SAP Cloud Platform cockpit**
  This web-based frontend provides you with the capability to manage all your account-related resources and extension applications.

The SAP Cloud Platform offers a rich set of capabilities that can be leveraged to build client-specific solutions (see Figure 13.5). One example is SAP Cloud Platform document service that provides solutions with the capability to build a repository to store and manage unstructured and semistructured data. More information regarding the current available capabilities can be found at *https://cloudplatform.sap.com/*

capabilities.html. Aside from these capabilities, standard API packages are available, for example, for SAP S/4HANA or SAP SuccessFactors, that can be used to consume business functionality via the platform. All available APIs can be discovered via the SAP API Business Hub (*https://api.sap.com*).

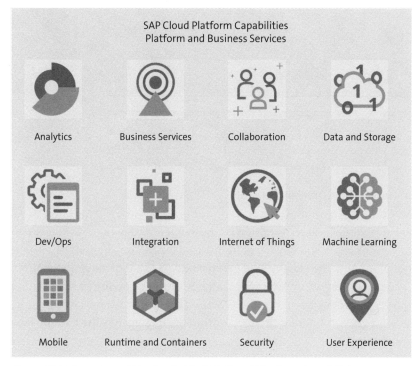

Figure 13.5 Overview of the Available SAP Cloud Platform Capabilities

13.3   Extensibility Options for the Intelligent Suite

Based on the current SAP strategy, the SAP Cloud Platform is the standard choice for building extension for any SAP Cloud solution or the intelligent suite. But what are the different choices available to extend SAP S/4HANA?

As you can see in Figure 13.6, there are different extensibility options available for the different user types. While business users need to make smaller personal adjustments, key users need a broader set of enhancement capabilities, and developers or partners need the full set of extensibility options. All of these different extensibility options are now separated into two major clusters for the extension of SAP S/4HANA as well as for any other LoB solution within the intelligent suite.

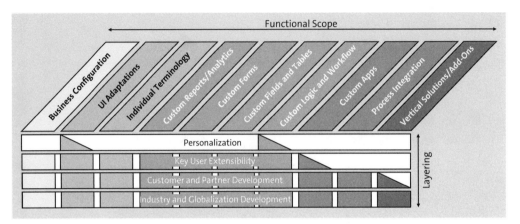

Figure 13.6 Overview of the Different Extensibilty Options

As illustrated in Figure 13.7, the first option is the in-app extensibility that focuses on supporting business users and key users in individualizing the application to their activities and processes. The side-by-side extensibility is the recommended option, especially when it comes to SAP S/4HANA Cloud, because it's preferred for building custom process extensions or additional functionality beyond the SAP core functions or when integrating different products within the intelligent suite to build new business models.

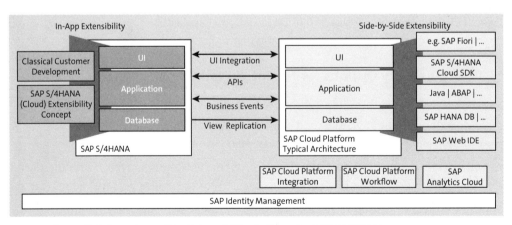

Figure 13.7 Overview of the Extensibility Options for SAP S/4HANA

The in-app extension possibilities are based on the different deployment options. The first option is the classical SAP extension strategy, which is only available for the on-premise edition and provides you with the already-available extension possibilities using the ABAP Workbench (SE 80) or Eclipse. It provides you with the freedom to modify SAP S/4HANA objects, but it's recommended to use the managed extensibility to ensure that the solution complies with future needs.

The second option is the classic extension strategy for SAP S/4HANA Cloud that is reflected by key-user tools and based on stable extension points and APIs. As you can see in Figure 13.8, the classical extension isn't available for the SAP S/4HANA edition because this would jeopardize the lifecycle management for the cloud-based solution and lead to instability and major efforts for adopting custom code.

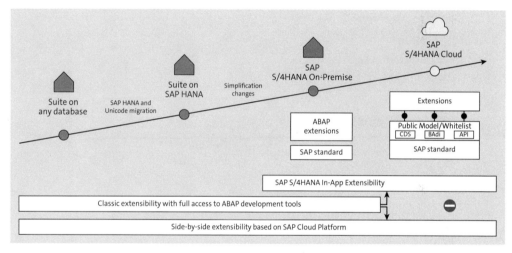

Figure 13.8 Extension Options on the Road to SAP S/4HANA Cloud

As described earlier, there are different use cases for different deployment scenarios. To support you in the decision process to build extension scenarios for SAP S/4HANA, Table 13.1 will help you evaluate the different options. In addition to the scenario you want to implement, you should also consider your current platform strategy and available technologies that you have in-house to ensure that you're not increasing the maintenance and development efforts. Other criteria include the availability of the developer skillsets within a company or generally in the market to ensure the delivery abilities of the solution build team. More information regarding SAP S/4HANA Cloud extension scenarios can also be found via the SAP Extensibility Explorer or the "SAP S/4HANA Extensibility for Customers and Partners" whitepaper.

Scenarios	SAP S/4HANA Classical/(Cloud) Extensibility Concept	SAP Cloud Platform Side-by-Side Extensibility
Target group: SAP S/4HANA user/employee	X	X
Target group: External/Consumer		X
UI design: Pattern based, SAP S/4HANA-like	X	X
UI design: Freestyle, native mobile app, etc.		X
Joined analytics with SAP S/4HANA objects	X	
Heavy usage of SAP S/4HANA data, extend SAP S/4HANA transaction, adapt a SAP S/4HANA process step	X	
Standalone/occasional SAP S/4HANA	X	X
Build data hub	(SAP S/4HANA-specific use cases)	X
Distributed scenarios loosely coupled		X
Integrate other cloud solutions		X
Big data (e.g., IoT)		X
Microservices		X

Table 13.1 Decision Matrix for SAP S/4HANA Extension

In the following sections, we'll take a closer look at the different available extension options that we've previously outlined.

13.3.1   In-App Extensibility

As outlined earlier, we differentiate between on-premise classical extensions and cloud extensions that are being reflected by key user in-app extensions.

The target group for this type of extension is typically made up of business experts who don't have a deep technical understanding but require a certain level of adjustment to fulfill their requirements. Those requirements will affect typically the LoB of the key user and are typically smaller changes. They can be classified in the categories shown in Figure 13.9.

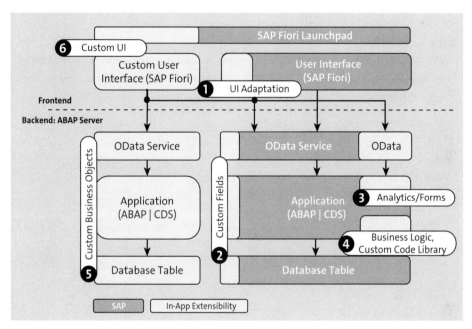

Figure 13.9 SAP S/4HANA Key User In-App Extensibility Scenarios

Let's explore each category, as follows:

❶ **UI adaptation**

The main purpose of the UI adaptation at runtime (RTA) is to provide key users with the ability to adapt the UI of apps so that it's tailored to their current tasks. Users can do the following:

– Add new fields

– Add new groups

– Add sections to an object page

– Rename fields and groups

– Move fields, groups, and object page sections

– Cut and paste fields and groups

- Split/combine fields
- Remove fields, groups, or object page sections
- Undo, redo, and discard changes
- Define new filter and table variants

All adaptation capabilities depend on the underlying SAP Fiori technology, and controls may vary from UI to UI.

❷ **Custom fields**

The custom field extension can be applied to database, application, Core Data Services (CDS), and OData services, and it allows you to reflect field extensions in the APIs of the extended applications (see Figure 13.10).

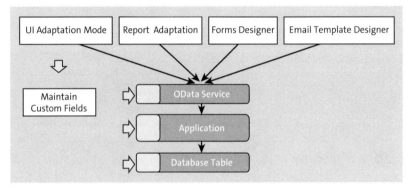

Figure 13.10 Key User Extensions for Custom Fields

The tool itself is easy to use and can be called directly from the UI of the extended application. You need to switch to **Adaptation Mode · Add Fields · New Custom Field** and then manage the usage of the custom field.

❸ **Custom analytics/forms/email templates**

You can create custom analytical queries just by copying standard queries, removing or customizing defined fields in the queries, applying filters, defining hierarchies, and finally previewing the report.

You can also build custom CDS views as a basis for the email templates and create new print forms based on the existing, new, or extended OData services.

All print forms will be extended/maintained via the Adobe LifeCycle Designer that consumes the underlying OData service (See Figure 13.10).

❹ **Custom business logic**

It's also possible to enhance existing functionality with additional business logic via a key-user friendly web editor. The editor provides the following possibilities:

- An easy way to explore existing APIs

- Perform a syntax check, syntax highlighting, and code completion check

- Creation of a draft version for local testing and comparison with the published logic

- Restricted usage of ABAP according to cloud qualities

❺ **Custom business objects**

The key user tool within SAP S/4HANA also provides you with the ability to create a custom business object that allows you to make a custom database table.

This is the baseline where you can start to implement determination and validation logic that should be applied to the business object. You can generate a UI to maintain the field values or generate a service so that an OData API is being created that can be consumed.

This can be easily consumed by using the SAP Cloud Platform and building a SAP Fiori UI on top of the OData service to execute simple create, read, update, and delete (CRUD) operations.

❻ **Custom SAP Fiori UIs**

As described in the previous section, it's possible to build custom SAP Fiori UIs with SAP Web IDE and deployed them into the ABAP SAPUI5 repository with a SAP predefined and released OData service or a custom OData service.

For transporting custom objects in an on-premise landscape, the Change Transport System (CTS) or enhanced CTS+ is still the right choice for lifecycle management. For the cloud version, the key user will be able to transport all his changes via SAP Fiori apps without any interference with the regular maintenance cycle.

If you want to assure a proper lifecycle management for SAP S/4HANA Cloud, the custom extension should not be affected by an update of the SAP core solution, and it must work after the update without any manual adjustments.

Now that we've looked at the in-app extensibility of SAP S/4HANA Cloud, let's take a quick look at the classical extensibility of the SAP S/4HANA. This won't be available after you migrate to the cloud (refer back to Figure 13.8).

13

13.3.2   Classic Extensibility

As already mentioned previously, the classical extensibility is only available for the on-premise edition and provides you with the extension possibilities that are already available using the ABAP Workbench or Eclipse. It provides you with the freedom to modify SAP S/4HANA objects, but it's recommended to use the managed extensibility by using enhancement features to ensure that the solution complies with future needs and that you can benefit from reduced maintenance costs.

To ensure that you don't face any challenges on your way to an SAP S/4HANA Cloud solution, we recommend you use business add-ins (BAdIs) as the enhancement technology for your future enhancements. As a guideline, you should follow those recommendations from SAP (refer to the "SAP S/4HANA Extensibility for Customers and Partners" whitepaper).

In general, if multiple options are available for your enhancement use case, choose the following (preference from top to bottom) for new implementations:

- New SAP S/4HANA BAdIs
- Explicit enhancement options, user/system exits, or application-specific enhancement frameworks
- Explicit enhancement options
- Modifications of SAP code
- Clone and adoption of SAP code

You might consider migrating existing code to new SAP S/4HANA BAdIs as well.

Now that we've introduced the possibilities for in-app extensions, we want to take a closer look at the possibilities and tools for side-by side extensibility.

13.3.3   Side-by-Side Extensibility

In the previous section, we outlined the key-user and classical in-app extension possibilities shown in Figure 13.11 on the left side numbered 1 to 6. In this section, we want to outline the right side of the picture and explain on which layer you can do an extension with the SAP Cloud Platform, why you should do it, and how it can be done.

If it comes to side-by-side extension scenarios, SAP recommends the SAP Cloud Platform. As described in the previous sections, an extension typically consists of four different layers:

- Frontend (UI)
- Business logic
- Persistence
- Connectivity

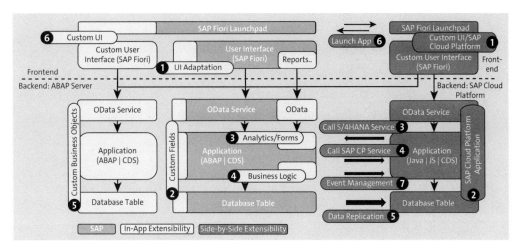

Figure 13.11 Side-by-Side Extensibility Overview

We'll take a closer look at each in the following sections.

Frontend

The recommendation for SAP S/4HANA UI enhancement is SAPUI5/SAP Fiori. SAP Fiori provides a consumer-grade, unified, intuitive, and persona/role-specific experience, which can be implemented based on the SAPUI5 Framework and is compatible with most of the SAP applications. The SAP Fiori frontend can be easily implemented via the SAP Web IDE, which provides you with the possibility to consume SAP Gateway services. These SAP Gateway services can be implemented via the SAP Gateway Service Builder for your own code, or you can use it based on existing business application programming interfaces (BAPIs) or CDS views. The SAP Gateway Service Builder projects can be created to be compliant with OData version 2 or OData version 4.

Business Logic and Connectivity

Following the previously described concept of ensuing the qualities of cloud solutions, SAP S/4HANA Cloud needs to expose all business functions and make them available for consumption. As illustrated in Figure 13.12, the following different methods are available to expose those functions:

- Public APIs that can be used to connect to SAP S/4HANA:
  - OData, REST, SOAP
  - Published APIs via the SAP API Business Hub where currently 203 APIs are published
  - BAPIs via the SAP S/4HANA Cloud SDK
  - Usage of SAP Cloud Platform Integration
- SAP S/4HANA extensibility concept
  - Released CDS views (read-only)
  - Custom business objects (read/write)
- SAP S/4HANA legacy APIs
  - BAPI (via cloud connector)
  - IDoc

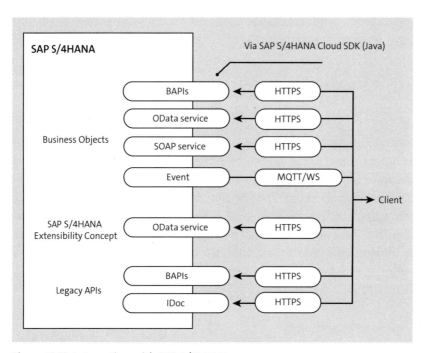

Figure 13.12 Integration with SAP S/4HANA

Persistence

For persistence, the SAP Cloud Platform provides services to utilize SAP HANA database services via Neo or to utilize database-as-a-service (DBaaS) for Cloud Foundry. Both Neo and Cloud Foundry environments provide a certain set of support, whereas Neo allows you to develop on HTLM5, Java, and SAP HANA extended application services (SAP HANA XS). Cloud Foundry supports SAP HANA extended application services, advanced model options and containers for Java, Node.JS, and Python. Regarding persistence, Neo allows you to use SAP HANA single container database systems and database tenants as well as SAP Adaptive Server Enterprise (SAP ASE). Cloud Foundry offers SAP HANA services, PostgreSQL, MongoDB, Redis, and Object Store. From an availability option, Neo is available on SAP's certified data centers within seven locations, and Cloud Foundry environments are offered by Amazon Web Services, Microsoft Azure, and Google Cloud Platform.

13.4   SAP Cloud Platform and SAP Leonardo

Referring to Figure 13.1 where we explained the key components of the intelligent enterprise, we saw that the digital platform enables intelligent technologies such as AI, machine learning, and IoT.

Those services are available via the SAP Cloud Platform as the foundation for SAP Leonardo to enable the enhancement of existing processes based on existing functionality from SAP S/4HANA. The SAP Cloud Platform resides on a multi-cloud infrastructure with the Cloud Foundry environment or Neo. The SAP Cloud Platform itself provides access to the SAP Leonardo services, for example, SAP Leonardo Machine Learning Foundation. With the machine learning API, you can enhance your processes with the natural language processing capabilities or analyze and forecast data.

While SAP Leonardo is a systematic approach toward digital innovation, the SAP Cloud Platform enables this approach with the availability of platform capabilities, for example, blockchain, IoT, and so on, to infuse existing processes and drive forward innovation.

Concrete examples of this infusion are the following solutions/scenarios:

- **SAP Predictive Maintenance**
  Avoid unplanned machine downtime and reduce maintenance costs using SAP S/4HANA asset management in combination with SAP IoT Application Enablement by SAP's Data Science services.

13

- **SAP Cash Application**
  Leverage SAP Leonardo Machine Learning capabilities empowered by the SAP Cloud Platform to learn from the accountants' past manual actions to process incoming payments and match them to the open invoice information on top of SAP S/4HANA Finance.

- **SAP Business Integrity Screening**
  Increase accuracy of fraud alerts based on SAP S/4HANA Finance and SAP Predictive Analytics.

These are just a view examples of how to connect existing processes and enrich them with advanced machine learning capabilities that help to recognize patterns and correlate the data in a way that wasn't possible before. We'll discuss SAP Leonardo capabilities further in the next chapter.

13.5   Summary

In this chapter, we outlined the importance of the SAP Cloud Platform as a fundamental part of the intelligent suite. We explained the different use cases on how to extend SAP S/4HANA and where clients can benefit from the platform capabilities. After that, we looked at in-app extensions and side-by-side extension possibilities and provided a guideline that helps you make the right decision regarding which technology to use for which use case. Finally, we provided you with an overview of SAP Leonardo and how the SAP Cloud Platform is providing the capabilities of an intelligent enterprise.

In the next chapter, we'll dive into SAP's next-generation solution portfolio, SAP Leonardo, and see how it intersects with SAP S/4HANA.

Chapter 14

SAP Leonardo

In this chapter, we'll show you how to extend your SAP S/4HANA landscape with SAP Leonardo with some real-world use cases.

As a continuation of Chapter 13, we'll take a deep dive into the SAP Leonardo offering, understand the various applications and technologies under the umbrella of the SAP Leonardo platform and how they intersect with SAP S/4HANA. SAP Leonardo powers the intelligent enterprise with intelligent technologies for every business process to create better outcomes. This enables businesses to leverage their data, detect patterns, process data intelligently, predict outcomes, and suggest actions. Thus, SAP Leonardo forms a core and vital component of the intelligent enterprise, which will transform the way IT interacts with business.

In this chapter, we'll break down what, exactly, the intelligent enterprise and SAP Leonardo are, and how they fit together in the SAP landscape. We'll then explore the major SAP Leonardo digital technologies, from the Internet of Things (IoT) to big data.

14.1 The Intelligent Enterprise and SAP Leonardo

The term "intelligent enterprise" refers to a management approach that applies technology and new service paradigms to the challenge of improving business performance.

In the past, the term "enterprise" has been associated only with large companies and organizations that have thousands of employees worldwide and generate billions in revenue. However, with mass digitalization of marketplaces; flexibility of cloud, subscription-based computation models; and high availability of game changer innovative solutions; the mid-sized companies are quickly adopting the digital bandwagon at a much faster pace compared to enterprise companies. Small-sized companies are already digitally competent and adopting the likes of machine learning, artificial intelligence (AI), deep learning, blockchain, predictive analytics, and prescriptive analytics to augment their businesses and stay ahead of the game. They are driving sustainable competitive advantage as quickly as they are converting data into insights that position them well for widespread market acceptance.

You can think of the intelligent enterprise as a virtual cycle, as shown in Figure 14.1, where business actions for segments (e.g., customer experience, manufacturing, and supply chain) are executed by the intelligent suite and are coupled with intelligence technology layer-generated data. And the data from these business processes is combined with external data sources in the digital platform where intelligent technologies can be applied to generate even better insights. These insights can then be embedded back into the intelligent suite for process automation or better decision support.

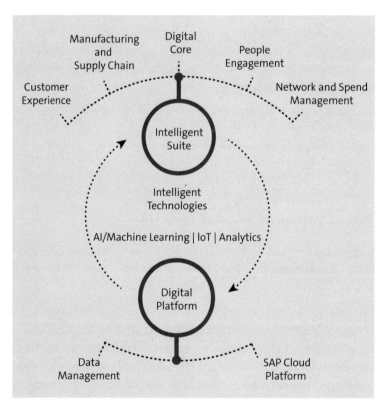

Figure 14.1 SAP Intelligent Enterprise with SAP Leonardo

SAP Leonardo, SAP's umbrella suite for the key digital technologies we've mentioned so far, is composed of three parts:

- **Intelligent business suite**
  SAP provides an intelligent suite that enables every line of business (LoB) to automate its day-to-day business processes and better interact with their customers, suppliers, and employees through applications that have intelligence embedded in them. This intelligence suite embeds intelligence in the application making the workflows smarter. The intelligence suite is quite modular in nature and is customizable per the customer's requirements. For SAP S/4HANA release 1809, 25 industries are covered under the SAP Leonardo intelligence suite.

- **Digital platform**
  The SAP Cloud Platform and the SAP HANA Data Management Suite together facilitate the collection, the connection, and the orchestration of data as well as the integration and the extension of processes within the intelligent suite.

- **Intelligent technologies**
  The intelligent technologies form the crux of the SAP Leonardo offering and basically encompass all the modern IT requirements. The intelligent services in SAP Leonardo enable customers across industries to have digital transformation.

As a lot has been mentioned about the intelligent suite and digital platform in the previous chapters; we'll focus more on the intelligent technologies in this chapter. Figure 14.2 details how SAP Leonardo allows customers to innovate, integrate, and scale their digital transformation projects by leveraging next-generation technologies such as the following:

- Machine learning
- IoT
- Big data analytics
- Blockchain
- Data intelligence

These technologies are built upon and integrated into the digital core of your business using SAP Cloud Platform, thus making the SAP digital core more powerful and more intelligent. These technologies are available on the SAP Cloud Platform and hosted on multiple cloud vendors, such as Microsoft Azure, Google Cloud Platform, and Amazon Web Services (AWS). IBM Cloud will host the private edition of SAP Cloud Platform, which will be available in 2019.

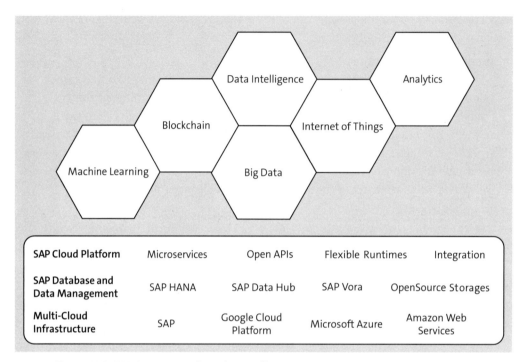

Figure 14.2 SAP Strategy: Deliver the Intelligent Enterprise

SAP Leonardo can be consumed in three ways. The first way to consume SAP Leonardo is through the SAP Leonardo technologies being embedded directly into the depth and the breadth of the SAP portfolio, including everything from SAP C/4HANA to SAP S/4HANA, to SAP SuccessFactors, to the entirety of SAP's portfolio.

The second way to consume SAP Leonardo is through industry innovation kits that combine the intelligent technology and the pre-integrated software with services into industry solutions for solving critical industry problems in an accelerated way. As of now, SAP Leonardo offers 23+ industry innovation kits that span more than 13 industry areas, including consumer products, life sciences, manufacturing, automotive, utilities, oil and gas, and sports and entertainment.

And the third option for consuming SAP Leonardo is by leveraging the intelligent technologies that are all available on SAP Cloud Platform. This method leverages a toolbox of intelligent technologies such as AI, machine learning, and IoT, together with microservices and data management tools. We'll describe these technologies in detail in the following sections.

14.2   Internet of Things

IoT is the intelligent connectivity of smart devices by which objects can sense one another and communicate, thus changing how business decisions can be made based on the "sensed" data. Many industries are implementing this intelligent connectivity of smart devices in their day-to-day business activities.

SAP Leonardo IoT is part of the overall SAP Leonardo digital innovation system. Leveraging information from sensors, microcontrollers, mobile communications, and other smart devices, SAP Leonardo IoT capabilities are transforming business models and processes across industries.

So how does it fit with SAP S/4HANA? SAP Leonardo IoT will enable digitization of end-to-end enterprises by capturing product/asset genealogy along the way. By running intelligent and predictive business models based on the captured sensors data, along with effective real-time responses for a variety of services, SAP Leonardo IoT will enable business outcomes by reducing operation costs and increasing revenue. For example, SAP Leonardo can be leveraged for industrial IoT (IIoT), which is a subset of IoT used in the manufacturing industry, for areas such as predictive maintenance of assets and analyzing critical operation cost drivers for streamlined operations of the digital factory.

SAP Leonardo IoT will also drive for better customer engagement and services for connected devices. It can provide end-to-end operations visibility and ways to automate business, increase revenue with new business models, and allow interoperability of Industry 4.0 and IoT across the enterprise, thereby forming one of the core components of the SAP digital core.

The ready-to-run enterprise scenarios along with the ready-to-build IoT application are the two entry points for using SAP Leonardo IoT. The ready-to-run enterprise scenarios use the SAP Edge Services, and the ready-to-build IoT application on SAP Cloud Platform uses SAP Leonardo IoT Foundation in conjunction with SAP Leonardo IoT Bridge (see Figure 14.3).

To aid in business operations, the SAP Leonardo IoT portfolio also offers built-in ready-to-run LoB solutions such as SAP Asset Intelligence Network, SAP Predictive Maintenance and Service, SAP Global Track and Trace, SAP Connected Goods, SAP Manufacturing Suite, SAP Vehicle Insights, and more, as shown in Figure 14.4.

14

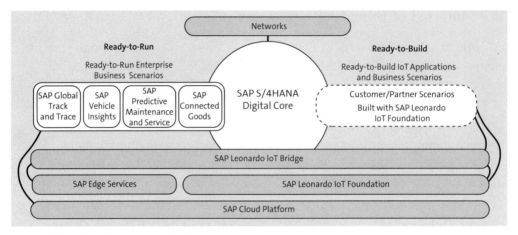

Figure 14.3 SAP Leonardo IoT 4.0

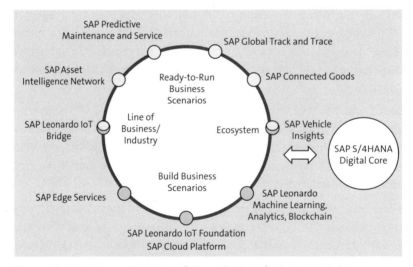

Figure 14.4 SAP Leonardo IoT Portfolio with SAP S/4HANA Digital Core

Let's take a look at each of these SAP Leonardo IoT solutions:

- **SAP Asset Intelligence Network**

   SAP Asset Intelligence Network is a cloud-based business network based on facilitating collaborative asset management.

   The aim of SAP Asset Intelligence Network is to maintain a global registry of equipment that uses common definitions, which can comprise asset performance feedback, analytics output, best practices for deployment strategies, and maintenance procedures. These common definitions are then shared between multiple business partners (e.g., manufacturers or original equipment manufacturers [OEMs]), operators, or service providers to deliver new collaborative business models resulting in operational excellence.

The four pillars of SAP Asset Intelligence Network are network, content, integration, and applications. This solution connects with other SAP solutions, such as SAP S/4HANA, to facilitate smooth data exchange across enterprise and plant systems as well. Applications in the SAP Asset Intelligence Network will also help customers share advanced analytics and collaborate on processes for equipment management and maintenance execution.

Using SAP Asset Intelligence Network, an OEM can make the content for all assets, including procedures, manuals, and maintenance requirements, available over a network. An equipment operator or a design engineer can tap into this network and access the shared data of a particular asset's configurations it's using (via data from SAP ERP and enterprise asset management) and combine it with the real-time information from the equipment itself (through smart sensor output attached to the equipment), enabling a streamlined maintenance and collaborative design of a complex installation.

- **SAP Predictive Maintenance and Service**
  SAP Predictive Maintenance and Service enables you to monitor vital parameters of an enterprise or shop floor assets in real time and perform timely maintenance of critical and required assets to incur low maintenance costs. It also helps to increase asset productivity by ensuring optimal scheduled asset downtime for maintenance rather than on-demand downtime. It also ensures shop floor and plant employee's safety and increases employee efficiency.

  SAP Predictive Maintenance and Service provides business users with a set of tools for managing equipment health. It also gives them decision-making support when maintaining schedules and optimizing resources based on health scores or anomaly detection.

  The Explorer and Details components are also provided by SAP Predictive Maintenance and Service. Business users can add analysis tools, such as the Equipment List, from the Analysis Tools Catalog to the Explorer and to the Details to analyze the equipment at the flexibility of the business scenario.

  SAP Predictive Maintenance and Service provides businesses with more time to respond, enabling greater flexibility to plan dynamic maintenance.

- **SAP Global Track and Trace**

  SAP Global Track and Trace is a cloud service solution based on the SAP Cloud Platform. It's enhanced with multitier logistics network capabilities to allow cross-company tracing of serialized objects (e.g., shipping containers or trucks), processes (e.g., delivery and/or shipment), and execution processes (e.g., changed temperature limits or faulty delivery environment).

  It captures, processes, and stores tracking information about tracked objects and business processes in a central repository of information for all involved stakeholders. They can query any tracked process and display its retrieved data from end to end. This solution is quite useful in supply chain management, retail management, and logistics.

- **SAP Connected Goods**

  SAP Connected Goods is a cloud-based IoT solution designed to maximize the value of products—such as raw materials and semifinished or finished goods—through insights derived from key indicators as to where, how, and how much the products are stored or utilized.

  In the supply chain, SAP Connected Goods helps logistics providers enhance replenishment processes. For instance, an organization responsible for supplying the raw materials for construction kept in different stock sites could use IoT-fed sensor data to monitor the current stock of cement at different construction sites and automatically replenish the required stock without human intervention.

  SAP Connected Goods features include customer engagement through insight on product utilization and usage patterns and product inventory optimization.

- **SAP Manufacturing Suite**

  The SAP Manufacturing Suite is a cloud-based SAP Leonardo solution for the discrete industries to enable a fully integrated production process from the top floor to the shop floor to minimize disruption, including machine integration into the production cycle. It can orchestrate highly automated production processes, enabling product variants with a lot size of 1 for addressing individual customer requirements. Variants and their production sequence can be changed automatically, quickly, and easily, enabling agile business operations.

  The SAP Manufacturing Suite is discussed in detail in Section 14.6.

- **SAP Vehicle Insights**

  This solution allows you to collect, map, store, and analyze increasing vehicle sensor data in real time. Once this vehicle data relates to existing business data, many superior agile business operations can be performed, such as digitizing moving assets insight, integrating moving asset insights to operationalize and optimize planning processes, and innovating by creating new processes to increase customer intimacy and create new revenue. In connection with real-time analytics and prediction capabilities of SAP Vehicle Insights, the solution generates valuable insights for companies and enables them to shorten their time to market for scenarios involving building connected vehicles.

If the business requirements aren't achieved by using the ready-to-run SAP Leonardo IoT solutions, the ready-to-build IoT application on SAP Cloud Platform allows custom development for customers and partners per their business requirements. SAP Cloud Platform is a base foundation for building, integrating, and extending new applications. It also provides design templates and prebuilt applications that help to expedite the development process for developers.

The SAP Cloud Platform IoT service provides interfaces for registering devices and their specific data types and sending data securely to a database running on the SAP Cloud Platform. In other cases, the sensor output data may require forwarding the data to a message broker, event stream processor, or even a document repository.

The IoT service cockpit is the main interface for users to interact with the Remote Device Management Service (RDMS) and can be used to register new devices, to define the schema of messages (device types and message types), and to establish the trust relationship needed by devices to interact with the Message Management Service (MMS). The IoT service cockpit and RDMS are provided as cloud services and can be used via subscription-based or consumption-based (paid using cloud credits) commercial models.

Let's do a technical dive into the various components of SAP Leonardo IoT. PLAT.ONE is an application enablement platform for IoT that SAP acquired in July 2016. PLAT.ONE forms a cornerstone of the IoT offering based on SAP Cloud Platform and, dubbed as SAP Cloud Platform IoT 4.0, has generally been available since May 2017 as a microservice on SAP Cloud Platform. SAP Leonardo IoT leverages SAP Cloud Platform IoT 4.0 microservices through Cloud Foundry. This feature is available for AWS (EU10/US10) and SAP data centers (EU1) on SAP Cloud Platform.

14

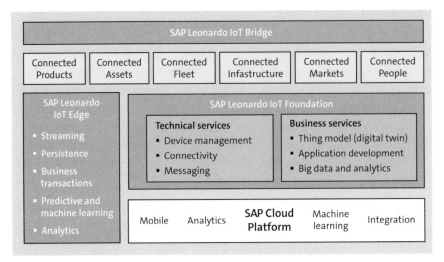

Figure 14.5 SAP Leonardo IoT Technical Architecture

The SAP Leonardo IoT architecture (see Figure 14.5) shows that SAP Leonardo IoT provides a full solution stack built on SAP Cloud Platform that includes the following:

- **SAP Leonardo IoT Bridge**
  A configurable cloud solution with a persona-centric work environment correlates business processes with data from IoT applications to provide intelligent business solutions in real time. Through an appealing frontend, it provides semantic integration of business solutions for collaboration between teams. SAP Leonardo IoT Bridge transforms experiences and interactions with systems and things in business networks based on real-time information and contextual intelligence.

- **SAP Leonardo IoT Edge**
  SAP Leonardo IoT Edge computing describes the capability of processing, storing, and analyzing sensor data, closer to the source of data, to enable faster decision-making and to operate with intermittent connectivity to the cloud. Offers data protocol conversion, persistence, and data analytics capabilities on devices or gateways for easy data ingestion to SAP Cloud Platform, irrespective of the type of connectivity. In addition, it allows you to execute business processes locally on edge gateways.

- **SAP Leonardo IoT Foundation**
  The best-of-breed business services enable developers to rapidly build IoT applications by leveraging digital twins, reusable application services, and predictive algorithms. It also provides core technical services to process a high velocity of device data, with streaming analytics and device management capabilities.

- **SAP Leonardo services**
  These services include SAP Leonardo Analytics, SAP Leonardo Machine Learning, SAP Leonardo Blockchain.

- **SAP Cloud Platform**
  The motherboard includes integration, security, and mobile services.

14.3   Machine Learning and Robotic Process Automation

SAP Leonardo Machine Learning is the new branding for SAP's entire portfolio of intelligent applications and services. SAP Leonardo Machine Learning is at the core of SAP Leonardo. Embedded into enterprise systems, machine learning lets customers augment and automate repetitive tasks and unlock entirely new kinds of digital innovation by learning from data, rather than programming explicit rules. Natively integrated into SAP applications, cloud, and business networks, SAP Leonardo Machine Learning ensures digital intelligence can be easily consumed across the entire business to create better customer service, optimize business operations, improve employee job satisfaction, reimagine existing business processes, and more.

It ranges from well-established product offerings, such as SAP HANA's Predictive Analytics Library (PAL) and SAP Predictive Analytics to services offered through the SAP Leonardo Machine Learning Foundation (see Figure 14.6).

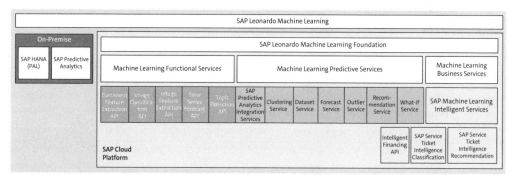

Figure 14.6 SAP Leonardo Machine Learning Components

SAP Leonardo Machine Learning offers a variety of intelligent applications, each designed to precisely meet a unique business need:

- **SAP Leonardo Machine Learning Foundation**

  This application provides an enterprise-grade platform for machine learning in the cloud. It enables simple consumption and tight integration with SAP's enterprise software combined with openness toward various machine-learning technologies. Developers can benefit from a scalable and secure platform to augment business processes with machine learning technology and infuse applications with intelligence.

  A SAP Leonardo Machine Learning Foundation demo web page is available that contains live demos for the facial detection, text processing, smart ticket processing, and API help page links at *https://leo-mlp-demo-solutionexper-v3.cfapps.eu10.hana.ondemand.com*.

  The SAP Leonardo Machine Learning Foundation allows you to deploy, publish, and run a machine learning model as a service. The lifecycle of the machine learning model is shown in Figure 14.7.

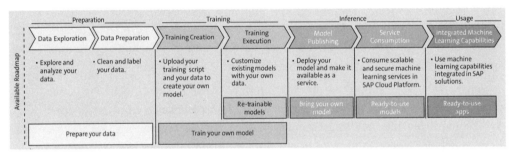

Figure 14.7 SAP Leonardo Machine Learning Foundation: Machine Learning Lifecycle Management

- **SAP Conversational AI**

  Formerly known as Recast.AI, this is the leading AI bot platform for enterprises. With more than 30,000 developers building more than 60,000 bots, SAP offers a world-class technology, an end-to-end bot platform, and off-the-shelf customer support bots to lead the revolution of customer relations around the world and enable the intelligent enterprise. SAP Conversation AI can be used to integrate with multiple platforms, such as Facebook, Twitter, Slack, and so on, to create seamless social connectivity.

- **SAP Cash Application**

  This automates the process of matching incoming payments to open receivables, reducing the time required.

- **SAP Service Ticket Intelligence**
  This application builds a model based on successful past ticket completion, using it to automatically categorize service tickets and provide recommended solutions to service agents.

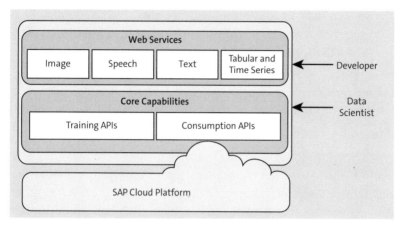

Figure 14.8 SAP Leonardo Machine Learning Services

Figure 14.8 shows the most important functional web services currently available as described here:

- **Natural language and text processing**
  Translate and analyze natural language content that is stored in documents, websites, and emails related to business data. These are further subdivided into the following features:
  - Text classification
  - Text feature extraction
  - Language detection and machine translation
  - Translations
  - Topic detection
- **Image processing**
  Processes the images to find the visual content that the intelligent system can understand. This is further subdivided into following features:
  - Image classification
  - Object detection

- Image feature extraction
- Image segmentation
- Optical character and scene text recognition

- **Speech**
  Processes the spoken data to find meaningful insights, such as sentiment of speech, tone of the speech, and so on, which can be combined with the business data to gauge product sentiment, customer retention, and customer satisfaction scenarios.

- **Tabular and time series**
  Processes large amounts of tabular and time series data without being explicitly programmed.

Another SAP machine learning solution that has been making headlines since SAP-PHIRE 2017 is SAP CoPilot. SAP CoPilot was available from SAP S/4HANA 1705 as a first step toward a digital assistant, and it supports daily tasks by offering relevant action options based on consumer's role, context, and business situation. For example, it allows the user to search for business information or chat in business context with experts to help find solutions to a current problem. Based on the context of the screen, a user can create, collect, and share artifacts such as notes, objects, messages, screenshots, and quick actions. Features of SAP CoPilot include the following:

- **Digital assistant**
  Advancements include Natural Language Interaction (NLI).

- **Notes and screenshots**
  Create notes and capture screenshots from apps, and then navigate to the app from the screenshot. Annotations can be added, and areas can be blacked out.

- **Recognizing business objects**
  Business objects within the current application context as well as those referred to in notes or chats are recognized.

- **In-context chat**
  Chat with other users from your business application context, sharing notes, screenshots, and business objects. You can also save the conversation for later use.

How does SAP Leonardo Machine Learning fit into the backend processes of SAP ERP? With SAP Leonardo Machine Learning, SAP enables its customers to reimagine the backend processes more efficiently, more securely, or more transparently as a new solution or as a middleware intelligence product. Singular business processes that can have a heavy impact in each business segment are coupled with machine learning to make them more intelligent and autonomous. Some of the examples are as follows:

- **Procurement**
  Goods and services classification, product category normalization, invoice payment block, and image-based detection of invoice.

- **Sales and marketing**
  Brand impact analysis, quotation conversion probability rate, customer retention, sales forecast, selling recommender, and more.

- **Operations**
  SAP Predictive Maintenance, quality inspection through image processing, and stock substitution.

- **Finance**
  SAP Cash Application, accounts payable, remittance advices, cash and liquidity management, dispute proposal, and cash collection reminder.

- **Service**
  Conversation commerce, service ticketing, customer support, and solution recommender.

- **Human resources**
  Learning recommender, career path recommender, simultaneous training content translation, job standardization, and resume matching.

- **Master data**
  Semantic search, text analysis on master data, business rule mining, and deduplication of records.

14.4 Blockchain

Blockchain is a technology that has raised many eyebrows lately. Some believe that it has the potential to disrupt the IT industry in the same manner that the invention of the telephone and Internet did to the traditional mailing and communications industries. Every business is based on transactions, and these transactions are often routed through third-party intermediaries, making processing time-consuming and expensive. Blockchain records data across a peer-to-peer network. Every participant can see the data and verify or reject it using consensus algorithms. Approved data is entered into the ledger as a collection of "blocks" and stored in a chronological "chain" that can't be altered. SAP Leonardo Blockchain simplifies the complex business transaction process using a distributed ledger.

Blockchains create excellent platforms for new ways of working. Another way to think of them is as springboards, capable of launching organizations in new directions. Currently more than 24 countries are investing in blockchain technologies, and more than $4.5 billion has been invested in the past three years. The global market for blockchain is at $2.1 billion as of January 2018 and is anticipated to reach $60.7 billion in 2024. That is a growth of 30 times its current size. Of CxO-level leaders, 33% actively use or consider blockchain and believe it plays a key role in advancing the technology and reestablishing industry standards.

Blockchain is a new protocol for distributed ledgers in multiparty business processes. Because of its huge footprint in the enterprise landscape, many ERP providers, such as SAP, IBM, Oracle, Microsoft, and even the tech evangelists Google, Tencent, and Baidu have invested in blockchain. SAP is taking more of an agnostic approach to the underlying ledger technology, whether it's the open source *Hyperledger Project* (SAP is a platinum sponsor), *MultiChain*, or any decentralized distributed ledger technologies. Features of SAP Leonardo Blockchain include the following:

- **Hyperledger Fabric on SAP Cloud Platform**
  SAP's blockchain-as-a-service (BaaS) offering allows businesses to explore the technology, integrate it into their SAP landscapes, and capitalize on its potential.

- **MultiChain on SAP Cloud Platform**
  The MultiChain service enables you to create, delete, monitor, and maintain individual MultiChain nodes and connect them to a blockchain network.

- **Blockchain application enablement**
  As of October 2018, this is available as a beta shipment for customers to experience in the BaaS with the existing SAP software portfolio. Some of the examples are track and trace goods in transit, track and trace pharmaceuticals, and transportation and logistics management using BaaS.

- **SAP HANA Blockchain service**
  This service connects external blockchain networks to SAP HANA and is accessed through SAP Cloud Platform blockchain application enablement. This service enables developers to use the SAP HANA platform to build applications incorporating blockchain data without dealing with the complexities of blockchain technology. SAP HANA Blockchain service is shown as part of the SAP Leonardo Blockchain portfolio in Figure 14.9.

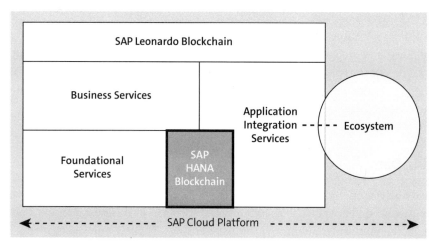

Figure 14.9 SAP Leonardo Blockchain Portfolio

In the areas of the blockchain application enablement, some of the notable applications developed by SAP are as follows:

- **Transportation management**
  Created for all transportation modes and industries, this application drives a blockchain case for international trade. Sellers, buyers, banks, and authorities share, review, and sign documents electronically; track process statuses; and hand over ownership of the e-bill of lading. A secure container release process will be evaluated to reduce fraud and stolen freight.

- **SAP Global Track and Trace**
  This application provides unified, end-to-end tracking, monitoring, and reporting of objects and business processes across supply chain networks. Blockchain technology is used to help make tracking information immutable and tamper-proof for product authenticity and providence. In addition, information stored in the blockchain can be positively traced back to the author/customer/business entity, building the basis for fully automated payment and settlement processes.

- **Advanced Track and Trace for Pharmaceuticals**
  This application enables pharmaceutical supply chain members to comply with global antidrug counterfeit regulations and to facilitate collaboration between supply chain partners in conjunction with SAP Information Collaboration Hub for Life Sciences.

- **Farm to Consumer**
  With this application, food producers and retailers come together to improve compliance and safeguard brand reputation by increasing confidence in food safety. The effort explores blockchain across the broader food ecosystem both as an effective remedy to product counterfeiting and as a way to boost supply chain integrity and efficiency.

14.5   Big Data

We already discussed big data in Chapter 8 in the context of analytics, so we'll keep our discussion brief here. With an exponential increase in business context data through digital platforms, data from "connected things" is posing new IT challenges to customers. The challenges aren't limited to just storing and processing this huge amount of data but more into harnessing the true potential of this business-sensitive data. The increased number of connected devices can alone generate terabytes of data per quarter. Although there are distributed technologies on Hadoop using predictive models to ingest this data, the data is still in silos, and it's difficult to integrate them with SAP ERP and non-SAP ERP solutions. Apart from this, a high level of effort is required to move from descriptive to prescriptive analytics on big data. To strengthen the conjunction of the otherwise siloed big data, machine data, social data, IoT, and SAP S/4HANA, SAP provides SAP Leonardo Big Data solutions.

The big data solution on the SAP Leonardo platform transitions from centralized, relational, on-premise data warehouse approaches to a serverless containerized, and distributed data platform. The big data portfolio ensembles new Hadoop/Spark Cloud Storage (i.e., AWS S3), machine learning components (Python, Spark, TensorFlow), and containers (Kubernetes, Docker) into the existing business systems to have a distributed system in a distributed landscape (see Figure 14.10).

SAP Leonardo Big Data provides critical tools for data cleansing, quality, and transformation using machine learning, graph computation, and stream processing, giving users the ability to utilize refined data in real time. Ingestion functions for big data processing are handled by an array of SAP solutions across enterprise and Hadoop data. Open source solutions can be used for ingestion to the SAP Distribution for Hadoop software. SAP ingestion solutions can ingest data to an SAP HANA stack or to Hadoop, depending on analytics requirements.

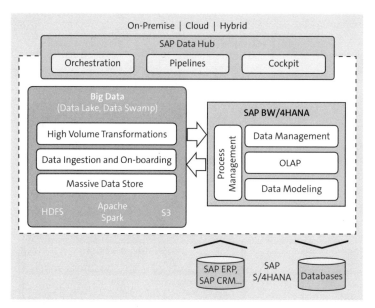

Figure 14.10 SAP Leonardo Big Data Portfolio

A new feather in the cap of the SAP Leonardo Big Data is the SAP Data Hub (which we already touched on in Chapter 8 but will review here in the context of SAP Leonardo). SAP Data Hub is a pipeline-driven, cloud container-based data integration, operations, and governance solution. All the necessary components are fully containerized, and deployment is on cloud environments with managed Kubernetes. It has a built-in metadata catalog to discover, define, and understand sources and search for metadata attributes and tags, and it allows automated metadata crawling for SAP HANA, cloud stores, and SAP Vora. The metadata can be visually evaluated using an SAP Data Hub metadata explorer. SAP Data Hub also encompasses a unified modeling tool for workflows, pipelines, and data transforms called the Pipeline Modeler. It enables data sharing, pipelining, and governance of all data in the connected landscape. Figure 14.11 shows the complete SAP Data Hub portfolio architecture.

SAP Data Hub enables self-service data preparation with SAP Agile Data Preparation and a comprehensive monitoring and diagnostic framework. From a connectivity point of view, SAP Data Hub has enhanced connectivity to databases, big data stores, and cloud native technologies, as well as integration into SAP S/4HANA, SAP C/4HANA, SAP MDG, and so on. SAP Data Hub is an open data architecture that works across Hadoop, data lakes, cloud object storage, relational databases, enterprise applications, and more.

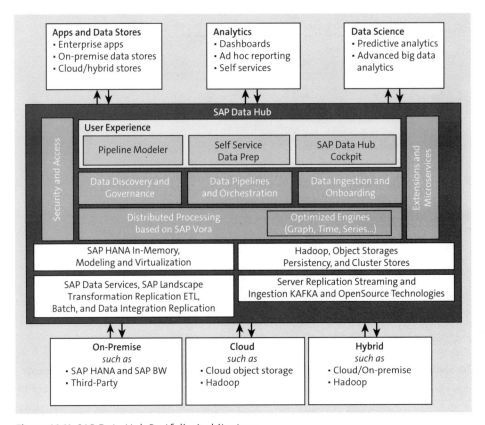

Figure 14.11 SAP Data Hub Portfolio Architecture

One or more components of SAP Leonardo can be integrated with business processes to enable solutions such as SAP S/4HANA to provide an integrated and more intelligent offering. Custom applications residing on SAP S/4HANA can also be built that can leverage the out-of-the-box SAP Leonardo capabilities. For example, various solutions, such as text processing and training of models in SAP Leonardo portfolio, coupled with data pipelining from SAP Data Hub can be used for an intelligent data governance. It can utilize heterogenous data managed by SAP Data Hub and orchestrate enterprise data with big data to feed machine learning models (see Figure 14.12).

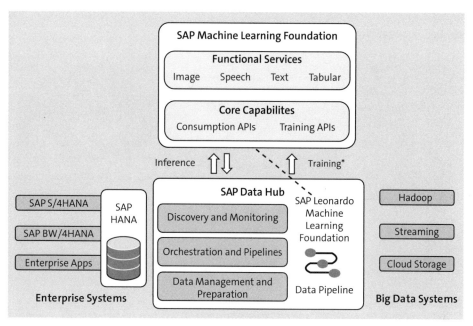

Figure 14.12 Concordance between SAP Leonardo Machine Learning Foundation and SAP Data Hub

14.6   SAP Leonardo Use Cases

With SAP Leonardo, industries can experiment with new business models with emerging technology put into action at lesser risk, quicker turnaround, and without huge up-front capital for the computing storage on the cloud. In this section, we'll try to bring to life a couple of use cases and highlight where and how SAP Leonardo and SAP Cloud Platform components are used along the workflow of the products and services in their respective industries.

14.6.1   Use Case 1: Consumer Packaged Goods Industry

SAP Leonardo IoT and SAP Cloud Platform combined offer several accelerators to jump-start your innovations on the cloud or offer tools to create your own application to bring innovations into play with your own business model. Figure 14.13 illustrates the convergence of IoT with the Industry 4.0 revolution and how it moves from external scenarios to in-house industrial operations to cater to the markets. We'll illustrate a consumer packaged goods (CPG) use case to see how this approach is applied in a real-world scenario.

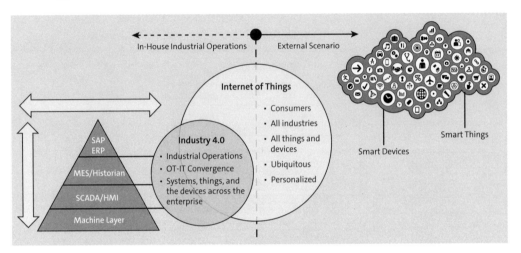

Figure 14.13 Convergence of Industry 4.0 and IoT

The marketing teams of the organization are planning for the campaigns that are based on the big data analytics driven by inputs from the data streams flowing in from previous marketing campaigns, clicks/comments/sentiments analysis flowing in from regional to global reach ecommerce sites and social media, TV advertisements, demand forecasts from the core systems, and probably the seasonal variations with weather data to throw in another factor to make sense from the huge data lake (Hadoop, Spark, or SAP Vora) formed of these data objects. The SAP Predictive Analytics engine applied to the data is predicting an increase in demand in coming weeks due to the seasonal change, that is, a heat wave across the European region.

The marketing teams spring into action and devise offer campaigns that will drive sales during the season and engage with customers through the loyalty program for consumers via apps integrated with SAP C/4HANA using the SAP Cloud Platform Integration combined with SAP Cloud Platform Mobile Services to push notifications in a specific region. The consumers of the app start getting offers to buy their beloved beverage at a discounted price with a "buy one and get another at 50% off" deal. With the marketing teams using the SAP Commerce Cloud platform for multichannel framework for promotion, they also use the digital media at major public places to push the brand with a message to stay hydrated in the hot season. The loyalty app also helps point to the nearest vending kiosks or a retailer where these offers can be redeemed.

The vending machines are connected assets and are represented in the IoT enablement layer as a digital twin of the asset along with every single parameter based on the sensors built into the machine. Instances of these defined twin structures represent every single machine in the market or a region tracked through a global dashboard if required. The sensors can track the temperature, stock type, and stock levels and are connected to other vending machines in the area, helping route consumers to the vending machine with their chosen flavor in stock. The consumers use kiosks/machines with touch-enabled interfaces to invoke a friendly SAP Conversation AI-based digital assistant that will help them select their drink flavors in their chosen form, that is, bottled, can, or glass, with different sizes to choose from.

As the vending machines are equipped with SAP Edge Services from SAP Leonardo IoT, they are using the vending rate and stock by type and flavors with SAP Leonardo Machine Learning models and weather insights to predict the stock levels required in the next few hours to serve the local market. The machine learning models also help decide the temperature levels for the machine to maintain the flavor of the beverages per stock levels and product categories/types.

Machine learning and IoT SAP Edge Services issue stock replenishment orders back to the SAP S/4HANA digital core and to the suppliers connected to the digital core. On receiving notification on the SAP Fiori dashboard (enabled by a side-by-side extension for SAP S/4HANA and exposed to all supplier networks), the supplier dispatches the order to mobile stock vans in the field with a few voice commands to the voice-enabled digital assistants (SAP CoPilot) and sends the replenishment orders to the van crew over their mobile apps (SAP Cloud Platform Mobile Services). They are quick to action and the stock levels across the market are replenished just in time (JIT).

The depleting stock levels at the warehouse are already being fed into the SAP S/4HANA digital core from the mobile van stock, supplier stock, and the connected assets in the field. This gives a live view of how the market is reacting to the campaigns that were announced a couple of hours or a couple of days previous. MRP Live kicks in on SAP S/4HANA and starts requisition planning runs across the regions from where the demands are emerging. No sooner is a batch size met for a region, then the digital supply chain processes take over the new requisition coming from different regions of the state/country. The product demands from the markets are fed into the bottling plants, which are using the SAP Manufacturing Suite to give a live status of each production lines, a precise timeline of when the demand can be met, and notification regarding whether there are any more lines to be activated to meet the demand in the short term.

The key components of the SAP Manufacturing Suite of applications, such as SAP Overall Equipment Effectiveness Management (SAP OEE Management) for batch manufacturing and SAP Manufacturing Execution for discrete manufacturing, connect with the underlying layer of SAP Plant Connectivity, taking care of the integration with the Supervisory Control and Data Acquisition (SCADA)/Human Machine Interface (HMI) or other sensing equipment or devices. On the overarching layer, SAP Manufacturing Integration and Insights on-premise will give dashboards with KPIs for the plant operators on how all the production lines are functioning. The CxO office uses SAP Digital Manufacturing Cloud insights to collaborate across corporate boundaries and get visibility into real-time working capital and revenue flow with cost and delivery performance. The SAP Leonardo IoT Bridge is further used to mash up all the data that is flowing through the digital supply chain, status of all the connected assets, and goods in market and connected manufacturing KPIs to visualize key insights to adjust the manufacturing to market strategies on the fly.

Once out of the manufacturing plant, the SAP Networked Logistics Hub takes over the logistics along with SAP Global Track and Trace for the shipped goods. All the key processes of picking, packing, shipping, and goods receipt at the supplier warehouses are flowing through the SAP S/4HANA digital core to update the status of the goods throughout the digital supply chain.

After the warehouse supplier stocks are replenished, the confidence of CxO office is bolstered to execute and plan for further marketing campaigns to cater to the needs and demands of the market by leveraging all the insights from the shop floor to the top floor. This convergence of Industry 4.0 and IoT is made possible using SAP Leonardo and SAP Cloud Platform to their fullest potential.

14.6.2   Use Case 2: Oil and Gas Asset Maintenance for Upstream Plants

Oil and gas companies deal with the challenges of maintaining the assets not only at the extraction sites but also at the processing plants. The maintenance of the key assets in these plants is a major cost factor, and upkeep of the inventories for spare parts and reducing the downtime of key assets and visibility of the statuses on each asset and spare parts is of great value to avoid overstocking or understocking the inventories affecting the uptime and productivity of the plant.

With SAP Leonardo IoT, there are exciting new ways of dealing with the high-value asset information that open the door to enthralling new service opportunities. Imagine a social network for assets where you can centrally collect track and trace information of high-value machines across their entire life span. That's exactly what SAP Leonardo IoT-based accelerators will provide with the SAP Asset Intelligence Network, a cloud platform that brings together manufacturers, operators, and service providers. Manufacturers of industrial assets, for example, contribute maintenance strategies and manuals, specifications, recommendations, and other information to the network, which benefits the companies running these assets as operators. In turn, they help manufacturers by updating the network with asset configuration modifications and constantly transmitting usage and failure data along with product improvement recommendations. Not only does this allow the manufacturer to improve its service offerings and enhance products in the long term, it allows the operator to optimize the assets utilization rate and prevent maintenance issues.

With a new business model where the oil and gas company buys the equipment as a service with a "pay for what you use model," the OEM is responsible for the service and uptime to maximize its return on investment (ROI). With SAP Asset Intelligence Network being used, the manufacturer also can track the functional location, usage, status, and any KPIs for the asset with the sensor data being sent to the manufacturer in real time. The manufacturer can arrange for an in-house or third-party service provider that will also have a view of the asset details over the network. Any service maintenance that is carried out on the assets is visible to the operator, manufacturer, and future service personnel as the history over the life span of the asset is available over the SAP Asset Intelligence Network. This information is used by the manufacturer to better its products and services via R&D and offering more competitive business models.

Combine the SAP Asset Intelligence Network with SAP Predictive Maintenance and Service using IoT to create digital twins off all high-value assets and IoT core services solution on the cloud, and we have a complete solution for asset maintenance and planning in which all involved parties can proactively work on ensuring maximum utilization and uptime of all the assets. With SAP Predictive Maintenance and Service, service providers can precisely predict when the equipment or part of the equipment needs to be replaced or serviced to keep the uptime intact. Let's bring it to life with an example flow:

14

1. The SAP Edge Services gateway in SAP Leonardo IoT is deployed on-site in a processing plant detects that one of the oil pumps is overheating, based on sensor values it's reading in real time. The SAP Edge Service raises a work order based on the crossed threshold, which it derived from heat thresholds the pump can handle from the SAP Asset Intelligence Network data that the OEM maintained.

2. The work order is sent immediately to the service provider to assign an engineer and get the work started before the pump goes down.

3. The SAP Predictive Maintenance and Service solution provides a deep dive into the incident with a detailed history, graphs, and predictive analytics. Combined with machine learning and SAP Asset Intelligence Network, the data predicts that the pump shaft coupling has worn out and needs replacing before a certain date.

4. A requisition to procure the spare part, with availability dates fetched from SAP Asset Intelligence Network from the OEM, is raised in the SAP S/4HANA digital core as part of the business process. If the operator prefers to procure it from its preferred vendors, this triggers the material requisition in the SAP S/4HANA environment, which then can be integrated using the Code Inspector with SAP Ariba to send out a bid request or, for that matter, procure from the verified and selected suppliers and vendors from the catalog.

5. In our case, the pay-per-use service model authorizes the manufacturer to be the selected vendor for procuring the part and so it's dispatched based on the dates requested on the work order combined with the specifications of spare part available on the SAP Asset Intelligence Network.

6. On the service provider side, the SAP Predictive Maintenance and Service solution also offers a dashboard for scheduling and planning, which can be configured with SAP Multiresource Scheduling. The planner schedules the order with a voice command to SAP CoPilot digital assistant on the SAP S/4HANA system, which, in turn, uses the robotic process automation (RPA) with SAP Multiresource Scheduling or other scheduling software if required.

7. The work order gets real-time information updates on the spare part being dispatched from the SAP Asset Intelligence Network. The lockers on-site are sensor enabled and can read the asset tags and work order QR codes. Based on the confirmation spare part asset being dispatched, the tag information is captured on the work order, and one of the lockers is reserved for the part to be received into.

8. Asset tags are scanned on receipt to open the locker. Once placed in the locker and locked, a GR is issued by the SAP S/4HANA system, and the inventory and stock

levels are updated with the status code on the spare part, that is, **New and Available**.

9. The service engineer reaches the site and uses the work order QR code to open the locker and use the spare part. The GI is done, and the inventory levels updated to have the spare part in the engineer van stock.

10. The engineer carries out his work updates on the work order with necessary details on the SAP Mobile Asset Management app on his phone using SAP Cloud Platform Mobile Services and puts the old coupling back into the locker using the old asset tag to open the locker that was recorded against the work order. The stock levels are again updated with the spare parts, but this time, the part is marked as **Old and Refurbishment** or **Scrap**.

11. Once done, the SAP Asset Intelligence Network is updated with the new spare part in the SAP Asset Intelligence Network BOM for the equipment, and the manufacturer can then use the refurbished part from the locker and the data from the SAP Asset Intelligence Network to understand what went wrong and use it for further R&D.

14.7   Summary

In this chapter, we've seen how SAP Cloud Platform provides the integration services to quickly support and adapt business applications and offers services that create the foundation for SAP Leonardo, such as analytics, big data, blockchain, data intelligence, machine learning, and IoT scenarios, with secure and scalable connectivity and integration across complex, multivendor, and hybrid landscapes.

We walked through the major SAP Leonardo offerings, from IoT, to machine learning, to blockchain, to big data. We've seen two compelling use cases of how SAP Leonardo fits with SAP S/4HANA for the intelligent enterprise.

In the next chapter, we'll switch gears and look at the various adoption paths you can take to launch your SAP S/4HANA implementation.

Chapter 15
Adoption Paths

SAP S/4HANA provides multiple adoption paths for SAP customers. Whereas a traditional upgrade to SAP S/4HANA would seem the most common path to take, many SAP customers are considering their options to meet business requirements. It's clear that the adoption of SAP S/4HANA is more a question of when than if, but the level of complexity around how to get there remains.

With the release of SAP S/4HANA, SAP has provided a digital core for its customers to leverage the latest technologies, ranging from big data and analytics to integration with cloud applications. SAP aims to improve user experience (UX) by increasing the use of mobile applications with simplified user interfaces (UIs) based on SAP Fiori. This transformation, with SAP S/4HANA as the digital core, integrates with innovative technologies, such as the Internet of Things (IoT) and machine learning, to fundamentally change the way we do business today.

In this chapter, we'll help you map your deployment path, including technical steps and associated restrictions. We'll help you determine whether a new implementation, system conversion, or landscape transformation is the right option for you and provide additional information about the steps you can take to get ready for SAP S/4HANA.

This chapter outlines the technical steps for adopting SAP S/4HANA. Due to the impact of digital transformation on the global IT market, every organization that uses SAP should be considering an SAP S/4HANA implementation strategy. Moving to SAP S/4HANA is the foundation of digital transformation, but this transformation can be confusing and disruptive. With different transformation paths to SAP S/4HANA (see Figure 15.1), defining your own SAP S/4HANA transformation strategy is critical for success.

Which of the three transformation options you choose—system conversion, landscape transformation, or new implementation—will depend on your objectives. Answers to the following questions will influence your decision:

- What is your starting point? Is this an SAP or non-SAP system?
- What pain points are you trying to address with SAP S/4HANA?
- What time to value do you need? How quickly do you need to benefit from the SAP S/4HANA solution?

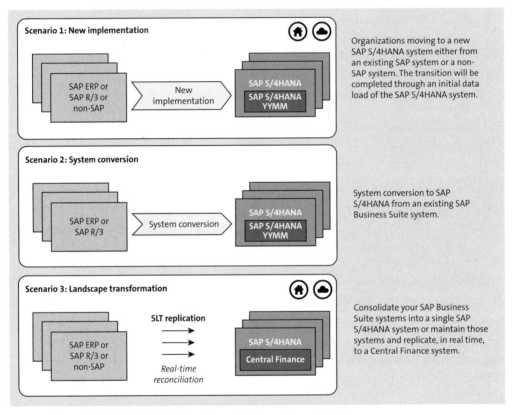

Figure 15.1 SAP S/4HANA Transformation from Current State

Throughout this chapter, we'll focus on all three transformation options: new implementation, system conversion, and landscape transformation. We'll address the key technical and functional considerations to be considered before moving to SAP S/4HANA. You'll need to decide whether to convert your current SAP landscape to SAP S/4HANA or perform a new implementation that will consist of migrating your data from your legacy system to a new SAP S/4HANA system. Moving to SAP S/4HANA provides an opportunity to redefine and improve your current business processes. The new implementation adoption scenario may provide more flexibility to perform business process standardization, or you may be looking for a mix of new implementation and system conversion with the landscape transformation scenario.

After considering the adoption scenarios, we'll discuss some prerequisites and considerations to think about prior to moving your SAP system to SAP S/4HANA. We'll include an overview of the accelerators and techniques available to make your SAP S/4HANA transformation project a success.

15.1   Assessing Your Adoption Options

There are multiple options to start your SAP S/4HANA journey, and understanding your options is the first step. Whether you know you want to move to SAP S/4HANA, you're trying to define a business case, or even if you want to highlight why now isn't a good time to go, starting with a SAP S/4HANA assessment is a great way to start. You can initiate this through a self-service assessment with the SAP Readiness Check or work with a consulting firm that will provide you with a more detailed analysis, business case, and road map when moving to SAP S/4HANA.

In this section, we'll explore the various SAP tools that help you assess SAP S/4HANA in terms of system conversion, business scenario impacts, associated value, and more.

15.1.1   SAP Readiness Check

To support the adoption of SAP S/4HANA, SAP has released the SAP Readiness Check to help customers understand the readiness of their current SAP ERP system for the move to SAP S/4HANA. This also provides a centralized view of most of the checks that are required prior to moving to SAP S/4HANA.

The SAP Readiness Check helps customers answer the following questions:

- Are my add-ons compatible with SAP S/4HANA?
- Which transactions are affected by SAP S/4HANA?
- Are my business functions compatible with or supported by SAP S/4HANA?
- Will my custom code work after I move to SAP S/4HANA?
- Which SAP Fiori applications are relevant for me?

You can find out more about the SAP Readiness Check for SAP S/4HANA via *https://help.sap.com/viewer/product/SAP_READINESS_CHECK/200/en-US*.

> **Note**
>
> The SAP S/4HANA Readiness Check can be implemented using SAP Note 2290622 (Setting Up the SAP Readiness Check for SAP S/4HANA).

If you're looking for a more in-depth analysis of your SAP system, additional consulting services can be provided to support your road map definition. Whether this is from SAP with the SAP System Transformation, Assessment, and Realignment consulting services or companies such as IBM through the IBM HANA Impact Assessment (HIA), a detailed road map, change management impact, and analysis can be provided to support your SAP S/4HANA adoption (see Figure 15.2).

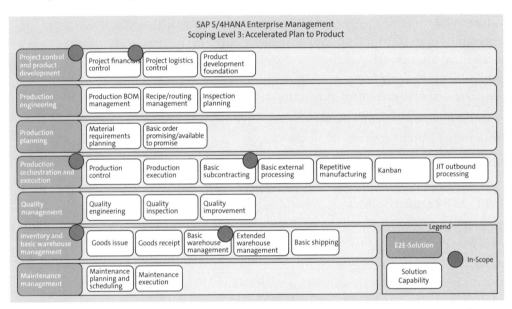

Figure 15.2 Sample Output from SAP System Transformation, Assessment, and Realignment Report

In addition to the above, the business scenario recommendation (BSR) report, SAP S/4HANA value advisor, and SAP Transformation Navigator can help identify the business scenarios impacted and associated business cases for SAP S/4HANA relevant to your organization. However, with detailed assessments like these, identifying your existing pain points and possible areas of improvement through a series of workshops will be vital to ensure you fully benefit from the value of SAP S/4HANA.

15.1.2 Business Scenario Recommendations

The implementation of SAP S/4HANA, whether a system conversion, new implementation, or landscape transformation, is an opportunity to reassess your business processes and identify where the simplifications provided by SAP S/4HANA can support your business objectives.

To understand the business benefits that are available when moving from an existing SAP system, you can leverage SAP's BSR report. This detailed report output provides a set of recommendations for new simplified business scenarios as part of SAP S/4HANA, including benefits associated with the SAP Fiori UX. It also provides recommendations for how to benefit from the SAP HANA in-memory platform to speed up your business transactions (see Figure 15.3).

This report runs using production usage statistics that allow SAP to provide output tailored to your specific business and organization requirements.

If you're interested in running the BSR report, additional information is available at *www.s4hana.com.*

Executive Summary – Top Recommendations

SAP S/4HANA simplifies and accelerates key business scenarios with in-memory technology. The table below shows the business scenarios in your system that could be simplified or improved and impact your business value.

LINES OF BUSINESS	BUSINESS SCENARIO		RELEVANCE FOR YOU	IMPROVED / RELEVANT TRANSACTIONS
Supply Chain	Basic Warehouse Management	Simplified	100%	114
Finance	Cost Management	Simplified	95%	87
Finance	General Ledger	Simplified	91%	59
Finance	Accounts Receivable	Simplified	86%	43
Finance	Profitability and Cost Analysis	Simplified	81%	38
Finance	Asset Accounting	Simplified	76%	35
Sourcing & Procurement	Purchase Order Processing	Simplified	72%	31
Services	Technical Assets, Structures, History		67%	25
Finance	Accounts Payable	Simplified	62%	27
Services	Service Execution and Delivery		62%	23
Sourcing & Procurement	Procurement Analytics	Simplified	58%	18

Figure 15.3 Sample Output from the BSR Report

15.1.3 SAP S/4HANA Value Advisor

Defining the value associated with SAP S/4HANA can be challenging, but there are several accelerators to help you identify which areas to focus on. SAP has released the

SAP S/4HANA value advisor (see Figure 15.4), which allows you to discover the value associated with your digital journey based on a series of value drivers.

Leveraging this interactive, online tool, you can select one or more industry solutions that you currently use or that you plan to use. In addition to the industry solutions, you'll need to select your line of business (LoB) and answer questions related to focus areas and priorities to generate your SAP S/4HANA value advisor report.

The SAP S/4HANA value advisor report will provide a high-level overview of some of the business benefits associated with SAP S/4HANA and identify client success stories that highlight the benefits other customers have achieved by moving to SAP S/4HANA.

If you're interested in running the SAP S/4HANA value advisor report, additional information is available at *http://s4value.com*.

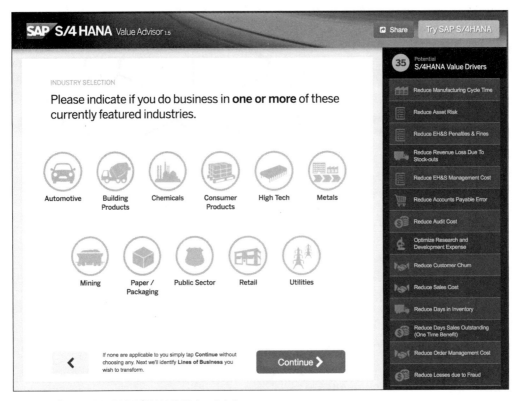

Figure 15.4 SAP S/4HANA Value Advisor

15.1.4 SAP Transformation Navigator

Navigating through the SAP S/4HANA world can be challenging, and the large number of SAP products available can make choosing the right ones seem overwhelming. Therefore, SAP has released a self-service tool called SAP Transformation Navigator (see Figure 15.5) to help define the strategic business and IT road map for SAP products. SAP has reviewed 2,100 of its products to provide clear guidance on the strategic path and the way forward, how its wider portfolio integrates with SAP S/4HANA, the impact on SAP licenses, and the business value of these applications.

If you're interested in running the SAP Transformation Navigator, additional information is available at *http://news.sap.com/navigating-to-your-digital-transformation.*

Figure 15.5 SAP S/4HANA Transformation Navigator

15.1.5 Sizing Requirements

With every SAP S/4HANA project, getting the sizing right for your SAP HANA database can be challenging; however, it's crucial for supporting your business operations after you're up and running. For those of you unfamiliar with the term, *sizing* refers to establishing the right hardware requirements for an SAP system, such as physical memory, I/O capacity, and CPU power. Getting this right is important to ensure that you can meet your business needs while trying to keep a low total cost of ownership (TCO).

SAP provides the Quick Sizer tool to size SAP HANA correctly and ensure that business requirements can be met after project go-live. If you're moving from an existing SAP environment through a system conversion, you can look to run the SAP HANA database sizing note that will allow you to define the database capacity you'll need once on SAP S/4HANA (see Figure 15.6). Although the questions asked during the Quick Sizer assessment may seem time-consuming and sometimes excessive, it's important to complete the steps accurately to avoid future sizing issues arising during production start. SAP also provides some sample configurations that can help define your SAP HANA sizing.

```
SIZING RESULTS IN GB
Based on the selected table(s), the anticipated maximum requirement are

for Suite on HANA:
- Memory requirement                                            706.4
- Net data size on disk                                         462.0

- Estimated memory requirement after data clean-up             625.2
- Estimated net data size on disk after data clean-up          420.9

Other possible additional memory requirement:
- for an upgrade shadow instance                                39.7
```

Figure 15.6 Sample SAP HANA Sizing Requirements

While assessing the SAP S/4HANA adoption options may provide you with an overview of functionality impacted or business benefits introduced, deciding how to adopt the next generation ERP solution from SAP will depend on your current state of operations and how you want to embrace this transformation. In the next three sections, we'll explain in more detail what options are available to adopt SAP S/4HANA based on the various paths available.

15.2   New Implementation

A new implementation is one of the three options provided by SAP to move to SAP S/4HANA. This scenario is valid for both existing SAP customers and new SAP customers. This scenario requires the implementation of a new SAP S/4HANA system with an initial data load.

As you learned in Chapter 1, Section 1.4, there are three deployment options for new implementations: SAP S/4HANA, SAP S/4HANA Cloud (public option or single tenant), and the hybrid model. In this section, we'll focus on the on-premise SAP S/4HANA, ending with a look at SAP S/4HANA Cloud.

15.2.1   Adoption Approach

As with other SAP applications, SAP has made installation guides available for SAP S/4HANA that provide a list of the necessary tools and documentation for your new installation. These guides also provide the follow-up activities required after the installation and, of course, a system landscape and product overview for the version of SAP S/4HANA you're planning to install. Access these guides at *http://help.sap.com/s4hana* to help support the installation process.

Like other IT implementation projects, SAP S/4HANA implementation can be split into three main project phases:

1. **Plan**
   Plan the scope of the migration effort and identify key business scenarios.

2. **Install**
   Install the SAP HANA database and SAP S/4HANA application.

3. **Import**
   Import and migrate data from legacy environments.

The output of these phases will start to feed the target architecture required to support the SAP S/4HANA implementation. In addition, you'll start to understand the scope of data migration work that will be required to move the master and transactional data from your legacy systems to the new SAP S/4HANA environment.

Each organization will have a set of business requirements that need to be met following these workshops. Figure 15.7 provides an overview of how the SAP S/4HANA architecture should be set up to support these requirements. This target architecture is valid whether your goal is to improve the UX via SAP Fiori apps, to provide more flexibility for the workforce by leveraging SAP Mobile Platform, or even to enhance reporting requirements when Core Data Services (CDS) views can be leveraged.

In addition to getting the architecture right, a key part of the new implementation will be defining the right data migration strategy to ensure that the data moved from

15

the legacy system to the new SAP S/4HANA system is in good condition—that is, cleansed, relevant, and timely.

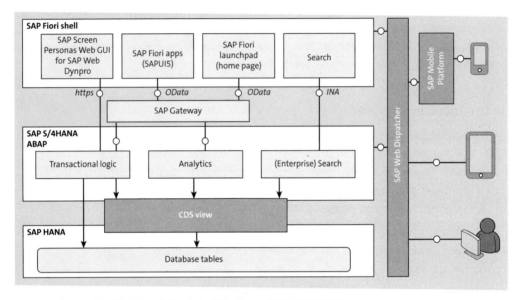

Figure 15.7 High-Level Stack Architecture of SAP S/4HANA

To accelerate the data migration process, SAP provides the SAP S/4HANA migration cockpit to support requirements for data migration to SAP S/4HANA.

The SAP S/4HANA migration cockpit comes with ready-made data migration templates that can be used to kick-start the data migration process. Additional cleansing functionality is also available to support business user review during the migration process. Loads can be simulated and account for system field settings and configuration, allowing the data migration team to quickly identify issues without impacting the SAP system and having to reverse data out after it has been posted.

The SAP S/4HANA new implementation scenario is also a great way to start over, especially if you want to benefit from SAP S/4HANA functionalities and industry best practices. Alternatively, you may want to remove your custom code that you've been keeping around for years and no longer use, or you may want to take the opportunity to realign your data governance and quality to leverage SAP S/4HANA as the core for your digital transformation journey. There are many considerations that may encourage you to embrace a new implementation, which we'll discuss next.

15.2.2 Considerations

The move to SAP S/4HANA is a great opportunity to simplify certain business processes and ways of working in your organization and to redesign the way you do business. If this is something you're considering, and you want to perform business process standardization, a new implementation may be the right option for your organization. Although starting with a new implementation may seem a bit daunting, a series of accelerators based on SAP Activate (which we'll discuss further in Chapter 16) provide configuration packs and best practices to set up the new system and complete the data migration required to get the new system up and running in a short time frame.

As part of the move to SAP S/4HANA, you should also take into consideration your current release level. SAP S/4HANA currently runs on SAP NetWeaver 7.5 (or above) on an SAP HANA database. For some organizations on older releases, such as SAP R/3 4.6c, a new implementation of SAP S/4HANA could be the perfect option to get back to the latest release while avoiding the challenges faced during the upgrade process and conversion to SAP S/4HANA. For organizations on SAP ERP 6.0, a one-step approach is available for system conversion, but a greenfield approach may still be preferable due to business considerations.

Items such as custom code should be factored into the decision of whether to choose a new implementation or system conversion. In an average SAP ERP system, between 25% and 50% of custom code isn't used, and up to 50% of modifications are considered obsolete. Adapting custom code to SAP S/4HANA can be very time-consuming and result in few benefits.

For a new implementation, this is a good opportunity to start again by leveraging SAP Best Practices and standard functionality. SAP Activate supports these activities. Any custom code that is still required can be leveraged from the legacy system and adapted on the fly to be incorporated into the new SAP S/4HANA system.

In certain cases, specific functionalities and features, such as industry solutions or SAP add-ons, may no longer be available or required. If clear business benefits have been identified that are driving the immediate move to SAP S/4HANA, it may be an opportunity to consider redesigning some of the existing business processes and start with a new implementation rather than waiting for the technology restrictions to be resolved. For functional restrictions, see Section 15.3.2. Report /SDF/RC_START_CHECK, discussed in Section 15.3.3, will let you know if any of your current functionality will be impacted.

15

Finally, you must consider the impact on your data with a new implementation:

- You'll have more flexibility to cleanse your data during the implementation if you decide to go down the new implementation route. This is an opportunity to restore data quality as a key part of your organization's governance procedures.

- If the effort and time associated with cleansing the data in your systems seems excessive to make your SAP environment "conversion ready," then, again, a new implementation may be the best option for you because it provides greater flexibility around data cleansing during the conversion process. You'll also be able to define the amount of data you want to move to the new SAP S/4HANA system. This option can considerably reduce the effort associated with the move to SAP S/4HANA based on the volume of data that requires cleansing.

- If you have a large volume of data and don't want to undergo a data-archiving project, you may want to follow the new implementation route and perform your data migration on a select set of data based on your future business and system requirements. This will also help reduce your system downtime, which can be considerable with a system conversion based on database size.

As part of a new implementation, excluding the design phase, data migration will be the critical part of setting up your new SAP system to support your business requirements. The following section highlights how the SAP S/4HANA migration cockpit can support your business transformation requirements.

15.2.3   SAP S/4HANA Migration Cockpit

SAP has released the SAP S/4HANA migration cockpit to support customers with the adoption of SAP S/4HANA via new implementations, and it has been embedded as part of the solution. This cockpit is available for both SAP S/4HANA and SAP S/4HANA Cloud and doesn't require any additional license costs.

Like previous data migration software, the SAP S/4HANA migration cockpit requires data extracts from the legacy systems, whether SAP or non-SAP systems, and leverages embedded migration tools to complete the data migration process (Figure 15.8).

The cockpit provides preconfigured content mapping for data migration objects, automated mapping, and self-generated programs based on predefined templates.

In the following sections, we'll take a closer look at the SAP S/4HANA migration cockpit functionality for both on-premise and cloud systems.

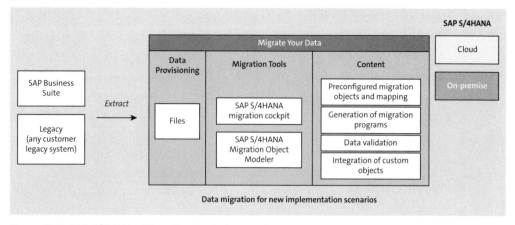

Figure 15.8 SAP S/4HANA Migration Cockpit Overview

SAP S/4HANA On-Premise

With the flexibility and custom development capability provided with on-premise SAP S/4HANA, the SAP S/4HANA migration cockpit also needs to cater for custom objects, including custom fields and enhancements that need to be incorporated into the data-migration process. The SAP S/4HANA migration object modeler (refer to Figure 15.8) provides the flexibility to support these business requirements.

Under the source structure, it's possible to perform the adjustments required to add fields into the standard structure so that data can be transferred easily to the SAP S/4HANA system. The same adjustments can be completed in the target structure to accommodate the transfer of data without any development required.

After the adjustments have been completed in both source and target structures, the structure mapping needs to be completed to accommodate the custom fields included as part of the migration process. The field mapping can be completed through a simple drag and drop of the fields to complete the mapping requirements.

The following is the list of standard objects available with the SAP S/4HANA migration cockpit (additional data objects will be included in future releases):

- Accounts payable (vendor open item)
- Equipment task list
- Accounts receivable (customer open item)
- Exchange rate
- Activity price

- Fixed asset (including balances)
- Activity type
- Functional location
- Bank master data
- General Ledger (G/L) account balances (classic G/L); G/L account open item
- Batches
- Internal order
- Bill of material (BOM)
- Inventory balances
- Characteristic
- Material (including long text)
- Class
- Material consumptions
- Contracts (purchasing)
- Profit center
- Cost center
- Purchase order
- Customer
- Purchasing info record
- Equipment
- Routing
- Sales order
- Supplier
- Work center

SAP S/4HANA Cloud

For SAP S/4HANA Cloud, public option, the SAP S/4HANA migration cockpit is embedded into the guided configuration menu. You'll need to create a migration project to start the data transfer from your legacy system to the target SAP S/4HANA Cloud system.

After your migration project is created, you'll need to select the data objects in scope for the migration and generate the corresponding templates to perform the loads.

The cockpit will support load simulations and allow you to monitor the data-migration process through a central cockpit dashboard.

The simulation allows you to perform data-load checks against the Customizing setup in your SAP S/4HANA Cloud system.

The following is the list of standard objects available with the SAP S/4HANA migration cockpit for SAP S/4HANA Cloud (additional data objects will be included in future releases):

- Accounts payable (vendor open item)
- Exchange rate
- Accounts receivable (customer open item)
- Fixed asset (including balances)
- Activity price
- Functional location
- Activity type
- G/L account balances (classic G/L); G/L account open item
- Bank master data
- Inspection method
- Batches
- Inspection plan
- BOM
- Internal order
- Characteristic
- Inventory balances
- Class
- Maintenance plan
- Code/code group
- Maintenance task list
- Commercial project management
- Master inspection characteristic
- Contracts (purchasing)
- Material (including long text)
- Cost center

- Material inspection type
- Customer
- Material commodity code
- Equipment
- Sales contract
- Material classification material price change pricing condition
- Sales order
- Profit center
- Scheduling agreement
- Purchase order
- Selected set and selected set codes source list
- Purchasing info record
- Supplier
- Routing
- Work center

The SAP S/4HANA migration cockpit will accelerate your move to SAP S/4HANA for new implementations. With predefined content and mapping for each migration object, no programming is required to create the load programs. Data validation is enabled through simulation loads and ready-made reports with flexible data structures, allowing easy integration of custom data structures for on-premise solutions.

However, if you've been heavily investing in your SAP ERP environment for many years or have recently implemented an SAP ERP environment that is customized for your business, a new implementation may not be the right option. The SAP S/4HANA conversion scenario will be more suitable for your requirements, as you'll see in the following section.

15.3 System Conversion

This section addresses the conversion options and approach to SAP S/4HANA for organizations that are already using SAP and want to move from their classic SAP Business Suite system to SAP S/4HANA. The system conversion scenario is only applicable for SAP customers already using a previous SAP ERP version that want to move to SAP S/4HANA. It's not possible to perform a system conversion to SAP S/4HANA Cloud.

Note

The section assumes that a migration scenario is the logical progression for you. If you're considering a new implementation, refer to Section 15.2.

In this section, we'll cover the adoption road map based on your current starting point by taking into account the SAP system upgrade and conversion scenarios; what to expect from code HANAtization, including SAP HANA code optimization; and how to perform the migration of data from the old data structures to the new simplified structures.

SAP provides a clear road map and sequence to move to SAP S/4HANA while adopting the system conversion transformation scenario (see Figure 15.9). Preparation is key when converting to SAP S/4HANA, and a set of tools and accelerators are available to download via SAP Notes to assess the impact of the move to SAP S/4HANA and determine whether this transformation scenario is an option for you. The tools and related SAP Notes were provided in Section 15.1. Given that some functionalities within SAP S/4HANA aren't currently supported or are supported with restrictions, a system conversion may not always be possible.

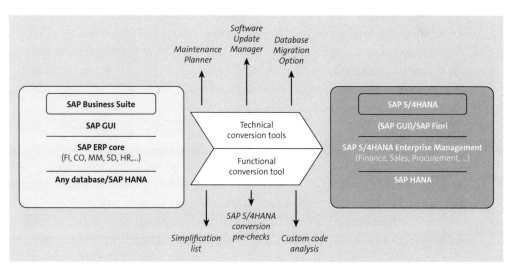

Figure 15.9 On-Premise SAP S/4HANA: System Conversion Sequence

Depending on your current SAP landscape, there are various steps to your SAP S/4HANA adoption. If you're running on one of the versions in the following list, you'll be able to convert in one step to SAP S/4HANA. If you're on a lower version, a new implementation or landscape transformation may be the best approach.

- SAP ERP 6.0, any EHP on a non-SAP HANA database
- SAP Business Suite powered by SAP HANA

We'll look at each of the adoption scenarios mentioned and evaluate the most suitable option based on your current starting point in the following sections.

15.3.1   Adoption Approach

Depending on your current landscape, several paths can help you reach the end state of SAP S/4HANA. However, it can be challenging to understand which conversion path is the correct one for your organization. Assuming a conversion scenario is the logical progression for customers running on SAP ERP 6.0 on any non-SAP HANA database, the objective is to move to either SAP Business Suite on SAP HANA or SAP S/4HANA.

For SAP customers that decide to move to SAP Business Suite on SAP HANA as an interim step, enabling the SAP S/4HANA innovations, such as SAP S/4HANA Finance or SAP S/4HANA's logistics functionality (e.g., manufacturing, supply chain, sales and marketing, and sourcing and procurement, discussed in Chapters 3 to 6) is the next step. Depending on the existing SAP ERP version in your SAP landscape, there are different approaches to perform the conversion from an SAP ERP 6.0 system running on a non-SAP HANA database to the SAP S/4HANA end state. However, based on the latest releases and more mature versions of SAP S/4HANA, its recommended to move in a single step from SAP ERP 6.0 to SAP S/4HANA.

With the past release of SAP S/4HANA 1605, SAP created two SAP S/4HANA adoption paths (see Figure 15.10) for SAP customers. SAP S/4HANA Finance 1605 contains the finance-only simplifications, whereas SAP S/4HANA 1809 contains the full SAP S/4HANA Enterprise Management solution. Note that SAP S/4HANA 1605 isn't part of the target SAP S/4HANA architecture and is only supported until 2025, given that most of the functionality is built on SAP ERP. SAP customers should look at moving to the latest SAP S/4HANA version (e.g., SAP S/4HANA 1809) and only look at alternative options if specific restrictions are in place for the target SAP S/4HANA version they are trying to move to.

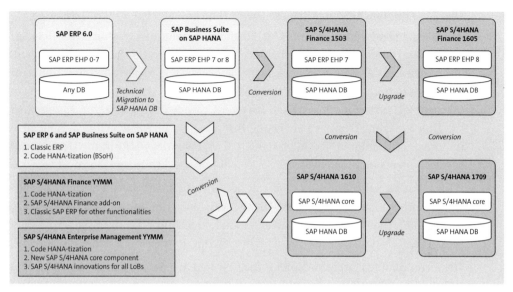

Figure 15.10 System Conversion Scenarios for SAP S/4HANA

Based on your business case, your organization will need to assess whether SAP S/4HANA Finance or SAP S/4HANA Enterprise Management is the right option. SAP S/4HANA Finance could be used as a stepping-stone to benefit from some of the SAP S/4HANA functionality while reducing the change impact associated with the overall move to SAP S/4HANA Enterprise Management. Although this may seem like an attractive approach, SAP customers looking to benefit from SAP S/4HANA's logistics functionality and other SAP S/4HANA simplifications soon will still have to undertake a second system conversion to benefit from these features, which should not be underestimated.

With all these different scenarios, it's hard to define which option may be best for you. The decision will need to be backed by a business case, but if you're currently running SAP ERP 6.0, it's technically possible to migrate in one step to SAP S/4HANA, assuming the downtime window is acceptable for your organization. If downtime is a challenge, customers that want to move to SAP S/4HANA by leveraging a system conversion should explore options using the Near-Zero Downtime (NZDT) approach or SAP Landscape Transformation approach (which we'll discuss in Section 15.4).

The following sections describe the two most common system conversion options available based on the SAP ERP release you're currently running on: the two-step approach and the one-step approach.

Two-Step Approach: Source Release Lower Than SAP ERP 6.0 on Any Database

If you're currently running your SAP ERP environment on a version lower than SAP ERP 6.0, and you want to pursue the system conversion route, you'll need to upgrade your existing SAP system to a release that will allow you to perform the system conversion in one step using the Database Migration Option (DMO) of Software Update Manager (SUM). If your SAP system isn't yet Unicode-compatible, you can perform the Unicode conversion as part of the first upgrade phase, which is a mandatory requirement to migrate to SAP S/4HANA. If you want to perform the Unicode and system conversion in one step, see Section 15.4 on SAP Landscape Transformation.

With a traditional conversion, you can perform the Unicode conversion at a later stage; however, if your target SAP S/4HANA version is running on SAP NetWeaver AS for ABAP 7.5, the DMO won't be able to handle the Unicode conversion at the same time. Therefore, you should complete the Unicode conversion as early as possible.

The recommended target version for the first step in a two-step approach is to move to SAP ERP 6.0 EHP 7 or above and perform the Unicode conversion at the same time. If you have a non-Unicode system, it isn't possible to move directly to SAP ERP 6.0 EHP 8 given that EHP 8 runs on SAP NetWeaver 7.5 and the system requires a Unicode source system, as mentioned previously.

One-Step Approach: Source Release SAP ERP 6.0 or Higher on Any Database

If your SAP system currently runs on SAP ERP 6.0, performing the conversion to SAP S/4HANA and the technical database migration to SAP HANA can be combined, again assuming the downtime window is acceptable for the business.

If the downtime window isn't achievable, you should consider downtime optimization. Various options are detailed in Section 15.3.3. The alternative is to separate these two activities. As a first step, you can perform the upgrade and SAP HANA database migration by taking your current SAP ERP system to SAP Business Suite on SAP HANA.

The second activity consists of converting your system from SAP Business Suite on SAP HANA to SAP S/4HANA. This activity transfers your data from the old data structures to the new simplified data structures, allowing your organization to benefit from the new simplified processes available within SAP S/4HANA.

The SAP S/4HANA system conversion scenario is also a great way to leverage your existing investment, especially if you want to benefit from SAP S/4HANA functionalities quickly while limiting change management and business disruption. In the following section, we highlight some of the considerations that may encourage you to embrace a system conversion.

15.3.2 Considerations

A system conversion will provide you with less flexibility to enhance your business processes compared to a new implementation; however, you'll still benefit from the mandatory simplifications SAP provides as part of the move to SAP S/4HANA. This can be a difficult decision to make, especially for customers who have spent many years investing in their existing SAP ERP environment; for others, it will be a no-brainer.

If most your custom code is still in use or required, a system conversion may be the correct approach for your organization. Under these circumstances, you can pursue a system conversion and implement a small code-cleansing project prior to the conversion start to help reduce the system code base and return to SAP's standard functionality. This also reduces the TCO of your SAP system further down the line.

Functionality restrictions linked to industry solutions or SAP add-ons not yet supported by SAP S/4HANA can be problematic if you're using these functionalities within your existing SAP environment and looking to convert your existing SAP system to SAP S/4HANA. You may want to delay your system conversion until they are made available. In the meantime, SAP has started to provide options to remove some additional add-ons, which will help with the transition to SAP S/4HANA.

> **Note**
>
> More information about currently unsupported industry solutions and add-ons is available in SAP Note 2011192 (Uninstalling ABAP Add-Ons).

> **Note**
>
> SAP also provides compatibility packs that allow SAP customers a limited-use right to run classic SAP ERP solutions on an SAP S/4HANA installation. The use right currently expires on December 31, 2025.
>
> Additional information and the scope matrix for SAP compatibility packages for SAP S/4HANA can be found in SAP Note 2269324 (Compatibility Scope Matrix for SAP S/4HANA On-Premise).

15

Finally, you may want to consider the impact on your data with a system conversion:

- A system conversion requires a high level of data quality, and you'll need to perform some cleansing activities during the conversion project if you want to successfully migrate your data from the old data structures to the new SAP S/4HANA data structures. This is even more applicable if you want to move from classic G/L directly to SAP S/4HANA.

- If you've been running your SAP ERP system for multiple years and have undertaken many upgrades, the system conversion process will be more complicated. In this case, allocating the right amount of time and effort to data cleansing is key, especially up front. This data cleansing can be initiated as part of the system conversion phase during the sandbox conversion. You can address any challenges or issues that occur and cleanse the data during the sandbox conversion. More importantly, these adjustments and cleansing activities need to be replicated accordingly into the production environment to ensure that the data issues don't occur when performing the same activities on the other environments after refresh—especially in production.

- While performing a system conversion, there is no way to limit the amount of data that will be moved from the old data structures to the new ones (for selective data migration, Section 15.4 on SAP Landscape Transformation). If you've been running your SAP systems with no data-archiving policy for several years, then this can add up to a lot of data! The amount of data in your system impacts the downtime required to perform the system conversion, in addition to other factors, such as the number of company codes for batch parallelization. To alleviate this issue, you must introduce a data-archiving project prior to starting your system conversion to reduce data volumes.

Both new implantations and system conversions have their benefits and downsides regarding time, effort, and speed to implement SAP S/4HANA. However, because organizations will have invested differently in their existing SAP environments, these elements will be a key part of the decision-making process.

15.3.3   SAP Conversion Software, Tools, and Accelerators

The conversion to SAP S/4HANA is split into two main parts (see Figure 15.11):

- The technical conversion, which consists of installing the new SAP software and/ or migrating to the SAP HANA database

- The functional conversion, which requires a clear understanding of the simplification list, performing the simplification item check, and assessing the impact that SAP S/4HANA may have on your custom code and enhancements

In this section, we'll look at how these tools can support the conversion and what outputs they provide.

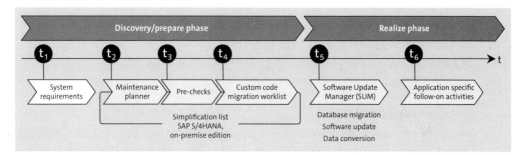

Figure 15.11 System Conversion Tasks for SAP S/4HANA

Technical Conversion Tools

SAP has been supporting its system upgrades and migrations for many years. This has given SAP the opportunity to build a well-established set of tools to support these types of transformation projects. Although SAP S/4HANA introduces additional complexity associated with the simplifications introduced with the new code line, the technical migration remains straightforward and relies on tools that many of you have used in the past.

Maintenance Planner

Most SAP technical architects or SAP Basis consultants are familiar with SAP's maintenance optimizer; however, this tool is no longer used directly for system conversions to SAP S/4HANA. Running the maintenance planner is now the prerequisite for executing the system conversion to SAP S/4HANA.

The maintenance planner is the successor to the maintenance optimizer and is hosted by SAP to help SAP customers manage their landscape transformation changes. The maintenance planner also generates the stack XML that used to be obtained via the maintenance optimizer.

Before the conversion to SAP S/4HANA starts, the maintenance planner checks the system for add-ons, business functions, and even industry solutions. If any restrictions are identified, the maintenance planner stops the conversion from moving ahead. You don't have to wait to start the system conversion project before running the maintenance planner; it should be run as part of the preparation phase to identify any issues as early as possible. Any remediation items can be managed before the SAP S/4HANA conversion project starts, if the system conversion is still a viable option based on the results provided.

Software Update Manager

As in SAP upgrades, SUM is used in the conversion to SAP S/4HANA. The latest version of SUM must be used.

You'll need to run the maintenance planner before running SUM, as explained in the previous section.

Database Migration Option

For those of you already familiar with SAP Business Suite on SAP HANA and who have already migrated to an SAP HANA database, the DMO will be familiar.

The DMO allows SAP customers to move from SAP ERP 6.0 to SAP S/4HANA in one step. In combination with SUM, DMO performs the database migration from any database to SAP HANA. The combination of both tools is referred to as *the DMO of SUM*.

The DMO of SUM will be used for SAP customers moving to SAP S/4HANA that are running SAP ERP 6.0 on any database. For SAP customers already using SAP Business Suite on an SAP HANA database, only SUM is required to move to SAP S/4HANA.

The technical conversion is only one part of the overall conversion process required as part of the SAP S/4HANA conversion journey. Additional functional checks must be completed to assess the impact of the new SAP S/4HANA code line and simplification items on your existing SAP environment.

Functional Conversion Tools

This is the area in which the conversion becomes challenging, but SAP now provides additional tool sets to support the SAP S/4HANA conversion. Although multiple tools are available, don't underestimate the time and effort required to get the solution right. Multiple challenges can be expected along the way.

Planning is key to a successful SAP S/4HANA conversion, and the tools described ahead can help get you started at an early stage.

Simplification List for SAP S/4HANA

The *simplification list* is a document provided by SAP that helps SAP customers understand the impact of the simplifications associated with SAP S/4HANA. Hence, the simplification list facilitates the planning and effort estimation associated with an SAP S/4HANA conversion project.

> **Note**
>
> The simplification list is version dependent. Each time SAP releases a new Feature Package Stack (FPS) for a given SAP S/4HANA version, a new simplification list is delivered for that version. Therefore, you need to make sure you have the correct simplification list based on your target SAP S/4HANA conversion version.

In this list, SAP describes the functional impact that SAP S/4HANA has on business processes, individual transactions, and associated solutions. In certain cases, solutions may have been merged or simplified with a new architecture compared to the source systems from which you're performing the conversion.

The document also provides a set of recommendations for how to adjust your custom code based on a series of SAP Notes provided within the document.

Simplification Item Check for SAP S/4HANA

As part of the system conversion, SUM runs a set of pre-checks to ensure that all the activities required to convert to SAP S/4HANA have been completed. If any activities haven't been carried out, SUM stops the conversion process.

To provide additional time and flexibility to carry out these pre-checks, SAP has provided the *Simplification Item Check report* (available from SAP S/4HANA 1709) as a standalone executable that you can complete prior to starting the SAP S/4HANA conversion. Again, like the simplification list, this report helps plan the activities and efforts associated with the move to SAP S/4HANA.

> **Note**
>
> From SAP S/4HANA 1709, the Simplification Item-Check (SI-Check) replaces the pre-checks available with earlier SAP S/4HANA releases. The SI-Check identifies all simplification items relevant for the current system. They will be called by the SUM tool to ensure that the system is in a consistent state.

Report /SDF/RC_START_CHECK is available within SAP Notes 2399707 and 2502552. SAP Note 2399707 delivers the new check report; SAP Note 2502552 delivers the check classes via transport-based correction instructions (TCI) and prerequisite notes. This SAP Note needs to be implemented in your source system, as well as the SAP Notes mentioned in the manual activities of the same document.

You can run the report as often as needed in simulation mode without creating any logs. With the simulation mode inactive, the report logs are saved in the application log and can be displayed at a later stage if required. Figure 15.12 provides a sample output of the SAP SI-Check report (report /SDF/RC_START_CHECK). At this point, you analyze the output and act accordingly. The green lights (squares) don't require any specific action, but you must address red lights (circles) before moving forward with the SAP S/4HANA conversion. The error messages in this report may not necessarily need to be addressed. Some of these items will require you to read and understand the information provided by the message provided in the list. You may, for example, be highlighted with an error loss if you proceed with the conversion that may or may not be an issue. These errors can be ignored or processed by adding an exception to the conversion process. They will be visible in the report output.

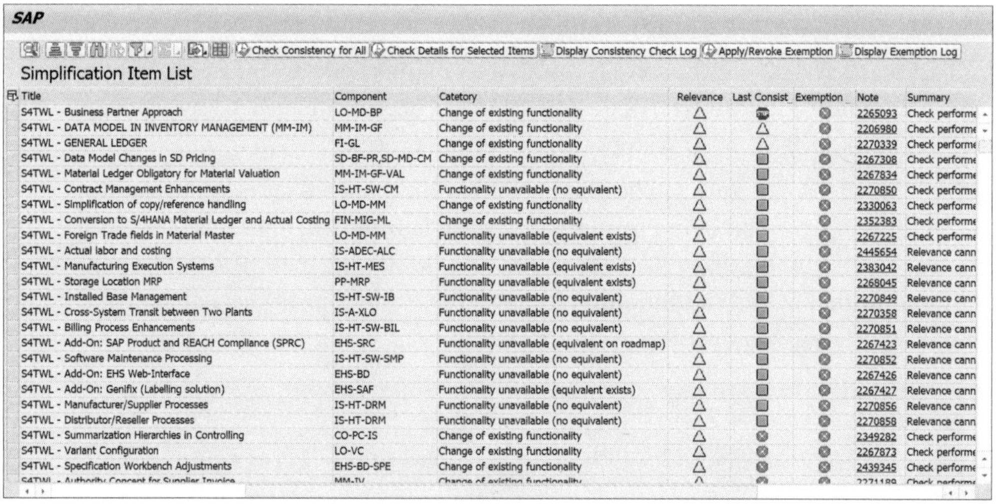

Figure 15.12 Sample Output for Report /SDF/RC_START_CHECK

After you've addressed all the simplification item issues, you can move ahead with the conversion to SAP S/4HANA.

Simplification Database for SAP S/4HANA

With the release of SAP S/4HANA Enterprise Management, SAP has created the *simplification database*, which is based on the same concept as the simplification list. The simplification database will be updated for each SAP S/4HANA Enterprise Management version. The simplification database helps identify the simplification impact SAP S/4HANA has on the existing custom code running in your system.

The simplifications are downloaded in a ZIP file from SAP Service Marketplace and need to be imported into an SAP NetWeaver 7.5 system.

> **Note**
>
> Information on how to download the simplification database is available in SAP Note 2241080 (Custom Code Check Content for SAP S/4HANA, On-Premise Edition). These simplifications have also been included in SAP's Code Inspector checks for SAP customers already running on SAP NetWeaver 7.50 or above.

To understand how these simplification items impact your existing SAP system, an extraction of your custom code may be required in the source system that you plan to convert to SAP S/4HANA. This won't be the case if you're running on a higher enough version of SAP NetWeaver.

After the custom code extraction program has been run, the ZIP files generated from the output need to be loaded into the SAP NetWeaver 7.5 evaluation system into which you previously imported the simplification database.

When the load is complete, report SYCM allows you to select the ZIP file that contains the extract of your custom code and run it against the simplification database. An example of the extraction process and output is shown in Figure 15.13.

The output of the report is also referred to as the *custom code migration worklist*.

Similar to the simplification list, the output from the custom code migration worklist report will provide you with a series of SAP Notes explaining how to adjust your custom code. In addition, drilldown functionality is available to analyze which code line is impacted in the custom program and to which functional area the simplification is associated.

This list of tools will help you understand the impact of SAP S/4HANA on your custom code, but it won't replace areas covered as part of the Code Inspector, which we'll discuss in the following section on code remediation, HANAtization, and optimization.

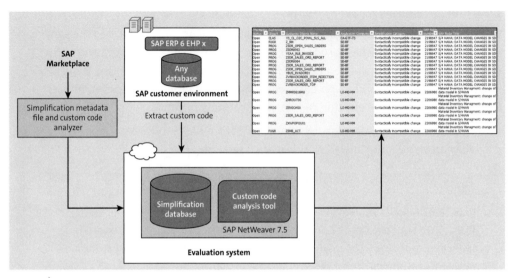

Figure 15.13 SAP S/4HANA Custom Code Migration Worklist

Code Remediation, HANAtization, and Optimization

As part of the move to SAP S/4HANA, code adjustments will be required; the amount of adjustments will vary based on the volume of custom code and the source version you're converting from. These code adjustments fall into three main categories: code remediation, code HANAtization, and code optimization.

Code remediation is required following an SAP upgrade. The upgrade contains code changes and introduces new functionality that can impact the existing ABAP code in your SAP system. Certain features may also become obsolete and may need to be replaced as part of the code remediation process.

Standard SAP code should work as usual; however, custom code may need to be remediated to ensure that it's still working as expected. Code remediation may be required due to additional fields added in a primary key of a table associated with a sequence of screen changes in a batch data communication (BDC) program, obsolete function modules, or even prior changes to SAP programs using access keys that conflict with the new upgrade code.

Like SAP upgrades in the past, adjustments with Transaction SPDD and Transaction SPAU will also be required as part of your move to SAP S/4HANA. These adjustments are required when existing SAP standard objects are overwritten with the objects delivered as part of the higher SAP version you're converting to. During the SAP

S/4HANA conversion, the developer responsible for the code remediation adjustments can decide, in agreement with the business, to retain or overwrite the objects based on any adjustments that may have been made in the previous SAP releases.

As mentioned, these adjustments are split into two categories: Transaction SPDD and Transaction SPAU. Transaction SPDD adjustments pertain to the list of all modified Data Dictionary objects, tables, data elements, and so on. Any adjustments required to these objects can be addressed within Transaction SPDD.

Transaction SPAU adjustments pertain to note corrections and modifications with or without the modification assistant. A developer needs to decide whether to adopt these modifications or reset them to the original statuses. All objects then need to be activated after the change.

Whether you're running SAP Business Suite on SAP HANA or SAP S/4HANA, an additional type of adjustment is required to allow the ABAP code to run on the SAP HANA database. This is referred to as *code HANAtization* and is required to make sure the code is compatible with the SAP HANA database. Previously, most of the code that consumed a lot of the system resources was managed within the application layer. However, to benefit from the in-memory architecture available within the SAP HANA database, the code needs to be adjusted.

With the conversion to SAP S/4HANA, the ABAP code adjustments can be split into two categories:

- **HANAtization**
  These are the mandatory adjustments required to run the existing ABAP code on an SAP HANA database.

- **Code optimization**
  Modifications to the ABAP code make it optimal and make it run faster to benefit from the SAP HANA functionalities. SAP HANA code optimization leverages items such as SAP HANA modeling with code pushdown, which delegates data-intense calculations to the database layer.

SAP provides a set of standard tools to help with code analysis for HANAtization. The Code Inspector (see Figure 15.14) and ABAP Test Cockpit identify the existing SAP code that needs to be HANAtized. SAP provides a set of variants within these tools that helps identify the mandatory requirements associated with code HANAtization.

The Code Inspector performs the code analysis based on the selected variant that contains the list of SAP development objects. The **Check Variant** area of the screen contains the information to perform the analysis—for example, "FUNCTIONAL_DB"

15

in the **Name** field in Figure 15.14. The **Object Set** area defines the ABAP objects for which the HANAtization inspection needs to be performed.

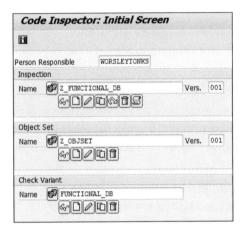

Figure 15.14 SAP Code Inspector Screen Selection

> **Note**
>
> You should use the FUNCTIONAL_DB variant in the Code Inspector. This check variant is delivered with SAP Note 1935918 (Downport Code Inspector Check Variants for HANA Migration), and it helps initiate the HANAtization process.

The FUNCTIONAL_DB variant contains checks that are mandatory for the analysis of ABAP custom code required as part of the move to SAP HANA.

The HANAtization requirements are classified into seven categories: native SQL, database hints, location of ABAP Database Connectivity (ADBC) usages, location of special ABAP Dictionary function modules, database operations on pool and cluster tables, problematic SELECT/OPEN CURSOR by statements and depooling/declustering, and location of nonrobust ABAP code. A few examples of these categories are described in detail in the following list:

- **Native SQL**
  Native SQL refers to the custom code that uses native SQL statements specific to an underlying database. Native SQL bypasses the synchronization of the SAP table buffers and can potentially cause data inconsistencies. An example of a native SQL statement is provided in Listing 15.1.

```
EXEC SQL
  SELECT WERKS,ALAND,WKREG,WKCOU
    INTO :w_vbrp
    FROM vbrp
  WHERE VBELN = :lv_vblen
ENDEXEC.
```

Listing 15.1 Example Native SQL Statement

The adjustments for native SQL as part of the HANAtization process mean that they must be rewritten as Open SQL in ABAP. These corrections can be made either before or during the project to migrate to the SAP HANA database.

- **Database hints**
  Database hints contain specific database code. In Figure 15.15, the database hint refers to an Oracle database and should only be used in exceptional cases. This can force the underlying database to work in a way different from what is expected as part of the standard SAP functionality.

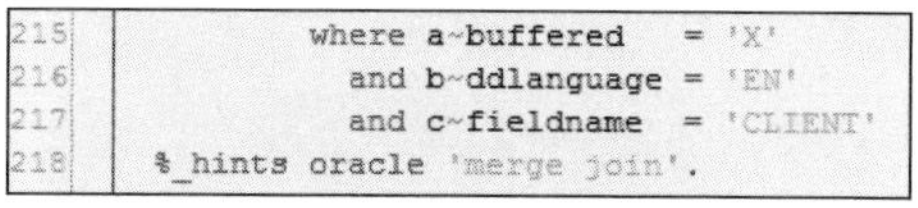

Figure 15.15 Example Database Oracle Hint

The adjustments for database hints are straightforward. These can be commented out, but this activity can only be completed after the migration to SAP Business Suite on SAP HANA or after SAP S/4HANA has been completed.

- **Database operations on pool and cluster tables**
  Database operations on pool and cluster tables refer to the ABAP code having direct access to the physical pool. After depooling/declustering, these accesses become hard errors. An example of a database operation on pool and cluster tables is shown in Figure 15.16.

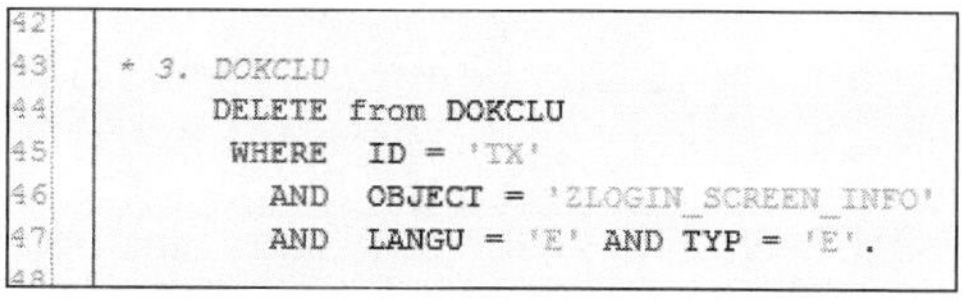

Figure 15.16 Example Database Operation on Pool and Cluster Table (Table Clusters)

After depooling/declustering is complete, the logical table is converted to a transparent table; however, the physical pool or cluster is still there but remains empty. This allows you to benefit from the SAP HANA analytical capabilities.

Per SAP's ABAP best practices, database operations should be avoided on these physical tables but not on logical tables.

The adjustments for database operations on pool and cluster tables require a rewrite of the code to avoid database operations. These corrections can be completed prior to the SAP HANA migration start.

- **Problematic by statements and depooling/declustering**
  Depooling/declustering requires a search for SELECT and OPEN CURSOR statements for pool or cluster tables for which no ORDER BY clause is specified. This becomes an issue when the order of the returned database entries changes if the database table is modified into a transparent table. An example of depooling/declustering is shown in Figure 15.17.

```
65        SELECT * FROM MSKU into table it_msku
66              WHERE MATNR = MATNR
67              AND    KUNNR = KUNNR
68              AND    SOBKZ = KONSIKUNDE.
69    ◊ elseif werks ne ' ' and matnr eq ' '.
```

Figure 15.17 Example of Depooling/Declustering

Per SAP's ABAP best practices, results should be sorted when the result is stored manually in an internal table. These corrections can be made prior to the start of the SAP HANA migration.

In the previous examples, we captured a few areas that require adjustments to run on the SAP HANA database platform. These issues will be flagged by the Code Inspector and classified into three categories (see Figure 15.18):

- Errors (red)
- Warnings (yellow)
- Information (green)

Some of these modifications will be mandatory, such as for the errors in Figure 15.18; others will just be recommendations.

For the SAP conversion scenarios described in Section 15.3.1, modernization and optimization of the remaining custom code is a separate activity, possibly driven by other business change requirements or transformational requirements. For new implementations, SAP S/4HANA-enabled custom code is the default.

Tests	Error	Warn...	Infor...
List of Checks	94	97	1320
Security Checks	0	0	0
Robust Programming	94	97	1320
Search DB Operations in Pool/Cluster Tables	0	0	0
Search problematic statements for result of SELECT/OPEN CURSOR without ORDER BY	94	97	1320
Errors	94	0	0
Warnings	0	97	0
Information	0	0	1320
Search Functs.	0	0	0

Figure 15.18 Sample Code Inspector Output

> **Note**
>
> For SAP HANA code remediation best practices and considerations, additional information can be found in SAP Note 1912445 (ABAP Custom Code Migration for SAP HANA—Recommendations and Code Inspector Variants for SAP HANA Migration).

Application-Specific Conversion Steps

In addition to the assessments completed with the simplification list, the simplification database, and the SAP S/4HANA SI-Checks, some application-specific conversion activities are required to complete the data conversion to SAP S/4HANA after the installation of the software.

The activities required for each of these applications will vary based on the target SAP S/4HANA version you're converting to. For example, if you're converting to SAP S/4HANA 1709, you may not benefit from the wider simplifications and innovations available in SAP S/4HANA 1809; therefore, some of the conversion steps and prerequisites may be different.

SAP S/4HANA Finance Data Conversion

The SAP S/4HANA Finance data conversion process is tied closely to the overall SAP S/4HANA system conversion and can't be executed in isolation.

Prior to performing the application-specific follow-on activities, it's important to ensure that the steps already addressed in this chapter have been completed, as follows:

1. Complete the SI-Checks to ensure that SAP S/4HANA Finance can be installed.

2. Execute the functional SI-Checks to ensure the completeness of the financial data.

3. Assess and perform any adjustments to custom programs that may be required to ensure a smooth execution of the finance functions after go-live.

In addition to these checks, you must have completed the system reconciliation between the different finance applications. This will ensure the data will be merged into the Universal Journal (table ACDOCA) without any issues. Month-end activities for the previous period also must be completed prior to starting the data migration from the old data structures to the new ones that are available with SAP S/4HANA.

Additional migration and configuration requirements are required for the following FI functions:

- SAP General Ledger (G/L)
- Asset Accounting (FI-AA)
- Cash Management

After the configuration steps are completed for these items, the execution of the data conversion can proceed from the old data structures to the new ones.

Note

If you're migrating from classic G/L to table ACDOCA, although the migration is technically possible, additional steps may be required or discrepancies may occur due to the SAP S/4HANA conversion process (e.g., profit centers from profit center accounting may not be carried across to table ACDOCA – Universal Journal).

SAP S/4HANA Logistics Data Conversion

Like for the SAP S/4HANA Finance application-specific conversion activities, SAP S/4HANA's logistics functionality requires some additional steps as well, although these steps aren't as manually demanding.

During the SAP S/4HANA logistics preparation, you must complete the activities that are included as part of the SI-Checks. For example, a conversion to the new data structure for the material number may be required, as the material number can change from 18 to 40 characters based on options selected when moving to SAP S/4HANA.

In addition to the material number extension adjustments, a fundamental change in SAP S/4HANA logistics functionality is the introduction of the mandatory business partner approach. This requires additional Customizing settings to be completed and checks to be performed to ensure customer and supplier integration is complete, as all customers and vendors are set up as business partners in SAP S/4HANA Enterprise Management. Additional features such as credit management, warehouse management (WM), revenue recognition, foreign trade, or other features may also be impacted based on current usage of the existing SAP ERP system.

The detailed step-by-step conversion requirements are available within the target conversion guides for the associated target SAP S/4HANA version. This includes the associated FPS that you've decided to convert to. These documents are available on the SAP help forum at *http://help.sap.com/s4hana*.

15.3.4 SAP S/4HANA Conversion Prerequisites

A direct conversion path to SAP S/4HANA isn't necessarily available for all SAP customers. A series of prerequisites needs to be met before it's possible to convert to SAP S/4HANA. Based on the business functions, SAP add-ons, or industry solutions that are currently installed in your SAP ERP environment, some features may not be supported. You either must remove these features (e.g., an SAP add-on) or perform a new implementation without these functionalities if you want to move to SAP S/4HANA and can't afford to wait for them to be made available in a future release of SAP S/4HANA. With the latest releases of SAP S/4HANA (SAP S/4HANA 1809 and above), most features and solutions are now supported; however, each item still needs to be checked prior to starting your system conversion.

You'll need to address multiple simplification items during the technical conversion to SAP S/4HANA. The conversion approach must also be tailored depending on the business's capability to accommodate system outages and overall project timelines.

The prerequisites required to convert to SAP S/4HANA should not only focus on the mandatory requirements but also ensure that your SAP environment is in the best possible shape prior to the conversion start. This reduces the overall project risk and ensures a smooth transition to SAP S/4HANA.

Some of the key items to factor into your SAP S/4HANA conversion scenario are listed here:

- **Migration timelines**
  Given the disruptive nature of the SAP S/4HANA conversion, it's important to identify the right time for your business to make the move. The usually avoided

15

go-live dates, such as key business sales cycles and financial month-end or year-end close, should still be avoided.

- **Custom code**
  As part of the conversion to SAP S/4HANA, many code changes are applied to your SAP system. Although most code will work normally after the conversion, some of your custom code may require mandatory changes to ensure a smooth transition. This also includes database-dependent code. As discussed earlier, SAP HANA code remediation is also referred to as HANAtization. (See Section 15.3.3 for more details.)

- **Technical and functional implications**
  Before moving to SAP S/4HANA, it's important to understand the current functional limitations the conversion may have on your SAP system. For example, if you're currently using classic G/L in SAP ERP, it's possible to convert to SAP S/4HANA, but you won't benefit from the new G/L functionalities, such as parallel accounting and document splitting. In the past, if you wanted to use these functionalities, you had to first migrate to new G/L, and then perform the SAP S/4HANA conversion. With the latest releases of SAP S/4HANA, after-conversion parallel ledgers can be activated with SAP S/4HANA 1610 and document splitting from SAP S/4HANA 1709.

Note

It's also important to ensure that all your current systems are patched to the minimum level prior to starting the system conversion. The minimum requirements to move to SAP S/4HANA are listed in this section.

With the latest release of SAP S/4HANA Enterprise Management, there has been considerable enhancement to the functional scope, with key additional features mainly focusing on the logistics and finance areas. These additional features have led to a change in the technical prerequisites needed to run SAP S/4HANA.

This has also led to an adjustment in the technical architecture of SAP S/4HANA. The architecture now consists of the following (see Figure 15.19):

- SAP S/4HANA core components
- SAP NetWeaver 7.5 (or above)
- SAP HANA database

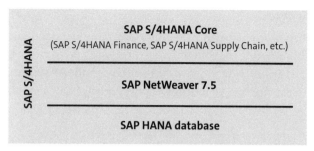

Figure 15.19 SAP S/4HANA Base Technology

SAP S/4HANA Application Prerequisites

While preparing to convert your SAP ERP system to SAP S/4HANA, you need to ensure that you're using the correct version of the Software Provisioning Manager (SWPM) for the installation and using SUM, with or without DMO, for the conversion. It's important to use the latest patch levels of SWPM and SUM that are available in the Software Logistics Toolset (SL Toolset).

Before you start using the SUM tool, make sure that you have the latest version of the corresponding guides:

- *Conversion Guide*: Converting SAP Systems into SAP S/4HANA Using SUM SP 15 (or above)
- *SUM Guide*: Updating SAP Systems Using Software Update Manager 1.0 SP 15 (or above)
- *DMO Guide*: DMO of SUM 1.0 SP 15 (or above)

In addition, there are different installation requirements depending on the SAP S/4HANA version that you want to convert to.

> **Note**
>
> On-premise deployment of SAP S/4HANA includes the component ST-A/PI. If this component isn't installed in your SAP environment, you'll need to use the add-on installation tool. If these add-ons are available, you need to make sure they are up to date. Use report RTCCTOOL, per SAP Note 69455, to ensure that the newest versions of add-ons ST-PI and ST-A/PI are implemented.

SAP S/4HANA Functional Restrictions

Prior to moving to on-premise SAP S/4HANA, it's important to understand the impact of the new SAP S/4HANA solution on your existing processes and to check if it's possible to convert based on the functionalities within your existing SAP system. The list of restrictions linked to moving to SAP S/4HANA continuously changes with the release of additional FPSs.

> **Note**
>
> For SAP S/4HANA 1809, see SAP Note 2659710 – SAP S/4HANA 1809: Restriction Note.

In the following sections, we'll explore the limitations of SAP S/4HANA in industry-specific functionality, finance, and logistics. We'll close the section with a brief overview of some of the technical limitations.

Industry Limitations

Although SAP continues to enhance its solution with additional industries supported in SAP S/4HANA, several restrictions need to be checked prior to performing the migration.

Table 15.1 lists areas and functionalities that are restricted in SAP S/4HANA 1809 and the SAP Notes that describe these restrictions. Table 15.2 lists the industries with limited and restricted functionality in SAP S/4HANA 1809.

Area	Restrictions SAP Note(s)
SAP Master Data Governance	2656712 2656693
LoB finance	2696359 2661581 2668594
LoB manufacturing	2668349 2668384
LoB supply chain – TM LoB supply chain – PP/DS LoB supply chain – EWM	2663403 2666947 2668150
LoB sales and distribution	2348936

Table 15.1 Restricted Areas in SAP S/4HANA 1809

Area	Restrictions SAP Note(s)
LoB commerce – SAP Hybris Billing	2351374
Advanced available-to-promise (AATP)	2642047
International trade	2669431
Globalization	2668307
SAP Best Practices content framework	2691784

Table 15.1 Restricted Areas in SAP S/4HANA 1809 (Cont.)

Industry	Restrictions SAP Note(s)
Aerospace & Defense (A&D)	2668085
Automotive	2668075
Banking	2661159
Catch Weight Management	2671323
Consumer Products	2668465
Defense and Security	2667104
Mill Products	2665709
Product Compliance	2667853
Public Sector	2662228

Table 15.2 Restricted Industries in SAP S/4HANA 1809

Note

For the restriction on SAP Patient Management (IS-H), see SAP Note 2689873. In addition to the current restrictions in industry solutions and additional areas, such as SAP MDG with SAP S/4HANA, several adjustments have been made to simplify the data model and business process within the finance and logistics areas. This has led to certain features being removed, impacting the conversion possibilities of SAP S/4HANA.

Functional Limitations

As with the Financial Accounting (FI) and Controlling (CO) modules, a simplification of the Sales and Distribution (SD) and Material Management (MM) modules has led to a certain number of restrictions within SAP S/4HANA.

First, the maximum material number length has been extended in SAP S/4HANA, from 18 characters to 40 characters. Therefore, restrictions have been introduced in the following areas:

- Archived data
- Application Linking and Enabling (ALE) generation for Business Application Programming Interfaces (BAPIs)
- Customer and supplier material numbers
- Logistics Information System (LIS)
- Integration with other SAP products

> **Note**
> Long material number–related restrictions are described in SAP Note 2233100. If you're using the extended material number, before converting to SAP S/4HANA, further information on the restrictions can be found in SAP Note 2384347 (Conversion for DIMP-LAMA).

SAP S/4HANA provides enhanced functionalities for material packaging, which creates restrictions for packaging material with more than 35 characters in combination with returnable packaging logistics:

- **Electronic Data Interchange (EDI) processing of returnable packaging account statement requests (message type ACCSTAREQ)**
  The IDoc type ACCSTA01 allows supplier and customer material numbers for packaging materials of up to 35 characters to be transmitted.
- **EDI processing of returnable packaging account statements (message type ACCSTA)**
  The IDoc type ACCSTA01 allows supplier and customer material numbers for packaging materials of up to 35 characters to be transmitted.

With SAP S/4HANA's logistics functionality, the business partner approach has also become mandatory, and restrictions have been applied for the number of fields that can be used. In addition to the business partner restrictions, the integrated solution of service parts management using SAP CRM Order Management with an active service parts management configuration (direct delivery scenario) in combination with SAP S/4HANA isn't released with SAP S/4HANA.

Additional restrictions associated with SAP business functions may occur while moving to SAP S/4HANA. When a business function is activated in the source system but defined as "always off" in the target SAP S/4HANA system, then system conversion won't be possible.

If the business function was switched off in the source release but is flagged as "always on" in the target release, then the business function will be automatically activated as part of the system conversion.

> **Note**
>
> For a full list of always-off business functions in SAP S/4HANA releases and feature packages, please refer to SAP Note 2240359 – SAP S/4HANA: Always-Off Business Functions.

Technical Limitations

Before migrating to SAP S/4HANA, you'll need to ensure that your add-ons are compatible with SAP S/4HANA. For standard SAP add-ons, Table 15.3 provides the name, component version, and software components that are compatible with SAP S/4HANA.

Name	Component Version	Software Component
SAP Access Control	SAP ACCESS CONTROL 10.1	GRCPIERP V1100_700
SAP Capital Yield Tax Management	SAP CYT MGMT FOR BANKING 8.0	CYT 800
SAP Capital Yield Tax Management	SAP CYT MGMT FOR BANKING 8.0	CYT 800
SAP Tax Declaration Framework for Brazil (SAP Note 2215394)	TAX MNGMT FRAMEWORK BR 1.0	TMFLOCBR 100

Table 15.3 SAP Add-Ons Compatible with SAP S/4HANA

Name	Component Version	Software Component
SAP Electronic Invoicing for Brazil (SAP Nota Fiscal Eletronica)	SAP NFE 10.0	SLL-NFE 900
SAP Decision Service Management	DECISION SERVICE MGMT. 1.0	DECSERMG 100
SAP Fraud Management	SAP ASSURANCE & COMPLIANCE 1.2	SAPFRA 120
SAP Enterprise Project Connection (SAP Note 2288953)	SAP ENTERPR PROJ CONN 3.0	EPROJCON 300
SAP Manufacturing Integration and Intelligence	SAP MII 15.1	OEE_ERP 150
SAP Access Control 10.1 for SAP S/4HANA	SAP PROCESS CONTROL 10.1 SAP AC 10.1 FOR SAP S/4HANA	GRCPIERP V1100_700 GRCFND_A V8000 GRCPIERP V1100_700 GRCPINW V1100_700 POASBC 100_731
SAP Risk Management	SAP RISK MANAGEMENT 10.1	GRCFND_A V1100
SAP Process Control 10.1 for SAP S/4HANA	SAP PC 10.1 FOR SAP S/4HANA	GRCFND_A V8000 GRCPIERP V1100_700 GRCPINW V1100_700 POASBC 100_731

Table 15.3 SAP Add-Ons Compatible with SAP S/4HANA (Cont.)

> **Note**
>
> For the list of latest add-ons available and compatible with SAP S/4HANA, refer to SAP Note 2214409 – SAP S/4HANA: Compatible Add-Ons.

For SAP standard custom-development add-ons, a list isn't yet available. SAP should be contacted at least three months before starting your SAP S/4HANA implementation to allow sufficient time for any adjustments if required. For supplier and partner add-ons, you'll need to check with them directly to see if their add-on has been released with SAP S/4HANA.

The list in Table 15.3 shows the current add-ons. If your add-on has been incorporated into the SAP S/4HANA solution, it will be considered part of the SAP S/4HANA Enterprise Management functionality and will no longer be considered an add-on.

Because SAP S/4HANA isn't supported with any code-page configuration other than Unicode, all SAP systems currently running on multiple or single code-page configurations need to be converted to Unicode. Based on the current level of your existing source release, the Unicode conversion can be combined with the migration using the DMO of SUM. Any language-related issues must be addressed prior to the migration start.

> **Note**
>
> If you're looking to convert your existing SAP system to SAP NetWeaver 7.5 or above, the source system also needs to be a Unicode system. Therefore, any SAP environments that currently run a non-Unicode system will need to perform a two-step approach to get to the end state of SAP S/4HANA running on SAP NetWeaver 7.5.

In addition, although SAP has removed dual-stack deployments with SAP NetWeaver 7.4, doing so is also one of the technical prerequisites prior to converting to SAP S/4HANA. Based on the current level of your existing source release, you may need to factor this into your conversion scenario. The SAP NetWeaver AS Java component needs to be separated from the SAP NetWeaver AS ABAP stack and deployed as a standalone system.

> **Note**
>
> With the latest release of SAP S/4HANA 1809, some of the restrictions associated with SAP S/4HANA 1709 or below are likely to change.

15.3.5   Minimizing Downtime

Although functional enablement of the SAP S/4HANA solution can be included in the same change window as the technical upgrade and database migration, you might want to keep the activities separate due to complexity, risk, and increased downtime requirements.

If two downtimes aren't acceptable, you have a few options to help minimize the system downtime during the cutover weekend. The following sections describe the traditional approaches available with the system conversion scenario; alternative options are available while using the SAP Landscape Transformation approach described in Section 15.4.

Data Volume Management

As mentioned in Section 15.3.3, it's important to maintain low data volumes via data archiving or by removing unnecessary data that may not require archiving. This is valid prior to moving to SAP S/4HANA, but it should also be considered as part of your best practices throughout the application lifecycle management (ALM) of your SAP and IT landscapes.

Data volume management (DVM) may not be specific to SAP S/4HANA, but it will support and help you manage your system data efficiently by reducing your data footprint. You not only reduce your system's complexity and cost but also avoid long downtime windows that the business can rarely afford and which continually delay these types of projects.

Before undertaking your conversion to SAP S/4HANA, you'll want to run your database as slim as possible to ensure minimized downtime. DVM can help you get rid of unnecessary data while ensuring that the relevant information is available to maintain your business processes.

DVM and the DVM work center run on SAP Solution Manager 7.1 SP 05 and above.

Optimizing Database Migration Option Performance

Several options exist to optimize the performance and minimize the downtime associated with the DMO. Once again, like in DVM, these improvements aren't specific to SAP S/4HANA and can also be applied on an SAP Business Suite on SAP HANA migration.

> **Note**
>
> More information on how to optimize downtime with DMO is available at *http://bit.ly/1Ub9OWK* in the SAP Community.

Use the benchmarking tool to assess the migration timelines for your SAP system to help you identify the optimal number of R3load processes and optimize table splitting.

If the overall performance of DMO still isn't sufficient to complete the SAP HANA migration within the expected downtime, you can enable the migration of selected application tables during the DMO uptime.

> **Note**
>
> SAP Note 2153242 (Estimation of Table Sizes and Downtime for SUM DMO with SLT) provides report RSDMODBSIZE, which helps optimize downtime by finding the largest tables in SAP and giving an estimation of their transfer time.

Near-Zero Downtime

The Near-Zero Downtime (NZDT) approach allows SAP customers to reduce system downtime from potentially days to only several hours.

The standard SAP S/4HANA conversion steps required during the project are listed in Figure 15.20.

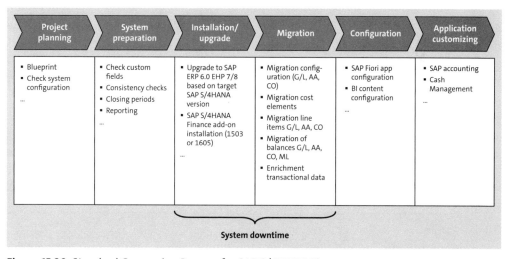

Figure 15.20 Standard Conversion Process for SAP S/4HANA Finance

Based on the database size, the SAP ERP source version (e.g., SAP ERP 6.0 EHP 8), the number of company codes, and so on, the activities associated with the system business downtime can vary considerably. To mitigate this risk and avoid a two-step upgrade and migration approach, SAP provides NZDT as part of the System Landscape Optimization (SLO) services. The NZDT version available for SAP S/4HANA works in a similar way to how it was used in the past, capturing log tables that are replicated at a later stage (see Figure 15.21).

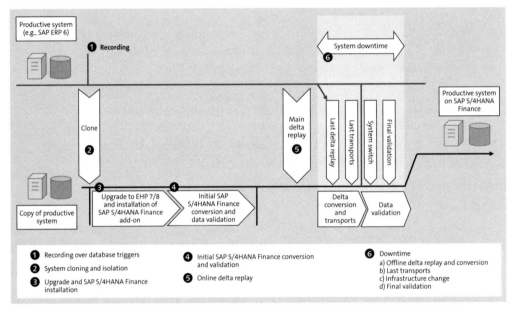

Figure 15.21 SAP S/4HANA Finance, Downtime Reduction with NZDT

All the SAP S/4HANA SI-Checks, consistency checks, closing activities, and reporting snapshots need to be completed in the production environment. After these steps are finalized, a clone of the production system is created, and the recording phase associated with the NZDT process can start.

Note

Like all other upgrade and conversion projects, the SI-Checks and consistency check activities are performed across the entire landscape prior to executing the same steps in the productive environment as part of the cutover activities.

During the recording phase, business activities are restricted and a "hard freeze" is put in place in the following areas:

- General (FI/CO/AA):
  - No archiving
  - No Customizing changes
  - No changes in the repository
  - No postings in closed periods
- Asset account-specific:
  - No data transfer for asset data (Transaction AS91)
  - No asset depreciation postings with old depreciation report RABUCH
  - No asset deactivations via asset transfer posting or full/complete retirement
  - No year-end closing activities via FI-AA (Transactions AJRW and AJAB)

All new records posted in the production system during the recording phase are captured in log tables and replicated during the downtime window. With the current SAP S/4HANA conversion steps, you can't select a timeline to define the amount of data that is transferred. NZDT allows customers to migrate only the delta postings captured during the recording phase during the business downtime window, hence considerably shortening the downtime window. All other activities are migrated while the production system is still up running.

15.4 Landscape Transformation

Most SAP customers believe that they only really have two options when moving to SAP S/4HANA, a new implementation or a system conversion. This isn't the case. With the landscape transformation scenario, SAP customers are provided with an opportunity to adopt SAP S/4HANA while leveraging their existing SAP ERP investment and transforming their business processes if needed.

SAP customers may think that the landscape transformation approach is only for customers that have multiple ERP systems, SAP or non-SAP, and want to consolidate them into a single target SAP S/4HANA system. Although this is one scenario, there are multiple suboptions that are available through this transformation approach as follows:

- **Scenario 1: Technical move to SAP S/4HANA**
  This scenario aims to help customers that want to move to SAP S/4HANA but have technical restrictions requiring them to perform multiple projects if they were to follow the traditional system conversion path. For example, if you're running on a SAP version prior to SAP ERP 6.0 or if you're not running on a Unicode system, this approach will allow you to get to SAP S/4HANA in one step. This approach will also support a minimized downtime approach or allow you to perform selective data migration, for example, the past three years, rather than the full history required as part of a system conversion.

- **Scenario 2: Functional move to SAP S/4HANA**
  This scenario aims to help customers that want to move to SAP S/4HANA but want to perform process redesign, organizational restructuring, master data harmonization, or new functionality activation. For example, if you want to move to SAP S/4HANA, perform a new G/L migration, chart of account harmonization, and process standardization, this can be completed in one step while moving to SAP S/4HANA.

- **Scenario 3: Consolidation of multiple landscapes into a target SAP S/4HANA system**
  This is the scenario that most customers think of when referring to landscape transformation. It allows you to consolidate multiple SAP or non-SAP systems into a target SAP S/4HANA system. This requires business process harmonization, configuration, and customization alignment. This is different from a new implementation in that one of the existing templates is used as the lead system and reconfigured to support the future business requirements (see Figure 15.22).

- **Scenario 4: Selective LoB or business split/carve out**
  This scenario enables a gradual transition to SAP S/4HANA while leveraging your existing investment from your SAP ERP system. This approach allows you to move, entity by entity, or region by region, your data from your source SAP ERP system to your target SAP S/4HANA system. The same would apply if you're trying to spin off part of the business into a target SAP S/4HANA environment. The complexity of running two productive SAP systems in this scenario should not be underestimated.

In the following sections, we'll explain in more detail the specific adoption approach that supports these transformation scenarios, as well as some considerations.

15.4.1   Adoption Approach

The underlying approach that differentiates the landscape transformation approach from a traditional system conversion is that the technical upgrade and transformation of the SAP ERP system is decoupled from the data transformation. This provides flexibility in terms of core system redesign, technical prerequisites, and data transformation.

The adoption approach is split into three key steps: creating a shell (empty copy) of your existing SAP ERP system, then converting that system to SAP S/4HANA, and finally moving the data back into the target SAP S/4HANA system using SAP Landscape Transformation or similar software that supports full historical migration. See Figure 15.22 for detailed steps.

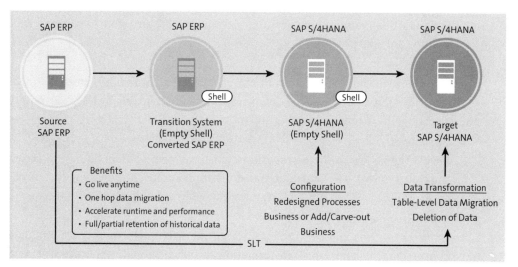

Figure 15.22 Landscape Transformation Adoption Approach

This approach provides greater flexibility to support system transformation requirements while leveraging your existing investment. This option is particularly attractive when there are specific areas target for transformation. However, additional risk and complexity may be introduced with this approach, and several items should be considered prior to starting this type of transformation.

15.4.2   Considerations

While considering your SAP S/4HANA adoption, the full picture needs to be assessed, and your target SAP S/4HANA end state must be defined. If the move to SAP S/4HANA means that you're going to have to perform back-to-back projects over the next three years, looking at alternative ways of adopting SAP S/4HANA should be assessed. This adoption process doesn't rule out traditional system conversion or new implementation adoption scenarios, and, based on your business requirements, both of these options may be still relevant for you. However, if you're looking to achieve any of the following scenarios, landscape transformation is probably your best option:

- **Transform**
  Transform and standardize your SAP business processes with SAP S/4HANA innovations while maintaining consistency through a lift and shift of some of your existing SAP ERP processes.

- **Harmonize**
  Harmonize master data (e.g., profit center, chart of accounts, etc.), organizational structures (e.g., company codes, plants, etc.), and Customizing by taking an empty shell of your current SAP system and moving this to SAP S/4HANA.

- **Consolidate**
  Enable the ability to merge repository (custom code) and configuration across multiple systems. The landscape transformation approach allows you to consolidate multiple SAP and non-SAP systems into a target SAP S/4HANA system.

- **Minimize downtime**
  Improve runtime and performance during the SAP S/4HANA upgrade and data conversion. The landscape transformation approach simplifies the SAP S/4HANA conversion as this is run on an empty production shell.

- **Reduce and cleanse data**
  Execute selective data migration and cleansing with full or partial historic data retention. This option also provides you with flexibility to perform a phased transition to SAP S/4HANA by moving entity by entity or region by region.

Note

An alternative option is to deploy SAP S/4HANA as a Central Finance system, which allows you to centralize all your financial data into one system in real time. The source systems can be SAP or non-SAP systems. This scenario is ideal for SAP customers looking to centralize their finance functions that can't achieve standardization in their existing systems due to a lack of global governance.

Central Finance will provide a consolidated view leveraging the Universal Journal. Although Central Finance requires a separate SAP S/4HANA license, it can be a stepping-stone toward your final SAP S/4HANA Enterprise Management solution. After your Central Finance system is up and running, you can look at incorporating carefully selected processes and/or legal entities into the SAP S/4HANA system, which will allow you to gradually decommission your legacy systems. The use of the original Central Finance system will gradually transition into a full-blown SAP S/4HANA system after all your business entities and processes have been incorporated into this system. This adoption scenario is equivalent to a new implementation scenario and will add complexity while you maintain two or more ERP systems throughout the transition. However, early value can be achieved with this adoption scenario by completing simple data mapping and real-time replication leveraging SAP MDG, which is provided with the Central Finance license.

The landscape transformation approach provides a real alternative to a lengthy new implementation while removing some of the constraints associated with a system conversion. With flexibility and options at the core of this approach, SAP customers should assess the option as part of their SAP S/4HANA business case and road map.

15.5   Housekeeping Activities

If you're considering a conversion or a landscape transformation to SAP S/4HANA, you have a prime opportunity to ensure that your existing SAP ERP installation is in a good state to convert to SAP S/4HANA. Volume of data, amount of custom code, and code quality are all factors that can disrupt your transformation to SAP S/4HANA. It's never too late to get your house in order, and we recommend that you start working on your housekeeping activities today to prepare your SAP ERP system for its transformation to SAP S/4HANA, especially if you're performing a system conversion.

Given that you're unable to limit or assign a time dependency to the amount of data migrated during the SAP S/4HANA conversion, it's important to ensure that you migrate only the relevant and required data. This is even more relevant for SAP systems that have been running for several years and for which there is no existing archiving strategy. Without archiving or data cleansing, all the data will be migrated to SAP S/4HANA, creating data issues during the conversion process. Archiving and cleansing your data not only avoids these data inconsistencies during your project but also reduces the system downtime during the cutover weekend.

Therefore, a detailed analysis of the data in the system that you plan to convert to SAP S/4HANA helps identify where inconsistencies and issues might arise and where you can reduce the database size. Consider performing the following:

- **Cleansing activities**
  Certain types of data that may not be relevant for archiving can be deleted soon after they are created. Data such as spool data, job logs, background jobs, and so on fall into this category. In a productive environment, jobs should be deleted on a regular basis.

- **Archiving activities**
  As the best practice approach, SAP standard data archiving is a free functionality to perform data management in an SAP system. You can use SAP data archiving to safely remove data from the database and store it in an attached archive.

In addition, SAP Information Lifecycle Management (SAP ILM) can be licensed to improve data-retention management (archived in SAP ILM–aware storage) by managing deletion based on defined retention policies.

To reduce the system downtime and optimize memory costs and hardware sizing, data archiving is a key part of the conversion to SAP S/4HANA. However, without an existing archiving strategy, it can be a challenge to delete or archive obsolete data from tables that show the largest growth in data volume in accordance with legal requirements and corporate policies. An appropriate data-archiving project should be started as soon as possible.

Note

SAP Notes 679456 (Reducing Data Volume before Unicode Conversion) and 1422822 (I18n Table Process Information) provide useful hints about which tables might be candidates for a size reduction that reduces data volume before a Unicode conversion.

> **Note**
>
> SAP Note 1659622 (SMIGR_BIG_ROW_STORE_TABS: Determine Tables from Database) provides the ABAP report SMIGR_BIG_ROW_STORE_TABS to identify large tables that will be stored as row-store tables in SAP HANA. The small memory footprint of the row store is beneficial to minimize the database startup time.

With a conversion to SAP S/4HANA, although your data footprint is meant to shrink due to the reorganization and column-store compression with SAP HANA, it's important to convert only the relevant data to in-memory storage. The price difference between in-memory and disk capacity is substantial.

The files archived before the system conversion are still supported and accessible after the system conversion to SAP S/4HANA.

15.6 Summary

Adopting SAP S/4HANA is clearly complex and requires a thorough assessment to understand which transformation path is right for you. Multiple considerations need to be assessed to understand whether a new implementation, landscape transformation, or system conversion is the right choice for your business. The adoption scenario needs to be aligned with your expected outcome and the benefits you're looking to achieve with SAP S/4HANA. SAP S/4HANA is clearly the way forward if you want to continue to use SAP and benefit from the latest innovations. You can start performing some of the housekeeping activities right away to reduce your overall project timelines and aim for a smooth transition to SAP S/4HANA.

In the next chapter, we'll explain how SAP Activate can support each of the SAP S/4HANA adoption scenarios and how to jump-start your journey with the SAP Model Company if you're looking to start again. We'll review the new SAP framework that supports the SAP S/4HANA implementation project, and we'll cover all aspects of the solution from agile methodology.

Chapter 16

Implementation Tools

This chapter focuses on SAP Activate, which is a framework based on an agile methodology that helps simplify the adoption of SAP S/4HANA whether it's for a new implementation, system conversion, or landscape transformation. In addition, we'll look at the SAP Model Company that provides a preconfigured template to start your implementation based on SAP Best Practices.

With SAP S/4HANA, SAP has introduced a series of accelerators and methods to jump-start your SAP S/4HANA journey and reduce the implementation timelines compared to previous SAP ERP implementations. Throughout this chapter, we'll explore the different methods and solutions available to guide you through your SAP S/4HANA implementation, leveraging learning from the past, and all embedded in a brand new methodology.

16.1   What Is SAP Activate?

SAP Activate is SAP's framework for SAP S/4HANA. SAP Activate is more than just a method; a series of SAP Best Practices and guided configuration come with the SAP Activate methodology to accelerate project delivery and lower implementation costs for SAP S/4HANA projects.

Throughout this chapter, we'll take you through an overview of SAP Activate, including how it's used and which aspects are best suited to the different types of projects you may be considering. We'll also perform a deep dive into some of the tools and accelerators SAP Activate provides to support your project delivery. We'll then demonstrate how the methodology and framework can help accelerate end-to-end project execution for your organization.

SAP Activate is a combination of methodology, SAP Best Practices, and the guided configuration packs that have been specifically designed for SAP S/4HANA (Figure 16.1).

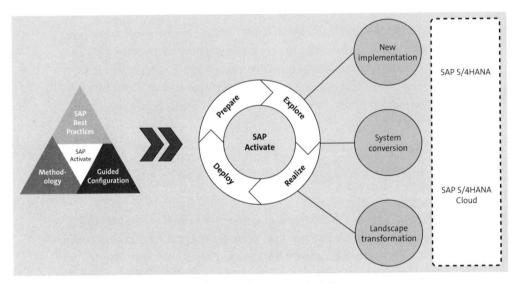

Figure 16.1 SAP Activate Overview and Deployment Options

The level of adoption of the SAP Activate framework will vary for each transformation scenario. You may choose to use only the methodology with templates and accelerators if you're performing a system conversion, whereas you can use the full suite, including SAP Best Practices, SAP Model Company, and guided configuration, for a new implementation. This is also true for the deployment scenario you decide to consider, be it SAP S/4HANA Cloud or SAP S/4HANA.

Although primarily aimed at SAP S/4HANA, SAP Activate can also be used for implementation projects such as SAP Business Suite for SAP ERP, SAP Customer Relationship Management (SAP CRM), SAP Supply Chain Management (SAP SCM), and so on. In addition, you can use it for some SAP Cloud Platform solutions, such as SAP SuccessFactors, SAP C/4HANA, and SAP Ariba.

SAP Activate is a flexible framework, given that it supports different starting points and different adoption and deployment scenarios based on the type of SAP S/4HANA scenario you're looking to implement. As noted earlier, this can be a new implementation, a system conversion, or even a landscape transformation.

For those of you familiar with SAP's ASAP methodology, SAP Activate is the successor to ASAP.

The SAP Activate framework also comes with a set of functionalities ready to support your SAP S/4HANA project. Based on the adoption scenario, certain features may not be available within the SAP Activate framework. These restrictions also vary for on-premise and cloud deployments. Table 16.1 highlights the features of SAP Activate available for each adoption and deployment scenario.

		New Imple-mentation	System Conversion	Landscape Transformation
Scenario characteristics		Data migration to SAP S/4HANA	Technical conversion from SAP ERP to SAP S/4HANA	IT transformation (consolidate or carve out) of SAP systems or a Central Finance scenario
Target audience		New or existing customers	Existing customers	New or existing customers
Deployment Option				
SAP Activate	SAP Best Practices	Yes	Migration and cloud integration	Migration and cloud integration, ready-to-run business processes based on use cases
	SAP Activate methodology	Yes	Yes	Yes
	SAP guided configuration	Yes	No	Applicable if ready-to-run business processes are used

Table 16.1 How SAP Activate Supports SAP S/4HANA Adoption Scenarios

16

As explained in Table 16.1, under the deployment options, the SAP Activate framework is split into three key areas (see Figure 16.2):

- SAP Best Practices
- Tools for guided configuration
- Methodology

Currently, self-service and expert configuration are available only for SAP S/4HANA Cloud versions.

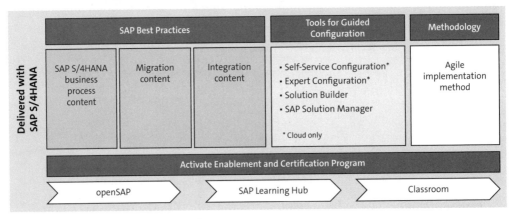

Figure 16.2 SAP Activate Accelerators

We'll perform a deep dive into these three key areas in the following sections. However, in addition to SAP Best Practices, guided configuration tools, and the agile implementation method, SAP Activate also provides a series of ready-to-use templates and accelerators that you can leverage throughout your project-delivery cycle. These accelerators are adapted to each phase of the SAP Activate methodology, and templates range from guidebooks to checklists or even questionnaires to support the delivery of your SAP S/4HANA project.

The agile implementation method accelerates product development and focuses on shippable releases, also referred to as *sprints*. The techniques used enable more efficient and higher-quality delivery execution while reducing the overall implementation risks. The agile approach differs from the traditional *waterfall* approach, in which each phase of the project (e.g., design, build, testing, etc.) was sequential. With the agile method, these phases become incremental.

Nevertheless, the use of these templates isn't mandatory. One of the benefits of SAP Activate is the flexibility it provides based on the complexity and size of your implementation project. How many times have we all struggled while trying to adopt a method or template before realizing that more than 50% of it doesn't fit the project or our organization's requirements? One of the benefits of SAP Activate is that it provides a set of standard deliverables for each work stream. You can either adopt or adjust these deliverables according to your specific requirements, as demonstrated in Figure 16.3.

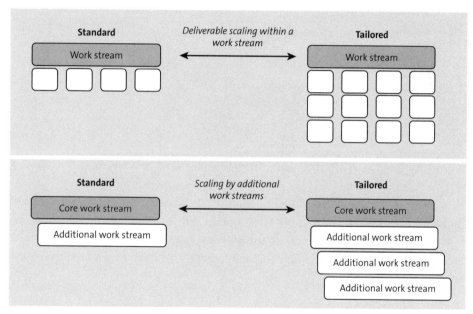

Figure 16.3 SAP Activate Flexible Methodology

If you want to explore some of the SAP Activate templates in more detail, sample versions are provided as part of the SAP Activate framework. These are available on the SAP road map viewer for SAP Activate at *http://bit.ly/2afat9p*.

Prior to finding the right templates for your project, you'll need to select the deployment scenario (i.e., cloud or on-premise) and the methodology (agile or waterfall) that you intend to use. In each deployment and methodology section, a set of accelerators and their associated templates are available to be downloaded, as shown in Figure 16.4.

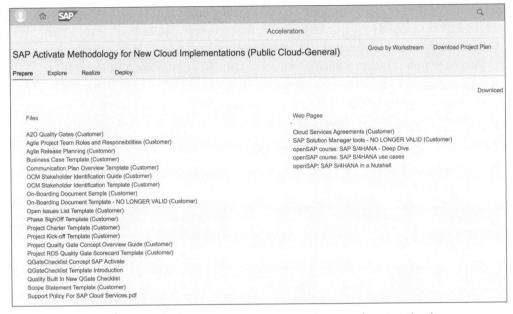

Figure 16.4 Sample List of SAP Activate Accelerators for SAP S/4HANA Cloud

Now that you have a better understanding of the ways SAP Activate can be used, including the scope and impact of each adoption and deployment scenario, in the following sections, we'll explain how to use SAP Best Practices, how to leverage the tools for guided configuration, and how the methodology needs to be adopted to achieve successful project delivery.

16.2   SAP Activate Methodology

The SAP Activate methodology is built on an agile delivery approach using SAP Best Practices that have been built to provide structure while delivering sufficient space for specific customer requirements.

The objective of SAP Activate is to accelerate the implementation or system conversion project you're undertaking. It provides structure and a foundation to adopt SAP S/4HANA with the methodology built around six key characteristics:

- **Start with SAP Best Practices**
  Use ready-to-run business processes.

- **Validate solution**
  Use SAP Best Practices to validate your process through fit/gap workshops.

- **Modular, scalable, and agile**
  Structure your project to deliver in sprints.

- **Cloud-ready**
  Leverage cloud-based solutions to provide flexibility and speed.

- **Premium engagement ready**
  Use SAP control centers to support building and running your SAP solution.

- **Quality built-in**
  Identify risk early with a total quality approach.

In addition to these characteristics, SAP Activate is divided into four phases known as *prepare, explore, realize,* and *deploy*. The phases and the activities associated with each phase support the project execution to adopt SAP S/4HANA (see Figure 16.5).

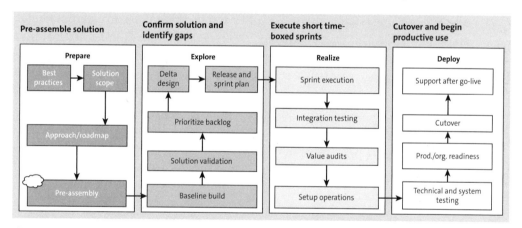

Figure 16.5 SAP Activate Methodology Phases

In the next few sections, we'll provide a detailed overview of each phase of the SAP Activate methodology before closing with a brief discussion of quality gates.

16.2.1   Prepare

The prepare phase is the foundation of the overall project kickoff and planning activities. You should start with SAP Best Practices to accelerate your SAP S/4HANA adoption. Doing so ensures process standardization and is based on business processes that have been adopted, tested, and tried for many years. The objective here is to provide faster time to value for SAP customers—that is, to allow them to benefit from SAP S/4HANA more quickly. The journey to adopt the SAP S/4HANA solution is already complex. Complexity will vary based on your starting point, but SAP Best Practices will help speed up the overall delivery.

These SAP Best Practices also provide a baseline for the overall solution, defining the scope of work to be adopted as part of the SAP S/4HANA implementation. Model companies also can be used that come with a full set of ready-to-use business processes, organizational structures, and sample data to support faster adoption. Additional detail on the SAP Model Company is provided in Section 16.5.

To get started with SAP Best Practices, you need an SAP S/4HANA system—either an on-premise sandbox system or a ready-to-use SAP S/4HANA Cloud solution—to explore the content. This is referred to as *preassembly* in Figure 16.5.

For preassembly, the recommendation is to use a cloud-based SAP system that will allow you to jump-start your project with a system that can be up and running in a short time frame. This system includes SAP Best Practices and is aimed at supporting the validation steps during the explore phase. This helps clarify any process requirements or gaps in a live system before starting any work in the development environment.

During the prepare phase, the target environments are set up, and you can leverage the preassembled solutions using SAP Rapid Deployment solutions, SAP Best Practices, and the other prebuilt assets.

16.2.2   Explore

Coming out of the prepare phase, you should now have your baseline solution initiated using the tools and SAP Best Practices identified in that phase.

During the *explore* phase, you validate your baseline and identify if any of the business processes differ from that baseline. This phase is used to play back and validate the business processes with the key stakeholders. The business process validation and the associated detailed analysis are completed during the fit/gap workshop (see Figure 16.6).

Two types of workshops will help define the target business processes to be incorporated into the SAP S/4HANA solution. First, the SAP Best Practices reviews, known as *solution validation workshops*, will ensure that most processes are covered with the

SAP Best Practices solution. This will also provide you with the opportunity to flag any gaps associated with SAP Best Practices and align the SAP solution to your specific business process requirements.

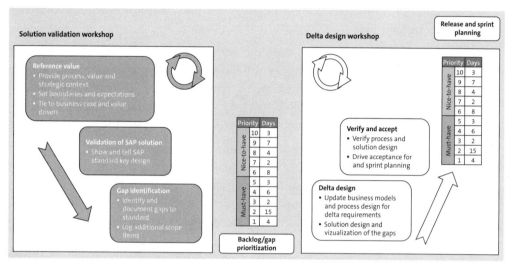

Figure 16.6 Fit/Gap Analysis and Workshops

After the solution validation workshops have been completed, a series of delta design workshops will be initiated, taking into account the number of gaps identified and the associated complexity of each of these gaps.

The target business processes then will need to be updated to be in line with the latest agreement coming out of your delta design workshops.

The fit/gap workshops should also leverage the preassembly solution put together during the prepare phase. In addition to the preassembly system, SAP Best Practices and SAP Solution Manager can be leveraged to initiate the documentation of your business processes. The starting point should be to leverage the SAP standard business processes and documentation, driving standardization across the board. However, any process changes identified during these workshops can be documented and maintained in SAP Solution Manager, as explained later in this chapter.

As an output of these workshops, the project team should have a clear understanding of the process gaps and the recommended solutions to remediate these gaps. After these gaps have been captured, the project management team can finalize the release and sprint plans that define the build and test activities per release, prior to moving into the realize phase.

16.2.3   Realize

Although the *realize* phase is also sometimes referred to as *build and test*, the agile methodology backbone of SAP Activate means you can expect shorter configuration and build cycles that are better integrated with the business functions to receive feedback on the fly.

The realize phase will vary based on the SAP S/4HANA adoption you've decided to undertake. Although the activities will be considerably different depending on whether this is a new implementation, a system conversion, or a landscape transformation, all the activities are still supported by the SAP Activate framework. You can find additional information on how to adopt SAP S/4HANA in Chapter 15.

After validating the business solution and undertaking the delta design workshops in the explore phase to flush out any additional business requirements, it's now time for your target solution to be configured, developed, and tested. This phase also provides the opportunity to execute testing and peer review to ensure the solution build is up to standard. In line with the overall SAP Activate method and agile delivery, the objective of this phase is to ensure that a minimum viable product (MVP) is ready to use. Additional features can be added through additional sprints. This will accelerate the deployment of your SAP S/4HANA solution and guarantee better time to value.

16.2.4   Deploy

The *deploy* phase supports the final preparation before you move all your transports into the production environment and execute the cutover activities during the go-live weekend. All testing activities must be completed prior to initiating these activities. During this phase, end-user training and execution of the change communication occurs. The project leads will prepare the sites for transition, and any data-migration activities are executed in the productive environment before handing the system back to the business users.

Prior to executing the live cutover activities, a dry run should be performed to capture timelines and understand and identify any challenges that may occur during the actual cutover. It's also a good opportunity for you to make all the project teams and business teams familiar with the activities they will execute during the cutover, ensure integration across these teams, and align expectations for the big weekend.

The cutover will consist of a ramp down of the legacy system and ramp up in the new SAP S/4HANA system. Interfaces need to be redirected to the new productive environments, and all the build activities completed during the realization phase should now be moved to production.

After all these activities are complete and smoke tests are executed, the system can be handed over to your business users. *Hypercare activities*, which entail supporting the production system after a new release has been moved to that environment, will start right after the project go-live, and it's important to ensure that your operations teams receive a handover to maintain the systems during the run phase. Handover activities should be initiated well in advance to guarantee a smooth transition.

16.2.5   Quality Gates

In addition to the four project phases in the SAP Activate method, a minimum of four quality gates are mandated as part of SAP S/4HANA implementation projects (see Figure 16.7). For more complex implementation programs, additional quality gates may be required.

A *project preview* session at the beginning of the prepare phase is strongly recommended to give the project team time to influence the next phase and perform any necessary adjustments. *Review* sessions at the end of each phase are mandatory to guarantee project standards and to ensure the agreed approach has been followed. It's possible to combine the preview and the review sessions for each phase to accelerate the overall process.

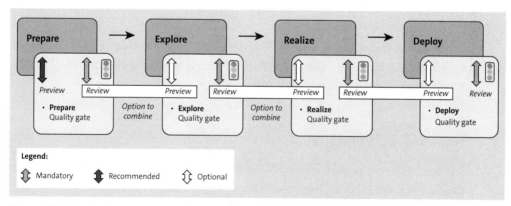

Figure 16.7 Mandatory Project Quality Gates and Recommended Review Phases

If you want to explore the SAP Activate methodology further, you can do so through SAP Jam for SAP Activate. There, you can access SAP Activate content and templates and interact with other SAP Activate subject matter experts in the SAP community (see Figure 16.8).

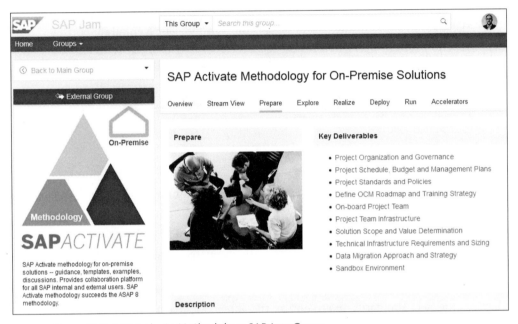

Figure 16.8 SAP Activate Methodology SAP Jam Group

To request access to the SAP Methodologies group on SAP Jam, submit your request at *http://bit.ly/SAPActivate*.

Now that you have a better understanding of how the SAP Activate method and project structure support the SAP S/4HANA project delivery, we'll dive into the SAP Best Practices and configuration tools that support the method.

16.3 SAP Best Practices

SAP Best Practices provided with SAP Activate are made available to help kick-start the overall SAP S/4HANA implementation project. They provide ready-to-run business processes for SAP S/4HANA that also integrate with SAP cloud solutions such as SAP Ariba, SAP C/4HANA, and SAP SuccessFactors (see Figure 16.9).

The SAP Best Practices were built using SAP's deep industry and business process expertise to provide out-of-the-box processes, data, and template organizational structures to support strategic business imperatives and accelerate the adoption of SAP S/4HANA.

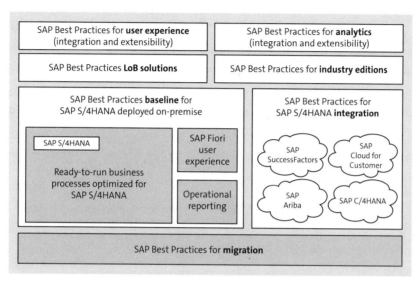

Figure 16.9 SAP Best Practices for On-Premise Deployment

SAP Best Practices content is made ready and available in your SAP S/4HANA system. However, it's worth checking if a more recent version of SAP Best Practices content has been made available before you start your implementation.

> **Note**
>
> SAP Best Practices content will vary based on the SAP S/4HANA version you're trying to implement. Content can be checked in SAP Note 2614075 – SAP Best Practices for SAP S/4HANA (on-premise) (Germany; DEV5) or SAP Note 2614077 – SAP Best Practices for SAP S/4HANA (on-premise) (US; USV5), depending on whether you need DE or US localizations. Additional country best practices are also available.

SAP Best Practices not only kick-start the build process but also provide a baseline for the preparation phase and support the fit/gap workshops. SAP Best Practices should be activated in the sandbox system to demonstrate the solution while supporting fit/gap analysis to flush out any specific requirements you may have as part of your business processes.

SAP Best Practices should drive rapid adoption of the standard SAP processes and solutions, which will help you eventually avoid additional customization requirements, thus reducing the overall maintenance cost for your SAP system.

Using the information from the fit/gap workshops, any delta requirements that aren't covered by SAP Best Practices will be prioritized to plan the realization effort and timelines.

After the scope of the solution has been agreed on and the related SAP Best Practices identified, the reference content associated with SAP Best Practices can be imported and activated in the development system.

> **Note**
>
> The procedure for activating reference content in the development client is available in SAP Note 2247743 (SAP Best Practices for SAP S/4HANA, on-Premise Edition [US; USV2]).
>
> You'll need to select your SAP S/4HANA version to identify the relevant SAP Note for your best practice activation.

Prior to importing the SAP Best Practices content, the client associated with SAP Best Practices needs to be set up so that you can activate and deploy the content.

> **Note**
>
> Additional information on how to set up the SAP Best Practices client is available in the "SAP Administration Guide for the Implementation of SAP S/4HANA" at *http://bit.ly/29aQhUn* (S-user ID required).

After the SAP Best Practices content has been imported, you can select the SAP Best Practices that you want to activate. SAP Best Practices are organized by business process—for example, period-end closing, make-to-stock production, accounts payable, and so on. This makes it easy to select the specific business processes you're looking for, as shown in Figure 16.10.

Each **Scope Item** has a series of dependencies that are referred to as *building blocks*. Additional information on the SAP solution builder tool and the building blocks are provided in Section 16.4.3. The building blocks will contain items such as sample master data, customization sets, and templates (e.g., process documents or reports).

Scope Items	
Scope Items	**Description**
• ☑ US_BD3_OP	Sales Processing using Third Party (w. Shipping Notification)
• ☑ US_BD6_OP	Credit Management
• ☑ US_BD9_OP	Sales Order Processing: Sale from Stock
• ☑ US_BDA_OP	Free of Charge Delivery
• ☑ US_BDD_OP	Returns and Complaints
• ☑ US_BDG_OP	Sales Quotation
• ☑ US_BDH_OP	Sales Order Processing for Prospect
• ☑ US_BDK_OP	Sales Processing using Third Party (without Shipping Notificat
• ☑ US_BDN_OP	Sales of Nonstock Item with Order specific Procurement
• ☑ US_BDQ_OP	Debit Memo Processing
• ☑ US_BDW_OP	Returnables Processing
• ☑ US_BEA_OP	Revenue Planning
• ☑ US_BEG_OP	Standard Cost Calculation (Plan)
• ☑ US_BEI_OP	Period End Closing "General" Plant

Figure 16.10 Scope Selection in SAP Solution Builder

The SAP solution builder tool allows you to activate the SAP Best Practices package you specifically require for your SAP S/4HANA project. The selection of these SAP Best Practices packages will be defined by your business processes and are generated from the output of the validation and delta design workshops.

SAP Activate also provides model companies that help get the configuration process going within SAP S/4HANA. We'll discuss the SAP Model Company further in Section 16.5.

Note

SAP Activate provides SAP Best Practices for industries by leveraging the existing SAP Rapid-Deployment solutions for SAP S/4HANA. SAP is building multiple country localizations as a priority, but it will continue to enhance LoB scenarios and industry best practices on top of the existing SAP S/4HANA baseline.

16.4   SAP Activate Tools

SAP Activate isn't just a method; it also contains accelerators and tools that can be used by the entire project team during each phase of the SAP Activate framework. The SAP Activate accelerators vary from best practices guidebooks to delivery templates, checklists, and project management deliverables.

To support guided configuration of the SAP S/4HANA solution, SAP provides four key tools for the implementation of SAP S/4HANA:

- Self-service configuration (available with cloud deployment only)
- Expert configuration (available with cloud deployment only)
- SAP solution builder tool
- SAP Solution Manager

There are a few differences between SAP Best Practices and tools that are available with SAP S/4HANA versus SAP S/4HANA Cloud. The main discrepancies center on preconfiguration and content lifecycle management services, as described in Table 16.2.

SAP S/4HANA Cloud	SAP S/4HANA
SAP Best Practices, including business and integration processes optimized for SAP S/4HANA Cloud	SAP Best Practices, including business and integration processes optimized for SAP S/4HANA
Starter system for initial scoping and fit/gap	Project jump-start with on-premise software appliance
Self-service configuration for initial setup	N/A
Scope extension through expert configuration	Scope extension through the classic Implementation Guide (IMG) approach
Content lifecycle management enabled by SAP	Content lifecycle management unavailable
SAP Solution Manager in the cloud, including SAP Best Practices business process and project content	SAP Solution Manager in the cloud or customer location, including SAP Best Practices business process and project content

Table 16.2 SAP S/4HANA Best Practices Based on Deployment Options

We'll now look at the functionality and benefits provided by the guided configuration solutions, the SAP solution builder tool, and the integration with SAP Solution Manager.

16.4.1   Self-Service Configuration

Self-service configuration is currently only available with SAP S/4HANA Cloud. The initial SAP S/4HANA system is preconfigured with sample data that provides a jump-start to system configuration and supports the prepare phase and the fit/gap workshops during the explore phase. The preconfigured system also comes with ready-to-run business processes provided with the SAP Activate framework and SAP Best Practices, as mentioned in previous sections.

Self-service configuration enables you to adjust the out-of-the-box solution to your specific business requirements. It leverages the SAP Fiori UX, making the overall solution easier to use than the IMG normally accessed via Transaction SPRO. The new UI, focused on simplification and ease of use, will only display configuration activities added as part of the SAP Best Practices preselected scope, described in Section 16.3.

The new UI considerably reduces the time and complexity associated with performing the configuration tasks by simplifying the number of screens required to complete the system configuration requirements (e.g., company code setup). However, the self-service configuration doesn't allow you to change the business process flow. It does allow you to adjust the existing business processes to support your organizational structure requirements. Process adjustments fall under the umbrella of expert configuration, covered in the next section.

16.4.2   Expert Configuration

Expert configuration is primarily aimed at advanced SAP users who are responsible for maintaining business process configuration within their organizations. Again, this is only for SAP S/4HANA Cloud.

This functionality provides both SAP customers and partners the ability to build on top of the standard SAP business processes while also ensuring consistency with the standard SAP business processes. The modeling of your solution needs to be completed via expert configuration, either to adapt standard SAP processes or to build your own new processes.

16.4.3   SAP Solution Builder Tool

The SAP solution builder tool is used to activate the SAP Best Practices content provided with SAP Activate for SAP S/4HANA.

After all the installation data files and solution scope files have been downloaded from the SAP Service Marketplace for the selected countries and release, you can import them into the SAP solution builder tool.

After importing SAP Best Practices, the installation data that contains the installation settings associated with configuration and data for the SAP S/4HANA solution can be uploaded into the system.

An SAP solution builder profile has been created to import all SAP Best Practices; however, if your project scope has already been defined, it's possible to select the SAP Best Practices content that you're looking to activate, as mentioned in Section 16.3. This defines the solution scope file that contains the technical structure, scope items, building blocks, and technical objects for the SAP S/4HANA solution.

In addition, the selected scope items are assigned to building blocks. Certain scope items may have dependencies related to the building blocks, which means that some items will need to be deployed in a predefined sequence because the building blocks have reusable content, such as business configuration, sample master data, and so on, that is used cross-scope.

After all the configuration is complete, including your specific business configuration requirements, it's recommended that you separate the transports among SAP Best Practices, the changes to SAP Best Practices, and your own specific configuration.

16.4.4   SAP Solution Manager

SAP Solution Manager 7.2 is designed to support SAP Activate. You can import SAP Best Practices for SAP Activate into SAP Solution Manager 7.2.

It's possible to review some SAP Best Practices content in SAP Solution Manager 7.1 by activating the solution package via Transaction SOLAR_PROJECT_ADMIN; however, the information provided isn't identical to the SAP Best Practices available with SAP Solution Manager 7.2.

> **Note**
>
> Throughout this book, when we refer to SAP Solution Manager, we're referring to SAP Solution Manager 7.2, as it's the version designed to support the implementation of SAP S/4HANA using SAP Activate.

SAP Activate provides templates, in addition to the SAP Best Practices described in Section 16.3, that can be imported into SAP Solution Manager to support project management timelines and activities, as well as business process design.

In addition, for any of your business processes that differ from the standard SAP Best Practices, adjustments can be made and documented in SAP Solution Manager via Business Process Model and Notation (BPMN 2.0). This will help you consolidate project documentation and process modeling within your SAP Solution Manager system.

Along with the other benefits SAP Solution Manager usually provides while managing the application lifecycle of your SAP system, SAP Solution Manager 7.2 provides a centralized access point for project templates, SAP Best Practices, business process models, and documentation supporting the overall implementation of SAP S/4HANA.

16.5   SAP Model Company

In this section, we'll discuss how SAP helps customers accelerate their SAP S/4HANA implementation by leveraging preconfigured solutions, known as the SAP Model Company. The SAP Model Company combines SAP Best Practices with end-to-end business processes based on SAP customers' implementation experiences. It's an additional service on top of SAP Best Practices and comes with associated business processes, master data, and organizational structures.

This solution provides you with a complete end-to-end solution based on an industry template, a LoB, or an enterprise foundation to accelerate your SAP S/4HANA implementation project. The SAP Model Company is available to SAP customers on-premise or as virtual appliances on cloud solutions such as AWS or Azure.

While leveraging the SAP Model Company, you can benefit from ready-made and preconfigured country or industry solutions. The country and industry solutions also can be activated via the SAP solution builder tool.

This can significantly reduce the implementation effort required as part of the implementation of SAP S/4HANA. Ultimately, this reduces risk and cost by accelerating the adoption process in discovery, preparation, realization, and explore, as described earlier in Figure 16.5. The SAP Model Company is embedded into the overall transformation road map and is delivered as a service by SAP. It's provided for different industries and LoBs (see Figure 16.11).

> **Note**
>
> You can find the full list of SAP Model Companies per industry or LoB via *www.sap.com/services/preconfigured-industry-solutions.html*.

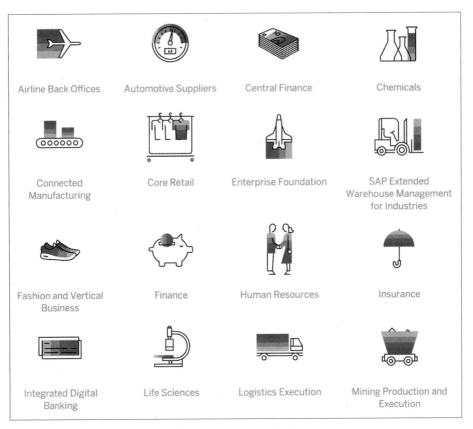

Figure 16.11 SAP Model Company for Your Industry or LoB

So, what are the benefits of the SAP Model Company? Regardless of the industry, the SAP Model Company helps you propel your SAP S/4HANA implementation by providing the following:

- **Faster time to value**
  Get to SAP S/4HANA faster by providing early "show and tell" to your business users to enable quick decision-making and accelerated implementation timelines.

- **Accelerated adoption**
  Leverage the preconfigured solution with access to a tailored SAP Model Company based on your industry or LoB, enabled by a cloud-based deployment.

- **Proven solution**
  The solution is enabled through a reliable architecture, SAP Best Practices, and proven implementation guides.

The SAP Model Company is defined by building blocks as highlighted in Figure 16.12.

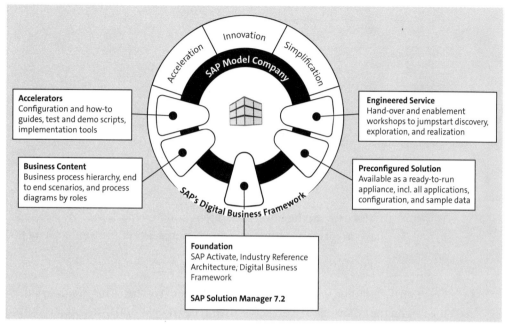

Figure 16.12 SAP Model Company for SAP S/4HANA

Let's take a closer look at the building blocks, as follows:

- **Foundation**
  The initial building block is related to the foundation based on SAP Activate (refer to Section 16.2), and the SAP Digital Transformation Framework, including SAP applications such as SAP S/4HANA, SAP C/4HANA, SAP SuccessFactors, and so on. In addition, the overall foundation building block is underpinned by industry reference architectures that consist of application maps, process models, and solution architectures for digital transformation (see Figure 16.13).

- **Accelerators**
  The second building block relates to the accelerators provided as part of the SAP Model Company. This building block consists of user guides, implementation tools and accelerators, configuration and implementation guides, training material, and test scripts.

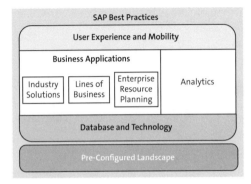

Figure 16.13 Building Block 1: Foundation

- **Business content**
  The third area focuses on the business content building block that provides end-to-end business models, including, reports, sample workflows, enhancements, and forms.

- **Engineered service**
  The fourth building block relates to engineered service. This building block focuses on the enablement workshops to initiate the SAP S/4HANA project during the discovery, exploration, and realization phases. This service has been enhanced over the years, taking into account the feedback from best practices, SAP Rapid-Deployment solutions, and today's SAP Model Company, as shown in Figure 16.14.

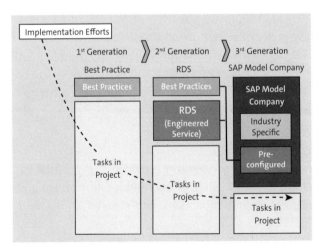

Figure 16.14 Building Block 4: Engineered Service

- **Preconfigured solution**

  The last building block focuses on the preconfigured solution that is a fundamental accelerator to the overall SAP S/4HANA implementation. The preconfigured solution provides end-to-end processes, with configuration and sample data. This preconfigured template allows SAP customers to adopt and adjust the core solution, providing training material and automated test cases based on the industry template that has been selected (see Figure 16.15).

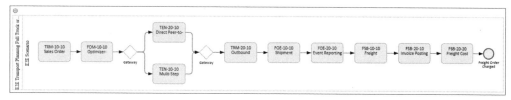

Figure 16.15 Building Block 5: Preconfigured Solution

These building blocks are the foundation of the SAP Model Company that will provide you with a reduced cost of implementation and help you kick-start your digital transformation. The template will enable you to benefit from the latest innovations in terms of business software based on SAP S/4HANA, and it will reduce your build timelines due to minimized configuration.

In addition to all of this, it's not a one size fits all. SAP provides specific templates for your industry or LoB to respond to specific business requirements and challenges, with multiple more industries to come as shown in the SAP Model Company road map in Table 16.3.

	Available	Planned
Industry	<ul><li>Airlines Back Offices</li><li>Analytical Banking</li><li>Automotive Suppliers</li><li>Chemicals</li><li>Integrated Digital Banking</li><li>Insurance</li><li>Life Sciences</li><li>Oil & Gas</li><li>Omnichannel Retail</li><li>Utilities</li></ul>	<ul><li>Rule-based Mill Production</li><li>Mining Production Execution</li><li>Fashion Management</li><li>Heavy Equipment Management</li><li>Trade Management for Consumer Products</li></ul>

Table 16.3 Available and Planned SAP Model Company Templates

	Available	Planned
Line of business	<ul><li>Connected manufacturing</li><li>Finance</li><li>Human resources</li><li>Logistics execution</li><li>R&D/Engineering</li><li>Subscription billing</li><li>Supply chain planning</li></ul>	<ul><li>Extended warehouse management (EWM) for industries</li></ul>
Generic	<ul><li>Enterprise Foundation</li></ul>	N/A

Table 16.3 Available and Planned SAP Model Company Templates (Cont.)

> **Note**
>
> You can find the latest information regarding the SAP Model Company, its assets, and accelerators, or even which industry-specific solutions are currently available via *http://sapsupport.info/offerings/model-company.*

16.6   Summary

In this chapter, we explored various tools to help you on your implementation journey: SAP Activate, SAP Best Practices, and the SAP Model Company.

SAP Activate is the framework designed to support your SAP S/4HANA adoption, regardless of the transformation scenario or deployment method you decide to follow for your SAP S/4HANA implementation. Certain restrictions are currently in place based on these decisions; however, SAP will continue to develop the SAP Activate framework to support and accelerate the adoption of SAP S/4HANA based on these scenarios.

The SAP Model Company aims to jump-start your SAP S/4HANA implementation and is tightly integrated with the SAP Activate framework, enabling a seamless UX in terms of SAP S/4HANA adoption.

Let's now move on to Chapter 17, which will unpack the idea of digital transformation and making a business case.

Chapter 17

Building the Business Case

In this chapter, we'll walk through key considerations for moving from your current environment to the future mode of operation. We'll outline the key steps to building a business case for SAP S/4HANA as a digital core, and we'll provide a balanced road map for value realization.

The traditional approach for building a business case for enterprise resource planning (ERP) applications has been well documented and even automated in some cases. Companies that have been successful in making a compelling case for SAP S/4HANA this way typically have one or more of the following attributes:

- No ERP system in productive operation
- Fragmented ERP landscape (often due to mergers and acquisitions)
- Low process maturity (aligned to SAP S/4HANA scope)
- High cost of IT operations
- Risk aversion to maintaining unsupported SAP systems post-2025

Fundamentally, ERP value propositions involve matching current pain points to existing solution enablers and then quantifying the potential impact of closing these gaps. There are multiple options available from SAP and its partners to create a business case this way, including business scenario comparisons, performance benchmarks, value calculator tools, and business case advisors.

For enterprises with mature ERP environments, however, making the business case for SAP S/4HANA is more challenging. The benefits considered in the traditional approach (simplification, real-time, analytics, deployment choice, agility, and consumer-grade user experience [UX]) aren't adequate to justify a multi-year investment of leadership. In these situations, a more strategic approach is required to make a successful case for change.

17

For enterprises that don't fit the attributes outlined previously, the question is what to do when the traditional ERP business case approach doesn't work. Evidence from enterprises already on their SAP S/4HANA journey suggests a higher probability of success shifting from a bottom-up, product-centric focus to one focused on the following principles:

- Stakeholder centric
- Value led
- Outcome based

In this chapter, we'll outline the process of building a business case for business transformation using SAP S/4HANA as the digital core. We'll unpack the various challenges and value dimensions, and walk through the major steps. We'll close with a look at some valuable lessons and tips that can help you throughout this process.

17.1   Common SAP S/4HANA Business Case Challenges

There are several common challenges experienced in developing a business case for SAP S/4HANA. The following lists a few of the primary ones:

- **Same benefit areas used in original ERP business case**
  The business case templates and value tools developed for SAP S/4HANA rely on the same benefit areas as earlier SAP ERP versions. This creates two potential problems. First, the degree of impact may be compromised if the original business case is used as a baseline. More significantly, however, is the credibility of realizing the benefits this time if the targeted improvements weren't realized in the past.

- **Reduced scope compared to previous SAP ERP solutions**
  Much of the core ERP functionality used by procurement and human resources (HR) has been transported from SAP S/4HANA into software-as-a-service (SaaS) applications such as SAP Ariba, SAP Fieldglass, SAP Concur, and SAP SuccessFactors. This can result in reducing the number of value drivers if products with comparable capabilities aren't included in the software bill of materials (BOM) since they're no longer in the SAP S/4HANA scope.

- **Quantifying indirect impact of analytics and UXs**
  New features related to transactional analytics and the SAP Fiori user interface (UI) are enablers of benefits that require someone to take an action, refine a plan, or change a decision. These second-degree value drivers can be difficult to quantify

especially if the primary value drivers (operators, planners, decision makers) aren't included in the discovery, value analysis, or future state solution design.

- **Business outcomes that require more than SAP S/4HANA software alone**
The specific contribution of SAP S/4HANA is hard to determine when business process designs, organizational structures, new skills and competencies, and performance management systems are also required to deliver the desired business outcomes. New software is one component of a more complex solution set for enterprises pursuing business transformation, so understanding the capability differential and incremental benefit contribution is critical for value attribution when SAP S/4HANA is the targeted end state.

- **Delayed time-to-value with a "Big Bang" investment profile**
Business executives and their board of directors are under intense scrutiny to act in their shareholders' best interest. As such, the implementation timing and investment profile for SAP S/4HANA can be prohibitive even when a persuasive value proposition exists. A balanced road map that provides quick fixes, early wins, and optionality is critical to gaining consensus. It's no longer acceptable to approve a multiyear ERP program with a 2 – 3 year payback without a solid understanding of tradeoffs and potential exit ramps.

17.2   Value Dimensions

The best business cases do more than just calculate the benefits, costs, and return of investment (ROI) of a proposed investment. They also clarify the connection to enterprise strategies and the reasoning for initiating a project now. In some cases, they will consider other value dimensions more difficult to quantify, such as the following (Figure 17.1):

- **Risk and compliance**
Includes the following benefits:
  - Lower risk of business disruptions from IT
  - Faster recover of supply and downtime issues
  - Reduced regulatory and tax noncompliance
  - Improved visibility to acquired businesses
- **Growth enablement**
Includes the following benefits:
  - Agility to enable organic and inorganic growth

- – A more flexible and learning organization
- – Business model adaptability to industry trends
- – A more connected and scalable organization

- **Innovation**
  Includes the following benefits:
  - – Real-time visibility to product profitability
  - – Improved time-to-market for new programs
  - – Business planning based on trusted information
  - – A connected and collaborative platform for growth

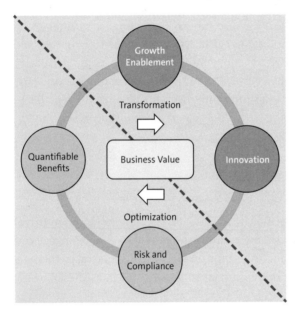

Figure 17.1 Dimensions of Value

Most chief information officers (CIOs) today don't have the authority to spend IT budget without formal approval by other business executives. The line of business (LoB) growth strategies prompted by cloud application providers have created more sophisticated buying behavior and increased complexity for business-IT alignment, architecture design, and value governance.

Many strategic imperatives are vying for the same sources of capital, operating budget, and staffing; the truth is that there is significant opportunity cost related to requests that draw on all three areas over a multiyear time frame. Expanding the business case to include risk and compliance, growth enablement, and innovation provides leverage when investment decisions include other competing options, including non-IT-related investments.

17.3 Alignment to Stakeholders and Business Outcomes

Given the cross-functional nature of ERP, the business case must be tailored to different stakeholder needs and desired business outcomes across the enterprise. The language used in daily operations is quite different from what is discussed in the boardroom, so the specific discussion themes and value drivers will change depending on who is involved in the decision process. In any case, the business case must address a few basic questions:

- What challenges and opportunities will be addressed?
- What are the key capabilities of the recommended solution(s)?
- What are the expected benefits, costs, and time frames?
- Why should we do this now?

Table 17.1 shows the various opportunity types and their associated decision makers, discussion themes, and key value drivers.

Opportunity Type	Decision Makers	Discussion Themes	Key Value Drivers
Technology renovation	<ul><li>CIO</li><li>Enterprise architects</li><li>System managers</li></ul>	<ul><li>Product features</li><li>System performance</li><li>Data inputs/ integration</li></ul>	<ul><li>Personnel productivity</li><li>Total cost of ownership (TCO)</li><li>Time to deploy</li></ul>
Process optimization	<ul><li>Function leader</li><li>Process owner</li><li>Key small and medium enterprises (SMEs)</li></ul>	<ul><li>Process effectiveness</li><li>Resource efficiency</li><li>Cost per unit</li></ul>	<ul><li>Revenue/cost/ return on assets (ROA)</li><li>Process efficiency/cycle time</li><li>Specific operational key performance indicators (KPIs)</li></ul>

Table 17.1 Different Stakeholders and Desired Outcomes

Opportunity Type	Decision Makers	Discussion Themes	Key Value Drivers
Business transformation	▪ Board of directors ▪ Company owner(s) ▪ CEO/CFO	▪ Competitive advantage ▪ Future growth ▪ Structural change	▪ Operating profit (earnings before interest and taxes [EBIT]) ▪ Earnings per share (EPS) ▪ Enterprise valuation multiple

Table 17.1 Different Stakeholders and Desired Outcomes (Cont.)

Let's take a closer look at each opportunity type:

- **Technology renovation**

  The decision to upgrade an existing ERP environment is typically focused on decreasing TCO. For global enterprises, reducing the complexity and associated risk via landscape consolidation, legacy system replacement, and decommissioning unsupported applications can be compelling. Often, the decision to move now can be influenced by contract compliance issues, expiring discounts, and other commercial terms.

  The ability to move SAP workloads to the cloud is an emerging opportunity to further reduce the TCO. SAP has partnerships with most of the leading hyperscale providers and offers its own cloud infrastructure for private hosted environments. Given this is a dynamic market, these experts should be consulted if this is a viable value driver for SAP S/4HANA.

- **Process optimization**

  Performance improvement initiatives usually target operational excellence from optimizing current processes. The classic ERP value proposition is based on gaining enterprise synergies by integrating cross-functional transaction processing. With a strong ERP foundation, shared service operating models can also be delivered when standardization and automation are deployed at scale. Typical value drivers include headcount reduction, labor arbitrage, and productivity improvement.

  Quantifying the potential of process optimization requires considering benefit areas beyond IT TCO and process efficiency. Proper discovery is needed to understand and position SAP S/4HANA capabilities that can enable process effectiveness as well. Specialized expertise may also be required to articulate the SAP S/4HANA value premium in industry-specific domains beyond back-office processes.

- **Business transformation**

  Most business transformations are focused on delivering competitive advantage and are led by a CEO, CFO, or other senior business executive. The desired outcome of business transformation can involve new operating models, acquisitions/divestures, emerging technologies, and go-to-market partnerships beyond a new ERP system. Similarly, the scope includes core operating processes designed for growth and competitive, sustainable advantage.

  A business transformation vision is based on opportunities to create new sources of value beyond optimization of current processes. Common transformation themes include integrated value streams, digital operating models, touchless workflows, and new pricing models designed to disrupt the current state. Leading enterprises are applying emerging technologies—automation, prediction, artificial intelligence (AI), and blockchain—to amplify the impact and fill the voids in what capabilities are enabled by SAP S/4HANA.

17.4   Proven Process for Building a Case for Change

A more contemporary process is evolving from the traditional ERP business case approach for enterprises seeking transformational business outcomes. In these situations, SAP S/4HANA can be positioned as a digital core to enable strategic imperatives that require continuous innovation and value delivery after the initial go-live date. This approach (shown in Figure 17.2) has proven to work in almost every customer situation when a qualified opportunity exists and each of the steps are followed in sequence.

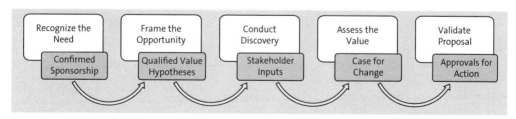

Figure 17.2 Proven Process for Building a Case for Business Transformation

The overall methodology is relatively straightforward, but leading a customer engagement is rarely simple. Cross-disciplinary expertise and tacit knowledge is required to balance the right mix of influencing factors and managing various trade-offs throughout the cycle.

As noted previously, the three core principles that are inherently different with this process are as follows:

- **Stakeholder centric**
  Focus on issues and needs from the buyers' perspectives.

- **Value led**
  Establish strong value hypotheses to manage scope and priorities through the journey.

- **Outcome based**
  Provide the vision and strategy for a better future.

The following sections will walk through each of the five steps in order for building a business case (refer to Figure 17.2).

17.4.1 Recognize the Need

There is a proven method to gain access to business executives, understand their priorities, and secure sponsorship for a collaborative path forward. Reframing the way customers think about their business and their needs helps to communicate capabilities and differentiators in the context of their environment. This two-step approach allows open pursuit of shared objectives in a direct but nonaggressive way to overcome increased risk aversion throughout the buying cycle.

The first step is to deliver new insight to establish credibility, via the following actions:

- Educate them on what is happening in their market or with similar enterprises.
- Acknowledge symptoms and root causes of a known problem they need to address.
- Challenge their current thinking or approach to a strategic imperative.

Next, you must present a plan for action to secure sponsorship for collaborative engagement:

- **Validation of their specific opportunity**
  Perform activities, analyses, and data necessary for assessment.

- **Resources and time commitments**
  Outline the participants involved at each stage and for how long.

- **Keys to success**
  Discuss active sponsorship and open participation from key stakeholders.

This method has been described as "easy to present, yet very difficult to do well" without proper preparation and delivery. To prepare, you must ask yourself several questions: What is your value hypothesis and linkage to your unique differentiators? What relevant insights can you share? Do you have specific examples, both good and bad?

There are multiple steps you can take to ensure a proper delivery of your pitch:

- Identify the few things that can deliver unique value.

- Share practical examples to start the conversation.

- Highlight provocative insights (what don't they know).

- Ask questions that lead to your unique capabilities.

- Propose a plan to validate the opportunity with them.

17.4.2   Frame the Opportunity

Framing an opportunity based on the unique customer situation provides context for defining the specific capabilities that will enable strategic business objectives, benefit areas, and value drivers. A common practice is to define and document the scope, objectives, and outcomes in an engagement charter:

- **Scope**
  Processes, organizations, systems, and geographies.

- **Objectives**
  Technology renovation, process optimization, and business transformation.

- **Outcomes**
  A calculation, report, presentation, demonstration, or decision.

Socializing this charter along with a few provocative value hypotheses can better prepare participants and build excitement in advance of actual engagement. Often, a kick-off event is necessary, especially when opportunities span geographic locations and existing functional boundaries.

It's also important to confirm what roles the business case will play in the program lifecycle. Leading companies understand the vital role a business case can have after initial program approval. In fact, active value governance has proven to also improve on-time and on-budget program performance. Figure 17.3 unpacks the continuous value governance process into three sequential phases:

- Value discovery
- Value enablement
- Value realization

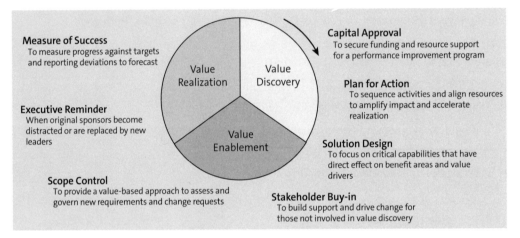

Figure 17.3 Role of a Business Case across the Program Lifecycle

17.4.3   Conduct Discovery

Discovery is a process to drive active input and collaboration from multiple parties and is a critical step in building the case for change. When done well, it can be a powerful way to deliver a personalized experience that builds stakeholder trust and ownership over time. Individual interviews and group sessions are typically conducted to complete the following:

- Understand current business strategy and processes gaps.
- Identify opportunities for strategic and economic impact.
- Match impact to solution capabilities and differentiators.
- Evaluate priorities by scale and accessibility.

Often business case creation is a mechanical exercise centered on "doing the math" to create an initial estimate of potential value. Without proper discovery, you miss the chance to uncover latent demand, establish solution differentiation, and convey the value premium over other alternatives. Different tools and techniques will be required depending on the business architecture scope and level of change, as shown in Figure 17.4:

- **Business model**

  Topics of interest include the following:

  - Competitive forces and change drivers
  - Vision, mission, and strategy
  - Strategic objectives
  - Business competencies

  The discovery tools and techniques include the following:

  - Five forces/strengths, weaknesses, opportunities, and threats (SWOT)/industry context map
  - Cover story/game plan vision
  - Balanced scorecard/stakeholder map
  - Business model canvas/competency matrix

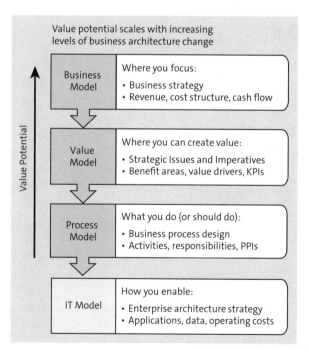

Figure 17.4 Shape Discovery to Business Scope and Level of Change

- **Value model**

  Topics of interest include the following:

  - Value chain/enterprise models

  - Revenue/margin breakouts

  - Total delivered cost (fixed/variable)

  - Scenario/sensitivity analysis

  The discovery tools and techniques include the following:

  - Value proposition canvas

  - Pro forma models

  - Investment portfolio map

  - Decision optimization/solver logic

- **Process model**

  Topics of interest include the following:

  - Process efficiency/effectiveness

  - Performance improvement targets

  - User adoption and training

  - Continuous improvement

  The discover tools and techniques include the following:

  - Process maturity models/benchmarks

  - Customer references/third-party content

  - Journey maps/day-in-the-life scenarios

  - Performance scorecards/dashboards

- **IT model**

  Topics of interest include the following:

  - Functionality/need assessment

  - Productivity drivers

  - TCO

  - Technical risk

  The discover tools and techniques include the following:

  - Business case templates

- Value calculators/ROI tools
- TCO models
- Risk profiles

There are many trade-offs made in a collaborative value assessment that require expertise in managing expectations. Proper discovery can help create constructive tension that can be leveraged throughout the engagement to keep things on track and ensure a quality outcome.

17.4.4 Assess the Value

The purpose of any value-based assessment is to highlight potential benefits as determined by key decision makers in the final selection process. In many business transformation programs, the case for change is ultimately determined by the value dimensions beyond ROI (i.e., risk and compliance, growth enablement, innovation). The information gained from discovery will help shape the structure and narrative for how value is positioned with executive sponsors, process/function owners, and operational subject matter experts.

Aligning and managing stakeholder expectations across the enterprise is one of the key success factors in any business transformation program. Too often, shortcuts are made using more simplistic approaches (value calculators, outside-in benchmark analyses, educated guesstimates) that will create problems later. The most compelling business cases not only demonstrate the real opportunities presented but also create pressure to force a decision and act now. They also lay the foundation for ongoing value governance beyond the initial software transaction or go-live date.

Figure 17.5 shows the value helps that establish proper expectations across the enterprise. It aligns the key stakeholders and core focus areas with strategic, tactical, and operational drivers.

The conventional ERP business case approach can be appropriate for enterprises that have no ERP solution deployed, a fragmented ERP landscape, low maturity of processes aligned to SAP S/4HANA scope, or high cost of IT operations now. In these cases, a product-centric value proposition is usually adequate and can be conveniently calculated based on standard ERP templates, value calculators, and benchmarking data. SAP and many of its partners offer solutions to help accelerate business case creation in these cases.

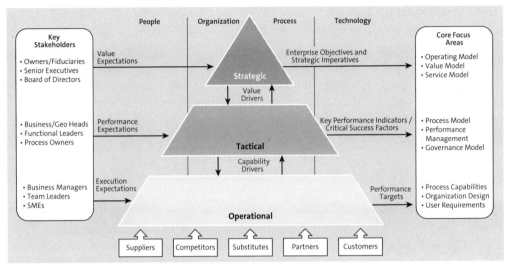

Figure 17.5 Value Helps Establish Proper Expectations across the Enterprise

The Selling, General, and Administrative Expenses Value Trap

There is a "value trap" that many have experienced when trying to conduct a bottom-up functional comparison to SAP ERP, as shown in Figure 17.6.

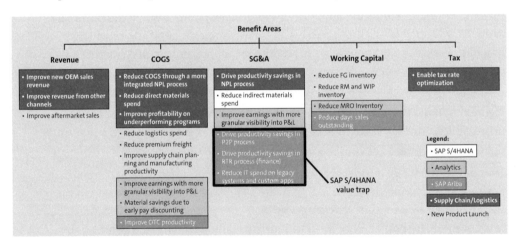

Figure 17.6 Avoid the SAP S/4HANA Value Trap to Make a Compelling Business Case

For large global enterprises with mature SAP environments, the typical benefit areas are constrained to theoretical productivity gains and TCO savings. In these situations, there are typically not enough people or legacy systems to eliminate to provide a meaningful value proposition. This is especially challenging when selling, general, and administrative expenses (SG&A) costs only represent a minor percentage of the overall cost structure of the enterprise.

Many decision processes get stuck when incremental improvements from simplified, faster back-office transaction processing aren't enough to make a compelling case for acting now. In lieu of a "no decision" and reverting to the status quo, too many are asking what should we do now? Fortunately, there is a proven alternative for those that require a better alternative to the conventional ERP business case approach.

Step 1: Focus on Value from the Start

An early value focus helps concentrate thinking on potential benefit areas and shape assessment before diving into specific SAP S/4HANA features and functions. This top-down mind-set allows more effective identification of new sources of opportunity and avoids the SG&A value trap.

There are inherent beliefs in every organization that guide the thinking of how value can be created. The natural tendency is to focus on addressing pain points in the current state to identify incremental improvements. In operations-intensive environments, reimagining how to work is often overruled by the daily firefight of running the business. This can also be true in public companies with a short-term business strategy directed by delivering quarterly results.

Taking more of a growth mind-set helps stretch conventional value propositions into opportunities that offer step-change performance improvement and sustainable competitive advantage. There is some "art" to constructing sound value statements that can be supported by real-world evidence and simple, yet realistic, calculation logic. Most expert practitioners begin by validating a set of value hypotheses before chasing data to "run the numbers." Let's take a look at a few examples of initial hypotheses created for different business value pools:

- **Finance and accounting productivity**
  Improve productivity of finance operations by leveraging the Universal Journal, reduction of manual processes, faster processes, and real-time analytics. Streamline parallel ledgers, reduce complexity, and ensure data consistency and accuracy.

- **Sales productivity**
  Improve productivity of sales through one integrated order management system, process automation, improved process compliance, and better data analytics.

- **Manufacturing productivity**
  Increase manufacturing productivity by shifting to demand-driven material requirements planning (MRP), advanced available-to-promise (AATP), and other SAP S/4HANA-enabled innovations. Integrated shop floor analytics will provide additional gains.

Step 2: Adjust Scope to Enterprise Value Streams and Jobs-to-Do

The first step in most value assessment methodologies is to assess current state performance to identify pain points and performance gaps. This approach relies on two foundational assumptions:

- The desired outcome is to incrementally improve the efficiency of existing work practices.
- The target solution already exists, and a road map can be reverse engineered for deployment.

Neither of these assumptions are valid for business transformation because most programs are defined by new outcomes with step-change performance goals. A fundamentally new approach is required that reframes the opportunity to more than SAP S/4HANA alone. In these cases, the potential value depends on how back-office data in SAP S/4HANA is strategic to the overall business model of the enterprise.

Building a business case for business transformation combines the potential of SAP S/4HANA as an ERP upgrade *and* a digital core for broader business operations, beyond the back office. There is much more value potential when the assessment scope can be adjusted along two dimensions:

- Extend classic ERP mega-process definitions (record-to-report, order-to-cash, procure-to-pay, plan-to-produce, hire-to-retire, acquire-to-retire) to value streams that run across the enterprise.
- Elevate the stack-of-work above transaction processing to include advanced technologies like analytics, decision support, automation, machine learning, prediction, and AI.

Shifting the initial focus to critical characteristics and design principles for the future state can guide discovery activities to a more strategic perspective. Consider jobs-to-do in the future that will require more than transaction processing alone. Also, consider an integrated business architecture that also includes data, insights, plans, decisions, and performance measures. Identifying blind spots, value stream disconnects, and unknown business requirements can also be more effective than simply targeting pain points when assessing total value potential.

Step 3: Define Linkage between Capabilities and Value Drivers

Defining the linkage between benefit areas, value drivers, and enabling SAP S/4HANA features is essential to supporting any quantifiable estimates. Understanding what SAP S/4HANA can and can't do in the context of enterprise value streams is critically important when a new business/operating model is the desired outcome. Let's take procure-to-pay, one of the well-known ERP mega-processes, as an example. SAP S/4HANA supports processing of purchase orders, invoices, and financial settlements with suppliers, similar to earlier versions of SAP ERP. However, this only represents part of the transaction processing component of the source-to-pay value stream in most companies (see Figure 17.7).

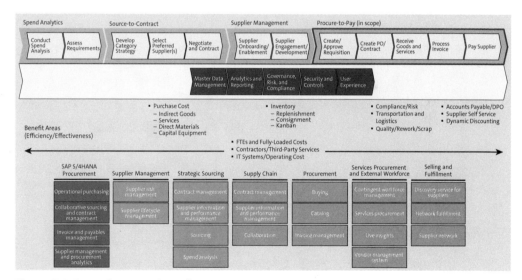

Figure 17.7 Example Enterprise Value Stream: Source-to-Pay

SAP S/4HANA provides that ability to simplify and speed up the processing of purchase orders, invoices, and supplier payments, which can benefit enterprises that don't do this well today. However, the value proposition can increase by a scale order of magnitude when processes beyond the scope of SAP S/4HANA are considered.

Better management of spend (direct, indirect, and services), supply market dynamics, and supplier risk are typically richer value pools than back-office efficiency gains. Note, however, that many other SAP (and non-SAP) applications, modules, and services will be required to deliver these benefits.

Step 4: Phase Expected Value to the Deployment Road Map

Even when the value proposition makes sense, the value realization plan can be problematic. The multiyear ROI profile and opportunity cost of conscribing critical resources recall unpleasant memories of Big Bang ERP programs. To avoid this requires a balanced plan that includes three distinct phases of value creation (as shown in Figure 17.8):

- **Optimize**
  Standardize and simplify how work is done today.

- **Enhance**
  Make existing work practices more useful and effective.

- **Transform**
  Change the structure/composition of future jobs-to-do.

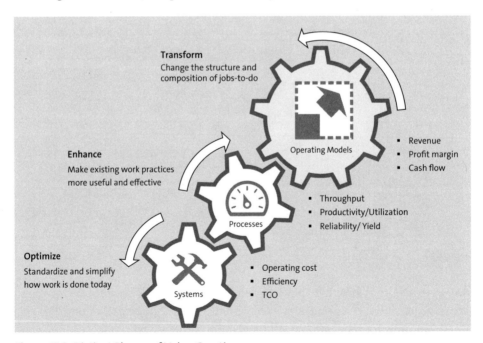

Figure 17.8 Distinct Phases of Value Creation

An increasing number of enterprises have moved their SAP workloads to hyperscale cloud providers as part of their SAP S/4HANA implementation. While this can provide short-term IT cost savings, the value potential is suboptimized without a longer-term perspective. These new platforms offer a new model for continuous innovation and value delivery that is very different from traditional enterprise applications. Understanding current capabilities and what is realistically possible in the next three to five years can help shape a more aspirational vision. Experienced business transformation leaders can help construct a balanced road map to activate new sources of value and competitive advantage before and long after the SAP S/4HANA go-live.

17.4.5   Validate Proposal

Presenting a compelling business case is about more than sharing expected benefits, costs, and ROI analyses. This step is when all the data, insights, and opportunities from the previous four steps need to come together. Specifically, the business case must address the following questions:

- What challenges and opportunities will be addressed?
- What are the key capabilities of the recommended solution(s)?
- What are the expected benefits, costs, and time frames?
- Why should we do this now?

In a collaborative engagement, validation is embedded into each step of the process. The final decision should be inevitable unless shortcuts were taken, shareholder expectations weren't satisfied, or the price-to-value ratio is out of proportion. An effective method is to require the functional process owners to present their business case to executive decision makers.

The business case summary can be a formal report or briefing document that follows the structure shown in Figure 17.9 (the benefits presented were removed). This transformation program was structured around three discrete value propositions—technical, functional, and innovation—enabled by SAP S/4HANA as a digital core.

Differentiating value propositions are based on specific customer needs and articulate unique benefits, capabilities, and delivery assurances as determined by the decision makers involved. Lack of differentiation in building the business case can result in price being the most important decision factor.

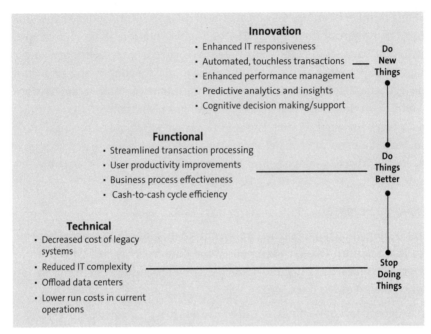

Figure 17.9 Example Enterprise Value Plan: SAP S/4HANA Plus Ongoing Innovation

Another area for differentiation is ensuring value management continues past the initial transaction. This is especially true when subscription pricing models, managed services, or gain/risk share agreements are involved. There are three main components for sustainable value management:

- Value model: Aligns strategic objectives, benefits areas, and operational value drivers.
- Value plan: Links improvement opportunities, capability enablers, and execution plans.
- Value governance: Outlines portfolio priorities, mitigation of issues/risks, and investment allocations.

Validation of the proposed value model, value plan, and value governance process is necessary to gain agreement in moving forward. The strategy-to-execution framework in Figure 17.10 can be a powerful way to structure a proposal for sustainable value management.

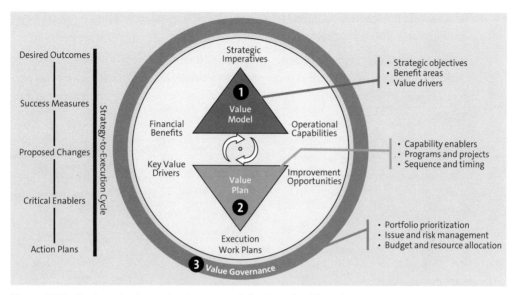

Figure 17.10 Strategy-to-Execution Framework for Sustainable Value Management

17.5   Develop Your IT Road Map

In addition to creating your value road map as we've outlined in Section 17.4, it's important to also define your IT development road map, which lays out specific application, architecture, and implementation details with realistic sequencing based on known constraints.

Figure 17.11 shows the overall approach for creating a transformational IT road map. The move from the current mode of operations (CMO) is based on a combination of IT and business inputs, industry best practices, benchmarks, and a target industry model company for assessment. In addition, the journey to a future mode of operations (FMO) follows a series of iterative steps or dynamic operating models. One of the key principles in defining the road map is understanding the building blocks (i.e., solutions) that will form the FMO and understanding the priorities, sequences, and dependencies to ensure that any throwaway costs are understood and minimized.

For example, if a move to SAP BW/4HANA is a predecessor to SAP S/4HANA, there will be operational analytics already deployed that will subsequently be replaced by embedded analytics in SAP S/4HANA. Once this is understood, then the data flows and reports designed in SAP BW/4HANA can be addressed to minimize rework when moving back into SAP S/4HANA at a later stage.

There are typically immediate benefits from optimizing the existing assets already in production. Advanced automation, predictive analytics, and artificial intelligence can improve both the efficiency and effectiveness of existing transactional processes.

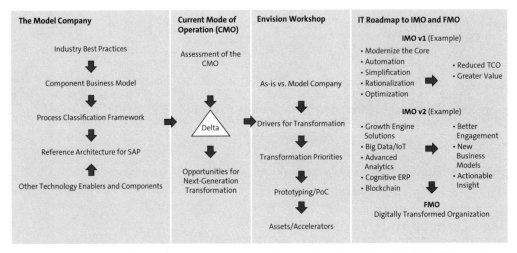

Figure 17.11 Understanding Business Imperatives to Move from Current Mode of Operations to Future Mode of Operations

We'll use extracts of the IBM Better Transformation method as a guide and basis for road map definition. The IBM Better Transformation method (illustrated in Figure 17.12) for road map *definition* and *execution* provides a framework that leverages assets to help with "as is" analysis and "to be" envisioning. This framework has proven to create a comprehensive approach to transform the organization beyond an application go-live. The resulting road map addresses strategic priorities, individual initiatives, dependencies, options, value drivers, sequencing/timing, and activities for practical execution.

The road map development stage includes the following four distinct phases that are described in detail in subsequent sections:

❶ **Engage**
Analyze the CMO.

❷ Envision

Explore the target operating model (TOM).

❸ Evaluate

Dive deep into the transformation approach.

❹ Enable

Build the road map.

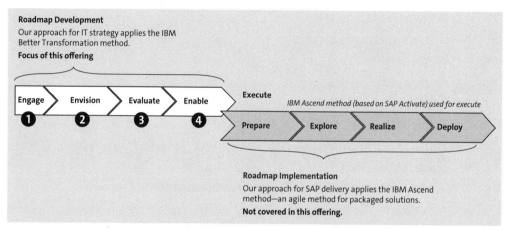

Figure 17.12 Complete End-to-End Approach from Road Map Definition to Execution

After the transformation road map has been defined, the hard work of execution can begin. The IBM Ascend methodology leverages SAP Activate methods and tools to accelerate road map definition through the deployment of the target solution. The integration of IBM Ascend and SAP Activate provides a complete and integrated end-to-end approach to deploy SAP S/4HANA as a platform for business transformation.

> **Note**
>
> As you work through the phases, it's important to keep in mind that the move from the CMO to a target state FMO needs to travel via multiple iterations or IMOs. In fact, the FMO is a state that's never actually achieved because it's a moving target that will be reviewed and revised during the transition journey at the different IMO stages and then tested against the ever-evolving business strategy.

17.5.1 Engage Phase: Analyzing the Current Mode of Operations

The first phase of the IBM Better Transformation framework is known as the *engage phase*, in which you look at and analyze the application landscape as-is and propose a vision for the desired end state.

The activities of this phase are as follows:

- Collect the following data in the current environment:
  - The as-is IT landscape
  - Application portfolio
  - IT strategy
- Understand the following parts of the business vision:
  - TOM
  - Pain points
- Compare CMO versus target FMO of the model company for a specific industry by doing the following:
  - Identifying opportunities for digital transformation initiatives
  - Setting up the envision phase workshop to identify participants, logistics, and so on

The goals for this phase are as follows:

- Documented understanding of the current IT landscape and application portfolio
- Gaps identified between the CMO and the FMO
- Workshop to be run in the envision phase driven by the identified gaps

17.5.2 Envision Phase: Exploring the Target Operational Model

The second phase of the IBM Better Transformation framework is known as the *envision phase*, in which we explore the TOM in the context of the business and IT strategy, the current pain points and business expectation gaps, and the business case for digital transformation.

The activities of this phase are as follows:

- Explore the findings of the engage phase.
- Explore the opportunities identified in the context of the client's business ambition and IT strategy.

- Demonstrate how current business expectation gaps are closed.
- Establish digital transformation priorities around key technology components.
- Decide to proceed with the evaluate phase.

The goals for this phase are as follows:

- Envision the workshops completed.
- Align qualified digital transformation opportunities with technology enablers and value propositions.
- Decide to proceed and set the contract in place to move into the evaluate phase.

17.5.3   Evaluate Phase: A Deep Dive into the Transformation Approach

The third phase of the IBM Better Transformation framework is known as the *evaluate phase*, in which you define an approach to address the priorities identified in the envision phase to modernize the core of the enterprise applications and deliver digital transformation. During this phase, you demonstrate solutions and iteratively build agile proofs of concept (POCs) and proofs of value.

The activities of this phase are as follows:

- Evaluate the current IT strategy and its ability to deliver the FMO and identify gaps.
- Run initiatives to dive deep into the identified transformation opportunities.
- Model business components to identify operational versus differentiating applications.
- Identify application consolidation opportunities.
- Identify application rationalization opportunities.
- Define key architecture principles and decisions for the IT road map.
- Identify alternative options, and make assessments based on business- and IT-ranked evaluation criteria.
- Run iterative POCs/proofs of value based on immediate priorities.

The goals of this phase are as follows:

- Assess current strategy, identify improvements, and articulate business values.
- Define a prioritized set of actions to deliver business value.
- Identify tools and accelerators for road map delivery.

17

17.5.4   Enable Phase: Build Your Road Map

The fourth phase of the IBM Better Transformation framework is known as the *enable phase*, during which you define the road map to introduce the FMO and close business expectation gaps based on prioritization of business capabilities.

The activities of this phase are as follows:

- Develop a prioritized portfolio and IT road map to achieve business objectives.
- Develop a supporting business case.
- Develop a plan to deliver the transformation and associated business objectives.
- Plan the approach for architectural vitality.

The goals of this phase are as follows:

- Define the road map and supporting plan showing the path to the FMO via an IMO.
- Define the approach for periodic application reviews of the road map against business ambition and needs.

17.6   Valuable Lessons Learned

One would be naïve to believe there is a standard playbook that works every time for something as complex as business transformation. That said, the process outlined in this chapter has proven successful for enterprises of different sizes, in different industries, and in different regions of the world.

However, there are two big risks that can adversely impact of this approach:

- **Wrong opportunity**
  - Relationships not aligned at the right levels
  - Lack of proper sponsorship—business AND IT leadership
  - IT-only focus (prohibits proper discovery and value assessment)
  - Client seeking free advisory/consulting services
- **Wrong timing**
  - Business priorities not aligned to opportunity type
  - Lack of urgency/funding to ensure decision closure
  - Unwillingness or inability to secure resources, data, or time
  - Relationship controlled via a third party (indirect client access)

Incorporate these points into opportunity validation and initial discovery to identify risks early and drive to resolution quickly. Table 17.2 shows a few leading examples of early SAP S/4HANA adoption.

Industry	Summary Overview of Business Case Drivers
International technology and e-commerce company	With a new CEO and stagnating growth, a technology and e-commerce company partnered with IBM to transform the business using SAP and other advanced technologies as enablers. The initial phase involved building a business case for the multiyear transformation program. With deep understanding of how the enabling technologies can lead to streamlined and lower cost processes, IBM worked with C-level global process owners to identify significant quantified benefits in each major process area across the enterprise. Approved by the board of directors, the resulting business case provided the foundation for value realization efforts throughout the transformation.
Global Internet-related services and products firm	Client's growth in scale and complexity was placing increasing pressure on business processes and system solutions across their $100 billion enterprise. IBM worked with the client to build a business case to assess investment in an SAP S/4HANA transformation. The joint team identified pain points by business process, quantified SAP S/4HANA-enabled benefits, and identified opportunities to leverage advanced technologies such as AI and RPT. The team defined and quantified eight key value pools that, together, generate positive ROI and serve as guideposts to value realization.

Table 17.2 SAP S/4HANA Adoption Examples

17.7   Summary

In this chapter, we discussed alternative approaches to developing a compelling business case for SAP S/4HANA. The traditional product-centric method of aggregating the incremental gains from closing the gap between current pain points and existing SAP S/4HANA functionality works when the original ERP value proposition still exists.

For enterprises seeking transformational business outcomes, however, a more contemporary process that is stakeholder centric, value focused, and outcome based is required. In these situations, SAP S/4HANA can be positioned as a digital core to enable strategic imperatives and step-change performance improvement across enterprise value steams.

Differentiating value propositions are based on specific customer needs, so there are no simple playbooks, services, or tools that work without proper discovery, value assessment, and client validation. Specialized expertise is required to navigate different stakeholder expectations and the complexities of aligning strategic, tactical, and operational objectives.

The five-step methodology outlined has proven to work when the traditional ERP business case isn't enough to make a compelling argument for change. Developing a comprehensive value model, value plan, and value governance approach is required for continuous innovation and sustainable value management after the initial SAP S/4HANA go-live. Expect more evolution as the SAP S/4HANA product road map matures and emerging technologies become mainstream.

In our next and final chapter, we'll explore how SAP S/4HANA has been utilized in several use cases.

Chapter 18

Customer Case Studies

Many SAP ERP customers still find it difficult to define the business case for SAP S/4HANA. In this chapter, we'll show you the value that was realized by SAP S/4HANA in real-world projects to help you build your own business case.

Don't forget that implementing SAP S/4HANA and taking advantage of the IT, finance, and logistics business benefits it offers isn't the destination, but simply a stepping-stone that will help you along your journey to digital transformation. Technological advances are disrupting the status quo and creating huge turbulence. Industries are converging, and new competitors are emerging at breakneck speed. The pressure to innovate has never been greater, nor has managing the risks been more difficult. How are CxOs carving a path through the chaos and helping their enterprises pursue profitable growth?

Let's look at a series of case studies that help showcase recent and ongoing SAP S/4HANA implementation projects. Of course, it's important to mention that for each business case, the focus should be not only on the cost of implementing SAP S/4HANA but especially on the business benefits it brings (e.g., the finance organization becoming a real business partner that supports the CEO with real-time insights).

18.1 Multinational Industrial Company

A multinational industrial company is operating in a *multi-ERP system landscape*, which means that instead of having a single ERP instance running its business, the company has a landscape with multiple versions of SAP instances and non-SAP instances. To report financials on a global scale, the company usually develops global financial data standards, such as a global chart of accounts, or develops a common definition of profit centers, cost centers, and so on.

However, this approach requires a high degree of governance and reconciliation between all systems that use common global master data. The only place where financial data comes together on a global scale is in a financial information warehouse and the consolidation system itself. However, this isn't a real-time process; data can be accessed one day later after a nightly upload or, sometimes, only after a month-end closing process has been finished. Further, most of the time, this consolidated financial information is delivered on an aggregated level only and not always uploaded via an automated interface to the consolidation system; this makes it impossible to drill down to the details behind these consolidated figures. In many cases, the closing process timelines are jeopardized as well because the upload to the consolidation system fails due to master data issues.

This kind of financial architecture and data flow is common in many multinational organizations. In this architecture (see Figure 18.1), an SAP Business Warehouse (SAP BW) system is often used as a kind of *financial data warehouse* to collect financial information from various source systems before sending the data to the corporate consolidation system.

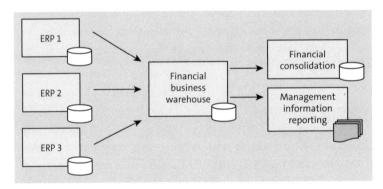

Figure 18.1 Typical Financial Architecture and Data Flow

However, because the load of data to a central system is irregular, this architecture causes the following problems:

- Because inconsistencies can only be detected late in the closing process, intercompany reconciliation issues arise that add to the time needed for the closing processes.

- There is a lack of instant insight into cash flow and working capital movement on the group level.

- With financial data in the local ledgers *and* in the consolidation ledger, there are multiple versions of truth, which causes transparency issues.

- Most of the time, the load to the consolidation system is a nonstandard solution containing massive data-mapping constructs, which results in high total cost of ownership (TCO).

Can this be rectified with SAP S/4HANA? Let's find out.

18.1.1   Vision

To overcome these problems, this customer was looking for a way to consolidate its financial system environment and create a single source of truth for finance by implementing SAP S/4HANA Finance via the Central Finance deployment model. The company envisioned that the end-state architecture would look like Figure 18.2.

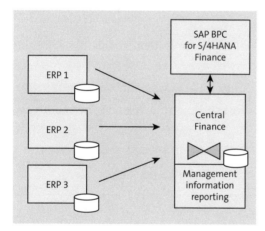

Figure 18.2 SAP S/4HANA Finance End-State Architecture

In this architecture, detailed financial transactions will be *replicated* in real time to a Central Finance box. In this process, the mappings needed between source and target systems will be handled by SAP Master Data Governance (SAP MDG) functionalities. This function can be used, for example, to make source data that employs different financial data standards compliant with global financial data standards. (In this scenario, we can assume that consolidation functionalities are provided by SAP BPC for SAP S/4HANA Finance.)

Therefore, in this architecture, we expect that most of the management information reporting requirements can be satisfied from the Central Finance system in real time, which would eliminate the need for management information reporting via SAP BW.

18.1.2 IT Project

The main driver for this Central Finance project was to implement SAP S/4HANA without any disruption, which is only possible using the sidecar approach. This also enabled the client to integrate and consolidate multiple SAP ERP systems into one SAP S/4HANA system. The client was able to test the SAP S/4HANA Finance simplification (Central Journal) easily, paving the way to upgrade existing SAP ERP systems to SAP S/4HANA Finance in the future. A lot of large corporations are looking at Central Finance as a noninvasive way to introduce SAP S/4HANA into the landscape.

18.1.3 Benefits

Having all financial transactions in one SAP S/4HANA system provides the following benefits:

- Instant insight into cash flow and working capital movements on the group level
- Intercompany reconciliation process in real time to accelerate the month-end close process
- Improved transparency due to the realization of a single source of truth for finance via the Universal Journal concept

> **Universal Journal**
>
> Recall from Chapter 2 that the Universal Journal acts as the single source of truth in an SAP S/4HANA Finance system and needs to be based on your global and local operational financial reporting requirements.

- Improved user experience (UX) with SAP Fiori screens for core finance functionality in SAP S/4HANA
- Soft close in SAP S/4HANA as opposed to hard close in SAP ERP
- Operational reporting directly in SAP S/4HANA
- Better insight into costs and revenues due to the introduction of account-based Profitability Analysis (CO-PA) as part of the Universal Journal

18.1.4 Path Forward

Central Finance can be activated without a lot of risk. One option is to activate Central Finance using a sidecar scenario (see Figure 18.3), meaning that it would act initially as the source for feeding the current consolidation and corporate finance reporting environments for a limited number of sources only.

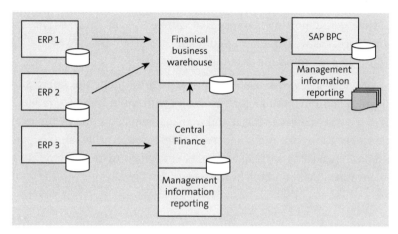

Figure 18.3 Central Finance as Sidecar Scenario

Later, when more organizations are connected to the Central Finance box and it works satisfactorily, we could route all sources via Central Finance, so it will become the single source for feeding the consolidation and group reporting systems.

Next, many of our customers today manage their cash position using Microsoft Excel. Because they operate multiple ERP systems rather than one ERP system, they don't have a standard process for long-term cash planning; the result is manual cash planning and laborious reconciliation efforts. The effect is that many customers lack insight into their daily cash positions, which makes it very difficult to centrally manage risk and exposure across regions/geographies.

This customer and many others show a lot of interest in bringing cash data together in a central repository such as Central Finance. To solve the issue of the lack of a centralized financial system environment, various proofs of concepts (POCs) started to explore this capability of SAP S/4HANA Finance in more detail. It can provide global cash positions in real time—even in the presence of heterogeneous backend systems. New analytical capabilities provide detailed analysis of forecasted cash flows to bring

18

greater levels of consistency to cash balances, cash requirements, and liquidity strategies.

Many large organizations are considering the Central Finance scenario as a viable option for optimizing their system landscapes. Some of them already started the journey because having all their General Ledger (G/L)-level data in one system was already enough of a business benefit to choose this scenario. Central Finance offers a centralized, real-time data-reporting instance that can be used as single source for the consolidation process as well. It allows a company to harmonize data on the fly and will support full data mapping and document drill-back.

Central Finance provides a low-risk, nondisruptive path to adopt the latest SAP finance simplification and innovations for customers with multi-ERP system landscapes. It provides a consolidated financial and management reporting instance to centralize process execution, planning, and reporting based on the same (single source of truth) data. Central Finance is also an excellent vehicle to implement financial shared services more quickly and will be a fast track for digitally reinventing your finance function.

18.2   Multinational Service Company

The customer in our next case study recently embarked on a multiyear transformation program to enable improved reliability, agility, and efficiency across all of its business segments. This global SAP implementation project for SAP S/4HANA Finance included the following functional domains: corporate finance, supply chain, customer engagement, manufacturing, quality management, human resources, enterprise asset management, and product and services delivery processes.

18.2.1   Vision

Due in part to a continual series of acquisitions, this customer had a lack of consistent structure and streamlined business processes across different segments, functions, and business units. The company needed to integrate key processes across multiple functions, including corporate finance, supply chain management, customer engagement, manufacturing, human resources, enterprise asset management, and product and service delivery. To do so, the company selected SAP S/4HANA.

18.2.2   IT Project

The client was already running its SAP Business Suite on SAP HANA and getting the benefits of being on the latest suite from SAP, so it was natural to upgrade to SAP S/4HANA to benefit from further simplification and innovation. The key to TCO was reducing the data footprint, which was achieved due to the simplified data model.

18.2.3   Benefits

Let's look at some of this customer's pain points and how SAP S/4HANA was deployed to overcome them through the lens of the following financial business elements.

Financial Reporting and Analysis

Running detailed operational reports, such as CO-PA reporting, on the SAP ERP system had an unacceptable impact on system performance. It forced the company to extract this operational data to an SAP BW environment, which caused a delay in reporting. During a given month, extracts to SAP BW normally occurred only once per day, and during month-end, they could be performed on demand. Furthermore, not all business data required was available on the spot; the company often had to run month-end closing jobs to make the data available on the level needed to satisfy financial reporting requirements. The company also needed to perform a complex reconciliation task to guarantee reliable financial reporting because it had no single version of truth in its SAP landscape. Instead, the company had to deal with various ledgers such as the G/L, asset ledger, Material Ledger (ML), CO-PA ledger, and so on. A lack of access to real-time data led to significant manual effort being required in internal financial reporting and analysis.

SAP S/4HANA took away most of these pain points by providing one access point for all financial reporting requirements. Now, finance team members never need to wonder where to report their financial data from; the Universal Journal contains all the financial information they need. It took away the necessity of reconciling the various ledgers as well.

Next, due to SAP S/4HANA's technical capabilities, such as in-memory processing and columnar storage, this service company no longer needs to run operational reporting in an SAP BW environment. The company can simply define and run operational reports in the SAP ERP system without jeopardizing its performance.

18

In a nutshell, SAP S/4HANA combines financial and management accounting, as well as profitability data, into one Universal Journal. It abolishes totals, indices, and other predefined aggregates and relies on line items as a single source of truth to provide an intuitive UX, reduce operational reporting efforts, and accelerate financial processes. It significantly reduced the finance business operation and analysis costs for this specific customer.

Managing Month-End Close

Beyond the described financial reporting and analysis pain points, the customer experienced more month-end misery:

- End-of-period bottlenecks due to many activities needing to be run at the same time, but not enough manpower available to execute all tasks in parallel
- Manual workarounds for loading data in the system due to lack of automation
- High cost of audit due to lack of transparency of the data and audit trail

The good news is that a soft close with SAP S/4HANA Finance supports the following:

- Real-time execution of closing activities
- Intramonth execution of month-end activities, such as intercompany reconciliation
- Accelerated month-end batch processes and real-time reporting
- Self-service analytics, which eliminates the requirement to develop specific reports to satisfy reporting needs

This customer eliminated one-third of its month-end closing processing. By combining financial, management accounting, and profitability data into one Universal Journal and offering a real-time intuitive UX, SAP S/4HANA reduced operational reporting efforts considerably.

Managing Receivables

This customer was struggling with the fact that accounts receivable (AR)-related data is only visible within the AR department. Sales and account managers talking to their clients were often equipped with outdated open item and payment history reports, making it cumbersome to discuss open item issues with their customers.

SAP S/4HANA offered all this information in real time and easily accessible via mobile applications. Next, it provided a lot of analytical SAP Fiori apps that enable exception-based management reports, allowing for proactive responses and decisions. In addition, SAP S/4HANA offers the following:

- Real-time simplified analysis to help determine a customer's top-line contribution
- Improved search facilities to support detailed analysis

Receivables management functionality in SAP S/4HANA improved working capital and financial health by using real-time receivables data to assess customer credit risk, streamline billing, resolve disputes, and prioritize customer collections.

Managing Payables

As in the receivables process, payables processing suffered from delays caused by batch-oriented processes in SAP ERP. The multinational service company was bogged down by the following obstacles:

- Often manual, error-prone, and time-consuming invoice processes
- Open items only visible within accounts payable (AP) teams, which causes delays in the issue-resolution process
- Inaccurate view of days payable outstanding (DPO) due to lack of understanding of exceptions and duplicates
- Missed opportunities to take advantage of cash discounts

SAP S/4HANA Finance boosted the payables process significantly by allowing real-time, detailed information. It offered our customer the following benefits:

- Automating invoice management and increasing speed of payment proposal runs
- Full visibility of relevant AP invoice content
- Real-time insight into AP open items and details
- On-demand forecasting of available cash for using discount opportunities and payment term adjustments
- Improved working capital and financial health via real-time payable data

Managing Assets

The current architecture of SAP ERP was causing inefficiencies in financial asset processing and required a reconciliation between the asset subledger and the G/L. The details of this customer's assets weren't visible in a central place, which caused the following problems:

- Lack of hierarchical views of depreciation areas

- Cost center asset postings only on the accumulated level, meaning the customer couldn't drill down to the individual asset

- A complex way of running deprecations for the various depreciation areas

The Universal Journal in SAP S/4HANA Finance removed the need for reconciliation. All detailed asset data can be viewed from here, and depreciation can be run much more simply due to simplified processing logic and data structures. Multiple parallel documents for all valuations are posted in real time to ensure correct values from the beginning.

18.2.4 Path Forward

For both customer engagements, SAP S/4HANA showed clearly it has the potential to remove pain points that couldn't be resolved with SAP ERP functionality. This client was one of the very early adopters of SAP S/4HANA; the next step is the planned upgrade to SAP S/4HANA 1809, and the client will eventually migrate to the latest version of SAP S/4HANA and start enjoying the benefits of logistics simplification and innovation as well as leveraging SAP Leonardo to extend its digital core.

18.3 Manufacturing Company

This next logistics case study will describe the implementation of SAP S/4HANA Enterprise Management for a manufacturing company.

The company wants to run its business processes through an integrated and standardized platform that offers transparency and accountability across its different lines of business (LoBs): manufacturing, procurement, and order-to-cash. The company also wants to drive margin-efficiency improvement through cost-optimization.

This company was experiencing some of the common key challenges associated with these LoBs. In manufacturing, this meant the following:

- Lack of real-time inventory data and inaccurate inventory stock levels, resulting in inaccurate production planning and stock-out situations

- Inability to report on costs, resulting in incapability to optimize costs

- Process and data redundancies, resulting in inefficiencies (e.g., long lead time for running material requirements planning [MRP] process)

In procure-to-pay, the company was burdened by the following obstacles:

- Lack of transparency and inability to hold and track supplier information
- Inefficient and error-sensitive process due to manual intervention and usage of different documents through the entire process

Finally, in order-to-cash, the company needed to overcome the following problems:

- Inability to see issues over the entire end-to-end process quickly, resulting in late actions for order exceptions, which can lead to customer complaints
- Lack of collaboration due to lack of real-time data and inability to run analytics across the entire process

18.3.1   Vision

The company's vision is to gain operational efficiencies by enhancing critical processes across various departments in the company and to drive growth by using real-time data insights, with the ultimate goal of gaining market share. Due to the capabilities of SAP S/4HANA as the digital core, the company has selected it as its preferred solution to manage the day-to-day operations and to support the company's strategy for growth.

The implementation project for SAP S/4HANA Enterprise Management took six months, and SAP S/4HANA was deployed across multiple plants and distribution centers simultaneously.

18.3.2   IT Project

The client is benefiting from faster MRP because it can now run across multiple plants—something that wasn't possible in SAP ERP. Real-time operational reporting is driving the business, which is something else that wasn't possible earlier when transactional data had to be sent to SAP BW servers overnight. The company has reduced its legacy ABAP code, and many of its business processes are now using the SAP S/4HANA standard code and configuration. This has reduced the company's TCO for maintenance. Many similar clients are using the SAP S/4HANA transformation to go back to standard and reduce their custom-development footprint.

18

18.3.3   Benefits

SAP S/4HANA offers functionalities that will support some of the company's key requirements at a lower TCO. The company has gone live very recently, so it's still early to quantify the benefits. However, following are some of the key benefits of SAP S/4HANA, which will resolve some of the key pain points of the company by LoB per the business case. In manufacturing, the company made the following gains:

- Real-time inventory reporting, resulting in more accurate production planning and fewer stock-outs
- Increased transparency due to the availability of real-time analytics, enabling the company to make better decisions based on real-time business insights
- Improved performance due to several simplifications and elimination of process and data redundancies (e.g., MRP is running more than 10 times faster)

There were two key benefits reaped by the SAP S/4HANA implementation in the procure-to-pay area:

- Standard integration with SAP Ariba, enabling seamless collaboration scenarios and improved process transparency
- Improved process efficiency due to better integration, less manual intervention, and usage of only a single document

Finally, there were much-needed improvements in order-to-cash:

- Introduction of the order cockpit, allowing the company to monitor issues across the entire end-to-end process easily via dashboards, enabling internal sales representatives to get full insight into the order-fulfillment process and immediately take action (e.g., orders that are on credit block, incomplete orders, and delays in delivery and shipping)
- Real-time inventory levels and data across the entire chain, allowing more accurate order promise dates and better collaboration among manufacturing, sales, and the supply chain

With SAP S/4HANA, SAP offers an integrated platform through which the company can optimize its processes across different LoBs and use real-time business insights to make better decisions and drive growth.

Embedded production planning/detailed scheduling (PP/DS) and SAP Extended Warehouse Management (SAP EWM) was activated. This has enabled the client to decommission its current SAP Supply Chain Management (SAP SCM) system and further reduce its TCO.

18.3.4 Path Forward

The client will continue to upgrade to SAP S/4HANA 1809 to benefit from new functionalities. The client also plans to activate the embedded transportation management (TM) functionality that it needs. This will enable the client to decommission its current SAP TM system and further reduce its TCO.

18.4 Food Industry Group

This group is one of the major players in the food industry. The company has been involved in a quick growth path by acquisitions that led to a very broad product portfolio distributed in more than 80 countries. The group had multiple local ERP systems and spent a lot of time trying to reconcile and consolidate its financials and optimize its supply chain. With SAP S/4HANA, the company has built one global template that works for all 80 countries, which will reduce their month-end closing to several days. In addition, with visibility of stocks and manufacturing capacity across multiple locations, the company can decide on move or manufacture at a click of an SAP Fiori button.

18.4.1 Vision

A project was launched last year as a strategic initiative to support the company's transformation and innovation strategies. This project is paramount to foster the group growth strategy that will lead to double the product turnover by 2025. The company will benefit from the project in many ways: streamlining and redesigning the core processes, defining the new organization, and implementing leading-edge SAP solutions that will enable the company to compete and win in the marketplace.

The company aimed to achieve the following:

- Increase the efficiency of its activities.
- Rethink processes, starting from the needs of the client and factoring in best practices of its sector and products.
- Make real-time information available to support its activities and decision-making process.

- Measure process performance via key performance indicators (KPIs).
- Be flexible and quick in response to change.
- Comply with international financial standards such as International Accounting Standards/International Financial Reporting Standards (IAS/IFRS).

The company has successfully completed the first two phases of the project, comprising the following initiatives:

- Business process reengineering
- Review of the organizational model
- Design of the performance-management system, on both an operational and a management level
- Change-management support
- Design and implementation of the transactional SAP S/4HANA enterprise system
- Design and implementation of the operational reporting and planning of the SAP S/4HANA enterprise system

Through the functionality of the SAP S/4HANA Enterprise Management system, the company activated the following processes: finance and administration, controlling, purchasing and related invoice verification, sales invoicing, management of non-product-related sales orders, production management, stock management, quality management, and material movements. It has rolled out its solution to India after the template was extended to incorporate India's goods and service tax (GST).

Operational reporting, including real-time analysis, was implemented directly in SAP S/4HANA by activating the embedded business intelligence models via SAP Business-Objects and SAP Fiori. Finally, the purchase requisition and order-approval processes were activated using SAP Fiori apps, enabling the company managers to approve purchase requisitions and purchase orders from their smartphones or tablets.

18.4.2   IT Project

The company implemented SAP S/4HANA to replace its legacy ERP system to leverage the digital core and integrate with cloud solutions such as SAP SuccessFactors. The company will also gain real-time insight into business performance via SAP Fiori and embedded analytics, which reduces TCO; operational reporting via SAP S/4HANA (no SAP BW required); and mobility via SAP Fiori (SAP Fiori frontend server and SAP Gateway server required).

18.4.3   Benefits

This initiative has supported the company in its transformation into an organization focused on streamlining processes, eliminating paper and manual activities, and enabling specific processes to be performed in full mobility (smartphones and tablets). The company has also optimized its target operating model, centralizing SAP processes and various systems and releasing reporting tools in areas formerly not covered by any application (e.g., analysis of purchasing services).

The implemented financial model ensures full compliance with international financial standards and supports the company's globalization strategy.

The controlling model is an advanced multidimensional model that uses the block-postings capability in table ACDOCA to simultaneously synchronize the sales, procurement, and financial data flows. This enables the company to manage its complex analytical dimensions in real time.

18.4.4   Path Forward

Further rollouts are planned for 2019 when more countries come on board. There is an ongoing plan to upgrade to the latest version of SAP S/4HANA with every new deployment to benefit from new functionalities.

18.5   Automotive Company

18

Our next case study follows a manufacturer, assembler, distributor, and importer of vehicles, spare parts, and accessories. The company operates a vast dealership network and generates gross annual revenues exceeding $1 billion. Most of the work was done on Excel and disconnected systems, and lots of paper was used in the manufacturing shop floor. Implementation of SAP S/4HANA enabled a digital manufacturing process. This truly enabled connectivity to suppliers and dealers with real-time data on what is in stock and what needs to be manufactured. This has helped improve customer experience for both after sales as well as for new vehicles.

18.5.1   Vision

To compete with a surge of foreign entrants to the market, the company wanted to improve customer experience by delivering high-quality vehicles rapidly and at the lowest cost. It had a legacy SAP ERP system that was batch-driven and didn't provide its managers with visibility into stock or production. The company needed a system that would be online and enable its management to make instant decisions.

18.5.2   IT Project

For more than a decade, the company had relied on SAP ERP enterprise applications to manage its workflows for manufacturing, production planning, finance, and controlling. To achieve its business goals, it decided to build on its success with SAP ERP solutions by seamlessly integrating its entire value chain using SAP S/4HANA.

18.5.3   Benefits

The company achieved the following general benefits from its SAP S/4HANA project:

- A 10% improvement in sales order accuracy will ensure that the company can manufacture the optimal quantity of each model—reducing the risk of a customer's chosen model being out of stock and delivering a seamless purchasing experience.
- A 20% reduction in defects per unit will reduce the risk of delivery delays and nurture increased customer satisfaction. Instrumented vehicles will enable the company to track customer deliveries in real time, ensuring they are within service-level agreements—delighting customers with a highly responsive service.
- 95% faster MRP will enable greater agility to switch to alternate vendors in the event of supply-chain disruption, reducing sourcing risks. Instrumented manufacturing equipment will help reduce unplanned downtime, maximize manufacturing capacity, and minimize costs.
- In the past, it took months to deliver reports to managers about what was happening on the ground, which was simply too long to make competitive decisions. The company realized it needed to collect information about forecasting, manufacturing, and suppliers faster and—crucially—deliver reports to decision makers immediately. SAP S/4HANA was the answer; it delivered both online transaction processing (OLTP) and online analytical processing (OLAP) without any lag.
- Embedded analytics enabled real-time operational reporting.
- SAP Fiori apps enabled access to the system via mobile devices.

18.5.4 Path Forward

With its new business systems now live, the company will ensure complete front-to-back integration—enabling sales forecasts from its dealerships to flow seamlessly to the primary suppliers and manufacturers in its value chain. Combined with real-time insight into the results of parts inspections, the company will gain the ability to detect defects at the earliest possible opportunity, reducing the risk of costly delays downstream in the manufacturing process. Regular upgrades to the latest versions of SAP S/4HANA will enable the company to leverage the latest innovation from SAP, which includes embedded PP/DS, EWM, product lifecycle management, and transportation management. This will further reduce the TCO because additional hardware and integration won't be required.

18.6 Summary

This chapter has explored several recent and ongoing SAP S/4HANA implementation projects to showcase real companies' paths to digital transformation. The number of SAP customers beginning these transitions is growing every quarter, and we expect the trend to continue in the coming years.

18

The Authors

Devraj Bardhan is an accomplished global leader for SAP Innovations at IBM. He has led several large transformation projects, driving business growth agenda through innovation and digital efficiencies. He is an established subject matter expert (SME) for SAP S/4HANA, SAP Ariba, and SAP Leonardo, growing IBM's digital transformation capability by designing and implementing global templates. He heads the SAP Garage and is part of the global SAP Center of Competence at IBM. Devraj can be reached via Twitter *@devbard* or via *www.linkedin.com/in/bardhan*.

Axel Baumgartl is part of the Center for Digital Leadership at SAP, where he leads the area of asset and method development. In his current role, he provides thought leadership and best practices for C-level customers based on his more than 19 years of experience with SAP transformation projects. He is the author of several publications and books about SAP products and developed a method for enterprise architecture blueprinting.

Nga-Sze Choi is the SAP S/4HANA Sales and Logistics Expert working for SAP Business Transformation Services. She has more than 14 years of experience in global business transformation programs, leading the design and implementation of SAP solutions in the order-to-cash and procure-to-pay areas. Her main area of expertise is in the life sciences, consumer products, and industrial industries.

Mark Dudgeon is the global SAP CTO of IBM Global Business Services, SAP Service Line. He has more than 21 years of experience in architecture, design, and delivery for some of IBM's largest SAP deployments. Mark's role includes ensuring that IBM has the right partnerships, capabilities, and offerings to support its customers in their digital transformational journey with SAP at their core. Mark can be reached via Twitter *@MarkPDudgeon.*

Asidhara Lahiri is an SAP Enterprise Architect in IBM India, working on complex SAP implementations for global clients in industries such as consumer products, oil & gas, airlines, and utility. She has more than 22 years of work experience, out of which 18 are in SAP. She advises client executives on digital road maps for their SAP landscape, and is a global subject matter expert (SME) in SAP HANA in IBM. She has also led the SAP HANA competency for IBM India, designing and reviewing client architecture, defining IBM services, and growing IBM's SAP HANA capability. Asidhara has filed two patents and is a member of the IBM Academy of Technology. She is also a coauthor for the book *SAP Cloud Platform: Cloud-Native Development* (SAP PRESS). Asidhara can be reached via Twitter *@AsidharaL* and *www.linkedin.com/in/asidharalahiri.*

Bert Meijerink is the SAP S/4HANA Finance lead in the IBM SAP Global Center of Competence. He has more than 30 years of working experience in implementing financial systems worldwide and over 20 years of experience in designing and implementing SAP global templates.

Andrew Worsley-Tonks is SAP Chief Architect and global SAP S/4HANA transformation lead for IBM Services. He has extensive experience in complex SAP upgrades, modernization, and business transformation projects. In his current role, he delivers multiple SAP S/4HANA projects while also helping existing SAP ERP customers define their SAP S/4HANA adoption strategy and business case. Andrew can be reached via Twitter *@A_WorsleyTonks*.

Contributors

David Breaugh is a partner in IBM's Global Enterprise Transformation practice with over 25 years of business strategy and process operations expertise. He has led many cross-functional teams to deliver performance improvements and bottom line results on large scale business transformation programs. He brings valuable experience across various industries including automotive, industrial manufacturing, distribution, consumer products, retail, and life sciences. He is also a recognized expert in value lifecycle management, and a founding member of the Value Selling and Realization Council, a professional organization dedicated to helping companies maximize value from investments enabled by information technology.

Piotr Gorecki is a program manager and enterprise architect working at IBM Global SAP Center of Competence. He has over 20 years of experience in planning and delivering complex business transformation programs based on SAP solutions. Piotr has been working on global and local SAP projects in several industries, including consumer products, life sciences, retail, and telecommunications. In his current role, he helps customers define their road maps to SAP S/4HANA and identify new solutions and technologies that enable reaching their business goals.

Index

U

Interested in reading more?

Please visit our website for all new book
and e-book releases from SAP PRESS.

www.sap-press.com